AFRICAN HISTORICAL DICTIONARIES
Edited by Jon Woronoff

Historical Dictionary

of

Nigeria

by
A. OYEWOLE

African Historical Dictionaries,
No. 40

The Scarecrow Press, Inc.
Metuchen, N.J., & London
1987

Library of Congress Cataloging in Publication Data

Oyewole, A.
   Historical dictionary of Nigeria.

   (African historical dictionaries ; no. 40)
   Bibliography: p.
   1. Nigeria--History--Dictionaries.   I. Title.
II. Series.
DT515.15.O94   1987   966.9'003'21   85-1792
ISBN 0-8108-1787-X

To my wife, Mary
and
my children: Adebayo, Ayodele and Adenike

ACKNOWLEDGEMENT

I want to thank a number of people for making this work possible. In the first place is Professor Thomas O'Toole of Western Carolina University, Cullowhee, North Carolina, USA, who first suggested to me the idea of undertaking the work. My colleague, Professor Oye Ogunbadejo of the Department of Political Science, University of Ife, for his invaluable assistance. Messrs. M. A. Oyinlola, Kayode Ola, Rotimi Oyeniran all graduates of the University of Ife, who assisted in no small way in the research on the work. Mr. Okon Essien a Youth Corper on National Service from the University of Calabar who also helped in the final arrangement of the bibliography. Finally Mrs. M. M. Salawu, Messrs. J. B. Taiwo and Murtala Agbaje, all secretarial staff of the Department of Political Science, for helping me in the final typing and other secretarial services.

A. Oyewole
Ile-Ife, Oyo State

CONTENTS

v

EDITOR'S FOREWORD

Africa's most populous country, one of the largest in size, and with a talented and energetic population, Nigeria seemed destined to lead and conceivably even dominate much of the continent. Yet, perhaps because it was so large and heavily populated, and its peoples were so diverse and ebullient, this has not happened. Nigeria is still trying to find itself, to define a suitable political structure and organize its economy.

These strivings are not easy to follow, passing through several democratic phases interrupted by military coups and assorted plans to make its peoples work together, these often revised to meet regional or ethnic demands which once took it into a civil war. The approach to economics has varied nearly as much, although avoiding the extremes of state capitalism or socialism, and ultimately depending excessively on a fickle resource: oil.

To get a handle on what Nigeria was, is, and can be, it is extremely useful to have a guide to its many political parties, ethnic groups, civilian and military leaders as well as its cultural heritage, economic endowment and much more. That is the purpose of this Historical Dictionary which should help newcomers--and specialists--get their bearings in an exceptionally variegated and often confusing nation. While the individual entries are designed to clarify just one aspect or another, together they give a rather complete view of the situation.

The author of this volume, Dr. A. Oyewole, probably had the most challenging task in the series. But he accomplished it admirably due to a knowledge of and concern for his country. Although busy as Senior Lecturer and Acting Head of the Department of Political Science at the University of Ife, he devoted the indispensable time and effort so that others would find it much easier to proceed. In so doing, he has made a notable contribution toward facilitating the study of Nigeria.

Jon Woronoff
Series Editor

SELECTED CHRONOLOGY

1788	The African Association was founded.
1795	Mungo Park started his first expedition to trace the course of River Niger.
1796	Mungo Park became the first European to discover the eastern course of River Niger.
1803	The Jihad, Muslim Holy War, began in Northern Nigeria.
1807	Parliament in England abolished the slave trade.
1841	Anglican Church sent its first Missionaries to Nigeria.
1842	Methodist Missionaries reached Badagry.
1846	The Presbyterian Missionaries landed in Calabar, as the first group of Missionaries.
1849	John Beecroft was appointed British Consul for the Bights of Benin and Biafra, thus opening up the first diplomatic link between Britain and Nigeria.
1853	King William Dappa Pepple was exiled.
1861	Lagos was ceded to the British Crown under King Dosumu and became a British Crown Colony.
1865	The British established a consulate at Lokoja.
1879	The United African Company was formed by George Taubman Goldie.
1882	The United African Company changed its name to National African Company.
1885	The Berlin Conference.
1886	British Government granted the National African Company, formerly known as the United African Company, a Royal Charter giving the Company political authority over the area under the Company's influence and the Company became known as the Royal Niger Company.

1887	The British proclaimed the delta region of the River Niger and its surroundings The Oil Rivers Protectorate.
1890	The Anglo-French Agreement
1893	Oil Rivers Protectorate became Niger Coast Protectorate.
1895	The Akassa Massacre.
1897	The Name "Nigeria" appeared in the London Times.
1898	Railway Construction began in Nigeria.
1898	The Anglo-French Convention.
1899	The name Nigeria received its first official recognition in London.
1900	The Royal Niger Company's charter was revoked and the Oil Rivers Protectorate together with the areas near it became the protectorate of Southern Nigeria. In the North, area under the Royal Niger Company's administration became the protectorate of Northern Nigeria.
1900	The Charter of the Royal Niger Company was revoked and Nigeria came under full British Authority.
1901	The Establishment of the West African Frontier Force.
1903	The Fulani Empire came under British rule.
1906	The Colony of Lagos was merged with the protectorate of Southern Nigeria to become the Colony and Protectorate of Southern Nigeria.
1914	The Colony and protectorate of Southern Nigeria was merged with the protectorate of Northern Nigeria to become the Colony and protectorate of Nigeria.
1922	The Clifford Constitution came into being.
1926	The Establishment of the Nigerian Daily Times.
1929	Aba Riot.
1934	Yaba Higher College was established, followed by the formation of the Lagos Youth Movement.
1936	The emergence of the Nigerian Youth Movement.
1939	The Southern Nigeria was divided by Governor Bourdillon into the Eastern and Western provinces, each of which later became regions.

1944	Ibo Federal Union was formed.
1944	The National Council of Nigeria and the Cameroons was formed.
1945	The General Strike took place.
1946	The Richards Constitution came into being.
1947	The founding of the University College of Ibadan associated to the University of London.
1947	Northern Representatives sat with the Southern Representatives in the Legislative Council in Lagos for the first time.
1948	Egbe Omo Oduduwa was founded in Ile-Ife.
1948	Ibo Federal Union became Ibo State Union.
1950	The formation of the Action Group (AG) Party.
1951	Macpherson Constitution came into being.
1953	Eastern Regional Crisis.
1953	"Self-Government in 1956" motion in the National Assembly.
1953	Kano Riot.
1953	First Constitutional Conference to be held in London.
1954	The Lyttelton Constitution which turned Nigeria into a federation of three regions.
1954	Lagos Constitutional Conference.
1954	COR State Movement was formed.
1955	Free Primary Education in Western Nigeria was launched.
1957	Second London Constitutional Conference. The British Government set up the Minority Commission known as the Willink Commission.
1957	Both the Eastern and the Western Regions became self-governing.
1958	Third London Constitutional Conference.
1959	Northern Region became self-governing.

1960   The fourth and the last London Constitutional Conference took place.
University of Nigeria Nsukka was founded.
Nigeria became Independent on October 1.

1961   University of Ife was founded.

1962   University of Lagos and Ahmadu Bello University in Zaria were established.

1962   The Action group crisis in the Western Region and the Declaration of a State of Emergency in that region.

1962   Coker Commission of Inquiry was set up to look into the affairs of certain Statutory Corporations in the Western Region.

1962   Nigeria abrogated the Defense Pact between her and Britain.

1963   Mid-Western Region was created from the then Western Region.

1963   Nigeria became a republic.

1963   A National Census was taken, leading to the Census crisis. This Census still remains the basis for the national planning.

1964   The Federal Election Crisis.

1965   Western Regional Election Crisis.

1966   First Military Coup d'état took place on January 15 and the second Military Coup d'état took place on July 29.

1967   Creation of Twelve States by which Nigeria became a federation of twelve states.

1967   Col. Odumegwu Ojukwu, Governor of the Eastern Region, declared that region the sovereign Republic of Biafra.

1967   The civil war began in July.

1967   Interim Administrative Council was established.

1968   Kampala Peace Talks and Addis Ababa Peace Talks.

1968   Interim Common Services Agency was established for the Northern Region.

1970   Colonel Odumegwu Ojukwu fled the country to the Ivory Coast.
The end of the civil war.

1970	The Eastern States Interim Assets and Liabilities Agency Decree was promulgated.
1973	Nigeria changed from the pound sterling to the Naira.
1975	Economic Community of West African States came into being.
1975	Third Military Coup which overthrew General Gowon and General Murtala Muhammed came to power.
1975	The Constitution Drafting Committee was set up.
1976	Nigeria became a Federation of Nineteen States.
1976	Federal Capital Territory was created in Abuja.
1976	Attempted coup, staged by Col. B. S. Dimka, February 13, in which General Murtala Muhammed was killed.
1976	Local government was recognized as the third tier of governmental activity in the Nation.
1976	Universal Primary Education was launched.
1977	Federal Electoral Commission established.
1978	Land Use Decree was promulgated.
1979	The Presidential Constitution came into being.
1980	Deportation of Alhaji Shugaba Abdurrahman Darman, the majority leader of the Great Nigerian Peoples Party in the Borno State.
1981	Governor Abubakar Balarabe Musa of Kaduna State was impeached by the State House of Assembly.
1983	The first and the last general elections were held under the Second Republican Constitution.
1983	The Fourth Military Coup d'état on December 31st, which overthrew the Alhaji Shehu Shagari administration and brought General Muhammadu Buhari to power.

ABBREVIATIONS AND ACRONYMS

ABU	Ahmadu Bello University
ACB	African Continental Bank
ACSTWU	African Civil Servants and Technical Workers' Union
AG	Action Group
ANTUF	All Nigerian Trade Union Federation
AWAM	Association of West African Merchants
BDPP	Benin Delta Peoples Party
BCGA	British Cotton Growing Association
BYM	Bornu Youth Movement
CAC	Christ Apostolic Church
CBE	Commander of the British Empire
CDC	Constitution Drafting Committee
CMB	Commodity Marketing Boards
CMG	Companion of the Order of St. Michael and St. George
CMS	Church Missionary Society
COLA	Cost of Living Allowance
COR	Calabar-Ogoja-Rivers State
CWTC	Central Water Transportation Company
DO	District Officer
DPNC	Democratic Party of Nigeria and Cameroons
ECA	United Nations Economic Commission for Africa
ECN	Electricity Corporation of Nigeria
ECOWAS	Economic Community of West African States
ESIALA	Eastern States Interim Assets and Liabilities Agency
FAO	Food and Agricultural Organisation
FBS	Federal Broadcasting Service
FCT	Federal Capital Territory
FCTA	Federal Capital Territory Authority
FEC	Federal Executive Council
FEDECO	Federal Electoral Commission
FESTAC	African Festival of Arts and Culture
FIIR	Federal Institute of Industrial Research
FRCN	Federal Radio Corporation of Nigeria
GCE	General Certificate of Education
G. C. E. A Level	General Certificate of Education, Advanced Level
GCON	Grand Commander of the Order of a Niger
GDP	Gross Domestic Product
GMT	Greenwich Mean Time
GNPP	Great Nigerian People's Party
HND	Higher National Diploma
ICFTU	International Confederation of Free Trade Unions

xiii

ICJ	International Court of Justice
ICRC	International Committee of the Red Cross
ITP	Ilorin Talaka Parapo
IULC	Independent United Labour Congress
ITT	International Telephones and Telegraphs
JAC	Joint Action Committee
JAMB	Joint Admissions and Matriculation Board
JPC	Joint Planning Committee
KBE	Knight of the British Empire
KCMG	Knight of the Companion of St. Michael and St. George
KNC	Kamerun National Congress
LYM	Lagos Youth Movement
MBPP	Middle Belt Peoples Party
MDF	Mid-West Democratic Front
MPC	Mid-West People's Congress
MPP	Mid-West People's Party
MZL	Middle Zone League
NA	Native Authority
NAB	Nigerian Agricultural Bank
NAC	National African Company
NANS	National Association of Nigerian Students
NAP	Nigeria Advance Party
NBC	Nigerian Broadcasting Corporation
NCTUN	National Council of Trade Unions of Nigeria
NDC	Niger Delta Congress
NEC	National Economic Council
	National Executive Council
NEPA	National Electric Power Authority
NEPU	Northern Element Progressive Union
NET	Nigerian External Telecommunications Limited
NICON	National Insurance Corporation of Nigeria
NIIA	Nigerian Institute of International Affairs
NIP	National Independence Party
NIPC	National Investment and Properties Company Limited
NISER	Nigerian Institute of Social and Economic Research
NLC	Nigerian Labour Congress
NNA	Nigerian National Alliance
NNDP	Nigerian National Democratic Party
NNFL	Nigerian National Federation of Labour
NNOC	Nigerian National Oil Corporation
NNPC	Nigerian National Petroleum Corporation
NPA	Nigerian Ports Authority
NPF	Northern Progressive Front
NPN	National Party of Nigeria
NPP	Nigerian People's Party
NNPC	Nigerian Printing and Publishing Company
NTA	National Television Authority
NSO	Nigerian Security Organization
NTUC	Nigerian Trade Union Congress
NUC	National Universities Commission
NUNS	National Union of Nigerian Students
NUT	Nigerian Union of Teachers
NYC	Nigerian Youth Congress

NYSC	National Youth Service Corps
NYM	Nigerian Youth Movement
OAU	Organization of African Unity
OBE	Order of the British Empire
OFN	Operation Feed the Nation
OFR	Order of the Federal Republic of Nigeria
OND	Ordinary National Diploma
PPA	Progressive Parties Alliance
PRP	People's Redemption Party
PWD	Public Works Department
QPM	Queen's Police Medal
RAF	Royal Air Force
RNC	Royal Niger Company
RWU	Railway Workers Union
SAN	Senior Advocate of Nigeria
SMC	Supreme Military Council
SPC	Southern People's Congress
SUM	Sudan United Mission
SWAFP	Socialist Workers and Farmers Party
TUC	Trade Union Congress
TUC(N)	Trade Union Congress of Nigeria
UAC	United African Company
ULC	United Labor Congress
UMBC	United Middle Belt Congress
UNESCO	United Nations Educational Scientific and Cultural Organization
UNIA	Universal Negro Improvement Association
UNIP	United National Independence Party
UPGA	United Progressive Grand Alliance
UPE	Universal Primary Education
UPN	Unity Party of Nigeria
UPP	United People's Party
WAAC	West African Airways Corporation
WAEC	West African Examination Council
WAFF	West African Frontier Force
WAISER	West African Institute of Social and Economic Research
WAPCB	West African Produce Control Board
WASU	West African Student Union
WNBS	Western Nigeria Broadcasting Service
WNDC	Western Nigeria Development Corporation
WNTV	Western Nigeria Television Service

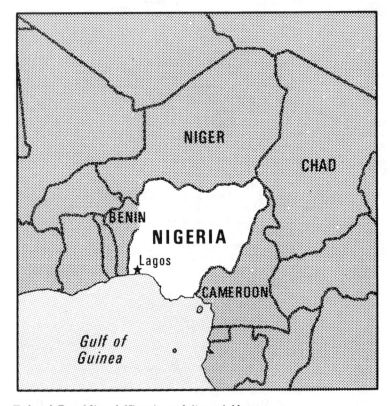

Federal Republic of Nigeria and its neighbors

Federal Republic of Nigeria

INTRODUCTION

Nigeria, with an area of 923, 768 square kilometers (356, 669 square miles), lies at the inner corner of the Gulf of Guinea in West Africa. The longest distance from the eastern to the western boundaries is 1, 126 kilometers (700 miles) while the distance from the northern boundaries to the Atlantic sea is 1, 046 kilometers (650 miles). It is bounded on the west by the Republic of Benin (former-ly known as Dahomey), on the north by the Republic of Niger and the Chad Republic, on the east by the Republic of Cameroon and on the south by the Atlantic Sea.

The most southern part of the country in the Delta area is about $4°$ north of the equator and the northern boundary is about $14°$ north. The western and the eastern boundaries lie north and south between $3°$ and $15°$ east meridian. The official hour is one hour ahead of the Greenwich Mean Time (GMT).

The country can be said to have four main vegetational re-gions: The first is the coastline, which is intersected by a network of creeks and rivers, and the delta of the Niger River which con-sists of a belt of mangrove swamp extending about 100 kilometers inland. After this comes the region of tropical forest in undulating land with scattered hills. The third region is the open woodland, the deciduous forest, stretching through an undulating plateau and hills of granite and sandstone at a general elevation of about 610 meters. The fourth region is the savannah grassland which spreads towards the Sahara Desert.

Nigeria takes its name from its most important feature: the River Niger. River Niger rises in the mountains northeast of Sierra Leone and flows through the republics of Guinea, Mali and Niger be-fore it enters Nigeria from the west and then runs southeasterly to Lokoja, about 540 kilometers to the Atlantic Sea, where it joins its main tributary, the River Benue. From Lokoja, the Niger flows southwards, to the delta where it splits into numerous channels be-fore emptying itself into the sea. The Benue on the other hand takes its source from the Cameroon Republic and flows south west-erly to its confluence with the Niger. River Niger is about 4, 169 kilometers in length. Nigeria gets much of its electricity from the hydroelectric dam built on River Niger at Kainji, about 112 kilo-meters north of Jebba.

In addition to the Niger and the Benue, the second major

1

drainage system in Nigeria flows northeast from the central plateau into the Yobe River which flows into the Lake Chad through which the boundary between Nigeria and the Chadian Republic passes.

The climate of Nigeria varies from the south to the north. In the coastal areas of the south, the mean maximum temperature is about 30. 55° C while it is 34. 44° C in the north. Maximum temperatures are generally highest from February to April in the south, while they are highest in the north between March and June. In the whole country, the temperatures are lowest in July and August. The average minimum temperature in the south is about 22. 2° C and in the north it is about 18. 88° C. As such, the mean range of temperature is higher in the north where it averages about 7° C than in the south, where the average is about 4. 77° C. The maximum relative humidity near the coast is between 95 percent to 100 percent through most of the year and usually decreases to between 70 percent and 80 percent in the afternoon. As one goes north, the humidity steadily decreases.

Nigeria can be said to have two main seasons, the rainy season and the dry season. This is due to the two principal wind systems in Nigeria: the southwesterly wind current and the northeasterly wind current. The southwesterly wind current is warm and very moist after its passage over the Atlantic Ocean. It therefore causes cloudy weather and frequently results in rain. Thus the rainfall is usually heavy in the south averaging about 177. 8 cm a year in the western end of the coast and increasing to about 431. 8 cm in the eastern section of the coast. The rainfall decreases sharply as one goes inland. It falls to about 127 cm in the central part of the country and to about 50. 8 cm in the north. The rainy season generally begins in April and ends in October or November.

The northeasterly wind current is hot and dry after its passage over the Sahara Desert, and it is frequently laden with dust from the desert. The wind and the dust is generally referred to as the Harmattan. Under the influence of the wind, current weather is dry and generally cloudless. Day temperatures are high in the afternoon, and low at night and in the early morning. The weather is often hazy and visibility is reduced. The dry season is generally between November and April.

Nigeria has a wealth of mineral resources among which are petroleum, limestone, tin, columbite, gold, silver, coal, lead-zinc, marble, iron ore and uranium. The ownership and control of all minerals is vested in the federal government.

In spite of these mineral resources and the exploitation of the oil resources which has made Nigeria an important oil exporting country, Nigeria is basically an agricultural country for farming is still the principal economic activity of most Nigerians. Before the civil war in 1967, agricultural products used to be the principal export earner but since the war, petroleum oil has taken that pride of place. As a result of the growth in the foreign exchange earnings from oil and the efforts to diversify the nation's economy by investing in other sectors of the economy (such as building and construction), mining and quarrying, transport and communication, and industry have expanded considerably, while for a long time agriculture appeared to have been benignly neglected. However owing to Nigeria's growing dependence on food imports, the military government before handing over to a civilian administration in 1979 began an agricultural recovery program known then as Operation Feed the Nation (OFN), designed to make the country self-sufficient in food and agricultural products for the growing local manufacturing industries. To make land readily available for large-scale commercial farming, the government in 1978 also issued the Land Use Decree which vested all land in the state government. The commitment of the national government to self-sufficiency has continued under the civilian administration of Alhaji Shehu Shagari who renamed the OFN program the Green Revolution. Under the Fourth National Development Plan 1981-1985, the agricultural sector was to receive about 13 percent of the total capital investment of all governments of the federation, which stood about N70 billion.

This objective is, however, unlikely to be achieved, for Nigerian economic well-being has been badly affected in recent years by the world oil glut which has led to a rapid decline in the country's foreign exchange earnings. As a result of this, the government in 1982 had to resort to austerity measures under the Economic Stabilization (Temporary Provision) Act. Under the Act the government began to reduce the level of imports to conserve foreign exchange and to take other measures to encourage and protect local industries.

Nigeria is a nation of many nationalities or ethnic groups, each occupying a separate geographic area, and having its own culture and tradition. These various groups speak different languages which are mutually unintelligible one to the other. The major ethnic groups are Hausa, Fulani, Ibo, Yoruba, Kanuri, Ibibio, Tiv, Itsekiri, Ijaw, Edo, Annang, Nupe, Urhobo, Igala, Idoma, Igbirra, Gwari, Effik, Birom and Yergam. The population of Nigeria according to the 1963 census was put at 55.7 million, making it the most populous country in Africa. The estimated rate of growth is about 2.5 percent per year, which makes the present population to be about 80 million people. The truth about Nigeria's population figures is that they are most unreliable. The problem is that population census has become too political. Since the sharing of the national pie has for long been tied to the population of the constituent parts of the federation (i.e., to the various groups occupying these areas), each part has tried to outperform the other in manipulating its figures to its own advantage.

Before the British came to Nigeria, these various groups had organized themselves into village or clan groups, emirates, kingdoms and states. Some of these were even organized into empires like the Kanem-Bornu empire around the area of Lake Chad from the eleventh to the fourteenth century, the Oyo Empire in Western Nigeria from the thirteenth to the eighteenth century and the Fulani Empire which started with the Jihad (Holy War) of Usman Dan Fodio in 1803, and was broken up by Lord Lugard in 1903.

Even though there was no central authority for present-day Nigeria before the British came, there were commercial and cultural contacts between the kingdoms, emirates and states. However the growth of the slave trade at the coast set back the development of this peaceful, cultural and commercial development. Nigerians at the coastal areas became intermediaries in the slave trade. Kingdoms rose against Kingdoms for the purpose of capturing slaves for sale to the European slavers transporting them to the Americas. As a result Benin, Lagos, Bonny and Calabar became thriving centers of slave trade from which more than 20,000 able-bodied men and women were transported annually to the New World from the sixteenth century to the nineteenth century. Even when major European powers had put an end to the trade and British naval ships patrolled the West African waters in the nineteenth century, millions of Africans were still being sent out as slaves many of whom were from Nigeria. Nigeria was therefore for centuries deprived of its able-bodied men and women.

Toward the end of the eighteenth century, when public opinion was growing against this inhuman trade, some British merchants began to look for markets in Africa for the products of their industries and for new sources of raw materials for those industries. This led to the founding of the African Association in 1788 which later organized the exploration of the interior of Africa, most especially the exploration of the Niger River, and the pioneering work of explorers like Mungo Park, Clapperton, the Lander Brothers, Barth and Baikie.

In 1807 Parliament in England abolished the slave trade and forbade its ships from trafficking in the trade. Britain soon set up a naval patrol to stop the continuation of the trade but it was discovered that this alone was not enough to stop the Africans from offering their people for sale to the Europeans. There had to be a new type of legitimate trade to take its place and efforts should be made to Christianize the Africans. The belief gained ground, and when the British Navy patrolled the seas, her merchants began to trade in palm oil, gold, ivory and other goods, and Christian missionaries began to set up mission houses in the country and to build schools.

The British effort to expand its trading interest by opening up the interior of Nigeria to European free traders instead of going through middlemen at the coast in Lagos and at the Delta area created great conflicts between Nigerian traditional rulers in those places and the British, leading to British interference in the politics of the areas. In 1851, the British consul for the Bights of Benin and Biafra, John Beecroft supported the deposed Oba of Lagos,

Akitoye, to regain his throne which in 1845 had been usurped by
Kosoko who was well known for his slave-trading activities. Akitoye signed a treaty abolishing slavery in his domain, guaranteeing
missionaries freedom to carry on their activities and giving the
British special trade concessions. In the delta, when the activities
of King William Dappa Pepple were seen as interfering with the interest of British traders in the area, he was exiled in 1853.

In 1853 the British government had two consuls in Nigeria,
Beecroft for the Bight of Biafra and Benjamin Campbell for Lagos.
In 1861, the son of Akitoye, Dosumu, who succeeded his father in
1853 and who was supported by the British Consul as being the most
amenable to British interest among all the contestants for the throne
was made to cede Lagos to the British Crown and so Lagos became
a Crown Colony. From Lagos and the delta area as base, the British extended their influence further inland and began an active process of trade, missionary activity and interference in local politics.
Until the 1870's, trade in the delta area and in the interior of the
country was dominated by British merchants. However the French
soon began to offer them a serious competition. At this critical
time Nigeria was saved for the British by the activities of George
Dashwood Goldie Taubman who welded all the major companies in
the area into the United African Company (UAC) and by underselling
the French companies, forced them out of the area. He then began
a series of treaties of British protection and free trade with the local chiefs. In 1885 at the Berlin Conference, the area under the
company's influence was recognized as being under the British influence. The British later proclaimed a protectorate over the Niger
Districts from the area around the confluence of Rivers Niger and
Benue to the sea. In 1886, Britain granted the UAC which had
changed its name in 1882 to National African Company a Royal Charter and it became the Royal Niger Company. Under the charter the
company obtained political authority over the areas under its influence. In 1900 the company's charter was revoked and Nigeria,
made up of the Colony of Lagos, the Protectorate of Southern Nigeria and the Protectorate of Northern Nigeria came under direct
British rule.

From the above brief history of the British acquisition of Nigeria it is clear that Nigeria was the creation of the British imperial authorities. Furthermore, its boundaries were determined not
on the basis of community of interest between the various peoples
that inhabited the area, but rather on the basis of European economic interests and power politics. In fact the name "Nigeria"
which first appeared in the London Times in 1897 received its first
official recognition in 1899 during the debate in the House of Com-
mons on the revocation of the charter of the Royal Niger Company.

The central political problem which Nigeria has always had
to face from its very creation is that of national unity, the problem
of uniting the various groups within its borders under one administration while at the same time allowing each group a sufficient degree

of autonomy to satisfy its cultural aspirations. In 1906 the British authorities made their first effort to unite the two southern administrations: the Colony of Lagos was merged with the protectorate of southern Nigeria to become the Colony and Protectorate of Southern Nigeria. In 1914 the second major effort was made when the Colony and Protectorate of Southern Nigeria was merged with the Protectorate of Northern Nigeria becoming the Colony and Protectorate of Nigeria.

However the amalgamation of 1914 was more on paper than in reality. The administrative system that emerged was more federal than unitary for it recognized the existence of two autonomous units called the Northern Provinces and the Southern Provinces, each being the same as the former northern and southern protectorates respectively. Over each group of provinces was a Lieutenant Governor with responsibility for certain matters. Each had a separate secretariat and was required to submit a separate annual budget for incorporation into the national budget. What is most remarkable was that the north, except insofar as the national budget was concerned, was administered as a separate unit. The legislative council only legislated for the colony and the southern group of provinces while the governor continued to legislate for the north by proclamation. The only representatives of the north on the council were the Lieutenant Governor and some senior colonial officials. This isolation of the north from the south continued until 1947 when northern representatives sat side by side for the first time with southern representatives in the legislative council in Lagos.

The unity of the country has often been threatened: in 1953 over the self-government-in-1956 motion and over the Lagos issue after the 1953 constitutional conference in London; in 1964 over the federal election crisis, and in 1967 when the Eastern Region decided to secede, and declared itself the Republic of Biafra. It was won back after 30 months of civil war, and even today, 14 years after the civil war, many Nigerians still worry about the precarious nature of their unity.

Nigeria has passed through a long period of constitution making. There was the Clifford Constitution of 1922 which introduced the elective principle into the constitutional development of the country and spurred on the emergence of political parties like the National Democratic Party of Herbert Macaulay, and the establishment of nationalist newspapers like the Daily Times in 1926. In 1936 a truly Nigerian nationalist organization came into being when the Lagos Youth Movement, founded in 1934, became the Nigerian Youth Movement. But in 1941, a crisis within the movement ensued which soon made the organization moribund. In 1944, the National Council of Nigeria and the Cameroons (NCNC) was formed with Herbert Macaulay as its president and Dr. Nnamdi Azikiwe its General Secretary. In 1946 the Richards Constitution came into being, and although it conceded majority membership of elected Nigerians on the legislative council, it fell far short of the nationalist expectations and was strongly criticized by the NCNC, which sent a delegation to the Secretary of State for the colonies in London to protest the inadequacies of the constitution. Because of the failure of the constitution to meet the nationalist expectations, Macpherson Constitution followed in 1951, but in spite of the care taken in its preparation, it was crisis-ridden, especially the Eastern Regional crisis of 1953 and the self-government-in-1956 motion crisis of the same year. What, however, was important during this period was the founding of the Action Group Party (AG), led by Chief Obafemi Awolowo and the Northern People's Congress (NPC) under the leadership of Sir Ahmadu Bello, the Sardauna of Sokoto. Furthermore party government began to emerge.

As a result of the crises that took place in 1953, there was a constitutional conference in London which decided on setting up a federal system of government in 1954 made up of three regions: Northern, Eastern and Western. In 1957 both the Eastern and the Western Regions became self-governing and the Northern Region joined suit in 1959. National independence finally came in 1960 with a parliamentary system of government at the federal and regional level. In 1963 Nigeria became a republic with a ceremonial head of state. It also became a federation of four regions after the Mid-Western Region was created from the Western Region.

After the euphoria of independence was over, the country went through nerve-racking crises, beginning with the Action Group crisis of 1962, the census crisis of 1963, the federal election crisis of 1964 and the Western Regional election crisis of 1965 which finally led to the military takeover of January 15, 1966.

The military government under the command of General Aguiyi-Ironsi who became the Head of State suspended certain parts of the constitution and asserted the supreme authority of federal military government decrees over any regional edict. In May 1966 the Ironsi government issued the Unification decree which abolished the federal structure and set up a unitary system of government. Though done with good intentions, the act provoked a lot of protest and resentment especially in the northern region which saw it as a means for the south, especially the Ibo people, to dominate the country. In July 1966 another coup staged by northern elements took place in which General Ironsi was killed and General Yakubu Gowon was brought to power.

Colonel Odumegwu Ojukwu, the head of the military government in Eastern Nigeria refused to accept the authority of General Gowon because he was not the next in line to succeed Ironsi. In September of 1966, a wave of killing of people of Eastern Nigerian origin in the north swept through the area and Ibos who escaped the killing went back to the eastern region, their home of origin. This intensified the problem between the federal government in Lagos and the Eastern Nigeria Government in Enugu. When all efforts to resolve the various issues in dispute had ended in failure, the Eastern Region seceded from the federation and a civil war broke out, which lasted till January 1970 after Colonel Ojukwu had fled to the Ivory Coast where he stayed in exile until 1982.

Before the civil war began, the government of General Gowon made an important decision to divide the country into twelve states. The north was divided into six states and the south was divided into six states. The big mistake then was to preserve the old line between north and south, which in essence has helped to sustain the old dichotomy between them. However the creation of states helped in no small way to allay the fears of the minority ethnic groups who had struggled since the 1950's for their own separate states. It also freed the south of the fear of domination by the monolithic and impregnable north.

In 1975 General Gowon was overthrown, and was succeeded by General Murtala Muhammed who, within the short time of his administration, decided to increase the number of states from twelve to nineteen, move the federal capital to Abuja, purge the public services of old and incompetent officers, set up the Constitution Drafting Committee to return the nation to civilian rule and set in motion efforts to reform the local government system. Murtala Muhammed was killed in an abortive coup in February 1976, but his program to disengage the military from politics went on as planned. A new constitution was drafted, debated by the Constituent Assembly, and was approved by the military government in September 1978 to take effect from October 1, 1979. With the approval of the constitution, the ban on political activities was lifted and the contest for the 1979 elections began. Out of more than 50 political associations that sought recognition as political parties, only five of them--The National Party of Nigeria (NPN), Unity Party of Nigeria (UPN), Nigerian People's Party (NPP) Great Nigerian People's Party (GNPP) and the People's Redemption Party (PRP) were recognized by the Federal Electoral Commission (FEDECO) as fulfilling the requirement of the electoral law.

Under the 1979 constitution, Nigeria changed from a parliamentary system of government to an executive presidential system, with a popularly elected president, and a bicameral national legislature. Alhaji Shehu Shagari was declared the winner in the 1979 general elections, and was reelected in 1983 for his second and last term. He was sworn in on October 1, 1983 but on December 31, 1983 a military coup d'état, the fourth successful one in the history of Nigeria, toppled his government and brought Major General Muhammadu Buhari to power.

The new administration declared all borders closed and began to arrest and detain both federal and state governments' functionaries during the Second Republic in an effort to make them account for their stewardship. Those found clean of corruption or ill-gotten wealth were released but others were kept in detention, awaiting their trial by military tribunals set up in five different locations in the country. Those who were found guilty were sentenced to varying lengths of imprisonment. Among those who escaped to Europe and America were multimillionaires like Dr. Umaru Dikko, former Transport Minister in the Shagari administration who became the most wanted person in Nigeria, Chief Adisa Akinloye, the National Chairman of the ruling National Party of Nigeria, Chief Richard Akinjide, former Attorney General in Shagaris' administration and Dr. Joseph Wayas, the former President of the Senate.

THE DICTIONARY

ABA RIOT. The immediate cause of the riot was the belief, though mistaken, that the colonial government was ready to tax women. As far back as 1926, the government had decided that people in the Eastern Region and parts of the west who were not then paying tax should be made to pay in the form of a poll tax. This was to be levied on adult males only. But in 1929 a warrant chief by the name of Okugo of Oloko near Aba, while assessing the taxable wealth of the people of the area began to count women, children and their animals. Rumors spread that this was the beginning of the policy to tax all women. The women in Aba and Owerri divisions rose up in arms against the administration. Chiefs and Europeans were attacked and there was a lot of destruction of property and goods belonging mainly to expatriate trading firms. As the riot grew in intensity and expanse, the police were asked to open fire, leaving over 30 persons dead and many more wounded.

Two commissions of inquiry were set up to look into the causes of the riot. The first, an official one, tended to exonerate the officials involved. But the second one which included two Nigerian barristers was critical of the way the administration handled the uprising. It attributed the causes of the riot to: the low prices received by the people for their farm produce and the high prices they had to pay for imported ones; discontent arising from the taxation of men; and the persecution, corruption and extortion practiced by the native court members; and finally to the belief that government was about to impose tax on women. The Secretary of State for the Colonies accepted the second report and blamed the riot on faulty intelligence. According to him the government had insufficient knowledge of the indigenous institutions and the life of the people.

ABAYOMI, SIR KOFOWOROLA ADEKUNLE. An eye specialist and a politician. Born on July 10, 1896 in Lagos. He attended the University of Edinburgh and the Moorefield's Eye Hospital in London where he specialized in ophthalmology. He returned to Nigeria in 1930 and set up a private practice which he combined with politics.

In 1933 he was a foundation member of the Lagos Youth Movement (LYM) which later became the Nigerian Youth Movement (NYM), the first truly Nationalist Organization. In 1938, he took over the Presidency of NYM after the death of Dr. J.C.

Vaughan. In the same year he was elected as an NYM member to the Legislative Council in Lagos. After serving for two years, he resigned and went to Britain for further studies. He later served in many public positions including: Yaba Higher College Advisory Board and the Board of Medical Examiners; he was a member of the University College of Ibadan Council up to 1961. He was the President of Nigeria's Society for the Blind in 1948. He was made the Chairman of the University Teaching Hospital Board in 1951; and in 1964, he was the Chairman of the Federal Electoral Commission but resigned a few months later. He died in January 1979.

ABDULLAHI BAYERO COLLEGE, KANO. Formerly known as Ahmadu Bello College, Kano, it was set up in 1960 by the Northern Regional Ministry of Education to prepare high school graduates for advanced level General Certificate of Education (G. C. E. A Level) in Arabic, Islamic History, Hausa and English. In 1962 the Ahmadu Bello College became incorporated into the new University of Zaria, Ahmadu Bello University (ABU) and it changed its name to Abdullahi Bayero College, named after the former Emir of Kano, Abdullahi Bayero. Thus the post-secondary courses offered by the college became preliminary courses for entry into ABU. The college grew as a center for Arabic and Islamic studies and in 1969 the center for Hausa studies was established in it. In 1975, it became a full-fledged University known as Bayero University, Kano, owned and financed by the federal government.

ABDUSALAMI. The first Fulani Emir of Ilorin about 1824 to 1830. His father Alimi, a Fulani muslim priest, had helped Afonja, the Yoruba ruler of Ilorin to fight for Ilorin's independence from the Alaafin of Oyo. Later on Afonja's troops, mostly Hausas and Fulanis, revolted against him and Abdusalami seized power and was recognized as an Emir by Muhammed Bello, who was then at the head of the Fulani Empire in Sokoto. He died about 1830.

ABEOKUTA. The capital city of Ogun State since 1976, it is located about 106 kilometers north of Lagos, the federal capital, and about 80 kilometers southwest of Ibadan, capital of Oyo State. Abeokuta was said to have been founded in 1830 by one Sodeke who led a party of refugees fleeing from Ibadan during the Yoruba intertribal wars. Abeokuta, meaning in Yoruba language "under the rock" derived its name from the cave dwellings of the Egba refugees under huge overhanging rocks. Later on, new groups of refugees from different parts of the Yoruba land followed them. At Abeokuta the refugees were kept together in separate communities and in different parts of the area. This explains why today there are many towns within the city of Abeokuta and why each has its own traditional ruler. The various towns in Abeokuta are Ibara, Ijaiye, Owu, Oke-Ona, Gbagura while the traditional rulers are Alake of Abeokuta, the Oshile of Oke-Ona, Agura of Gbagura, Olowu of Owu and

the Olubara of Ibara.   However because of the belief that the
first Alake was the first settler in Abeokuta, the Alake has
been given a central position among the Obas.
　　　　The people of Abeokuta have been prominent in the acquisition of western-type education.   They came in contact with
white missionaries as early as 1842 who began the process of
educating Nigerians.   In 1846, Mr. and Mrs. Townsend and
Rev. Ajayi Crowther a Nigerian clergyman went to the town
and were given three acres of land at Ake for their first church.
Abeokuta was the home of the first secondary grammar school
in Western Nigeria; the Abeokuta Grammar School opened in
1908.   However in spite of this early acceptance of Western education, Abeokuta was for decades a depressed area.   Things
began to change rapidly when the city became the capital of the
newly created Ogun State in 1976.

ABIKU.   "Abiku" in Yoruba language means "Born-to-die."   It has
　　　an Ibo equivalent "Ogbanje."   In Yorubaland Abiku children are
believed to belong to a group of evil spirits that live in the
woods.   When each is coming to the world, he is believed to
have arranged beforehand when he would come back to join his
comrades.   In Iboland, the belief is that a wicked spirit takes
the form of a child.   Consequently the child dies and even
though he is constantly being reborn, he dies again.   In Yorubaland, parents sometimes resort to charms to thwart the plans
of the children so that they may not die again.   Some children
are given some marks below the eyes; these are not the same
as "tribal" marks which are on both cheeks.
　　　　Abiku appears to be the explanation for the unknown
disease of sickle-cell anemia.

ABIODUN.   Said to be the last great ruler of the Oyo empire, he
　　　ruled 1770-1789.   Abiodun deposed Gaha, the Basorun (head
of the Council of State known as Oyomesi) who himself had deposed other rulers of Oyo empire.   During his reign there was
peace, and trade flourished.   But the army declined during the
period for it was defeated in 1783 by the Borgu Army.   He
died in 1789 and Oyo empire rapidly declined afterwards.

ABIOLA, MOSHOOD KASHIMAWO OLAWALE.   A chartered account-
　　　ant, born on August 24, 1937 in Abeokuta, Ogun State.   He
was educated at the Baptist Boys' High School, Abeokuta, and
later proceeded to the University of Glasgow in Scotland to
study accountancy in 1961.   In 1965 he became deputy chief
accountant of the University of Lagos Teaching Hospital and
in 1967 he became the controller of the Pfizer Products Ltd.
In 1969 he was the Comptroller of the International Telephone
and Telegraph (Nigeria) (Limited) (ITT).   He was later appointed vice-president of the ITT for Africa and the Middle-
East and also Chairman and Chief Executive of the ITT Nigeria
Limited in 1971.
　　　　Chief Abiola became very wealthy, but rather than use
his wealth for personal aggrandizement, he used it for

philanthropic purposes like donating and building public institutions and community development efforts, opening up educational institutions and other such activities. He is popularly known for his philanthropic efforts.

When the ban on politics was lifted in 1978, Chief Abiola became a member of the National Party of Nigeria (NPN), a true believer of its objectives and its methods of uniting the country, especially giving every major or minor ethnic group a share in the national decision making through the system of zoning. He set up the Concord Press of Nigeria Ltd., the publisher of the National and Sunday Concord and Isokan, a Yoruba counterpart.

In July 1982, Chief Abiola became disillusioned when his aspiration to become the NPN presidential candidate for the 1983 elections was thwarted. He said he could no longer interact in the party where he could not contest his right. He resigned from the NPN and from all partisan politics.

ABOYADE TECHNICAL COMMITTEE ON REVENUE ALLOCATION.
Set up in June 1977 to examine the then existing revenue allocation formula with a view to determining its adequacy in the light of the factors of population, equality of status among the states, derivation, geographical peculiarities, even development, national interest and any other factors bearing on the problem. The committee was to recommend new proposals for the allocation of revenue between the federal, state and local governments, and make recommendations on measures necessary for effective collection and distribution of the federal and state revenues.

The committee rejected the old principles of revenue allocation which it found either as politically controversial or as lacking in statistically concise definitions, and suggested new principles of allocating federally derived revenue. These were equality of access to development opportunities, national minimum standards for national integration, absorptive capacity, independent revenue and minimum tax effort, and fiscal efficiency. It also recommended that 30 percent of the federally derived revenue should be shared among the states and 10 percent be shared among the local governments.

The report was accepted by the federal military government but was rejected by the civilian government that succeeded it in 1979 on the basis that it was too technical and out of tune with the present political realities. As a result of this when Alhaji Shehu Shagari became President, he set up another revenue allocation commission known as the Okigbo Commission. (q. v.)

ABURI MEETING. A meeting of the Supreme Military Council of Nigeria between January 4 and 5, 1967 at Aburi, Ghana, under the auspices of the Ghanaian Head of State, General Ankrah, when the conflict between the federal military government headed by General Yakubu Gowon and the former Eastern Regional government, headed by Lieutenant Colonel Odumegwu Ojukwu could not be amicably resolved.

The meeting agreed to renounce the use of force for settling conflicts between the two sides, and to reorganize the armed forces. The army was to be governed by the Supreme Military Council, the Chairman of which would be known as Commander-in-Chief and Head of the Federal Military Government. There would be a military headquarters with equal representation from each of the regions, and headed by a Chief of Staff. Each region was to be constituted into an area command under an Area Commander. The personnel of the Area Command was to be drawn wholly from the people of the region and as long as military rule lasted, Military Governors were to have control over internal security in their respective areas. Furthermore all matters of policy including appointments and promotions of persons in executive posts in the armed forces and police were to be dealt with by the Supreme Military Council.

They also agreed that all decisions on matters affecting the whole country would be determined by the Supreme Military Council with the concurrence of every member of the council; they agreed to set up a committee to look into the problem of rehabilitating displaced persons and recovering their property. Civil servants who had left their posts because of the disturbances should continue to receive their normal salary until the end of March 1967 provided they had not found alternative jobs.

Finally, all appointments to diplomatic and consular posts, and to senior posts in the armed forces and the police, together with those carrying superscale salaries in the federal civil service and federal corporations required the approval of the Supreme Military Council.

These agreements were important for at least two reasons: the agreement that a region should constitute an area command under the control of the regional Military Governor in internal security gave the Military Governor of the Eastern Region control over the military unit in his area. Secondly, by introducing the principle of unanimity in decision making on matters that concerned the whole country, the Military Governors were each granted a veto power which was tantamount to a regional veto.

As was expected, interpretations of these provisions differed on both sides and there could be no agreement in carrying them out. The decree supposedly issued to implement the agreements was rejected by Colonel Ojukwu and from then on relations between the two sides worsened, leading progressively to the civil war.

ACHEBE CHINUA. A writer, born in November 1930 at Ogidi, near Onitsha in Anambra State where his father was teaching at a mission school. He received his secondary education in Umuahia, in Imo State and he later went to the University College, Ibadan. In 1954 he became a producer of the Nigerian Broadcasting Corporation in Lagos and in 1959, he was the regional controller of the Enugu Station of the Corporation. In 1961 he became the first Director of the Corporations External Broadcasting Service known then as the "Voice of Nigeria," in Lagos.

In 1967 he became a Senior Research Fellow at the University of Nigeria, Nsukka. During the Nigerian civil war, he supported the Biafran cause. In 1971 he became the director of African Studies at the University of Nigeria, Enugu Branch, as well as the editor of a literary journal, Okike.

In 1972 he was a visiting professor of English at the University of Massachusetts at Amherst, and in 1975 he was at the University of Connecticut at Storrs. Upon his return to Nigeria, he was appointed professor of English at the University of Nigeria Nsukka. At the same time he was Director of the Heinemann Educational Books Nigeria Limited.

Professor Achebe has written many books among which are Things Fall Apart (1958), No Longer at Ease (1960), Arrow of God (1964), A Man of the People (1966), Chike and the River (1966), How the Leopard Got His Claws (1973) and Morning Yet on Creation Day (1975).

For his literary achievement he was the recipient of many national and international honors and awards including the Nigerian National Trophy (1961), the Jock Campbell New Statesman Award (1965), the Commonwealth Poetry Prize (1972), honorary fellowship of the Modern Language Association of America (1974), honorary doctorate degrees of the University of Stirling in Scotland and University of Southampton, England in 1974. In 1975 he won the Lotus International Prize for Afro-Asian Writers and the Neill International Prize of the Scottish Arts Council in 1975. He was also an honorary fellow of the Ghana Association of Writers. Professor Achebe was a member of the People's Redemption Party (PRP) and the Deputy National President of the party in 1983.

ACHUZIE, COLONEL JOE "HANNIBAL." A Biafran soldier who before the Biafran War ran an electrical business in Port-Harcourt. During the war, he played a leading role in the recapture of Owerri from the federal troops and was said to have inspired great fear and respect in his men.

ACTION GROUP CRISIS OF 1962. The crisis originated partly from the fact that Chief Obafemi Awolowo surrendered the premiership of the Western Region to a deputy whom he did not like to see suceed him and partly from his failure, contrary to his expectations, to secure enough seats in the federal parliament in 1959 to become the first Prime Minister of an independent Nigeria. This failure reduced him to continuing as the National President of the party and leader of the opposition in the federal parliament in Lagos. As party leader Chief Awolowo believed that he should exercise power of supervision over all the activities of the Action Group including those under the authority of the government of Western Region. He asked that he should be duly consulted before major changes in policy and major appointments should be made. Chief S. L. Akintola, his Deputy, and Premier of the Western Region bitterly resented this.

Other areas of disagreement included the question of

whether or not the Action Group should join in a National Government which the Prime Minister Alhaji Tafawa Balewa believed would strengthen national unity, but which would considerably limit the Action Group opposition to the NCNC and the NPC in their own regions. Even though Chief Akintola supported the idea, Chief Awolowo did not like it. He would prefer the formation of a progressive alliance that would dislodge the Northern People's Congress from its grip on the north. He therefore wanted a policy of collaborating with the NCNC with the hope that more states would be created in the north.

On an ideological basis, the two men were not in agreement. Chief Awolowo supported the ideology of democratic socialism while he, as the Coker Commission of Inquiry showed, allowed party leaders close to him to amass wealth. Chief Akintola would prefer to leave things as they were for the time being. Finally there was the undying belief of Chief Awolowo that Chief Akintola wanted to supplant him as the party leader. This Chief Awolowo regarded as perfidy.

The crisis came to a head at the party Congress in Jos, Plateau State in February 1962. Because Alhaji Sir Ahmadu Bello, Premier of the Northern Region, was then visiting Ibadan, the capital of Western Nigeria, Chief Akintola and some of his close associates left the Congress to give a courtesy reception to the Northern Premier. After Chief Akintola's departure, the Congress decided to amend the party constitution to exclude regional ministers from membership in the Federal Executive Council of the party and to provide for the removal of any parliamentary leader by the body that put him in office. At the Congress, Awolowo's supporters gained control of the party and they began to move to oust Chief Akintola. In spite of several "peace" efforts to reconcile the two leaders and their factions, and in spite of the public apology of Chief Akintola to the party, Awolowo was determined to press the issue to a definite conclusion. On May 19, 1962, at a joint meeting of the Western and Mid-Western Regional Executive Committee, Chief Akintola was asked by a vote of 81 to 29, to tender his resignation as Premier of the region and as deputy leader of the party. This decision was later confirmed by the Federal Executive Committee. Consequently, Chief Akintola was deposed as deputy leader of the party and since he would not voluntarily resign from the post of Premier, the Governor of the region was asked to remove him. This he did when he received a petition signed by 65 members of the House of Assembly out of a total of 117 members purporting to say that they no longer had confidence in the Premier. To replace him Alhaji D. S. Adegbenro was appointed as Premier. But Chief Akintola argued that the only vote that could remove him from office was a majority vote in the House of Assembly, and so he went to court.

On May 25 Alhaji D. S. Adegbenro summoned a meeting of the House of Assembly and requested for a vote of confidence in his new government. But suddenly a member began to throw chairs and there was disorder in the House. Police dispersed them with tear gas. Both sides had telephone conversations with the Prime Minister of the Federation in Lagos who acknowledged the right of the House to meet but refused to provide police protection within the Chamber, and said that the federal government would not accept any decisions reached in the course of their deliberations if the police guarded them. Later when fighting again broke out in the house, the "honorable" members were dispersed and the House was locked up. Later a meeting of the Federal Parliament was summoned for May 29. At its meeting, a motion was carried that a state of public emergency existed in the region. Existing emergency regulations then came into operation while some others were passed. The federal government appointed Dr. M. A. Majekodunmi who at the time was a Senator and the Federal Minister of Health to administer the affairs of the region for six months. Immediately he assumed office, the governor, premier, ministers and other government officials were removed from office. Leaders of both factions were detained in various places but Chief Akintola and his supporters were released in less than two months, giving rise to the accusation that the administrator and the federal government were not evenhanded. As the emergency period passed by, the Supreme Court in July ruled that the ex-governor of the Western Region had acted unconstitutionally when he removed Chief Akintola as Premier without a vote of no confidence being passed on the floor of the House of Assembly. Furthermore in December the Coker Commission of Inquiry set up by the federal government during the period to look into the affairs of statutory corporations in the Western Region reported. It found incidence of malpractices and illegal syphoning of money to the Action Group Party with the knowledge of the party President. But it exonerated Chief Akintola from any blame. Before this report was released, however, the police unearthed an alleged plot to overthrow the federal government. The plot involved some top members of the Action Group, some of whom had fled the country. Sam Ikoku, the National Secretary of the party went to Ghana. Chief Anthony Enahoro, the second Vice-President of the party and a member of the tactical committee sought asylum in Britain but was later brought back into the country, tried and sentenced. Chief Awolowo and many of his followers were found guilty and sentenced to varying terms of imprisonment. Chief Awolowo was given 10 years. In December 1962 the Prime Minister, seeing that the Action Group party members in the House of Representatives had dwindled from 75 to 20, declared that he would no longer recognize Chief Awolowo as leader of the opposition. When the emergency administration came to an end on January 1, 1963 Chief Akintola was reinstated as Premier of the region, leading a coalition of his own faction which had then formed itself into United People's Party and the NCNC whose parliamentary leader was Chief R. A. Fani-Kayode, popularly known then as "Fani-Power," who became the Deputy Premier. At this juncture only 38 of the 82 members of the party in the regional house remained loyal to the Action Group

Party under the leadership of Alhaji Adegbenro who then became the leader of opposition. But when in May 1963 the Judicial Committee of the Privy Council in London, to which appeals from the Supreme Court in Nigeria lay, accepted the appeal of Adegbenro against Akintola and reversed the Supreme Court decision, the Western Regional House of Assembly hurriedly amended the regional constitution retroactively, that the Premier could not be removed without a vote of no confidence in the House of Assembly. The Federal Parliament endorsed this amendment and abolished all appeals from thenceforth to the Privy Council.

ACTION GROUP PARTY (AG). A party formed in March 1950 by Chief Obafemi Awolowo. At the meeting during which it was formed, eight members including the founder were present, and they decided to name it "Action Group" (a group that was disciplined and that meant action, not words). It operated in secret for a whole year after which it was publicly launched on March 21, 1951. Its aims were

1. To bring and organize within its fold all nationalists in the former Western Region so that they might work together as a united and disciplined group and
2. To prepare and present to the public, programs for all government departments and to work hard to see them carried out.

Its undeclared aim was to capture political power in the Western Region under the electoral system that was to operate under the 1951 constitution.

Its slogan was "Freedom for All and Life More Abundant." According to them there was freedom for all when colonial rule was terminated; and there was life more abundant when there was education for all school-age children and general enlightenment of all illiterate adults. Furthermore there was life more abundant when there was provision of health and general welfare for all, and total abolition of want in the society. Between 1951 and 1957, the party had become firmly established in the Western Region. Having become secure in its own region, the AG turned its mind to winning the federal government election of 1959. This it failed to do. The net effect of this was that Chief Awolowo became leader of opposition in the Federal Parliament while he reluctantly agreed that the Deputy Leader of the Party Chief S. L. Akintola should become the Premier of the Western Region.

In 1962 a crisis ensued during which Chief Akintola was removed from the positions of Premier and Deputy Leader of the party. After the state of emergency in the Western Region and Chief Akintola's United People's Party was installed in government, the AG became the opposition party under the leadership of Alhaji D. S. Adegbenro. In 1964 the party went into an alliance with the National Council of Nigerian Citizens (NCNC) and formed themselves into the United Progressive Grand

Alliance (UPGA) to fight for the 1964 general elections. There were too many reports of election malpractices but in the end Nigerian National Alliance (NNA) made up of the Northern Peoples Congress (NPC) and Nigerian National Democratic Party (NNDP) was declared the winner. People, especially in the Western Region, the stronghold of the Action Group, hoped to deal a death blow to the Akintola's NNDP party in the October regional election of 1965 but it came and was more brazenly rigged than ever before. The people then took the law into their hands and there was a serious breakdown of law and order. On January 15, 1966 the army came into power and by Decree Number 34 of 1966 the Action Group and all other political parties were banned.

ADEBAYO, MAJOR-GENERAL ROBERT ADEYINKA. Born in 1928 in Ile-Ife, Oyo State but his hometown is Iyin-Ekiti, Ondo State. He was educated at Christ's School, Ado-Ekiti and at Eko Boys' High School, Lagos.

He was enlisted in the Nigerian Army in 1948. He attended various military courses both in Ghana and in Britain. He served in the Congo under the United Nations Peace-Keeping Force between 1961 and 1963. Between 1964 and 1965, he was Chief of Staff of the Nigerian Army. In August 1966, he was appointed the Military Governor of Western Nigeria after the death of Adekunle Fajuyi in the July 1966 coup. After the civil war, he was the chairman of the commission that was established to look into the conduct of all officers who fought on the Biafran side with a view to readmitting into the Nigeria army those who were not involved in the mutiny or convicted of any sadistic behavior. In 1971 he was posted to head the Defence Academy at Kaduna with promotion as Major-General. He was retired from the army in August 1975 by the late General Murtala Muhammed's regime.

After the ban on political activities was lifted in 1978, he joined the National Party of Nigeria (NPN) and became the National Vice-Chairman of the party.

ADEBOLA, ALHAJI HAROUN POPOOLA. A trade unionist, born on October 1, 1916 at Ijebu-Ode, Ogun State. After his primary education, he went to Abeokuta Grammar School and Ijebu-Ode Grammar School. He joined the Nigerian Railway Corporation in 1941 and became an elected member of the Western House of Assembly between 1952 and 1954. In 1959 he was elected President of the Nigerian Union of Railway Staff and in 1960 he was President of the Trade Union Congress of Nigeria. In 1962 he became the President of the United Labor Congress of Nigeria, a position he occupied till 1969. He was a member of the Western House of Chiefs from 1963 to 1965 and was Vice-President of the International Confederation of Free Trade Union (ICFTU) from 1965 to 1970. In 1977 he was nominated to serve on the Constitution Drafting Committee.

ADEBO, SIMEON OLAOSEBIKAN (CMG). A lawyer and a diplomat. Born on October 5, 1913 in Abeokuta, capital of Ogun State, he attended St. Peter's Day School in Abeokuta, and Abeokuta Grammar School, and finished his secondary education in King's College in Lagos in 1932. In 1933 he became a clerk at the Nigerian Railway Corporation. He later in 1945 went to study law in London and was called to the Bar at Gray's Inn in 1948. Upon his return to Nigeria he became an administrative officer and rose to become the permanent secretary in the Ministry of Finance Western Region from 1957-1959 and in the Treasury from 1959-1960. He became Head of the Civil Service and Chief Secretary to the government of Western Nigeria in 1961. In 1962 he was appointed Permanent Representative of Nigeria to the United Nations in New York, USA. In 1968 he was made the United Nations Under-Secretary-General and Executive Director of the UN Institute for Training and Research. After the civil war in 1970 he was appointed Chairman of the salary review commission known as Adebo Salary Review Commission. The Commission granted interim salary increases to the workers to offset the effect of the inflation that followed the civil war. In 1973 he became Chairman, National Universities Commission but resigned in 1979 when he was appointed Chairman of the National Institute of Policy and Strategic Studies of Nigeria.

ADEDEJI, ADEBAYO. Professor Adebayo Adedeji was born on December 21, 1930 at Ijebu-Ode, Ogun State. He attended Ijebu-Ode Grammar School and later the University College, Ibadan 1953-1954 and then went to Leicester University in Britain 1955-1958 where he took a B. Sc. degree in Economics. He returned home and became an Assistant Secretary in the Ministry of Economic Planning in Western Nigeria 1958 to 1960. He then went to Harvard University (1960-1961) where he received a Masters degree in Public Administration. He later returned to Nigeria as Principal Secretary (Revenue) at the Treasury Department of the Ministry of Finance in Western Nigeria. In 1963 he joined the University of Ife as Deputy Director, Institute of Administration and in 1967 he became the Director of the Institute. In 1968 he was made Professor of Public Administration, University of Ife. In 1971 he became the Federal Commissioner for Economic Development and Reconstruction and in June 1975 he left the service of the federal government to become the Executive Secretary, United Nations Economic Commission for Africa (ECA).

Professor Adedeji is the author of many articles and books. He edited the Nigerian Administration and its Political Setting (1968), Problems and Techniques of Administrative Training in Africa (1969) and Nigerian Local Government Finance; Development Problems and Prospects.

ADEDOYIN, PRINCE ADELEKE. A politician born on March 3, 1912 in Lagos, he attended the Methodist Boys' High School in Lagos. He later studied law and was called to the bar at the Inner

Temple in 1940. In 1942 he was appointed as magistrate, first
in Lagos and later transferred to Ikot-Ekpene in Eastern Nigeria. He was also then appointed Commissioner of the Supreme Court and was put in charge of many towns in the Eastern Region. He resigned his appointment in 1944 to enter into
politics. In 1947, he became a member of the Lagos Town
Council and in the same year was elected as member of the
legislative council under the Richards Constitution. In the same
year he was the Secretary of the National Council of Nigeria
and Cameroon (NCNC) and was one of the party's pan-Nigerian
delegation to London to protest against the Richards Constitution
of 1946 and to demand self-government for the country. In
1951 he was elected into the Western House of Assembly on the
platform of the NCNC and in 1952 he was elected from the
Western House of Assembly to the House of Representatives in
Lagos. However by 1956 he had changed his party allegiance
and was elected into the Western House of Assembly as an Action Group member. In 1957 he became the Speaker in the
Western House of Assembly. In the 1960 Western Regional
election he was also elected and kept his position as Speaker.
He was in this post during the Action Group crisis of 1962,
but during it he joined the Akintola faction which later formed
itself into the Nigerian National Democratic Party (NNDP). In
1964 he was elected on the platform of this party into the Federal House of Representatives. After the military came to
power in 1966, little was heard of him until the ban on politics
was lifted in 1978. He then became one of the foundation members of the National Party of Nigeria. He contested the national chairmanship of the party but lost to Chief A. M. A. Akinloye.

ADEGBENRO, ALHAJI DAUDA SOROYE. A politician, born at Ago-
Owu, Abeokuta in 1909 in Ogun State, he was educated at the
Baptist Boys' High School, Abeokuta and Abeokuta Grammar
School. He worked for the Nigerian Railway 1930-1937, United
African Company (UAC) 1937-1940 and rejoined the railway in
1943. He became a businessman in 1945 and remained there
till 1951 when he was elected as an Action Group (AG) member
into the Western House of Assembly. As member of the House
he held many ministerial appointments, including Minister of
Lands and Housing and Minister of Local Government. During
the Action Group crisis of 1962 he was chosen to replace Chief
S. L. Akintola as Premier of Western Nigeria, but the declaration of a state of emergency in the region by the federal government, and the appointment of an Administrator prevented
him from acting in that position. In 1963 when Chief Akintola
was reinstated in power as Premier of the region, Alhaji Adegbenro became the leader of the opposition, a post he occupied
until 1966. In 1967 when the military decided on inviting civilians into their administration, Alhaji Adegbenro was appointed
Commissioner for the Ministry of Trade and Industry until 1971.
Since then he remained a private citizen in Abeokuta,
where he died in 1975.

ADEKUNLE, BRIGADIER BENJAMIN MAJA ADESANYA. A retired soldier born on June 26, 1937, he was educated at Dekina Primary School and Government College, Okene 1951-1957. He enlisted in the army and was sent to the Officer Cadet Training School at Teshie in Accra in 1958. In 1959 he proceeded to the Officer Cadet Training School, Aldershot, England and thence to Sandhurst Military Academy in England in 1960 and 1961. He was aide-de-camp to the Governor of Eastern Nigeria from 1962 to 1963. Between 1964 and 1965 he was at the Defence Services Staff College, Wellington, in India. He was promoted to Adjutant-General, Nigerian Army in 1966 and became a Brigade Commander in 1967. During the civil war he commanded the 3rd Marine Commando which made seaborne assaults on Bonny and the Mid-West early in the war. Under him the third Marine Commando had some spectacular successes by taking Calabar, Port Harcourt, Aba and Owerri.

Brigadier Adekunle was seen as a man with the great talent of getting things done. After the war, this talent was again put to use when he was appointed by the government to relieve the congestion at the Lagos ports, a task which again he accomplished with great success. Brigadier Adekunle is said to have inspired great respect and fear in his men during the war. He was otherwise known as the "Black Scorpion," a name given to him as a result of his brilliant performance on the war front. He was retired from the Nigerian Army in 1975. When the ban on political activities was lifted in 1978 he identified himself with the Nigerian People's Party (NPP). But he has since left the party to join the National Party of Nigeria (NPN).

ADELABU, ALHAJI ADEGOKE ODUOLA AKANDE. A politician born in 1915 in Ibadan, the capital of Oyo State. He had his elementary education at the Mapo Central School, Ibadan and later went to Ibadan Government College in 1931 on government scholarship and graduated from there in 1935. He went from there to Yaba Higher College in Lagos, which then was the highest educational institution in the whole country, under the United African Company (UAC) scholarship. He did not complete his studies there, for in June 1935 he returned to Ibadan and was appointed secretary to the UAC Regional Manager and became in 1936 an Assistant Produce Manager. In 1939 he resigned his appointment and joined the Union of Cooperative Societies as Produce Inspector. He later came back in 1945 to the UAC where he was appointed as Assistant Production Manager in Lagos. By this time he was becoming keenly interested in politics and he decided to leave the UAC for good in 1946. In 1951 he joined the National Council of Nigeria and Cameroons (NCNC) under the leadership of Dr. Nnamdi Azikiwe. He was then elected the party's Assistant Secretary for Western Nigeria from which he later rose to be the first National Vice-President and a member of the party's Executive Committee. In the 1951 elections to the Regional House of Assembly the NCNC won the majority, but owing to the practice of carpet

crossing begun then by some members of his party the Action
Group Party (AG) became the majority party and the NCNC became the opposition party in the House. In 1954 he was elected
to the Federal House of Representatives in Lagos and was appointed Minister of Natural Resources and Social Services in
the national government under Alahaji Sir Abubakar Tafawa Balewa. He was also elected to the Ibadan District Council where
he became the Chairman, thus holding two public posts. In
1956 he resigned from both posts following allegations of administrative irregularities in the Ibadan City Council but he
was reelected into the Western House of Assembly where he
again became the leader of the opposition.

He was a good orator and a hardworking politician. He
was very popular in Ibadan. He led the Western Nigeria NCNC
to the Constitutional Conference in London in 1957 but on March
23, 1958, he died in a motor accident. Because of the circumstances surrounding his death, his supporters believed that his
political enemies had a hand in his death and they went into
rioting, later known as the Adelabu Riot.

ADELE II, ADENIJI, OBA OF LAGOS. Born in 1893, Oba Adeniji
Adele was the grandson of Adele I who reigned as Oba of Lagos
before Lagos was ceded to the British in 1861. He attended
the Church Missionary Society (CMS) Grammar School in Lagos
and later worked as a surveyor for the colonial government.
As a surveyor he travelled to different parts of the country.
During the First World War, he volunteered for service and
was with the Royal Engineers in the Cameroons from 1914 to
1915. He later worked in the government service in various
capacities, while he was working in Kano as Provincial Treasurer
in 1949, he was nominated as Oba of Lagos, but he was not
crowned until three years later as there were challenges to his
nomination. In 1952 he became a member of the Western House
of Chiefs, for at that time until 1954, Lagos administratively
was part of Western Nigeria. He was at the same time the
President of the Lagos Town Council under the 1953 Local
Government Law. He died in 1964 and was succeeded by Oba
Oyekan.

ADEMOLA, SIR ADETOKUNBO ADEGBOYEGA. Retired Chief Justice of the Supreme Court of Nigeria, Sir Adetokunbo Ademola
was born on September 1, 1906 at Abeokuta, Ogun State. The
son of Oba Ademola II, he received his education at St. Gregory's Grammar School and King's College, all in Lagos. He
later proceeded to the University of Cambridge, England to
study law and was called to the bar at the Middle Temple in
London in 1934. Between 1934 and 1935 he was a crown counsel, but later went into private legal practice. He was made
a magistrate in 1939 and became a judge in 1949. In 1955 he
was appointed Chief Justice of Western Nigeria and in 1958 he
became Chief Justice of the Federal Republic of Nigeria from
which position he retired due to health reasons in 1975.

Sir Adetokunbo Ademola played many important roles in

the politics of Nigeria after independence and during the First Republic. In the Action Group crisis of 1962 (q. v.) during which Chief S. L. Akintola was removed as premier of Western Nigeria, he presided over the court cases that emanated from the crisis. He also featured prominently in the effort to bring together the two factions into which the Action Group had been divided by merging the two then existing Yoruba Cultural groups --Egbe Omo Oduduwa and Egbe Omo Yoruba into Egbe Omo Olofin. Also in January 1965 during the election crisis, when the President refused to call on Sir Abubakar Tafawa Balewa to form a new government, Sir Adetokunbo Ademola was then quietly mediating between the President and the Prime Minister until the President finally decided to perform his constitutional duty. Again in May 1967, in an effort to avoid military confrontation between the federal government and the Eastern Region which was itching for a secession, Sir Adetokunbo Ademola was one of the people who convened the National Reconciliation Committee which sent a delegation to Lt. Col. Ojukwu in Enugu to attend the next Committee meeting in order to discuss pressing problems and ensure that the country did not disintegrate.

In addition to these mediating roles he was also called upon to serve the nation on many important occasions. He was Chairman of the Federal Census Board from 1972 and it was under his chairmanship that the ill-fated 1973 census was conducted. It was later cancelled in 1975 by the regime of Murtala Muhammed because it did not command general acceptance. In 1976 he was Chancellor, University of Nigeria, Nsukka. He won many foreign honors including the Knight Commander of the Order of the British Empire in 1957 and in 1963 he was made the Queen's Privy Councillor.

ADEMOLA II, OBA SIR LADIPO SAMUEL, THE ALAKE OF ABEO-
KUTA. Born to Oba Ademola I in the Ake palace in Abeokuta in September 1872, Oba Ademola II received his education at Igbore and Ikereku schools and later at St. Paul's School, Breadfruit Street in Lagos. After being in business for some time, he became a printing apprentice to Mr. Richard Beale Olamilege Blaize, before going back into business. In 1920 after the death of Oba Gbadebo, Prince Ademola was chosen as the Alake of Abeokuta, and crowned on September 27, 1920. It was during his time that Abeokuta celebrated the 100th anniversary of its founding in 1930. In 1937 he was awarded the Commander of the British Empire (CBE) and in 1937 he attended the coronation of King George VI of England.

In 1948, there were riots by market women organized by Mrs. Funmilayo Ransome Kuti (q. v.), wife of Reverend J. Ransome Kuti. As a result of this, the Alake was forced into exile for some years. Later when peace had returned, he was allowed to come back into the city and he ruled with greater support of his people. He died in 1962.

ADEREMI I, OBA ADESOJI TADENIAWO. A traditional ruler born

on November 15, 1889 in Ile-Ife, Oyo State, he belonged to
the Oshinkola ruling house, one of the four ruling houses in
Ile-Ife. Sir Adesoji Aderemi was one of the first pupils to
enter the first school in Ile-Ife, St. Phillips, in 1901. Leaving the school in 1907, and being unable then to enter the secondary school of his choice, he began to attend evening schools
in Lagos, where he was working on the staff of the Nigeria
Railway and he also took correspondence courses from overseas. By 1925, he had become a businessman. He was so
successful that by 1927 he was being called "Obalola" or "king-
to-be."

When the ruling Oba died on June 24, 1930, Oba Aderemi vied for the throne and he got it. On August 23, 1930,
the Governor of Nigeria assented to the choice of the kingmak-
ers and he became Oni-Elect. On September 2, 1930 he was
installed and crowned as the Oni of Ife.

Sir Adesoji Aderemi was a modernizer. He modernized
many of the traditional customs in Ile-Ife and saw to the economic and social development of the town. In 1932 he founded
the Oduduwa College, the first secondary school in the whole
of Ife Division. In 1934 he founded the Ife Central School and
in 1938 the Origbo Central School, two primary schools meant
to supply students to Oduduwa College. From then to his passing away on July 1, 1980, Ife Division abounded with numerous
high schools and primary schools and the town is blessed with
the prestigeous University of Ife which was opened in 1962.

Oba Aderemi played an important role in the politics of
Nigeria. When the Richards Constitution came into existence
in 1946, Oba Aderemi became a member of the Nigerian Legislative Council in 1947. In 1948, he attended the African Conference in London and in the same year he hosted the conference at which Egbe Omo Oduduwa was founded. (This Egbe
later became the nucleus of the Action Group Party.) Between
1951 and 1954 he was a member of the House of Representatives
in Lagos where he was a Minister without portfolio. In 1953
he led the Nigerian delegation to the coronation of Queen Elizabeth II and in the same year he was a delegate to the Nigerian
Constitutional Conference in London, and all later ones in Nigeria, in 1954 and in London in 1957 and 1958. Between 1954
and 1960 he was President of the Western House of Chiefs.
In 1960 he became the first Nigerian Governor of the Western
Region of Nigeria but was suspended from office in 1962 when
a state of emergency was declared in the region during the
Action Group crisis. From then to his death he became what
he himself called "an elder statesman playing the role of adviser in many aspects of the nation's administration."

During his 50-year reign, Oba Aderemi was showered
with many honors. In 1943 he was awarded the Companion of
the Order of St. Michael and St. George (CMG) for his sound
common sense, his statesmanlike ability and his invaluable advice to the British Chief Commissioner. In 1950 he was
awarded Knight of the British Empire (KBE) by King George VI

of England and in 1962 Queen Elizabeth II made him Knight of the Companion of St. Michael and St. George (KCMG).

AD HOC CONSTITUTIONAL CONFERENCE. After the second coup d'état of July 1966 which brought General Yakubu Gowon to power, the new Head of State announced to the nation that he would set in motion the process to review "our national standing" and return to civilian rule as soon as it could be arranged. His first step to bring this about was to set up a meeting of representatives of all the regions on August 9, 1966 and the meeting among other things recommended the setting up of an ad hoc constitutional conference of delegates from all the regions to review the constitutional future of the federation.

The conference met from September 12 to 30, 1966. There were many proposals from each regional delegation and the conference reached agreement on a number of problems, but it could not complete its task because of the massacre of the Ibo people in the northern region which began on September 29, 1966. The conference later adjourned for three weeks, and when the conference resumed on October 24, the Eastern Regional government was not represented. All efforts aimed at persuading the east to resume participation failed.

ADUBI WAR (1918). This was a revolt by the people in Egbaland, in which a European and a traditional chief were killed. The revolt was a result of the loss of independence enjoyed under treaties with the British by the Egbas and terminated by the administrative innovations of 1914 and the consequent introduction of the indirect rule. Other causes of the revolt were resentment of the imposition of direct taxation on the people in 1918 and the grievances felt by Egbas abroad over the termination of their independence. It was quickly crushed. Investigations later showed that educated Egba people resident in Lagos played a significant role in the revolt.

ADVISORY COMMITTEE ON NATURE EDUCATION IN THE BRITISH TROPICAL AFRICAN DEPENDENCIES See MEMORANDUM ON EDUCATION IN BRITISH TROPICAL AFRICA

ADVISORY JUDICIAL COMMITTEE. Created under Decree Number 1 of 1966 it consisted of the Chief Justice of the federation who was the Chairman, the Chief Justices of the four existing regions and the Chief Justice of Lagos, the Grand Kadi of the Sharia Court of Appeal and the Attorney General of the federation with the Solicitor General of the federation acting as the Secretary to the Committee. Its function was to advise the military government on judicial matters.

AFONJA. Afonja, ruler of Ilorin province at the end of the eighteenth century, was posted there by the Alafin of Oyo to guard and defend the northern outpost of the Yoruba kingdom against the threatened invasion by the lieutenants of Usman Dan Fodio during the Holy War (Jihad) from Sokoto. He however revolted

against the Alafin by proclaiming Ilorin independent of Oyo in
1817. To strengthen his position, he incorporated into his
army some Hausa slaves and received assistance from Alimi,
a Fulani moslem priest. As such he was able to repel all
attacks by the Oyo Army. Later on relations between him and
his neighbors strained and in his effort to seek reconciliation,
he angered his Hausa troops who revolted and had him killed.
The town thus fell to Abdulsalami, one of the sons of Alimi.
The Emir of Sokoto, Mohammed Bello recognized the new ruler
and thus began Fulani rule in Ilorin, a Yoruba town.

AFRICAN ASSOCIATION. The African Association was formed in
1788 by British merchants who were desirous of exploring
trade possibilities in the interior of Africa. The association
was therefore prepared to finance the expedition of any person
who would come forward for that purpose. One of the many
volunteers was Mungo Park who in 1795 had his offer accepted
and started on his first expedition to trace the course of the
river Niger. In this first expedition he saw that river Niger
flowed eastwards but he later turned back and arrived in England in June 1797. He later on undertook a second journey
during which he died at Bussa in Nigeria without accomplish-
ing his mission. Later on, other British expeditions followed
the successes of Mungo Park. Among the explorers of river
Niger were Clapperton, Richard Lander, John Lander, Baikie
and McGregor Laird who in 1832 accompanied a commercial
expedition from the Niger Delta up the Niger River to Lokoja
where River Niger meets with its biggest tributary, River Benue.
Soon after, the British government became interested in the exploration of Africa, but most of its efforts were frustrated owing to the attack of malaria fever. It was not until quinine was
discovered that loss in life was reduced to a minimum.

AFRICAN BANKING CORPORATION. African Banking Corporation
was the first commercial bank to be established in Nigeria.
It became the sole distributor of British silver coins in Lagos
and the sole repatriating agent in 1872 and started banking
business in Lagos in 1891. Being a pioneering private company in a country where money economy was yet to develop
and receiving no government subsidy, the corporation had many
problems. Sir Alfred Lewis Jones, a shipping magnate from
Elder Dempster Company came to its rescue by agreeing to
take it over, hoping that by extending credit facilities to small
businesses his own shipping business would continue to grow.
Later the British government asked that the company be made
a joint-stock bank, and having reached an agreement, the company was registered in England as a limited liability company
under a new name of the Bank of West Africa in May 1894.
Before this time, in 1892, the colonial administration in Nigeria had transferred its account in Lagos to the company's
account. The bank is now known as the First Bank. It is
today one of the leading commercial banks in the country, and

because of the Indigenization Decree, a large equity share of the bank is now held by Nigerians.

AFRICAN CHURCH. The African church was founded in protest against the practice of color prejudice (racism) in the Anglican church, the imposition of foreign culture and customary practices on the people, the effort to translate and enforce the principles of the church of England on the Africans and the colonial government's denial of self-government to the people. On October 13, 1901, about 800 worshippers of the Anglican church, St. Paul's Breadfruit Church in Lagos broke away to form the African church. From there the church spread to other parts of the country and outside it. The church was active in the educational and economic development of the nation. Its first school was built in 1902 and can boast of many primary and secondary schools together with teacher training colleges all over the nation. It was also through the activities of its evangelists like J.K. Coker that the cultivation of cocoa spread to places like Ondo, Owo and Ekiti provinces. The African church is remarkable for its protest against the imposition of alien culture and rule. The founding of the church was no doubt the beginning of nationalist movements within the Christian church in Nigeria.

AFRICAN CONTINENTAL BANK (ACB). Founded in 1948 by Dr. Nnamdi Azikiwe, the then leader of the National Council of Nigeria and the Cameroons (NCNC) it started operating in September of the same year. As the Foster Sutton Commission of Inquiry, set up to investigate the relationship existing between Dr. Azikiwe and the bank found out in 1954, Dr. Azikiwe together with members of his family and the companies controlled by him were the principal shareholders of the bank. The commission therefore concluded that Dr. Azikiwe's conduct in connection with the affairs of the bank left much to be desired. Dr. Azikiwe later transferred all his rights and interests in the bank to the former Eastern Regional government. The bank presently has branches in many cities and towns all over the country.

AFRICAN EDUCATION CONFERENCE OF 1952. The conference met at King's College, Cambridge in 1952 to study educational policy and practice in British Tropical Africa. The conference considered five major themes: responsibility and control, the expansion of the educational system, the teaching profession, organization and curriculum, and education and adult education. The recommendations of the conference were of great importance in setting up the aims of primary education in Western Nigeria.

AFRICAN EDUCATION INCORPORATED. African Education Incorporated was an educational scheme launched by Dr. Nwafor Orizu in 1946, and designed to give scholarship to young Nigerians and to secure places of admission for them in American universities. Between 1947 and 1950, it was recorded that about 100 students had benefitted from the program. But beginning from 1949 the scheme began to have serious financial and other difficulties due to poor management and inexperience. This brought great hardship to many of the students, and the Nigerian government together with some American foundations came to the rescue of the financially handicapped students by giving them loans, bursaries and other financial assistance.

AFRICAN FESTIVAL OF ARTS AND CULTURE (FESTAC-77). The First World Festival of Negro Arts and Culture was organized in Dakar, Senegal in April 1966 and the Second World Black and African Festival of Arts and Culture popularly known as FESTAC-77 was held in Nigeria from January 15 to February 12, 1977. The aims of FESTAC-77 were to ensure the revival, resurgence, propagation and promotion of black and African culture and black African cultural values and civilization; to work towards better international and interracial understanding, encourage and facilitate periodic return of black artists outside Africa to the cultural sources, bring to the attention of the world the artistic and cultural achievements of the black man, and to give black artists in Africa the opportunity of sharing their experiences and problems with other black artists operating outside of Africa.

AFRICAN STUDENTS' ASSOCIATION OF THE UNITED STATES AND CANADA. Organized in 1941, it had close association with West African Students Union (WASU) in London. Its aim was to fight for the independence of African countries. It asked the British government and its allies to grant internal self-government to the colonial peoples of Africa. It asked that the fundamental principles of democracy in the Atlantic Charter be applied to the African peoples immediately. Many members of the Association, like the late Dr. Kwame Nkrumah of Ghana, later became leaders in their countries. The association published a monthly paper called The African Interpreter.

AGBEBI, DR. MOJOLA. Dr. Agbebi Mojola was formerly called Mr. David Brown Vincent, a name given to him by his Sierra-Leonean creole parents who had come back to Nigeria, their original home country. He was born at Ilesa, in the present Oyo State in April 1860. He went to CMS Day School, Faji, Lagos. In 1874, he entered a CMS Teacher Training School and after three years, he was appointed as Schoolmaster of Faji Day School. He worked not only for the CMS but also for other denominations like the Catholic, the Methodist and the American Baptist missions. He also worked with the first Independent Native Baptist Church of which he became a leader in 1888. In 1903, he left that church and founded his own Aroromi church but he later joined the American Baptist church and remained there until his death in 1917.

     He edited many papers during his life time. He worked with R.B. Blaize on The Lagos Times, and later he worked

for the Lagos Observer, Lagos Weekly Times, Lagos Weekly
Record and he edited the Iwe Irohin Eko. Dr. Agbebi was a
close friend of Edward W. Blyden who invited him to spend
some years in Liberia where he was awarded honorary degrees
of Master of Arts and Doctor of Philosophy for his literary
ability. He also received an honorary degree of Doctor of Divinity from the University of New York in 1903.

Dr. Agbebi may be regarded as the forerunner of the
later-year cultural nationalism, for he dropped his European
names for Yoruba ones and he was said to have abandoned
European dress for Yoruba clothing.

AGE GROUPS. An age group was constituted of children of about
the same age. In some Yoruba towns, men were divided into
age grades, each age grade being under the control of a slightly
older person. Among the Ibos, as each age group reached
manhood, the members would select one of them as the group
leader or head. Each age group performed important functions.
They maintained discipline within the group and saw to it that
each member obeyed the customary law of the community.
The age groups were the only effective means of enforcing the
law. The older age groups formed the governing age grade,
while the younger ones carried out the orders of the elders
be it in judicial or other matters. The age group was also
a means of organizing the young people for war and for public
work like cleaning footpaths. In short, the age-group system
combined the function of defending the community, ensuring
law and order and providing for public labor. They also were
initiators of many useful community programs and projects.

Age grouping is also common among the Nupe, Ibibios,
the Beni and the Fulanis. Age is an important element in the
life of many ethnic groups in Nigeria. For example among
the Yorubas, reverence for those who are older is very great.
In traditional Yoruba society, a younger man normally pros-
trates to an older person, woman or man, when greeting them,
and a younger woman kneels or genuflects before an older person.

AGRICULTURAL CREDIT GUARANTEE SCHEME FUND. Established
in March 1977 to increase the volume of banks' lending to agriculture, and minimize the risks to which banks are exposed
in lending for agricultural purposes. The scheme encourages
banks to lend to all those who intend to or are engaged in the
establishment or management of plantations for the production
of crops like rubber, oil palm, cocoa, coffee, tea and similar
crops. It is also to be given to those who want to produce
cereal crops, tubers, fruits of all kinds, cotton, beans, groundnuts, benniseed, vegetables, bananas, pineapples and plantain
and for people who want to engage in animal husbandry like
poultry, pig and cattle rearing, and fish farming. The extent of the liability of the fund in respect of guaranteed loans
is 75 percent of any amount in default, subject, in case of a

loan to an individual, to a maximum of ₦50,000 and in case of
a loan to a cooperative society to a maximum of ₦1 million.
Under the scheme thousands of people have benefitted.

AGRICULTURE.   Nigeria, in spite of its oil resources and decades
of industrial development, is still an agricultural country.
Even though there are no reliable figures, about 70 percent
of the adult population are farmers, most of whom are subsistence farmers, each cultivating an average of about two hectares of land.   Most often the only implements used are hand
hoes, cutlasses, machetes and other such tools, and some of
the crops they grow are yams, corn, guinea corn, cassava,
beans, groundnuts, plantain, cotton, cocoa, coffee, palm trees
and rubber.
     Agricultural production is low and Nigeria still has to
import much of its food from abroad.   Because of the country's
overdependence on food import, the military government decided in 1976 to launch the Operation Feed the Nation Program
which was designed to make the nation self-sufficient in food.
The government also created many farming schemes through
the institution of River Basin Authorities for irrigation and
other agricultural purposes, provision of fertilizer and seeds
at subsidized rates, and the provision of credit to farmers.
The civilian administration that succeeded the military also
accepted the challenge and tried to improve on the old program by setting up what it called the Green Revolution, believed to be capable of making Nigeria self-sufficient in essential food materials by 1985.
     Another important step taken by the military to solve the
country's food problem was the reform of the traditional land
tenure system which for long had inhibited in many places the
development of mechanized farming.   The principle governing
traditional land tenure system was that the right to use a piece
of land lies in perpetuity with an individual and his hiers, but
the ownership of the land lies with the community, family, or
clan of which the individual is a member.   As such an individual cannot sell the land he uses.   This system has under-
gone considerable modifications as a result of the introduction
of nonagricultural uses in the towns and the introduction of the
British legal system, but not enough land was yet available
for large-scale mechanized farming.   To remove this impedi-
ment the military government in 1978 issued the Land Use Decree which vested the ownership of land in the state government.   While the decree did not disturb the rights of users of
land already occupied or developed, it gave the governments
power over undeveloped lands which could be allocated to people who want to use them for commercial farming and other
purposes.
     Finally the government has taken some important steps
to provide agricultural products for the growing industrial sector.   Before oil became the nation's most important foreign
exchange earner, agricultural exports used to play that role.
Nigeria was the largest exporter of groundnuts and palm products,

and second largest producer of cocoa. She also exported rubber, timber and cotton. The government has reorganized the system of marketing boards which used to buy those products from the farmers for export. At present marketing boards are now required to provide for home industries before the products are offered for export.

AGUDA COMMITTEE. Set up in August 1975 to examine the dual role of Lagos City as a federal and state capital and advise on the desirability or otherwise of Lagos continuing in that role. The Committee recommended that Lagos should no longer maintain the dual role as a federal and Lagos state capital, and that the federal government should move its capital to an area of about 8,000 square kilometers in the central part of the country. The federal government later chose Abuja as the new capital.

AGUIYI-IRONSI, MAJOR-GENERAL JOHNSON THOMAS UMUNANKWE. Former Head of State, born on March 3, 1924. After his elementary and secondary education he enlisted in the Nigerian Regiment in 1942. He was promoted to Captain in May 1953 and as Captain, he came into prominence. In 1956 when Queen Elizabeth II was visiting Nigeria, he was chosen among others as Equerry to the Queen. In 1958 he became Lieutenant Colonel. In 1961 he served as Military Adviser to the Nigerian High Commission in London and was later promoted to the rank of Brigadier. During the Congo crisis, he was the first African Force Commander of the United Nations Peace-Keeping Operation. In February 1965 he became a Major-General and was appointed General Officer Commanding the Nigerian Army. After the 1966 coup d'état, General Ironsi became the head of the federal military government and Supreme Commander of the Armed Forces. He held this position till he was kidnapped and killed on July 29, 1966 during the second military coup. It was his regime that issued the Unification Decree of May 1966, which abolished the federal structure and set up a unitary form of government for Nigeria.

AHIARA DECLARATION. On June 1, 1969, Lt. Col. Odumegwu Ojukwu, as the Commander-in-Chief of the Armed Forces of the Republic of Biafra launched the Biafran Revolution in a village called Ahiara. The main principles of the revolution were that the people were supreme while the leaders were their servants. Biafrans from different parts of the country were to live together, work together, suffer together and pursue together a common cause of national survival. The revolution believed in the sanctity of human life and the dignity of the human person and it placed a high premium on love, patriotism and devotion to the fatherland. One of the cornerstones of the revolution was social justice in Biafra: "all property belongs to the community." Whatever a person had, either in talent or material wealth was held in trust for the community. This did not mean the abolition of personal property, but the state, acting on behalf of the community could intervene in the disposition of property to the greater advantage of all. While the revolution would foster private economic enterprise and initiative, it was constantly alive to the dangers of accumulation of large private fortunes. Biafran revolution would create possibilities for citizens with talent in business, administration, management and technology, and it would create a society not torn asunder by class consciousness and class antagonisms. It was to be an egalitarian society.

AHMADU BELLO UNIVERSITY. Established in October 1962 by the Northern Regional government, it incorporated the Zaria branch of the Nigerian College of Arts, Science and Technology, the Ahmadu Bello College, Kano, which later became (Abdullahi Bayero College, Kano), the Institute of Administration in Zaria and the Institute of Agricultural Research at Samaru together with the Veterinary Research Institute at Vom. The University was taken over by the federal military government in 1975.

AHMED ALIMI. Ruler of the Kanuri state of Bornu about 1791 to 1810 who tried to defend his domain against the Jihad (Holy War) initiated by Usman Dan Fodio. In 1805, the Fulani people in Bornu province, in reply to the call to join the Jihad, attacked, and Ahmed counterattacked and ordered a full-scale campaign against the Fulani attackers. He had correspondences with Muhammed Bello in Sokoto, the son of Usman Dan Fodio, asking to know why a muslim should wage a muslim holy war against a muslim state, but to no avail. The Fulani had a number of important victories and Ahmed had to abdicate in favor of his son Dunama. He died a few months later. His abdication divided his followers into various factions, a fact that helped Al Kanemi in later taking over power in the state.

AIRSTRIP ANNABELLE. The Airstrip Annabelle was the Uli Airfield, a road sufficiently widened to be used as an airfield by the Biafrans during the civil war. The airstrip was where most of the relief planes were landed. It was later captured by the federal troops and for many years after, the remains of burnt airplanes bore evidence to the fact that it was one of the centers of activity during the war.

AJASA, SIR KITOYI. A lawyer and a journalist, born in 1866 and originally named Edmund Macaulay, the son of a Thomas Benjamin, a Sierra-Leonean slave freed from a slave ship, he received his education at Dalwich College in London and was called to the bar in 1893. Following the cultural nationalism of dropping foreign names for Yoruba ones common then among many Lagos people who came from Sierra-Leone to Nigeria, he too changed his name. In 1894, he was party to the launching of the Lagos Standard, but he soon fell out with the owner, George Alfred Williams who was for him too critical of the British government. The British rewarded him for his loyalty --in 1902 he was appointed to the Board of Health and in 1906 he was appointed to the Legislative Council in Lagos. He was a good friend of Lord Lugard and in 1914 when the ineffective Nigerian Council was created after the amalgamation of the Southern and Northern protectorates, he was appointed to that body. In the same year (1914) he established a new weekly newspaper, Nigerian Pioneer, in partnership with some European businessmen. The paper, believing in moderate and loyal criticism of the colonial government, was disliked by other nationalists and their newspapers. In 1923 when the elective principle was conceded to Lagos and Calabar to send elected representatives to the Legislative Council, Sir Kitoyi Ajasa was nominated by the governor to sit with the elected representatives. In the same year, 1923, he was awarded the OBE by the British government. In 1929, he became a Knight. He died in August 1937.

AJASIN, CHIEF MICHAEL ADEKUNLE. An educationist and a politician, first governor of Ondo State in the Second Republic. Born in Owo on November 28, 1908 he attended Saint Andrew's College in Oyo and later went to Fourah Bay College, Sierra-Leone and the University of Durham, in Britain 1943-1946 where he obtained a Bachelor of Arts Degree in English, History and Economics. In 1947 he obtained a Diploma in Education from the Institute of Education of the University of London. In the same year he became the first Principal of Imade College in Owo, a post he occupied till December 1962. In January, 1963 he became the founder, proprietor and first principal of Owo High School.

Chief Ajasin's interest in politics has an early history. He was the initiator and cofounder of the Nigerian Union of Students of Great Britain and Ireland in London in 1947. He was also the first Vice-President of the former Action Group Party when it was founded in 1951. He was also the President of Egbe Omo Oduduwa, an organization named after the mythical ancestor of the Yorubas, before it was banned by the military administration in 1966.

Chief Ajasin has also functioned in many public offices. He was chairman of Owo District Council 1954-1959 and a member of the House of Representatives, 1960-1966. Following the reform of local government by the military administration in 1976, he was Chairman of Owo local government in 1977, a post he held till 1978 when the ban on political activities was lifted. He became a member of the Unity Party of Nigeria (UPN) and was later elected Ondo State Chairman of the party and a member of the party's National Executive Council. In 1979 he was elected Governor of Ondo State, and was reelected in 1983 for a second term. After the military takeover of December 31, 1983, he was arrested and detained. He was tried with Governor Bisi Onabanjo of Ogun State and Governor Bola Ige of Oyo State by a military tribunal on the charges of receiving a kickback of ₦2.8 million and passing it to the Unity Party of Nigeria but he was acquitted. He was nonetheless still detained, awaiting further investigations on whether or not he had corruptly enriched himself while in office as Governor of Ondo State. He was released in August 1985 by the Babangida administration.

AKASSA MASSACRE 1895. When the Royal Niger Company obtained its charter from the British government in 1886 the Brassmen on the lower part of the River Niger, who had from the very beginning resented the visits of European traders among them, saw that the customs regulations being made and vigorously enforced by the company were excluding them from their traditional markets. They in 1889 made a formal complaint to Mr. Macdonald, a British officer, who was then the Special Commissioner sent to investigate certain complaints against the company. However nothing resulted from this and the company continued to apply its regulations as strictly as possible. When the people saw that their complaint fell on deaf ears, they organized a force of about 1500 men which attacked and destroyed the company's property at Akassa. There followed a punitive expedition in which many people were killed. The Foreign Office then sent Sir John Kirk as a Special Commissioner to investigate the Akassa massacre. In its report the commission noted that the rules in force were practically prohibitory of native trade and the Brassmen were right in saying this was so.

AKENZUA II OBA OF BENIN. Oba Akenzua II was born in Benin in 1899, the son of Oba Eweka II who ruled Benin between 1914 and 1933. As a young man, the Oba was educated at Benin Government School and at the King's College in Lagos. He later became a transport clerk in the Benin Native Authority. In 1925, he worked under Oba Ademola II, the Alake of Abeokuta and was later appointed as head of the Ekiadolor District, a position he was in when his father died and he became the reigning Oba in 1933. As Oba, he was appointed to many important public positions. He was a member of the Western House of Chiefs when that house was founded in 1946, and became a cabinet minister later. He was instrumental to the carving out of the Midwestern Region from the old Western Region by sponsoring organizations and parties that agitated for this, and when the Midwestern Region was created in 1963, he became the first President of the House of Chiefs in 1964.

As Oba of Benin he was the custodian of the culture and tradition of the people of Benin. To promote this culture and tradition he readily made available many ancient bronze and ivory carvings that the Festival of Black Arts and Culture (FESTAC) needed in 1977. For his many contributions to the political and the cultural development of his people, he was honored with the insignia of Commander of the Republic of Nigeria and was also appointed Chancellor of Ahmadu Bello University in Zaria. Oba Akenzua died in 1978 succeeded by Oba Erediauwa I of Benin in 1979.

AKIN-DEKO, GABRIEL. Born on October 30, 1913, he attended Higher College, Yaba and the Brixton School of Building, England to qualify in building technology. He was a schoolteacher from 1937 to 1947. He then set up a private civil engineering firm in 1950. He was later elected as a member of the Western House of Assembly and was appointed Minister of Agriculture of Western Nigeria from 1952-1961. He later became chairman of the Western Nigeria Development Corporation after which he was appointed the Regional Representative for Africa on the Food and Agricultural Organization (FAO) in 1962. He was appointed the Pro-Chancellor, University of Benin. He was also a former Chairman of National Sports Council of Nigeria. He has served as a top member of the National Party of Nigeria. (NPN). He was later appointed as the Pro-Chancellor of the newly established Federal University of Technology, Abeokuta, Ogun State.

AKINFOSILE, OLUFEMI. A lawyer, born on March 5, 1926 at Igbolako Ikale in Ondo State, he attended Baptist Academy, Lagos from 1934 to 1944, Birbeck College, University of London in England from 1948 to 1952 and the Northwestern Polytechnic in London in 1953. He was called to the bar at the Lincoln's Inn in London. He came back to Nigeria, and in 1959 contested the federal elections as a member of the National Council of Nigeria and the Cameroons (NCNC) and was later made the Federal Minister of Communication. From 1962 to 1966, he was Chairman, Western Working Committee of the party. He was a member of the Ad Hoc Constitutional Conference called by General Gowon 1966 to 1967. He also was a member of the Constituent Assembly 1977 to 1978. In 1978 he was appointed national chairman of the Nigerian People's Party and played a prominent role in the negotiation that led to the Accord reached between his party and the presidential party, the National Party of Nigeria (NPN) in October 1979.

AKINJIDE, RICHARD OSUOLALE ABIMBOLA. A Senior Advocate of Nigeria, born on November 4, 1931, in Ibadan, Oyo State he was educated at St. Peter's School, Aremo, Ibadan, Oduduwa College, Ile-Ife and at the University of London in England 1952-1956. He was called to the bar at the Inner Temple in London in 1956. Upon returning home he was elected member of Parliament in 1959 and became Federal Minister of Education in 1965. He was President of the Nigerian Bar Association from 1970 to 1973 and a member of the Governing Council of the University of Ife, Ile-Ife, 1975-76. He was appointed Pro-Chancellor and Chairman of Council, University of Jos, 1976. In 1978 he became a member of the National Party of Nigeria NPN and its legal adviser. As Legal Adviser he became more famous by his interpretation of the constitutional requirement that for a candidate to be elected as President where there were more than two candidates, he must have the highest number of votes cast in the election and he must have not less than one quarter of the votes cast at the election in each of at least two-thirds of all the states in the federation. As there were 19 states in 1979, he interpreted the two thirds

of 19 states to mean 12-2/3 states and not 13 states as had
previously been believed. His interpretation was upheld by
the Federal Electoral Commission (FEDECO), the Election
Tribunal and the Supreme Court and so Alhaji Shehu Shagari,
his party's candidate became the first executive president of
Nigeria. He was later appointed Minister of Justice. He was
however nicknamed Mr. Twelve-Two-Thirds. He was not reappointed as Minister of Justice during the Shagari's second
term of office, but after the December 1983 military takeover,
he escaped to Britain.

AKINRINADE, MAJOR-GENERAL IPOOLA ALANI. A soldier born
on October 3, 1939 at Yakoyo Oyo State, he attended Offa
Grammar School, Royal Nigerian Military Forces Training
College, Kaduna, and the Royal Military Academy, Sandhurst
in England 1960-62. He later went to the United States Army
Infantry School, Fort Benning Georgia, 1965-1966, and the
Staff College, Camberley, England 1971. He served in many
important positions in the army including Rear Commander and
Sector Commander of units of the Nigerian Army. In the February 1976 abortive coup staged by Colonel B.S. Dimka, in
which the late Head of State, General Murtala Muhammed was
killed, he refused to allow the First Division of the army under him in Kaduna to join, thereby causing the coup to fail.
In 1979, he was appointed Army Chief of Staff, a post from
which he later retired. He was nationally honored as Commander, Order of the Federal Republic.

AKINSANYA, OBA SAMUEL. Traditional ruler, born August 1, 1898,
he was educated at Ishara Anglican School. He worked as a shorthand typist 1916-1931. He was the Organizing Secretary of the
Nigerian Produce Traders and the President of the Nigerian
Motor Transport Union 1932-1940.

He was a foundation member of the Lagos Youth Movement which later became Nigerian Youth Movement (NYM) (q.v.).
He rose from general secretary of the organization to being
its Vice-President. He contested in 1941 with Ernest Ikoli the
election within the movement to fill the vacancy in the Legislative Council created by the resignation of Sir K.A. Abayomi
who was then the President of the NYM, but he lost to Ikoli.
The same year he was appointed the Odemo of Ishara.

Oba Akinsanya was also a foundation member of the
former Action Group and remained faithful to the party even
during the party's crisis of 1962. For example in 1963 his
salary as a traditional ruler was reduced to a penny (1p) by
the government of Western Nigeria simply because he refused
to join the government party.

In 1966 after the military takeover, the military government ordered that his salary should be paid in full together
with all the arrears since 1963. He died in January 1985.

AKINTOLA, CHIEF SAMUEL LADOKE. A politician born on July
6, 1910 at Ogbomosho in Western Nigeria, he received his

primary and secondary education in his hometown, Ogbomosho, and after it, he became the editor of the Nigerian Baptist, published then by the Baptist mission in Lagos. He worked as a clerk for the Nigerian Railway and later as editor of the Daily Service which was at the time the organ of the Nigerian Youth Movement (NYM). He went to the United Kingdom to study Public Administration at Oxford in 1946 and later received a law degree. He came back to Nigeria in 1949. He served as the legal adviser to the Egbe Omo Oduduwa, a Yoruba Cultural Society (Society of the Descendants of Oduduwa) and joined the Action Group early in its foundation.

Under the Macpherson Constitution, Chief Akintola was a member of the Central Legislative Assembly and one of the four Action Group ministers that tendered their resignation on the "self-government in 1956" crisis in April 1953. He, in May 1953, led the Action Group tour of the Northern Region which precipitated the Kano Riots of 1953.

In 1955, Chief Akintola became deputy leader of the party while Chief Obafemi Awolowo was leader. As deputy leader of the party he served in many important positions. He was the leader of the Action Group parliamentary group in the Federal House of Representatives in Lagos and served there as Minister of Communication and Aviation in the national government formed by Alhaji Tafawa Balewa in 1957.

In preparation for the 1959 general elections which were to lead the nation into independence in 1960, Chief Awolowo decided to vie for the topmost position in the country. He left the Western Regional government to go to the center. Chief Akintola then became Premier of the region. The Action Group party did not win the majority of the seats to the national assembly and could not find a coalition partner. As such the party became the opposition party while Chief Awolowo became the leader of the opposition. In 1962 a crisis erupted within the party as a result of disagreement between him and the party leader, which led to fractionalization of the party. On January 1, 1963, after the state of emergency in the Western Region had been lifted, Chief Akintola's newly formed party, United People's Party (UPP) formed a coalition government with the National Council of Nigerian Citizens (NCNC) in Western Nigeria.

In March 1964, Chief Akintola was the leader of a new party, the Nigerian National Democratic Party (NNDP) which consisted of his United People's Party, some former members of the NCNC and the Southern People's Congress, with the hand as its symbol. In the same year and in preparation for the 1964 federal elections, the NNDP came into an alliance with the Northern People's Congress (NPC) known as the Nigerian National Alliance (NNA) while the NCNC and the remnants of the Action Group together with other so-called progressive parties formed an alliance called United Progressive Grand Alliance (UPGA). The NNA won the election which was marred by many allegations of election malpractices. In October 1965, there were to be the Western Regional elections, which many people believed

would oust Chief Akintola out of power. But the elections were
so rigged that Chief Akintola was back into power. There followed three months of bloody rioting in Western Nigeria, including arson, and killing, until January 15, 1966 when the
army staged a coup d'état. In the exercise, Chief Akintola
was killed.

AKINYELE, CHIEF THEOPHILUS ADELEKE. Born in Ibadan Oyo
State on February 29, 1932. Chief Akinyele attended St. Peter's
School, Aremo and Mapo Central School in Ibadan. He also attended Ibadan Grammar School, University College, Ibadan and
the University of Connecticut. Apart from his university degree, he also possessed a Diploma Certificate in Financial
management. Chief Akinyele joined the western regional civil
service as an Administrative Officer from which he rose to the
rank of Permanent Secretary in 1974. He had served in various ministries. In 1975, he was seconded to the University
of Ife as a Registrar. It was while he was serving in that
capacity that he was appointed the Secretary to the Oyo State
military government and head of service in 1976. He resigned
from that post in 1978. In 1979, he was appointed the Presidential Special Adviser on Budgetary Matters. Chief Akinyele
has published and contributed articles on Modern Management
Techniques in many Journals and he was a coeditor of a book,
Programme Budgeting in Nigeria.

AKITOYE. King of Lagos from 1841 to 1853, during whose reign
the British Consul began the practice of effectively interfering
in local affairs. When Oba Oluwole of Lagos died in 1841
without an issue, rival claims arose between Oluwole's cousin
Kosoko and his uncle Akitoye, who with the assistance of the
Oba of Benin was crowned as the Oba (king) of Lagos in that
year. Kosoko resented this and in 1845, drove out Akitoye
from the throne. Akitoye went to Badagary, put pressure on
the British to reinstate him with the promise that he would put
an end to the slave trade still going on under Kosoko. When
that was not successful, he made an alliance with Domingo
José, a notorious Brazilian slave trader, to help him regain his
throne, but that also failed. In 1849 Beecroft was appointed
Consul to the Bights of Benin and Biafra and Akitoye agreed
with him that if he were restored to the throne of Lagos, he
would put an end to the slave trade in Lagos. In 1851 Beecroft moved against Kosoko, expelled him from Lagos and reinstated Akitoye. Akitoye agreed to prohibit human sacrifice
and stop the sale of slaves in his domain. Akitoye died in
1853, succeeded by his son, Dosumu, who among other contestants the newly appointed Consul of Lagos, Benjamin Campbell, believed would be more amenable to the British interest.
It was Dosumu who ceded the city of Lagos to the British in
1861.

AKRAN, OBA C.D. A former traditional ruler of Badagry, Lagos
State and a member of the banned Action Group Party (AG)

until that party's crisis in 1962. In 1963 he was instrumental in bringing about some kind of reconciliation between Chief S. L. Akintola, leader of the United People's Party (UPP) and premier of Western Nigeria, and Alhaji D. S. Adegbenro, AG parliamentary leader, together with their supporters. They issued a statement to the effect that they had resolved to collaborate in order to usher in an era of unity, peace, tranquility, progress and the welfare of the people of Western Nigeria. They also resolved to evolve an all-embracing democratic organization to which all the people would belong. The agreement was criticized by opposition parties and so it was short-lived.

ALAAFIN. The title of the ruler of the City of Oyo, the capital of the old Oyo Empire.

ALAKIJA, SIR ADEYEMO. A lawyer and a founding member of the Daily Times of Nigeria, Sir Adeyemo Alakija was born on May 25, 1884 to a Brazilian family, which, remembering their ancestral origin to be Egbaland in Nigeria, had previously come back home. He was named Placido Adeyemo Assumpçao. He attended St. Gregory's Catholic School in Lagos and later went to the Church Missionary Society (CMS) Grammar School for his secondary education. In 1900 he became a clerk in the government service and was for many years with the Post and Telegraph Department. He married in 1907. In 1910 he went to London to study law and was called to the bar in 1913. In that year he abandoned his Brazilian name and became Adeyemo Alakija. He was a successful lawyer, but soon became interested in politics. He was a good friend of Herbert Macaulay, but the two men fell apart in the 1920's over the issue of British government treatment of the Oba of Lagos. In 1923 and 1926 he ran for one of the Lagos seats in the Legislative Council but he lost. In 1933 however he was appointed member of the Council as a member representing Egba Division.

Sir Adeyemo Alakija's greatest contribution to the development of Nigeria was the part he played in the founding of the Nigerian Daily Times in 1926. He, together with Ernest Ikoli and Richard Barrow, who was an agent of Jurgen's Colonial Products Limited and the Chairman of the Lagos Chambers of Commerce, planned the paper. They then formed the Nigerian Printing and Publishing Company (NPPC) to start the publishing of the Daily Times. The new paper took over Ikoli's own paper, African Messenger which Ikoli was editing. Ikoli became the first editor of the Daily Times which started on June 1, 1926. Sir Alakija was the Chairman of the Board of NPPC. In 1936 the NPPC was merged with the West African Newspapers Limited of London which used to publish the West Africa magazine and the West African Review. In 1948, the International Publishing Corporation of London took over the Daily Times.

Sir Alakija won traditional titles from Abeokuta and Ile-Ife and was many times honored by the British government.

In 1945 he became a knight with the KBE. Though not very successful in politics, he contributed a great deal to the founding of Egbe Omo Oduduwa (society of the sons of Oduduwa) a Yoruba cultural organization. In 1948 when the Egbe was officially launched in Ile-Ife, Sir Alakija was made its first President and Chief Obafemi Awolowo its General Secretary. This Egbe later became the nucleus of the Action Group Party. Sir Adeyemo Alakija died on May 10, 1952.

ALEXANDER, SIR DARNLEY ARTHUR RAYMOND K.G., C.B.E., LLD. A former Chief Justice of Nigeria Sir Alexander was born on January 28, 1920 at St. Lucia, West Indies. He was educated at St. Mary's College in St. Lucia and later at the University College, London. In 1938 he was at the Middle Temple and was called to the bar in 1942. He practiced law in Jamaica between 1944 and 1957 and in Western Nigeria 1957-1960. He was Solicitor-General and Permanent Secretary, Ministry of Justice in Western Nigeria 1960-1963. In 1964 he became a judge of the High Court of Lagos, the position he occupied till 1969. During this period he was appointed Chairman of the Public Inquiries into the Owegbe Cult in the former Mid-West Region (now Bendel State) in 1965, and in 1968 he also was chairman of the Public Inquiries into Examination Leakages in Nigeria. In 1969 he became Chief Justice of the South Eastern State (now known as the Cross River State). He remained in this position until 1975 when he was appointed the Chief Justice of the Federal Republic of Nigeria and served in that position until 1979 when he retired. He is a member of many learned societies among which are the Nigerian Society of International Law. He was knighted Commander, Order of the British Empire (CBE) in January 1963.

AL-KANEMI, SHEIKH MUHAMMED EL-AMIN. Al Kanemi was a scholar and a religious and political leader who helped contain the Fulani empire from engulfing Bornu. He was the son of Sheikh Ninga. He became a Moslem scholar, went to Mecca, and upon his return saw that the Jihad of Usman Dan Fodio had spread to the Capital of Bornu, Birni Ngazargamu in 1808. He quickly organized some forces to help the defeated Mai, the King of Bornu. In 1809, Birni Ngazargamu was recaptured and Al-Kanemi became a most important personality in Bornu. In 1811 Ibrahim Zaki was given the right to take whatever part of Bornu he could capture. As a result, Birni Ngazargamu was occupied again, but Al-Kanemi's forces, together with that of Mai Dunama drove Ibrahim Zaki back to Katagum, thus preventing the Fulani empire from spreading to Bornu. In 1814, Mai Dunama tried to free himself from the authority and power of Al Kanemi, but he was caught and deposed, and Al-Kanemi became the most powerful person in Bornu, exercising all the powers of the old Mai. When D. Denham and Hugh Clapperton visited Bornu in the early 1820's they saw Al Kanemi to be the effective ruler of Bornu, who was feared, though loved and respected, a ruler who substituted laws of reason for practices of barbarity. Al Kanemi died about 1835, succeeded by his son Sheikh Umar, who took the title of Shehu, and ruled through Mai Ibrahim. In 1846, Mai Ibrahim wanting to take advantage of the revolt of the state of Zinder tried to shake off the control of Sheikh Umar over them. Mai Ibrahim was killed in the attempt, just like his sons. After his death Sheikh Umar established the Al Kanemi Dynasty of Shehus of Borno.

ALL-NIGERIA TRADE UNION FEDERATION (ANTUF). Inaugurated in August 1953 in an effort to form a central labor organization after the disintegration of the Nigerian Labour Congress (NLC), its aims were to improve the position and the living conditions of the workers, organize and unite all the trade unions in the country, encourage the spirit of oneness and collective security among workers, fight for the social and economic security of workers and secure for workers improvement in wages and in their conditions of service. The leaders of the organization were M. A. O. Imoudu, who was President and Gogo Chu Nzeribe, the General Secretary.

The organization did not last long for it disintegrated on the issue of its international affiliation. At the 1956 Conference of the Union, it was agreed that the union could affiliate with an international organization. However in the 1957 conference, some members wanted the Federation to affiliate with the International Confederation of Free Trade Unions (ICFTU), while others wanted affiliation with the World Federation of Trade Unions (WFTU) which was communist-oriented. The motion for affiliation with ICFTU was made and defeated. But the General Secretary of the ANTUF ruled that since the conference voted against affiliation with ICFTU, it meant it approved affiliation with WFTU. Many unions left in disgust and they went to form the National Council of Trade Unions of Nigeria (NCTUN). In 1959 through the effort of the government and some union leaders the ANTUF and the NCTUN came together to form the Trade Union Congress of Nigeria [TUC(N)].

AMALGAMATION OF NIGERIA. The Amalgamation of Nigeria was the process of uniting the various parts of the country under one colonial administration.

Nigeria, before the amalgamation, was made up of many parts. There was the Crown Colony of Lagos which was ceded to the British Crown in 1861. From Lagos the British authorities extended their jurisdiction to the hinterland as they developed their trading interest in the area. After the Berlin Conference of 1885, the zone of interest which British traders had established in the coastal areas became the Oil Rivers Protectorate. In 1893 the protectorate was extended further to the interior and renamed the Niger Coast Protectorate and when in 1900 the charter of the Royal Niger Company was revoked it became the Protectorate of Southern Nigeria. In 1906 the Crown Colony of Lagos was amalgamated with the Protectorate of Southern Nigeria and was then called Colony and Protectorate

of Southern Nigeria.   This was really the first process in the
unification of the various parts of Nigeria.

But while progress was going on in the south, Lord
Lugard's administration was also busy consolidating its power
in the north.   On January 1, 1900 the Protectorate of Northern
Nigeria replaced the administration of the Royal Niger Company.
Between 1900 and 1914 with the use of the Royal West African
Frontier Force, Lord Lugard was able to attack and defeat all
centers of resistance to British rule and pacify the north.   On
January 1, 1914, the two administrations of the southern and
northern protectorates were amalgamated and named the Colony
and Protectorate of Nigeria with Lord Lugard as the Governor-
General, and two Lieutenant Governors were put in charge of
the former areas of the former protectorates.

Certain factors were responsible for the amalgamation,
one of which was that before 1914 the Northern Protectorate
was always in a deficit and it had to be subsidized by annual
grants from the Imperial Treasury and from the southern administration which was having surpluses from the import duties
on liquor and other goods.   Thus, amalgamation was a means
of relieving the Imperial Treasury of its burden.

The amalgamation did not mean complete unification of
the former two administrations.   Important departments like
Health, Public Works, Forestry, Education, Agriculture, Police
and Prison were still administered separately.

As a result of the amalgamation, the provincial system
of government in the north was extended to the south, each
province was then headed by a resident.   The government set
up, in addition to the Executive Council, a deliberative body
known as the Nigerian Council, composed of official and non-
official members including traditional rulers from both the
north and the south.   The Council was designed to give expression to African public opinion but the chiefs who were in the
majority of the nominated African members rarely attended its
meetings.   Lastly, after the amalgamation, the system of Indirect Rule was extended to the southern provinces.   However
the Colony of Lagos was recognized as a separate unit from
the southern provinces and was placed under an administrator.

AMINA, QUEEN OF ZARIA.   According to oral tradition, Amina
was the Queen of Zaria about 1588.   She is believed to have
fought many wars and expanded her jurisdiction as far as to
the River Niger in the south, and Kano and Katsina to the north.
She is also remembered for the walled camps she established
wherever she halted during her extensive campaign, like the
wall around Katsina; and the famous Zaria wall is attributed to
her reign.   It is not certain whether or not she ever married
but tradition has it that she used to take new lovers wherever
she stopped during her wars and had them disposed of when
she left.   During her reign Zaria achieved considerable influence in Hausaland.

ANAMBRA STATE.   One of the two states carved out of the former

East Central State in February 1976, the Anambra State of about 17,675 sq. km. in area is bounded on the north by Benue State, on the West by the River Niger, on the south by Imo State, the second state created from the East Central State, and on the east by the Cross River State. The people of the state are ethnically Ibos who speak the Ibo (Igbo) language. The people are farmers, craftsmen and traders.

Culturally, the state is famous for many festivals. The Mkpokiti Acrobatic Dance Group from Umunze in the state is popular in Nigeria where it won gold medals in the All-Nigeria Festivals of Arts in Lagos and Ibadan in 1970 and 1971 respectively. There is the Odinani Museum at Nri in Njoka Division, which serves as a showpiece of the archaelogical past of the people of the area.

The state is well connected with every part of the country. There is the famous Niger Bridge which links the state to Bendel and the western part of the country, and there are roads, railroad and waterways in the state connecting it with other parts of the country.

The state is also rich in mineral deposits which include iron ore, coal, clay, marble, silica sand, lead, zinc petroleum, natural gas and others. Agricultural resources include cocoa, oil palm, maize, rice, cassava, banana and plantain.

Industrially, the state is moving up pretty fast. There are the Nkalagu Cement Factory, burnt brick industry, gas factory, steel industry, asbestos industry and many others.

The state capital is Enugu, the base of the nation's coal industry. Enugu also contains a campus of the University of Nigeria, Nsukka, the second university to be built in Nigeria.

The population of the state according to the 1963 census is about 3.5 million people. The main towns in the state are Enugu, Abakaliki, Nsukka, and Onitsha with its famous market.

ANGLO-FRENCH AGREEMENT OF 1890. After the agreement at the Berlin Conference of 1885, recognizing British claims to areas along the Niger River, the French were still pushing hard in an effort to penetrate Nigeria through the west below the Niger. The two countries signed an agreement in 1890 which greatly strengthened British position in northern Nigeria and effected a settlement of the northern boundaries. Under the agreement, Britain recognized French influence from her Mediterranean possessions south to a line drawn from Say on the Niger to Barrawa on the Lake Chad. Britain was to claim all the territories of the Royal Niger Company that fell within the Kingdom of Sokoto, the exact units of which were to be determined by a joint commission. The French were not happy about this treaty since it strengthened British claim to Borgu which the French were very much interested in getting.

ANGLO-FRENCH CONVENTION OF 1898. The struggle for territories in parts of West Africa continued to engender serious tension between the French and the British after the Anglo-French Convention of 1890. The French still wanted to extend their power to Borgu, an area which included Bussa, but the British who had already signed a treaty with the ruler of Borgu, were determined to resist. To prevent the tension from leading to hostility between the two nations the Anglo-French Convention of June 14, 1898, also known as the Borgu Convention, was called. Under the agreement reached, the French were granted the entrepôt on the Niger River; the frontiers of Dahomey, now the Republic of Benin, were extended to the Niger above Ilo; the Kingdom of Sokoto was awarded to Britain; the lease of ground below Bussa was approved, and the British guaranteed equality of treatment on all matters dealing with navigation, commerce and tariffs. They further agreed that the delimitation of the West African territories should be entrusted to a joint commission. By this treaty, British claim to Nigeria became more secure.

ANI, MICHAEL OKON NSA. Former Chairman of the Federal Electoral Commission--which declared Alhaji Shehu Shagari as the nation's first Executive President. Born on November 30, 1917 in Calabar, Cross River State, he was educated at the Sacred Heart School and at the Sacred Heart College all in Calabar. He later went to the London School of Economics and Political Science in England. Upon his return to Nigeria he joined the Federal Civil Service and rose to the position of Permanent Secretary in 1960. In 1963 he was appointed UN expert on Public Administration for proposed Federal Civil Service for Uganda, Kenya and Tanganyika. In 1967 he was appointed Administrator of the liberated areas of Eastern Nigeria under federal command during the civil war of 1967-1970. He was Director of the Flour Mills of Nigeria 1973-1975 and member of the Federal Public Service Commission 1975-1976. In 1977 he became Chairman of the Federal Electoral Commission and it was his responsibility to conduct the first election that ushered in the Second Republic in 1979. He held this position till 1980 when the commission was dissolved.

ANTI-INFLATION TASK FORCE. When the administration of General Murtala Muhammed took over in July 1975, it was faced with some major problems, one of which was how to reduce the ever growing rate of inflation which was a menace to the economy of the country. The government therefore set up the Anti-Inflation Task Force, headed by Professor H. M. A. Onitiri of the Nigerian Institute of Social and Economic Research (NISER).

The task force made many recommendations, one of which led to the decision to set up the Rent Control Panel.

ANTI-SABOTAGE DECREE. See EXCHANGE CONTROL DECREE

ARIKPO, DR. OKOI. Born in September 1916 he was educated at the Church of Scotland Mission, Ugefa. In 1923 he entered Hope Waddell Institute, Calabar, and in 1927 he went to the Government College, Umuahia. From 1934 to 1938 he was a student at the Higher College, Yaba and he later left for Britain to study anthropology at the London University. He was Assistant Lecturer in Anthropology, University College, London 1949-1951. After his studies in London, he came back to Nigeria and in 1952 he was Minister of Lands, Survey and Local Development, and in 1953 Minister of Mines and Power. He later became Commissioner for External Affairs during the regime of General Yakubu Gowon. As Commissioner, he worked hard to restore better harmony with some African and other countries with which relations had been impaired during the civil war.

ARMED FORCES. During the civil war the Nigerian armed forces grew at a very rapid rate. Before the military took over the government in January 1966, the army was about 10,500 men, but at the end of the civil war in January 1970, the army was about 250,000 men. After the war, efforts were made to demobilize some of these soldiers and by the time the military was handing over to the civilian administration more than 50,000 men had been demobilized while over 250 officers had retired. In 1980, the armed forces were estimated to be about 150,000 men strong, and in 1984, there were about 100,000 men. See also NIGERIAN ARMY.

ARMED PLOT. On October 1, 1962, Prime Minister Alhaji Sir Abubakar Tafawa Balewa announced to the nation that government had foiled an armed plot to forcibly overthrow the government by staging a coup d'état. He announced that some persons who were principally implicated had absconded and were abroad. Many others had been arrested and were being detained under the emergency regulations powers of May 1962. On October 5, 1962, the police, after searching the homes of some Action Group (AG) members, discovered three stores of arms including submachine guns, tear gas, pistols, revolvers and other weapons. On November 2, 1962 Chief Obafemi Awolowo, leader of the Action Group party and leader of opposition in the Federal House of Representatives, was charged with 26 other persons with a treasonable felony, conspiracy to overthrow the federal government by force. Some of the persons implicated and who were outside the country were Chief Anthony Enahoro in London, Mr. Samuel Ikoku, the Federal Secretary of the party in Ghana and Mr. Ayo Adebanjo.

AROS. The Aros were an Igbo subgroup which had generally set themselves apart from other groups as a trading group. Before the British had extended their sway over the area, the Aros had traded in slaves and palm oil. To perpetuate their monopoly in these trades, they developed a religion which claimed that God (Chukwu) had appointed them as his agents on earth, and had put them in charge of their famous fetish, the "Long Juju" known popularly as Aro-Chukwu through which God revealed himself to men. This was not all; the Aros did not put all their confidence in the divine, they also entered into alliances with many other warlike clans within the Ibos and the Ibibio peoples. By these two means they were able to control not only the slave trade but also the trade in palm oil. Their dominant economic position began to be challenged when British officials began in the late nineteenth century to enter into treaties of friendship with various chiefs in the area, and they began to assert their authority over the whole country.

ASHBY COMMISSION. The official name of this commission is "The Commission on Post-School Certificate and Higher Education in Nigeria." There were nine members: three from the United States, three from Great Britain and three from Nigeria. The Commission was set up in 1959 by the Minister of Education; it was the first such commission on higher education that Nigerians had an opportunity to set up to look into higher education needs of the country. Its mandate was to look into the country's needs in the field of postschool certificate and higher education for the following 20 years (up to 1980). The Commission's report, based upon the objective of upgrading employed Nigerians who needed further training and of designing a system of postsecondary education that would meet the manpower needs of the country, drew much information from the Harbison's Report on High-Level Manpower for Nigeria (q. v.). The Commission's recommendations were extensive. It made recommendations on primary and secondary education, on teacher training, on technical and commercial education, on agriculture and veterinary education and on university education. The government accepted the Commission's report on principle and declared that with some amendments the report would constitute the basis for the development of postschool certificate and higher education in Nigeria.

ASIKA, ANTHONY UKPABI. A political scientist, born on June 2, 1936 in Jos, Plateau State, he attended St. Patrick's College; Calabar in 1949 and Edo College in Benin in 1951. In 1953 he was a clerk at Onitsha Town Council and later a clerk at the Department of Marketing and Exports, Lagos and also at the Northern Nigerian Marketing Board in Kano. In 1956 he went to the University College, Ibadan and later in 1961 he obtained a Rockefeller scholarship to study at the University of California, Los Angeles. In 1966 he was appointed lecturer in Political Sociology at the University of Ibadan. In 1967 after the government of General Yakubu Gowon had divided the country into twelve states, he was appointed the Administrator for the East Central State, one of the three states into which the former Eastern Region was divided. He was the only civilian member of the Supreme Military Council until July 1975, when another coup d'état overthrew the regime of General Gowon, and all state Military Governors together with the Administrator of the East Central State were compulsorily retired. He later went into private business. He was awarded an honorary degree of Doctor of Laws in 1970 by Ahmadu Bello University and a Doctor of Literature by the University of Nigeria, Nsukka in 1971.

ASQUITH COMMISSION. The Commission on Higher Education in the colonies was set up in 1943 under the chairmanship of Hon. Mr. Justice Cyril Asquith. It was asked to consider the principles that should guide the promotion of higher education, learning and research, and the development of universities in the colonies. It was also to explore ways by which universities in the United Kingdom could cooperate with the higher education institutions in the colonies. The areas to be covered by the Commission included Asia, Africa and West Indies. The most important recommendation for the universities that were later founded in the African colonies was that there should be an interuniversity council for higher education in the colonies, and that all colonial universities and university colleges should be under its jurisdiction. Members of such a council should be made up of representatives of all the universities in the United Kingdom and the council should keep in touch with the development of the new colonial institutions through regular visits of its members and should help in the recruitment of staff and in encouraging their staff members to take up appointment in the new institutions.

ASSOCIATION OF EUROPEAN CIVIL SERVANTS IN NIGERIA. Formed in 1919 for the purpose of putting pressure on the colonial government to regrade the salaries of all European public servants in Nigeria with the exception of the medical staff and the West African Frontier Force. As a result of the activities of the association, the government not only regraded their salaries upward but granted them many concessions like travelling, transport and bush allowances, and travelling allowance on home leave. The government also agreed to pay a year's salary to the estate of a confirmed officer who died in the service.

ASSOCIATION OF NIGERIAN RAILWAY CIVIL SERVANTS. A splinter union from the Nigerian Civil Service Union, its objective was to take care of matters affecting railway office employees.

ASSOCIATION OF WEST AFRICAN MERCHANTS (AWAM). An association of European firms operating in the West African countries, formed during the Second World War to facilitate import agreements among the member companies and allocate export quotas to members. The member firms were the principal purchasers of export products at low fixed prices and principal importers of European goods at high and extortionist prices, leading to a lot of unrest in Ghana and Nigeria after the war. Government later withdrew support from the organization, leading to its demise.

ATIBA. Ruler of Oyo kingdom 1836-1859, he was the son of Abiodun, a former ruler of Oyo who was said to be the last great ruler of the empire. In 1858, Atiba abolished the traditional practice of the Crown Prince committing suicide at the death of his father, and therefore became one of the few obas in

Yorubaland to modernize traditional chieftaincy system. Upon
his death in 1859 he was succeeded by his eldest son, Adelu.
Because this was a breach of tradition, tension rose in Yorubaland; some important towns like Ijaye refused to recognize
him but other towns like Ibadan recognized him. This led to
the outbreak of a civil war which lasted for a very long time.

ATTAHIRU, AHMADU. Ruler of the Sokoto Caliphate at the time
of the British conquest of the area. Attahiru had succeeded
Abdurrahman who died in 1902, shortly after Frederick Lugard
had begun the British conquest of Northern Nigeria. Because
of dissension in the Sokoto Army, Attahiru forces could not put
up a strong defense against Lugard and Attahiru was forced to
flee to Burmi in 1903. Lugard entered the capital and persuaded the people to elect a new ruler, Muhamadu Attahiru II,
son of Aliyu Babba, who then became a new Sultan of Sokoto on
March 21, 1903. In Burmi, Attahiru (who had been joined by
some deposed chiefs including the ex-Emir of Bida and the
Magaji of Keffi, under whom Captain Maloney, British Resident
in Keffi, died) was able to persuade a lot of people to go with
him on a pilgrimage to Mecca in protest against British interference in the affairs of the Muslim empire of Sokoto. On his
way British forces followed and after Attahiru's men had put
up a gallant show against British forces, his army was finally
defeated and he himself was killed in July 1903.

AWOKOYA, PROFESSOR STEPHEN OLUWOLE. An educationist
and a great supporter of adult education, born on July 9, 1913,
in Awa, Ijebu-Ode in Ogun State, he was educated at St. Andrew's College, Oyo, Yaba Higher College, Lagos and the University of London in England. He was former Principal of Molusi
College, Ijebu Igbo before getting into politics. Between 1952
and 1956, he was Minister of Education in Western Nigeria and
it was during his term of office that Western Nigeria launched
its free primary education scheme, for all primary school children in the region. In 1958 he became the Principal of the
Federal Emergency Science School in Lagos and in 1961 he
was Permanent Secretary and Chief Federal Adviser on Education in Lagos. In 1967 he became Director, Department of
Application of Science to Development, UNESCO and in 1968 he
was Director, Department of Scientific and Technological Research and Higher Education of UNESCO. In 1973 he was appointed a research professor of education in the University of
Ife. He was a member of the Action Group 1950-1956. He
was honored with traditional and other titles: Aseto of Awa
and Commander of the Order of the British Empire. In 1966
he published his book, Science of Things Above Us.

AWOLOWO, CHIEF OBAFEMI. Born at Ikenne in Ijebu-Remo
in Ogun State on March 6, 1909, he had his elementary education at Imo Western School, Abeokuta and also attended Wesley College, Ibadan. He began to work in various capacities
from 1926 while at the same time he began to take correspond-

ence courses in English, commercial knowledge, bookkeeping, business methods and shorthand. He wanted very much to be a journalist, a lawyer, a wealthy man and a politician. Accordingly, in 1934 he joined the staff of the Daily Times of Nigeria as a reporter-in-training. When he left the Daily Times, he became a freelance journalist while at the same time he was studying by correspondence courses for a Bachelor of Commerce Degree of the University of London, a degree which he successfully passed as an external student in 1944. The same year, he went to study law in London; he got his LL.B degree in 1946 and was called to the bar at the Inner Temple in London on November 18, 1946. During his short stay in London, he wrote Path to Nigerian Freedom in which he said that every national group in Nigeria had its indigenous constitution which had been corrupted under colonial rule. He then advocated that the constitution of each cultural nationality should be its own domestic concern and every such nationality should be entitled and should be encouraged to develop its own political institutions within the framework of a Nigerian federation. He further maintained that it was the right of the educated minority of each cultural group to lead their fellow men into a higher political development. His belief then was that there should be political reforms at the local level and that there should be political unity at the cultural level and a federal constitution at the national level. This belief he has restated in The Peoples' Republic and Thoughts on Nigerian Constitution.

While in the United Kingdom, he founded the Egbe Omo Oduduwa (Society of the Descendants of Oduduwa which had as its objective the unity and cultural development of the Yorubas.

He returned to Nigeria in 1947 and became a practicing lawyer and a politician. He was one of the leading nationalists and has had great impact on the constitutional development of Nigeria. In 1948, at a conference hosted by the then Ooni of Ife, Sir Adesoji Aderemi, in Ile-Ife, the mythical cradle of the Yorubas, the Egbe Omo Oduduwa was inaugurated with Awolowo as its General Secretary.

In 1949, he started the Nigerian Tribune, a daily newspaper which later became the organ of his political party, the Action Group, and the main organ of the Unity Party of Nigeria. In March 1951 he publicly announced the forming of the Action Group (AG) Party which had in reality been in secret existence for about a year. He was elected the party's President, the position which he held until 1966 when the military banned all political parties. In the same year Awolowo was elected into the then Western House of Assembly. In 1952 he became leader of Government Business and Minister of Local Government and Finance. In 1954 he assumed office as the first Premier of the Western Region. In 1955 he introduced in the region free primary education for all school-age children. In 1959 he gave up his position as Premier to run for the federal government election into the House of Representatives with the hope of becoming the first Prime Minister of independent Nigeria. He conducted a very well-organized and vigorous campaign but his party was unable to win a majority of the seats in Parliament or to make other parties join in a coalition with him. He then became the leader of the opposition in the Federal Parliament. In 1962 a quarrel arose between him and his deputy leader Chief S. L. Akintola who became Premier after Chief Awolowo had left for the center. The quarrel grew into a serious crisis in the then-Western Region, which led to the declaration of an emergency in the region and his detention and that of many party members. He was later charged along with about 26 other party members with plotting to overthrow the federal government. He was found guilty and sentenced to ten years imprisonment. In August 1966 when Lt. Col. Yakubu Gowon became head of the federal military government, he was pardoned and set free from prison. In May 1967, he was appointed the First Chancellor of the University of Ife and in the following month he was appointed Federal Commissioner for Finance and the Vice-Chairman of the Federal Executive Council. He held this post until the end of June 1971 when he resigned.

In September 1966, he led the Western Nigerian Delegation to the Lagos Ad-Hoc Constitutional Conference and served on the Ad-Hoc Committee charged with finding a workable constitution for Nigeria. Before this conference met, some Yoruba intelligentsia had chosen him as "Leader of the Yorubas." When the government of Eastern Nigeria, led by Lt. Colonel Odumegwu Ojukwu refused after the September 1966 massacre of the Ibo people in Northern Nigeria to continue participation in the conference and to attend regular meetings of the Supreme Military Council, Chief Awolowo led a delegation of the National Reconciliation Committee to Enugu in May 1967 to persuade the government of Ojukwu to send representation to the National Reconciliation Committee.

After his resignation in 1971, he went into private practice. In 1975 General Murtala Muhammed appointed him one of the 50-member Constitutional Drafting Committee (CDC) but he declined to serve. When the ban on political activity was lifted in September 1978, he was the first to form his new political party, Unity Party of Nigeria (UPN). As always, Chief Awolowo put up a hard but uncompromising campaign. His party captured the five states that made up the former Western Region but he failed to win sufficient support in other states to make him the first civilian Executive President of Nigeria. He also contested the 1983 Presidential election, but he lost again.

Chief Awolowo is one of the few who are hard-working and intelligent; most straightforward of all Nigerian politicians of his time. Even though much of his life ambition has been realized (he is well educated, with professional standing as a lawyer and a politician and he is very wealthy), one ambition he has not been able to realize is that of leading Nigeria. He failed in 1959 to become the first Prime Minister of independent Nigeria and, 20 years later, failed to become the first Executive President of the Second Republic. This is partly due to his straightforwardness, his uncompromising attitude in politics, to a well-founded fear people have that he is vindictive and does not forgive, as shown in the Action Group crisis of 1962 and the many harsh references he has made to the late Akintola 15 to 17 years after the latter had been killed in the 1966 coup d'état.

In the pursuit of this last and overriding ambition of his, he has been in the forefront of the Progressive Parties Alliance (PPA), which hoped to wrench power from the National Party of Nigeria (NPN) in 1983. The alliance however failed to get off the ground.

Chief Awolowo has been showered with many traditional titles. He is Asiwaju of Ijebu-Remo, Losi of Ikenne, Apesin of Osogbo, Odole of Ife and Odofin of Owo. In 1982, he was awarded the highest national honor of Grand Commander of the Order of the Federal Republic of Nigeria. He has honorary degrees of LL.D from the University of Nigeria, Nsukka and Ibadan, D. Litt. from the University of Lagos and D. Sc. from the University of Ife. Among his many publications are: Path to Nigerian Freedom (1947), Awo, An Autobiography (1960), Thoughts on Nigerian Constitution (1968) and The Strategy and Tactics of the Peoples Republic of Nigeria (1970).

AZIKIWE, CHIEF (DR.) NNAMDI. First President of the Federal Republic of Nigeria and first indigenous Governor-General of Nigeria. Born in Zungeru in Northern Nigeria on November 16, 1904 where his father was serving as a clerk in the Nigerian Regiment, he attended Mission Schools in Onitsha, Lagos and Calabar and he later became a clerk in the Treasury Office in Lagos. He sailed for the United States in 1925, where he enrolled in Storer College, but he later transferred to Lincoln University and later still to Howard University in Washington, D.C. He lectured in Political Science at the Lincoln University and later went to the University of Pennsylvania where he obtained a Master of Science degree. He returned to Nigeria in 1934 but he soon moved to Accra, Ghana, where in 1935 he became the editor of the Accra African Morning Post. In 1938 he returned to Nigeria where he established the now defunct West African Pilot, a daily newspaper. He was a member of the Nigerian Youth Movement (NYM) but owing to the disagreement between him and other members of the movement as to who should fill the position left vacant in the Legislative Council by the resignation of Dr. Abayomi in 1941, he pulled out of the movement. In 1944 he, with Herbert Macaulay, the leader of the Nigerian National Democratic Party (NNDP), founded the National Council of Nigeria and the Cameroons (NCNC), a party which came to be known for its nationalist agitations.

In June 1945, there was a general strike which many people believed was engineered by "Zik." On July 8, 1945, two of his daily papers--the West African Pilot and the Daily Comet--were banned by the government for allegedly misrepresenting facts that related to the strike. A few days later Dr. Azikiwe wrote what he called his "last testament" and fled

to Onitsha.   In the testament he alleged that some unknown
persons had planned to kill him.   He then sent cablegrams to
important personalities, news media and organizations in the
United Kingdom imploring them to prevail upon the government
to give him police protection.   The assassination plot increased
his popularity among the rank and file but he was criticized by
the NYM members for propagating falsehood and inventing a
story to make him a martyr and gain cheap popularity.   In
1947, Zik led his party's delegation of seven people including
a woman, Mrs. Funmilayo Ransome-Kuti, to London to protest against the Richards Constitution but the Secretary of State
for the colonies, Rt. Hon. Arthur Creech Jones, told them to
go back home and try to cooperate to work the new constitution.   Dr. Azikiwe was also at the head of his party's delegation to all the constitutional conferences both in London in 1953,
1957, 1958 and in Nigeria in 1954.

Dr. Azikiwe was the Premier of the Eastern Region
from 1954 to 1959 but he resigned in December 1959 to take
up the position of President of the Senate in January 1960.
When Nigeria became independent in 1960 he became the first
indigenous Nigerian Governor-General of the Federation and in
1963, when the country became a Republic, he was made the
first President of the Federal Republic of Nigeria, a position
that was mainly ceremonial.

His term of office as President of the first Republic
was not without its crisis.   After the 1964 election which was
riddled with irregularities in various parts of the country,
President Azikiwe at first refused to appoint Sir Abubakar Tafawa Balewa as Prime Minister to form a new government.
However after a lot of discussions and compromise and the
legal advice given to him that he had no constitutional power
to order the army about, he performed his constitutional duty.
On January 4, 1965 he stated that the constitution left him no
alternative but to call on Alhaji Tafawa Balewa to form a new
government.

In 1966 when the military seized power, Dr. Azikiwe
was relieved of his post.   Later, when the civil war broke
out, he supported the Biafran cause and used his great influence all over the world to seek diplomatic recognition and
support for Biafra.   However when it became apparent that the
federal side was winning the war he began to look for a compromise solution with the federal government on ways to end
the war.   He later retired to his hometown but when the ban
on politics was lifted in 1978 he was persuaded to come back
into politics by joining the Nigerian People's Party (NPP).   He
contested the position of the First Executive President of the
Federal Republic of Nigeria but he lost to Alhaji Shehu Shagari.   As such he remained the NPP leader.   His party
later on began to work together with three other parties, the
Unity Party of Nigeria (UPN) led by Chief Obafemi Awolowo,
a faction of the People's Redemption Party (PRP) and a faction
of the Great Nigerian People's Party (GNPP) in an effort to
form the so-called Progressive Parties Alliance (PPA).   But

in the choice of who should be the PPA presidential candidate
to beat the NPN in 1983, neither Azikiwe nor Awolowo could
step down for the other.   The PPA therefore decided to field
the two men as their presidential candidates, a fact which
greatly weakened their support among the people, and led to
the defeat of both candidates.

Dr. Azikiwe's contribution to Nigerian development is
well recognized by the many honors bestowed on him. He is the
Owelle of Onitsha, and was the Grand Commander of the Order
of the Federal Republic of Nigeria in 1980.   He has many honorary degrees of LLD. and D. Litt.   He also has written many
books including Renascent Africa (1939), Political Blue Print of
Nigeria (1943), Zik: A Selection of Speeches (1961) and My
Odyssey (1970).

Though a Nigerian nationalist, Dr. Nnamdi Azikiwe was
always conscious of the fact that he was an Ibo man.   In 1948,
in his address as the President of the Ibo State Union, he said
that it would appear that the God of Africa had created the Ibo
nation to lead the children of Africa from the bondage of the
ages and the Ibo nation could not shirk its responsibility from
its manifest destiny.   In 1978, he attributed his tax problem
with the Federal Electoral Commission to the fact that he was
an Ibo.

-B-

BABALOLA, APOSTLE JOSEPH AYO.   Born in 1904 at Ilofa, Kwara
State, he, after his primary education, joined the Public Works
Department (PWD) where he worked as a Caterpillar operator.
He left the PWD in 1930 to begin his missionary activities in
Oke-Oye in Ilesha.   He founded the Christ Apostolic Church
(CAC) in 1930 but he later moved to Efon Alaye which he made
the base of his missionary activities.   Believing him to be an
instrument of healing the sick, people flocked to him for healing.   He travelled all over Nigeria and outside to Ghana, preaching the word of God and healing the sick.   In 1955 he founded
the Christ Apostolic Church Teacher Training College at Efon
Alaye, the second oldest teacher-training college in Ondo State,
to train teachers who would teach in his mission schools.   He
died in 1959 in Ede, Oyo State but was buried in Efon Alaye
where he had wanted to be buried.   CAC was one of the first
indigenous churches in Nigeria and was a demonstration of revolt against Christian churches dominated by white value systems.

BABANGIDA, MAJOR-GENERAL IBRAHIM GBADAMOSI.   First military President of Nigeria, born on August 17, 1941 in Minna,
capital of Niger State, he received his elementary education in
Minna and proceeded to the Government College in Bida where
he successfully obtained his High School Diploma in 1962.   In
1963, he enrolled in the Nigerian Military Training College and
later in the same year he was sent to the Indian Military Academy in India.   (Continued on p. 385.)

BAIKIE, DR.   A Niger explorer asked in 1854 to command the
Pleiad, a ship built by Macgregor Laird to go up the River
Niger and open up trade with the people in the interior.   The
expedition was very successful, and no life was lost.   Baikie
explored the Benue, almost getting up to Yola, and trade was
opened up with people of the area.   In 1857, he was also asked
to command the Dayspring, a steamer which again sailed up
the River Niger.   Among the people on board was Samuel Ajayi
Crowther who later became the Bishop of the Niger.   The Dayspring was wrecked near Jebba but the crew members began
to make contacts with the local people.   Baikie installed himself at Lokoja which he hoped could become a permanent commercial site and a center of trade.   Baikie travelled to many
parts of Nigeria including Bida, Zaria and Kano.   He died in
1864.

BALEWA, SIR ALHAJI ABUBAKAR TAFAWA.   The first Prime Minister of Nigeria, born in 1912 at Tafawa Balewa Town in Bauchi State, northeast of Nigeria.   He attended the Bauchi Provincial School for his elementary education and later went to
the Katsina Higher College, in 1928, where he received a teacher's certificate in 1933.   He then went to Bauchi Middle School
to teach.   In 1945 he was awarded a scholarship to study in
the Institute of Education of the London University in Britain.
Upon his return, he was appointed an education officer in
charge of Bauchi Province.
        Soon after, he became involved in the politics of north-
ern Nigeria.   He was one of the foundation members of the
Bauchi General Improvement Union in 1943.   When the Richards
Constitution came into effect in 1947, he became a member of
the Northern House of Assembly from which he was elected to
the Legislative Council in Lagos.   In 1949, following the pattern of cultural organization going on in the south, he, along
with Mallam Aminu Kano and some other leaders of the defunct
Bauchi Improvement Union, joined together to form the Jami'
yya Mutanen Arewa, a Northern People's Congress.   However
because of the conservative attitude of the organization and its
deference to the traditional political system, some members,
led by Mallam Aminu Kano broke away to form the Northern
Element Progressive Union.   In 1951, Alhaji Tafawa Balewa
joined Alhaji Sir Ahmadu Bello, the Sardauna of Sokoto, in the
reorganization of the Northern People's Congress into a political party with Sir Ahmadu Bello as the leader and Alhaji Tafawa Balewa as the deputy leader.   After the implementation of
the Macpherson Constitution of 1951, Alhaji Tafawa Balewa became Minister of Works in the central government.   In 1954,
when the country became a federation, he was appointed Federal Minister of Transport.   Following further constitutional
developments, on September 2, 1957, being the parliamentary
leader of the Northern People's Congress (NPC) which had
more representatives than any other party in the Federal House
of Representatives, he was appointed the first Prime Minister
of Nigeria.   He went on to form a national government, con-

sisting of all the major parties; six ministers from the National Council of Nigeria and Cameroons, four from the NPC, two from the Action Group (AG) and one from the Kamerun National Congress (KNC). His belief was that all the major parties needed to cooperate on matters of planning and policy if Nigeria was to achieve independence at the appointed time. After the 1959 elections, the NPC still won a plurality of seats in the Federal House of Representatives. Forming a coalition with the NCNC, Sir Tafawa Balewa was again appointed the Prime Minister and on October 1, 1960, he became the first Prime Minister of Independent Nigeria.

After independence Sir Abubakar Tafawa Balewa's administration was plagued by many crises. He worked as hard as he could for Nigerian unity but that unity eluded him. In May 1962, there was the Action Group crisis (q.v.) in which the federal coalition government apparently took sides with the Akintola faction in an effort to weaken the Action Group led by Chief Obafemi Awolowo. There was also the census crisis of 1963 which made for the final disintegration of the coalition between the NPC and the NCNC at the center. Following this in rapid succession was the election crisis of 1964 which led to open conflict between him and the President, Dr. Nnamdi Azikiwe, a former member of the NCNC.

The straw that broke the camel's back was the Western Regional election of October 1965 which was followed by a complete breakdown of law and order in the region. Many supporters of the jailed AG leader, Chief Awolowo, had thought that under the new leadership of Alhaji D.S. Adegbenro, they would deal a deathblow to the Akintola government, but the elections were rigged more than ever before and Chief Akintola was back in power. Three months of rioting, arson and killing followed, until January 15 when the army decided to intervene. Some dissidents in the army led by Chukumah Nzeogwu staged a coup in which Sir Abubakar Tafawa Balewa was killed.

Sir Abubakar Tafawa Balewa received many honors from the British government. He was made Officer of the Order of the British Empire (OBE) in 1952, Commander of the Order of the British Empire (CBE) in 1955, Knight Commander of the British Empire (KBE) in 1960 and in 1961, he was appointed a Privy Councillor.

BALOGUN, CHIEF (DR.) KOLAWOLE. A lawyer and politician, born on April 11, 1922 in Otan Aiyegbaju in Oyo State, he attended Government College, Ibadan and the University of London from which he graduated with an LL.B. degree. He was called to the bar at the Lincoln's Inn in London. While in London, he was the secretary of the London Branch of the National Council of Nigeria and Cameroons (NCNC) party. He became a chief in 1956, having been installed Ajaguna of Otan Aiyegbaju. He also has chieftaincy titles from Osogbo and Akure.

In 1953, he was a member of the Western House of Assembly as an NCNC member. From there he was, under the 1954 constitution, sent to the Federal House of Representatives in Lagos and became the Federal Minister of Research and Information, 1956-1958. In 1958 he and some others joined Dr. K.O. Mbadiwe in a petition to get Dr. Nnamdi Azikiwe, the NCNC party leader, to resign, accusing him of splitting the party asunder and of losing interest in it. The National Executive of the party expelled the leaders of the group including Chief Kolawole Balogun. He and Dr. Mbadiwe later resigned from the federal government.

In 1959, he was Nigerian High Commissioner to Ghana and in 1962 he became the Chairman of the Nigerian National Shipping Lines. In 1967 he was appointed Commissioner for Economic Planning and Social Development and Commissioner for Education in 1968. Chief Balogun was also a journalist and an author. He was Assistant Editor of West African Pilot, 1946-47, and Editor of Spokesman, Ibadan 1948. He is a lawyer and he has authored numerous books which include the following: My Country Nigeria and The Growing Elephant. Balogun founded the magazine called the Social Reformer in 1966. In 1971 he became Chairman, Sketch Group of Newspapers.

He was also a lecturer at the Faculty of Administration, University of Ife, and when the ban on political activities was lifted in 1978, he left the institution to go back into politics. He was a foundation member of the Nigeria People's Party (NPP) and when the party broke into two factions, he left the NPP in the company of Alhaji Waziri Ibrahim to form the Great Nigeria People's Party (GNPP) where he was chosen as the National Vice-Chairman. He was expelled from GNPP together with some few others on the ground of antiparty activities. He later joined the National Party of Nigeria (NPN).

BANJO COMMISSION. Appointed in 1960 to review the educational system of Western Nigeria, with regard to the structure and working of the primary and secondary grammar schools, the adequacy or inadequacy of the teacher training program and the interrelationship between primary and secondary education.

The Commission gained the impression that the standard of education was falling in the region because of the rapid expansion of primary education without corresponding increase in facilities for teacher training. It recommended among other things more trained and better-qualified teachers, strengthening of the local education authorities to perform their duties more efficiently and enlarging the Inspectorate of Education to match increased number of schools.

BANKING AMENDMENT DECREE. This was Decree Number 5 of 1966. The national military government on February 16, 1966 issued the decree empowering the government to order an investigation into the account of any person, including legal persons in the country, when there was reasonable cause to suspect that such a person had enriched himself through bribery, corruption, extortion or abuse of office.

BANK OF BRITISH WEST AFRICA. Formerly known as African
Banking Corporation. Established in 1872 but reorganized as
a limited liability company under the new name of Bank of British West Africa in May 1894, the bank was the first expatriate
commercial banking institution in Nigeria. See also AFRICAN
BANKING CORPORATION.

BAPTIST CHURCH. The American Baptist church sent its first missionary to Nigeria, Reverend Thomas J. Bowen, who arrived
in Badagry in August 1850 with the objective of setting up missions in the interior of the country. The church established
mission houses and schools in Ijaye, Ogbomoso, Oyo, Shaki,
Igboho and in many other places. In the history of education
in Nigeria, the Baptist church is one of the most prominent.
The church also established hospitals to provide health care
for people in many towns.

BARTH, HEINRICH. A German sent with two others to report on
the general conditions of the countries in central Africa. Barth
travelled hundreds of kilometers in the former northern part of
Nigeria. In 1852 he reported that he had crossed the Benue
and speculated that it was the same river that flowed to the
Niger at Lokoja. An expedition was financed by the British
government to ascertain this fact. The expedition went as far
as Yola with no loss of life, for the use of quinine against malaria had been found to be very effective.

BAUCHI GENERAL IMPROVEMENT UNION. Formed in 1943 by
three young northerners then living in Bauchi: Mallam Sa'ad
Zungur, the first northern Nigerian to attend the Yaba Higher
College where he came in contact with nationalist activities in
the south, Mallam Aminu Kano, a Fulani schoolteacher who
later became the leader of the Northern Element Progressive
Union and Mallam Abubakar Tafawa Balewa, also a teacher,
who later became the first Prime Minister of Nigeria. The
Emir of Bauchi, realizing its political importance, became
hostile to the Union and it soon became defunct. The Union
is important however for it started such pressure group activities in the north which had long been protected by the British against nationalist activities in the south.

BAUCHI STATE. Created in 1976, Bauchi State is situated on the
Bauchi Plateau which stretches into the Gongola and Borno
States. It is bounded on the north by Kano and Borno states,
on the west by Kaduna State, on the south by Plateau State and
on the east by Gongola state.
     The population of the state is about 2,431,296 million
people occupying about 64,605 sq. km. of land. The people,
as in most other states of the federation, are made up of many
ethnic groups including Tangale, the Waja, the Fulani, and the
Hausa. Most of the people of the state are farmers growing
crops like millet, guinea corn, maize, yams, tomatoes and

vegetables. They also produce coffee and cotton and some of
them rear cattle.

The state is rich in minerals like columbite, cassiterite,
coal, limestone, iron ore, antimony and marble. It is also
growing industrially: it has meat canning factories, groundnut
processing factories, oil mills, cotton ginneries and a cement
factory. Bauchi State could be one of the most promising tourist attractions if only the resources could be developed. There
is the Yankari Game Reserve, about 207,800 hectares of open
woodland where a large variety of wildlife is collected. There
is also another game reserve at Lame Burra which contains
some rare types of animal not found in the Yankari Game Reserve.

The state capital is Bauchi, and other main towns in
the state include Gombe, Azare, Misau, Jama'are, Ningi Bi-
liri and Dass.

BAYAJIDDA. He was the mythical ancestor of the Hausa people.
His sons and grandsons were said to have founded the following
seven Hausa city-states: Daura, Rano, Bina, Gobir, Kano,
Katsina and Zazzau (Zaria).

BAYERO, ABDULLAHI, EMIR OF KANO. Born in 1881, the son of
Emir Muhammadu Abbas who ruled in Kano between 1903 and
1919. Before he was appointed Emir of Kano in 1926, he was
the District Head of Bichi. As Emir, he carried out some
reforms of the government of the emirate, and saw to the development of the Kano Native Authority. By the time of his
death in 1953, the Authority was spending well over £1m annually. He visited Britain in 1934 and was received by King
George V. He went to Mecca in 1937 and again in 1951. The
Bayero University in Kano was named after him. He was succeeded by his son Muhammad Sanusi.

BAYERO, ALHAJI ADO. Traditional ruler, born on July 25, 1930
in Kano, Kano State, he was educated at Arabic Schools in
Kano, Kofar Kudu Elementary School in Kano, Kano Middle
School and at the School for Arabic Studies. After his education he joined the Bank of West Africa Limited, now the Standard Bank of Nigeria in Kano. He resigned in 1955 to become
a clerk in the Native Authority in Kano. He went to the Clerical Training College in Zaria and was later promoted to the
post of clerk to the Kano City Council. He was in 1955 elected
into the Northern House of Assembly but he relinquished this
post in 1957 when he was appointed Chief of the Native Authority (NA) Police Force. In 1962 he was appointed Nigerian Ambassador to Senegal, but he had to leave when he was made
Emir of Kano in 1963. He was Chancellor of the University
of Nigeria, Nsukka in 1966 and Chancellor of the University of
Ibadan in 1975.

BEECROFT, JOHN (1790-1854). He was appointed the British Consul for the Bights of Benin and Biafra by Lord Palmerston in

1849, thus opening up the first diplomatic link between British government and Nigeria. It was he who established the pattern of British intervention in Nigerian affairs. Before his appointment he was a British Resident on the island of Fernando Po which, with Spanish consent, had come under the British rule in 1827. Fernando Po was then used as a base for the suppression of the slave trade and the establishment of "legitimate" trade with the people of Benin, Calabar, Bonny and the Cameroons.

In 1851 the deposed King Akintoye of Lagos petitioned him to restore him to his throne, promising to abolish the slave trade, which was still being carried on under Kosoko in Lagos, and to begin to carry on lawful trade especially with the British merchants. Beecroft accepted the petition, visited Lagos the same year with a naval force and deposed King Kosoko and restored Akintoye to the throne. In 1852, he had a treaty signed by Akintoye who undertook to abolish the slave trade in his territory and afford protection to missionaries. In 1853 he presided over the exile of William Dappa Pepple, King of Bonny. He later died at Fernando Po in 1854.

BELLO, SIR AHMADU, THE SARDAUNA OF SOKOTO. A politician born on June 12, 1910 in Rabbah near Sokoto, he was the grandson of Usman Dan Fodio, the leader of the Fulani Islamic revolution in northern Nigeria during the nineteenth century and the founder of the Fulani empire. He graduated from Katsina Higher College in 1931 and he became a teacher in Sokoto at the Sokoto Middle School. In 1938 when the then reigning Sultan of Sokoto died, he vied for the position, which was the most powerful in the Northern Region at the time. But he lost to Abubakar who later appointed him the Sardauna of Sokoto (leader of war).

In 1948 he had a scholarship to study local government in England. In 1949 he was chosen by the Sultan of Sokoto to represent Sokoto in the Northern House of Assembly which was established under the Richards Constitution. In 1951 Sir Ahmadu Bello was instrumental in forming the Northern People's Congress (NPC) (q.v.) which the north later used to dominate not only the region of origin but the politics of the country up until 1966.

In 1954 when the country became a federation composed of three regions, Sir Ahmadu Bello became the Premier of the Northern Region. Because he preferred to remain in the north rather than go to the center in Lagos, the position of leader of the government fell to his able Lieutenant, Sir Abubakar Tafawa Balewa who was then the NPC Vice-President. After the federal election of 1959, the NPC went into a coalition with the NCNC and Balewa became the first Prime Minister of independent Nigeria. Ahmadu Bello remained in the north, preferring to direct the affairs of the country through his lieutenants. During the first few years of independence, the belief was widespread that Sir Ahmadu Bello was the effective ruler of the country because the federal Prime Minister had to constantly have consultations with him on major policy issues. In 1962 during the Action Group crisis, Sir Ahmadu and his party supported Chief S. L. Akintola's faction against Chief Obafemi Awolowo's faction and later formed an alliance with Akintola's faction to fight for the 1964 elections. In the dawn coup of January 15, 1966 he was assassinated together with Alhaji Tafawa Balewa the Prime Minister, Chief S. L. Akintola and some others. Sir Ahmadu Bello was knighted in 1959. The first university in the north, Ahmadu Bello University, founded by his government, was named after him.

BELLO, SULTAN MOHAMMED. Son of Usman Dan Fodio, the initiator of the Jihad (Holy War) of the early nineteenth century, he was born in 1797 and when his father died in 1817, he succeeded him as the Moslem religious leader and took the title of Commander of the Faithful. Administratively, the Fulani empire, which had been divided into the eastern and western sectors, remained so divided while he was in charge of the Sokoto sector.

Sultan Bello led his men in battle against forces in Hausaland and in Bornu. It was through his good sense of government that the various autonomous Hausa States were brought under a centralized system of government covering much of northern Nigeria.

He was also a distinguished Moslem scholar who invited scholars from other countries to visit with him. He saw the need to adapt Islam to the social, cultural and the administrative life of the people. He died in 1837.

BENDEL STATE. This state is substantially the same as the former Mid-Western Region. It was created in 1963 from the former Western Region and became the fourth region in the Nigerian federation. In 1967 when the country was divided into 12 states, the region remained intact but its name was changed to Mid-Western State. However in 1976 when some of the states were further subdivided, the Mid-Western State became the Bendel State, and it underwent some boundary adjustments in which some areas of the state were merged with the Rivers State while some others were merged with Ondo State.

The state shares common boundaries with Ondo, Anambra, Kwara and Rivers states with the River Niger being the natural boundary between it and Anambra State. It has about 128 kilometers of coastline in the south, and the southwest is bounded by the Bight of Benin on the Atlantic Ocean.

The state capital is the ancient city of Benin known as Benin City. The city was surrounded by a moat several meters deep some of which is still extant today.

The population of the state is 2,535,839 according to the 1963 census. It has a density of 17 people to 2.6 sq. km. The main ethnic communities that compose it are the Edos, Urhobos, Igbos, Ijaws and the Itsekiris.

The state is rich in petroleum, rubber, cocoa and palm oil, and supplies about 60 percent of the nation's total timber.

There are other resources, such as natural gas, limestone and lignite.

BENIN CITY. Benin City is the heart of the ancient Benin empire and one of the nation's centers of art and culture. Bini artworks and carvings are some of the best in the world. Some of the famous arts are kept in the national museum situated on the Ring Road.

The Binis have great respect for the institution of the Oba, a fact which explains why many of their carvings relate to Obas and why many ancient streets and institutions are named after past Obas.

One of the still extant tourist attractions in Benin is the old moat, a fortification dug around the ancient city about the fifteenth century. The depths in some places are still about three to four meters.

Benin City became the capital of the Mid-Western Region in 1963 and today it is the capital of the Bendel State. The population of the city was about 100,694 in 1963 and has probably more than doubled since then. The people of the town are mainly Edo speaking. The city is one of the cleanest towns in Nigeria with wide streets and some very good roads. It is also a university city, being the home of the University of Benin, established in 1970.

BENIN DELTA PEOPLES PARTY (BDPP). Formed in 1953 under the leadership of His Highness, Akenzua II, the Oba of Benin, its aim was to seek a separate state for the Mid-Western Region. In the 1954 federal elections the BDPP in alliance with the National Council of Nigeria and the Cameroons (NCNC) won most of the seats but was soon absorbed by the NCNC.

BENNS FISCAL REVIEW COMMISSION. Set up in June 1964 with Mr. K. J. Binns, an Under Secretary and State Commissioner of Taxes in Tanzania as the sole Commissioner. The Commission was to review and make recommendations with respect to the provisions of Sections 140 and 141 of the Constitution of the Federal Republic of Nigeria on mining royalties and rents, and on the distribution of funds in the Distributative Pool Account. In doing its work, it was to take into account the experiences of the various governments of the federation in the working of the revenue allocation that was then in force, the recent creation of the Mid-Western Region and proportion of revenue allocated to it, the sources of revenue available to each of the governments and the legitimate requirements and responsibilities of each of the governments. It was also to consider the financial implications of the nonavailability of promised foreign aid for university education and other unfulfilled pledges for financial assistance to Nigeria and make recommendations on all the above matters. The commission recommended that:

1. The amount of 30 percent credited to the Distributable

Pool Account in accordance with the constitutional provision of Section 136(i) on import duties on certain commodities and Section 140(2) Mining Royalties and rents should not be altered.

2. The portion of the Distributable Pool Account payable to each region in accordance with Section 141 of the constitution should be altered as follows: Northern Nigeria and Eastern Nigeria were to continue to have a share of 40 percent and 31 percent respectively and the Western Region was to get 21 percent instead of the existing 18 percent and the Mid-Western Region was to get 8 percent instead of the existing 6 percent. The federal government should introduce a Bill to provide a payment of £3.75m to the regions on an annual basis from 1965 to 1969. The federal government should discontinue as from 1965-1966 financial year the practice of paying to the regions a share of General Excise Revenue but in doing so the federal constitution should be amended to provide that when an Excise Duty was imposed on locally produced motor spirit and diesel oil, the federation would pay to the regions the proceeds of that duty on consumption in the regions to be divided among them in proportion to consumption in the several regions.

BENSON, CHIEF THEOPHILUS OWOLABI SOBOWALE. A lawyer and politician popularly known as TOS Benson, born on July 23, 1917 at Ikorodu, Lagos State. He attended the CMS Grammar School in Lagos, University College, London, Inns of Court School of Laws and was called to the bar at the Lincoln's Inn, London in January 1947. When he came back to Nigeria, he enrolled as a barrister and solicitor at the Federal Supreme Court. In 1951, he was elected into the Western House of Assembly as a member of the National Council of Nigeria and the Cameroons. In 1953, he became the leader of opposition in the Western House of Assembly. In 1954, he was elected into the Federal House of Representatives and later became its Chief Whip from 1954 to 1959. In 1955, he was a member of the Lagos Town Council and in 1959 having won another election to the Federal House, he was appointed the Federal Minister of Information and Broadcasting, a post he occupied till the military came to power in 1966 when he went into private practice.

Chief Benson has played a significant role in the development of Nigeria. He was a delegate to all the constitutional conferences from 1953 to 1962. He was a delegate to the Commonwealth Prime Ministers Conferences and to the UN General Assembly from 1960 to 1965. He was a foundation member of the Organization of African Unity and at many times acted for the Prime Minister.

He was a staunch NCNC member who started as a legal adviser, then rose to be the Chairman of the party's Western Working Committee, the party's National Secretary and the post of Third National Vice-President of the party.

After the ban on politics was lifted in 1978, he became a member of the Nigerian People's Party (NPP). He supported the efforts of the minority parties--the NPP, the Unity Party of Nigeria (UPN), the Great Nigerian People's Party (GNPP) and the People's Redemption Party (PRP)--to form the Progressive Parties Alliance (PPA) to fight the National Party of Nigeria (NPN) in the 1983 general elections.

BENUE PLATEAU STATE. One of the six states carved out of the former northern region in May 1967 when Nigeria became a federation of 12 states, the state was in 1976 further divided into two separate states, Plateau and Benue states.
    The capital of Benue Plateau State was Jos. See also BENUE and PLATEAU states.

BENUE STATE. Deriving its name from the River Benue, Benue State is one of the two states created out of the former Benue Plateau State in 1976. It is bounded on the north by Plateau State, on the west by Bendel and Kwara states, on the south by Anambra and Cross River and on the east by Gongola State. It is about 45,174 sq. km. in area and has a population of about 2,427,017 people.
    The major ethnic groups in the state are Igala, Tiv, Idoma, Etulo and Igedde. Other linguistic groups include Junkus, Idah, Katsina-Ala, Kwande, Oturkpo, Okpolwu and Vandeikya. The peoples of the state are mostly farmers growing crops like beniseed, soya beans, groundnuts, rice, yams, millet, cassava, bananas, cotton, oil palm, cocoa and coffee. They also keep large herds of sheep and goats and they get fish from River Benue and some other rivers.
    Among the mineral resources of the state are coal, limestone, marble, tin and columbite.
    The capital of the state is Makurdi on River Benue and other main towns include Gboko, Katsina Ala, Oturkpo, Idah, Dekina, Ankpa, Abade and Vandeikya.

BERLIN CONFERENCE. As a result of the European scramble for territories in Africa, a lot of frictions developed. Rather than allow the situation to become explosive, the Berlin Conference was called in 1884 and it finished its work in 1885. The agreements at the Conference greatly influenced British acquisition of Nigeria. At the Conference, Britain made claim to all the territories under the Royal Niger Company and the Conference recognized them as being under her influence. They also agreed that navigation on the River Niger must be free to all merchant ships of all nations, and they agreed on the important principle of effective occupation for delimiting the boundaries of their territory. The interpretation of this principle was not clear but claims to sovereignty, maintained by sufficient military power to guarantee order, protection of foreigners and control over the indigenous population were considered. Treaties of protection made by the Europeans with the local chiefs were also considered as evidence of a valid title of sov-

ereignty.   After this conference the British moved ahead rapidly to acquire the whole of Nigeria.

BIAFRA.   The name given to the former Eastern Region when Lt.
Col. Odumegwu Ojukwu declared the secession of the region
from the rest of the country on May 30, 1967 as the "Independent Republic of Biafra." As a result of this secession,
a civil war ensued in 1967 which ended in January 1970 after
the surrender of the Biafran soldiers.   See also CIVIL WAR.

BIAFRAN ORGANIZATION OF FREEDOM FIGHTERS (BOFF).   In
the last year of the civil war, Lt. Col. Odumegwu Ojukwu
launched a guerrilla operation composed of paramilitary young
people under his own control.   The group had some political
education and ideological motivation.   It was designed to move
freely among the civilians in the federally controlled areas
north of Biafra, and along the west bank of the Niger in the
Mid-West.   Though fairly successful, it was unable to help
dislodge the federal troops from the areas they had occupied.

BLAIZE, RICHARD BEALE.   Born in 1845 in Freetown, Sierra
Leone to Yoruba liberated slave parents, he was raised as a
Christian and was educated in mission schools.   After school-
ing, he became apprenticed to a printer.   In 1862 he came to
Lagos and started to work for Robert Campbell, as editor of
the then Anglo-African newspaper.   In 1863 he took up an appointment in the government printing office where he became
Head Printer.   In 1875 he left government service to start his
own business as a merchant.   Towards the end of the century
he was regarded as the wealthiest native businessman in Lagos.
He was a member of the Lagos Chamber of Commerce and the
owner of the Lagos Weekly Record which J. P. Jackson, a
Liberian-born journalist and a nationalist, edited.   The Lagos
Weekly Record was well known for its criticism of the British
colonial authorities.   Having become very successful as a merchant, Blaize began to be active in church and also in politics.
He died in 1904.

BLYDEN, DR. EDWARD WILMONT (1845-1904).   Born in Charlotte-
Amalie, capital of St. Thomas in the Virgin Islands in the West
Indies on August 3, 1832, he in 1849 wanted to join the ministry and went to the United States to enter a theological training college but he was rebuffed because he was black.   He left
the United States and migrated to Liberia in 1851.   In Liberia
he became the editor of the Liberia Herald, for which he had
been a correspondent.   In 1856 he wrote his famous pamphlet,
"A Voice from Bleeding Africa on behalf of Her Exiled Children" which later had tremendous influence on black nationalists everywhere.   In it he sought to restore pride and self-
respect in the black race and disproved the myth of black man's
inferiority to whites.   He wanted to rediscover black history
and correct many of the misrepresentations in books published
by the white people.   He also aimed at preserving African

customs, culture and institutions and to develop what he called the "African personality." Dr. Blyden was not happy with colonial partitioning of Africa into ministates and advocated large groupings of people. Though himself a Christian, he was disenchanted with the racial discrimination practiced in the churches and so said that Christianity was unsuitable for Africans. In his book, Christianity, Islam and the Negro Race published in 1887, he criticized the established Christian churches for their attitude on African culture and their intolerance of certain African customs like polygamy. According to him Christianity had retarded the emergence of African personality while Islam had in fact worked in the opposite direction.

He visited Nigeria in 1876 and was one of the people who at the time agitated for the establishment of higher educational institutions in the country. In 1896 he was again in Nigeria. He recommended the establishment of a training college and an industrial institute in Nigeria to the Governor of Lagos. His writings together with his presence in Nigeria and his appeal to prominent African Church leaders that they should establish a native church modelled on black churches in the United States, a church which would be composed of native Africans who would support it and govern it, helped a great deal to bring about the first religious protest movements against white dominated Christian churches and the secession of United native African church from the Anglican church. He died in 1912.

BORNO STATE. The largest of all the nineteen states of the federation, it is 116,400 sq. km. in area, and has a population of about 2,997,498 people according to the 1963 census. It shares borders with the Republic of Niger to the North, the Republic of Chad to the northeast and the Republic of Cameroon to the east. It is bounded in the west by Kano and Bauchi states and in the south by Gongola State.

The linguistic groups making up the state are the Kanuri, Bolewa, Ngizim, Karai-karai, Ngamo, Fulani, Babur, Bedde, Waha, Guduf, Marghi and Shuwa. The most important geographical feature in the state is Lake Chad situated in the extreme northeast corner of the state and the state wealth comes from fisheries, cattle and agriculture, with about three-quarters of the population in agriculture. They produce such crops as groundnuts, cotton, guinea corn, millet, rice, wheat and others. Gum arabic is also tapped in the state. Industrially the state is advancing. Oil mills to produce groundnut oil and cakes, and tanneries to produce pickled skin for export, together with other industries, are being set up

The state is investing quite a bit in education. For instance, primary and secondary schools have been multiplied and there are technical schools and the University of Maiduguri, owned by the federal government. The capital of the state is Maiduguri, with a population of over 200,000 people and well connected by road and air to all the parts of the country. Other important towns include Borno, Bedde, Fika, Biu, Dikwa,

Nguru Gwoza, Geidom, Gashua, Konduga, Monguno, Potishum, Bama and Damaturu.

BORNU YOUTH MOVEMENT. Formed in 1954 by young Kanuri people who were dissatisfied with the system of Native Authority in the area, and the corruption they saw around them. Its major objective was the creation of a North-Eastern State which would consist of Bornu, Adamawa, Bauchi and Plateau provinces. The ruling Northern People's Congress (NPC) moved quickly to weaken the BYM by making efforts to eradicate corruption in the area, and as a result the party gradually declined enough so that the BYM did not make any representation to the Minorities Commission (q. v.) in 1958.

BOUNDARY ADJUSTMENT COMMISSION. Set up on February 12, 1976 to examine the boundary adjustment problems identified by the Irikefe Panel, which looked into the creation of more states in addition to the 12 states created in 1967. The Commission, headed by Justice Muhammadu Nasir, was also to specify areas to be merged, and to define interstate boundaries especially where there were intergovernmental disputes.

BOURDILLON, SIR BERNARD. Born in 1883, he served in India, Iraq, Ceylon and Uganda before coming to Nigeria as Governor of Nigeria in 1935. It was he who laid the foundation for the constitutional proposals which bear the name of his successor, Sir Arthur Richards. During his term he became convinced that the policy of isolating the north from the rest of the country had to change. He worked hard to convince the Northern Emirs about the advisability of coming to join the southerners in the Legislative Council of the country. But rather than recommend increasing the number of the members on the Legislative Council by members from the north, he, realizing the north's shortcoming with the use of English as a language of communication in the Legislative Council, proposed the setting up of regional councils with a central council in Lagos to which the deliberations of regional councils would be sent. This idea gave rise to the concept of regionalism which Arthur Richards embodied in the 1946 Constitution. In fact it was Bourdillon who in 1939 divided the south into the Eastern and Western Provinces. What he did later was to substitute region for province. He returned home in 1943 and died in 1948.

BOWEN, THOMAS I. An American Baptist missionary sent to Nigeria in 1850 with the objective of setting up missions in the interior of the country. He built his first station in Ijaye, and in 1854 he established another station in Ogbomoso. He wrote his Yoruba Grammar and Dictionary which was published in 1858 by the Smithsonian Institution.

BRIDE PRICE. The bride price is the money paid by a bridegroom or his parents to the family of his would-be bride. This was part of traditional marriage custom. Part of the rationale for

the parents paying it was to assert their authority over who the
bride was going to be. The price varied from place to place.
In Yorubaland, the amount was not that much but among the
Ibos of Eastern Nigeria, the price has always been high, so
high sometimes that appeals are often made over the mass
media for its reduction.

BRITISH COTTON GROWING ASSOCIATION (BCGA). The British
Cotton Growing Association (BCGA) was founded in 1902 with
a capital of £50,000. It then began to conduct research into
whether any British West African countries could be suitable
or adaptable to cotton growing. The objective was to supply
British markets with cotton grown within the commonwealth
rather than from America. Experiments were then begun in
both southern and northern Nigeria and cotton ginneries were
erected along the railroad at Abeokuta, Ibadan, Iwo and Osogbo
in the south and Ilorin, Kano, Zaria, Kaduna and Sokoto in the
north. The Moore Plantations at Ibadan were said to have been
founded by the BCGA as an experimental farm for cotton growing. The experiment in the south did not succeed too well as
the interest in cocoa plantations occupied the minds of most
farmers. However the experiment was very successful in the
north. The BCGA supplied cotton seeds to farmers free of
charge in an effort to increase production. The Association
not only opened up profitable employments for people in the
cotton-growing area, but offered the country another of its
cash crops and so helped in the diversification of the Nigerian
economy.

BROADCASTING CORPORATION OF BIAFRA. When Eastern Nigeria
declared itself a Republic of Biafra in 1967, the Eastern Nigeria broadcasting service, "Radio Enugu," was renamed the
Broadcasting Corporation of Biafra. The corporation played a
very prominent role in the secessionist propaganda.

BUHARI, MAJOR-GENERAL MUHAMMADU. Head of State, born on
December 17, 1942 in Daura in Katsina Province of Kaduna
State, he attended the Katsina Middle School from 1953 to 1956
and later went to the Katsina Provincial Secondary School, now
Government College, Katsina. He joined the army in 1962 and
was trained at the Nigerian Military Training College in Kaduna,
Mons Officer Cadet School, Aldershot, in the United Kingdom
and was commissioned Second Lieutenant in January 1963.
General Buhari had served in many important positions
before December 31, 1983 when he became the Head of State
and Commander in Chief of the Armed Forces. He served
with the 2nd Battalion Nigerian Army in the Congo, now Zaire
in the early 1960's. In April 1964 he was posted to the Corps
of Supply and Transport where he served until August 1966.
He later served in many staff and command positions in the
army. In 1972 he attended the Defense Service Staff College,
Wellington, India. He was Director of Supply and Transport
of the Nigerian Army from September 1974 until July 30, 1975,

when he was appointed Military Governor of the North-Eastern State. When the state was broken up into three different states in February 1976, he was named Military Governor of one of them, Borno State. In March 1976, he was reassigned as Federal Commissioner for Petroleum and Energy. On December 31, 1983, after the administration of President Shehu Shagari had been overthrown by a military coup d'état he became the Head of State and Commander in Chief of the Armed Forces. He was ousted from power on August 27, 1985, after twenty months in office, and was retired in September 1985.

-C-

CALABAR. Calabar, the capital of the Cross River State is a coastal town which has always enjoyed a special place, like Lagos, in the political development of Nigeria. It was one of the earliest British trading posts in the Eastern part of the country. The first Consul-General, Major Macdonald was appointed there in January 1891. The people traded in palm oil with the Royal Niger Company. After the coming into operation of the Clifford Constitution of 1922, Calabar enjoyed the status of a municipality with an elected member to represent her in the Legislative Council of 1923. Calabar and Lagos were the first two cities where elections were held for members of the Legislative Council.

Calabar has also been famous for being an early place for missionary activities. The first group of missionaries to land there were the Presbyterians who came in 1846. Calabar is now a university city.

CALABAR-OGOJA-RIVERS STATE (COR). With the constitutional changes into a federal system coming into effect, non-Ibo speaking groups in the former provinces of Calabar, Ogoja and Rivers who were minority ethnic groups in the Eastern Region began to agitate for a state separate from the numerically dominant Ibo areas of the region. The demand for the Calabar-Ogoja-Rivers State was made first in 1953 at the conference of chiefs and representatives of the areas. In 1954 the Calabar-Ogoja-Rivers (COR) Movement was formed and inaugurated at Uyo in Calabar province. The leader of the movement was Dr. Udo Udoma, a member of the House of Representatives for Opobo, and a member of the United National Independence Party and the President of the Ibibio State Union.

The proposal for a separate state became an important issue in the Eastern Regional election of 1957. It was supported by the United Nigeria Independent Party, but was opposed by Dr. Nnamdi Azikiwe and his party on the ground that it would break up the Eastern Region and that the agitators for it were motivated by anti-Ibo sentiments and hate. However in 1967, their demands became a reality when the 12-state structure came into being. But rather than a COR State, there were the Rivers State and the South-Eastern State. The South-Eastern State was later changed into the Cross River State in February

1976 when seven more states were created from the old 12 states.

CALIPHATE. The Caliphate was the administrative division into which the Moslem areas of the Northern Region were divided. After the death of Usman Dan Fodio, who initiated the Holy War (Jihad), the areas under his lieutenants were divided into two Caliphates: Sokoto and Gwandu. Bello, the son of Usman Dan Fodio ruled in Sokoto while his uncle, Dan Fodio's brother Abdullahi, ruled in Gwandu.

CAMERON, SIR DONALD CHARLES. Governor of Nigeria 1931-1935, born in 1875, he served in British Guiana, Newfoundland and Mauritius before he joined the colonial administration in Nigeria. He became interested in Lord Lugard's idea of indirect rule. From Nigeria he was sent to Tanganyika (now Tanzania) 1925-31, where he organized the country's Civil Service and introduced a Legislative Council and successfully opposed the effort to unite Tanganyika, Kenya and Uganda. He then returned to Nigeria where he served as Governor, 1931-1935. His one great objective was the reform of the administrative system then operating, which he believed was deviating from the original idea of the founder. He was concerned about the slow progress in the north where he felt the government had too long permitted the development of a system of fiefdom. He abolished the system whereby British administrators sat as judges. He abolished the Provincial Courts, where lawyers were not allowed to appear, and replaced them with the High Courts and Magistrate Courts where lawyers could appear. He also set up a system for a Native Court of Appeal and subordinated all types of courts in the country to the authority of the Supreme Court. Cameron did not believe in the policy set up by Lord Lugard of developing the north and the south on separate lines. He encouraged northern rulers and their staff to visit the south and the United Kingdom. His ideas were articulated in his "Principles of Native Administration and their Application" in 1934. He opened the Yaba Higher College which was the first postsecondary institution in Nigeria. He left Nigeria in 1935, and was succeeded by Sir Bernard Bourdillon. He later served as a member of Asquith Commission in 1943. He died in 1948.

CAMEROONS. In 1884, Germany hoisted her flag over the Cameroons, just a few days before the British arrived to declare it a British Protectorate. The Germans ruled it till the end of the First World War when it came under the mandate of the League of Nations, and was placed under the British administration in 1922. The British government then brought it under the administration of the government of Nigeria and administered it as part of Nigeria. In 1947, the League of Nations mandate was replaced with a Trusteeship Agreement between the United Nations and Britain.

However as Nigeria moved toward independence, demands

were being made that the Cameroons should be granted autonomy from Nigeria. This demand became intensified in 1953 after the Eastern Regional Crisis. Cameroons' representatives in the Eastern Region began to demand Cameroon autonomy from the Eastern Region. In 1953 they submitted a memorandum to the Secretary of State for the colonies asking for a regional legislature of their own. At the Lagos Conference of 1954, Southern Cameroon was granted an autonomous status and so ceased to be a part of the Eastern Region of Nigeria but it remained as a quasi-federal territory of the Federation of Nigeria. By this means the Federal Legislature and the Federal Executive Council would still have jurisdiction in the territory over matters in the federal and concurrent lists. Northern Cameroons on the other hand did not opt to break away from the Northern Region and pull out of the Federation. The view of the leadership was that they wished to remain part of the Northern Region.

According to the 1954 Constitution, the House of Assembly of the Southern Cameroons consisted of the Commissioner of the Cameroons, who was President of the House, three ex-officio members, 13 elected members, six members representing the Native Authorities of the Southern Cameroons, and not more than two special members appointed by the Governor-General to represent interests or communities not otherwise adequately represented. In 1957 the status of Southern Cameroons was raised to that of a region within the federation and provisions were made for the position of Premier as in other regions but the ultimate responsibility for the territory still rested with the Governor-General. In 1961, after Nigeria became independent, there was a referendum in the whole of Northern and Southern Cameroons under the British administration to determine whether or not both north and south or any of them should opt out of the Federation of Nigeria or stay in it. The results of the referendum showed that Northern Cameroons preferred to stay in the Federation while Southern Cameroons opted out to join the Republic of Cameroon.

CANAIRELIEF. A Canadian relief organization which played an important role in giving relief materials to the war-affected areas of the country during the civil war, 1967-1970.

CARPET CROSSING. Carpet crossing denotes the movement of a parliamentarian from one party to the other. It might be from the opposition party to the government party or vice versa. The practice started in the Western Region after the 1951 regional election which the National Convention of Nigeria and Cameroons (NCNC) apprently won. But when the house met, some members of the NCNC crossed to the Action Group party (AG) giving the AG the majority it needed to form the government of the region.

After independence and during the first Republic, carpet crossing was a common feature of Nigerian politics. The period witnessed a constant drift of opposition members in parliament or in the regional Houses to the government side. As a result of this practice, the Action Group, which won 75 seats in the Federal House of Representatives in Lagos in 1959, was by 1963 (after the 1962 crisis) reduced to only 21 members.

To prevent this practice which was open to great corruption from continuing, the 1979 Constitution section 64(1a) provides that a member of any legislative house loses his seat when, "being a person whose election to the House was sponsored by a political party, he becomes a member of another political party before the expiration of the period for which that House was elected." The only exception to this was if a party breaks into two factions or two parties merge into one.

CARR, HENRY RAWLINGSON. Born on August 15, 1863 in Lagos, he was the son of an immigrant from Sierra Leone who originally was from England. He attended St. Paul's (Breadfruit) School and Olowogbowo Wesleyan Elementary School, all in Lagos, from 1869-1873. In 1874, he went to the Wesleyan Boys' High School in Freetown, Sierra Leone, and in 1877 he was admitted to Fourah Bay College where he obtained a Bachelor of Arts degree in 1882, being the first student of the institution to obtain an honors degree. He then went to Britain and enrolled at the Lincoln's Inn, St. Mark's College in Chelsea and at the Royal College of Science in South Kensington in London. He returned to Nigeria in 1885 and joined the Church Missionary Society (CMS) Grammar School in Lagos as a Senior Assistant Master. In 1889 he joined the civil service as a Chief Clerk and became the first sub-Inspector of Schools in Lagos. In the following year he became an Assistant Secretary for Native Affairs. He was later transferred to the Department of Education as a Provincial Inspector and later as Chief Inspector of Schools in the southern part of the country. Before he retired in 1924 he was the Commissioner for the Colony of Lagos.

Henry Carr believed that education was most necessary for the development of the individual, and therefore he devoted his life to the advancement of education in Nigeria. In 1928 he was appointed to the Legislative Council as an adviser on education until 1941. For his contribution to the development of education in the country he was honored with honorary degrees of Master of Science and Doctor of Civil Law and Commander of the British Empire (CBE). He died on March 6, 1945.

CATHOLIC CHURCH. As early as 1472, Portuguese merchants had visited Lagos and Benin. By 1515, some Catholic missionaries had established a school in the palace of the Oba of Benin for his sons and those of his chiefs, some of whom were converted to Christianity. As such the Catholic missionaries were the first to enter Nigeria. However their initial effort was almost completely destroyed by the slave trade which lasted for almost 300 years.

The second coming of the Catholic church was in 1868. The church set up mission schools in Lagos and from there it moved inland. Most of the adherents of the Catholic faith in the country are in the Eastern part of the country. The Catholic church is one of the major churches that have advanced the course of educational development in the country.

CATTLE TAX. This is a tax payable by cattle owners in the former Northern Nigeria. This tax was imposed because the nomadic herdsmen normally did not pay community tax. Generally herds were counted from June of each year and collection of the tax used to begin in July and close in November unless extensions of periods were granted by the Ministry of Local Government.

CENSUS. There have been four censuses in Nigeria from 1952 to 1983, but only two of these have been accepted and used. The colonial authorities carried out the 1952-53 census with the following results for the main divisions into which the nation had been divided: east 7,215,251, west 6,685,065, north 16,835,582, federal territory of Lagos 267,407. Total: 30,403,305. Many people criticized this census because it was said to be inaccurate: many people avoided being counted because they thought the purpose was to impose taxation on them. It was also criticized on the ground that the enumerators did not visit many villages. Nevertheless the figures became the basis of the allocation of federal seats to the regions and Lagos.

The 1962 census started on May 13, but because of the apparent inflation of the figures in some of the regions, and the controversies arising from it, both the federal and the regional governments agreed in September 1963 to cancel it and authorize a new one. This started on November 5 and ended on November 8, 1963. The operation was to be in the hands of regional officials, but each region was to send teams of inspectors to the other regions to observe the procedure and carry out checks. Demographic tests would also be applied to the figures when they arrived at the Lagos headquarters. The outcome of the census was announced on February 24, 1964 with the following figures: north 29,777,986, east 12,388,646, west including the newly created Mid-Western Region 12,811,837 and Lagos 675,352. The total was 55,653,821. There was a lot of uproar over these figures, for many people believed them to have been rigged and grossly inaccurate. When the Eastern Region, which appeared most aggrieved, could not persuade the federal government and the other three regions to cancel it, it went to the Supreme Court asking that because of the many irregularities in the process of the counting, the court should declare the exercise invalid. But the court refused to accept its plea and so dismissed the case. The figures were finally accepted and they became the basis for the allocation of seats to the states in the federal legislative houses and the basis for the national development planning.

In 1973, the Military administration under General Yakubu Gowon carried out another census, but it was more widely
rigged than ever before. As such it generated a lot of debate
and hot blood, to the extent that General Murtala Muhammed
on his accession to the headship of the nation in July 1975 had
to say that it was clear that whatever results were announced
with regard to the 1973 population census, they would not command general acceptance throughout the country. The 1973 census
was therefore declared cancelled and the 1963 figures would
continue to be used for national planning.

The major problem with census in Nigeria is that it
has become too politicized--the people have been made to believe that census is used to allocate seats to their regions or
states in the national assembly, and also that it is the basis
for the sharing of the national pie whether at the national,
state or local level.

CENTRAL BANK OF NIGERIA. Established in 1958 with the sole
right to issue currency, maintain the country's external reserves, control commercial banks, safeguard the international
value of the naira, promote monetary stability, administer exchange control in Nigeria and to serve as the financial adviser
and banker to the federal government. The bank already has
branches in all the 19 states headquarters like Ibadan, Benin,
Enugu, Jos, Kaduna, Kano, Port Harcourt, Abeokuta, Maiduguri, Sokoto and Calabar.

CENTRAL WATER TRANSPORTATION COMPANY (CWTC). Established in 1970 by six shareholding states of Benue-Plateau,
East Central, Midwest, Kwara, North-Western and North-
Eastern states, with its base in Onitsha, the capital of the present Anambra State which is one of the states created out of
the East-Central State. The CWTC operates river transportation, with a fleet of tugs and barges, from the Warri and Burutu
ports in Bendel State and Port Harcourt in the Rivers State to
the river ports of Onitsha in Anambra State and to other places
on rivers Niger and Benue. The company also offers ferry
and passenger services at Idah in Benue State to connect the
town with Agenebode in Bendel State.

CENTRAL-WEST STATE. The Central-West State was carved out
of the former Northern Region in May 1967 and comprised of
Kabba and Ilorin provinces. In March 1968, the name of the
state was changed to Kwara State. See also KWARA STATE.

CHAHA, MR. BENJAMIN AKARI. Speaker, House of Representatives,
October 1983 to December 1983 during the second term of the
Second Republic. Born in 1940 at Zaki Biam in Katsina Ala/
Ukum, Benue State, he was educated at Zaki Biam and later
attended Teachers Training College at Mkar 1952-1954 and
Higher Teachers College at Gindiri, 1957-1958. He later
served in many different positions including Education Officer,
Supervisor of Education, and teacher. In 1978, when the ban

on political activities was lifted, he joined the National Party of Nigeria under the banners of which he was elected to the National House of Assembly. In 1983, after his reelection into the house, he became the Speaker of the House, a post he occupied until December 31, 1983 when the military took over power.

CHICK COMMISSION. After the Constitutional Crisis of 1953, there was need for the review of the 1951 Constitution. The regions wanted greater autonomy for themselves and they also began to make demands for fiscal autonomy. Sir Louis Chick was therefore appointed as Sole Commissioner by the Secretary of State for the Colonies to review the financial effect of the proposed federal constitutional agreement. The Commission was to draw up a revenue allocation scheme in which the principle of derivation would be followed to the fullest degree compatible with the needs of the central and regional governments.

The commission proposed that the system already in existence, under which revenue from the sale of tobacco and petrol were allocated to the regions, should be continued. Half of excise duties on beer should also go to the regions in proportion to their consumption. Also half the net proceeds of export duties should go to the regions of origin of the products. Personal tax should go to the regions where the taxpayer resided. Mining royalties should go to the regions where the minerals were extracted. Regional High Court fees and fines together with fees for licenses on regional matters should go to the regions. Furthermore one half of the net proceeds on import duties, with the exclusion of tobacco and petrol should be given to the regions and it should be divided as follows: 30 percent each to the Eastern and the Northern regions while the Western region would have the remaining 40 percent. The regions were to pay the federal government a proportion of the cost of collecting revenues that they shared and the federal government was given power to make grants to any regional government that might have financial difficulties arising from circumstances beyond its control.

The recommended principle of derivation was accepted. The west and the north did better under the principle, but the east did not do as well and it had to complain that the commission did not adequately take note of the needs of the centre and the needs of each of the regions.

CHIEF AND COUNCIL. Under the 1914 Native Authority Ordinance which made provisions for the peculiarities of traditional administrative systems existing in the various provinces, the colonial authorities set up two types of native administration in the north: Chief-In-Council and Chief-and-Council. The paramount chief in both cases had to consult with his council on all matters except where the matter was not of much importance or was too urgent to allow for consultation of his council. In such cases he could consult with two members, act and later report to the Council on what he had done. Where a difference came up was that under the Chief-In-Council system, the chief could disagree with the decision of his council and even act contrary to its decision if he believed this to be in the interest of his people. However he had to make a report of his action to the regional government which would assess whether or not his action was justified. On the other hand, under the Chief-and-Council system, the chief could not act contrary to the decision of his council. This type of system was generally associated with areas where chiefs had been "artificially created," i. e. , where tradition did not recognize such paramount chieftaincy. The Chief-In-Council system obtained generally where there was a system of traditional paramount chieftaincy like an Emir in his emirate. But where a chief abused his power by misgoverning his people, he could be reduced to a Chief-and-Council to curb such abuses in the future.

During the military regime, most native authorities in the north were reduced to Chief-and-Council system, but in 1976, the two systems were replaced with the local government system when the federal military government came up with its guidelines for the reform of local governments in the country.

CHIEFS. Chiefs are known by various names in different parts of the country. They are called Emirs among the Hausa/Fulani people, Oba among the Yoruba/Edo and Itsekiri people, and Obi among the people of Onitsha. The system of chieftaincy and the powers of Chiefs vary from one ethnic group to the other.

Among the Yorubas for example, in every town, the administration is hierarchical from the Oba or Bale at the top to the lowest-ranking Chiefs at the bottom. Each town has a number of Chiefs who help the Oba in the daily administration of the town. There are different kinds of Chiefs in each town. These range from quarter-heads to the head messenger. For each quarter of the town, there is a Chief who is responsible to the town council. There are War Chiefs like the Baloguns, Ritual Chiefs like the Arabas and so on. The chiefs are of grades with the most senior ones as the king-makers. The chiefs confer with the Oba on many issues affecting the town. They are also members of the Oba's Council otherwise called Town Council. They enjoy a great respect within the society.

The chiefs perform some judicial functions like settling quarrels or disputes that emanated within their area of jurisdiction. However, difficult cases are referred to the Paramount Chief or the Oba for final arbitration and settlement. It should be noted that during the colonial rule, the Chiefs were involved in the administration of Nigeria through the system called "indirect rule. " In the north, Emirs or Chiefs of various grades functioned as the Sole Native authorities and in the west, by 1939, five of the Ruling Chiefs or Obas had been appointed sole native authorities. In the east the situation was different. Because most people there did not have indigenous centralized authority like the Hausas or the Yorubas, the colonial authorities in pursuance of the system of indirect rule had to appoint what they called "Warrant Chiefs" and gave them great powers. This was resented and it led to series of crises and riots, especially the Aba Riot, in which many people were killed.

Today, in addition to traditional title holders like the above, there are Honorary Chiefs especially in the southern part of Nigeria where politicians, businessmen, professional people and even academicians actively seek to be honored with a chieftaincy title.

CHURCH MISSIONARY SOCIETY (CMS). The evangelization of Nigeria by the church missionary society first originated in London and in Freetown, Sierra Leone where the church had been active among slaves who were settled there beginning from 1787. The church, known in England as the Anglican church, sent its first missionaries to Nigeria in 1841 in the persons of Rev. J.F. Schön and Ajayi Crowther. In 1842 Henry Townsend and two freed Yoruba slaves, Andrew Wilhelm and John McCormack, arrived in Badagry, Lagos State and moved on to Abeokuta, Ogun State to explore the possibility of establishing a mission in the town to cater to the immigrant ex-slaves settling in the city. They arrived in the town in January 1843 and they began to work in earnest, building churches, mission houses and schools in Abeokuta and Badagry and opening up the country to Christian missionaries. By 1858, Rev. Samuel Ajayi Crowther had reached Onitsha on River Niger, in Anambra State.

In the field of primary, secondary and postsecondary education the church was pioneer and leader. It established primary and secondary schools and teacher training colleges in many parts of the country. The first postsecondary institution, Fourah Bay College in Sierra Leone, which helped greatly in the education of Nigerians was established by the church in 1827. The church is still growing strong. In 1979 the Anglican church of Nigeria was carved out of the Province of West Africa and became a full-fledged province of Nigeria with its own Archbishop.

CIRCULATION OF NEWSPAPERS DECREE. Before the military came to power, the circulation of some newspapers was restricted in some local government areas of the federation. This Decree lifted the bans on any such newspapers and prohibited such bans anywhere in the federation in the future.

CITIZENS' COMMITTEE FOR INDEPENDENCE. The Citizens' Committee for Independence was formed in Lagos in 1956. It was a small group of intellectuals and professionals like Chief R.O.A. Akinjide, a lawyer, Eme O. Awa, a lecturer, D.A. Badejo, an engineer, H.A. Oluwasanmi, a lecturer and A.B. Fafunwa, then a businessman. The Committee published a pamphlet entitled "Forward to Freedom" in 1957 and distributed a free copy to the Nigerian delegates going to the 1957

Constitutional Conference in London. The group asked for the creation of more states in the country based on the old provinces so as to place the new federation of Nigeria on a more harmonious basis to make for national unity. In the pamphlet, the committee also asked that the federal government have residual powers and that in the allocation of revenue, need should have greater weight than derivation. Furthermore they asked that primary, secondary and technical education in the nation should be funded by the federal government.

CITIZENSHIP. According to the 1979 Second Republican Constitution, the following are Nigerian citizens: Any person born in Nigeria before October 1, 1960, either of whose parents or any of whose grandparents belonged or belongs to a community indigenous to Nigeria; any person born in Nigeria after that date either of whose parents or any of whose grandparents is a citizen of Nigeria and any person born outside Nigeria either of whose parents is a Nigerian.

A woman married to a citizen of Nigeria or any person of full age and capacity born outside Nigeria, any of whose grandparents is a citizen of Nigeria may be registered as a citizen of Nigeria if the President is satisfied that he is a person of good character, with clear intention to be domiciled in Nigeria and takes the Oath of Allegiance. Furthermore, a person of full age and capacity, who satisfies the above conditions can be a citizen of Nigeria by naturalization if the Governor of the state where he or she lives believes that such a person is acceptable to the local community, he or she has made or is capable of making useful contribution to the progress and well being of the country and has immediately preceeding the date of application either resided continuously in Nigeria for a period of 15 years or has resided in Nigeria continuously for a period of 12 months, and during the period of 20 years immediately preceeding that period of 12 months has resided in Nigeria for periods amounting in the aggregate to not less than 15 years. A person with dual citizenship, i.e., a citizen of Nigeria by birth who is also a citizen of another country, does not forfeit his Nigerian citizenship if when he attains the age of 21 years he renounces the citizenship or nationality of the other country.

CIVIL COMMISSIONERS. After one and a half years of military rule, the Supreme Military Council (SMC) decided in July 1967 to invite civilians as full members of the federal and state executive councils (cabinet). These civilians were called Civil Commissioners to distinguish them from military men who were also members of the executive councils.

Even though they were supposed to be in charge of the ministries just as ministers used to be under the First Republic, their effectiveness was very limited. Many of them suffered from what may be called a crisis of identity: they were neither military men who naturally belonged in a military administration nor civil servants without whom the military could not function. Their position depended on the fiat of the Governor or the Head of State. They could not effectively supervise the activities of the civil servants and their effectiveness gradually waned.

CIVIL WAR. The Nigerian civil war came about mainly as a result of ethnic suspicion and leadership tussle. In the first place, the Hausa/Fulani people saw the January 15, 1966 coup as a plot by the Ibos to dominate the country. The reactions of the northerners towards the January 15 coup led to a counter coup on July 29, 1966 which was led by the northern military officers. A lot of high-ranking Ibo officers were killed including the Supreme Commander of the Armed Forces and Head of the national military government, Major General J. T. U. Aguiyi-Ironsi who was an Ibo. Also, a lot of civilians who were Ibo were murdered in Kano and Kaduna. All this made the Ibos feel that they were victims of genocide. The Ibos then felt that they could no longer be secure within the Federation of Nigeria. Also, General Gowon who emerged as the nation's leader after the second coup of July 1966 was unacceptable to Lt. Col. Odumegu Ojukwu who was then the Military Governor of Eastern Nigeria. According to him, there were officers superior to Gowon and as such he would not agree to the leadership of Gowon.

On January 4, 1967, Ghana's Head of State, General Ankara, organized a reconciliation meeting between the federal government and the Eastern Region at Aburi, Ghana. But the meeting failed to end the crisis because the resolutions reached at the meeting were interpreted differently by both parties.

On April 1, 1967, Ojukwu announced that all revenues due from any source whatsoever in Eastern Nigeria which were being collected for or on behalf of the federal government would be paid to the government of Eastern Nigeria. This edict also empowered the Eastern Regional government to take over all the federal government departments and statutory corporations situated in the region. The federal government reacted by suspending all flights between all parts of Nigeria and the Eastern Region and ordered the blockade of all the ports in the east. Furthermore postal services to the east were grounded.

On May 27, 1967, General Yakubu Gowon declared a state of emergency throughout the federation and announced the division of Nigeria into 12 states. On the 30th of May 1967, Lt. Col. Ojukwu proclaimed the independent Republic of Biafra on the ground that the people of Eastern Nigeria believed that they could no longer be protected in their lives and property by any government based outside Eastern Nigeria.

The federal government described the action of the Eastern Regional government as a rebellion and promised to crush it. On July 6, 1967, fighting broke out. The federal government described it as a "police action" against Ojukwu's act of rebellion. The end of the war however came on January 12, 1970 when Lt. Col. Effiong announced, after Lt. Col. Ojukwu had fled the country, the surrender of Biafra. On the second

day General Gowon accepted the surrender of the Biafran soldiers and promised an amnesty for secessionist supporters.
During the war many efforts were made to reconcile
the two sides. There was the Kampala Peace Talk of May
23 to 31, 1968, the Niamey meeting between July 16th and
26th of 1968, and the Addis Ababa talk of August 5th to 13,
1968. All these meetings did not yield any appreciable success. Biafra put up a strong propaganda effort to achieve
international recognition, but in spite of this, only four African countries, Tanzania, Gabon, Ivory Coast and Zambia in
Africa and the Republic of Haiti recognized her.

CLAPPERTON, HUGH. One of the leading pioneering explorers of
the interior of Africa for the purpose of opening up trade with
the people of the area, he together with Denham and Oudney
left for Nigeria from Tripoli across the Sahara in 1821. They
arrived at Lake Chad in 1823 and from there they went to
Bornu where they were received by Al Kanemi. From there
they went to Kano, and later to Sokoto where Sultan Bello received them well and expressed desire to establish commercial
relationship with Britain. Clapperton then returned to England.
The report made the government equip another expedition led
by Clapperton with the object of reaching the interior from the
sea through River Niger. When he got to the coast, he did not
discover the port which the Sultan Bello had told him would
lead him up the Niger River, and so he decided to go by foot
from Badagry to Sokoto. Upon arrival in Sokoto he saw that
the attitude of the Sultan to him had changed. He soon fell
ill and died in 1827.

CLIFFORD CONSTITUTION (1922). The Clifford Constitution came
after strong pressure from organizations like the National Congress of British West Africa for greater representation in the
Legislative Council. Under the constitution there was a Legislative Council for the Colony of Lagos and the Protectorate of
Nigeria made up of 46 members, 27 of whom were officials
and 19 unofficials. Out of the 19 unofficial members 15 were
nominated by the Governor while four were elected on the basis
of three members to represent Lagos the capital city and one
to represent Calabar. The Legislative Council legislated for
the Colony and the Southern provinces while the Governor extended parts of the legislation that were relevant to the Northern provinces by proclamations. What the country generally
had in common was the annual budget which was prepared for
the whole country. In addition to the Legislative Council,
there was an Executive Council which was an advisory body
to the governor. The Executive Council was composed of officials who at the time were all expatriates since there were
no African principal officials or heads of departments at the
time. The constitution was remarkable for one thing: its introduction of the elective principle into the composition of the
Legislative Council. However, the exclusion of the Northern
provinces from its overall authority helped to exacerbate the
north-south dichotomy.

COAL. Coal, one of the important mineral resources of Nigeria, was discovered in 1909 in Enugu, Eastern Nigeria, the present capital of Anambra State in the former Eastern Region of Nigeria. By 1915, the first colliery in West Africa was opened there. In the past the Nigerian Railway used to buy most of the coal produced but the introduction of diesel engine locomotives has depressed the business considerably.

COCOA. Cocoa was introduced into Nigeria in the nineteenth century, and for many years Nigeria was second only to Ghana as a cocoa producing and exporting country. In 1965 the country produced almost one quarter of all the world total but this production has been rapidly falling partly as a result of the aging of the old trees and failure to substitute them with new ones, and partly due to the oil boom which attracted farmers away from not very profitable farms to the cities where they could earn wages in the construction and other works going on in the country. The government through the reorganization of the Cocoa Marketing Board has tried to encourage farmers to produce more, but there is no sign yet that the effort is succeeding. In spite of this however, cocoa is still the most important Nigerian export after oil. It is grown mostly in Ondo, Oyo and Ogun States.

COCOA MARKETING BOARD. Established in 1947 for the purpose of controlling all exports of cocoa. The establishment of the Board removed the purchase of cocoa from the West African Produce Control Board (WAPCB). The Board was to recommend the fixed price of cocoa to the government. The Board was dissolved in 1954 when the Western Nigeria Marketing Board was established to take charge of the purchase of cocoa and other agricultural produce in the region.

CODE OF CONDUCT. At the outbreak of the civil war, General Yakubu Gowon, believing that he was taking only a police action against the rebellion of Lieutenant Colonel Odumegwu Ojukwu and his clique, issued a Code of Conduct to his armed forces. He referred to the international reputation of the Nigerian Army before the civil war, and went on to give reasons for going to war. He demanded loyalty, patriotism and discipline from officers and their men alike and exhorted them to behave humanely. He stressed the political nature of the war and told them that they were not fighting a war against a foreign enemy, nor were they fighting a Jihad or religious war--they were only subduing Ojukwu's rebellion. He then went on to outline how civilians, churches, foreigners, mosques and properties and prisoners of war should be treated. However he said mercenaries were their worst enemies and should not be spared. The troops must always remember that other nations of Africa and the whole world were looking at the country to see how well it could solve its problem. He concluded by reminding them that some of the soldiers they were fighting against were forced to fight against them by Ojukwu, and that

they were their old comrades in arms and would like to remain so. As such they should be treated with respect and
dignity, except those that were hostile to them.

COKER COMMISSION OF INQUIRY. Set up by the federal government in June 1962 after a state of emergency had been declared in the Western Region, its purpose was to look into
the affairs of certain statutory corporations in Western Nigeria.
The Chairman of the Commission was Justice G. B. A. Coker.
    The report of the Commission was a serious indictment
of the Action Group Party administration of the region. The
Commission found that the National Bank owned by the government of the region made unsecured loans to the Action Group
through the medium of fictitious accounts, and that on one occasion it concealed the actual indebtedness of the party to the
bank from federal government examiners. Further still it
found that the National Investment and Properties Company
Limited (NIPC) created in 1958 apparently to develop properties owned by the National Bank was in fact owned by four
leading members of the Action Group, who also happened to
be its directors. However the chief purpose the company
served was to subscribe or guarantee money for charitable
political causes. The commission found that the shares held
by the four directors were in fact purchased with funds diverted from the company itself. More still, the company bor-
rowed freely from the Western Region Marketing Board which
had the responsibility of purchasing export crops from farmers
at stabilized prices for sale abroad and was empowered to supply
capital to statutory corporations in an effort to further the economic development of the region. Thus the company received
from the Board over £6 million. Still more strange was the
finding that over £2 million allocated to the Western Development Corporation by the Board had also been diverted to the
NIPC and that the NIPC was making great profit over the sale
of property to the Western Regional government at inflated
prices.
    On March 17, 1963, the Western Nigerian government
announced that it would acquire for public purposes all property
owned by the National Investment and Properties Company in
the region, in accordance with the recommendation of the Commission.

COLONIAL DEVELOPMENT CORPORATION. The Corporation was
created by the United Kingdom's Overseas Resources Development Act of 1948. Its purpose was to formulate and carry out
projects for the development of the colonial resources. The
corporation played a significant role in the development of Nigeria: it invested in engineering, industry, housing development and sawmills. It permitted and encouraged participation
by commercial firms and by the government and its agencies
so that these could eventually assume full responsibility for
them.

COLONIZATION. With the abolition of slave trade, the intensification in the search for legitimate trade, and the increased growth of the palm oil, the British government in 1849 appointed John Beecroft as the Consul for the Bight of Benin and Bonny, with the task of regulating commercial relations with the coastal people. However Beecroft was not satisfied with such a modest assignment; he began to interfere in the internal affairs of the coastal states, and backed by the British gunboats, he began the process that finally led to the imposition of British colonial rule on the whole of the country. In 1861, as a result of the internal conflicts in Lagos and the pressure brought to bear on the British authorities by commercial and missionary interests, the British had Lagos Island ceded to them and proclaimed it a Crown Colony. From there the British began to spread their tentacles to the hinterland.

    Because of the pressure of competition brought to bear on the British by the French and the Germans in the area, the British government had to abandon its earlier policy not to expand their colonial possession in the area. Thus through the initiative of the United Africa Company, formed by George Goldie by the amalgamation of a number of British firms in 1879, which had secured trading rights in parts of the country that subsequently became Northern Nigeria, Nigeria was recognized as being under a British sphere of influence during the Berlin Conference of 1885. In 1886 the UAC received a Royal Charter to administer the territory but in 1899, the charter was revoked and the British government began to directly administer it under the name "Protectorate of Northern Nigeria."

    Similarly in 1885, the delta area of the country was proclaimed the Oil Rivers Protectorate after many treaties had been signed between the local rulers and the British consular officials. In 1893, the protectorate had been extended inland and was then known as the Niger Coast Protectorate. In 1906, Lagos Colony was merged with this protectorate and became known as the Colony and Protectorate of Southern Nigeria. In 1914, the two British administrations, the Protectorate of Northern Nigeria and the Colony and Protectorate of Southern Nigeria were merged to form a single unity known as Nigeria under British rule.

COMET, THE. On July 14, 1933 Duse Mohammed Ali, an Egyptian internationalist, launched his weekly Comet which D. Nnamdi Azikiwe acquired in 1945 and turned into a daily newspaper. The paper which was then published in Lagos was transferred by him to Kano, making it the first daily newspaper in Northern Nigeria.

COMMISSIONER. The term "Commissioner" has been used to refer to the occupier of different offices in the history of Nigeria. It referred to the administrative head of each of the Northern and Southern protectorates (1900-1909), and under Sir Donald Cameron (1931-1935). In this sense it is equivalent to a Lieutenant Governor, which the head of each unit was called from

1909 to 1931. It has also referred to political appointees like Commissioners of Native Courts and Provincial Commissioners. Under the military administration a Civil Commissioner was a civilian member of the military cabinet known then as the Executive Council. Under the 1979 Constitution, a Commissioner is a political appointee of the State Governor and a member of the Governor's cabinet. The term can also refer to a member of a federal or state commission, be it an ad hoc commission as a commission of inquiry or a full-time commission like the Public Service Commission.

COMMODITY BOARDS. Following the creation of states in Nigeria, the reorganization of the various states marketing boards became a pressing problem, more so since the increasing expenses and administrative overheads of each board were eroding the income that was coming to the farmers and which could still be worse if each state had its own marketing boards. The military government therefore in 1976 set up a committee to study the operation of the state marketing boards system and the Nigerian Produce Marketing Company. Following the report of the Committee the government began a thorough reorganization of the system on a nationwide basis. The government set up a new commodity marketing system made up of a price-fixing authority and seven commodity boards, each responsible for different commodities--cocoa, groundnut, cotton, palm produce, rubber, grains and root crops. The objective of the new boards was not only to market raw materials for the world market as previously done but more importantly to encourage the production of the commodities and organize the marketing of such commodities for local consumption and local processing, with maximum benefit to the farmers. As a result of this reorganization, the Nigerian Produce Marketing Company and the then-existing state marketing boards were phased out in 1977.

COMMON SERVICES see INTERIM COMMON SERVICES AGENCY and EASTERN STATES INTERIM ASSETS AND LIABILITIES AGENCY and page 99.

COMMONWEALTH. An international organization made up of Britain and some members of the old British empire, who have now become independent including many countries in Asia, Africa and North and South America. When Nigeria became independent in 1960, it became a member of the organization and is still an important member of it. In addition to their common imperial bond, the member countries cooperate on economic, social and political matters.

COMMUNITY TAX. Community tax was formerly called Haraji in the north where it was in practice. It used to be paid by persons who were not salary earners, including those whose income did not exceed ₦800 per year. In some places, it was a flat rate on everybody but in others, a fixed amount was levied on a community or village and the community or village head would decide how much each tax payer would pay. Under the British, the Native Authority kept 7/8 of the tax collected while it handed over the rest to the government.

CONSTITUENCY DELIMITATION COMMISSION. At the 1957 constitutional conference, agreement was reached that the country should be divided into 320 single-member constituencies for the purpose of federal elections on the basis of about one member to 100,000 people. As such a Delimitation Commission headed by Lord Merthyr a deputy Speaker of the House of Lords was appointed. The commission recommended 174 seats to the Northern Region, 73 seats to the Eastern Region, 62 seats to the Western Region, eight seats to the Cameroons and three seats to Lagos.

CONSTITUENT ASSEMBLY. On September 14, 1976, the Constitution Drafting Committee (CDC) submitted its report and on October 7, 1976 the Constituent Assembly was set up to receive and collate comments from the public on the draft constitution and in the light of these, revise the draft. The Assembly was made up of 203 elected members. Each state had five members on the basis of equality while the remaining seats were computed on the basis of population. Members of the Assembly were elected by the various local government councils which constituted themselves into electoral colleges. In addition to the elected members, 20 other members were appointed to the assembly to represent interests that were inadequately represented through the election process. These included women, labor, commerce, press, education, students, public servants and traditional rulers. Justice Udo Udoma, a Judge of the Supreme Court of Nigeria was appointed Chairman of the Assembly by the Supreme Military Council on September 11, 1977. When the Assembly met on October 6, 1977 it totalled 230 elected and nominated members. On August 29, 1978, after 11 months of open debate, it submitted its report and was then formally dissolved.

CONSTITUTIONAL CONFERENCES. The calling of constitutional conferences was the British government's method of involving public opinion and most vocal political groups in their overseas territories in the discussion of the kind of government that they would like to live under. In the constitutional history of Nigeria, there were many such conferences.

The first took place in Ibadan, capital of the Western Region, to review the Richards Constitution which was strongly criticized for lack of consultation with the people before it was drawn up; Sir John Macpherson decided that full consultation should be made in its review. The procedure for its review went through village meetings, provincial conferences, regional conferences and finally the general conference which was composed of all unofficial members of the Legislative Council together with additional representatives of the Regional Conferences and the Colony and Lagos conference. The general conference agreed on a number of issues which became incorporated into the Macpherson Constitution of 1951.

The Macpherson Constitution, however, was not destined to last, for in its operation, many unforeseen problems like the Eastern Regional Crisis of 1953 cropped up. As such there was need for another review of the constitution. The Secretary of State for the Colonies announced the Macpherson Constitution would be redrawn to provide for greater regional autonomy and for the removal of powers of intervention by the center. He therefore invited Nigerians to come to London for a constitutional conference. The conference met in London from July 30 to August 22, 1953 under the chairmanship of the Secretary of State for the Colonies, Lord Chandos, to consider the defects of the Macpherson Constitution, changes that would be required to remedy the defects, steps that would be taken to put the changes into effect and the question of self-government in 1956. Before the conference adjourned, it agreed to reconvene in Lagos in January 1954 to consider the advice of Fiscal Commissioner Sir Louis Chick, appointed by the Colonial Secretary with regard to the allocation of financial resources to the regions and the central government. The 1953 conference agreed on a federal system of government with residual powers in the hands of the regions. It agreed that the regions should be more independent of the center. It drew up a list of specific functions to be allocated to the center and a concurrent list. It also agreed on neutralizing Lagos, the capital city, instead of merging it with the west. On the question of self-government, the British government agreed to grant any region self-government on regional matters in 1956.

On January 19, 1954, there was the Lagos Conference which could be regarded as a continuation of the 1953 London Conference. The Conference reached decisions on fiscal agreement under the new constitution, regionalization of the public services and the judiciary and on granting a quasi-federal status to Southern Cameroon.

In 1957 there was another constitutional conference in London. It took place from May 23 to June 26. It was attended by all political parties and chaired by the Secretary of State for the Colonies, Mr. Lennox-Boyd. This conference agreed on a Senate for the Federal Parliament and the enlargement of the House of Representatives to 320 members. The position of the Chief Secretary was to be abolished. There was to be a House of Chiefs for the Eastern Region and the Southern Cameroon, and an all-African executive council for both the Eastern and the Western regions. It agreed on setting up an independent civil service commission, the retention of the police as a federal subject and on setting up commissions of inquiry to look into the fears of minorities, and on revenue allocation. It agreed on the Western and Eastern regions becoming self-governing that year provided they would do nothing to prejudice the functions of the federal government. The Governor was to appoint as premier the person who appeared to

him to command a majority in the House of Assembly and the
Queen's power to disallow regional legislation was to remain.
Southern Cameroon was to be raised to the status of a region.
The Northern Region was to be self-governing in 1959, and
election to the federal legislature was to be by universal adult
suffrage in the Eastern and Western regions, and the Southern
Cameroon, while it was to be by adult male suffrage in the
Northern Region. There was also agreement that the office
of the Prime Minister for the Federation should be created
and the Governor-General was to appoint as Prime Minister
any member who appeared to him to command a majority in
the House of Representatives. Before the conference closed,
the Secretary of State said that if a new Nigerian Parliament
to be elected in 1959 would pass a resolution asking for independence on a date in 1960, the British government would do
its best to implement it.

In 1958, another constitutional conference was held in
London from September 29 till October 27 to consider the reports of the Fiscal and Minorities Commissions appointed in
1957 and other outstanding matters from the previous constitutional conferences. It was also to discuss the request for
independence which Nigerian delegates were making to the
British government at the 1957 conference.

The Conference made decisions on matters like the inclusion of the Fundamental Human Rights in the constitution,
the police, self-government for Northern Nigeria, the position
of Lagos, the position of the Southern Cameroons, electoral
arrangements, fiscal arrangements, the minorities problems,
Nigerian independence and other pertinent matters. There was
to be a single police force under an Inspector-General of Police responsible to the federal government, but each regional
contingent was to be under the control of a commissioner who,
though under the general supervision of the Inspector-General
of Police, would be responsible for the recruitment of the force
under his charge within the region. The Conference accepted
the main recommendations of the Fiscal Commission chaired
by Sir Jeremy Raisman. It also agreed on a uniform set of
electoral qualifications for all future elections to the Regional
Houses of Assembly and the Federal House of Representatives.
On state creation, the Conference, rather than throw away the
opportunity to become independent in 1960 agreed to accept the
Minorities Commission's report that there was no need to create
new states. With this accepted, the Colonial Secretary announced the willingness of Her Majesty's government to grant
full independence to Nigeria on October 1, 1960.

The final Nigerian constitutional conference under the
colonial administration opened in London from May 10 to May
19, 1960. The Conference authorized a committee of legal
draughtsmen to submit a draft of the Independence Constitution
to the conference for approval. There was agreement on military cooperation between Britain and Nigeria, which would be
of mutual advantage to both countries and it was agreed that
if Northern Cameroon joined Nigeria, it would form part of

the Northern Region, but if Southern Cameroon joined, it would have the status of a fully self-governing region like other regions in the federation.

CONSTITUTIONAL REVIEW STUDY GROUP. This group was set up in March 1966 by General Aguiyi-Ironsi, the first Military Head of State. It had a membership of ten under Chief F. R. A. Williams a distinguished constitutional lawyer. The group was to identify those problems which militated against the unity of the country and which might make for the emergence of a strong central government. In addition it was to look into the extent to which territorial division of the country into constituent parts of the federation and the division of powers between the center and the regions fostered regionalism and contributed to the weakness of the center. Furthermore, it was to look into the merit of a unitary versus a federal system of government and a one-party system versus a multiparty system. The group met in June when specific assignments were given to individual members to study and report on. Before members had enough time to do the work assigned to them there was the July coup in which the General and others were killed.

CONSTITUTION DRAFTING COMMITTEE. The Constitution Drafting Committee (CDC) was set up in September 1975 under the distinguished chairmanship of Chief Rotimi Williams, a prominent constitutional lawyer. The Committee was initially composed of 50 members but it was later reduced to 49 members when Chief Obafemi Awolowo declined to serve. The Committee was chosen on the basis of at least two members from each of the then-existing 12 states. Beyond this state and geographical representation there were no other criteria for the selection of members except to see that major professional and other groups were represented. Thus, there were lawyers, businessmen, professional men, administrators, university lecturers and so on. The committee was assigned the job of drafting a constitution that would be federal and democratic, in which basic human rights would be guaranteed and which would make for political stability and the development of the principle of constitutionalism. The Committee was not unanimous in its recommendations. Dr. Segun Osoba and Mr. Yesufu Usman submitted a minority report which was not contained in the official report of the Committee. In spite of this, the report generated a lot of debate all over the nation.

CONSTITUTIONS. Nigeria has gone through a long and tedious route in constitution making. There was the Clifford Constitution of 1922, the Richards Constitution of 1946, the Macpherson Constitution of 1951, the Lyttelton Constitution of 1954--each of which progressively made certain concessions to the nationalist demands--and finally before independence, the Independence Constitution which conceded full sovereignty to Nigeria.
    The Independence Constitution followed very closely the British constitution in that it was parliamentary, but it differed from it in that it was a written constitution. At the time of

independence in 1960, Nigeria was a federation of three regions. The Head of State was the Governor-General who was ceremonial head and represented the Queen of England. There was the Prime Minister, the leader of the majority party or coalition in parliament, who was responsible for the national government and who appointed members of his cabinet, which was collectively responsible to the parliament. Parliament, which was under a firm control of the majority party or coalition, was said to be supreme. In 1963 the country became a republic. The only major change to the Independence Constitution was that the Head of State was no longer the Governor-General but the President, who still was a ceremonial head as before.

In 1966, following the military takeover, much of the republican constitution was suspended, but in 1979 a new constitution came into being known as the Second Republican Constitution. This Constitution set up an executive presidential form of government. The president was popularly elected for a term of four years and could serve for only a second term. The President appointed his cabinet members with the approval of the Senate. Members of the cabinet were not members of the legislative assembly which was made up of the Senate and a House of Representatives. The Constitution guaranteed individual freedom of thought, conscience, association, movement, and expression. After the 1983 military coup d'état, parts of the Constitution were suspended and other parts could be amended by decrees.

CONSTITUTION (SUSPENSION AND MODIFICATION) DECREE NUMBER 1 OF 1966. After the military came to power in 1966, the first decree issued suspended certain provisions of the Republican Constitution, especially those dealing with the legislative and executive branches of the regional and national governments. Other provisions not suspended were to continue to have effect. Section six of the Decree stated that the validity of a decree made by the federal military government or an edict made by the regional governors could not be questioned by any court of law in the country.

CONTRACTS PANEL. On December 14, 1979, President Shehu Shagari appointed a six-man ministerial committee to study the award, costing the execution of federal government contracts and services throughout the nation. The President complained that the excessively high cost at which government contracts for works and services were executed was causing him great concern.

The committee was headed by the Minister of Finance, Professor S.M. Essang. Its terms of reference included a critical examination of the current procedures and conditions relating to the award of government contracts, the determination of how fair and realistic the prices arrived at for works and services compared with the ongoing rates in other countries and finding out if the costs of works and services in Nigeria were above the average in other countries. The committee was to make recommendations for an alternative system to the current procedure and suggest ways of eliminating or reducing areas of unjustifiable cost escalation in contract for works and services.

CONTRACT SYSTEM. This is the system which allows the employer, be it public or private, to hire a person on a contract which could be periodically renewed for as long as the employee's services are needed, that is as long as no "indigenous" replacement could be found for him. This means a person on this kind of contract cannot expect to be confirmed or allowed to have tenure. Effective use of this system by many state governments has greatly limited the geographical mobility of labor in the country and deprived various agencies of the expertise readily available in the country. In fact, many states prefer to hire expatriate Indians and Pakistani over Nigerians who may wish to settle down where they work.

COOPERATIVE MOVEMENT. With the growth of cocoa crop in Nigeria in the early part of this century, farmers in Western Nigeria began in the early 1920's to organize collective sale of their cocoa under the supervision of the Department of Agriculture. In the early 1930's the organization had become fairly well established in many places, so the government had to appoint an administrative officer as registrar of cooperative societies. Later a Cooperative Department was created, and made responsible for the affairs of cooperative societies. The new department saw to the training of Nigerian officials to teach the various associations how they could apply the basic principles of cooperation to solving practical problems and teach them a sound and simple system of accounting. Farmers who desired to form cooperative societies were also encouraged.

The cooperative society was based on the principle that the share capital of the society was provided by its members, the principle of one man, one vote regardless of capital holding, and the society did not make profit. Surpluses were allocated at the end of the financial year to members in accordance to the proportion of their sales or their purchases.

Other forms of cooperative associations came into being. There was the Association of Nigerian Cooperative Exporters which became a licensed buying agent for the Western Region Marketing Board and was responsible for selling the products supplied by the Produce Marketing Societies. There were also the Cooperative Thrift and Loan Societies which catered primarily to salary earners. Members of Thrift and Loan Societies were encouraged to save part of their salary with the society and could borrow from the society. Other cooperative associations also grew up like the Cooperative Thrift and Credit Societies for nonsalary earners and the Cooperative Consumer Societies. The movement even went into banking, with the establishment of the First Cooperative Bank in Western Nigeria in 1953. To improve efficiency of the various societies, government in 1953 opened a Cooperative Training School in Ibadan, the capital of Western Nigeria, to train cooperative inspectors, auditors and other staff.

COST OF LIVING ALLOWANCE (COLA). A sum of money granted in 1941 by the colonial government to civil servants, employees of native authorities and teachers on account of the rising cost of living caused by the Second World War.

COTTON. Cotton was one of the local crops which gave the Europeans the idea that Nigeria might be a great country for raw materials for their factories at home. The production of cotton is now concentrated in a few northern states and the present production falls far short of local needs of the textile factories. To encourage farmers to increase production, the government set up the Cotton Marketing Board with adequate money to pay the farmers for their cotton.

COUNCIL OF CHIEFS. Under the Richards Constitution of 1946, there were houses of chiefs in the north and in the Western Region. At the Constitutional Conference of 1958, it was also agreed that the east should have its own House of Chiefs. These houses constituted second legislative chambers in the regions. When the military took over power in 1966, and the legislative houses were dissolved, the chiefs in each region (and later each state) formed themselves into a council known as Council of Chiefs, with different names in each region like the Council of Obas in the west and Emirs Council in the north. The main function of the Council of Chiefs is to advise the state government on chieftaincy and other related matters. The council is made up of the first-class and in some places, second-class chiefs.

COUNCIL OF MINISTERS. The Council of Ministers was the principal instrument of public policy. It was established under the Macpherson Constitution of 1951. The Council consisted of the Governor, six official members and 12 ministers appointed by the Governor. Of these ministers, four were appointed from each of the regions from the members of the House of Representatives chosen by the regional legislatures to represent them.
    The ministers were not responsible for any ministries. Their responsibility was limited to dealing in the legislature with matters concerning their "subject" or "subjects" or introducing in the Council of Ministers matters concerning their subject or subjects. Furthermore, when a decision concerning their subject had been taken in the council of ministers, they were to ensure, in association with the appropriate officials, that effect was given to such a decision.
    Under the 1954 Federal Constitution, the Council of Ministers consisted of the Governor-General, three official members and three ministers from each region and one from the Cameroons. They were appointed by the Governor-General on the advice of the Regional Executive.

The Council of Ministers during this period served as a kind of a second chamber while at the same time it was the only policy-making body for the whole country. One of the weaknesses of this arrangement was that the council of ministers had regional basis and they were beholden to the regional executives by whose grace they were appointed. This necessarily facilitated the drift to the regionalism that later became characteristic of later politics.

COUNCIL OF STATE. The Council of State was originally created in 1975 by the military regime of General Murtala Muhammed. Before that time, military governors used to be members of the Supreme Military Council which was the highest policy-making body. In 1975, the Supreme Military Council no longer included the military governors. It was therefore thought necessary to set up an advisory body in the Council of State where each state would have an input into decisions of major political importance.

Under the 1979 Constitution, the Council of State is a federal agency, composed of the President who is also the Chairman, the Vice-President, all former Presidents and Heads of the Government of the federation, the Chief Justice of Nigeria, President of Senate, Speaker of the House of Representatives, all state governors, the Attorney General of the Federation and one person from each state appointed by the Council of Chiefs of each state. Its function is to advise the President on the national population census, the grant of prerogative of mercy, award of national honors, appointment to the Federal Electoral Commission, the Federal Judicial Service Commission and National Population Commission. It also can advise the President when requested on the maintenance of public order and any other matters that are put before it.

COUP D'ETAT. Nigeria has witnessed five successful coups d'état and one attempted coup. The first coup occurred on January 15, 1966 when a section of the Nigerian Army revolted in Lagos, Enugu, Ibadan and Kaduna and killed many army officers and many leading politicians including the Prime Minister, Sir Abubakar Tafawa Balewa, the Premier of Northern Nigeria, Alhaji Sir Ahmadu Bello, the Premier of Western Nigeria, Chief S. L. Akintola and the Federal Minister for Finance, Chief Festus Okotie-Eboh. The leader of the coup, Major C. K. Nzeogwu, said that they seized power to stamp out tribalism, nepotism and regionalism. However, rather than he becoming the head of government, it was the General Commanding Officer of the Nigerian Army, Major-General Johnson Thomas Umunankwe Aguiyi-Ironsi, who became the head of the Federal Military Government and Supreme Commander of the Nigerian Armed Forces.

He immediately announced decrees for the suspension of the offices of the President, Prime Minister and Parliament. He decreed that there should be military governors to head the governments of all the regions and that regional military government would be responsible to the federal military government.

The first coup was seen by some people as having been staged for the single purpose of bringing about Igbo domination. This impression was sadly reinforced by certain appointments and actions of the Ironsi regime. A good example of such actions was the Unification Decree of May 24, 1966 which abolished the federal structure of the country and set up a unitary form of government in its place. People from the Northern Region saw this as a concrete evidence of the Igbo people's attempt to dominate the rest of the country, and there were demands for secession to avoid such domination.

After the promulgation of the Unification Decree, violent protest demonstrations began in the Northern Region. Many Igbos were killed and their properties destroyed. This hostility towards the Igbos continued until July 29, 1966 when the Ironsi regime was overthrown by northern elements in the army. Their intention was to lead the north out of Nigeria, through secession. Their keyword was "araba," the Hausa word for secession. This second coup claimed the lives of Major General Ironsi, Lt. Col. Adekunle Fajuyi and many other military men. After a lot of negotiation, Lt. Col. Yakubu Gowon became the new Head of State. Gowon repealed the Unification Decree and brought back the federal structure.

The third coup, a bloodless one, took place on Tuesday July 29, 1975. It toppled the government of General Gowon, and General Murtala Muhammed emerged as the new Head of State. Many reasons were advanced for this coup:

1. In 1974, General Gowon in his National Day address to the nation dismissed as "unrealistic" the 1976 deadline previously made to return the government to civilian rule.

2. As the coup makers put it, the nation had been groping in the dark and the situation inevitably would result in chaos and bloodshed unless it was arrested. The administration had been characterized by indecision, indiscipline, lack of consultation and neglect. The Head of State had become inaccessible even to his official advisers and when advice was given, it was often ignored.

The coup brought Brigadier Murtala Muhammed and Brigadier Olusegun Obasanjo to power.

On February 13, 1976, there was an attempted coup, organized by Lt. Col. B.S. Dimka and others. In it, General Murtala Muhammed was killed, but it failed to gain support. All the organizers still in the country were apprehended, tried and those found guilty were publicly executed.

The next successful coup occurred on December 31, 1983 after Nigeria had experimented with the presidential system of government for four years and three months. It was a bloodless coup which brought Major General Muhammadu Buhari into the leadership of the country. The coup was sequel to the farcical electoral processes the nation went through in the second half of 1983, mismanagement of the economy which turned an oil-rich country into a beggar nation filled with corruption and indiscipline.

One major contribution of this coup to the political development of Nigeria was the insistence that past and present leaders must be made accountable for their stewardship. As soon as the coup became successful, past political leaders, beginning from the former Executive President of Nigeria, Alhaji Shehu Shagari, the Vice-President of Nigeria, Dr. Alex Ekueme, State Governors, Ministers and Commissioners who were in Nigeria, were arrested and detained. Their accounts were all frozen and investigations began on them to find out whether or not they had corruptly enriched themselves while in office. Many of these were found guilty and sentenced to varying terms of imprisonment. (Continued on p. 386.)

COURTS OF EQUITY. The Court of Equity was first set up at Bonny. It was a commercial association organized by some merchants in the Oil Rivers. It was composed of both white and black traders but the whites occupied the chair in monthly rotation. All trade disputes came before the court and with the consent of the traditional rulers, fines were levied on defaulters and collected. Similar courts composed of agents of various firms were set up in other areas like Calabar, Brass, Akassa and Opobo. Initially the courts possessed no legal status but its rules were submitted to the British government for approval or disapproval. In 1872 the courts were legalized by the Order in Council which helped to strengthen the administrative and judicial powers of the Consul by giving him power to inflict fines of a limited amount and to imprison for 21 days or even banish for one whole year from an area for a breach of the regulations set up between the British and the people.

COWAN INQUIRY. Set up in 1948 to investigate and report on the methods of negotiation between government and its employees on questions affecting conditions of service in government industrial establishments. In his report Mr. T.M. Cowan of the United Kingdom Ministry of Labor and National Service stressed the need for improving industrial relations by improving the organization of trade unions, continuity of leadership, and the need for discipline and education of the workers on the principles of trade unionism. The report also laid down the duties of government with regard to labor relations as being those of making laws that give room for union development, improving its own side of labor-management relations by employing the right kind of personnel officers in some of the principal industrial developments, provision of independent assistance to the growing trade union movement and the need to have adequate consultation and negotiation between government, its departmental representatives and the unions.

COWRY SHELLS. Cowry shells were used before the advent of the
Europeans as a medium of exchange among the Yorubas, Igbo
and the Benin peoples of Southern Nigeria. Even when the
British came with the circulation of British coins, cowry shells
were still being converted or being equated with British coins.
Among the Yorubas, six pence used to be equated with 2,000
cowries (Egbaa) and 1 shilling was 4,000 cowries (Egbaaji,
Egbaa meji), three pence was 1,000 cowries (Egberun). Cowry
shells were generally used for small exchanges locally while
costly beads were used on distant journeys for trade. The
shells used to be collected from the coast and especially along
the Indian Ocean. Cowries gradually faded out as commerce
grew more complex with modern technicalities and expanded
scope. Today the shells can be found as ornamentations
in palaces, shrines, museums, and they are even used for
decorative purposes in various houses, both public and private.
They are also used as part of Yoruba musical instruments
called sekere and dundun.

CROSS RIVER STATE. One of the three states carved out of the
former Eastern region in 1967 under the name of South-Eastern
State, it assumed its new name of Cross River State in 1976
because of the federal government policy of eliminating the old
idea of designating any state with its old geographical name of
West, East or North.
    The Cross River State lies within the Cross River basin;
the state has an area of 28,685 sq. km. It is bounded in the
north by the Benue State and shares common borders with the
Cameroon Republic in the east, the Atlantic Sea in the south
and is bounded by the Imo and Rivers states in the west. The
major ethnic groups inhabiting the state are the Efik/Ibibio,
the Annang, the Ejagham and smaller groups like the Ibeno,
Adoni, Yalla/Yache, Ukete and others. In spite of the differ-
ing dialects among these people, the linguistic root is Bantu.
    The Cross River State has concentrated into about
12,000 sq. km. of its land area, about one third of the nation's
forested land which produces the bulk of the nation's industrial
wood for domestic and export markets. The forests also abound
in rare wildlife such as gorillas, chimpanzees, leopards, buffa-
loes, snakes and monkeys. It has limestone, calcium, clay,
salt, lead and zinc and it is also oil producing.
    The state capital is Calabar. Following the Clifford
Constitution of 1922, which allowed the cities to elect four
representatives to the legislative council in Lagos, Calabar
elected one of them to the council while Lagos, the second
city, elected the remaining three.
    The state is well connected by road, sea and air to the
rest of the country. Among the most important holiday resorts
in the state are the Obudu Cattle Ranch, the Agbokim Falls,
the Obam Hills and the Calabar Zoo.

CROWN, THE. The Crown in Nigeria under the colonial rule legally
meant the Nigerian government which was subject to policy di-

rection and the power of disallowance exercizable by His/Her Majesty's Government in London. However, because that government was alien, the Crown came to mean, for many people, British imperialism.

CROWN COLONY. This is a colony under the power and authority of a king or queen. Its main characteristics are that the legislature of the colony is subordinate to its executive council and the colonial government is subordinate to the imperial government. Lagos became a Crown Colony when it was ceded to the British crown in 1861. From there as base, the British extended their jurisdiction into the interior.

CROWTHER, BISHOP SAMUEL AJAYI, 1809-1891. The first African Bishop of the Anglican church in Nigeria, he was an explorer and a missionary. He was born in Yorubaland about 1809 but was captured in 1821 during the civil war that devastated the area in the early nineteenth century and sold into slavery to the Portuguese slave traders. But the ship transporting him to America was seized by the British antislavery patrol ship and was released in Freetown, the capital of Sierra Leone. He was educated there by the Church Missionary Society (CMS) and was baptized in 1825. He later went to Fourah Bay Institute and after graduating, he became a schoolteacher. Due to how devoted, hardworking and intelligent he was, he was invited to join the British Niger expedition in 1841. He later went to England where he was ordained in 1844. He was then sent back to the west coast as a missionary. His first post was Badagry in Nigeria before being sent to Abeokuta in 1846. In 1854 and later 1857 he joined the W. B. Baikie expedition up the Niger River. The CMS later decided to create a West African diocese with indigenous African pastorate and selected Crowther to be the first indigenous Bishop in 1861. He was very successful in promoting Christianity and missionary education along the Niger River. Owing to his hard work and enthusiasm, he was able to attract many people to the church and the clergy. But not being able to supervise all the men and women working under him, discipline waned. He was criticized by white missionaries who opposed the setting up of an indigenous African pastorate and people like Sir George Goldie who believed that missionaries in Nigeria should help to extend British political influence, but he did not heed these criticisms very much. He resigned in 1890 and died the following year. Bishop Ajayi Crowther was known not only for his religious activities but also for his intellectual and scholarly achievements. His work included the translation of the New Testament into Yoruba. He was given an honorary degree of Doctor of Divinity by Oxford University.

    Bishop Ajayi Crowther was also an African nationalist. He had the strong belief during his missionary days that Africa needed to be saved by Africans.

CRUDE OIL SALES COMMISSION OF INQUIRY. The Commission,

headed by Mr. Justice Ayo Irikefe, a Judge of the Supreme
Court, was appointed by the federal government on April 16,
1980 to probe the alleged loss of ₦2.8 billion by the Nigerian
National Petroleum Corporation. The Commission found that
all crude oil sold by NNPC and payments therefrom were in
all respects made in accordance with the terms of their contract, that no proceeds of any sales were missing or improp-
erly accounted for, that no person had been found guilty of
fraud or wrongdoing with regard to the auditing or accounting
for the sales of crude oil, that no proceeds of sales of crude
oil were ever paid into the NNPC account with the Midland
Bank, International Division in London and that the corporation
as set up was extensive and far beyond normal span of management control. The government accepted the report and stated
that no ₦2.8 billion was ever missing from the account of the
company. Following this the government began to study necessary changes in the organization of the company.

CURRENCY. From January 1, 1973 Nigeria changed from the pound
sterling to the decimal currency known as the Naira which is
subdivided into 100 kobo. The word naira written with the
symbol N was adapted from Nigeria and Kobo has always been
a popular name for a penny in the old currency. Both terms
are the same in singular and plural forms. The naira is
presently issued in the ₦20, ₦10, ₦5, ₦1, and ₦0.5k denominations of notes, while the coins presently in use are in the
1 kobo, 5 kobo and 10 kobo denominations. Other denominations of coins not much in use are 1/2 kobo and 25 kobo. When
the new currency was issued, the naira was to be equivalent
to 10 shillings (£0.5) in the old currency and to be worth about
1.5 American dollars. The Nigerian government still exchanges the naira for the British pound or American dollar at
a rate not too far below this exchange rate even though the
price of the naira in the world money market has fluctuated
from day to day.

CURRICULUM CONFERENCE OF 1969. The report of this conference marked the beginning of the nation's action in the history
of educational research. The report reviewed the objectives
and purposes of primary, secondary, teacher training and university education and made recommendations on each sector.
It also examined the role of science and technology in national
development, and also the role of women in education. As a
result of the report, in 1972 the Nigerian Educational Research
Council was formed, charged with the duty of encouraging, promoting and coordinating educational research programs carried
out in Nigeria.

CUSTOMARY COURTS. Before the advent of colonial authorities in
Nigeria, cases of disputes over land and family matters were
heard in the courts of the Paramount Chiefs, Obas, Obis and
the Emirs. When the British came, rather than destroy the
system which they saw had existed since time immemorial and

which worked fairly efficiently, they decided only to reform it
and allow it to exist side-by-side with the British types of
courts, Magistrate and High Courts. These indigenous courts
were first called "native courts" but later came to be known
as "customary courts. " These courts still exist to administer
customary laws dealing with such matters as divorce contracted
in the traditional manner. In the Moslem areas of the north,
Moslem law is administered as customary law. The Sharia
Courts in the Moslem areas of the north are the courts to
which appeals lie from the Alkali or Moslem courts.

CUSTOMARY RIGHT OF OCCUPANCY. Under the Land Tenure Law
of 1962 in Northern Nigeria, one of the ways an individual or
a community could hold land was by the Customary Right of
Occupancy, which means the right of a member of an indigenous community or such a community to use or occupy a piece
of land in accordance with customary law prevailing in the
community. This right however could be revoked by the Minister if the land was needed for public use, but in such cases
compensations must be paid not for the land itself but for the
improvements and crops on it. In 1978, under the Land Use
Decree, all the land in a state was then vested in the Governor
of the state as a trust for the people but the right of occupancy
already acquired, either under customary law or under statute
law especially in the south where land was allowed to be purchased in "fee simple, " was recognized.

COMMON SERVICES. When Nigeria was divided into 12 states in
1967, there came the problem of sharing the assets and liabilities of the former Eastern and Northern regions by the new
states. To solve the problem, the federal military government
promulgated two decrees establishing agencies that could take
care of these assets and liabilities.
    The first decree was the Decree Number 12 of 1968
which established for the Northern Region the Interim Common
Services Agency to take care of the assets and liabilities of
the former Northern Region which was then divided into six
states. According to the decree, the Agency consisted of one
person from each of the six states of the former region appointed by the head of the federal military government. The
Chairman was to be appointed by the members from amongst
their members. The Agency was charged with the control,
operation and general management of the services, statutory
bodies and institutions, jointly owned by the states which were
inherited from the former Northern Region. It was empowered
to dispose of property that it no longer required on such terms
as it thought fit; to erect, provide, equip and maintain and keep
in repair buildings necessary for carrying out its duties and
invest its funds in Government Securities in Nigeria or in any
other manner approved by the Agency.
    Among the services, institutions and statutory bodies
that were vested in the Agency were Ahmadu Bello University
and its affiliated Schools and Services, Advanced Teachers

Colleges in Kano and Zaria, Government Press Kaduna, Sharia Court of Appeal, Kaduna Polytechnic, Livestock and Meat Authority, Northern Nigeria Housing Corporation, Northern Nigeria Marketing Board and the Northern Nigeria Radio Corporation. The Agency was dissolved in 1976 with the promulgation of Decree Number 19 of 1975. The decree made the term of the Agency to expire on the 31st of March 1976.

The second decree on the Common Services was promulgated in 1970 and titled "Eastern States Interim Assets and Liabilities Agency Decree 1970 (ESIALA). It was Decree Number 39 of 1970. According to the decree, the Agency consisted of the military Governors of South-Eastern State and Rivers State together with the Administrator of East-Central State. The office of Chairman of the Agency was to be held by each member in rotation for such periods as members might agree among themselves. All the assets and liabilities of the former Eastern Region which were vested in the Agency in trust for the Eastern States included statutory corporations established by law for the former region of Eastern Nigeria, the University of Nigeria, Nsukka, former government-controlled limited-liability companies and those jointly owned by the former government and any person corporate or incorporate.

-D-

DAILY EXPRESS. A daily newspaper formerly known as the Daily Service which was the official organ of the Nigerian Youth Movement (NYM) with its first editor being Ernest Ikoli. With the dissolution of the NYM, the Daily Service then became the official organ of the Action Group party (A. G.). The Daily Express was used throughout the first Republic as the official organ of the Action Group Party.

DAILY TIMES. One of the leading national newspapers, it was established in 1926 by Richard Barrow, Sir Adeyemo Alakija, a Nigerian barrister and some European businessmen. The first publication of the paper came out on June 1, 1926. Originally it was an independent newspaper, but in 1977, the federal government bought the largest share in the company, thus bringing the paper under the control of that government. Though still a national daily, it has come to be regarded as a government paper.

DANTATA, ALHASSAN. Said to be the wealthiest Nigerian in his time, Alhaji Alhassan Dantata's date of birth is not certainly known but it is said to be about 1880. As early as 1912, he had developed a business in kola nuts, trading in Kumasi, Ghana, from where he shipped kola nuts to Nigeria by sea. He returned to Nigeria in 1912 and turned his attention also to groundnut purchasing and became the main supplier of groundnuts to the Royal Niger Company. He went to Mecca after the First World War, via London where he was presented to King

George V. His businesses in kola nuts and groundnuts continued to grow. He even became one of the two major agents
buying groundnuts for the marketing board. He founded with
other merchants the Kano Citizens' Trading Company for industrial enterprises. It was he who started the Kano Textile
Mill in 1950. Before he died, he was appointed to some important positions including being a Director of the Railway
Corporation, and a member of the Emir of Kano's Council.
He died in October 1955.

D'AVEIRO, JOHN AFFONSO. A Portuguese explorer, he was recorded to be the first Portuguese explorer to visit Benin City
in 1485. Upon his return to Portugal, he reported to the King
of the great possibilities for opening up trade in ivory and
pepper with the people of the area and of evangelizing them.
He later on returned to Benin, to establish a trading post, where
he later died.

DAVID-WEST, PROFESSOR TAMUNOEMI SOKARI. An educationist
and newspaper columnist, born on August 26, in 1936 at Buguma, Kalabari in the Rivers State, he was educated at Kalabari National College in Buguma, University College, Ibadan,
Michigan State University and Yale University in the U.S. and
McGill University in Canada. Upon returning to Nigeria he
joined the staff of the University of Ibadan and rose to the position of Professor of Virology. He served as Commissioner
for Education and was later a member of the Constitution Drafting Committee. He has received many academic awards including a WHO Fellowship and Commonwealth Medical Research
Fellowship, and he is a member of many national and international organizations. In January 1984, after the military had
overthrown the government of President Alhaji Shehu Shagari,
he was appointed by the new Head of State as Minister for Petroleum and Energy.

DAVIES, CHIEF HEZEKIAH OLADIPO. A lawyer and businessman,
born on April 5, 1905, he was educated at the Methodist Boys'
High School, Lagos, King's College Lagos and at the London
School of Economics and Political Science in England. He was
called to the bar at the Middle Temple in London in 1946.
　　　　Chief Davies started as a teacher at the King's College
in Lagos from 1925 to 1926. In 1934, he became a cofounder
of the Nigerian Youth Movement (NYM) the first really nationalist organization in the country. And while in London he was
President of the West African Student Union (WASU), 1944-1945,
and in 1946, its Secretary General. Upon his return to Nigeria,
he was made Chairman of the NYM from 1946 to 1948. Also,
when the Egbe Omo Oduduwa which gave birth to the Action
Group Party was founded in 1948, he was its Legal Adviser.
He was also Legal Adviser to the Lagos and Colony State Movement from 1953 to 1956. He became a Queen's Counsel in
1958 and Fellow of the Institute of International Affairs of Harvard University. He later joined the Nigerian National Democratic

Party (NNDP) led by Chief S. L. Akintola and was elected member for Ekiti West Constituency into the Federal House of Representatives; he was later appointed Minister of State in the Federal Ministry of Industries from 1964 to 1966. He is at the head of many business companies: he is Chairman of the Board of Directors, Arbico Limited, Director of the Total Oil Products (Nigeria) Limited, Chairman of Safrap (Nig.) Ltd. and Chairman of the Hassan Transport Limited.

DECIMAL CURRENCY BOARD. The Board was established to supervise and superintend the changeover from the pound currency which had been in operation in Nigeria since the colonial period to decimal currency. In 1971 the federal government issued Decree Number 21 of 1971 establishing a decimal currency for Nigeria. The unit of the currency was to be and still is the naira (written ₦) divided into 100 kobo. One naira would be equivalent to ten shillings (half a pound) of the old currency.

Internationally the ratio of the naira to the pound varies from time to time but many people in Nigeria, especially older or uneducated people still talk of the pound as being equal to two naira.

DECOLONIZATION. The city of Lagos was ceded to the British in 1861 and from there they extended their influence and jurisdiction to the hinterland. This process of extension of jurisdiction met with a lot of resistance from the traditional chiefs, Obas and Emirs all over the country, but because the British had the "maxim" guns, they overcame the resistance, though at great cost. Thus by 1903 they had asserted their power over Sokoto, the capital of the Fulani empire.

Even though the country was subjugated, resistance to British rule continued. However, it took a new turn. Various nationalist organizations, newspapers and political parties took up the struggle. The first of these was the formation of the National Congress of British West Africa, founded in the Gold Coast (Ghana) in 1917 by Caseley Hayford, a lawyer, with a branch in Lagos. The aims of the Congress included putting pressure on the British Government to grant its four West African colonies, Nigeria, Gold Coast, Sierra Leone and the Gambia, the right of self-determination. Its branch in Nigeria was critical of the composition and the role of the Nigerian Council set up by Lord Lugard after the 1914 amalgamation.

In 1921, the first militantly nationalist newspaper, the Lagos Weekly Record of Mr. John Payne Jackson was formed, followed by Herbert Macaulay's Lagos Daily News. The same Macaulay founded a political party, the Nigerian National Democratic Party (NNDP), in 1923, which, though concentrated in its activities on parochial Lagos affairs, nonetheless put pressure on the colonial authorities at the seat of government. In 1926, the Nigerian Daily Times was also founded, which together with the West African Pilot became the forum for nationalist expression of discontent and agitation.

In London there was also the West African Student Union

(WASU), formed in 1925 by Ladipo Solanke, which acted as a pressure group.

In 1934 the Lagos Youth Movement (LYM) was formed in opposition to the colonial government educational policy with regard to the alleged deficiencies of the Yaba Higher College. The LYM in 1936 changed its name to Nigerian Youth Movement (NYM) and was therefore the first really nationalist organization in Nigeria. It quickly superseded the NNDP but was short-lived.

Between 1944 and 1951, the development of political parties was rapid. Beginning with the formation of the National Council of Nigeria and Cameroons (NCNC) in 1944, the Action Group (AG) in 1951 and the NPC in 1951--all which fought relentlessly to gain independence for Nigeria--Western and Eastern Nigeria became internally self-governing in 1957, and Northern Nigeria in 1959. National independence finally came on October 1, 1960.

DEFENCE ACADEMY. The Nigerian Defence Academy was established in Kaduna in January 1964 to cater for the joint training of potential officers belonging to the three Services--army, navy and air force. The Academy runs regular commission courses. In the regular army courses, cadets pursue two and a half years of training at the end of which successful candidates are commissioned as second lieutenants. The naval and air force cadets do only a one-and-a-half-year joint training program at the end of which successful candidates leave for further specialization training in their respective services. The Academy also runs short-service commission courses of six months duration for men who rise from the ranks. At the end of the training, the cadets are commissioned as Second Lieutenants.

DEFENCE PACT. As far back as 1958, Nigerian political leaders had initialled an agreement for mutual defense arrangements between Britain and Nigeria. This agreement became a matter of great debate and in the 1960 Constitutional Conference in London, the Colonial Secretary had to assure Nigerians that the granting of independence was without any strings attached. At the Conference, agreement was reached that each country would give the other assistance in mutual defense--Britain to give help in training, equipment and supplies while the two countries would give each other staging facilities for aircraft in their respective areas. The agreement was to be laid after independence before the Federal Parliament.

Immediately after independence, the defense agreement was put before the House. It was to afford each other such assistance as may be necessary for mutual defense and to consult together on the measures to be taken jointly or separately to ensure the fullest cooperation between the two countries. Britain was to help in training the Nigerian Army while Nigeria was to provide overflying rights and facilities for the Royal Air Force (RAF). The pact generated a lot of heat both at the House of Representatives where the opposition party strongly attacked it as an attempt to swindle Nigeria out of its sovereignty. Both the press and university students were critical of the agreement, and as a result of adverse opinion against it, the agreement had to be abrogated in 1962.

DE GRAFT, WILLIAM. A Methodist missionary who accompanied Reverend Thomas Birch Freeman to Badagry (Lagos State) in September 1842. When Reverend Freeman returned to the Gold Coast in 1843, de Graft and his wife built the first western-type school in Badagry named "Nursery of the Infant Church."

DELEGATION TO LONDON. The Richards Constitution of 1946 was bitterly criticized by Nigerians, especially by the National Council of Nigeria and the Cameroons (NCNC), on the grounds that by formalizing the regional concept into the Nigerian constitutional development, it might lead to the disintegration of the country. Further they criticized it as being the work of only one man without seeking the consent of the people who were to live under it. The NCNC also said that the Constitution should not only secure greater participation by Africans in the discussion of their own affairs, but more importantly it should secure for them greater participation in the management of their own affairs. Finally the party objected to the continuation of nominated members in the legislative council. They asked that nominated members should be replaced with popularly elected members.

Because the colonial government would not yield on these matters, the NCNC began a tour of the country to secure a kind of a mandate to go to London and present the people's grievances against the Constitution. The delegation to London was received by the Secretary of State, Rt. Hon. Arthur Creech Jones, who advised them to go back home and cooperate on making the Constitution work.

DELIMITATION COMMISSION see CONSTITUENCY DELIMITATION COMMISSION

DEMOCRATIC PARTY OF NIGERIA AND CAMEROONS. Formed out of a split in the National Council of Nigeria and the Cameroons (NCNC) in 1958 by Dr. K. O. Mbadiwe, Federal Minister of Commerce and Industry, Chief Kolawole Balogun, Federal Minister of Information, Mr. U. O. Ndem, Parliamentary Secretary to Dr. Mbadiwe and Mr. O. Bademosi, Parliamentary Secretary to Chief Balogun.

On June 14, 1958, 31 NCNC members petitioned Dr. Nnamdi Azikiwe, the National President and Eastern Regional Premier to resign from the government and the party because, as they alleged he was splitting the party asunder and was losing interest in the party. They referred to the findings of the Foster-Sutton tribunal against him and they also blamed him for the failure of the universal free primary education scheme.

The National Executive Committee of the party expelled the four members from the party and they then formed a new organization called the NCNC Reform Committee. In July 1958 Dr. Mbadiwe, Chief Kola Balogun, and their parliamentary secretaries resigned from the federal government and on August 4, 1958, the Reform Committee turned itself into a new political party known as the Democratic Party of Nigeria and the Cameroons under the leadership of Dr. Mbadiwe. It advocated a federal form of government based on socialist ideology.

The new party found little support. It could not secure a footing in the Western Region and so found itself limited to the Eastern Region where Dr. Mbadiwe could not adequately compete with Dr. Azikiwe. The new party met with complete failure in the federal elections of December 1959, and in 1960, Dr. Mbadiwe became reconciled with Dr. Azikiwe and the DPNC was dissolved.

DEMOCRATIC SOCIALISM. Democratic socialism was adopted as a political ideology by the Action Group Party (AG) at the Jos Conference in 1962. The ideology envisaged the construction of a mixed socialist economy that would combine elements of both public and private enterprise within the framework of a comprehensive national plan. The adoption of the ideology split the party into two: those who supported the ideology were led by the party leader and the National President Chief Obafemi Awolowo, while those who did not support it were led by the Western Regional Premier and Deputy Leader of the party, Chief S. L. Akintola. See also ACTION GROUP CRISIS.

DEVELOPMENT PLANS. Since independence in 1960 Nigeria has had four Five-Year Development Plans--1962-1968, 1970-1974, 1975-1980 and 1981-1985. The first National Development Plan (1962-1968) aimed at a growth rate of at least 4 percent per annum as against the 3.9 percent per annum achieved in the preceding ten years. To achieve this objective, the plan aimed to invest 15 percent of the country's GDP and raise per capita consumption by 1 percent per year.

The Second National Development Plan (1970-1974) was drawn up by the military administration of General Gowon. It aimed at the transformation of the whole society. The planners recognized the possibility of using planning as a weapon of social change and as a means for correcting existing defects in production, distribution and exchange. To this end it sought to make Nigeria a united, strong and self-reliant nation; a great and dynamic society; a just and egalitarian society; a land bright and full of opportunities for all its citizens, and a free and democratic society. The third plan retained the objectives of the second plan but broadened its scope. It aimed to invest ₦30 billion, which was ten times the level of investment for the Second Plan. Every aspect of government endeavor was provided for. For example ₦7 billion was allocated to transport; education ₦2.5 billion, Agriculture ₦2.2

billion, urban development ₦1.8 billion and Health ₦700 million.
The private sector's participation stood at ₦10 billion of the
total planned expenditure.

   The Fourth Plan (1981-1985) envisaged the expenditure
of about ₦82 billion of which ₦70.5 billion would be accounted
for by the various governments of the federation while ₦11.5
billion would be added from the private sector. This plan came
at a time when the revenue from oil on which the plan heavily
depended was rapidly declining as a result of the world oil
glut. It would therefore be impossible to achieve many of the
objectives of the plan during the plan period.

DIKE, PROFESSOR KENNETH O. Born on December 17, 1917, he
   received his education at the Dennis Memorial Grammar School
   Onitsha, Achimota College, Ghana and Fourah Bay College,
   Sierra Leone. He went for further studies at the Universities
   of Durham, Aberdeen and London where he obtained his M.A.,
   Ph.D. and L.LD degrees. He returned to Nigeria and became
   a lecturer at University of Ibadan from 1950 to 1952 and Senior
   Research Fellow, West African Institute of Social and Economic
   Research from 1952 to 1954. He was made Chairman, Ni-
   geria Antiquities Commission in 1954 and in 1955 he was made
   President, Historical Society of Nigeria and became a professor
   of History in 1956.

      In 1960, he was chosen as the Vice-Chancellor, Univer-
   sity of Ibadan, a post he occupied till 1966. He was also the
   Director of the Institute of African Studies, University of Ibadan
   from 1962 to 1967. Professor Dike published many articles
   and books including Trade and Politics in the Niger Delta from
   1830 to 1895, A Hundred Years of British Rule in Nigeria and
   the Origin of the Niger Mission.

DIKKO, DR. RUSSELL ALIYU BARAU. A Fulani, converted to
   Christianity, the first university-educated person and the
   first medical doctor from northern Nigeria, Dr. Dikko was
   born on June 15, 1912 in Zaria. He was educated at the
   Church Missionary Society (CMS) School at Wusasa outside
   Zaria from 1922 to 1929. He then went to King's College in
   Lagos from 1929 to 1931 and then to the University of Birming-
   ham, England.

      Upon his return to Nigeria, he joined the government
   medical service in 1940. Because of his educational attain-
   ment in the Northern Region, Dr. Dikko could not but take
   part in the political activities going on in the north and in the
   country as a whole at the time. In 1949, he, together with
   people like Mallam Aminu Kano, Tafawa Balewa and Yahaya
   Gusau created a pan-Northern Nigeria cultural organization
   known as Jamiyyar Mutanem Arewa which later became the
   Northern People's Congress (NPC). Dr. Dikko headed the organization for two years until 1951 when the NPC became a
   political party, and he, being a civil servant, had to resign.

      In 1960, Dr. Dikko was posted to the Curative Service
   Division in the Northern Region and in 1962 he became a

Permanent Secretary in the Ministry of Health. In June 1967 during the military rule he became the Federal Commissioner for Mines and Power and in 1971 he became Commissioner for Transport. He retired from the federal government services in January 1975 and died in 1977.

DIKKO, DR. UMARU. Born on December 31, 1936 in Kaduna State, he attended the Barewa College in Zaria (1949-1954), the Nigerian College of Arts, Science and Technology in Zaria (1954-1958) and the University of London, where he obtained a degree in 1965. In 1967 he was appointed Commissioner for Finance in the North Central State (1967-1972) and later made Commissioner for Information (1972-1975). In 1979, he was appointed by President Shehu Shagari to be Minister of Transport and he later became the Chairman of the Presidential Task Force for the importation of essential commodities like rice. He became suddenly a very wealthy person.

After the military takeover on December 31, 1983 he went underground and later surfaced in London where he preferred to stay. In London he was reported to have threatened the overthrow of the government of General Buhari. In Nigeria, he was accused of large-scale corruption, hoarding of essential commodities and illegally enriching himself. He became the most wanted man among the many wealthy Nigerian fugitives in Europe and America. In July 1984, there was an attempted abduction of Dr. Dikko but the attempt failed some time before the crate in which he in a drugged condition, was loaded into a Cargo plane that would have flown him to Nigeria.

DIMKA, LT. COLONEL B.S. An officer of the Physical Education Corps of the Nigerian Army, he with others made an attempt to overthrow the government of General Murtala Muhammed on February 13, 1976. The attempted coup led to the death of the Head of State, General Murtala Muhammed. Immediately the coup was aborted; Dimka went into hiding but was later arrested on March 5, 1976 at a checkpoint at Abakaliki in Anambra State. He was tried by a military tribunal which found him guilty and sentenced him to death by firing squad. He was executed along with six others on March 15, 1976.

DINA COMMITTEE. Set up in 1968, during the civil war and after the country had been divided into 12 states, to look into and suggest changes in the then existing system of revenue allocation in the country. It was also to suggest new revenue resources for both the federal and the state governments. In its effort to foster national unity through fiscal allocations, the Committee recommended among other things, a uniform income tax legislation for the whole country and federal government assumption of full responsibility for the financing of higher education. Mining rents were to be distributed on the basis of 15 percent to the federal government, 10 percent to the states of derivation and 70 percent to the distributable pool account; offshore rents and royalties were to be distributed on the basis of 60 percent to the federal government, 30 percent to the distributable pool and 10 percent to a special account. It also suggested that the pricing and financial policies of marketing boards should be harmonized, and recommended the setting up of a permanent national planning commission for the whole country. The report was, after thorough examination, rejected because it was said to have exceeded its powers and in some cases ignored its terms of reference.

DIPCHARIMA, ZANA BUKAR SULOMA. Born in 1917 in Dipcharima Village in the Bornu Province of Northern Nigeria (Borno State), he was educated at the Maiduguri Middle School and later trained as a teacher at the Katsina Teacher Training College. He taught from 1938 to 1946 when the Richards Constitution came into being and when he decided to go into politics. He first joined the only party existing then, the National Council of Nigeria and Cameroons (NCNC) under the leadership of Dr. Nnamdi Azikiwe. He was a member of the NCNC delegation to London in 1947. In the same year he left the party and joined the John Holt Company. In 1954 he came back to party politics by joining the dominant party in the north, the Northern People's Congress (NPC), and was elected on its platform to the Bornu Native Authority, and won a seat to the Federal House of Representatives in Lagos in the same year that he was made a Parliamentary Secretary in the Ministry of Transport. His popularity made him rise very fast. He became President of the NPC branch in the Bornu Province and was appointed the head of the Yerwa District with the title of Zana in 1956. In 1957 he was made Minister of State without Portfolio and later Minister of Commerce and Industry. In 1964 he accepted the portfolio of the Ministry of Transport. When the military took over power in January 1966 he was still in this position, and in the absence of the Prime Minister, Alhaji Tafawa Balewa, who had then been abducted, it was his fate to preside over the cabinet meeting which handed over power to the armed forces. He died in 1969 in an air accident.

DISTRIBUTABLE POOL ACCOUNT. This was the account where all revenues which were to be shared by all the states were paid. Some percentage of federally generated revenue, like import duties on certain commodities, and mining royalties, were paid into this account while some percentage was paid to the federal government and some percentage paid to the state of origin. The proportion of distributing this money to the regions or states varied from time to time. For instance in 1958 it was shared in the ratio of 40 to the north, 24 to the west and 31 to the east. In the 1963 Constitution the north received 40, the east 31, the west 18 and the mid-west (which was in 1958 part of the west) 6, with five percent always being left in the account. But under the 1979 Constitution, the Distributable Pool Account is called the "Federation Account" into which all revenues collected by the federal government, with some few exceptions, are paid. The amount in this account is distributed among the federal, state and the local government councils in accordance with the prescription of the National Assembly. In 1982 the National Assembly agreed on a ratio of 55 percent to the federal government, 35 percent to the state governments and 10 percent to local governments.

DISTRICT COMMISSIONERS. Colonial administrative officers appointed to be President of Native Councils and performing many other administrative duties. For many years before the amalgamation of 1914, the former Eastern Nigeria, and the Mid-Western Nigeria were subject to direct administration by the so-called native councils which were native courts with legislative, executive and judicial powers. The council was generally made up of influential members selected from the various communities in each area. The British then appointed a District Commissioner to each of the Native Councils as President and Chairman. However when Lord Lugard introduced the Indirect Rule system to the area, believing that native courts should really be native, he removed the district commissioners from the chairmanship of the native councils and appointed warrant chiefs, hand-picked from the community without caring about their acceptability to the people, as chairmen of the councils. However the councils were under the supervision of the District Officers who replaced the District Commissioners.

DISTRICT HEADS. In the Northern Region, these were Senior Native Authority Officials who were responsible for collecting taxes and other forms of revenue, with the exception of court fines, and for maintaining law and order in their districts.

DISTRICT OFFICERS. Under the system of Native Administration, the Resident was the political officer in charge of a province while the District Officer was in charge of one of the divisions or districts within the province. The District Officer generally had a university education and was given special training in administration. He was required to perform all the functions of all the departments. These included judicial, postal, customs, police and engineering. He saw to the enforcement of ordinances, kept records and issued licenses. He was the medium of communication between the military or departmental officers and the native chiefs on a number of matters. He rendered assistance to missionaries, miners and traders in his area. He also undertook regular tours to administer justice, settle disputes, and correct any injustices that came to his notice.

DOSUNMU. The ruler of Lagos (1853-1885) under whom Lagos was ceded to the British Crown in 1861. When his father Akitoye (q. v.), died in 1853 he ascended to the throne of Lagos with the help of the British Consul of Lagos, who believed him among other rivals to be more tractable to the British interest. Like his father, he was a weak ruler who heavily depended on the British, thereby allowing them to interfere more and more in local affairs. Thus in 1861, with their warship steaming at the Lagos harbor, the British demanded that Dosunmu sign the treaty ceding Lagos to them. When he refused, he was threatened with force and three days later August 6, 1861 he yielded. In return the British gave him a pension. He was allowed to continue to use his title as King of Lagos and was permitted to continue to decide disputes between the inhabitants of Lagos with their consent, but subject to appeal to British law. He died in 1885, succeeded by his son Oyekan.

DUAL MANDATE, THE. According to Lord Lugard in his book The Dual Mandate, the British had a dual purpose in Africa: to promote the interests of the British industrial class and those of the native races in their progress toward self-government.

DUDLEY, BILLY J. Professor of Political Science, one of those pioneers in the study of Nigerian politics, and a national figure who was often called to serve in important positions in the affairs of the country. In 1966 he was Adviser to the Mid-Western Delegation to the Ad Hoc Constitutional Conference, and while other regions were thinking of a breakup of the country, or a confederal arrangement, his delegation was the only one that stood firmly by the idea that the country should remain a federation. He was also in 1975 appointed to the Constitution Drafting Committee and was a member of the subcommittee on Citizenship, Citizenship Right, Political Parties and the Electoral System. In 1977 he became the Director of Nigerian University Commission in London where he later died at the age of 49 in December 1980. Among his books are Politics and Parties in Northern Nigeria, Politics and Crisis in Nigeria and An Introduction to Nigerian Government and Politics.

DUNAMA, MAI LEFIAMI. Ruler of the Kanuri State of Bornu, he in 1810 succeeded his father Ahmed Alimi, who had abdicated as a result of the Fulani attack on his territory during the Jihad (the Holy War) begun by Usman Dan Fodio. In 1911, Dunama was attacked by the Fulani led by Ibrahim Zaki, and he and Al-Kanemi, a Moslem priest, joined forces and drove the Fulani attackers back to Katagum, thus protecting Bornu against the Fulani suzerainty.

After the war, Al Kanemi became recognized as the savior of Bornu, and became very powerful. In 1814, Dunama decided it was time to shake off his dependence on Al Kanemi. He conceived of a plan to kill Al Kanemi, which came to be known to Al Kanemi. In the ensuing battle, Dunama was killed, in 1820, and though he was succeeded by his brother Ibrahim, Al Kanemi virtually exercised all the powers of the old Mai.

-E-

EAST-CENTRAL STATE. Created out of the former Eastern Region

of Nigeria on May 27, 1967, it covered an area of about
28,459 sq. km. with a population of about 7.5 million. In
October 1967 when the Biafran rebellion was thought to be
nearing an end after the fall of Enugu, Mr. Anthony Ukpabi
Asika, a lecturer in political science at the University of Ibadan was appointed the Administrator of the State, a position he
occupied till the fall of General Gowon in 1975.

The state, for all practical purposes could be said to
have existed for six years because the period between 1967
and 1970 was a period of civil war when the administrator
could not take up effective administration of the state. He
frequently stayed in Lagos, till the end of the civil war in January 1970.

The state was rich in agricultural resources like oil
palm, yams, cassava, plantain, maize, citrus and others including cocoa. There are many industries like the coal industry, cement factory, asbestos, pottery and oil-processing industries.

The state capital was Enugu, best known as an administrative center of the former Eastern Region, and presently
of Anambra State. The state commercial centers were Aba
and Onitsha with its famous market. Some of the major towns
in the state were Aba, Enugu, Onitsha, Owerri and Abakaliki.
The state was on February 3, 1976 divided into two--Anambra
and Imo states.

EASTERN HOUSE OF ASSEMBLY. The Eastern House of Assembly
was created under the Richards Constitution of 1946 which divided the country for administrative purposes into three regions
--Eastern, Western and Northern. The Eastern House of Assembly was composed of the Chief Commissioner as President,
13 official members and 15-18 unofficial members, 10-13 of
which were selected from the native authorities and five of
whom were to be nominated by the Governor to represent interests and communities that were inadequately represented.
The House was intended to be a link between the native authorities and the legislative council in Lagos, and it was to advise
the governor on any matter referred to it or introduced by a
member in accordance with the Constitution.

In 1951 the house became a truly legislative body. It
was however dissolved in 1966 when the military took over
power.

EASTERN HOUSE OF CHIEFS. Eastern Nigeria did not have a
House of Chiefs under the 1946, 1951 and 1954 constitutions
as the Western and Northern regions had done. However realizing that this kind of institution could be helpful in getting
control over voters, the politicians decided that the region too
would have a House of Chiefs.

At the 1957 Constitutional Conference in London, it was
agreed that the Eastern Region should also have a House of
Chiefs. The House met in January 1960, but in 1966 it was
dissolved by the military administration just as all other legislative bodies had been dissolved.

EASTERN REGION. The Eastern Region extended from the East of
River Niger to the boundary with the Cameroon, and from some
miles south of the Benue River to the Atlantic Ocean in the
south.   The region was about 29,484 square miles in area with
about 12,388,000, inhabitants according to the 1963 census.
The pressure of population on the land was very great,
which partly accounted for the fact that many people in the region readily left the area to look for employment in other parts
of the country.   The dominant ethnic group in the region was
the Igbo but there were other important groups like the Ibibio,
Efik and the Ijaws who were generally looked at as the minority groups in the area.   The people of the region like all the
other regions were mostly farmers, with palm oil being their
chief agricultural export product.   The region was also blessed
with coal and petroleum which has today become Nigeria's most
important foreign exchange earner.
    The first premier of the region was Dr. Nnamdi Azikiwe,
1954-1959, and the dominant party in the region up to the military takeover in 1966 was the National Council of Nigerian Citizens (NCNC) founded and led by Dr. Nnamdi Azikiwe till he
became the Governor-General of Nigeria in 1960, but led after
him by Dr. Michael Okpara.
    Some of the main towns of the region were Enugu, the
regional headquarters, Calabar which according to the 1922
Constitution was allowed to elect and send a representative to
the legislative council in Lagos, Port Harcourt with its harbor,
Onitsha, famous for its markets, Owerri, Aba, Abakaliki and
Nsukka, which became a university town, the seat of the University of Nsukka in 1960.
    Even though the region had always fought for a united
Nigeria which was propitious for its citizens in other parts of
the country, in 1964, following the outcome of the 1963-64 census which the region described as unacceptable, and the emergence of petroleum as the most important foreign exchange
earner, it threatened to secede from the rest of the country.
In 1967, following the vendetta against the Ibos in the north in
1966 and the failure of the federal government and the Eastern
Regional government to peacefully resolve the differences between them, the region under Lt. Colonel Odumegwu Ojukwu
declared itself as independent Republic of Biafra on May 30,
1967 a few days after the region had been divided into three
separate states by the federal government as part of the exercise that created 12 states out of the four previously existing
regions.   The "rebellion" was however crushed in January 1970
after a 30-month war.

EASTERN STATES INTERIM ASSETS AND LIABILITIES AGENCY
    (ESIALA).   When Nigeria was divided into 12 states in 1967,
    the civil war which started did not allow the federal military
    government to concentrate its effort on how best to solve the
    problem of sharing the assets of the former Eastern Region
    which had been divided into three different states.   After the
    end of the war in 1970, the federal government issued Decree

Number 39 of 1970 which set up the Eastern States Interim Assets and Liabilities Agency (ESIALA). In this Agency was vested all the assets and liabilities of the former Eastern Region. These included all statutory corporations, the University of Nigeria, Nsukka and government-controlled companies. The Agency ceased to exist in 1976 by the promulgation of Decree Number 19 of 1975. See also INTERIM ADMINISTRATIVE COUNCIL.

ECONOMIC BLOCKADE. One of the weapons used by the Nigerian government against secessionist Biafra during the civil war was to impose economic sanctions. After Colonel Odumegwu Ojukwu had declared the secession of the former Eastern Nigeria as the "Republic of Biafra," the Nigerian government ordered the closure of all the ports in the region. Communication links to the region from outside Nigeria and from other parts of the country were cut off. Later during the war, the federal government imposed restrictions on transportation or the sending of food to the region, and it instructed the oil companies not to pay any royalties due to it to the secessionist region. All these measures helped in no small way to later bring an end to the civil war.

ECONOMIC COMMUNITY OF WEST AFRICAN STATES (ECOWAS). A 16-nation association of West African states, ECOWAS came into being in 1975 following the signing of the ECOWAS Treaty by 15 of the members including Nigeria, Niger, Benin, Togo, Ghana, Ivory Coast, Liberia, Sierra Leone, Guinea Bissau, Upper Volta and Cape Verde Island. The ECOWAS Treaty was the result of the initiative of both Nigeria and Togo and its aim is to unite the countries in West Africa into one large economic community patterned on the European Economic Community. As such ECOWAS is to be a common market of West Africa and a Customs Union. It is to promote free flow of persons, property and capital within the community. This implies an integration of the economic policies and programs of member states and an indigenization of the ownership and control of capital in the area. The two main organs of ECOWAS are the Summit of the Heads of State which is the highest body, and the Council of Ministers. Like the OAU Council of Ministers, ECOWAS Council of Ministers makes recommendations to the Summit and gives direction to subordinate institutions of the organization. The Summit meets at least once a year while the Council of Ministers meets about twice a year. The headquarters of the organization is in Lagos, Nigeria.

Many ECOWAS citizens who took advantage of the free flow of persons came to Nigeria and decided to stay and work beyond the time permitted so as to take advantage of the apparent oil boom in the country. In February 1983, these illegal aliens were asked to go back while those who were still legally in the country were allowed to stay.

EDET, INSPECTOR GENERAL LOUIS OROLA. Born on August 29,

1913 at Duke Town Calabar, Cross River State, he obtained his elementary education at the Sacred Heart in Calabar and his secondary education at the Bonny Government Grammar School. He joined the Nigerian Police Force in 1931 as a clerk, and later proceeded to the Police College in Hampshire in England. He became a Sub-Inspector in 1945 an Assistant Superintendent of Police in 1949. He again attended a senior training course at the Rython-on-Dunesmore in Britain between 1953 and 1957 and later in 1960. In 1957 he was promoted Senior Superintendent of Police. In 1960, he led and commanded the first contingent of the Nigerian Police Force to the Congo under the United Nations auspices. Edet returned to Nigeria in 1961 and became a Commissioner of Police in Lagos. In 1962 he was promoted Deputy Inspector-General of Police and became Inspector-General of Police in 1964, being the first Nigerian to hold such a high post.

When in 1966 the military took over power, he was a member of the Federal Executive Council. After the second military coup in July 1966, General Gowon, on taking over power accepted the retirement of the Inspector-General who was of Eastern Nigerian origin. After his retirement he was appointed as recruitment attaché in the Nigerian High Commission in London. In 1968 he was appointed Commissioner for Home Affairs and Information in the South-Eastern State, one of the 12 states newly created in 1967. Inspector-general Edet was a highly honored person. He was awarded Order of the Federal Republic of Nigeria (OFR), the Queen's Police Medal (QPM), Commander of the British Empire (CBE) and was also awarded a medal by Pope Paul VI. He died on January 17, 1979.

EDO PEOPLE. The Edo people constitute one of the major communities in the Bendel State of Nigeria. The word Edo corresponds to the language spoken by the various groups in the state whose dialects are similar to each other. These are the Etsakos, Ishans, Owans and the Urhobos. These people are centered in the old kingdom of Benin. Yoruba tradition says that the various peoples were offshoots of the Yorubas; however the Edo and Yoruba languages are today mutually unintelligible. By the time the Europeans came to Benin in the fifteenth century the place had become a powerful kingdom.

EDUCATION. The foundation of education in Nigeria was laid by the European missionaries who came to Nigeria in the nineteenth century. Even though the aim of the missionaries was to save souls by making converts, they saw that they had to teach the people how to read and write, thus opening up opportunities for young men and women to enter schools. Prominent among the missionary groups that led in this field were Wesleyan Methodist missionaries who visited Badagry and Abeokuta in 1841, the Church Missionary Society (CMS) who landed at Badagry in 1842, the Presbyterians who began work in Calabar, Eastern Nigeria in 1846, the Baptist and the Catholic missionaries. Even when the need of expatriate commercial firms and the government for literate people to staff their agencies, departments and companies became felt, government still considered it cheaper to subsidize mission schools rather than set up its own schools. Thus until 1898 all education in Nigeria was under the direct control of missionaries and as late as 1942 missionaries controlled more than 90 percent of the schools.

But while the south readily accepted the education that white missionaries brought, the Moslem north appeared to identify that education with the Christian religion and so were reluctant to accept it. In 1903, Lord Lugard, realizing how sensitive the issue was, promised the Emir of Sokoto that government would not interfere with the Moslem religion and the colonial government kept out missionaries from most of the Moslem north. This explains why the north, even today lags behind the south in western education and many of the states in the north are still officially regarded as educationally backward states.

But while missionaries led in the field of primary and secondary education, the government has had a virtual monopoly of postsecondary education. Beginning in 1934 with the establishment of the Yaba Higher College, government went on in 1947 to set up the University College of Ibadan in association with London University, with Yaba Higher College becoming a nucleus of the new University College. Later on, the regional governments stepped into founding universities. In the east was the University of Nigeria, Nsukka founded in 1960, in the west was the University of Ife founded in 1961 and in the north was Ahmadu Bello University founded in 1962. The federal government in 1962 set up another university, the University of Lagos while making the University College, Ibadan an autonomous university. Today there are many universities in the country most of them federally owned and financed, many technical colleges and teacher-training colleges. Education today has a high priority in the country's development plan. There has been free primary education in Western Region since 1955 and universal primary education (UPE) all over the nation since 1976. What this meant is that parents whose children went to public schools did not pay tuition. University education also is tuition free.

EDUCATION, NATIONAL POLICY ON. Published in 1977 as a result of the Nigerian Educational Research Council, the policy has as its major objective the improvement of the productive capacity of the nation so as to consolidate the nation's independence while reducing its dependence on the outside sources for most of its needs.

The proposals for executing it were made in 1979 in the Blueprint of the Implementation Committee. According to the blueprint, secondary school education would be reorganized into junior and senior secondary schools each providing a three-year course in 1982 when the graduates of the Universal

Primary Education would be ready to enter the high school. It was estimated that about 40 percent of the children would enter junior secondary schools while about 40 percent of these would go to the senior secondary schools.

EFIK see IBIBIO

EGBA. The Egbas are a subgroup of the Yoruba people, who during the Yoruba civil war in the early nineteenth century left Ibadan in 1830 under their leader, Sodeke, a hunter, to a place which is now known as Abeokuta, meaning "under the rock," which has become the chief town of the Egbas. The rock is the Olumo Rock which is at the outskirt of Abeokuta and which served as a protective device for the Egbas during any war or invasion.

One important thing to note about the Egbas is that they provided places for refugees from other parts of Yorubaland during the Yoruba civil war. For instance refugees from Ijaiye and Owu were given settlement by the Egbas. Each section of the Egbas has their own traditional ruler but the supreme head of all the Egbas is the Alake of Egbaland.

The Egbas were the first Yoruba people to have contacts with the European Christian missionaries. It is also important to note that western civilization spread from Abeokuta to other parts of Yorubaland, and because of their early contact with western civilization, they were able to preserve the autonomy of the Egba kingdom until 1914 when their independence was taken away by the British taking full control of the country after the amalgamation of the Northern and Southern protectorates. In 1918 there was a revolt in Egbaland called the Adubi War which was caused partly because of resentment over the termination of Egba independence and partly over the system of indirect rule newly introduced to the area. The Egbas are mostly farmers and because of their proximity to Lagos, many of them have become successful businessmen. One important thing to note about this people is that all their traditional rulers (Alake, Osile, Gbagura, Olubara and Olowu) now live in Abeokuta in peace with each other.

EGBA UNITED GOVERNMENT. In 1893 the British entered into a treaty with the Egba Chiefs stipulating that all disputes between Egba and the British were to be settled by the Governor, and roads were to be closed only with the consent of the British. By this treaty the British recognized some degree of independence of the Egba people. The people aided by some missionaries and British officials set up a government known as Egba United Government modeled on the British Colonial system. When Lord Lugard became Governor-General of Nigeria after the 1914 amalgamation, he looked for an opportunity to bring Abeokuta the Chief Town of the Egbas in line with what went on in other Yoruba kingdoms, i. e., introducing the system of indirect rule to the town. The opportunity soon came when the people demonstrated against the united government over a person

arrested and who died in prison.   Government troops had to
be called in from Lagos leading to loss of lives, and Lord Lugard with the Alake's agreement had to abrogate the 1893 treaty,
and so he brought Egbaland under firm British control.

EGBA UPRISING see ADUBI WAR

EGBE OMO ODUDUWA.   Egbe Omo Oduduwa (the Descendants of
Oduduwa, the mythical ancestor of the Yorubas) was a Pan-
Yoruba cultural society founded in 1945 by Chief Obafemi Awolowo when he was in the United Kingdom.   Its main objectives
according to its constitution were to promote the unity and the
social progress of the Yoruba people, and to cooperate with
other regions in the country so that the aims set out for the
Yorubaland would be applied to the whole country.   It also
aimed at fostering the study of Yoruba language, culture and
history and to accelerate the emergence of a virile, modernized,
and an efficient Yoruba State with its own individuality within
the federal state of Nigeria.

In June, 1948, the society was inaugurated at a conference held in Ile-Ife, Oyo State of Nigeria under the auspices
of the late Ooni of Ife, Sir Adesoji Aderemi.   Sir Adeyemo
Alakija was made president of the organization while Chief Awolowo was chosen as the General-Secretary.   The society had
among its members many important people including Obas,
Chiefs, businessmen and politicians.   The society had branches
in many Yoruba Towns.   It promoted the study of Yoruba language, culture and history and awarded scholarships to deserv-
ing students in secondary schools and universities.

Although the Egbe was said to be nonpolitical, the National Council of Nigeria and the Cameroons (NCNC) saw it as
a threat and therefore it launched a vigorous campaign against
it through the West African Pilot.   The Egbe later became the
nucleus of the Action Group Party formed in 1951.

EIGHT-POINT PROGRAM.   Consequent on the Constitutional Crisis
of 1953 at which Chief Anthony Enahoro moved in the National
House of Assembly a motion for self-government in 1956 and
the northern representatives moved an amendment "as soon as
practicable" the Action Group and the NCNC members walked
out of the House in protest.   The Colonial Secretary in London
called Nigerian leaders for a constitutional conference in London.   While preparations for the conference were being made,
the Northern People's Congress put forward its Eight-Point
Program which they believed would remedy the defects in the
constitution.   The program proposed that each region should
have complete legislative and executive autonomy in all matters except defense, external affairs, customs and some research institutions.   They asked that there should be no central legislative and executive or policy-making body for the
country.   A nonpolitical body that would have no legislative
or executive power operating in a neutral territory should constitute a central agency for the country and should be responsible

for matters not allocated to the regions. Matters like rail-
ways, air services, ports, electricity posts and telegraphs
and coal mining should be organized on an interregional basis
and all revenues except customs duties should be collected by
the regions. Finally, each region should have its own separate public service. This program, if accepted, would have
created three independent states rather than a federal state.
In the 1953 Constitutional Conference in London, the north
abandoned the Eight-Point Program.

EJOOR, MAJOR GENERAL DAVID AKPODE. Retired soldier, born
on January 10, 1934 at Ovu in Bendel State, he was educated
at the Government College, Ughelli and joined the army in 1953.
He did his officer's training in Accra Ghana before going to
Sandhurst in England. He returned to Nigeria and was commissioned in 1956. He was Company Commander in the Cameroons in 1960 and was with the Nigerian Peace-Keeping Mission to the Congo under the UN Peace-Keeping Force 1960 to
1961. He was the military governor of the Mid-Western Region from 1966 to 1967.

When the civil war broke out, he was firmly on the side
of the federal government but some of the men he trusted
double-crossed him by allowing the Biafrans to invade the Mid-
West. He escaped to Lagos. In 1969, he became Commandant of the Nigerian Defense Academy and Chief of Staff of
the Nigerian Army in 1972. He retired in 1975.

EKANDEM, HIS EMINENCE DOMINIC. First West-African Catholic
Bishop and first Nigerian Cardinal, born 1917, at Obio Ibiono,
Itu in Cross River State, he was educated at the Christ the
King College, Onitsha, Senior Seminary Okpala Ngor, Owerri
and the Bigard Memorial Seminary in Enugu. He was ordained
a priest December 1947 and served at St. Andrew's Parish and
was later appointed Rector of the Queen of Apostles Seminary,
Afaha Obong. He was consecrated Auxiliary Bishop of Calabar
by Pope Pius XII February 1954 and was consecrated Bishop
of Ikot Ekpene 1963. He was made a Cardinal by Pope Paul
VI April 1977. He is the President of the National Episcopal
Conference. He is honored with the Commander, Order of the
Niger and he is a member of the Order of the British Empire.

EKWUEME, DR. ALEX IFEANYICHUKWU. First Vice-President of
Nigeria, born on October 21, 1932, in Oko, Anambra State,
he attended Anglican School, Oko, Anglican Central School,
Ekwulobia, King's College, Lagos and later studied Sociology,
Architecture and Urban Planning at the University of Washington in the United States, and had his Ph. D. from the University of Stratholyde, Glasgow, Scotland. When the ban on political activities was lifted in 1978, he joined the National Party
of Nigeria (NPN) and was elected Vice-President of Nigeria
with Alhaji Shehu Shagari who was President. After the December, 1983 military takeover Dr. Ekwueme was arrested
and detained, and investigations went on to determine whether

or not he had corruptly enriched himself while in office as
Vice-President of the country.

ELECTORAL MALPRACTICES. Electoral malpractices are devices
by which elections are made unfair and most often farcical.
In Nigeria the popular expression is "rigging" and this includes
falsification of election results, double voting, voting by under-
age, or unregistered persons. For example, in the federal
elections of 1964 and the Western Regional election of 1965,
there were allegations of electoral malpractices by politicians;
it was alleged that government parties in many constituencies
prevented other party candidates from filing their nomination
papers or that when such candidates presented the papers in
the office of the electoral officer, the officer would not be
available. The result was that in many constituencies government candidates were declared unopposed. Furthermore there
were charges of falsification of election results in many constituencies and that ballot boxes were stuffed with "fake ballot
papers." At the 1979 general elections to usher in the presidential system of government, all the parties complained of
electoral malpractices in the states where their parties failed
to win. Worse still was the allegation that the gubernatorial
primary elections of the Unity Party of Nigeria in 1982 were
rigged in four out of five states, a situation which rocked the
solidarity of that party. The losers like Chief S.M. Afolabi
and Chief Busari Adelakun in Oyo State, and Chief Akin Omo-
boriowo in Ondo State opted out of the party. In the 1983 national and state elections allegations of electoral malpractices
were common, which led to many court cases in which the pe-
titioners asked the court to nullify the results.

ELECTRICITY. Production and transmission of electricity was formerly in the hands of the Electricity Corporation of Nigeria
(ECN) but in 1972, the company was merged with the Niger
Dams Authority which was then producing hydroelectric power
from the Niger Dam at Kainji, to become National Electric
Power Authority (NEPA).
    In 1970, the original capacity of the four generating
units at Kainji 647 megawatts was sufficient to double the then
installed capacity in the country, but owing to the rapid economic development consequent on the oil boom, the demands
soon outstripped the supply.
    In 1970, the original capacity of the four generating units
at Kainji, 647 megawatts, was sufficient to double the then
ding," to see that each part of a town or city got electricity
some part of the day. However owing to gross inefficiency,
shortage of technically qualified staff, problem of having to
import all parts from abroad, some areas remained without
electricity for days and weeks. To remedy the production
side of this problem, new hydroelectric projects have been
set up in some other places and gas-fired stations have also
been set up in Ughelli, Afam and Sapele. The Fourth National
Development Plan, 1981-1985 envisaged a maximum supply of
4,600 megawatts by 1985.

ELECTRICITY CORPORATION OF NIGERIA. Established in 1951, the Corporation was empowered to generate or acquire the supply of electricity and provide bulk supply of electricity for consumers in Nigeria. In 1972 it was replaced with the National Electric Power Authority (NEPA).

ELIAS, DR. TASLIM OLAWALE. A scholar and a jurist, former Chief Justice of the Federation, he was born on November 11, 1914 in Lagos and was educated at the CMS Grammar School in Lagos, Igbobi College, Yaba, Lagos and at the University College, London. He was called to the bar at the Inner Temple in London in 1947. After receiving his Ph. D. in Law at the London University, the first Nigerian to have done so, he taught law at the Manchester University from 1951 to 1953 and was the recipient of many research fellowships among which were the Oppenheim Research Fellow, Institute of Common Wealth Studies, Queen Elizabeth House and Nuffield College. He was in 1956 a Visiting Professor to the University of Delhi where he helped to establish a Department of African Studies. Returning to London, he was appointed Governor of the School of Oriental and African Studies 1957 to 1960.

Back in Nigeria he became Attorney General and Minister of Justice from 1960 to January 1966 when the military took over. In the same year he became Professor and Dean of the faculty of Law, University of Lagos, but in October 1966, he was reappointed Attorney General and later Commissioner of Justice from 1967 to 1972. In 1972 he became the Chief Justice of the Federal Republic. In 1975, he was appointed a Judge of the International Court of Justice (ICJ) at the Hague and in 1979, he was elected Vice-President of the ICJ, and later became the President of the Court.

Professor Elias has in addition held many important national and international posts including membership of the Governing Council of the University of Nigeria, Nsukka 1959 to 1966, and being the Chairman of the Committee of the UN Conference on Law of Treaties 1968 to 1969.

Dr. Elias has honorary degrees of D. Litt. from the University of Ibadan 1969 and LL. D. from the University of Hull in England 1980. His publications include: Nigerian Land, Law and Custom (1951), Nigerian Legal System (1954), Ghana and Sierra Leone: Development of their Laws and Constitution (1962), British Colonial Law: A Comparative Study (1962), Nature of African Customary Law and Nigeria: Development of its Laws and Constitution (1965).

ELLIOT COMMISSION. Set up in 1943 to look into higher education in West Africa, the commission, headed by Sir Walter Elliot, with three African educationists and members of the Conservative, Labor, and Liberal parties made a fairly comprehensive survey of higher education in West Africa and reported in 1945. The Commission agreed on the urgent need for the extension of higher education and university development in West Africa. The majority agreed that there should be a university college established in Nigeria and in Ghana respectively and that higher educational development should also be carried through in Sierra Leone in connection with the Fourah Bay College. The Commission suggested the faculties that should be set up in each institution. They also recommended how the colleges were to be administered and financed. This report was finally accepted, leading to the establishment of the University College in Ibadan in 1947, and it opened in January 1948.

EMERGENCY ADMINISTRATION IN WESTERN NIGERIA. The disorder in the Western House of Assembly in May 1962 arising from the Action Group Crisis made the federal government invoke sections 64 and 65 of the 1960 Constitution by declaring that a state of emergency did exist in the region. The regional government was suspended and an administrator in the person of Dr. M. A. Majekodunmi was appointed to look after the affairs of the region. The administrator restricted most of the leading politicians to places outside Ibadan, the regionl capital, but by the end of two months, virtually all the members of the Akintola factions and those of the National Council of Nigerian Citizens were released while Action Group members remained restricted. The period of the emergency witnessed two important events: the setting up of the Coker Commission of Inquiry to look into the affairs of certain statutory corporations in Western Nigeria, and the Treason Trial of Chief Awolowo and many other Action Group leaders charged with the plan to overthrow the government of Nigeria. At the end of the emergency, a new government headed by Chief S. L. Akintola was installed in office.

EMIR. The title Emir is that of the Fulani rulers in the northern parts of Nigeria, including the Yoruba town of Ilorin. It is an Arabic title referring to a governor.

ENAHORO, CHIEF ANTHONY ERONSELE. Journalist and politician, born on July 22, 1923 at Uromi in Bendel State, he was educated at the King's College, Lagos. In 1942, he took up journalism, and became Editor of the Southern Nigerian Defender in 1944. In 1945 he joined the Daily Comet in Kano and became Associate Editor of the West African Pilot in 1949. In 1951 he was appointed Editor-in-Chief of the Nigerian Star.
    Chief Enahoro was a foundation member of the Action Group (AG) Party in 1951. He was elected under the AG ticket to the Western Regional House of Assembly in 1951 and from there was later sent to the House of Representatives in Lagos. As a member of the Central Legislature, he moved the "self-government-in-1956" motion, asking that the British give self-government to Nigeria in 1956. While this motion eventually led to self-government for the regions and the country it immediately created a crisis leading to the resignation of the four Action Group ministers from the government and a temporary alliance between the AG and the National Council of Nigeria and Cameroons (NCNC) and the northern loss of confidence in

the legislative assembly. It also speeded up the demise of the Macpherson Constitution.

Back in Western Nigeria, Chief Enahoro was made Minister of Home Affairs in 1954 and in 1957 he added the portfolio of the Mid-Western Affairs. After the 1959 federal elections in which his party became the opposition party, Chief Enahoro was the opposition spokesman on foreign affairs from 1959 to 1963. He attended all constitutional conferences beginning in 1953 to independence.

During the AG crisis in the Western Region in 1962, and the declaration of emergency following it, Chief Enahoro was arrested and detained along with Chief Awolowo and was to be tried with others for treasonable felony but he escaped, first to Ghana and finally sought asylum in Britain. He was arrested in Britain and detained when extradition proceedings were going on. After a lot of row in the press and in the British Parliament over the decision to extradite him, and after many court cases to keep him in Britain, he was extradited to Nigeria on May 16, 1963. He was then tried for treasonable felony, found guilty and sentenced to seven years' imprisonment. However he did not stay that long in jail for on August 2, 1966, two days after General Gowon became head of state, he released Chief Enahoro and Chief Awolowo at the same time.

Chief Enahoro led the Mid-Western Delegation to the Ad Hoc Constitutional Conference of September 1966 and served on the committee that was charged with finding a workable constitution for the country. In 1967, he was appointed Federal Commissioner for Information, Labor, and Cultural Affairs. As such he worked hard to keep Nigeria united. He ensured that Nigeria got its arms supply from Britain and from Russia and presented the federal case at the Kampala Peace Talks in May 1968 when the Biafrans were asked to give up secession and accept the new order in the federation. He also later led a delegation to Addis Ababa, Ethiopia to present similar proposals. In 1975 he was made Federal Commissioner for Special Duties, to prepare for the Festival of Art and Culture (FESTAC). The July 1975 coup relieved him of his duties and he went into private business. When the ban on politics was lifted in 1978, Chief Enahoro became a member of the National Party of Nigeria, NPN, and was made Chairman of the party's branch in the Bendel State. Chief Enahoro received an honorary degree of D. Sc. from the University of Benin in 1972. He published the Fugitive Offender in 1965.

ENDELEY, DR. EMMANUEL MBELA LILAFFE. A Cameroonian physician and politician, born on April 10, 1916 at Buea in the Cameroons, he was educated at the Bonjongo Government College, Umuahia from 1931 to 1934 and in 1935 he entered the Yaba Higher College to study medicine. After his training he served in many places as a medical officer. He later founded the Cameroons National Federation which later became the Kamerun National Congress (KNC) and was its President.

He was leader of the South Cameroons Delegation to the 1957 Constitutional Conference in London and became the first Premier of the Southern Cameroons in 1958. He successfully fought for the separation of his country, the Southern Cameroons from Nigeria.

ENGLISH. Nigeria is made up of many nationalities or ethnic groups whose languages are mutually unintelligible. And even though Hausa is the lingua franca of most of the former northern Nigeria, the only common language between the peoples of the south and north, and the language of communication between one group and another is the English language, inherited from the British colonial authorities. English is learned as a second language and is spoken by a growing portion of the population.

ENUGU. Enugu is one of the new towns east of the Niger River. It is presently the capital of Anambra State. The city owes its origin to the discovery of coal east of the Nguro village in 1909. In 1917 Enugu attained the status of a township and in 1929 it was made the administrative headquarters of the Southern Provinces. In 1939 it became the headquarters of the eastern provinces. In 1951 it became the capital of the Eastern region and in 1967, the capital of the East Central State. In 1976 it became the capital of Anambra State.

With a population of about 138,457 people according to the 1963 census, Enugu is well served by trunk roads which run west to Onitsha and east to Abakaliki. It is linked to the north through Opi junction, near Nsukka. There is a modern airport linking Enugu with other parts of the country, and there is a railroad that runs down from Jos in the north to Port Harcourt in the south. Enugu is a thriving city. It has many institutions of higher learning like the Enugu Campus of the University of Nsukka and the College of Technology. Besides the coal mining industry, there is the steel-rolling mill, the asbestos product factory and many other factories.

ESIGIE, OBA OF BENIN. He ascended the throne of Benin about 1504. During his reign, trade in ivory, Benin cloths and beads flourished between his people and the Portuguese who came to his kingdom as traders and missionaries.

Esigie was the first Oba in West Africa to establish diplomatic relations with a European country. His son was the first accredited black envoy to Portugal.

It is believed that Onitsha was founded by his people who immigrated there from Benin and this may explain the fact that like Benin, with an Oba, Onitsha has an Obi. His mother, Idia, was a warrior Queen who became immortalized in the ivory carving of her face, adopted as the FESTAC symbol.

Oba Esigie contributed much to the arts and culture of Benin, and he encouraged the brass work which his predecessors had introduced into the kingdom, all of which continue to make Benin such a tourist attraction.

ETHNIC GROUP. Generally, a group of people who have a common language and common cultural values. In Nigeria there are ethnic majority groups and ethnic minority groups. In the old regional arrangement, the ethnic majority groups were those groups which constituted a majority in each region like the Hausa-Fulani in the north, the Yorubas in the west and the Ibos in the east. Ethnic minority groups were the other smaller ethnic groups in each region. Because each ethnic majority group controlled the parties that controlled the regional government, fears of domination by the ethnic majority groups began to be felt in each region by the ethnic minority groups as independence drew nearer. The minorities then began to agitate for their own separate states, to be carved out of each region. See also MINORITIES PROBLEM.

EXCHANGE CONTROL DECREE. Foreign exchange transaction in Nigeria is done by the commercial banks with the approval of the Central Bank. In an effort to conserve the nation's foreign reserves, the government has put a limit on the amount a tourist or any person travelling out of Nigeria can change into foreign currency and carry out of Nigeria. In order not to sabotage this policy the federal military government enacted a decree in 1977 called Exchange Control (Anti-Sabotage) Decree, Number 57 of 1977. According to this decree it is an offense for a person resident in Nigeria to make any payments to persons outside Nigeria without the permission of the appropriate authority by going through the foreign exchange process.

EXECUTIVE COUNCIL. The Executive Council, now known as the Cabinet in both the state and the federal governments has its origin in colonial administration. Under the British colonial system, when a colony is set up there is a Legislative Council and an Executive Council. The Legislative Council legislates for the colony while the executive council formulates government policy and carries out the law. The relationship between the Legislative and Executive councils was based on clearly defined principles, according to which the Legislative Council is subordinate to the Executive Council, and the colonial government itself is subordinate to the British government in London. When Lagos became a Crown Colony, there was a Legislative Council and a small Executive Council set up. The Executive Council was an advisory body to the Governor and it consisted of the governor and some departmental heads of the government. After the 1914 amalgamation, the Lieutenant Governors of the Northern and Southern provinces and the Administrator of Lagos were also included. The first African to be a member of the executive council was appointed in 1943. Under the 1951 Macpherson Constitution, the executive council became the Council of Ministers and the policy-making body for the government. In the first Republic, the Executive Council, known as the Cabinet, was collectively responsible to Parliament for its actions. This lasted till January 1966 when the military took over power. During the military regime, the

Executive Council for the federal government was known as the Federal Executive Council, while for the states, it was called Executive Council. Under the Second Republican Constitution, the Executive Council was called the Cabinet, made up of the President and his ministers. The ministers were responsible only to the President who appointed them and not to the legislative assembly.

EXERCISE DAMISA. This was the term used by the plotters of the January 15, 1966 coup to designate the coup. When translated from its Hausa language, it means "Exercise Tiger."

EXERCISE HARMONY. During the tense period before the December 30, 1964 federal elections, Sir Abubakar Tafawa Balewa on December 28 announced that the troops would make country-wide tour to give the people of the country an opportunity to see their army, and show the people that the army was at the ready in case there was any trouble anywhere. This show of force and military readiness for troublemakers was termed "Exercise Harmony." The exercise did show that things were not well in the country, that the politicians could not conduct their business by negotiation and compromise, and it put ideas in the minds of young army officers who were politically minded to later begin to plan for a coup which finally came in January 1966.

EX-OFFICIO MEMBERS. During the colonial administration, membership in the Legislative and Executive councils were made up mostly of officials and some few nonofficials. The official members of these councils were known as Ex-Officio members, that is, they were there because of the posts or offices they held. For example, the Executive Council of Nigeria before World War II consisted of entirely official members like the Chief Secretary, Lt. Governors of the Northern and Southern provinces of the protectorate, the administrator of the colony, the Attorney-General, and the Commandant of the Nigeria Regiment. The Legislative Council consisted of officials (ex-officio members) as majority, and nominated nonofficials together with four elected members. However as Nigeria advanced towards independence the number of the ex-officio members of the legislative houses and executive councils gradually dwindled and they were almost completely eliminated at independence.

-F-

FADAHUNSI, SIR ODELEYE. A former governor of Western Nigeria, Sir Odeleye Fadahunsi was born in 1901 at Ilesha, Oyo State. He was educated at Osu Methodist School and Wesley Teacher Training College, Ibadan. He was a teacher at Methodist schools at Ikorodu and Lagos between 1925 and 1926; he also worked as a produce buyer, a storekeeper and a salesman in the GBO, UAC and UTC companies from 1927 to 1948.

He formed and was the Managing Director of the Ijesha United Trading and Transport Company Ltd. in 1948. He was also a member of the Nigerian Cocoa Marketing Board from 1948 to 1953 and the Director of Nigeria Produce Marketing Company from 1952 to 1953; Chairman of Ijesha Divisional Council from 1955 to 1960; and Chairman, Nigeria Airways Corporation in 1961.

Sir Odeleye Fadahunsi was a member of the Western House of Assembly and deputy leader of the National Council of Nigeria and Cameroons (NCNC) the opposition party in the House from 1951 to 1961.

After the state of emergency was lifted in January 1963 and Chief S. L. Akintola was reinstated, Sir Odeleye was appointed Governor of Western Nigeria, a position he held till the military took over power in January 1966.

Sir Odeleye was knighted by Queen Elizabeth II in 1963 and was earlier awarded the Queen's Coronation Medal in 1953. He also is a traditional Chief and has been the recipient of a national honor, the Grand Commander of the Niger.

FAJEMIROKUN, CHIEF HENRY OLOYEDE. Born in Ile-Oluji in Ondo State on July 14, 1926, he attended the CMS Grammar School in Lagos and Ondo Boys' High School in Ondo. In 1944 he joined the Royal West African Frontier Force and in 1945 served during the war in India. From 1946 to 1956, he served in many positions as a civil servant. In 1956 he left the government service to start his own business. He was a successful businessman, and by his death in 1978, his business, known as Henry Stephens and Sons, included insurance, engineering and shipping firms. In 1970 he became President of the Lagos Chamber of Commerce and Industry. In 1972 he was President of the Nigerian Association of Chambers of Commerce, Industry and Mines and was also elected the President of the Federation of West African Chambers of Commerce. In 1974 he was elected Vice-President of the Federation of Commonwealth Chambers of Commerce. He was also a Co-President of the Nigerian British Chamber of Commerce and a member of the Board of Governors of the Nigerian American Chamber of Commerce. In recognition of his contribution to his home areas, he was honored with chieftaincy titles: Yegbato of Ile Oluji and the Asiwaju of Okeigbo. The University of Ife conferred on him the honorary degree of Doctor of Science.

FAJUYI, LT. COL. ADEKUNLE. Born in Ado Ekiti, Ondo State on June 26, 1926, he was educated at St. George's Catholic School, Ado Ekiti. He later enlisted in the army, received military training at the Command Training School at Teshie, Ghana, and went for a course at the Officer Cadet School at Chester in England. He was commissioned in 1954. He later returned to Nigeria and joined the 3rd Battalion of the Queen's Own Nigeria Regiment. He was appointed to a number of posts between 1955 and 1960, and also went back to Britain for further training. He served in the United Nations Operations in

the Congo where he won a military cross for his performances
as head of his company in North Katanga. He even became
Military Assistant to the Supreme Commander of the UN forces
in the Congo. Back in Nigeria in 1964, he was made Commander of the 1st Battalion of the Second Brigade of the Nigerian Army in Enugu. He was later sent on a Senior Military Tactical Course in Pakistan. Before the January 1966
coup, he was at Abeokuta to command the Abeokuta Garrison.
After General Aguiyi-Ironsi took over the government in 1966,
Lt. Col. Fajuyi was appointed Military Governor of the Western Region. On July 29, 1966, while the Supreme Commander
and Head of State, General Ironsi was his guest at the government house in Ibadan, a second coup was staged. Both Lt.
Col. Fajuyi and General Ironsi were arrested and killed. The
coup makers would have spared his life, but he told them if
they took General Ironsi, they should take him too, and so they
did and killed both of them.

FANI-KAYODE, CHIEF REMI ADE. A legal practitioner and politician, born on December 22, 1921 in London. He was educated
at the C.M.S. Grammar School and King's College in Lagos,
and later proceeded to the Cambridge University where he obtained M.A. and LL.B degrees. He was called to the bar at
the Inner Temple in 1945. He later went into politics, becoming a member of the Federal House of Representatives in 1954
and a member of the Western Regional House of Assembly in
1960, and the NCNC opposition party leader. After the state
of emergency in the Western Region was lifted in January 1963,
he came to the height of his power as the Deputy Premier of
the region during the coalition government of his party with
the United Peoples' Party, and played an important role in the
postemergency politics. He was popularly known then and after
as "Fani-Power." In 1966 after the military took over power,
he went into private legal practice and business. In 1978 when
the ban on politics was lifted, he became a member of the National Party of Nigeria (NPN). He was later chosen as one of
the National Vice-Presidents of the party.

FEDERAL CAPITAL TERRITORY (FCT). Until the creation of the
Federal Capital Territory (FCT) in 1976 by Decree Number 6
of 1976, Lagos was the federal capital of Nigeria. As from
that date, Lagos became a "Special Area" along with Port Harcourt and Kaduna, and at the same time continued to play the
role of the nation's capital.
    Because of the social, environmental and traffic prob-
lems that have accompanied the population explosion in Lagos,
it was decided in 1975 to set up a panel, headed by Justice
T.A. Aguda, to look into the desirability or otherwise of maintaining Lagos as the federal capital. The panel recommended
movement of the capital to a geographically centrally located
area of the country. The military government of Murtala Muhammed accepted the recommendation and excised an area of
about 800 sq. km. from Kwara, Plateau and Niger states, but

the FCT is not part of any of the states--it is independent of all of them.

The administration of the Territory is carried on by the federal government through the instrumentality of the Federal Capital Territory Authority (FCDA). The capital was to be built in about 15 to 20 years from the time of its establishment, and it was then estimated to cost about ₦10 billion.

The work that the military administration began was continued with vigor by the administration of President Shehu Shagari and the 22nd Independence Day anniversary, October 1, 1982 was celebrated there, with all political party leaders present. Efforts were being made to move ministries and departments there gradually.

The name of the territory is Abuja.

FEDERAL CHARACTER. In an effort to promote national unity the 1979 Constitution provided that appointments into positions in the federal government and federal agencies must reflect the federal character of the country. This meant that there should be no predominance of persons from a few states or from a few ethnic or sectional groups in the government or its agencies. The same requirement applied to the executive organs of political parties. This provision made sure that no major ethnic group or no state was left out in decision making at various levels of government.

FEDERAL COUNCIL OF MINISTERS. Under the 1951 constitution there was a Council of Ministers, the principal instrument of policy for the central government. Under the 1954 Federal Constitution, the Council of Ministers became the Federal Council of Ministers and was made up of the Governor-General, three ex-officio members and 10 ministers, three from each of the three regions and one from the Southern Cameroon. During the first republic, 1960-1966, the Federal Council of Ministers consisted of the Prime Minister and the Cabinet Ministers which, following the British system, was collectively responsible for the policy of government.

FEDERAL COURT OF APPEAL. Established in 1976 by the military administration, it is an intermediate appellate court. Under the 1979 constitution, appeals lie from it to the Supreme Court while appeals lie to it from the State High Courts, Sharia Court of Appeal, Customary Court of Appeal Code of Conduct tribunal and other tribunals. The court has jurisdiction all over the nation and is composed of not less than 15 members, of which not fewer than three members must be learned in Islamic personal law and not fewer than three must be learned in customary law.

FEDERAL DEPARTMENT OF ANTIQUITIES. The Nigerian Antiquities Services was set up in 1945 under Mr. K.C. Murray who was then the Surveyor of Antiquities. In 1953 the Federal Department of Antiquities was established by an ordinance, and following this law, a 17-member Antiquities Commission was set up with powers to control archeological excavations and export of antiquities. The Department of Antiquities acts as the executive arm of the Commission in its effort to prevent illegal export of valuable works of art from the country. In addition, the Department is responsible for discovering and preserving traditional cultural materials all over the country. It has responsibility for studying these and publishing the results of its work. As a result of the work of the Nigerian Antiquities Services, the Commission and the Department Museums were built in many parts of the country: Owo and Esie in 1945, Jos in 1952, Ile-Ife in 1954, Lagos in 1957, Oron in 1958, Kano in 1960, Kaduna in 1972 and Benin City in 1973. The National Museum in Lagos houses most of the collections of the Department. It holds over half a million such collections but only a few of them are on display to the public.

FEDERAL ELECTIONS. Federal elections refer to elections to the Federal Houses of Representatives before and during the First Republic. The results of these elections determined which party leader would be called upon as Prime Minister to form the government. The first truly federal election took place in December 1959 with the following results: NPC 142 seats, NCNC 89, AG and allies 72 and Independents 9. With a total of 312 seats. As such, a coalition government was formed by NPC and NCNC with NPC presenting the Prime Minister. Another federal election took place in 1964, which was said to have been riddled with abuses, and which the UPGA Party boycotted in many places, leading in 1965 to a little federal election in places where there were boycotts in 1964.

    In the 1979 elections, the distinction between the federal and state elections was not that pronounced partly because the same body, FEDECO, handled both and they took place within the same four-to-five-week period. During this period, there were three separate "federal" elections to the Senate, House of Representatives and to the presidency, and two separate "State" elections to the Houses of Assembly and to the Governor's offices.

FEDERAL ELECTORAL COMMISSION (FEDECO). Established in 1977 it consisted of 24 members with Chief Michael Ani, a retired civil servant as its Chairman. The Commission was to register political parties and conduct elections into the State and Federal Legislative Houses in an effort to return the country to civilian rule in 1979.

    The Federal Electoral Commission was one of the federal commissions established under the 1979 Second Republican Constitution. It was empowered to organize, undertake and supervise all elections to the offices of the President and Vice-President, Governors and members of the Federal and State Legislative Houses. It had power to arrange for the annual examination and auditing of the accounts of political parties and to publish a report for public information. It was responsible

for the registration of voters and for making the list ready
and available for all elections even to local government councils.

FEDERAL EXECUTIVE COUNCIL (FEC). Established under Decree
Number 1 of 1966 as the executive organ of the federal military government, it consisted of the Head of the Federal Military Government who was the President of the Council, the
Heads of the Nigerian Army, Navy and the Air Force, Chief
of Staff of the Armed Forces, the Chief of Staff of the Nigerian
Army, the Attorney General of the federation and the Inspector-
General and the Deputy Inspector-General of the Police. In
1967 the Secretary to the federal military government and other
appropriate officials of the federal and regional governments
could attend the meetings of the council in an advisory capacity. Later, civilian and military commissioners (ministers)
were added to the council.

FEDERAL GOVERNMENT. Under the 1954 constitution, Nigeria,
which had been run as a unitary government since 1914, became a federation made up of three regions, the Eastern, the
Western and the Northern. Since then, with only a brief period from May 1966 when the Unification Decree was issued to
July 1966 when the second coup took place, Nigeria has
remained a federal state. Accordingly the powers of government are shared between the center and the regions/states.
The exclusive legislative list spells out federal government
powers, the concurrent legislative list relates to areas where
the center and the constituent parts can exercise powers but
in case of conflict federal laws would prevail. Residual powers
are left for the states to exercise. The government at the
center is the federal government. The chief executive during
the first republic was the Prime Minister, but during the Second Republic, he was called the President, who was popularly and
nationally elected. He freely chose his cabinet provided that
all the states of the federation were represented in it. His term
of office was four years and could be reelected into office for a
second term only. The seat of government is in Lagos but it
will move to Abuja, when the new federal capital being built
there is completed.

FEDERAL HIGH COURT see FEDERAL REVENUE COURT

FEDERAL HOUSE OF REPRESENTATIVES. The Federal House of
Representatives was one of the legislative chambers for the
federal government. During the First Republic the house was
made up of 312 members but during the Second Republic it was
made up of 450 members, with the Speaker as its leader. The
only difference between the House during the First and the Second Republic was that they were working under different political systems. The First Republic operated under the West-
minister type of parliamentary democracy while the second
operated under the executive presidential system.

FEDERAL INSTITUTE OF INDUSTRIAL RESEARCH (FIIR). Established in 1956, it was given the function of furthering the government policy of diversifying the nation's economy by encouraging businessmen to set up industries which especially relate to the processing of the nation's raw materials. The Institute also offers help to anyone wishing to set up new industries based upon Nigerian raw materials and it offers technical advice to existing industries through provision of laboratory facilities for analyzing samples of products and seeking solutions to basic technical problems. The major criteria used for the choice of its research projects are import substitutability, primary processing of raw materials for local industries and the development of native technology. Contract research is however acceptable at any time.

FEDERAL JUDICIAL SERVICE COMMISSION. Under the 1960 constitution, the appointment of judges of the superior courts was the responsibility of a body known as the Judicial Service Commission. Before a Judge could be removed from office, it was provided that his case should be examined by a tribunal whose membership was restricted to Judges and ex-Judges. However in 1963, the Judicial Service Commission was abolished when Nigeria became a Republic; it was then the Prime Minister who advised the President on the appointment of Federal Judges, and whether or not any of them should be removed from office was left to a two-thirds majority vote on the floor of the two Houses of Parliament. This was a retrogressive step which affected the independence of the judiciary.

When the military took over in 1966, they established the Federal Judicial Service Commission charged with the responsibility of appointment and disciplining Judges of the superior courts in the country. But it was the responsibility of the Head of State to appoint the members and Chairman of the Commission.

Under the 1979 Constitution, the Judicial Service Commission became entrenched. It was then responsible for advising the President on nominations for appointment of Justices to the Supreme Court including the Chief Justice of the Federal Court of Appeal, Judges of the Federal High Courts and members of the code of Conduct Tribunal. However such nominations required the approval of the Senate. It could also recommend their removal for inability to discharge their duties, misconduct or contravention of the code of conduct.

FEDERAL LOANS BOARD. Established in 1956, it succeeded the Colony Development Board. Its objectives were to help finance projects that were designed to further industrial development of the country. It could give a loan up to £50,000. The Board was to provide medium-term loan capital to indigenous entrepreneurs who appeared to have the ability to use it profitably. Furthermore, it was to help those whose capital fell short of their demonstrated ability.

FEDERAL PUBLIC SERVICE COMMISSION. The 1954 constitution
provided for the establishment of the Public Service Commission of the federation, with the power to appoint, promote and
discipline public servants in the federal public service. Under
the 1979 constitution, the scope of the commission was limited
to the civil service. It was then called the Federal Civil Service
Commission, composed of a chairman and not more than nine
members. Its responsibilities were to appoint persons to offices
in the federal civil service and to exercise disciplinary control
over them.

FEDERAL RADIO CORPORATION OF NIGERIA (FRCN). The name
Federal Radio Corporation came to be used in 1978 for the
Nigerian Broadcasting Corporation (NBC) after the latter had
been reorganized. The NBC was established by an act of Parliament in April 1957. It was owned and financed by the federal government. Before the corporation came into being in
1957, its functions used to be carried out by the Federal Broadcasting Service (FBS) which was a government department.
  Among the major functions of FRC are to provide broadcasting services by radio for reception in Nigeria, based on
the national objectives and aspirations, and to areas outside
the country in accordance with Nigeria's foreign policy. Its
broadcasting is to contribute to the development of Nigerian
Society and to promote national unity by ensuring balanced pres-
entation of views from all parts of the country. It is also to
provide commercial and educational broadcasting services.
  The Corporation has a policy-making body, known as
the Board of Governors, made up of nine members. Its headquarters is in Ikoyi Lagos, but its zonal broadcasting houses
are in the former regional capitals of Ibadan, Enugu and Kaduna.

FEDERAL REVENUE COURT. The Federal Revenue Court was set
up in 1973 with jurisdiction over all revenue matters. It handles both civil and criminal matters relating to companies,
taxes, banking, copyright, merchandise marks, trademarks and
cases of admiralty, relating to ships within the country's waters. The Federal Revenue Court became known as the Federal High Court under the 1979 constitution and it is given
power to hear all cases pertaining to the revenue of the government of the federation and any other matter which the National Assembly may by law prescribe.

FIRST BANK see AFRICAN BANKING CORPORATION

FIRST REPUBLIC (1963-1966). Generally refers to the period between independence on October 1, 1960 and the military takeover on January 15, 1966, but the First Republic formally came
into being only on October 1, 1963. By becoming a republic,
Nigeria broke the few remaining legal ties to Great Britain.
Instead of the Governor-General, who legally represented the
Queen of England, the country had a President who was more

or less a figurehead. Secondly, appeals which used to lie to
the Privy Council in London were abolished. The Federal Supreme Court became the final Court of Appeal for Nigeria.
The short period of the Republic was filled with crisis--in fact
one can say it was born in crisis, for events of military takeover of 1966 were the culmination of the events that started
with the Action Group crisis of 1962. These crises were:
the 1962-63 census controversy leading to alienation between
the federal coalition of Northern People's Congress NPC (representing the north) and the National Council of Nigerian Citizens (NCNC) (representing the East); the election conflict of
1964 among the various parties, again which led to two broad
political alliances: NNA, Nigerian National Alliance composed
of NPC and the NNDP (Nigerian National Democratic Party)
formed during the Action Group crisis by the Akintola faction
and the UPGA (United Progressive Grand Alliance) composed
of NCNC, Action Group (AG) and the United Middle Belt Congress (UMBC) and the Northern Element Progressive Union
(NEPU). The 1964 federal election created open disagreement
between the President, who, convinced that the elections were
grossly rigged in many places and having seen that the election was boycotted in parts of the country, refused at first to
call the leader of the majority party after the election to form
a new government. The differences were mediated and things
returned to "normal." But the Western Regional election campaign and the rigging of the election in 1965 led to a breakdown of law and order in the west. The government appeared
unable to put an end to the thuggery, killing and arson that
followed and so the military on January 15, 1966 had to put
an end to the life of the First Republic.

FOOT COMMISSION. After the Second World War, the government
finally yielded to the demand of the Nigerians for the Nigerianization of the higher civil service. As such in June 1948, Sir
John Macpherson, soon after his coming into Nigeria, set up
the Foot Commission of Inquiry headed by the Chief Secretary
to the Government Sir Hugh M. Foot. The Commission was
to look into the problem of recruiting Nigerians into the higher
levels of the civil service, and make recommendations with
regard to the steps that had to be taken to implement the government policy to appoint Nigerians to posts in the government
senior service as fast as suitable candidates were available.
The commission recommended among other things that no non-
Nigerian should be recruited for any government post except
where no suitable and qualified Nigerian was available. The
government accepted the recommendation and the process of
Nigerianization was speeded up. See also NIGERIANIZATION.

FOOT, SIR HUGH M. Born in 1907 he was educated at St. John's
College, Cambridge. He served as an administrative officer
in Palestine 1938-1939, assistant British Resident in Trans-
Jordan 1939-1942, in Cyrenaica in 1943, Colonial Secretary in
Cyprus in 1943-1945, as Acting Governor of Cyprus in 1944,

Colonial Secretary in Jamaica 1945-1947 and Chief Secretary
of Nigeria 1947-1951. He later went back to Jamaica. As
Chief Secretary, one of his first assignments was to head a
Commission on Nigerianization of the higher civil service with
the recommendation that only where no suitable and qualified
Nigerian was available should non-Nigerians be considered for
any government post. Furthermore in the process of reviewing the Richards Constitution of 1946, Sir Hugh Foot moved a
resolution in the Legislative Council, that there should be set
up a Select Committee of the Legislative Council to study the
methods of reviewing the constitution. He proposed various
ways to consult public opinion, through village meetings, divisional meetings, provincial meetings and other organizations.
He contributed in no small way to the making of the Macpherson Constitution of 1951. While still in Nigeria, on February
18, 1950, a member of the Zikist Movement made an unsuccessful attempt on his life, an incident that confirmed the colonial authorities' suspicion of the organization as dangerous
to the good government of the country and led to the banning
of the Movement in April 1950.

FORD FOUNDATION. Among the donors of aid to educational institutions in Nigeria, the Ford Foundation has played very significant roles. Between 1948 and 1964, it gave millions of naira
as research grants to the University of Ibadan. And when regional Universities of Ife, Ahmadu Bello and Nsukka were established in the early 1960's, the foundation was quick to come
to their aid. It helped to develop the Faculty of Education in
the University of Nigeria, Nsukka and in the building of the
former Institute (now Faculty) of Administration and the Institute of African Studies in the University of Ife.

FOREIGN TRADE. Nigeria maintains essentially nondiscrimina-
tory foreign trade relations with all the continents of the world.
She has bilateral trade agreements with various countries both
in Eastern and Western Europe, in Asia, America, and Africa,
and there is a thriving trade between her and her neighbors.
However most of her imports and her nonoil exports are still
from and to Western Europe.

FOSTER-SUTTON COMMISSION OF INQUIRY. The Foster-Sutton
Commission of Inquiry chaired by Sir Stafford Foster-Sutton,
Chief Justice of the Federation of Nigeria was set up in 1956
to inquire into the relationship between Dr. Nnamdi Azikiwe,
the then-Premier of Eastern Nigeria, the Government of Eastern Nigeria and the African Continental Bank (ACB). The Commission was to look into the allegations of improper conduct on
the part of Dr. Nnamdi Azikiwe in connection with the affairs
of the African Continental Bank Limited and examine the circumstances in which securities belonging to the Eastern Regional Marketing Board were transferred to the Eastern Region
Finance Corporation and the circumstances in which such proceeds were invested in or deposited with the African Continental

Bank by the Eastern Region Finance Corporation. It was also
to look into the relationship between Dr. Nnamdi Azikiwe and
the African Continental Bank, its directors, shareholders or
officers and the relationship between the Eastern Region Finance Corporation and the African Continental Bank. In addition it also looked into the relationship between any person or
organization, corporate or not in which Dr. Nnamdi Azikiwe
had some interest at any material time whether direct or indirect and the African Continental Bank Limited, and the use
made of the resouces of the ACB whether before or after the
investments and deposits referred to were made insofar as
such use appeared to the Tribunal to be material for the fore-
going purposes. Finally the Commission was to determine
whether in respect of any persons holding ministerial or other
public offices had infringed the standards of the conduct demanded of the holder of such offices and if so in what respect.
On January 16, 1957 the report of the Commission was published. After noting that Dr. Azikiwe's motives for founding
the bank were to make available an indigenous bank with the
purpose of liberalizing credit for the people of the country, it
still went on to conclude that his conduct in connection with
the affairs of the bank fell short of the expectations of honest,
reasonable people. As a means of contesting the findings of
the Commission and to test the support of the people for Dr.
Azikiwe, the Eastern House of Assembly was dissolved and
fresh elections were called. The people voted him and his
party back into power with a fairly large majority. Furthermore the Executive Council advised Dr. Azikiwe to transfer
all his rights and interests in the bank to the Eastern Regional
government which Dr. Azikiwe readily accepted.

FOURAH BAY COLLEGE. The Fourah Bay College was established
in 1927 in Sierra Leone by the Church Missionary Society
(CMS). Its original aim was to train teachers, priests and
layworkers for the church. However in 1876 the status of the
college was raised by affiliating it to Durham University in
England. As such it prepared students to take the external
examinations for the B.A. degrees awarded by Durham University. Furthermore the college offered diploma courses in
theology and education.
        Fourah Bay College has played a very significant role
in the history of higher education in Nigeria. As it was the first
higher institution in all British West Africa--Nigeria, Ghana,
Sierra Leone and the Gambia--the students came from the four
territories but for quite over a century Nigerian students constituted about 50 percent of all student population. In fact the
first graduate of the College was Bishop Ajayi Crowther, a
Nigerian, in 1828.
        Fourah Bay College has also grown not only in enroll-
ment and staff but in status, for in 1960 it was granted University College status even though it was still affiliated with
Durham University, and in 1966 it severed this legal bond by
becoming a constituent college of the University of Sierra Leone
which was granted autonomous status that same year.

FREEDOM MOVEMENT. When the colonial government in April 1950 declared the Zikist Movement unlawful because its purposes and methods were dangerous to the good government of the country, the group met in Port Harcourt the following month and reorganized itself into the Freedom Movement with the aim to destroy all forms of imperialism and to establish a free socialist Republic of Nigeria which would fight in and out of Parliament, employing nonviolent revolutionary tactics. Memberships were the same in both. Branches were set up mainly in the Eastern Region, even though there were some in the west. The Movement was short-lived, owing to waning enthusiasm among its members and the factional feuds between the leaders in Lagos and those in Port Harcourt. Its death was however hastened by the reorganization of the NCNC on the basis of individual membership rather than organizational membership in 1951.

FREEMAN, REVEREND THOMAS BIRCH. A Methodist missionary of mixed race. Accompanied by William de Graft, a Ghanaian, he was the first missionary to arrive in Badagry in September 1842. He built a mission house and started a small prayer service. In December of that year he visited Abeokuta and was well received by the Oba Sodeke and his people. In 1843 Freeman returned to the Gold Coast (Ghana) and left William de Graft behind.

FULANI EMPIRE. Founded by Usman Dan Fodio, the leader of the Islamic Holy War (Jihad) begun in 1804, which swept through the Hausa states. By 1808 most of the Hausa States had been brought under the Fulani rulers including Kano, Katsina, and Zaria. The empire was divided into two--the Western Sector with the headquarters at Gwandu came under the administration of Abdullahi who was the brother of Usman Dan Fodio, and the Eastern Sector with the headquarters at Sokoto came under Bello, son of Usman Dan Fodio who became the Sultan of Sokoto, the town which Usman himself had made his home, and which today gives Sokoto a focal point of Islamic religion in Nigeria.

The empire extended all the way to Ilorin, south of River Niger--a Yoruba town, Lokoja, Yola, Gombe but was checked by the Al-Kanemi and the forces of the Mai of Bornu. By 1830 most of the area, later known as the Protectorate of Northern Nigeria, with the exception of Bornu, the Tiv area and some part of Jos Plateau had fallen to the Fulanis. The empire gave unity to the whole of Northern Nigeria which for long had been torn asunder by local wars; it also set up a uniform system of government in the area, and made for easy flow of commerce in the empire.

The empire lasted for 100 years. In 1903 Lord Lugard told the conquered Fulanis in Sokoto that he, the British High Commissioner, was completely succeeding the right of Usman Dan Fodio to rule all of the empire. However Sokoto still retains its role as the Moslem religious center.

FULANIS. The Fulanis are one of the major ethnic groups in Nigeria and one of the first to accept the Muslim religion; they did much to spread it. Though their real origin is unknown they are said to have come from places like Senegal. They are found mostly in the northern part of the country. They first settled among the Hausas, and the educated ones among them occupied positions as teachers and moslem priests among the Hausas.

The Fulanis can be put in two categories, one being the cattle Fulani who are uneducated by western standards and constitute a normadic class that wander from place to place with their flocks and herd of cattle. They keep themselves fairly aloof from others. The other is the town Fulani who are settled down in cities and are traders.

With the rise of Usman Dan Fodio, they gained the political control of the Hausa states during the Holy War called the Jihad. As a result of the war the Fulanis were installed as Emirs in all the Emirates in the Northern Nigeria in place of the former traditional rulers.

The Fulanis and the Hausas have acculturated each other's values and it is now very difficult to distinguish an Hausa town from a Fulani town. This is because they live in the same environment with the Fulanis as the Emirs.

FUNDAMENTAL HUMAN RIGHTS. When Nigeria became a federation in 1954, the minorities in each region became restive: there were demands to create new regions in the three existing regions. The demand became so loud that the British government set up the Minorities Commission in 1957 to look into the fears being expressed. The Commission as was expected did not recommend the creation of new regions but it recommended some palliatives, one of which was that fundamental rights of the citizens everywhere in the country should be protected by the constitution. Accordingly in the 1958 Constitutional Conference, a proposal to include a list of Fundamental Rights in the Constitution was adopted. At present Chapter IV of the 1979 constitution deals with these fundamental rights.

-G-

GAMBARI, DR. IBRAHIM AGBOOLA. Minister of External Affairs, born on October 24, 1944 in Ilorin Kwara State, he was educated at the Provincial Secondary School, Ilorin, King's College, Lagos, London School of Economics, University of London and Columbia University in New York. Returning to Nigeria in 1977, he joined the Department of Political Science in the Ahmadu Bello University in Zaria. In October 1983 he was appointed Director-General of the Nigerian Institute of International Affairs, and in January 1984 after the December 1983 coup d'état, he was appointed Minister of External Affairs.

GARBA, MAJOR-GENERAL JOSEPH NAUVEN. Born on July 17,

1943 at Langtan near Shendam in Plateau State. He was educated at the Sacred Heart School, Shendam and later at the Nigerian Military School in Zaria from 1957 to 1961. In 1962,
he was sent to the Mons Officer Cadet School, Aldershot in
England from where he became a commissioned officer. In
1973, he was on the staff, College Camberley, England. From
1963 to 1968, he moved up very rapidly and served in many
capacities and places including Kashmir in India under the
United Nations Observer forces. From 1968 to 1975 when
General Gowon was toppled from power, he was the commanding officer of the Brigade of Guards at the Dodan Barracks in
Lagos. He participated actively in the 1975 coup and it was
he who announced the ouster of General Gowon from power in
a bloodless coup on July 29, 1975. He later became Commissioner for External Affairs. In 1978 he was commandant, Nigerian Defense Academy in Kaduna and was promoted to Major-
General in 1979. He retired from the army in 1980, but after
the December 1983 coup, he was appointed Nigerian Ambassador to the United Nations.

GENERAL STRIKE. During the Second World War, and as a result
of the austerity measures adopted by the colonial government,
the condition of life for the workers increasingly deteriorated.
In 1942 the government approved a cost of living allowance
(COLA) to workers, but this did not improve things much.
And as government price control efforts were also ineffective,
workers asked for a 50 percent increase in the cost of living
allowance and a minimum daily wage of 2/6d for a laborer.
When the demands were not met, union leaders called for a
strike by the railway workers, postal and telegraph workers,
and technical workers in government departments. The strike,
lasting 37 days, virtually paralyzed the economy. The government later set up the Davies Commission of Enquiry to examine
the workers' grievances. As a result of its submission, workers' salaries were regraded upward and the cost-of-living allowances were also increased. Nationalists like Dr. Nnamdi
Azikiwe and his newspapers gave strong support to the workers. And so, even though the colonial government helped the
development of labor organizations in Nigeria, labor unions
became one of the pressure groups fighting not only for economic betterment but also for social and political reforms.

GENOCIDE ALLEGATION. During the 1967-1970 civil war, the
former Eastern Nigeria, known as Biafra, mounted a series
of propaganda to arouse the sympathy of the people all over
the world to their cause. One such propaganda issue was
the allegation that they were seceding from Nigeria because
of Nigeria's determination to wipe out the Ibo people. They
alleged that their security could no longer be guaranteed by a
government outside their regional boundaries and they considered the war being waged against them by the federal government as a war of genocide. To disprove this allegation, the
federal military government had to allow international observers
to come to the so-called liberated areas.

GOLD COAST (GHANA). Gold Coast is the colonial name of the modern Ghana. The name was changed to Ghana in 1957 at the country's independence. In 1874, Lagos was brought under the administration of the Governor of the Gold Coast but in January 1886, Lagos was detached from the Gold Coast and became self-administering. In 1894, the Nana of Itsekiri was deported to the Gold Coast because of his resistance to the British. He stayed in the Gold Coast until 1906 when he was allowed to come back home.

Both Nigeria and the Gold Coast share the common colonial experience under the British colonial administration. During the nationalist struggle, the Gold Coast gave Nigeria the lead. One of the most popular nationalists in Nigeria, Dr. Nnamdi Azikiwe first worked in the Gold Coast as a nationalist before coming back to Nigeria. In 1957 the Gold Coast became the first of the British West African countries to become independent and changed its name to Ghana. Ghana was a sort of inspiration to Nigeria in its struggle for national independence. In 1959 Ghana hosted the Pan-African Conference at which nearly all the nationalist leaders in Africa were present.

In addition to the above common experiences, Ghana and Nigeria also share common experiences in agriculture for both are major cocoa-producing countries for the world market. However the two countries almost unconsciously see each other as rivals. This rivalry is best seen in their sporting activities which have for a long time been organized between the two countries. In fact one may say that it was this Nigeria-Ghana sports rivalry that gave birth to the All-West African Sports Competition.

Again during Nigeria's agonizing years in which great efforts were being made to bring about a reconciliation between the federal government headed by General Yakubu Gowon and the Eastern Regional government headed by Lt. Col. Odumegwu Ojukwu, it was Ghana among all African countries that first organized a peace talk at Aburi to settle the dispute. However relations strained later when in 1970 Ghana ordered thousands of Nigerians who had for decades lived and worked in Ghana to pack and go back to Nigeria. Nigeria then showed a sign of maturity by not reacting under such provocation. But with the coming into operation of the Economic Community of West African Countries (ECOWAS), many Ghanaians flooded to Nigeria to avoid the political instability and the economic hardship going on in the country, most of them staying in the country illegally. In February 1983, the government of Nigeria, itself suffering from economic recession due to the world oil glut, ordered illegal aliens to leave the country. This was a big blow to Ghana which was forced to make room for about two million citizens that had to go back home. The government of Lt. Jerry Rawlings calmly accepted the challenge and began the process of absorbing them.

GOLDIE, GEORGE TAUBMAN. Born in 1846 on the Isle of Man off

the British shore. As a youth in the early 1860's he trained
for two years at the Royal Military Academy, Woolwich, as
an engineer. Two years later a relation of his died, leaving
him a fortune and Goldie went straight to Egypt where he
learned from Hausa pilgrims and scholars on their way to
Mecca that the Egyptian Sudan was just the fringe of the vast
Sudanic belt extending from the Niger to the Nile. After three
years he left Egypt and returned to England. In 1871 he married. In 1875 the opportunity he had been looking for came
through his family connection. His eldest brother, the then-
head of the family, had married Min Amelia Grove-Ross whose
father, Captain Joseph Grove-Ross, was the secretary of a
small firm, Holland Jacques and Company which had been trading on the Niger since 1869. By 1875 the company was in financial difficulty and Joseph Grove-Ross appealed to his son-
in-law for help. The Taubman family then decided to take
over the company and Goldie decided to go back to Africa,
specifically to the Niger and if possible cross over through
the Sudan to the Nile. Within two years of his stay in Nigeria
he had created what may be called a trading empire on the
river. He saw to the amalgamation of the four competing
companies--Miller Brothers of Glasgow, James Pinnock, Holland Jacques Central African Trading Company and his own
West and Central African Company--into a United African Company (UAC). But the UAC was later found to be incapable of
coping with the situation and so in 1881 a new company, the
National African Company was formed. It took over UAC's
business in Central Africa and the Niger. The success of his
company attracted foreign competition by the French and the
Germans who were pursuing a vigorous colonial policy in Africa. By underselling the French companies he was able to
make them agree to merge with the National African Company
in 1884 or leave the scene. He concluded treaties with many
Chiefs along the Niger, all which later became the basis for
the British claim at the 1884-1885 Berlin Conference at which
Goldie was representing the British. In 1886, the British government granted a charter to his company which became the
Royal Niger Company. The charter empowered the company
to govern, keep order and protect the territories under it and
to acquire new ones subject to the sanction of the Secretary
of State. In 1900 the company's charter was revoked. The
British government took over the administration of the country
while the company concentrated on business. By this time
Goldie had become fairly wealthy. He died in August 1925.

GOMWALK, JOSEPH DESHI. Born on April 13, 1935 at Amper
Pankshin Division in Plateau State, he was educated at the
Sudan United Mission (SUM) School in Amper and in Gindiri
where he finished his secondary education in 1955. He then
went to the Nigerian College of Arts, Science and Technology
in Zaria in 1956 and University College, Ibadan in 1958 where
in 1961 he obtained a Bachelor's degree in Zoology, specializ-
ing in parasitology. He later worked as a research officer at

the Kaduna Veterinary School and after some time he was transferred to the Northern Nigerian administrative service from 1961 to 1965. In February 1966, he joined the Nigeria Police Force and quickly rose to the rank of Chief Superintendent. When states were created in 1967, he was appointed Governor of Benue-Plateau State. He was together with other governors compulsorily retired in 1975 when General Gowon's regime was overthrown. After the abortive coup of February 13, 1976, led by Lt. Col. Dimka in which General Murtala was killed, Mr. Gomwalk was said to be connected with the plot. He was arrested, secretly tried and found guilty. He was shot by firing squad on May 14, 1976, leaving behind a widow and three children.

GONGOLA STATE. Gongola State was created on February 3, 1976 out of the former North-Eastern State. In size, the state is the second largest in the federation with an estimated area of 91,390 sq. km. It has a population of about three million people. The State has a large variety of ethnic groups who live in segmented large and small communities speaking different languages. Most of the groups fall into two linguistic groups--the Afro-Asian group and the Niger-Congo family. Among the first group are people like the Higgi, Margi, Gude, Kilba and Bata/Bachama, and within the other group are the Chamba, Bura and Vere. There are others like the Fulani, Jukun, Mambilla, and some others.

The main towns in Gongola State are Yola, Mubi, Numan, Ganye, Jalingo, Gembu and Wukari. Gongola State has many secondary and postsecondary schools like Advanced Teachers' College, Federal College of Arts and Science, Advanced College of Preliminary Studies to prepare students for entrance into the universities and some other institutions. Being an agricultural land area, the state has farm training centers and many farms which produce food crops and livestock. The state is also rich in mineral resources like iron, lead, zinc, limestone and others.

The state capital is Yola.

GORSUCH COMMISSION. In 1954, agreements at the Constitutional Conference had been reached that Nigeria should become a federation of three regions, and that the civil service and the judiciary should be regionalized. Furthermore, the existing division of the civil service into senior and junior staff, where the senior staff were mainly expatriates and the junior staff were Nigerians, was most criticized and it called for a change, especially since independence was just a few years away. As such the government decided in 1954 to set up the Gorsuch Commission under the chairmanship of Mr. L. H. Gorsuch to inquire into the structure and remuneration of the public services with special reference to the problems arising from the constitutional changes proposed at the 1954 Conference on the Nigerian constitution. It was also to examine the problems from the individual aspects of the future federal and regional governments while taking into consideration factors of similarity and divergence that were involved, and make recommendations in a form that would be suitable for submission to the future federal and regional governments.

The Commission did not like the structure of the civil service which was broad at the top and at the bottom, but there was little or nothing at the middle level. In its place the Commission recommended a hierarchical structure similar to the one in the United Kingdom. The old classification was replaced by a new classification into generalist and specialist branches. The generalist branch in descending order was made up of the superscale, the administrative, the executive, the clerical and the subclerical. The specialist branch was made up of the superscale, the professional, higher technical, technical and minor technical. The Commission recommended advancement through training from one level to another.

These recommendations were accepted both by the federal and regional governments and they became the basis of the civil service structure until the Udoji Commission recommended the abolition of the many classes and substituted a single grading system for both generalist and specialist branches. The Commission was important for many reasons. It enabled the new regions to mold their services on a similar pattern, based on the system in the United Kingdom. By broadening the middle level, it freed the administrators and their professional counterparts from routine duties which people at the executive level could do.

GOVERNMENT. The frequent constitutional changes that Nigeria has experienced since her independence in 1960 have led to experiments with different types of government. At independence, Nigeria inherited the parliamentary system of government. The Queen of England, represented by the governor-general was the constitutional Head of State, while the Prime Minister was the head of government collectively responsible to parliament. In 1963, Nigeria became a republic. The Queen was no longer the Head of State. The Head of State became the President, elected by a secret ballot at a joint meeting of both houses of parliament. The President appointed the Prime Minister, a member of the House of Representatives who appeared to him likely to command the support of the majority of the members of the house, and other ministers on the advice of the Prime Minister. The Prime Minister and the other ministers formed the Council of Ministers, which was collectively responsible to parliament for any advice given to the President.

The first republic was riddled with many crises and it finally broke down in January 1966 when the military came to power. The Federal Military Government suspended certain provisions of the 1963 constitution especially those dealing with the executive and legislative institutions of government. In their place was the Head of State who was the Head of the Federal Military Government and the Commander-in-Chief of the Armed Forces. Under him was the Chief of Staff Supreme Headquarters, who served in a position analogous to that of a Prime Minister. (Cont'd. p. 387.)

GOVERNOR-GENERAL OF NIGERIA. Consequent upon the amalgamation of the Protectorate of Northern Nigeria with the Colony
and Protectorate of Southern Nigeria on January 1, 1914, the
post of Governor-General of Nigeria was created, with Sir
Frederick Lugard as its first incumbent. However, all his
successors beginning with Sir Hugh Clifford to Sir Arthur
Richards were all referred to as Governors of Nigeria. But
when the 1954 Federal Constitution came into being Sir John
Macpherson, who since 1948 had been Governor of Nigeria,
became the Governor-General. The Governor-General or the
Governor of Nigeria was the Queen's representative and all
his powers derived from Her Majesty's Government. Before
1957, the Governor-General combined the functions of Head of
State and the Chief Executive. In 1957, the position of Prime
Minister was created and the Governor-General became the
Head of State and a ceremonial Head of Government, for he
had to be advised by his responsible ministers.

   After Nigeria became independent on October 1, 1960,
Sir James Robertson, the then Governor-General, stayed on till
November 15, 1960 when he retired. As such Dr. Nnamdi
Azikiwe became the first indigenous Governor-General of Ni-
geria.

   In 1963 when Nigeria became a republic, the position of
Governor-General was abolished and the position of the President of the Republic was created. Dr. Azikiwe again stepped
into this new position. However he remained Head of State
and a Ceremonial Chief Executive only but he did not owe his
authority to the King or Queen of England.

GOWON, GENERAL YAKUBU. Head of the federal military government and Supreme Commander of the Nigerian Army from August 1966 to July 1975. Born on October 19, 1934 in the Lur
Pankshim division of Plateau State, he was educated at St.
Bartholomew's School, Wusasa and at the Government College
in Zaria. He enlisted in the army in 1954 and was sent to
take many officers' courses in Ghana and England. He served
twice with the Nigerian contingent serving on the United Nations
Peace-Keeping Force in the Congo, first from 1960 to 1961,
and second in 1963. He was promoted to Major in 1962 and Lt.
Colonel in 1963.

   Gowon was out of the country in January 1966 during
the first coup, and since he was not involved in it, the new
leader, General Aguiyi-Ironsi appointed him Chief of Staff of
the Nigerian Army and a member of the military government.

   In the second coup of July 29, General Ironsi was killed
and the coup makers, most of them from the north decided he
was the only leader acceptable to them even though Brigadier
Babafemi Ogundipe, a Yoruba man and his senior in rank was
available. As Head of State, his first priority was to restore
discipline in the army and allay the fear of the civilian population. On August 2, 1966, a day after he came to power, he
released from jail Chief Obafemi Awolowo, leader of the banned

Action Group Party, convicted of treasonable felony of planning to overthrow the federal government of Nigeria in 1962. He also released many other political prisoners.

The discipline he tried to restore in the army eluded him. Lt. Colonel Odumegwu Ojukwu, the Eastern Region Military Governor, believing that Brigadier Ogundipe should have assumed command refused to accept Gowon's leadership. In October 1966 a violent massacre of the Ibo people erupted in the north, causing them to flee home. It prepared the way for the movement towards the secession of Eastern Nigeria, later called Biafra. Efforts were made to reconcile the wishes of the two men, including the meeting at Aburi Ghana, but all failed. On May 27, 1967 Ojukwu was mandated by the meeting of the Consultative Assembly held at the instance of the Governor in Enugu to declare at an early practical date Eastern Nigeria as a free sovereign and independent state by the name of the Republic of Biafra. In the evening of the same day, General Gowon announced a state of emergency throughout the nation and a decree dividing the country into 12 states, thus removing the old fear of northern domination and assuring Gowon the support of the minority areas, two of which were in the Eastern Region, that had long agitated for their own states. Two days later, Ojukwu proclaimed the Republic of Biafra.

Hostilities started in July and General Gowon took what he called "a police action" to end the Biafran secession. But the war continued for two and a half years, after which Lt. Colonel Ojukwu fled the country to the Ivory Coast and the federal government accepted the surrender of Biafra.

During the civil war, to allay the fears of the Ibos who were being told that the federal government was waging a war of genocide against them, and to assure the world that there was no intention to commit such attrocities, General Gowon did two things: he issued a "Code of Conduct" to his troops, insisting that Biafran soldiers were not to be treated as external enemies but former comrades and the civilians were to be treated as Nigerians and cared for; he also allowed international observer teams to come to the war zone and observe his troops' conduct of the war. His only objective was to keep Nigeria one by bringing back Biafra. Once the war was over he began the process of rehabilitation and reconstruction of the war-torn areas.

On October 1, 1970, General Gowon announced the program that would lead to civilian rule in 1976. These included a new constitution, a new population census and elections. But on October 1, 1974, he told the nation that 1976 was no longer a realistic date to hand over government to civilian rule. This announcement was a great disappointment to a lot of people.

On July 27, 1975 General Gowon left Lagos for Kampala in Uganda to attend the 12th Summit meeting of the Organization of African Unity (OAU). Two days later on July 29, Colonel Joseph Nanven Garba, Head, Brigade of Guards announced at 6 am in a radio broadcast that General Gowon had been ousted from power in a bloodless operation. Brigadier Murtala Muhammed succeeded him as Head of State and Commander-in-Chief of the Armed Forces. General Gowon in Kampala pledged support and loyalty to the officers who ousted him and the new Head of State said that General Gowon would be retired in his rank with pension and he would be free to return home as soon as conditions permitted.

Leaving Kampala he went into exile in Britain and enrolled as a student of Political Science at the University of Warwick, Coventry in October 1975. In the abortive coup of February 13, 1976 staged by Lt. Col. B.S. Dimka in which General Murtala Muhammed was killed, it was alleged that one of the purposes of the coup was to restore General Gowon back to power, but General Gowon denied any knowledge of the coup. However Lt. Col. Dimka, after his arrest, confirmed that he had visited General Gowon in London and discussed plans with him. On May 15, 1976 the Head of State announced the dismissal of General Gowon from the army and he was declared a wanted person. However President Shehu Shagari, the first civilian Head of State of the Second Republic, pardoned him in 1981 and declared that he was free to come home from exile. He came back home in 1983, but soon went back to England to finish his Ph.D. thesis. He received his Ph.D. degree in Political Science at the University of Warwick in July 1984.

While in office, he was the recipient of many honorary degrees awarded him in Nigeria, the United States and Britain.

GRAHAM-DOUGLAS, NABO BEKINBO. Born on July 15, 1926 at Abonnema in the Rivers State, he was educated at Nyemoni School, Abonnema and at Kalabari National College, Bugama. He later went to the University College, Exeter, England, and to King's College University of London. He then went to the Institute of Advanced Legal Studies in London. He was called to the bar at the Inner Temple in London.

Upon his return to Nigeria he took up a successful law practice in Port Harcourt, the capital of the Rivers State. In 1966, after the first coup d'état and Colonel Odumegwu Ojukwu became the Military Governor of the Eastern Region, he was appointed Attorney-General for the Eastern Region. He became unpopular in the Ojukwu administration by advising against secession after the massacre of the Ibos in the north and he had to resign in September 1966. When Ojukwu finally declared secession in 1967, he was arrested and detained and his law library in Port Harcourt was burned by the Biafran troops. In 1968 he was liberated from detention and became federal government envoy touring Europe and America to explain the federal government side in the war. In 1972 when Teslim Elias succeeded the retired Chief Justice of the Federation, Sir Adetokunbo Ademola, Graham Douglas was appointed Attorney General of the federation, a position he occupied till 1975.

Mr. Graham-Douglas wrote Triumph or Turpitude, an account of his personal involvement in the civil war crisis and also Forensic Aspects of Nigerian Land Law in 1972.

GRAND KADI. The Grand Kadi is the judge who presides over the Sharia Court of Appeal which hears cases concerning Moslem private law. He has vast powers under Islamic laws.

GREAT NIGERIA PEOPLE'S PARTY (GNPP). A political party, one of the many parties formed when the ban on politics was lifted in 1978, and one of the five political parties recognized in 1979 elections. The GNPP was formed by the faction that broke away from the Nigerian People's Party on whether or not the same person should combine in himself the position of presidential candidate and the party leader. Alhaji Waziri Ibrahim, the party leader, believed that the two posts should be combined and held by himself while the other faction disagreed.

After the senatorial election on July 7, 1979 and the House of Representatives election on July 14, it became clear that the only party that all the other parties had to beat was the National Party of Nigeria (NPN). Alhaji Waziri Ibrahim on July 17, 1979 announced that the other four parties, the GNPP, the Nigerian People's Party (NPP) the Unity Party of Nigeria (UPN) and the People's Redemption Party (PRP) were making moves to work together to prevent the NPN from coming to power. In spite of the move, not only did he lose the presidency but the NPN was declared the winner of the presidential office. The GNPP won two gubernatorial elections in Borno and Gongola states and won 8 out of 95 senatorial seats and 44 seats out of 449 in the House of Representatives. It also won many seats in state legislatures. Although the party slogan during the campaign was "Politics Without Bitterness," the party leader was very bitter about the alleged rigging of the election especially in Sokoto State where the party believed it was most favored to win. The postelection politicking led the party and the Unity Party of Nigeria (UPN) to enter into an accord of some sort. In the 1983 elections, the party fared very poorly, for it could not win any state gubernatorial election, not to talk of the presidency. The party was banned after the coup d'etat of December 31, 1983.

GREEN REVOLUTION. In December 1979 President Shehu Shagari announced plans for a program to increase food production in an effort to provide food for every Nigerian. The government would speed up shipments of new materials and animal feeds and help each state to expand its productive areas. An additional 4,000 hectares of land would be tilled at the beginning of the program. The government, he said, was determined to establish a self-reliant economy. This program is popularly known as the Green Revolution.

Thus on January 31, 1980, the Operation Feed the Nation (OFN), launched in May 1976 by the military regime of General Obasanjo was abolished and replaced by the National

Council on Green Revolution. The National Council would consist of the federal Minister for Agriculture and State Commissioners for Agriculture and would be headed by the President himself. The government would harness the services of the Ministry of Science and Technology to provide necessary equipment for farmers with the services of the Ministry of Water Resources to provide water for farming and animal husbandry.

GROUNDNUTS. Groundnuts used to be one of the most important foreign exchange earners in Nigeria. They were grown mostly in the northern part of the country and when packed into sacks ready for transportation to the coast, they used to be stacked up into a beautiful pyramidal form in many places in northern Nigeria. However as a result of the 1972-1974 drought, which badly affected the crop, farmers were discouraged from continuing to grow them. Today Nigeria has no groundnuts for export, for the small amount that is produced is being locally processed and consumed. To encourage greater production, the government River Basin Projects are designed to ensure the supply of water to farmers all the year round, and the government has also provided fertilizer and other agricultural assistance at subsidized rate, and has reorganized the Groundnut Marketing Board. See also MARKETING BOARDS.

GWARRI. An ethnic minority group, it is located in the present Niger State. The people were said to have come from Bornu and to be indigenous to Nigeria. They were never conquered by the Fulani during the Jihad.

-H-

HABE KINGDOMS. The same as Hausa Kingdoms.

HARBISON REPORT. This report on high-level manpower study for Nigeria was submitted by Frederick Harbison of Princeton University in the United States to the federal government. Professor Harbison was required to estimate the country's manpower needs between 1960 and 1970. He divided what he regarded as high-level manpower into two categories--senior and the intermediate. He estimated that Nigeria would need 31,200 personnel in the senior category by 1970 and 54,000 persons in the intermediate category as opposed to the 30,000 personnel in both categories in 1960. He estimated that Nigerian universities would have to turn out at the rate of 2,000 graduates a year to meet these demands and other postsecondary institutions an estimate of about 5,400 graduates a year in the intermediate category. He therefore recommended upgrading the employed manpower through in-service training, and the establishment of a Manpower Development Board to coordinate other interregional machinery for manpower development. The government accepted Harbison's analysis of the country's manpower position but could not accept his estimates of future needs of the country. The government felt that the target set was too low.

HARRAGIN COMMISSION. Set up in November 1945 to review and make recommendations on the structure and remunerations of the civil services of the four British West African colonies. It was to look specifically at the standards of remuneration and superannuation payments, the relationship between the salaries and conditions of service of locally recruited and externally recruited officers, machinery for adjusting remuneration to variations in the cost of living, provision of suitable arrangements between governments and staff organizations, and provision by means of the Public Service Commission for regulating, selecting and promoting candidates for posts in the service.

Sir Walter Harragin who was then the Chief Justice of the Gold Coast (Ghana) was the sole commissioner. His report was published in 1947. It recommended substantial wage increases for government employees and a higher entry point of salary for African technical staff in an effort to encourage them to stay with the government for its many development programs. It recommended the introduction of expatriation pay for expatriates who were recruited outside Nigeria. It also recommended the setting up of an advisory council modelled on the British Whitley Councils in each territory to advise government on all matters like salaries and conditions of employment of civil servants.

Government accepted most of its recommendations but the Nigerian Civil Service Union and some others were strongly opposed to higher entry points for African technical officers.

HAUSA BAKWAI. Hausa Bakwai refers to the seven original Hausa states: Kano, Rano, Zaria, Daura, Gobir, Katsina and Zamfara, but owing to the destruction of records of Hausa history by the Fulanis who conquered them, authorities are not agreed on Zamfara as one of the seven original states. Some will substitute Biram or Yareem for Zamfara and include Zamfara as one of the Hausa Banza or Banza Bakwai which were the seven states which had great Hausa influence but were not the seven original states. These seven states are listed as Zamfara, Kebbi, Nupe, Gwari, Yauri, Yoruba and Kororofa by some authors while others say they are Zamfara, Kebbi, Nupe, Yauri, Yoruba, Borgu and Ghoorma.

HAUSA CONSTABULARY. The Nigerian Police, founded in Lagos in February 1861 as a consular guard of 30 men, was to maintain public peace in Lagos which had just become the Crown Colony. Two years later the police force became known as Hausa Police. In 1879 the colonial authority set up the Hausa Constabulary for the colony of Lagos, consisting of 1200 officers and men under the command of an Inspector-General. The Constabulary was mainly military in character but it performed some civil police duties also. In 1896, the Lagos

Police Force was created under the command of a Commissioner who also was responsible for the prisons and for the Fire Brigade. The Lagos Police Force was also equipped like the Hausa Constabulary.

HAUSAS. The Hausas are the largest ethnic group in Nigeria. They are found mostly in Sokoto, Kano, Bauchi, and Kaduna states. They trace their origin through Bayajidda, son of Abdullahi, King of Bagdad, who had journeyed first to Bornu, then to Daura where he begot Bawo. Bawo later had six sons who together with him founded the seven Hausa states or Hausa Bakwai. These seven states are Katsina, Kano, Rano, Daura, Zaria, Gobir and Zamfara.

The Hausas are Moslems who were greatly influenced by the Fulani Jihad of the early nineteenth century.

They possess an intense cultural consciousness and pride in themselves. Consequently the impact of Christianity upon them has been small. By virtue of their Moslem faith and proud tradition, they look with contempt upon non-Moslems and even regard the southern Christians as unbelievers--Kafiris.

Like many other Nigerian ethnic groups the Hausas trace their descent patrilineally and their marriages are patrilocal while inheritance is mainly by male heirs.

The Hausas are mainly farmers, artisans and traders. Among the crops planted by them are millet, sorghum, groundnuts, beans and rice. As artisans, they excel in the making and dyeing of cotton textile which in the precolonial days found a ready market across the Sudan belt to North Africa. Leather goods are also another of their specialities. They are also great blacksmiths and silversmiths, iron smelters, mat and basket makers. Being highly skilled traders, they have settled in almost all urban centers throughout West Africa and Central Africa.

The Hausa language is widely spoken, not only in Northern Nigeria where it has become a lingua franca for most part, but also in many parts of West Africa. Since the conquest of the Hausaland by the Fulani during the Jihad, the whole of Hausaland has been under the control of the Fulani Emirs.

HEAD OF SERVICE. The Head of Service is the head of all the civil servants of the state or federal government. During the colonial days, the Head of Service was known as the Chief Secretary, but during the First Republic and the military regime, the posts of Head of Service and Secretary to the government were concentrated in one person. However under the 1979 constitution the two posts were separated. The constitution made the Head of Service a civil service appointment while the post of secretary to the government was termed "political." The appointment of a Head of Service was made by the Governor in case of the state government and by the President in case of the federal government. The Head of Service, directly responsible to the governor or the president as the case may be coordinated the activities of the Permanent Secretaries in the various ministries.

HICKS-PHILLIPSON COMMISSION. During the period between 1948 and 1951, when the recommendation of Sidney Phillipson Commission that allocation of revenue to the regions be based on derivation and even progress was adopted, the north felt that it was receiving less than its just share of the central revenue. Thus, at the Ibadan Conference of 1950, a review was recommended. The government thus set up the Hicks-Phillipson Commission charged with responsibility to inquire into and submit proposals on how government revenue was to be divided over a period of five years. The Commission could not say whether or not the north had been unfairly treated. To cater to the principle of national unity and national well-being in which the well being of one part depended on the other, the Commission suggested that allocation should be based on the principle of independent revenue, needs, national interest and special federal grants. Thus the Commission recommended that all revenue already regional should continue to be regional together with taxes on petrol; half of the proceeds from duties on manufactured and nonmanufactured tobacco should be assigned to the regions in proportion to their rate of consumption. Furthermore to cater to national interest the federal government should make annual grants to the regions on population basis and refund part regional expenditure on the Nigerian Police Force and half of the expenses on the Native Administration Police Force. It also recommended special grants of £2 million to the Northern Region. The government accepted these recommendations with some modifications. The report was short-lived because the government set up another revenue allocation commission in 1953 known as the Chick Report.

HIGHER EDUCATION. Higher education in Nigeria has gone through a very rapid expansion in the past decade. Before 1960, there was only the University of Ibadan, but in the early 1960's, there were universities in Nsukka, Ile-Ife, Zaria, Lagos, Benin and Kano. In the 1970's, the federal military government established new universities in Jos, Calabar, Maiduguri, Sokoto, Port-Harcourt and Ilorin. During the Second Republic the federal government of Alhaji Shehu Shagari pledged to establish a university in any state that did not already have one. Furthermore, some state governments began to set up new state universities.

As a result of this expansion enrollment has risen sharply from about 10,000 in 1970 to over 60,000 in 1980. Admission to these universities is done through a central admission board known as the Joint Admissions and Matriculation Board (JAMB). The aim in setting up the Board was to avoid duplicate offers of a place and to "nationalize" the admission system, by taking account of the "federal character" of Nigeria. At present, admission through JAMB is based on the criteria of merit, catchment areas, and educationally backward areas. Every university is therefore expected to admit some candidates on merit no matter what states they come from, some candidates are to be admitted from the areas or states close to the university and from some states which are said to be educationally backward. Since university education is tuition free, financing this many universities has posed a great problem especially when the country slumped into a recession.

In addition to rapid expansion in university facilities, both the federal and state governments have set up polytechnical and technical schools to train people to operate the growing technical industries.

HOUPHOUET-BOIGNY, FELIX. Former President of the Ivory Coast. During the Nigerian civil war, he accorded diplomatic recognition to the "Republic of Biafra" after President Nyerere of Tanzania and President Albert Bongo of Gabon had done so. He also gave asylum to Lt. Col. Odumegwu Ojuku after he fled from Biafra before its surrender to the federal government.

HOUSE OF ASSEMBLY. A legislative House of Assembly was created for each of the three regions under the Richards Constitution of 1946. Each of the regional houses had both official and unofficial members but for the first time in the history of the country unofficial members were more than official members, and the number of official members gradually dwindled until they practically disappeared at independence.

HOUSE OF CHIEFS. The House of Chiefs was the second legislative chamber in each of the three regions constituting the Nigerian federation. Its history began in 1947 when the Richards Constitution created a Council of Chiefs for the Northern Region. In 1951 under the Macpherson Constitution, the west got its own House of Chiefs. In the Constitutional Conference of 1958, a recommendation for an upper chamber was made for the Eastern Region and in 1960, a second upper house was created for that region. Under the 1979 constitution there were no Houses of Chiefs. Each state legislative house was unicameral.

HOUSE OF REPRESENTATIVES. The House of Representatives was originally created under the Macpherson Constitution of 1951. It then consisted of a President, six ex-officio members, 136 representatives elected from the regional houses and six special members appointed by the Governor to represent interests and communities that were inadequately represented. Under the Independence Constitution of 1960 and the Republican Constitution of 1963 the House of Representatives consisted of 312 members, from whom the Governor was to choose a member who appeared to him to command the support of the majority of the members as Prime Minister, who together with his cabinet was responsible to the House. However, under the Executive Presidential system of the Second Republican Constitution, the House of Representatives was independent of the executive branch, for the President and his cabinet were not members of the House of Representatives.

HOWELLS, BISHOP ADOLPHUS WILLIAMSON, 1866-1938. Born in
Abeokuta on August 9, 1866, he attended the Ake School there
before he went to the CMS Training Institute in Lagos in 1882.
He later became a teacher at a mission school in Badagry.
In 1887 he was transferred to St. Paul's School on the Breadfruit Street in Lagos. In 1891 he went to study at Fourah Bay
College, Freetown in Sierra Leone and later to Durham University in England. He returned to Lagos in 1894 and was appointed a tutor at the CMS Grammar School, while at the same
time he supervised the CMS mission's training institutions in
Lagos. In 1897 he became a Deacon of the church and was
ordained Priest in 1899. He became Curate of the Christ
Church Pro-Cathedral in Lagos in 1900 and later was appointed
pastor of St. John's Parish, Aroloya. In 1919 he was appointed
the first African Vicar of the Pro-Cathedral Church of Christ.
His superiors did not fail to recognize his work and his worth
to the church, and in 1920 he was consecrated Bishop by the
Archbishop of Canterbury at St. Paul's Cathedral in London.
He was then posted to the Niger Diocese where he served until 1933. He returned to Lagos as assistant to Bishop Melville
Jones who was then the Bishop of Lagos. He had under him
the churches in Abeokuta, Ibadan and Ijebu. In the same year,
1933, he became a resident Bishop of Abeokuta, his hometown.
He served there till he retired. He lived long enough to or-
dain his own son, Rev. A. W. Howells, a priest at Onitsha
in 1931. He died on December 3, 1938.

-I-

IBADAN. Capital city and administrative headquarters of Oyo State,
Ibadan, according to the 1963 population census was the largest
city in the whole of West Africa and the most populous in Africa south of the Sahara. Its population then stood at 1,300,000
people.
    There are many versions of the founding of Ibadan, but
what is certain is that Ibadan was originally an Egba village
in the center of which was a market. This village was destroyed during the intertribal wars that destroyed Owu and
other places, and after the Egbas withdrew to Abeokuta and
settled there the conquering army occupied the village. The
leader of the army that settled in Ibadan was Lagelu, an Ife
warrior and a farmer, said to have been the founder of the
town. The place where he first pitched his camp was known
as "Eba-Odan," meaning "by the field" (in between the forest
and the savanna land). From this came Ibadan by which it is
known today. Some sources went further to say that this settlement was later destroyed by the Olowu, and Lagelu had to
move to Eleyele Hill, where they suffered a lot of hardship,
and had to feed on snails and a wild apple called "oro." Hence
the Ibadan are called "Omo a joro sun, omo a je'gbin yo, omo
a fikarahun fori mu,"--Ibadans eat oro for supper, feed on
snails and use the snail shells as bowls for eating corn porridge.

Because of the military foundation of Ibadan, the traditional titles and order of precedence in the town are mostly military. The traditional ruler of the town is the Olubadan, whose selection is through promotion from among a long line of hierarchy of Chiefs divided into two lines, one military and the other civil, instead of the usual succession of the Yoruba Obas. Hence there is not one family in which the previous title of Baale, now Oba, is hereditary, and until recently there was no official residence of the Oba. Thus succession to the throne in Ibadan is devoid of the acrimony seen in other towns where there are hereditary lines. In Ibadan, the Balogun always succeeds the Oba.

Ibadan is a commercial and an administrative town, but a good percentage of its inhabitants are farmers. The most important traditional festivals in the town are Oke'badan and the Egungun (masquerade). The town is blessed with many educational institutions. It has three teacher-training colleges, scores of secondary schools, hundreds of primary schools, a polytechnic and a university. Places of interest in the town are: University of Ibadan, which was founded in 1948; University Teaching Hospital, Nigerian Television (formerly WNTV first in Africa); Liberty Stadium which was opened on September 30, 1960; Cocoa House, a 27-story skyscraper reputed to be West Africa's tallest skyscraper; The Premier Hotel; Government Secretariat and a host of others.

IBEKWE, DAN ONUORA. Born in Onitsha, Anambra State he had his primary education at St. Mary's School, Onitsha and his secondary education at the Christ the King College, Onitsha. He later went to the Council of Legal Education Law School in London and was called to the bar in 1951. Upon his arrival in Nigeria, he and the late Justice J.I.C. Taylor became partners in a private legal practice in Lagos. In 1954 Mr. Ibekwe moved to Aba where he set up his legal practice. In 1956 he was legal adviser to the Premier of Eastern Nigeria, Dr. Nnamdi Azikiwe. In 1958 he was made Solicitor-General of Eastern Nigeria. During the constitutional crisis over the federal elections of 1964, he advised the President that he had no constitutional powers to form an interim government nor to assume power himself. He was strongly criticized for this advice and he resigned as Solicitor-General. He later became a Senator in the Federal Senate and was appointed Minister of Commonwealth Relations. He was in this post when the coup came in January 1966 after which he became solicitor to the firm of Messrs. Irving and Bonner. In 1966, he was arrested by the government of Eastern Nigeria and was detained until after the civil war in 1970 when he was released. He was later appointed Commissioner for Works, Housing and Transport in the East-Central State. In 1972 he was made a Justice of the Supreme Court of Nigeria. In 1975, he became Federal Attorney General and Commissioner for Justice. In 1976 he became President of the Federal Court of Appeal and also the Chairman of the Nigerian Institute of International Affairs in Lagos. He died on March 23, 1978.

IBIAM, SIR FRANCIS. Physician and a statesman, Sir Francis
    Ibiam was born on November 29, 1906 at Unwana, a town in
    Afikpo division of Anambra State. He was educated at Hope
    Waddell Training Institute, Calabar; King's College, Lagos; Uni-
    versity of St. Andrews, Scotland and the London School of
    Tropical Medicine and Hygiene, England. He returned to Ni-
    geria to become the medical missionary to the Church of Scot-
    land Mission (CSM), Calabar, from 1936 to 1966. He founded
    the Abiriba Hospital in 1936. He later became Medical Super-
    intendent, CSM Hospital at Itu from 1945 to 1948. In 1947 he
    became a member of the Legislative Council of Nigeria and a
    member of the Executive Council of Nigeria between 1949 and
    1952. Between 1952 and 1957, he was the Medical Superintend-
    ent, CSM Hospital at Uburu. In 1957 he became the Principal
    of the Hope Waddel Training Institute, Calabar and was also
    President of the Christian Council of Nigeria from 1955 to
    1958 and Chairman of the Provisional Committee of All-Africa
    Church Council from 1958 to 1962. Between 1958 and 1961,
    he was the Chairman, Council of University College, Ibadan and
    was appointed one of the six presidents, World Council of
    Churches in 1961.
        He became the Governor of Eastern Nigeria in 1960,
    the post he held till 1966 when the military took over, and
    was appointed adviser to the Military Governor of the Eastern
    Provinces from 1966 to 1967. He was the Special Adviser to
    the Biafran Head of State, Colonel Odumegwu Ojukwu from
    1967 to 1970.
        Sir Francis Ibiam was nationally honored as the Grand
    Commander of the Order of Niger (GCON). Foreign honors
    are Knight Commander of the Order of the British Empire
    (KBE) and Knight Commander of St. Michael and St. George
    (KCMG). He was awarded honorary LL. B. degree by the Uni-
    versity of St. Andrews, Scotland, D. Litt. by the University of
    Ibadan and an LL. D. by the University of Ife.

IBIBIO-EFIK. The Ibibio-Efik inhabit the southern part of the Cross
    River State and are the second largest population in the former
    Eastern Nigeria. The people were in long contact with the
    Europeans, especially the slave traders, a fact which led to
    the emergence of city-states like the Old Calabar. The Efik
    are a subgroup of the Ibibio and they speak the same language.
    Occupationally they are mainly farmers and traders.

IBO FEDERAL UNION. The Ibo Federal Union was founded in 1944
    as a cultural organization. It aimed mainly to promote soli-
    darity of the Ibos and their educational development. When
    the National Council of Nigeria and the Cameroons (NCNC) was
    founded later that year by Dr. Nnamdi Azikiwe, an Ibo man,
    the Ibo Federal Union was one of its member organizations.
    In 1948, the Union changed its name to Ibo State Union and
    redefined its purpose to include organizing Ibo linguistic groups
    into a political unit in accordance with the NCNC Freedom
    Charter. The Union gave its unflinching support to the NCNC

and elected the party leader, Dr. Azikiwe, its national President. The organization worked relentlessly to promote Ibo solidarity among the Ibos, especially outside the Ibo land and to provide for the educational advancement of the Ibo people through scholarship at home and abroad. The Union was banned in 1966 after the military seized power.

IBO PEOPLE. The Ibo people constitute the majority ethnic group in the former Eastern Region, and presently, Anambra and Imo states can be regarded as the nuclear area of Ibo people. The origin of the Ibos is not precisely known but it is a common belief that they migrated from the north around the confluence of the Niger.

Linguistically, the Ibos are said to belong to the Kwa subfamily of the Niger-Congo family. However numerous dialects are spoken, which reflect the small scale of their organizational setup. The two most used dialects are the Owerri Ibo and the Onitsha Ibo, even though neither coincided with the former provinces. Demographically, Ibo land has a high population density which accounts to a great extent for their willingness to migrate not only to other parts of Nigeria, but even outside it. Politically, the Ibo did not develop a highly centralized political organization, like the Yorubas of Western Nigeria with the institution of an Oba, Hausa/Fulani people of Northern Nigeria with their Emirs. The highest form of political organization was a collection of villages called village groups. The basic unit among them was the family while the largest was the village group. However the Ibo of Onitsha, on the east of River Niger have a tradition of kingship which is similar to that of the Yorubas or the Edos of Benin which shows the influence of Benin immigrants in the place. The government of each village was carried on by all the family heads or elders sitting together. Usually the most senior of the elders used to preside at meetings. Though the oldest man among the elders, he was not a chief in the usual sense, for he did not rule, and had not much authority outside his extended family.

The social unit among the Ibo is the extended family and their system of descent is patrilineal.

Some of the Ibo are traders but most are farmers, growing cash crops like rubber, oil palms and cashew. They also cultivate cassava, plantain and banana, maize and yams.

IBO STATE UNION. In 1948 the Ibo Federal Union became Ibo State Union. It consisted of representatives of all local unions. Many leading members of the National Council of Nigeria and the Cameroon (NCNC) were members of the Union. In fact Dr. Nnamdi Azikiwe, the NCNC president, was also President of the Union, 1948-1952. See also IBO FEDERAL UNION.

IBRAHIM, SIR KASHIM. An educationist, politician and the first indigenous Governor of Northern Nigeria. Sir Kashim Ibrahim was born in 1910 at Maiduguri Borno State. He was educated

at Borno Provincial School and at the Katsina Training College.
He became a teacher in 1929 and in 1933 he became the Senior
Provincial Visiting Teacher and Education Officer from 1949
to 1952. He was a founding member of the Northern People's
Congress (NPC) and became the Central Minister of social
services in Lagos from 1952 to 1955 and Northern Regional
Minister of Social Development from 1955 to 1956. He was
the Waziri of the Borno Native Administration between 1956
and 1962, Chairman of the Nigerian College of Arts and Science between 1958 and 1952 and Chairman of the provisional
council of Ahmadu Bello University, Zaria from 1960 to 1962.
He was appointed Governor of Northern Nigeria from 1962 to
1966 and when the military took over power, he was appointed
Adviser to the Military Governor of Northern Nigeria from
1966 to 1967. Additionally, he was Chancellor of the University of Ibadan, 1966 and in 1977 he became the Chancellor of
the University of Lagos. He was awarded several honors,
among them: Grand Commander of the Order of the Niger
(GCON); Knight Commander of the Order of St. Michael and
St. George (KCMG); member of the Order of the British Empire (OBE) and Commander of the Order of British Empire
(CBE). He was awarded honorary LL. D. degrees by the University of Nigeria, Nsukka, University of Ibadan and Ahmadu
Bello University, and a D. Litt. by the University of Lagos.

IBRAHIM, ALHAJI WAZIRI. Businessman and politician, born at
Yerwa, Borno State on February 26, 1926 he attended Maiduguri Middle School and Kaduna College in Kaduna. He worked
as a Labor Staff Manager at the United African Company (UAC)
in Benue Area between 1953 and 1954, and served in many
capacities under the UAC establishment until 1959 when he
was elected into the Federal House of Representatives where
he was appointed Federal Minister of Health, and later Minister of Economic Development between 1962 and 1966. He
went into business after the military came to power in 1966.
When the ban on political activities was lifted in 1978, he ful-
filled one of his life ambitions by forming a political party,
the Nigerian People's Party (NPP). But owing to dissension
on whether or not the same person should be Chairman of the
party and the presidential candidate, Alhaji Waziri, believing
that he should be both Chairman and presidential candidate left
to form a new party, the Great Nigerian People's Party (GNPP).
He contested the presidential election in 1979 under the banner
of his new party. He lost the election but his party won the
gubernatorial elections in Borno and Gongola states.

After the presidential defeat of 1979, the GNPP became
a close ally of the Unity Party of Nigeria (UPN) and both became the nucleus of the four-party alliance which was being
forged in 1982. But Alhaji Ibrahim later in 1982 became disillusioned and withdrew from the alliance effort. However a
faction of his party led by the two Governors of Borno and
Gongola continued to cooperate with the other parties to work
out a basis for the alliance known as the Progressive Parties
Alliance (PPA). Alhaji Waziri was also a candidate for the

presidency in 1983 but he again lost to Alhaji Shehu Shagari who was reelected for a second term.

IDIA. Idia was the Queen Mother of Oba Esigie of Benin who ruled at the beginning of the sixteenth century. Idia was said to be a great warrior, immortalized by an ivory carving of her face, adopted in 1977 as the FESTAC symbol.

IDIAGBON, BRIGADIER TUNDE. Chief of Staff, Supreme Headquarters and the number-two man in the military administration that replaced the Shagari administration. He was born in the Kwara State and had served in many important positions prior to the December 1983 coup. He was, for example, in 1978 the Military Administrator for Borno State in a preparatory effort to hand over power of the military to civilians in 1979. (Continued on p. 389.)

IFES see ILE-IFE.

IGBIRA. One of the minority ethnic groups that inhabit the areas north and east of the Niger-Benue confluence in the old Northern Nigeria, the people are now part of the Kwara State. Even though most of the north was subjugated by the Fulanis in the early nineteenth century, the Igbiras were never so subjugated.

IGBO. This is the same as Ibo but modern Ibo writers say Igbo is the more correct spelling of the Ibo ethnic group who occupy much of the parts of the country east of River Niger and South of River Benue. They also make up a substantial ethnic group in the Bendel State. See also IBO PEOPLE.

IGE, CHIEF BOLA. Lawyer, politician and the first Governor of Oyo State in the Second Republic, Chief Ige was born on September 13, 1930 at Esa Oke in Obokun Local Government Area, Ilesha Division of Oyo State and received his primary education at St. Joseph's Catholic School in Kaduna and his secondary education at the Ibadan Grammar School, 1943-1948. From 1949 to 1955 he attended the University College, Ibadan where he graduated with a Bachelor of Arts degree in Classics. He taught in Ibadan Grammar School from 1955 to 1956 when he proceeded to the United Kingdom where he graduated in law from the University College, London, and was called to the bar at the Inner Temple in 1961. He returned to Nigeria and set up a private legal practice.

His political activities started at the University of Ibadan where he took active part in the student union politics and also served as the Publicity Secretary and General Secretary of the Action Group Youth Club at the university. In 1962, he was elected Federal Publicity Secretary of the Action Group at the Jos Conference, a post he held till January 1966 when the military took over the government. During the 1962 emergency period in Western Nigeria, Chief Ige was one of those restricted. After his release, he was a delegate to the Nigerian Constitutional Conference held in Lagos in 1963.

Under the military administration, Chief Ige was appointed Commissioner for Agriculture and Natural Resources for the Western State from July 1967 to January 1970 when he became Commissioner for Lands and Housing till May 1970. He was a member of the Constitution Drafting Committee appointed to draft a new constitution for the country in 1975.

When the ban on politics was lifted in 1978, Chief Ige became a member of the Unity Party of Nigeria in Oyo State. He ran for the governorship of the state under his party's platform and won. He was also the Chairman of his party in the state. In the 1983 gubernatorial elections, he lost to Dr. Omololu Olunloyo, the candidate of the National Party of Nigeria (NPN).

After the December 1983 coup d'état, he was arrested and detained. He was tried with Governor Bisi Onabanjo of Ogun State and Governor Michael Ajasin of Ondo State for receiving a kickback of ₦2.8 million from a contract. He was acquitted, but he was later convicted on a two-count charge of conspiracy and corruptly enriching the proscribed Unity Party of Nigeria. He was sentenced to 21 years imprisonment.

IJAW. The Ijaw people make up a large part of the present Rivers State. Some of them are also found in the Bendel State. They occupy places like Bonny, Brass, Okrika, Kalabari and Akassa. Tradition says they came from the east and the north about the fifteenth century, but their language, compared to other Nigerian languages does not give credence to this.

Most of their land is in the Niger Delta which consists largely of mangrove swamps, and farmlands, divided by creeks and rivers. The Ijaws traditionally depended on fishing. They built small villages, with their houses built on stilts above the swamps. Because of their geographical location, many villages joined in the slave trade with the Europeans in the eighteenth century, and they became intermediaries between the Europeans at the sea and the hinterland.

Today the area inhabited by the Ijaws is being drastically changed by the exploitation of petroleum oil in the area and the emergence of some big cities like Port Harcourt. However in some places the traditional life of the people is still preserved.

IJEBU. A subgroup of the Yoruba ethnic group, the Ijebus, together with the Egbas make up most of the people of Ogun State. Because of their proximity to Lagos and the sea, the Ijebus like the Egbas played the role of middlemen between the white traders and the people in the interior, a position which they jealously protected. Thus during the Yoruba civil wars of the nineteenth century they occupied a better position than other Yoruba states in getting modern weapons from the coast. In 1891, the British finally secured a treaty abolishing human sacrifice, opening up the road to the sea from the hinterland and allowing trade to go through their territory. But in 1892, the Ijebus reneged and a war between them and the British

ensued in which they were defeated.   The defeat of the Ijebus
marked a significant event in the British occupation of the
Yorubaland.

    During the colonial era, the whole of Ijebu area was
constituted into a province with a Resident.   Important traditional rulers in Ijebu are the Awujale of Ijebu-Ode, Akarigbo
of Ijebu-Remo, Odemo of Ishara and Orimolusi of Ijebu-Igbo.

IJEMO MASSACRE.   Under the treaty of 1893 between the Egba
    Chiefs and the Governor of Lagos, Egbaland was a semi-
    independent state.   It therefore set up the Egba united govern-
    ment.   In 1914, Mr. Ponlade, one of the opponents of the Sec-
    retary to the united government, Mr. Edun, was arrested and
    died in prison.   People began to demonstrate against the death,
    and because the Egba united government could not contain the
    demonstration, additional troops were requested from Lagos.
    The troops had to fire on the people killing many demonstra-
    tors.   This was the Ijemo Massacre, and it led to the abroga-
    tion of the independence of Egbaland and the British assertion
    of authority over the land.

IKEJA.   Though historically distinct, Ikeja has become part of the
    metropolitan Lagos.   It used to be provincial headquarters in
    the former Western Region of Nigeria, and the industrial cen-
    ter of the region.   But by the creation of the Lagos State in
    1976, Ikeja became the administrative capital of the new state
    and still so remains.   Ikeja is where the Lagos International
    Airport, called Murtala Muhammed Airport so named after the
    late head of state killed in the 1976 abortive coup, is built.

IKOKU, ALVAN AZIMWA (1900-1971).   An educationist, born in
    Amanagwu in Arochukwu on August 1, 1900.   He was educated
    at the Government School, Calabar, Cross River State and later
    went to the Hope Waddell College to train as a teacher.   In
    1920, he joined the Presbyterian Church of Scotland in Itigidi
    and became a staff member of St. Paul's Teacher Training College
    in Awka in 1924.   While at the college, he took correspondence
    courses with the Wolsey Hall in London and earned the Univer-
    sity of London degree in Philosophy in 1928 with honors.   Be-
    lieving that education was essential to the development of the
    country, in 1931 he resigned from his work with the mission
    to establish his own college in Arochukwu, the Aggrey Memo-
    rial College, named after Dr. Aggrey, the Ghanaian education-
    ist.   When a branch of the Nigerian Union of Teachers (NUT)
    was opened in Calabar, Ikoku joined it and in November 1940,
    with his leadership capacity being recognized, he was elected
    the national Second Vice-President of the Organization.   In
    1944 he became one of the three men appointed to serve on
    the Board of Education for the Southern Provinces.   In 1946,
    following the Richards Constitution, Ikoku was nominated to
    the Eastern Nigeria House of Assembly and was appointed to
    the Ministry of Education.   1947, he became a member of the
    Legislative Council in Lagos, being one of the three people

who were representing the Eastern Region in the Council. As a member of the council, he used his position to advance the interest of NUT and education in the country.

Ikoku later became interested in politics, becoming the leader of the United National Party which won some seats in the former Eastern House of Assembly, but the party did not live long, owing to the Eastern Regional Crisis of 1953. In 1955 he became President of NUT, and under him as President, the organization made recommendations to the government to set up a uniform educational system for the country. The recommendations were rejected but when the military took over power in 1966, Ikoku was a member of the Study Group, set up to look into the feasibility of setting up a unified educational policy for the country. Unfortunately the civil war (1967-1970) interrupted their work. Ikoku died on November 18, 1971.

Ikoku was a dedicated educationist. Besides founding the Aggrey Memorial College, he established other schools and initiated private scholarship schemes for needy students. In 1965 the University of Ibadan awarded him an honorary degree of Doctor of Laws, and for his lasting contribution to the development of education in Nigeria, the federal military government declared him a national hero and his picture is engraved on the Nigerian ten naira note.

IKOKU, SAMUEL GOMSU. An educationist and a politician, born on July 24, 1924, he was educated at the Aggrey Memorial College, Arochukwu, Achimota College, Accra Ghana and at the London University where he received an M. Sc. degree in Economics. He later on in Nigeria joined the Action Group Party and in 1962 during that party's crisis, he was the Secretary General of the party as well as the leader of the party in the Eastern Region. He was one of those charged with Chief Obafemi Awolowo in 1962 as conspiring to overthrow the federal government by force. He fled the country to Ghana and became a wanted man. He was repatriated in March 1966 and detained but was later released by the military administration which later came to power. He was appointed East Central State Commissioner for Economic Development and Construction in 1970. When the ban on political activity was lifted in 1978, he became a member of the People's Redemption Party (PRP) and was later elected the National Secretary of the party.

IKOLI, ERNEST SESEI. A journalist born on March 25, 1893 at Brass in Rivers State. He was a son of a successful businessman and a western-educated mother. He attended the Bonny Primary School and was later a foundation student of the King's College in Lagos in 1909. After his secondary education, he was appointed a teacher at the school but resigned in 1919 to become an editorial assistant in the Lagos Weekly Record which was at the time being edited by Thomas Horatio Jackson, the son of the paper's founder, John Payne Jackson. In 1921 he left to found his own newspaper, the African Messenger, which he edited until 1926 when he became editor of the newly founded Daily Times of Nigeria. He wrote the first editorial of the paper on June 1, 1926. His own paper, the African Messenger, by this time had been taken over by the Daily Times. In 1928, he left the Daily Times to found the Nigerian Daily Mail and edited the Daily Telegraph for J. A. Doherty, the owner. In 1931, the Daily Telegraph became defunct.

Ikoli also played a prominent role in Nigerian political awakening. He was Secretary of the Lagos Branch of the Universal Negro Improvement Association (UNIA) set up by Marcus Garvey. In 1934, he, Dr. J. C. Vaughan, Chief H. O. Davies and Oba Samuel Akinsanya formed the Lagos Youth Movement (LYM) which was opposed to the colonial government education policy with regard to some alleged deficiencies of the Yaba Higher College. The LYM in 1936 in an effort to convert itself to a nationalist organization changed its name into Nigerian Youth Movement (NYM) under the leadership of Dr. J. C. Vaughan. Ikoli in 1941 vied with Oba Samuel Akinsanya for the vacancy on the Legislative Council, created by the resignation of Dr. K. Abayomi, and won. In 1943 he became the President of the NYM which could not fully recover from the schism created by the 1941 contest. He for six years (1938-1944) edited with Chief S. L. Akintola the NYM organ, the Daily Service. He was also reelected into the Legislative Council in 1946. He was later appointed Chairman of the Rediffusion Service, and became Public Relations Adviser to the Nigerian Railway Corporation. He was awarded the Order of the Members of the British Empire (MBE). He died on October 21, 1960, just a few weeks after Nigeria became independent.

IKOYI-LAGOS. Ikoyi-Lagos, a residential area in Lagos where colonial officials used to live. Today, it still remains the most prestigious residential area in Lagos.

ILE-IFE. Known as the "Cradle of the Yorubas," Ile-Ife is believed to be the final home of Oduduwa, the mythical ancestor of the Yorubas. In fact all the Yorubas regard Ile-Ife as their original home from where they all dispersed to various settlements.

Ile-Ife is located on longitude 4.6°E and latitude 7.5°N and is situated on an elevation of about 275 meters above sea level. It has a tropical temperature and is within the tropical rain forest zone.

The population of the town was about 130,050 people according to the 1963 census. The people of Ile-Ife are mainly farmers with cocoa and oil palms as their major cash crops.

The traditional ruler of the town is the Ooni of Ife, who according to history is the spiritual leader of all the Yorubas, a fact which is evidenced by the many shrines in the ancient city. But in spite of this fact, foreign religions like Islam and Christianity coexist amicably in the city.

Ile-Ife is blessed with a number of educational institutions ranging from a number of primary schools to about 15 secondary schools; a college of arts and science and a university.

The University of Ife Teaching Hospitals Complex manages two hospitals at Ile-Ife: the former Seventh Day Adventist Hospital and the former General Hospital.

Among the places of interest in the town are: Opa Oranyan, Ife Museum of Antiquities, the Afin, and the University of Ife.

The Ifes are the indigenous people of Ile-Ife and its district. They are predominantly farmers who live mostly in the villages except a few of them who are traders and craftsmen who reside in the township.

The Ifes are a subgroup of the Yorubas. Although the Ifes lay much importance on the indigenous religions, they also embrace the two foreign religions in Nigeria--Islam and Christianity.

ILORIN. A Yoruba town in the old Northern Region, and now the capital of the Kwara State. Originally, Ilorin was one of the military outposts of the Old Oyo empire under the Alaafin, but it came under the Fulani rule after the defeat of Afonja, who was posted there to guard and defend the northern outpost against the threatened invasion by the lieutenants of Usman Dan Fodio during the Holy War (Jihad) from Sokoto. Afonja himself, with the assistance of one Alimi, a Fulani herdsman, had revolted against the Alaafin of Oyo and proclaimed the independence of the town. However soon after, Alimi attacked Afonja and won, and so the town came under the rule of the Fulanis with the title of Emir of Ilorin, even to this day.

During the colonial era, Ilorin was part of the Northern Protectorate which in 1946 came to be regarded as a region. In 1967, when the then-existing four regions were divided into 12 states, Ilorin became the capital of the Kwara State. It is also a university town. The Ilorin people are famous for their pottery industry.

ILORIN TALAKA PARAPO (ITP). One of the small parties that combined to form opposition in Northern House of Assembly during the First Republic. In the 1956 Northern Regional election, ITP backed by the Action Group gained 2. 6 percent of the seats in the Northern House. In the 1957 elections the ITP captured the Ilorin District Council, but the Council had to be suspended after many clashes between it and the Emir aided by NPC politicians. The leaders of the ITP were Chief J. S. Olawoyin and Alhaji Sule Maito.

IMAM. A term in Nigeria which refers to the Moslem prayer leader; any Muslim with necessary theological education and sufficiently versed in the technique of the Sal'at can be an Imam.

IMO STATE. Created in February 1976 out of the former East-Central State, the state has a total land area of about 13,032 sq. km. and according to the 1963 census a population of about 3,658,125 people. It is landlocked and has boundaries with Anambra State to the north, Rivers State to the south, Cross River State to the east and Bendel State to the west, and therefore is connected to the parts of the country by roads and railroads.

The people of the state are mainly Igbo speaking. Most of them engage in agriculture, producing crops like yam, rice, cassava, plantain, palm oil, rubber and cocoa. The state is also rich in mineral resources which include petroleum, natural gas, lead, clay, limestone and salt.

Educationally, the state has many primary and secondary schools, teacher training colleges, one college of education and a university of technology.

The capital of the state is Owerri, and other important towns are Aba, Umuahia, Orlu, Okigwe, Oguta, Arochukwu, Afikpo and Abiriba.

IMOUDU, CHIEF MICHAEL OMINUS. A trade unionist and a politician born on November 20, 1902 at Ora in Bendel State. He was educated at the Government School, Ora, Catholic school, Onitsha and Agbor government school. In 1928 he joined the Nigerian Railway as a laborer and later became an apprentice turner. Chief Michael Imoudu played a prominent role in the establishment of the Railway Workers' Union in 1932.

In 1941, Imoudu was elected the Vice-President of the African Civil Servants Technical Workers' Union (ACSTWU) comprised of the Railway Workers' Union, P. & T. Workers' Union, the Nigerian Marine African Workers' Union and the Public Works Department Workers' Union. In January 1943, he was summarily dismissed for alleged misconduct and insubordination and was served with a detention order under the Nigeria General Defense regulations. He was accused of action prejudicial to public safety or defense and was immediately taken to Benin province. In March 1943, the detention order was replaced by a Restriction Order and he was required to report twice a week to the police in Auchi. The ACSTWU and the Railway Workers' Union began a vigorous campaign for his release. Their efforts later bore fruit. He was released from restriction and returned to Lagos on June 2, 1945 amidst the cheers of his supporters.

In the nationalist struggle after the Second World War, Chief Imoudu played a very important role. He led the nationwide strike of 1945 and was among the NCNC delegates who toured Nigeria between April and December to educate the people on the Richards Constitution of 1946 and the so-called "obnoxious bills." In 1949, Chief Imoudu was elected the President of the Nigerian National Federation of Labor (NNFL) and at the inauguration of the Nigerian Labor Congress on May 26, 1950, he became its President. In 1953, he was made the President of the All-Nigeria Trade Union Federation (ANTUF).

When the ANTUF and the National Council of Trade Unions of Nigeria (NCTUN) merged together in January 1959, to form the Trade Union Congress of Nigeria (TUC), Chief Michael Imoudu was also elected its President. In May 1962, he formed the Independent United Labor Congress (IULC) and became its President. In 1976, in an effort by the military administration to reorganize the Nigerian Trade Unions, he and other labor leaders were retired. In 1978 the University of Ife conferred on him an honorary degree of Doctor of Law. In the same year when the ban on politics was lifted Dr. Imoudu became one of the leaders of the People's Redemption Party, led by Mallam Aminu Kano. In 1980 when the party broke into two factions, on whether or not the party should acceed to National Party of Nigeria's (NPN) invitation to take part in a national government, Dr. Imoudu, believing that the two parties were not ideologically compatible led the breakaway faction and remained its leader. In the four-party alliance being worked out in 1982, Imoudu faction of the PRP was one of the parties. However, in the preparation for the 1983 elections, efforts began to be made to reunite the factions to improve the party's electoral chances in the states and in the nation as a whole. On May 18, 1983, just about a month after the death of Mallam Aminu Kano, the two factions were reunited and Chief Imoudu became a national Vice-President of the party.

INDEPENDENCE. In 1958 the British government agreed that if a resolution asking for independence was passed by the new Federal Parliament that was to come into being early in 1960, Her Majesty's government would agree to such a resolution. Accordingly, at the first meeting of the Federal Legislature in January 1960, both Houses of Parliament unanimously passed a resolution calling for independence. Her Majesty's government later introduced a bill known as the Nigerian (Constitution) Order in Council, 1960, in Parliament and it was passed on September 12, 1960. The Order came into effect on October 1, 1960 and Nigeria became an independent and sovereign nation as from that date.

INDEPENDENT UNITED LABOR CONGRESS. Formed on May 4, 1962 as a protest movement against the decision of the United Labor Congress to affiliate with the International Confederation of Free Trade Unions. The principal officers of the new group were M. A. O. Imoudu as president and Amaefule Ikoro as Secretary. The IULC preferred to affiliate only with the All-African Trade Union Federation.

INDIANS. The Indians began to come into the country as early as 1911, but beginning from the 1920's they began to arrive in increasing numbers and the influx was not arrested until the immigration restrictions of 1947. Originally they were retail traders, but today only few Indians can be found in commercial activities in Nigeria. Nigeria is presently experiencing a new influx of Indians who work as teachers in many schools, as doctors in hospitals and as engineers or architects all over the nation.

INDIGENIZATION DECREE see NIGERIAN ENTERPRISES PROMO-TION BOARD

INDIRECT RULE.   The system of ruling the indigenous population through the already existing traditional local structures, Chiefs, Emirs and native courts, adopted in all British West African territories by the colonial authorities.   When Britain took over the administration of Nigeria from the Royal Niger Company, in 1900 Lord Lugard became the High Commissioner of the then Northern Protectorate.   As Commissioner he was faced with two major problems: he lacked sufficient knowledge of the local population to be able to rule them effectively and effi-ciently and he had very limited financial and human resources to directly rule what he called a "vast" country.   He therefore decided to rule through the northern Emirs and the existing moslem courts so that his need for European officers would be limited to a supervisory role.   The system was based on the belief that Chiefs and Emirs were the rulers of their people and if the colonial authorities would officially recognize them as having authority to make laws, enforce them, punish offend-ers, collect local revenues and provide certain services they would be a great asset to the colonial authorities who only had to control the chiefs and emirs to control the people.

After the amalgamation of the Northern and Southern protectorates, the system was nationalized by extending it to the south, and the fallacy of the British assumption became clear.   In Western Nigeria, Chiefs did not have absolute au-thority and therefore could not always make the people do what they did not want to do.   In Eastern Nigeria, there were not such Chiefs in many towns and villages as in the north and in the west.   Thus, colonial authorities had to embark on a policy of creating chiefs by issuing them warrants--these were the Warrant Chiefs, who were very much resented by the peo-ple, a situation which partly accounted for the Aba Riots of 1929.

While the system for a long time protected the tradi-tional political and legal system from too much interference from the outside, it nonetheless worked against the principles that the British believed in.   It limited the participation of the educated elements in the government of their locality, made for fragmentation of the country into discreet cultural groups thereby making the problem of national integration a more ser-ious one, and while it strengthened traditional authorities vis-a-vis their people, these traditional rulers became mere pup-pets in the hands of colonial authorities.   Finally the system preserved the indigenous system of land ownership and so en-couraged a peasant and subsistence production system rather than freeing land for large commercial agricultural undertakings.

INDUSTRIAL RESEARCH COUNCIL OF NIGERIA.   Established in

1971, it is a federal government statutory body affiliated to
the federal Ministry of Industries.   Its principal functions are
to promote and coordinate all industrial research activities of
Nigeria, and develop and apply such industrial research results.   The 12 members of the Council come from faculties
of science and engineering of Nigerian universities, the public
and the private sectors of the economy, with four ex-officio
members made up of permanent Secretaries from the federal
Ministries of Trade, Communications, Works and Housing,
and Mines and Powers.

INTERIM ADMINISTRATIVE COUNCIL.   Established in May 1967 with
respect to the territories formerly known as Northern and Eastern Nigeria which were divided into new states.
        The Council, composed of the permanent Secretaries
of the territory or the newly created states, was charged with
responsibility to arrange the share to which each state was
entitled in the assets of the former region out of which the new
states were created.   It was responsible for establishing new
departments of government or other government institutions
which were necessary in the new states.   It was also to allocate members of the public service in the former regions to
the new states, and to consider from time to time problems
of general administration in all or any of the states.   By
further amendments the Council had vested in it all immovable
public property held in trust by the governors of the former
Northern and Eastern regions.   While the Council was able to
function in the north, the civil war that broke out immediately
after the states were created did not permit the decree to take
effect in the Eastern Region.   In 1968 the Council was succeeded by the Interim Common Services Agency (q.v.).   In the
Eastern Region, after the civil war in 1970, Decree Number
39 of 1970 which set up the Eastern States Interim Assets and
Liabilities Agency (q.v.) was promulgated.

INTERIM COMMON SERVICES AGENCY.   When Nigeria was divided
into 12 states in 1967 there came the problem of how best to
share the assets and liabilities of the former Northern and
Eastern regions where the new states were created.   To solve
the problem in the north, the federal military government issued Decree Number 12 of 1968 creating the Interim Common
Services Agency to take care of the assets and liabilities of
the former Northern Region which had then been divided into
six states.   The Agency was charged with the control, operation and general management of the services, statutory bodies
and institutions that were owned by the states which formerly
formed the Northern Region.   It had power to dispose of any
property that was no longer required by it, invest its funds
in government securities and maintain its various property.
Included under the authority of the Agency were Ahmadu Bello
University, in Zaria, the Government Press in Kaduna, Sharia
Court of Appeal, Kaduna Polytechnic, Northern Nigeria Housing
Corporation, Livestock and Meat Authority, Northern Nigeria

Marketing Board and Northern Nigeria Radio Corporation. The Agency was dissolved in 1976 with the promulgation of Decree Number 19 of 1975 which caused the term of the Agency to expire on March 31, 1976.

INTERNATIONAL COMMITTEE OF THE RED CROSS (ICRC). During the Nigerian civil war the Red Cross was one of the relief agencies that supplied relief materials to the war-affected areas of the country. The Committee made use of Fernando Po, a Spanish Island near Nigeria, as their storing depot where the relief materials were stored before onward transmission to the war areas.

The ICRC having received approval of the two sides to the war, it received donations from organizations and individuals throughout the world to enable it to carry out its humanitarian assignment.

However, the involvement of Carl Gustaf Von Rosen in the relief effort, who in May 1969 led an air raid on Port Harcourt, created problems for the organization. The federal government troops shot down a Swedish Red Cross aircraft in June 1969, after the aircraft, heading for Uli airport had refused to land, when asked, at the Port Harcourt airport. The government later formally banned all unauthorized night flights through its air space and ended the ICRC's mandate to coordinate the relief operations in the country. The government then handed over the ICRC's coordination effort to the Nigerian Red Cross, and expelled the ICRC's representative to Nigeria, August Lindt.

INTERNATIONAL CONFEDERATION OF FREE TRADE UNIONS (ICFTU). The International Confederation of Free Trade Unions sent a delegation to Nigeria in 1951 with a view to recommending a base in West Africa where the organization could begin its operations. The Nigerian Labor Congress was opposed to this and there were demonstrations against the visit at the airport in Lagos. As a result of this opposition the ICFTU left for Accra, Ghana where they were well received. The Gold Coast Trade Union Congress decided to affiliate with it and they recommended Accra to be the base of their operations in West Africa.

INTERNATIONAL INSTITUTE OF TROPICAL AGRICULTURE. Before the military came into power in 1966, the federal government had begun negotiations with the Ford Foundation and the Rockefeller Foundation to establish and maintain in Nigeria an international institute of tropical agriculture. A proposal to this effect had been submitted as far back as March 1965. The federal military government seeing the need for the establishment of the Institute in Nigeria issued Decree Number 32 of 1967 to set it up. Its functions were to undertake studies of and research into tropical agriculture and to provide information to authorized representatives of governments, or groups or bodies of persons, interested in tropical agriculture. It was to look for ways and means to increase the output and improve the quality of tropical food crops, to provide, in cooperation with universities and other educational institutions, high-level professional training to persons who were expected to become staff members of the institutions and organizations concerned with increasing food production and distribution in the tropics. The Institute was to publish its research findings and distribute improved plant materials to other research centers.

The Institute was governed by a board of trustees composed of the permanent Secretary of the Ministry of Agriculture and Natural Resources, two members appointed by the federal government, two members, one each from Rockefeller Foundation and Ford Foundation, both serving as ex-officio members, the Director of the Institute and another person chosen outside Nigeria but from tropical area of the world.

Its headquarters or principal office was in Ibadan.

INTERNATIONAL OBSERVER TEAM IN NIGERIA. During the civil war, the federal government, in order to counteract the effective propaganda of Biafra against the alleged federal government atrocities, resorted to allowing various groups of foreign observers to come and see for themselves and report on their experience in the war-zone. These were groups of military observers drawn from Britain, Canada and Poland to inspect the behavior of federal troops at the fronts and investigate Biafran charges of genocide.

The idea of an observer team was first suggested by the British government and accepted by General Gowon. It was opposed by some who saw the presence of such observers as an infringement on Nigeria's sovereignty and independence.

The team spent 16 months working at the fronts and producing objective reports on the conduct of federal soldiers' treatment of Biafran civilians, prisoners of war and the relief situation, and investigation of charges of brutality. The team was only on the federal side and did not go to the Biafran side because the federal government was opposed. The team exercised a moderating and cautionary influence on the federal troops but it undermined Biafran claims of genocide.

INTER-UNIVERSITY COUNCIL FOR HIGHER EDUCATION IN THE COLONIES. The Inter-University Council for Higher Education in the Colonies was set up in 1946 as a follow-up of the recommendation of the Asquith Commission. Members were representatives of all the universities in the United Kingdom. It was charged with the duties of keeping in touch with the development of new colonial institutions of higher learning through regular visits by its members. The Council was to help in the recruitment of staff and encourage members of the home universities to take up appointment in the colonial universities. The Council was also to strengthen cooperation between universities in the United Kingdom and those in the colonies and to foster the development of higher colleges in the colonies with a view to their advancement to university status. Members of the Council visited West Africa in 1946. Their purpose was to make recommendations to the Secretary of State for the Colonies on the issue of university colleges for West Africa. As a result of their recommendation two university colleges were established, one in the Gold Coast (Ghana) and the other in Ibadan, Nigeria in 1948.

INVESTMENT COMPANY OF NIGERIA LIMITED. The Investment Company of Nigeria Limited, organized by the Commonwealth Development Finance Company Limited in consultation with British and Nigerian business interests, was incorporated in 1959. Its objectives were to encourage and if necessary to sponsor the development of local industrial commercial and agricultural enterprises. It was to provide financial assistance to exploit the country's natural resources and attract expatriate investment capital to private enterprises. Furthermore it sought technical and managerial expertise and encouraged the development of stocks and shares market.

IRIKEFE COMMISSION. Set up by the Federal Military Government in August 1975 to examine the burning issue of creation of more states in the federation. The Commission, headed by Supreme Court Judge Ayo Irikefe, was, if it found a need for more states, to advise the government on the delimitation of such states, on the location of the administrative capital of the states to be created, on the economic viability of the states to be created and on all other matters that might appear to the Commission to be relevant to the exercise. The Commission submitted its report on December 23, 1975. On February 3, 1976 following some of the recommendations of the Commission, seven new states were created from the existing 12 states.

ISHAN. The Ishan people constitute an ethnic group in Bendel State. They form part of the Edo-speaking people of the state. See also EDO.

ISLAM. Islam is the earliest external influence to reach Nigeria. Islamic faith and idea began to come into the Kanem-Borno Area of North Africa around the ninth century and from there it spread to the Hausa states. It introduced a new way of life and brought with it literacy in the Arabic language to the area. As such the first written sources of historical study of the area were by Arabic scholars. However Islam remained until the Jihad of the early nineteenth century, a religion of a small elite found around the courts of the Hausa rulers. Today Islam is widely accepted and practiced, not only in Northern Nigeria but also in the western part. The only area it has not had many adherents in is Eastern Nigeria where Christianity has had a fairly firm root.

ITA, PROFESSOR EYO. Born in Calabar, Cross River State, he was educated first at Duke Town School and then at the Hope Waddell Training Institute to become a teacher. He taught at

the Baptist Academy in Lagos before proceeding to the United
States for studies. Upon his return from the United States in
1933, he founded the Nigeria Youth League Movement. He
taught for some time in Ogbomosho, but in 1938 he went back
to Calabar where he became the head of a national institute
founded by some educated people there. He later started his
educational institution known as the West African People's Institute. He set up a press which, among other things, published his many works.

Professor Eyo Ita was a member of the National Council of Nigeria and Cameroons (NCNC) and became in 1948 the
first National Vice-President of the party. In 1951 he was
elected to the Eastern House of Assembly and became Minister
for Natural Resources and Leader of Government Business for
the region. During the Eastern Regional Crisis of 1953 (q. v.),
he, together with some regional ministers and expelled NCNC
central ministers and their supporters, formed a new party
known as the National Independence Party (NIP). Professor
Eyo Ita became the President of the new party. In conjunc-
tion with the United National Party of Alvan Ikoku, they were
able to maintain themselves as opposition parties in the region. The two parties later joined together to form the United
National Independence Party (UNIP). When later in the year
the Calabar-Ogoja-Rivers (COR) Movement was launched, comprised of the non-Ibo-speaking minorities of the region, and
asking for a separate state of their own, Professor Eyo Ita
was a leading figure of this movement. In 1959 he went back
to the NCNC and after independence in 1960 he concentrated
his effort on the development of his school. During the civil
war, he supported the cause of Biafra. He died in 1972.

ITSEKIRIS. The Itsekiri people live on the western side of the Niger
Delta in the Bendel State. Traditionally they were fishermen
and traders and during the period of slave trade the Itsekiri
Kingdom of Warri (q. v.) was one of the major sources for the
supply of slaves as the people acted as middlemen between the
Europeans and the peoples in the hinterland. The kingdom was
said to have been founded in the fifteenth century by a Benin
prince, who with his followers migrated to Warri, and upon
getting there found a branch of the Yoruba people with whom
they intermarried. They later grew up to become a new group
speaking a Yoruba dialect modified by Benin influence, known
as Itsekiri. Today the area has become an important center
of the nation's petroleum industry.

IWO ELERU. Iwo Eleru was a rock shelter about 24 km. from
Akure, capital of Ondo State. Excavations have shown that it
was inhabited at recurring intervals thousands of years before
Christ. What the place however is most famous for are the
remains of the Late Stone Age covering a period of about
10, 000 years. It is said that the oldest Nigerian skeleton yet
discovered, and perhaps the oldest skeleton showing negroid
characteristics so far discovered in Africa, was found there.
It was dated at about 9, 000 B. C.

-J-

JACKSON, JOHN PAYNE. Born in 1848 in Liberia, and after his
formal education in his home country, he went into business,
travelling to Ghana and Nigeria, but he finally settled in Nigeria. After serving under J. S. Leigh, a businessman, he
set up his own business and became a palm produce trader.
He was later forced out of competition and he went to Lagos
in 1882 and took up a job with the Lagos Times which was
then owned by Mr. R. B. Blaize. In 1891, he founded his own
weekly newspaper, the Lagos Weekly Record, which became an
important force in the nationalist struggle. He was in the early
1900's critical of British administration and was very much involved in petitions and protest activities against the government
in Lagos. He died in 1915.

JAJA, KING OF OPOBO, 1821-1891. Born in 1821 in Amaigbo village group in the former Eastern Nigeria, he was sold as a
slave into the house of Anna Pepple of Bonny. In Bonny, he
joined the lowest rank of slave societies made up of those born
outside Bonny. He became a trader and made a success of it.
When his master died in 1863 he was elected to succeed him
as the new head of the house. His successes however aroused
the jealousy of other houses in Bonny. This led to a civil war
in which Jaja was victorious. But after the war, he decided
to move the members of his household to Opobo River where
he founded the Kingdom of Opobo on the Niger Delta.
As ruler of Opobo, he established plantations, built ports
and trading settlements and he got control of the flow of palm
oil to the European merchants. He became famous as a result
and the British had to make many treaties with him. However,
he began to have trouble in 1885 when the British proclaimed
the Protectorate of the Oil Rivers which included his kingdom.
Jaja did not like the idea of the free trade that the British
were peddling about and the British decided to get him out of
their way so as to have direct access to the market instead of
through him as middleman. By trickery, the British Acting
Vice Consul, Harry Johnston, invited him on board the gunboat
H. M. S. Goshawk with assurances that he would have safe conduct and no evil would happen to him. He was arrested, taken
to Accra, in the Gold Coast, now Ghana, tried and was ban-
ished in 1887 to the West Indies. The British, after petitions,
finally agreed that he should return back home. He died on
his way back on July 7, 1891. His body was taken home and
buried in Opobo.

JAKANDE, ALHAJI LATEEF KAYODE. A journalist and a politician
born on July 23, 1929 in Lagos. He was educated at the Ban-
ham Memorial Methodist School, Port Harcourt, Ilesha Grammar School and King's College in Lagos. He became a re-
porter for the Daily Service (1949-1950), subeditor (1950-1951)
and acting editor (1951-1952). He joined the Nigerian Tribune
as Editor in 1953 and became Managing Editor of the Nigerian

Tribune in 1954. In 1956, he became the Editor in Chief of the Amalgamated Press of Nigeria and Managing Director, Allied Newspapers of Nigeria in 1960. Later he became the Managing Director and Editor-in-Chief of the African Newspapers of Nigeria, Chairman of the Lagoon Book and Stationery Company Ltd. and Chairman of the John West Publications Ltd. He was the former Chairman of the Nigerian Institute of Journalism, former President of the International Press Institute, Patron of the Nigerian Union of Journalists in Lagos state and the Nigerian Guild of Editors. He is a member of the International Association for Mass Communications Research.

Alhaji Jakande was a prominent member of the defunct Action Group Party. He was also one of those tried and jailed with Chief Obafemi Awolowo for treasonable felony in 1963. He was also released and fully pardoned along with Chief Obafemi Awolowo in August 1966. With the coming of the Second Republic, he became a prominent member of Unity Party of Nigeria (UPN) under whose ticket he won the Governorship election of Lagos State in 1979. As Governor, Alhaji L. K. Jakande talked little but worked hard. This peculiarity earned him nationwide acclaim as the "action man" of Lagos State.

After the December 1983 military takeover, he was arrested and detained while investigation went on on how he had managed the financial resources of the Lagos State when he was governor. The Babangida administration released him August 1985.

Alhaji Lateef Jakande wrote many books including The Role of the Mass Media in a Developing Country and The Trial of Obafemi Awolowo.

JAMI'YYAR MUTANEM AREWA. The Jami'yyar Mutanem Arewa originally was a cultural organization meant to embrace all of the Northern Region. Its meaning is Northern People's Congress, and it was formed in 1949, as a way to provide for the cultural and educational development of the region just like the Ibo had done in 1944 by forming the Ibo Federal Union and the Yorubas in the west in 1948 by forming Egbe Omo Oduduwa. Its leaders included Mallam Aminu Kano, as well as Alhaji Sir Abubakar Tafawa Balewa and some others. Its aim was not to usurp the authority of the traditional rulers, the Emirs, but rather to enhance their authority whenever possible. Members would also help the traditional rulers in the discharge of their duties and the enlightenment of the masses of the people.

As election under the 1951 constitution was approaching, the Jami'yyar reorganized itself into a political party, the Northern People's Congress, which, from then on till 1966 when the military banned all political parties and cultural associations, controlled the pace of political development in the Northern Region.

JANGALI see CATTLE TAX

JEMIBEWON, MAJOR-GENERAL DAVID MEDAIYESE. A soldier, born on July 20, 1940 at Iyah-Gbedde in Kaba Division of Kwara

State. After his elementary education, he attended Offa Grammar School in Kwara State from 1955 to 1959. He later enlisted in the army and received military training in Nigeria, Britain and the United States.

During the civil war, he was the Assistant Adjutant and Quartermaster-General of the First Division based at Makurdi. He later commanded the 27th Infantry Battalion under the Second Section which liberated Abakaliki in March 1968. He fought in many other places during the war. After the war, he served in many capacities until 1975 when he was appointed Military Governor of the Western State to replace Captain Akintunde Aduwo who was reported to have been sent on an overseas course. In 1978 he returned to regular army service and was appointed Commander, Army School of Infantry in Jaji. He retired from the army in September 1983.

General Jemibewon was the recipient of many honors including Defense Service Medal, National Service Medal and the UN Congo Medal. He wrote A Combatant in Government.

JIHAD. The Jihad was the Moslem Holy War initiated in 1803 by Usman Dan Fodio, a Fulani Moslem priest and reformer. The aim of it was religious purification and social justice together with a desire to see improvement in the economy which was being adversely affected by the wars going on among the various Hausa city-states. To this end the Shehu selected 14 trusted Lieutenants to carry the flag to the 14 Hausa states. After they would have conquered they were to be installed Emirs there. The war was waged in the name of Allah and his prophet and was directed not only against the pagans (unbelievers) but also against lukewarm followers of the prophet Mohammed. During the war, Bornu, which was then a Moslem country, was attacked and conquered but later regained its independence under Al Kanemi, a fact which has always colored the relationship between the Hausa-Fulani and the Kanuri peoples. Usman Dan Fodio died in 1817 leaving the care of the state to his brother Abdullai and his son Bello, the grandfather of the late Sir Ahmadu Bello, the Saudauna of Sokoto. The Fulani empire, created by the Jihad included Katsina, Kano, Zaria, Hadeija, Adamawa, Gombe, Katagum, Nupe, Ilorin, Daura and Bauchi.

The war helped in the spread of Islam, and in giving Northern Nigeria a unity that it never had before. Sokoto, the city founded by Usman Dan Fodio became the focal point of Islam in Nigeria.

JOHNSON, SAMUEL. Born in 1846 in Hastings, Sierra Leone, Samuel Johnson came to Lagos, Nigeria with his parents in 1857 and later from there to Ibadan, now the capital of Oyo State. He was there during the Ijaye war till 1862 when he was sent to the Church Missionary Society (CMS) Training Institute in Abeokuta where he studied for three years. In 1866 he was appointed Schoolmaster in Ibadan, a position from which he rose to be the Superintendent of Schools at Kudeti and Aremo. He was made a Catechist in 1875 and mediated on behalf of the colonial government in the war between Ibadan, Ijesha and the Ekitis in 1885. In 1886 he became a Deacon and was ordained in 1888. He was later sent to Oyo where he remained until his death. He was a great historian and wrote The History of the Yorubas, a book which today remains the truest eyewitness account of the intertribal wars among the Yorubas in the second part of the nineteenth century. The book was completed in 1897 and sent in 1899 to the CMS in London for publication but the manuscript got lost. Johnson died in 1901. It was his brother Obadiah Johnson who compiled the present book from his notes.

JOINT ACTION COMMITTEE (JAC). Formed in September 1963 at a meeting of the United Labour Congress (ULC) for the purpose of prosecuting wage demands for the Nigerian workers. The pressure mounted by the JAC for the review of wages prompted the government to set up the Morgan Commission of Inquiry to look into the existing wage structure, remuneration and conditions of service in wage-earning employments. The Commission submitted its report in April 1964, and when the government failed to publish the report in time, the labor unions on June 1, 1964 began a general strike which prompted the government to release the report two days later. In 1965, the Committee was disbanded.

JOINT ADMISSIONS AND MATRICULATION BOARD (JAMB). Established by a decree in 1977, it is responsible for the general control of the conduct of matriculation examinations for admissions of undergraduate students into all Universities in Nigeria. It can appoint examiners, moderators and invigilators, and it can set up panels and committees with respect to matriculation examinations and other matters incidental to it. It is also responsible for the placement of successful candidates in the Universities and collection and dissemination of information on matters relating to admissions into the Universities. The Board however is not responsible for examinations or any other selective processes leading to postgraduate or professional courses.

Members of the Board, appointed by the Minister of Education, consist of a Chairman who is a Vice-Chancellor of a Nigerian university, the Vice-Chancellor of each university in Nigeria, or his representative, two representatives each of intermediate postsecondary institutions, teachers' colleges and the Nigerian Conference of Principals of Secondary Schools, the permanent Secretary in the Ministry of Education or his representative, the Registrar of the West African Examination Council which conducts High School Diploma examinations, the Executive Secretary of the National University Commission or his representative, the Registrar of the Board and three other persons representing interests not otherwise represented in the above list.

In practical terms, the Board sets examinations and sees to their marking, sends computer printout of the results to each university in accordance with the choice of candidates. Each university through its various faculties selects candidates on approved criteria, and presents its list of candidates to JAMB panels or committees for approval. Candidates so approved are duly notified by JAMB.

This system of recruitment of candidates to the universities was set up to make for national character in the admission of students to the various universities and prevent a student from being offered admission in two or more universities at the same time. In this way a university is sure that most of the candidates offered admission will take advantage of the offer there.

JOINT CHURCH AID. The Joint Church Aid was one of the humanitarian organizations that supplied relief materials to Biafra during the Nigerian civil war.

JOINT PLANNING COMMITTEE. The Joint Planning Committee (JPC) was established by the National Economic Council in 1958. The Committee was composed of all the permanent secretaries of all departments concerned with economic affairs, with the Economic Adviser to the federal government as Chairman. The Committee was saddled with the responsibility of drawing the national development plan for the whole country. Most of the work of National Economic Council was done by this Committee because the NEC barely functioned. For instance, it met only once throughout 1964. Most of the works, proposals and recommendations of JPC were submitted to the National Economic Council which would either amend, accept or reject such proposals. The Committee issued various reports among which is the Economic Survey of Nigeria, 1959.

JOS. The capital of Plateau State, with a population of about 100,000 people according to the 1963 census figures, Jos is relatively a young city having been officially founded as a township in 1915. It is situated on the northern edge of the Plateau named after itself (Jos Plateau). It is about 4,000 feet above the sea level and is famous for its fairly temperate climate. The yearly temperature ranges between 50° to 95° while the annual rainfall ranges between 40 and 70 inches. Jos is blessed with a large deposit of tin ore on the Jos Plateau, which has attracted the Makeri tin smelting company into the area. In 1972 a campus of the University of Ibadan was established there but this was later constituted into a full-fledged university known as the University of Jos.

JOSE, ALHAJI ISMAIL BABATUNDE. A distinguished journalist, born on December 13, 1925, he was educated in a Yaba Methodist school and the Saviours' Boys High School in Lagos. In 1941, he began to train as a printer with the Daily Times of Nigeria Limited. Between 1948 and 1952 he was the political correspondent for the same paper, and was in 1957 promoted to the position of Editor of the paper. In 1962 he became the

Managing Director of the company, but retired in 1975 when the federal military government acquired 60 percent of the company's share. He was honored with a Doctorate degree in 1980 by the University of Benin.

JUDICIAL COMMITTEE OF THE PRIVY COUNCIL. Before October 1, 1963, when Nigeria became a republic, the highest court of appeal for Nigeria was Her Majesty's Judicial Committee of the Privy Council in London, to which appeals lay from the Supreme Court in Nigeria. The privy council was famous for its impartiality and forthrightness, and was the defender of the legal rights of the citizens against the colonial administration. The court no doubt contributed immensely to the constitutional development of the country.

JUDICIARY. The judicial system is organized as follows: at the federal level, there are the Federal High Courts, Federal Court of Appeal and the Supreme Court. Appeals lie from the Federal High Courts to the Federal Court of Appeal and from there to the Supreme Court. On the state level there are three types of court: at bottom level are Magistrate Courts, Customary Courts and Sharia Courts. At the top are State High Courts, State Customary Courts of Appeal and State Sharia Courts of Appeal. Appeals lie from Magistrate Court to State High Court, from the Customary Court to the State Customary Court of Appeal and from the Sharia Court to the State Sharia Court of Appeal. However there is a link between the federal and the state judicial organizations: appeals lie from the State High Court, State Customary Court of Appeal and State Sharia Court of Appeal to the Federal Court of Appeal and from there to the Supreme Court.

JUKUNS. The Jukuns are one of the minority ethnic groups in the northern parts of Nigeria along the Benue valley. According to their tradition, they came from Yemil, east of Mecca, with one Agudu as their leader. But Hausa myth says that Kororofa, the ancestor of the Jukuns, was one of the seven illegitimate children of Biram. Therefore, another name for the Jukuns is Kororofa, which again was the name of the capital city of the Jukun kingdom.

The Jukuns were warlike. They subjugated many ethnic groups and towns including the Angaras and Miriam, and the towns of Zaria and Kano. The kingdom once extended to the south of the Cross River and the borders of Bornu. However the city of Kororofa was destroyed during the Fulani Jihad (Holy War) of the early nineteenth century.

-K-

KADUNA. The capital of the old Northern Region and now of the Kaduna State, it is one of the most important towns in Nigeria,

being the city in which most northern intelligentsia are concentrated. It is also the town in which are located the Defense
Academy, a modern military training institution and the Nigerian Airforce Tactical and Training Wing. Furthermore Kaduna
has become a booming industrial center in the north, having
located in it modern factories like the Peugeot Assembly Plant.

In 1900 Kaduna was selected as the headquarters of the
Northern Protectorate and when the old Northern Protectorate
became the Northern Region, it remained as the regional headquarters. In the First Republic, Kaduna, the home of the
Northern Regional government of the Northern People's Congress (NPC) which was the major coalition partner at the center, was the center of power in the federation. Even the Prime
Minister of the federation had to have constant consultation with
the party leader in Kaduna, Sir Ahmadu Bello, the Sardauna of
Sokoto and the Premier of Northern Nigeria.

"KADUNA MAFIA." A derogatory term referring to an assumed
clique of Kaduna elite and intelligentsia operating secretly behind the scene to get what it wants from the federal government. Because of the historical past of Kaduna as the regional
headquarters of the former Northern Nigeria, it has concentrated within it a good number of northern intelligentsia and
elite, who had worked there and now are retired and live in
the city, or who are presently working there.

KADUNA POLYTECHNIC. Established by the federal military government in 1968 it consisted of the College of Science and Technology made up of the Polytechnic of Kaduna and the Irrigation
School at Sokoto, and the Staff Development Center, made up
of the Staff Development Center in Kaduna, the Local Government Training Center in Zaria, the Cooperative Training Center in Zaria, the Social Welfare Training Center in Zaria and
the Community Development Institute. The Polytechnic was to
provide diverse instructions, training and research in technology, the sciences, commerce and the humanities. It was
also required to provide in-service training for members of
the public services in Nigeria. The institution was to be run
by a board of governors composed of members from all the
northern states appointed by the Governor of each state and
other members from some industries and the Ahmadu Bello
University.

KADUNA STATE. Created out of the former North-Central State in
February 1976. The state has a population of about 4,098,305
with an area of about 70,293 sq. km. The capital of the state
is Kaduna, thus occupying a unique position when one consid-
ers the role of Kaduna as the capital of the former Northern
Region. Today the state is still the commercial and industrial
nerve center of all the northern states.

The peoples of the state are Hausa, Fulanis, Kajes,
Gwans and the Pitis. The main towns of the state are Kaduna,
Katsina, Zaria, Funtua, Daura and Kafanchan.

Most of the people in the state engage in agriculture, which is being progressively mechanized to provide food and raw materials for the country. Cotton is the state's major cash crop, but it also produces groundnuts and ginger for export. Food crops include guinea corn, millet, maize, yams, beans and rice. The state is also rich in mineral resources like tin ore, columbite, sapphire, iron ore, graphite and gold.

A number of industrial projects are located in Kaduna state, which include a Peugeot assembly plant, a petroleum refinery, textile mills and a number of other projects. The state is blessed with a number of educational institutions which include the famous Katsina College which produced a high number of the early northern elites, and Ahmadu Bello University in Zaria.

The state is also rich in tourist attractions. There is the Regimental Museum of the Nigerian Army in Zaria, the famous Nok terra heads, polished iron axes and weapons believed to be over 2,000 years old and the palaces of the Emirs of the major towns. There are also good hotel services in Kaduna.

KAINJI RIVER DAM. River Niger was dammed at Kainji about 112 kms. north of Jebba for the purpose of generating hydroelectric power which is distributed to different parts of the country. The generating capacity of the dam at its inception in 1969 was 647 megawatts which doubled the installed capacity in the country. Nigeria was therefore able to supply electricity to the Niger Republic. In 1976 two more turbines were installed making the total six, thereby considerably raising the generating capacity of the dam. In spite of this, demand continues to outstrip the supply.

KAMERUN NATIONAL CONGRESS. A political party formed in the early 1950's under the leadership of Dr. E.M.L. Endeley, it began agitation for the separation of the Cameroons, a British trust territory, administered as part of Nigeria, from Nigeria. During the 1954 federal elections, the party won all the six seats allocated to the Southern Cameroons, and when the Southern Cameroons was given regional autonomy, the party was the governing party. In 1961, its objective was realized: Southern Cameroons became separated from Nigeria and joined the Republic of Cameroon while the Northern Cameroons preferred to remain as an integral part of Nigeria.

KAMPALA PEACE TALKS. The Kampala Peace Talks were held between May 23 and 31, 1968. The meeting was convened by the President of Uganda, Dr. Milton Obote, in an effort to find a political solution to the civil war then tearing the country into pieces. The two sides to the war--the federal government and Biafra--sent delegates to the talks. Dr. Milton Obote in declaring the meeting open appealed for an agreement on cessation of hostilities and a cease-fire as a basic preliminary stage for a broad understanding on the nature of the government

that would later be set up. His appeals fell on deaf ears.
Neither side was prepared to yield on their major demands.
During the talks a member of the federal government delegation, Mr. Johnson Banjo was reported abducted and later reported killed. When the talks resumed after this incident,
Chief Anthony Enahoro, the leader of the federal delegation,
put forward his proposals for a cease-fire and Sir Louis Mbanefo, a Justice of the High Court who led the Biafran side, had
to tell him that Biafra had not come to Kampala to surrender
to Nigeria. The meeting then broke up on May 31, 1968 without reaching any important agreement.

KANEM-BORNU EMPIRE. The earliest that came into being in the
    region of Lake Chad. It started towards the end of the tenth
    century, first with the kingdom of Kanem, north of Lake Chad,
    and it gradually extended south of the lake to Bornu. Islam
    came to the area in the eleventh century but the administrative
    system had been laid down by the King (Mai) of the kingdom.
    The influence of the empire was felt in many parts of North
    Africa including Egypt, but the empire broke down in the four-
    teenth century owing to the defects of the administrative sys-
    tem which entrusted provincial governorship positions to mem-
    bers of the royal family who often intrigued against the King.

KANO. The capital of Kano state and one of the most ancient and
    famous of Nigerian cities, Kano was for centuries the commer-
    cial center of the Western Sudan from which and to which many
    West African caravans took off or went to. It was also the
    southern terminus of the Trans-Saharan trade and was second
    only to Timbuktu in all of West Africa. With the coming of
    the British, Kano still maintained this trading role and is now
    the commercial center of the whole of Northern Nigeria.
        Being one of the seven historical Hausa states, Kano
    is predominantly Hausa-speaking and even though there are
    Fulanis and the Kanuris in the city, Hausa culture and tradi-
    tion are dominant and Hausa language is the lingua franca,
    even for most of the north. The traditional industries of weav-
    ing, embroidery of cloths, tanning of animal skins and the pro-
    duction of ornamental leather work, all of which in the past made
    Kano famous are still carried on today in the city.
        Kano is made up of the old walled city with 16 gates.
    The walls were built for the purpose of protection against any
    aggression. This area is about 21 sq. km. and contains the
    traditional markets which offer all kinds of goods including lo-
    cally made goods and foreign goods. The other part is the
    modern industrial and commercial center known as Sabongari
    (strangers' quarters) where mostly people of southern origin
    live. To the north of the old city and the edge of the Sabon-
    gari is the Mallam Aminu Kano international airport, the sec-
    ond in the nation.
        Kano city is famous for its groundnut pyramids, pyra-
    mids made up of groundnut bags ready for export to the world
    market.

KANO, ALHAJI MUHAMMED AMINU. Popularly known as Mallam
Aminu Kano, he was a teacher and a politician, the founder of
the Northern Element Progressive Union (NEPU) and the former
leader of the People's Redemption Party. A Fulani, born on
August 9, 1920, he was educated at the Shahuchi Primary
School, the Kano Middle School and at the Kaduna College,
from 1937 to 1942. He later received a Teacher's Certificate
from the Institute of Education in the London University in
England and taught at the Bauchi Middle School from 1942 to
1946. While at the school, he, together with Mallam Sa'ad
Zungur and Mallam Abubakar Tafawa Balewa, founded the Bauchi Improvement Union in 1943. He was also the founder of
the Northern Teachers' Association and he became its first
Secretary-General 1948-1953.

Following the pattern of group associations being formed
in the south, Mallam Aminu Kano, together with Alhaji Abubakar
Tafawa Balewa, Dr. Dikko and Yahaya Gusau founded the Jami'-
yyar Muten-en Arewa meaning Northern People's Congress in
1949. Because this organization was too conservative for Mallam Aminu Kano, he, together with people who felt like him
broke away from the organization and founded the Northern
Element Progressive Union (NEPU) in 1950. He remained the
leader of the party until 1966 when the military dissolved all
political parties. As such he led his party's delegation to all
the constitutional conferences both in London and in Nigeria.

Mallam Aminu Kano had many years of service to the
nation. In 1959 he was elected into the Federal House of Representatives, and his party being in alliance with the National
Council of Nigeria and Cameroons (NCNC), which was the junior
partner in the coalition government that emerged after the election, he became Deputy Government Chief Whip, 1959 to 1964,
while his party in the Northern House of Assembly continued
to maintain the radical proletarian image of the party in that
house. In 1963, with the coalition between NPC and NCNC
disintegrating, NEPU's alliance with the NCNC became stronger
and Mallam Aminu became first Vice-President of the NCNC.
In 1964, the coalition completely broke down and in the realignment efforts being made before the 1964 federal elections,
NEPU and some other progressive parties in the north and
south, including United Middle Belt Congress (UMBC), NCNC
and the Action Group (AG), formed the United Progressive Grand
Alliance (UPGA). UPGA lost and Mallam Aminu also lost his
seat in Kano.

During the military rule, Mallam Aminu Kano was appointed Federal Commissioner for Communications (1967-1971)
and Federal Commissioner for Health (1971-1974). He was a
member of the Constituent Assembly (1977-1978) and when the
ban on political activities was lifted in September 1978, Mallam Aminu Kano formed the People's Redemption Party (PRP)
under which he was nominated as candidate for the presidential
election in 1979. He lost the election to Alhaji Shehu Shagari.
In the effort to realign the parties that lost the presidential
election against the presidential party--National Party of Nigeria

(NPN)--Mallam Aminu refused to gang up against the NPN. In the process his party, the PRP, broke into two factions, one led by him and the other led by Chief Michael Imoudu, the old trade unionist. Just as Mallam Aminu Kano refused to gang up in 1979, in the same way he refused in 1982 to join the so-called Progressive Parties Alliance whose main objective was nothing other than to wrest power from the NPN. Aminu later worked hard to reunite the factions in his party and prepare it for the 1983 election. He was on the verge of doing so when death took him away on April 17, 1983. The factions became reunited on May 18, 1983.

Mallam Aminu Kano was a great nationalist, a defender of the poor and the downtrodden. The international airport in Kano, Mallam Aminu Kano Airport, was named after him.

KANO PEOPLE'S PARTY. A splinter party from the Northern People's Congress (NPC) formed in opposition to the NPC deposition of Alhaji Sir Muhammadu Sanusi, the Emir of Kano, in 1963, the party contested the 1964 elections and won seven seats in the Kano province of Northern Nigeria. The party was banned along with other political parties when the military came to power in 1966.

KANO RIOTS OF 1953. In 1953 Chief Anthony Enahoro tabled a motion in the National House of Representatives in Lagos for "Self-government-for-Nigeria-in-1956." The northern representatives wanted self-government "as soon as practicable." The motion generated a lot of heat and after it had been amended to read "as soon as practicable," Action Group members and some NCNC members walked out of the house. The two parties later decided to form an alliance to bring about self-government in 1956. To this end, they undertook to send delegations to tour the northern cities to campaign for self-government in 1956. One such delegation led by the late Chief S. L. Akintola, a member of the Action Group Party, went to Kano. The mission of these southern politicians was resented by the Northerners and the tense atmosphere that it generated resulted in a four-day riot at Sabongari Kano during which 36 persons died and over 200 were injured. At the Constitutional Conference in London in July 1953, Britain agreed to give self-government to any region wishing to have it.

KANO STATE. One of the 12 states created in May 1967, the state covers an area of about 43,285 sq. km. and has a population of over 5.8 million people according to the 1963 census and therefore is the largest state, population-wise, in the federation. It is predominantly Hausa-speaking, and most of the people in the state are farmers, but the residents of Kano City, the capital of the state are mainly traders and craftsmen. The city of Kano used to be for many centuries the greatest commercial center of the old Western Sudan.

The farmers of the state are predominantly groundnut producers and it was the storage of the final production of the

groundnut that resulted in the famous Kano groundnut pyramids.
The craftsmen engage in beautiful leather work; metal work,
colorful and decorated garments, wood and bone carving.

Educationally, the state is gradually correcting its educational imbalance with the rest of the country. Great strides
have been made since the beginning of the Universal Primary
Education in 1976. There are Teacher Training Colleges and
secondary schools. There is also the Bayero University in
Kano and the Baguda and Technical and Vocational Center.

Kano is well served by good communications and transportation systems. It is connected to the rest of the country
by road, rail and air, and Kano has the second international
airport in the country.

Tourist attractions include Kano Central Mosque, the
city walls, the city market, Baguda Lake Hotel and the famous
Tiga Dam.

KANURIS. An ethnic group living in the region of Lake Chad in
Borno State and the eastern part of the Niger Republic, they
are mostly farmers growing crops like guinea corn, millet,
groundnuts and cotton. The people live in small agricultural
villages and the traditional political authority is the chief advised by a council of elders. However the Kanuris have also
had large towns that were centers of commerce and trade, and
they have also had a tradition of centralized political authority
and organization. Mention should be made of the great Kanuri-
Bornu empire which was a major power in the Sudan between
the eleventh and the fourteenth centuries and their organizational power to resist the Fulani Jihad in the nineteenth century. The Kanuris are by religion Muslim which has greatly
influenced many aspects of their life.

KATAGUM. A town in Bauchi State, established in 1803 by Malam
Zaki who after the death of his father went to Shehu Usman
Dan Fodio in Sokoto, the originator of the Jihad of the early
nineteenth century, received a flag from him and became the
Emir of the town. The headquarters of the Katagum was re-
moved in 1910 for administrative convenience to Azare.

KATSINA. A town in Kaduna State, and the administrative headquarters of the former Katsina province in the old northern region.
Katsina is important in the north because of the Katsina Teacher
Training College which most of the northern elites attended.
Among the students of this school were Alhaji Tafawa Balewa, former Prime Minister, Sir Kashim Ibrahim, former
Governor of Northern Nigeria, and many others. When the proposed Katsina State is created, Katsina will most likely be its
capital.

KATSINA, MAJOR-GENERAL HASSAN USMAN. A soldier, born on
March 31, 1933 in Katsina, Kaduna State, he was educated at
Kankiya Elementary School, Katsina Middle School, Kaduna Col-
lege, the Institute of Administration in Zaria and at the Nigerian
College of Arts, Science and Technology in Zaria.

He joined the army in 1956 and trained as an officer in Ghana and in England. He later returned to Nigeria and in 1961 he was sent to the Congo as a member of the United Nations Peace-Keeping Force. In 1962, he was sent for further training on Infantry maneuvers in the U.S.A. at Fort Benning. He returned later and was appointed Company Commander of the Fifth Battalion. In 1964 he was at the Staff College, Camberley in England. In 1965 he became a squadron leader and later in the year a Regimental Commander.

General Katsina did not participate in the January 15, 1966 coup and was later appointed Governor of the Northern Region by General Ironsi, the Head of State. After the death of Ironsi in July 1966, General Gowon kept him in his place as Governor, and Katsina helped to keep the north behind Gowon and the federal government. When the north was divided into six states in 1967, he was the Chairman of the Interim Common Services Agency until 1968 when he became Army Chief of Staff and helped in the prosecution of the civil war. In 1971 he was appointed a Major-General and in 1973 he became a federal commissioner for establishment. He retired later from the army and became a businessman.

KING'S COLLEGE, LAGOS. Established in Lagos by the colonial government in 1909. It was the first government owned secondary school in the country. The college admits students from all over the nation. When the Yaba Higher College was established, parts of King's College served as temporary buildings for it. Today the college runs both secondary school certificate courses as well as higher certificate courses for those who would like to seek direct entry to one of the universities in the country.

KORANIC SCHOOLS. Koranic Schools are schools where the Holy Koran--the Moslem holy book--is learned, usually by young boys and girls. At the school they learn the Arabic alphabets and they can read the Koran in Arabic and interpret it. They are also trained in the correct method of worship and the basic rules of social conduct. In the past in many Moslem places, this was the only school that Moslem children were sent to. Today children go to secular schools and take lessons in the Holy Koran as well as in other subjects. This however does not mean the end of Koranic schools. They still exist, but their hours are now fixed for the evenings after the children will have come back home from the secular schools and also in the mornings during the weekends.

KOSOKO. The son of King Idowu Ojulari, who was born in Lagos and ruled over Lagos between 1819 and 1832, during the time the British were trying to put an end to slave trade and have legitimate trade substituted in its place. After his father's death in 1832, Kosoko did not support King Oluwole, who succeeded his father. He and others conspired to overthrow him but failed. He was deported from Lagos to Porto Novo where

he came in contact with Portuguese slave traders. Oluwole
died and Akintoye succeeded him in 1841. The new king allowed his nephew Kosoko to come back to Lagos in 1845. He
led a rebellion against his uncle Akintoye and being victorious,
he deported him to Abeokuta. Slave trading continued to flour-
ish during his reign. In 1851 the British Consul in the Bight
of Benin, John Beecroft, wanted to bring back Akintoye after the
latter had sent a petition to the consul to restore him to the
throne in return for which he would put an end to slave trade.
With a naval force of about 400 men, the Consul stormed the
city, drove Kosoko out from Lagos and restored Akintoye to
the throne. Kosoko was exiled to Epe where he continued his
campaign against the British. Akintoye died in 1853 and was
succeeded by his son Dosunmu. In 1862 Kosoko returned to
Lagos, but did not reclaim the throne.

KWARA STATE. Created out of the former Northern Region of Nigeria in May 1967 with the original name of Central-West State,
it is about 66,869 sq. km. in area and has a population of
about 2.4 million people according to the 1963 census. The
state is bounded on the north by the Niger River and Sokoto
State, on the south by Oyo, Ondo and Bendel states, on the east
by Benue and Plateau states and on the west by the Republic
of Benin. The unique position of the state has caused many people to refer to it as the gateway to the north and south of Nigeria.

The peoples of the state are Yorubas, Igbiras, Nupes,
Baribas and the Hausa-Fulanis. Islam is the dominant religion
in the state, but there are Christians and worshippers of other
religions. Agriculture is the most important industry in the
state. The people produce cotton, coffee, cocoa, kola nuts,
tobacco, benniseed and palm produce. The state also has many
mineral resources which are still to be developed. These include coal, limestone, marble, tin, gold, talc, and iron ore.
The major industrial projects in the state are sugar production
at Bacita, paper manufacturing at Jebba, steel industry in
Ajaokuta, a cloth-weaving factory at Okene and marble quarrying at Jakura and Lokoja.

Educationally the state is making great progress. In
addition to many primary and secondary schools, there is a
state college of technology and the University of Ilorin.

Tourist attractions include the Kainji Dam which supplies the bulk of the nation's electricity supply, Lokoja, the
confluence town of rivers Niger and Benue, the Borgu Game
Reserve and the Esie Stone Images at Esie/Iludun in Igbomina
Ekiti Division of the state.

The capital of the state is Ilorin and other main towns
are Lokoja, Jebba, New Bussa (Kainji) Okene, Esie, Offa,
Omuaran, Kabba, Lafiagi, Pategi, Bacita, Ajase-Ipo and Bode-
Sadu.

-L-

LAGOS. A Yoruba town and capital of Nigeria from 1914 to 1976.
The town was ceded to Britain in 1861 by King Dosumu (q. v.)
and it became a Crown Colony. In 1866 the colony was placed
under the British administration in Sierra Leone, but it retained
a separate legislative council and an administrator was responsible for its affairs. In 1874 it came under the governor of
the Gold Coast and in 1886, it was finally set up as a separate
colony under its own Governor. In 1914 Lagos became the
capital of all of Nigeria. In 1919 it became a first-class township with a representative Town Council. Under the Macpherson Constitution of 1951, Lagos formed part of the Western
Region, but in 1954, it was constituted a neutral federal territory. In 1967, Lagos served in the role of being the capital
of both the federation and of the Lagos State. In 1976, it was
constituted a "Special Area" along with Kaduna and Port Harcourt. Lagos is a big commercial and industrial center and
has the largest and main seaport. Though now a cosmopolitan
city, the tradition of the Yorubas, the original settlers, have
been preserved through the institution of Obaship.

LAGOS CHAMBER OF COMMERCE. Founded as a private organization in 1888 for the purpose of protecting all matters affecting
trade and industry and for the promotion of the economic growth
of the country. The Chamber of Commerce is financed by sub-
scription paid by members, the composition of which includes
Nigerians, Europeans and Asians all numbering well over 450.
Though not a government organization, it maintains close relations with the government and is frequently asked to express
its views on pertinent pending legislations and in fact to make
recommendations on such legislation and other matters affecting
the commercial and the industrial interests.

LAGOS ISSUE. The Lagos Issue was the controversy as to the position of Lagos, the capital of Nigeria in the federation that
was to emerge in 1954. Under the Macpherson Constitution
of 1951, Lagos was part of the Western Region, but owing to
the Constitutional Crisis of 1953 over the question of self-
government in 1956, the northern people who formerly did not
want to oppose the position of Lagos began to ask that the capital be neutralized so that in the event of the west seceding,
they would still be able to get their exports to Lagos which
was the most important Nigerian seaport. The NCNC, which
had never been in favor of Lagos being merged with the west,
supported the neutralization of Lagos but the Action Group
which controlled the west argued for the merging of Lagos
with the west as it had been since 1951. When the delegation
to the London Conference could not agree on the issue, they
appealed to the Colonial Secretary to arbitrate. The Colonial
Secretary supported the idea of a neutral Lagos, that is, the
federal capital being separated from the Western Region.

LAGOS STATE. Created with the other 11 states in the federation
on May 27, 1967, Lagos State covers an area of about 3,577
sq. km. with a population of over 1.5 million people, thus being the most densely populated state in the federation, with about
815 persons per sq. km.
　　　　The people of Lagos are mainly Yoruba, but since Lagos
City has been the capital of Nigeria since 1914, many other
ethnic groups from all over the country have found a home in
the state.　These people are mainly wage and salary earners
in the public and private sectors: businessmen, fishermen and
farmers.　In fact the state is the commercial and industrial
nerve center of the country and having the nation's chief port,
it handles the greatest percentage of the country's export and
import business.　Lagos State is the home of the Murtala Muhammed International Airport at Ikeja, which is about 24 km.
from the center of the city of Lagos itself.
　　　　Lagos State has rich cultural heritage.　The most popular festival on the Lagos Island is the Eyo.　There are many
tourist attractions like the Bar Beach at the Victorial Island,
the National Museum and the Festac building.
　　　　The state capital is Ikeja and other towns in the state
include Epe, Badagry and Ikorodu.

LAGOS TOWN COUNCIL. Established by ordinance in 1917, it had
power to have among its members elected Councilors to represent the various wards into which the town was divided.　The
election to the council was dominated from 1922 by Herbert
Macaulay's Nigerian National Democratic Party (NNDP) until
1938 when the Nigerian Youth Movement successfully challenged
the party's monopoly.　Because the Macpherson Constitution of
1951 placed the city of Lagos in the Western Region, the Western Regional Local Government Law of 1953 brought the Lagos
Town Council under the control of the region, abolished the
office of the Mayor and in its place put the Oba of Lagos as
the President of the Council.　Later the Town Council was
known as the Lagos City Council.　With the 1976 Local Government reforms, the Lagos City Council was dissolved and
new local governments were established.

LAGOS WEEKLY RECORD. Established in Lagos in 1891 by
John Payne Jackson who was its first Editor, the paper was
most popular among the Nigerian nationalists for its campaign
in defense of West Africans against alien white rule.　In 1915
when John Payne Jackson died, his son Thomas Horatio Jackson took over the editorship and the ownership of the paper.
The paper stopped publishing in 1930.

LAGOS YOUTH MOVEMENT. Lagos Youth Movement was formed
by four eminent Nigerian nationalists--Ernest Ikoli, Dr. J. C.
Vaughan, Oba Samuel Akinsanya and Mr. H. O. Davies--to
oppose the government education policy with regard to the deficiencies evident in the setting up of the Yaba Higher College
in 1934.　The institution was to award its own Nigerian diplomas

in medicine, arts, economics, agriculture and engineering without it being affiliated at least initially with any British university. This arrangement was attacked because it was believed that the institution would be inferior in status to British universities and its diplomas would be inferior even though the time taken to acquire the diplomas was longer than the time required for a university degree in the same subject. In 1936, the Lagos Youth Movement changed its name to the Nigerian Youth Movement.

LAIRD, MACGREGOR. After the Lander brothers returned to England with the news that the riddle of the Niger had been solved, Macgregor Laird, a Liverpool businessman financed an expedition from the coast to the interior of Nigeria in 1832. Many of the members of the expedition died of malaria. Out of the 48 Europeans that set sail, only nine survived. The failure of the expedition slowed down the efforts to open up the interior of the country to trade. In 1854 Laird built the Pleiad and sent out an expedition to the Niger under the command of Dr. Baikie. The expedition was a great success; trading posts were established in many places including Lokoja on the confluence of rivers Niger and Benue. In 1857, Laird was given a contract by the British government to maintain a steamer on the Niger for five years and again he placed Dr. Baikie in command. The first steamer was the Dayspring and the expedition included Samuel Ajayi Crowther who later became the first Bishop of the Niger. Laird met with a lot of opposition from the people of the area, who served as middlemen between the interior and the white men on the coast, and the Liverpool supercargoes who resented his efforts. In 1860 he was able to convince the British government to provide him with a naval escort, but the local Commander never provided any because he felt it was too risky at the time. As a result his expedition involved him in heavy losses of capital. However Dr. Baikie, who had been wrecked in the Dayspring, established himself in Lokoja and appeared to be doing well. Laird died in 1861.

LAKE CHAD. Lake Chad on the northeastern border of Nigeria lies partly within the boundary of Nigeria. The lake receives its waters from the Yobe and the Shari rivers. In spite of this, reports say that it is drying up even though there is no visible outlet, except evaporation. Lake Chad gave its name to the present Chad Republic.

LAMBO, PROFESSOR THOMAS ADEOYE. A neuropsychiatrist and an educationist, he was born on March 29, 1929 at Abeokuta, Ogun State and educated at the Baptist Boys' High School, Abeokuta. He later went to the University of Birmingham in England and later to the Institute of Psychiatry, University of London in England.

Back in Nigeria in 1950 he became a Medical Officer, Nigerian Medical Services, and Specialist-in-Charge at Aro

Hospital for Nervous Diseases and a Consultant Physician to
the University College, Ibadan, 1956 to 1963. In 1963 he became
Professor and Head of Department of Psychiatry and Neurology
at the University of Ibadan and Dean of the Medical Faculty in
1966. In 1968 he was appointed the Vice-Chancellor of the
University of Ibadan. While he was a Vice-Chancellor, he
was also the Chairman, West African Examinations Council
(WAEC).

Professor Lambo has held important positions in many
international organizations and has been the recipient of many
honors. In 1961 he convened the first Pan-African Conference
of Psychiatrists and was founder of the Association of Psychiatrists in Africa in 1961. He was Chairman, Scientific Council
for Africa from 1965 to 1970 and was a member of the Executive Committee, Council for International Organization for Medical Science (UNESCO) from 1965 to 1968. He was also Chairman, United Nations Advisory Committee for the Prevention of
Crime and Treatment of Offenders from 1968 to 1971. In 1971 he
was appointed Assistant Director-General of the World Health
Organization (WHO) and in 1973 he became Deputy Director of
the organization. He was also a member of the Royal Medico-
Psychological Association of Great Britain and a Fellow of the
Royal College of Physicians. Among the honors received were
Order of the British Empire OBE, honorary degrees of D. Sc.
and LL. D. from various universities. He also received Haile
Selassie African Research Award in 1970. He coauthored
Psychiatric Disorder Among the Yorubas in 1963.

LANDER, RICHARD. The servant of Hugh Clapperton, (q. v.) one
of the leading explorers of the interior of West Africa, he was
with Clapperton in the latter's journey from Badagry to Sokoto
in 1825. When Clapperton died in 1827, Lander tried to
reach the coast by going down through the River Niger. He
was captured by the local inhabitants at the confluence of Rivers
Niger and Benue and was made to go down to the coast by land.
He went back to England and persuaded the British government
to support his journey to Nigeria. In 1830 he and his brother
John travelled by land from Badagry to Bussa where Mungo
Park died. They got two boats there and sailed down the Niger until they reached Asaba where they were captured by the
local inhabitants, who agreed to hand them over to the master
of the English ship at Brass at the mouth of River Niger.
They journeyed down the Niger, thereby solving the riddle of
the Niger River. Lander died in 1834.

LAND TENURE SYSTEM. Traditional basis of land tenure was common ownership whether by the community as a whole or by
families, and the allocation of land was controlled by traditional
authorities who acted as trustees for the community. All the
members of the community or family had a right to the land
and once an individual was given a piece of land, he could use
it as he saw fit but he could not sell it or alienate it in any
way from the family or the community. The right an individual
had over the land in his possession was usufructuary.

When the colonial authorities came they decided to preserve as much as possible the traditional land ownership system. In the Southern Protectorate an alien, that is, an expatriate, was prohibited from acquiring an interest in land from a native or from a fellow alien except under an instrument previously approved by the Governor. This meant that some families that wished could collectively alienate their land to Nigerians. As such some community lands were divided up among families and some of these began to offer them for sale to other Nigerians in "fee simple" (absolutely). In the Northern Protectorate the government was empowered to hold all the land in trust for the natives and no title to the use and occupation of land was valid without the consent of the government.

The policy of preventing aliens from purchasing land in fee simple had two major effects. It prevented the growth of a white settler community in Nigeria and so deterred the investment of private European capital in the development of the economy. In the second place by defining an alien as a person whose father belonged to a tribe indigenous to Northern Nigeria, the law in the north inhibited freedom of migration and residence of Nigerians in their own country and therefore made the problem of national integration all the more difficult. See also LAND USE DECREE.

LAND USE AND ALLOCATION COMMITTEE. Set up by the Land Use Decree (now Act) of 1978 (q. v.) its responsibility is to advise the Governor of the state on matters connected with the management of land and with the resettlement of persons affected by the revocation of rights of occupancy on the ground of overriding public interest. It is also to determine the amount of compensation payable under the decree for improvements on the land.

LAND USE DECREE/ACT. As a result of the recommendation of the Rent Control Panel (q. v.), the federal military government set up the Land Use Panel headed by Justice Chike Idigbe. The outcome of the panel's recommendations was the promulgation of the Land Use Decree (now Act) in March 1978.

As a result of the traditional Land Tenure System (q. v.) as amended by different statutory laws in the Southern and Northern protectorates, certain problems which urgently needed solution arose. In the urban areas, there was too much speculation in land, and this made for the rise in land value all over the nation. Secondly, the governments of the federation were experiencing difficulty in acquiring land for public use, especially in the south where there was no coordinated tenurial system of land, which consequently led to endless land litigations. Finally the land tenure system as it operated in the country imposed great impediments on agricultural modernization and the effort of the nation to be self-sufficient in food. It was these impediments and other problems that the Land Use Decree was designed to remove and solve.

According to the decree, ownership of all land in each state of the federation is vested in the government of the state which holds it in trust for the people and administers it for the use and common benefit of all the people. By this decree a uniform system of land ownership for the whole country was established and an individual could no longer legally sell land in fee simple. All urban areas were further placed under the control and management of the governor of the state while rural lands were placed under the control and management of the local government that had jurisdiction in the area where the land is situated. As far as rural land areas were concerned, the decree did not disturb the right of users of land traditionally occupied or developed, but it transferred the right of allocating unoccupied land from traditional authorities like Chiefs and Heads of Families to local governments, which are empowered to grant customary right of occupancy to persons or organizations of not more than 500 hectares for agricultural purposes or 5,000 hectares for grazing purposes. By this decree, traditional authorities are deprived of the right to their undeveloped land and such land is opened to anyone who needed it for development, including strangers.

There is great resistance to this decree by traditional land owners, lawyers who lost income through the new system and some others. There are efforts to amend the decree, but an amendment of it cannot be easy since it is protected by the 1979 constitution.

The implementation of the decree has been woefully poor. Part of the problem is that the government of each state has not a survey map of unoccupied lands before nor even after the decree came into being. As such, land continued to be sold by traditional land owners and the receipts were backdated to a time before 1978.

LANLEHIN, CHIEF SAMUEL OWOOLA. Born in Ibadan, Oyo State on August 22, 1919, he attended Ibadan Grammar School. He became a member of the Western House of Assembly in 1951 as an Action Group member and, from 1953 to 1966, he was the Federal Treasurer of the party. In 1957 he became the Executive Director of the Western Nigeria Development Corporation and as such in 1962, during the Action Group crisis, his bank account was one of those that were examined by the Coker Commission of Inquiry.

LEGAL SYSTEM. With the exception of the courts which administer Islamic personal law in some parts of the northern states and courts which administer customary law in some other states, the Nigerian legal system conforms with the British legal system. There are the Magistrate Courts, State and Federal High Courts, Courts of Appeal and the Supreme Court. The head of the judicial system is the Chief Justice, who is appointed by the President with the consent of the Senate. A judge may retire at the age of 60 years but he has to retire at 65. Any judge who retires at 65 is entitled to pension for

life at the rate equivalent to his last annual salary in addition
to any other retirement benefits to which he may be entitled.

LEGISLATIVE COUNCIL. After the annexation of Lagos in 1861
    whereby Lagos became a Crown Colony, the colonial author-
    ities in accordance with the British policy in Crown Colonies
    set up a small body known as the Legislative Council. Its
    purpose was to advise the Governor in framing legislation for
    the colony but the Governor did not need to accept its advice.
    It was not a representative body. It was composed of the Gov-
    ernor, government officials and unofficial nominated members.
        In 1923, the Council was reorganized to provide for four
    elected African members, three from Lagos and one from Cal-
    abar. Its advisory role was to cover the whole of the South-
    ern provinces. This arrangement lasted until 1947 when the
    Richards Constitution came into force. The Council was re-
    placed by a more representative All-Nigerian Council in which
    both the northern and the southern representatives sat to dis-
    cuss Nigerian affairs.

LEGITIMATE COMMERCE. Owing to the many pressures put on
    the British government by many organizations and individuals
    to put an end to slave trading, parliament in London abolished
    the slave trade in 1807 and efforts from then on were directed
    at finding suitable substitutes, then called legitimate commerce;
    that is, trade in tropical produce like palm oil instead of the
    abolished slave trade. The desire to get such products made
    people in Britain want to penetrate into the hinterland and led
    to the exploration of the Niger River by people like Mungo
    Park, a Scottish doctor, and Richard and John Lander, who
    were brothers. By 1830, it had become clear that the Niger
    emptied itself into the Atlantic through the delta from which
    Europeans had been obtaining their slaves. This discovery
    encouraged the British government to sponsor trading expedi-
    tions to the lower Niger. The first of these failed in 1841 be-
    cause of the high mortality among the men on the ship as a
    result of the malaria fever. However when quinine was dis-
    covered, another expedition was launched in 1856, with no lives
    lost, thanks to the use of the new drug, entreprenuers like
    Macgregor Laird, a Liverpool businessman, began the pioneer-
    ing search for legitimate trade on the lower Niger. This they
    initially found in palm oil.

LIEUTENANT GOVERNOR. After the amalgamation of the Southern
    and the Northern protectorates, there were appointed one Lieu-
    tenant Governor for each of the former protectorates and he
    was responsible to the Governor-General in Lagos. Each Lieu-
    tenant Governor was charged with the administration of the
    former protectorate to which he was appointed. When Sir Don-
    ald Cameron became governor of Nigeria in 1931, he abolished
    the offices of Lieutenant Governors and renamed them Chief
    Commissioners. Under the Macpherson Constitution of 1951
    the office of Lieutenant Governor was reinstated and each

Lieutenant Governor was in charge of each of the three regions in which Nigeria was divided. Under the 1954 Federal Constitution, the Lieutenant Governors became Governors over their regions while the Governor at the center became the Governor-General.

LINGUISTIC GROUPS. In Nigeria there are many linguistic groups commonly referred to as ethnic groups or tribes. These groups range in size from a few thousand people to many millions of people. There are however three major groups: the Hausa-Fulani group predominantly inhabiting the northern part of the country, the Yorubas inhabiting the southwest, and the Ibos living in the southeastern part of the country. Besides these three major groups there are several other linguistic groups like the Edos, Gwaris, Ibiobios, Itsekiris, Kanuris, Tivs, Urhobos, Nupes and others.

LIPEDE, OBA MICHAEL MOFOLORUNSO OYEBADE (THE ALAKE OF ABEOKUTA). Born in 1915 in Abeokuta, Ogun State, Oba Oyebade Lipede, the only surviving son of his parents, attended St. Peter's School, Ake, Abeokuta and later went to Abeokuta Grammar School and the C.M.S. Grammar School in Lagos. In 1937 after his secondary school education, he joined the Department of Customs and Excise. He later worked in many parts of Nigeria, especially in Warri, Sapele, Port Harcourt and Calabar, as a staff of the Nigerian Produce Marketing Company Limited. While still under this company, he served also in England, Belgium, and Hamburg in Germany. In 1956, Oba Lipede was one of the first two Nigerians promoted as Shipping Officers and after 34 years in the government service Oba Lipede retired in 1971. He became an Oba, the Alake of Egbaland in 1972.

LITTLE ELECTION. The Little Election was held in March 1965 as a result of the UPGA's boycott of the federal elections of December 1964 in the former Eastern Nigeria. The boycott was occasioned by the then unprobed allegation of election malpractices in many parts of the federation, especially in the north and in the west and the government rejection of the call to postpone the elections.

LOCAL AUTHORITY POLICE FORCE. During the colonial period, up till the First Republic, there were Local Authority Police forces, which operated side by side with the Nigeria Police Force, but their jurisdiction was limited to their local authority areas. These forces were merged with the Nigeria Police Force during the military era.

LOCAL GOVERNMENT. Up until 1976, local government in Nigeria was within the complete authority of the state government, and as such, local governments had suffered continuous whittling down of their powers. They lacked adequate funds and appropriate institutions to carry out their functions efficiently and effectively, and excessive politicking characterized the life of local governments during the first republic. Furthermore, each state decided on the type of local government it wanted, and exercised the power of life and death over it.

In 1976, the federal military government decided to rescue local government from some of the problems that plagued it, by recognizing it as the third tier of governmental activity in the nation. The government then issued its <u>Guidelines for Local Government Reform</u> which laid down a uniform type of local government for the nation. Each local government was to have not less than 150,000 people except in exceptional cases, and each was given specific functions to be administered by a popularly elected council. Under the 1979 constitution, the system of local government by democratically elected Local Government Council was guaranteed. The constitution went further to assign them specific functions and to guarantee them a share in the public revenue collected by the federal government, which presently stands at 10 percent. However state governments still have the power to create local governments and to supervise their activities.

LOKOJA. A town in Kwara State of Nigeria, it is important geographically because of its position at the confluence of rivers Niger and Benue. The members of the 1841 expedition (which included Samuel Ajayi Crowther who, 23 years later became Bishop of the Niger territories), sent by the British government, bought a piece of land from the local chiefs and later set up what they called a model farm. Lokoja became the headquarters of British trade and influence and from there they established routes into the Hausa states of the north and to Lagos. In 1865 the British established a consulate at Lokoja but because of the hostilities of the Africans towards the white settlers, it had to be closed down in 1869. Lokoja was originally made the capital of the Northern Protectorate, but the capital was later moved to Jebba. Today Lokoja is a local government headquarters in Kwara State and a tourist attraction.

LUGARD, SIR FREDERICK. A British colonial administrator, born in India in 1858, he began a career in the army after his education. He served in Nyasaland (Malawi) in 1888, in Kenya in 1889 and in Uganda in 1890. He entered the service of the Royal Niger Company in 1894 and negotiated a number of treaties of protection with local rulers and succeeded in bringing Borgu under the Royal Niger Company. He later left Nigeria to lead an expedition to extend the pacification and trading role of the South African Company upon Bechuanaland (Botswana). In 1897 he was called upon by the British government to organize and command the West African Frontier Force with which to defend British interest and possession against the French and the German claims to territories in Northern Nigeria. In 1900 when the British government revoked the charter of the company, he was appointed the first High Commissioner of the northern territories. Between 1901 and 1903 he was engaged in the pacification and conquest of the Sokoto Caliphate which was created by Usman Dan Fodio. In 1903 he told the newly appointed Sultan of Sokoto that Fulani rule established in the territories during the Jihad had come under the British. He also annexed territories outside Sokoto.

In 1907 Lord Lugard left Nigeria to be governor of Hong Kong but in 1912 he was brought back to Nigeria with the task of unifying the north with the south. After the amalgamation of the two territories in 1914, he became the Governor General of the Colony and Protectorate of Nigeria. In addition to the legislative council which then existed he set up the Nigerian Council which was a larger body with the hope that the newly united country should have a larger advisory body which would be fairly representative of the Chiefs and other people, but with an official majority.

Lord Lugard is generally associated with the system of Indirect Rule which was later accepted by the British as the best method of administering Africa. He resorted to this method out of necessity: he did not know enough of the culture of the people and he did not have sufficient British officials to administer directly such a vast territory. According to the system, British officials ruled the people indirectly, through the chiefs. The British government assumed power to appoint Emirs and Chiefs who ruled over their people provided their rule was not repugnant to British moral standards. The chiefs were to collect taxes as appointed by the High Commissioner and they were to be advised by the British officials known as residents. The system succeeded fairly well, but met with opposition when extended to the south, especially in Eastern Nigeria where the people had not developed such centralized administration as existed under the Emirs or the Obas in Western Nigeria.

In 1919 Lord Lugard retired from public service and three years later he published his famous book The Dual Mandate in British Tropical Africa. The thesis of the book was that Europe was in Africa for the mutual benefit of her own industrial classes and of the native races in their progress to a higher plane. He argued that the benefit could be made reciprocal and that it was the aim of civilized administration to fulfill this dual mandate.

Thus, Lord Lugard has played a very prominent role in the making of modern Nigeria. He died in 1945.

LYTTELTON CONSTITUTION. The Lyttelton Constitution came in 1954 as a result of the two constitutional conferences held in London between July and August 1953 and in Lagos between January and February 1954. At the conferences, the defects of the Macpherson Constitution were highlighted and agreements were reached on major changes that were necessary to remedy those defects.

Under the constitution, Nigeria became a federation of three regions: Northern, Eastern and Western. Lagos, which was formerly part of the Western Region, became a federal

territory, while Southern Cameroon which was previously administered as part of the Eastern Region, ceased to be part
of that region; it however remained part of the federation of
Nigeria as a quasi-federal territory.

The federal legislature was unicameral and consisted of
a Speaker, three ex-officio members and 184 representative
members elected independently of the regional legislatures on
the basis of single-member district.   The north had 92 representatives while the west and the east had 42 representatives
respectively; Southern Cameroon sent in six members while
Lagos sent in two.   The House could legislate on the exclusive
and the concurrent legislative lists, while the regional houses
could legislate on areas not in the exclusive legislative list
and also on the concurrent list.   However, federal laws would
prevail over regional laws.

The Council of Ministers consisted of the Governor-
General who presided, three official members, three members
from each region and one member representing the Cameroon.
These ministers were appointed by the governor from members
directly elected to the House, on the advice of the Regional
Executive.

While the constitution did not provide for the post of a
Prime Minister for the federation, it however established the
position of a Premier for each of the regions.   The regional
governor was given the power to appoint the leader of the
party that commanded the regional house as Premier.

By this constitution, the public service in Nigeria and
the judiciary were also regionalized.

-M-

MABOLAJE GRAND ALLIANCE.   Organized in 1953 in Ibadan, the
then-capital of Western Nigeria, by Alhaji Adegoke Adelabu,
Mabolaje Grand Alliance was a political party with its base in
Ibadan and in alliance with the National Council of Nigerian
Citizens (NCNC) which at that time was the party in opposition
to the Action Group (AG), then gradually increasing its hold on
the region.   The alliance was very popular as can be seen from
the sweeping victory in the Ibadan District Council elections of
1954 and 1958 where it won 35 and 28 seats respectively out
of 43 seats, in spite of the efforts of the Action Group to win
substantial support in the capital.   Adelabu however died in a
motor accident in 1958 and the alliance broke into two factions,
one led by Adeoye Adisa who succeeded to the Adelabu's seat
in the regional house of assembly and the other by Mojeed
Agbaje, Chairman of Ibadan District Council, elected in 1958.
This spelled the end of the Alliance for, with Adelabu out of
the way, the Action Group increased its support and the NCNC
began to assert more and more its freedom and independence.

MACAULAY, HERBERT.   Born on November 14, 1884. He lost his
father at the age of 13 and graduated from Lagos Grammar

School at 14. He worked as a clerk with the Public Works
Department in Lagos. He was later granted a scholarship by
the Governor of the Colony of Lagos, Sir Alfred Moloney, to
train in England as a land surveyor and a civil engineer. Upon
returning from England, he took appointment with the colonial
government as a surveyor in Lagos. He resigned his appointment in 1898 after working for the government for five years
and set up his own private practice as a licensed surveyor and
civil engineer in Lagos.

Macaulay became interested in politics and successfully
opposed a number of unpopular measures proposed by the colonial government in Lagos. The one that made him most popular was the Apapa Land Case of 1920 in which a chief in Lagos, Chief Amadu Oluwa, demanded compensation for land compulsorily acquired by the government. Macaulay and the Chief
successfully fought the government in court up to the Privy
Council in London and he returned home a hero.

Herbert Macaulay was first in many ways. He was the
grandson of Bishop Ajayi Crowther, who was the first African
Bishop in West Africa, the son of the first Principal of the
first Grammar School in Nigeria, King's College and the first
Nigerian to be given a scholarship to have professional training in England. He founded the first political party in Nigeria,
the Nigerian National Democratic Party (NNDP) which had as
its goals local self-government, expanded educational and commercial opportunities for the people and Africanization of the
civil service. Strictly speaking however, it was a Lagos organization for it concentrated much of its efforts on Lagos affairs and received much of its support from the traditional
leaders. Macaulay also was the founder of the first daily
newspaper in Nigeria, the Lagos Daily News, which he used
effectively to arouse nationalist sentiments in the country and
which today remains a reference journal of the pioneering
phase of nationalist movement in the country.

Macaulay was the Chairman of the meeting held at the
Glover Memorial Hall in 1944, called at the instance of the
National Union of Students in connection with the King's College
Boys' Strike. This meeting gave birth to a new political party,
the National Congress of Nigeria and the Cameroons (NCNC).
Macaulay was elected the President of the party while Dr.
Nnamdi Azikiwe was General Secretary.

In 1945 when the Richards Constitution--which fell short
of nationalist expectations--was being proposed for Nigeria, the
NCNC led a campaign against it. In 1946 Macaulay and other
NCNC leaders began a campaign tour of the country against
the constitution, sought support of the people for the position
of the party and raised funds for a representation to London.
Macaulay fell sick in Kano and was rushed back to Lagos. He
died the second day on May 7, 1946. Before the military relinquished power in 1979, Herbert Macaulay had been declared
by the federal military government a national hero and his portrait is on every Nigerian naira.

MACPHERSON CONSTITUTION. Sir John Macpherson became Governor of Nigeria in 1948 and announced that rather than wait for nine years after the Richards Constitution of 1946 before making any changes, as was formerly proposed, he was prepared during the second three-year period to agree to constitutional changes if it was the wish of the country. Accordingly before the constitution was adopted there were series of conferences both at the provincial and regional levels and at the All-Nigerian Constitutional Conference at Ibadan in 1950. The constitution that ensued was thus named after Sir John Macpherson.

The constitution promulgated in 1951 provided for a Council of Ministers made up of six ex-officio members and 12 Nigerian ministers, four from each Regional House of Assembly. The responsibility of each minister was limited to dealing in the legislative assembly with matters concerning his ministry and introducing in the Council of Ministers matters concerning his ministry and to see that the decisions taken by the Council of Ministers were carried out by appropriate officials. The constitution did not make the Minister responsible for the framing of the policy of his ministry.

The constitution provided for a House of Representatives consisting of 142 members of which 136 were Nigerians. In both the north and the west, the constitution also provided for a bicameral legislature, the House of Assembly and the House of Chiefs, while in the east, there was only one legislative house, the House of Assembly. The constitution also provided for the Public Service Commission to advise the Governor on matters affecting the public service.

In spite of the consultations that went into its making, the constitution later proved unworkable and had to be replaced in 1954.

MACPHERSON, SIR JOHN. Born in 1898, Sir John Macpherson became the Governor of the Colony and Protectorate of Nigeria in 1948. His first major concern was the reform of the local government system. His government initiated first in the Eastern region the transformation of the Native Authority system to the Local Government Council system modelled on the British system. He then proposed that beginning in 1950 there would be a review of the 1947 constitution if the people so wished. This review led to the 1951 constitution, christened the Macpherson Constitution. Owing to the Constitutional Crisis of 1953, new efforts were initiated in 1953 to review the constitution in London and in 1954 in Lagos. This gave rise to the Federal Constitution of 1954, at which time Sir John Macpherson became the Governor-General of the federation. He officially opened the Ibadan branch of the Nigerian College of Arts, Science and Technology in 1954. He left Nigeria in 1955 and was succeeded by Sir J. W. Robertson.

"MAITATSINE" (MARWA, MUHAMMADU). Mahammadu Marwa, alias "Maitatsine" an illegal Cameroonian citizen in Nigeria, was a religious Muslim fanatic who claimed to be the right and true prophet of Allah, a claim which the orthodox Moslems believe is heretical since Prophet Muhammed was the last and greatest of all the prophets. From 1980 to 1985 Maitatsine religious disturbances occurred in many parts of Northern Nigeria. It first surfaced in Kano in December 1980 and later spread to Kaduna State in 1981 and Maiduguri in Borno State in 1982. During the disturbances thousands of people, including Maitatsine himself, were killed. When the police could not handle the disturbances, the army had to be called in. In November 1982, the Council of State meeting at Abuja, the new state capital, agreed to make an order proscribing the Maitatsine Movement. Accordingly in November 1982, President Shehu Shagari signed the Muhammadu Marwa alias Maitatsine Movement (Declaration) order which declared the movement to be unlawful.

However on February 27, 1984, The Maitatsine Movement struck again, this time in Yola, Capital of Gongola State. In this new wave of disturbances, more than 130 people, including antiriot police officers, civilians and the Maitatsine zealots were killed. Many houses, and marketplaces were also set on fire.

MAJA, DR. AKINOLA. A medical practitioner, a politician and one of the early Nigerian intellectuals. He was a foundation member of the Nigerian Youth Movement (NYM) and its President from 1944 to 1951. In 1949 after the shooting incident in Enugu during which many miners were killed, many leading Nigerians formed the National Emergency Council to investigate, report and see that justice was done. Dr. Maja was elected Chairman of the Council. He was also a foundation member of the Egbe Omo Oduduwa and later became its President. He used to be referred to as "Father" of the Action Group Party, and when the Action Group crisis was brewing in 1962, he was called upon to intervene. He was also one of the founders of the National Bank of Nigeria in 1933, and later became the Chairman of the Board of Directors of the Bank.

MAJEKODUNMI, CHIEF MOSES ADEKOYEJO. Physician and politician, born August 17, 1916 at Abeokuta Ogun State, he was educated at the Abeokuta Grammar School, St. Gregory's College, Lagos, Trinity College, Dublin where he received a Diploma in Child Health and Master of Obstetric Art. He then became a house physician at the National Children's Hospital in Dublin from 1941 to 1943. Upon his return to Nigeria, he was appointed federal medical officer from 1943 to 1949 and then a consulting obstetrician at the Massey Street Maternity Hospital in Lagos, General Hospital in Lagos and Greek Hospital in Lagos from 1949 to 1960. He was also appointed a Senior Specialist Obstetrician of the Nigerian Federal Government Medical Services.

In 1960, Dr. Majekodunmi became a Senator and leader of the Senate in the First Republic and was appointed Federal Minister of State for the army and in 1961 he was Federal

Minister of Health.   In 1962 during the Action Group crisis in
Western Nigeria, when a state of emergency was declared for
the Western Region, Dr. Majekodunmi was appointed Administrator for Western Nigeria.   In 1965 he was made the federal
Minister of Health and Information.
      Dr. Majekodunmi was the former Director of Barclays
Bank of Nigeria, former Director of the Westminster Dredging
Company Limited and was appointed a member of the Board of
Governors of St. Gregory's College in Lagos.   He was a Fellow of the Royal College of Obstetricians and Gynecologists and
a fellow of the Royal College of Physicians.   He was awarded
many honorary degrees including LL.D. from the University
of Dublin and D.Sc. from the University of Lagos.   His foreign
honors include Companion Order of St. Michael and St. George
(CMG).   He published many books including Premature Infants:
Management and Prognosis.

MALARIA.   Malaria was one of the most dreaded diseases by the
    white man in Nigeria.   Because of the number of Europeans
who died of the disease during the exploration of Nigeria, Nigeria and other West African countries were referred to as
the "white man's grave."   Malaria is caused by the bite of
anopheles mosquitoes, and it is characterized by chills and high
fever.   However the incidence of this disease has been greatly
reduced through the campaign on environmental hygiene to reduce stagnant water where mosquitoes breed and the use of
drugs that serve as prophylactics against malaria.   Furthermore
the effect of the disease has also been reduced through the use
of drugs like quinine and its many variations.   It is to be noted
that the dread of the disease helped in no small way to dis-
courage permanent white settlement in Nigeria in contrast to
many other places.

MALIKI, ALHAJI ABDUL.   Born in 1914, he was the son of the
    Atta of Igbira, a traditional ruler in the Kwara State.   He re-
ceived his education at the Katsina Training College and taught
for some years at Okene Middle School (1934-1935).   In 1936
he was appointed supervisor of Native Authority Works.   In
1939 he was Provincial Clerk in Katsina.   In 1940 he became
the Chief Officer of Igbira Native Authority and also Chairman
of Okene Town Council.   In 1950 he took a local government
training course in Britain.   On his arrival, he joined the Northern People's Congress (NPC) and became a member of the
Northern Regional House of Assembly, and in 1952 a member
of the Federal House of Representatives.   In 1955 he was appointed Commissioner to the United Kingdom for Northern Nigeria.   In 1958, he joined the federal diplomatic service and
after independence he became the first High Commissioner to
the United Kingdom.   In 1966 he was transferred to France as
Ambassador.   He died in 1969 while on leave at home.

MANUWA, SIR SAMUEL LAYINKA AYODEJI.   Born on March 4,
    1903 in Ijebu-Ode Ogun State, he received his education at

many schools including the CMS Grammar School and King's
College, all in Lagos. After his secondary education in 1921,
he went on to the University of Edinburgh to study medicine.
In 1926 he went to the University of Liverpool, England where
he received a diploma in Tropical Medicine and Hygiene. Upon
arrival in Nigeria in 1927 he was appointed a Medical Officer
and a Senior Surgical Specialist. He served in many capacities
and was a member of many scholarly associations. He served
on the Federal Public Service Commission and was Pro-
Chancellor and Chairman of the University Council of the University of Ibadan, 1961 to 1975. He published many books including Hernia in the West African Negro (1929), Mental Health
in Commonwealth (1967), and Mass Campaign as an Instrument
of Endemic Disease Control in Developing Countries.
He died in 1975.

MARIERE, CHIEF SAMUEL JERETON. The first Governor of the
Mid-Western Region, Chief Samuel Jereton Mariere was born
in 1907 at Evwreni, Urhobo Division of the Bendel State. He
was educated at St. Andrew's School, Warri. He then taught
at the African School at Okpari (1927-1928). In 1929 he began
to work for Mukoro Mowoe & Co., founded by Chief Mukoro
Mowoe, a relation of his, where he stayed until 1938. He
later joined the John Holt Company and stayed there until his
retirement in 1961.

Chief Mariere was active in political activities as far
back as the 1930's. He was a member of the Urhobo Progressive Union and became its Secretary-General in 1935. He later
joined the National Council of Nigeria and the Cameroons
(NCNC). He was elected an NCNC member of the House of
Representatives for Urhobo East in 1954 and later in 1959 for
Urhobo Central. When the Mid-Western Region was created
in 1963 he became its first Governor. When the military seized
power in 1966, he, like other Governors, lost his job, but was
later appointed adviser to the Military Governor. In 1968 he
became the Chancellor of the University of Lagos and also
Chairman, State School Board, Mid-Western State. He was
honored with many traditional titles and was awarded an honorary LL.D. degree of the University of Nigeria, Nsukka and
that of Ibadan, all in 1964. He died in 1971.

MARKETING BOARDS. Before the 1954 Federal Constitution, Marketing Boards were organized on a nationwide basis. The Nigerian
Cocoa Marketing Board was established by law in 1947, the Nigerian Groundnut (peanut) Marketing Board in 1949, the Nigerian
Oil Palm Produce Marketing Board in 1949, and the Nigerian
Cotton Marketing Board in 1954. These boards were set up
to secure a most favorable arrangements for the purchase and
evacuation of agricultural produce intended for export. As
such they were placed in a monopolistic position since they
had complete control of purchases of such agricultural export
products. The Board fixed the buying prices at the beginning
of each season. In the second place they generally adopted

different grades for the same products and paid different prices for each grade in order to improve the quality of the products. This system was much criticized because, while it stabilized prices of agricultural produce and so lessened the impact of price fluctuation on farmers, it nonetheless set and maintained producer prices throughout each season at a rate much below the world market prices and thus accumulated a lot of surpluses which should have gone to the farmers but which never did. Under the 1954 Federal Constitution agriculture became a regional matter and the purchase of agricultural produce was reorganized on a regional basis, leading to establishment of regional marketing boards and the division of the assets of the former Boards among the regional Boards. However the export of crops was a federal matter and therefore there was then a Central Produce Marketing Board to export the crops purchased by the Regional Marketing Boards.

In 1977, the military administration, in a reform effort, reverted to what used to be before the 1954 constitution. Seven new Commodity Marketing Boards (CMB), each operating on a nationwide basis, were set up.

It should be noted that the surpluses generated by the purchase and exports of the produce were used by regional governments to finance regional development corporations to further agricultural and industrial development and, as the Coker Commission of Inquiry showed, some of the surpluses indirectly found their way to party accounts.

MARKETS. In Nigeria, a market is a place where sellers and buyers go to sell or buy. They both bargain over prices in an effort to maximize their gains and satisfaction. Nearly all Nigerian towns have their own marketplaces. The markets are generally of two types: the daily markets and the periodic markets. The daily markets are common in all parts of Nigeria while the periodic markets are common in Southern Nigeria. The periodic markets are either open every four, five or nine days, weekly or fortnightly. The commodities common in Nigerian marketplaces are assorted types of foodstuffs, meat, vegetables, clothes and various other goods ranging from provisions to cosmetics. The various craftsmen use the marketday to display or carry on their trade such as blacksmiths, bicycle repairers, tailors, sewing mistresses and tinkers. The essential difference between the market in a southern town and in a northern town is that both men and women are sellers of commodities in the south but in the north, men predominate. This may be explained by the fact that in the north, Moslem women are expected to stay in their purdah.

There are other social activities that do take place in the Nigerian traditional markets, especially the periodic markets. They serve as centers of communication and information networks. Markets do provide opportunities for religious and ritual performances by people meeting on particular days and for political or other announcements by rulers and leaders. It also provides an opportunity for the exchange of views between friends and kinsmen from neighboring villages and towns. Also, both males and females utilize the market day and market-place as an opportunity for recruiting sexual partners.

MARKPRESS. Markpress, an abbreviation for Market Press, was the Biafran Overseas Press Service. It was Biafra's public relations firm based in Geneva to propagate the Biafran cause. The owner and director of Markpress was William Bernhardt, an American public relations expert. Though the first press release was made in February 1968, the effort was not successful until April, when the first organized group correspondents' reports about starvation in Biafra became a good propaganda issue.

The agency was linked by telex to Biafra via Lisbon, which was the main Biafran base and communications center. Markpress's success in selling Biafra to the world was due in part to the hard work and dedication of the owner, William Bernhardt, who also served as a kind of a roving ambassador for Biafra, attending the peace conferences, and meeting important personalities.

MASS PURGE. The massive retirement of public officeholders during the second half of 1975 is known as the Mass Purge. The decision to purge the public services in the federation of all undesirable elements was taken by the new military regime of Murtala and Obasanjo, which overthrew the Gowon regime on July 29, 1975. The second day, new Head of State Brigadier Murtala Muhammed announced the compulsory retirement of all officers of the rank of General and the equivalent in other services, the military governors, the Inspector General and the Deputy Inspector General of Police. He also announced the dismissal of all federal and state Civil Commissioners. The purge of other officers started on August 5, 1975 and it cut across various ranks, ranging from other senior army officers, senior public servants, including the Chief Justice of the Federation who was retired for health reasons, to junior staff all over the nation. Various criteria were used to decide the fate of those retired. These included divided interest (that is, public servants who still had their private businesses) old age, poor health, inefficiency, corruption, incompetence and confidential reports based on the public servants' records. Unfortunately, many people in power turned the whole exercise into a kind of witch-hunt and personal vendetta, and when the government saw that the purposes of the purge were being abused, it was called to a halt, but not until about 10,000 public officers had been retired or dismissed.

While the purge had its salutary effects, it nonetheless undermined the sense of security which had hitherto characterized seeking a career in the public services and it disposed any public servant to begin to look out for a greater sense of security for himself and his family. Some left the services, some of those who remained saw the period of service as a period to make as much money as possible and get out to start their own businesses, while some others continued their private businesses pari passu with their public services at the expense of the latter. Thus rather than reduce indiscipline and corruption in the public services, it appears to have increased them.

This corruption and indiscipline had a field day during the civilian administration that succeeded the military in October 1979. And when the military intervened again in December 1983, there were calls that many public officials should be investigated and retired, especially for the role many of them played in the general elections of 1983. The new military administration began a slow and quiet retrenchment of public officers, including teachers, which, after its completion, would be perhaps much more than the Mass Purge of 1975.

MBANEFO, SIR LOUIS NWACHUKWU. A jurist born in 1911, he went to St. Mary's School in Onitsha, the Methodist Grammar School and later to King's College, both in Lagos. In 1935 he obtained a Bachelor of Law degree from the University of London and was called to the bar at the Middle Temple. He then went to King's College, Cambridge where he got a B.A. in History, followed by an M.A. in 1937.

Upon arrival in Nigeria, he set up his law practice in Onitsha. In 1939, he became a member of the Onitsha Town Council. In 1950, he was a member of the Eastern House of Assembly and represented the Eastern Region at the Legislative Council in Lagos in 1950 and 1951. In 1952 he was appointed Judge of the Supreme Court, and in 1956, following the regionalization of the judiciary consequent on the adoption of a federal constitution in 1954, he became a Judge of the High Court of Eastern Nigeria. In 1958, he was transferred to Lagos as a Judge of the Federal Supreme Court of Appeal but he went back to the East in 1959 as the Chief Justice of the region. In 1961 he was appointed an Ad Hoc Judge of the International Court of Justice (ICJ).

In addition to his services on the bench, he was appointed to many important positions. In 1946, his hard work and devotion to the Anglican church earned him recognition and he was made the Chancellor of the Anglican Diocese of the Niger. He was Pro-Chancellor of the University of Ibadan, 1965-1967, Chairman of the Board of Governors of Iyi Enu Hospital in Ogidi, Anambra State and during the Biafran civil war, he represented Biafra on several trips abroad, including the meeting in Kampala, Uganda in 1968. In 1970, he took part in the formal surrender of Biafran soldiers to the federal government in Lagos. He was knighted in 1961 by Queen Elizabeth II and in 1963 he received an honorary degree of Doctor of Laws from the University of Nigeria, Nsukka. In 1972, he was made a Fellow of the University of London. He died in 1977.

MELLANBY, DR. KENNETH. The first Principal of the Ibadan University College. Appointed in May 1947, he worked hard to settle the college in its permanent site within a short time and saw to the rapid academic and physical development of the institution. In his honor, a hall of residence at the university was named after him. He left the institution in 1960.

MEMORANDUM ON EDUCATION POLICY IN BRITISH TROPICAL AFRICA. As a result of the 1922 Phelps-Stokes Report entitled Education in Africa, the British government felt it had to do something about the criticisms levelled against colonial government education policy. The Colonial Office in London therefore set up an advisory committee on Native Education in the British Tropical African Dependencies in 1923 to advise the Secretary of State on matters of native education. As a result of this, the government in 1925 issued its education policy contained in the Memorandum on Education in British Tropical Africa. Requirements of the policy include the following: government would encourage voluntary educational efforts, but it reserved to itself the right to direct education policy and supervise educational institutions by inspection and other means; education should be adapted to the aptitudes, occupations and traditions of the people while conserving as far as possible all sound and healthy elements in the social life of the people; religious training and moral instruction should be related to the condition of life and the daily experience of the people; there should be set up in each dependency an advisory board on education to advise the government; voluntary agency schools which conform to the standard laid down should be grant-aided and teacher training institutions should be guided by the provision of the memorandum; and technical and vocational training should also be carried out with the help of government department and supervision.

The memorandum, in short, accepted the report of the Phelps-Stokes Report and tried to adopt it.

METHODIST CHURCH. The Methodist missionaries were the first to reach Badagry in 1842, setting up a mission house there. They were also the first to set up a western-type school by the name of Nursery of the Infant Church after the slave trade had virtually wiped out the initial efforts of the Catholic church in the Benin kingdom in the early sixteenth century.

MIDDLE BELT PEOPLES PARTY (MBPP). A splinter party from the Middle Zone League (MZL). The MBPP was formed in 1953 in opposition to the decision of the MZL to ally itself with the Northern People's Congress (NPC), which was the ruling party in the north. The MBPP demanded the creation of a Middle Belt State in the Northern Region.

MIDDLE-BELT STATE MOVEMENT. In 1955 there was a movement, led by the late Joseph S. Tarka, leader of United Middle Belt Congress, an ally of the Action Group Party, demanding the creation of the Middle-Belt State out of the former Northern Region. The state was to comprise all the minority groups of Northern Nigeria, an area which was made up of the Benue,

Plateau and Kwara states. The Northern People's Congress (NPC), which was in power in the north with the motto of "One north irrespective of tribes or religion," was opposed to this idea. But in 1967, during the military administration, their wish came true: the Benue Plateau Area was created into a state and so was Kwara Area. In 1976, Benue Plateau State was further split into Benue State and Plateau State.

MIDDLE ZONE LEAGUE. A broad-based ethnic minority movement in the Northern Region. It was formed in 1950 to fight for the creation of a separate region from the Northern Region.

MID-WEST DEMOCRATIC FRONT. An alliance made up of the Mid-West People's Party (MPP), a branch of the Northern People's Congress (NPC), the regional branches of the United People's Party (UPP) and the Action Group (AG). The Front can be regarded as containing all the elements in the newly created region who were opposed to the National Council of Nigerian Citizens (NCNC), and who were struggling for their political life.

In the 1964 Mid-Western election, the parties did not field common candidates. Each of the parties, by fielding separate candidates, became very weak and they all lost badly to the NCNC, winning 11 out of the 65 seats. In the realignment for the 1964 federal elections, the Front joined the Nigerian National Alliance (NNA), made up of the NPC and the Nigerian National Democratic Party (NNDP) of Chief Akintola in the Western Region. In April 1965, almost all the members of the MDF crossed to the NCNC, the government party in the region, and the leader of the carpet-crossers announced the formal dissolution of the MDF.

In 1966, after the military takeover of government, the party was banned along with all the other political parties.

MID-WESTERN REGION. The Mid-Western Region is the name given to the first region created after independence. The region was originally part of the Western Region and while the Action Group controlled the politics of the region, the NCNC had a lot of support in the mid-west. The people of the mid-west being minorities in the Western Region had always made their intentions known to regional and federal governments that they wanted a region of their own, but it was not until the Action Group Crisis began in 1962 that they had their opportunity to get their own government. On August 9, 1963, the region was created. In 1967 when the 12-state structure came into being, the state became Mid-Western State and in 1976 when seven new states were created, it became the Bendel State, with minor boundary adjustments.

Mid-Western Region had an area of about 15,244 square miles with a population of about 2,536,000 people. The regional capital was Benin City with a population well over 200,000 people. Benin is well known all over the world for its bronze, brass and ivory works of art which visitors can always see in museums all over the world.

The Mid-Western Region produced most of Nigeria's lump and crepe rubber and supplied much of the country's timber. What is more, it supplies about 40 percent of Nigeria's crude oil. The mid-west area is fairly well endowed with natural resources including natural gas and limestone. The region is made up of five main ethnic groups: the Edos, the Ishans, the Urhobos, the Ibos and the Itsekiris. See also BENDEL.

MID-WESTERN STATE see BENDEL STATE.

MID-WEST PEOPLE'S CONGRESS (MPC). A political party formed in 1963. It was a branch of the Northern People's Congress (NPC) in the Mid-Western Region. After cracks in the coalition between the NPC and the National Council of Nigerian Citizens (NCNC) began to show, the NPC, in an effort to establish itself as a national party and extend its political support, decided to establish branches in the other regions of the country. The MPC was led by Apostle John Edokpolo who was then the Commissioner of Trade and Industries in the Mid-Western Interim government.

MID-WEST STATE MOVEMENT. An ethnic minority movement formed in 1956 under the leadership of Chief Dennis Osadebey, the leader of opposition in the Western House of Assembly, its aim was to see that the Mid-Western Region was created. Being led by members of the National Council of Nigeria and Cameroon (NCNC) it soon became a part of the NCNC and was later absorbed by it. However the Mid-Western Region was created in 1963.

MIGRATION. Population migration is the movement of people in and out of a country within a specific period of time. Within the country there is the usual rural-urban migration. Because of wage-earning employment and availability of many social services in the cities, people--young and old--do move from the rural areas of the country to the urban centers. Some of them look for employment while others start small trading businesses. This type of migration accounts for the rapid growth rate of cities like Lagos, Ibadan, Kaduna, Port Harcourt and Enugu.

Migration outside the country rose in the 1950's when some Nigerians emigrated to Ghana to work in the gold mines. Because of Ghana's prosperity at the time, migration between Nigeria and Ghana could be said to be one-way. Also some Nigerians went to Equatorial Guinea to work and many of them became successful there. However most of the citizens of West African countries living and working in Ghana in 1969 were ordered out of the country in that year during the rule of Dr. Kofi Busia.

In the latter part of the 1970's, the trend in migration began to change. As a result of the oil boom in Nigeria and the ECOWAS Treaty, which eliminated the need to obtain a visa before a citizen of a member country could travel to another member country, many immigrants from neighboring another member country, many immigrants from neighboring countries came into Nigeria in search of work; in construction companies, schools (as teachers) and in many other establishments. In 1982 the federal government saw the need to stem the tide and it ordered illegal aliens to leave the country. Most of them left, but many of them, taking advantage of the ECOWAS Treaty and corrupt custom officials, have since returned.

MILITARY COUPS. Nigeria has witnessed one attempted and five successful coups d'état. The first occurred on January 15, 1966; and the then-Prime Minister, Alhaji Tafawa Balewa; the Northern Premier, Alhaji Ahmadu Bello; the Western Premier, Chief S. L. Akintola, and Chief Festus Okotie-Eboh were killed. The late Major Kaduna Nzeogwu was the leader of the coup planners but Major-General Ironsi emerged as the leader of the government that was formed.

The second coup occurred on July 29, 1966, claiming the lives of Major General Ironsi, Lt. Col. Adekunle Fajuyi and many military men. This coup brought General Yakubu Gowon to the head of the army and also made him Head of State.

The third coup occurred on July 29, 1975. A bloodless coup, it toppled the government of General Gowon, and General Murtala Muhammed emerged as the new Head of State. The attempted coup, led by Col. B. S. Dimka, occurred on February 13, 1976, and claimed the life of General Murtala Muhammed. Since the coup failed, the right-hand man of General Muhammed, General Olusegun Obasanjo, became Head of State.

The fourth successful coup took place on December 31, 1983, ending the Second Republic and the country's first experiment in presidential system of government. The coup brought Major-General Muhammadu Buhari to power. However, his administration did not last long--just under 20 months--for on August 27, 1985, he too was overthrown in a palace coup that brought Major-General Ibrahim Babangida to power. See also COUP D'ETAT.

MILVERTON, LORD (SIR ARTHUR RICHARDS). A distinguished public servant and Governor of Nigeria, 1943-1947. Born on February 21, 1885 in England, he served in many posts in the Federated Malay States before he became Governor of Borneo in 1930. He also served as Governor of the Gambia (1933-1936), Governor of Fiji and High Commissioner for the Western Pacific (1936-1938) and Governor of Jamaica (1938-1944). He became Governor of Nigeria in 1943.

As Governor of Nigeria, he succeeded Sir Bernard Bourdillion, who, before his retirement in 1943, had laid the groundwork for the review of the 1922 constitution and had tried to persuade the people in the north to begin to take an active part in the affairs of the country. Sir Arthur Richards built upon the work of his predecessor by redrafting his constitution. In 1944, Sir Arthur Richards' constitutional proposals were submitted to the Secretary of State for the Colonies, Colonel Oliver Stanley, without consulting public opinion or letting people know what he was planning. His objective was to draw up a constitution that would promote the unity of Nigeria, provide adequately for the diverse elements within the country and secure greater participation by Africans in the discussion of their own affairs. He recommended that the constitution remain in force for nine years subject to a limited review every three years.

The constitution came into effect in 1947. For the first time it provided for an unofficial majority in the Legislative Council and set up three regional councils for each of the three regions of the northern, eastern, and western provinces, each also having a majority of unofficial members.

The constitution, though an advance over previous ones, provoked a lot of criticism. Sir Arthur Richards retired in 1947 to be succeeded by Sir John Macpherson, who immediately upon arrival began measures to review the Richards Constitution.

MINERAL RESOURCES. Nigeria is rich in mineral resources like limestone, tin, columbite, iron ore, lead, zinc, gold, marble, coal, petroleum, natural gas and uranium. Some of these are being mined and are fairly well developed, but some others, like uranium, are still not being developed.

MINISTRY OF OVERSEAS DEVELOPMENT. The Ministry of Overseas Development was a ministerial department in the British government. The Ministry, on behalf of the British government, was one of the overseas agencies that helped the Nigerian universities during the first six years of independence.

The Ministry, through the London University, supplied a number of lecturers in the main branches of science, physics, chemistry, zoology, botany and biology. The program was called VISTA (Visiting Scientists Teaching Abroad).

MINORITIES PROBLEM. Each of the former three regions of Nigeria had its own share of ethnic minorities. The minorities in each region formed themselves into movements, agitating for constitutional safeguards against oppression from the larger ethnic groups that dominated the affairs of each region. For example, the Edos, Urhobos and the Western Ibos agitated for the creation of the Mid-Western State from the Western Region, while the peoples of Calabar, Ogoja and Rivers Area asked for Calabar-Ogoja-Rivers State (COR State) to be created from the Eastern Region. In the Northern Region, the peoples of the Middle Belt made up of Niger, Ilorin, Kabba and Plateau provinces, with parts of Adamawa and Zaria provinces, also asked for a separate existence from the Northern Region.

The minorities problem became a major political problem when it became clear that Nigeria was going to adopt a federal system of government. Since each region was dominated by one ethnic group which in turn controlled the dominant party in that region, the minorities began to feel that if they were to avoid oppression they had better ask for their own separate existence. The issue became very important between 1954, when Nigeria became a federation, and the 1957 Constitutional Conference in London. The Conference devoted much attention to the problem and finally agreed on setting up

a commission of inquiry to ascertain the facts about the fears
of minorities in any part of the country and to propose means
of allaying those fears whether or not they were well founded.
However, the British government made it clear that recommendations for the creation of new states before independence
should be seen as a last resort. Accordingly on September
26, 1957 the Minorities Commission was set up and it later
held hearings throughout the country.

Reactions to minorities demands were mixed in the regions. The north refused any fragmentation or adjustment of
any boundaries. While the west supported the creation of the
Mid-Western State, it contended that such exercise could be
carried out if other regions would comply. The east was opposed to any dismemberment as a sacrifice either for the sake
of national unity or for administrative convenience. The Commission's report was published in July 1958. It did not recommend the creation of new states, but recommended some pallia-
tive measures to allay the fears which it found really existed
in many places. For example, it recommended that certain
councils should be set up for minority areas of Calabar and
Benin and that the Niger Delta Development Board be established for the area. It also recommended the inclusion of
fundamental human rights in the federal constitution to protect
and safeguard the interests of both the minorities and the majorities.

Even though the Commission did not recommend the
creation of any state, in 1963 the people of Benin and the Delta
provinces succeeded in securing their own region called Mid-
Western region. In 1967, the administration of General Yakubu
Gowon decided in an effort: (1) to resolve the minorities problem, (2) to allay the fear of northern domination of the rest of
the country and (3) to weaken the Eastern Region, should that
region declare a secession from the rest of the country, to
divide the country into 12 states. However the 1967 creation
of states did not end all minorities' agitation for their own
states and in 1976 Nigeria became a federation of 19 states
under the regime of General Murtala Muhammed. In spite of
this, agitation for more states has continued. More and
more minorities have been asking for separate state identity
and it appears the demand will continue until every ethnic group
or every town gets its own state.

MONGUNO, SHETTIMA ALI. Born in 1926 in Monguno, Borno State
in 1926, he attended Monguno Elementary School, Borno Middle
School and Bauchi Teacher Training College. He also attended
the Katsina Higher College and the Nigerian College of Arts,
Science and Technology in Zaria. In 1958 he went to the College of Education, Moray House, Edinburgh and to Edinburgh
University.

On his return to Nigeria he became Education Secretary
to the Borno Local Authority. He later became Chairman, Education Committee of Borno Local Education Authority. In 1959
he became a member of Parliament in Lagos and a member of

the Northern People's Congress (NPC). He was appointed Minister of State for the Air Force in 1965 and later became Minister for Internal Affairs in 1965.

When the military came to power and began to appoint civil commissioners in 1967, he was appointed Commissioner for Industry and Commissioner for Trade in the same year and of Mines and Power in 1971 till 1975. He was a member of the Constituent Assembly, 1977 to 1978.

MOREL, EDMUND DERE. A journalist, born in 1873 in Paris, France. He later became interested in West Africa, read about it and wrote about it. In 1911 he wrote a book, Nigeria, Its Peoples and Its Problems, in which he proposed what he called "an unauthorized scheme of amalgamation" of the northern and the southern protectorates. He proposed that the country should be divided into provinces corresponding as far as possible with natural geographical boundaries and existing political conditions. He therefore suggested that the country should be divided into four provinces. According to him, the rivers Niger and Benue were to be the natural boundaries of the Western and Eastern provinces from a third province which roughly corresponded to the old Middle Belt and which he called Central Province. The remaining part of the country was to be the Northern Province. Each province was to be headed by a Lieutenant-Governor. His objective was to put an end to the north-south dichotomy, open the landlocked north to the sea through the rivers Niger and Benue. His proposals were not accepted, but they certainly gave an impetus to the demand for a separate region for the Middle Belt Area in the 1950's.

MORGAN COMMISSION. The Morgan Commission, headed by Justice Adeyinka Morgan, was set up in 1963 as a result of an industrial strike embarked upon by Nigerian workers on September 27, 1963, agitating for a general upward revision of wages and salaries of junior civil servants as well as junior employees in private establishments. The Commission was asked to investigate the existing wage structure, remuneration and conditions of service in wage-earning employments in the country and to make recommendations concerning a suitable new structure, as well as adequate machinery for a wages review on a continuing basis. It was also to examine the need for a general upward revision of salaries and wages of junior employees in both government and private establishments, the abolition of the daily-wage system, the introduction of national minimum wage and to make recommendations on all these problems. Because of the government's delay to release the report, workers staged a demonstration in Lagos on June 1, 1964, followed by a general strike on the second day. On June 3, 1964 the government released the report and the government white paper on it. The Commission recommended that the workers be paid a living wage, that is, wages high enough to enable them to support themselves and their families. The Commission then decided to divide the country into four zones and to recommend for each one what it felt should be a minimum wage. The government accepted the recommendations with some modifications.

MOSLEM RELIGION. A follower of Islam is called a Moslem by people who are not adherents of Islam. Islam, meaning submission in Arabic, is the name given to the religion established by Prophet Mohammed in the seventh century. A Moslem believes that there is only one god, Allah, and that Mohammed is his prophet. Allah, is to them the most high, the absolute creator and ruler of all things. Moslems also believe in the Holy Koran, in angels, in the Day of Judgment and in predestination.

The five main duties of Islam which a Moslem must fulfill are: (1) that there is no god but Allah and that Mohammed is his prophet; (2) he must say his prayers regularly five times a day; (3) he must fast during the month of Ramadan; (4) he must give alms in money and goods to the poor; and (5) he must, if he can afford it, make a pilgrimage to Mecca.

The Moslem religion is an important social factor which, like the Hausa language, unifies most of the people of the northern part of the country.

MUHAMMED, GENERAL MURTALA RAMAT. Former Head of State, born on November 8, 1938 in Kano, Murtala Muhammed was educated at Gidan Makama Primary School in Kano and at the Government College in Zaria. He enlisted in the Nigerian Army in 1957 and was later sent to Sandhurst Royal Academy in Britain for training. He returned to Nigeria in 1961 as a commissioned Second Lieutenant and was posted to the Army Signals. He later served with the United Nations Peace-Keeping forces in the Congo, now Zaïre. On his return in 1962, he was appointed Aide-de-Camp (ADC) to the Administrator of Western Nigeria during the period of emergency in that region. In 1963, he was made Officer-in-Charge of the First Brigade Signal Troop in Kaduna and went to Catterick School of Signals in England for a course on advanced telecommunications techniques. In 1964, he was promoted to Major and in 1965 he became Acting Chief Signals Officer of the Army. When the military took over in 1966, and under General Ironsi, he became a Lieutenant Colonel. He took active part in the 1966 July coup which brought General Gowon to power.

In August 1967, when the Biafrans came within 70 miles of Lagos, the federal government hastily raised a new Second Division and appointed him as its commanding officer. He pushed the Biafrans back towards the east and retook Benin on September 20. Here he broadcast his message of liberation of the Mid-West State, appointing Major Samuel Ogbemudia Military Administrator. He captured Asaba on the Niger but was blocked by the retreating Biafrans who blew up the Niger Bridge. After three costly attempts to cross the river by boat, he turned north, crossed at Lokoja, which was firmly in federal hands, and began to advance down the river on the Biafran side, capturing Onitsha in March 1968.

He was appointed Inspector of the Nigerian Army Signal in April 1968 and came down to Lagos to assume the new office. He was promoted to Brigadier in October 1971 and became the Federal Commissioner for Communications in August 1974.

Following the coup that ousted General Yakubu Gowon on July 29, 1975, he became the Head of State and Commander. in-Chief of the Nigerian Armed Forces. General Murtala, as the new Head of State, said that the nation for too long had been groping in the dark and the situation would lead to chaos and bloodshed if not arrested. He accused the Gowon administration of indecision and indiscipline. He instituted mass retirement and dismissal of about 10,000 public officials, including people in the armed forces, civil service, parastatals, universities and even the judiciary, for incompetence, old age and corruption. He outlined a political program to hand over power to an elected civilian government. This included the creation of seven more states in February 1976, the drafting of a new constitution and the reform of local governments and the organization of national elections to pave the way for a civilian administration in 1979. He decided on moving the capital of the country from Lagos to Abuja, which is more central to the people of the nation. On the international plane, he recognized the MPLA government of Angola, and stated that Nigeria would no longer take orders from any country, no matter how powerful.

He was a simple man, beloved by most people, though not all, for he was ambushed and assassinated on the 13th of February 1976 during the abortive coup organized by Lt. Col. Dimka. Today he is one of the Nigerian Heroes. In order to immortalize his name, many places and institutions are named after him, including the International Airport at Ikeja, Lagos. His portrait is also placed on Nigeria's twenty naira currency note. He was succeeded by General Olusegun Obasanjo.

MUNGO PARK. Mungo Park was a young Scottish doctor, who, in 1796, became the first European to discover the easterly course of the River Niger and to take news back to Europe about this fact. In 1788, the African Association was formed in Britain for the purpose of the exploration of Africa and more particularly for finding out the route of the River Niger. Mungo Park offered his services to the Association and in 1795 he started his first expedition beginning from the Gambia. On July 20, 1796 he caught sight of the Niger and noted that it flowed east. He followed the river some distance and having lost his men and being short of food he turned back and reported what he had discovered. Later, the British government became interested and in January 1805, Mungo Park was entrusted with another expedition. He then sailed to Gorce to organize the expedition which started in April 1806 with over 40 Europeans including himself, his brother-in-law, Anderson, a priest and a guide. In August they reached the Niger but by then most of his men had died, leaving only Park, Anderson and eight other Europeans. By the time he actually started down the stream of the River Niger, he himself wrote that of the 44 Europeans that left the Gambia, only five were then alive. On November 19, 1806, his boat started down the stream and was never heard of again. He died with his men at the rapids of Bussa.

MUSA, ALHAJI ABUBAKAR BALARABE. A chartered accountant, politician and ex-Governor of Kaduna State, he was the first Governor under the 1979 constitution to be successfully impeached. Born on August 21, 1936 in Kaya, Kaduna State, he was educated at the Zaria Middle School, the Institute of Administration in Zaria and at various colleges in London. In 1978, he joined the People's Redemption Party (PRP) and was elected Governor of the Kaduna State. With the National Party of Nigeria (NPN) controlling more than two thirds of the majority in the State Legislative Assembly, disagreement between him and the House on ideology and policy soon arose but because of his uncompromising attitude, various charges were proferred against him in the House and he was later, in 1981, impeached, to be succeeded by the Deputy Governor Alhaji Aba Rimi.

MUSEUMS. Established in 1957 and situated in Lagos, the National Museum contains some of the finest collections of Nigerian art anywhere in the world. Other museums established by the Department of Antiquity include: the Ife Museum, established in 1954; Owo and Esie museums, opened in 1945; the Jos Museum, opened in 1952; Oron Museum, opened in 1958; Kano Museum, opened in 1960; Kaduna Museum, established in 1972 and the Benin Museum, opened in 1973. There is also the Museum of Natural History in the University of Ife. All these museums, perhaps the richest in sculptural art and tradition, offer great attraction to tourists visiting the country.

MUSTAPHA, ALHAJI MUHAMMED. Leader of the People's Redemption Party (PRP) in the House of Representatives under the second Republican Constitution. Born in 1939 at Zanguza Village, Kano, he had his early education at Islamiya Primary School in Zaria 1949-1955 and his secondary education at West African Collegiate School, Freetown in Sierra Leone, 1955-1961. He then went to Durham University in England where he obtained a B. Sc. in Economics in 1964. He also attended Fourah Bay College in 1968-1971, where he received a diploma in Public Administration. He served later as Assistant Registrar at the Ado Bayero University in Kano. In 1977 he resigned to set up an Economic Consultancy Company in Kano. He later joined the PRP and was elected into the House of Representatives and became the leader of the party in the House.

-N-

NANA OF THE ITSEKIRI. Born in 1852 at Jakpa, Mid-Western

State to Olomu, founder of Ebrohimi, Nana was a traditional ruler. His father was a wealthy trader and a member of the house of Ologbotsere who ruled for only four years before Nana succeeded to the throne. Nana, as a young man, began to work for his father, and because of his intelligence and ability he soon became his father's right-hand man. When his father died in 1883 Nana, at the age of 31, succeeded him not only as the head of his family but also as Governor of the Benin River. As Governor he, in 1884, signed a treaty with the British Consul, Hewett, bringing Benin River, Warri and other parts of Western Ijo under British protection. These treaties gave the British exclusive rights to trade in the area. In 1891, problems between him and the British began to arise when the British decided to extend the control of the Oil Rivers Protectorate to Itsekiri area under him. The British, interested in free trade in the area, did not want to accept the monopoly which Nana had created there. Nana was therefore accused of strangling trade on the Benin River and of defying the British authority in slave trading. He denied the accusations and remembering the infidelity of the British to Jaja of Opobo, refused to go to the British authorities to answer to those charges. The British, allied with his enemies among the Itsekiris, forbade the use of the river to his boats. Nana placed an iron barricade across the creek entrance. The British decided to blow it up and war broke out. Nana's men fought gallantly but were defeated. Nana escaped to Lagos where he surrendered to the British who deported him to Accra, Ghana. While in Ghana he sent numerous petitions to the British Government asking that he be returned home. In 1906, he was allowed to return home. He settled down as an ordinary man in Koko where he designed and built for himself and family what is now known as the Nana's Palace.

Nana was no doubt a great man. He opened up many oil palm markets employing thousands of people. He stood up and fought against the British for his rights and those of his people, and he was able to offer serious resistance to the British who were all too anxious to extend their power over his area. He died in Koko on July 3, 1916.

NASIR COMMISSION. After the creation of seven new states from the existing 12 states on February 3, 1976, the government on February 12, 1976, set up a six-man Boundary Adjustment Commission under Supreme Court Justice Muhammadu Nasir. The Commission was to examine the boundary adjustment problems identified by the Irikefe Panel on the creation of states, specify which areas of Andoni and Nkoro in Opobo Division of the Cross River State should be in the Rivers State and which areas of Ndoni should form part of the Rivers State or the Imo State. It was also to identify and define the boundaries of any other area, district or division that might be brought to the Commission, define interstate boundaries (especially in cases where there were intergovernmental disputes) and make recommendations.

NATIONAL AFRICAN COMPANY (NAC). Formed in 1882, the National African Company took over the assets of the United African Company (UAC) and carried out its work. Two years later the company had signed many so-called treaties with traditional rulers on both banks of River Niger up to Lokoja. During the 1884-1885 Berlin Conference, the areas under the control of the National African Company were recognized as being under the British government. In 1886 the NAC was granted a charter and renamed the Royal Niger Company. See also ROYAL NIGER COMPANY.

NATIONAL ANTHEM. Within two decades of Nigeria's independence, the country had adopted two different National Anthems.

The first one, composed by a British citizen, was adopted on the 1st of October 1960, but it ceased to be in use in 1978. A verse of the former anthem reads thus:

> Nigeria we hail thee,
> Our own dear native land,
> Though tribe and tongue may differ;
> In brotherhood we stand,
> Nigerians all are proud to serve,
> Our sovereign motherland.

In 1977, the then-military government announced their intention to change the anthem and a committee was appointed to look for the ways of composing the new anthem. The committee came out with a competition which was open to all Nigerians to send in entries for the lyrics for the anthem. The committee selected five of the entries and the five entries were synthesized into the present anthem. The music departments of the universities of Lagos, Zaria and Nsukka were invited together with some renowned classical musicians to give suitable music to the anthem. The anthem goes thusly:

> Arise, O Compatriot,
> Nigeria call obey
> To serve our fatherland,
> With love and strength and faith,
> The labour of our heroes past,
> Shall never be in vain,
> To serve with heart and might,
> One nation bound in freedom,
> Peace, and Unity.
>
> O God of Creation direct our noble cause,
> Guide our leaders right,
> Help our Youth the truth to know
> In love and honesty to grow,
> And living just and true,
> Great lofty heights attain
> To build a nation where
> Peace and justice shall reign.

NATIONAL ASSOCIATION OF NIGERIAN STUDENTS (NANS) see
   NATIONAL UNION OF NIGERIAN STUDENTS (NUNS)

NATIONAL BANK.   Established in 1933 by Chief Akinola Maja, T. A.
   Doherty and H. A. Subair to make loans more readily available
   to Nigerians than expatriate banks which discriminated against
   Nigerians.   By 1951 the bank had been officially recognized
   and it was appointed an authorized dealer under the Exchange
   Control Regulation and it became the banker to the Cocoa Marketing Board.   In 1961, owing to the banks financial difficulties,
   it was converted to an official bank of the Western Region.
         In 1976, when the Western State was divided into three
   states, the National Bank became a subsidiary of the Odu'a
   Investment Company, a holding company jointly owned by the
   three new states.   The bank has branches in many parts of
   Nigeria with its headquarters in Lagos.

NATIONAL CHURCH OF NIGERIA.   Established in 1948, it likened
   Dr. Nnamdi Azikiwe to Christ.   It was the religious wing of
   the Zikist Movement and membership of both were almost completely the same.   But while the Zikist Movement expressed
   protest against the political aspects of the colonial rule, the
   church expressed protest against white-dominated churches.
   Thus the church was one of the nationalist instruments to
   awaken racial and national consciousness in the minds of Nigerians.

NATIONAL COMMISSION FOR REHABILITATION.   Established in
   1969 by the federal military government, it had the function
   of supplying food, clothing, drugs and other essentials to needy
   persons in areas affected by the civil war and its aftermath.
   It was empowered to: determine priority for all emergency
   relief operations and rehabilitation work in all parts of the
   federation; coordinate the activities of voluntary agencies engaged in emergency relief operations and rehabilitation work;
   coordinate the activities of the states in the administration of
   properties abandoned by displaced persons in the federation;
   collect food and drugs and other humane gifts from foreign
   governments and receive financial and technical aid through appropriate federal ministries.   The Commission was composed
   of the Federal Commissioner for Rehabilitation, one member
   from each state, a member to represent each of the ministries
   of Finance, Economic Development, Health and Labor and not
   more than six other members.

NATIONAL CONCILIATION COMMITTEE.   After the September 1966
   massacre of the Ibos in Northern Nigeria and the return of the
   people of Eastern Nigerian origin to the Eastern Region the
   gap between the federal government, headed by General Gowon
   (a leader unacceptable to Ojukwu), and the Eastern Nigerian
   government, headed by Lt. Col. Ojukwu, began to widen.   Ojukwu's government was moving inexorably to the secession of
   the east from the rest of the country while the Gowon administration

was determined to keep Nigeria unified. Some people, including Chief Obafemi Awolowo, Sir Adetokunbo Ademola (the then Chief Justice of the Federation), Chief Mariere (the former Governor of the Mid-West and the then advisor to the Military Governor of the Mid-West), Professor Samuel Aluko, Sir Kashim Ibrahim, Alhaji Zana Bukar Dipcharima, Mr. Godfrey Amachree and some others, disheartened by events, decided to form a committee which would work to bring the two sides together again and look into the demands of all the regions with a view to making them work together in the same federation. At the first meeting of the committee, known later as the National Reconciliation Committee, things could not go very far because the Eastern Region was not represented. A committee, later known as the National Conciliation Committee, led by Chief Awolowo, was sent in May 1967 to Enugu for talks with Lt. Col. Ojukwu to persuade him to send delegates to the National Reconciliation Committee. The National Conciliation Committee was well received, but it failed to persuade Ojukwu to send representatives to the National Reconciliation Committee.

NATIONAL CONGRESS OF BRITISH WEST AFRICA. The National Congress of British West Africa was founded in 1917 in the Gold Coast by Caseley Hayford, a Gold Coast lawyer. It was composed mainly of the Gold Coast intellectuals, but it had branches in all the British West African countries--Nigeria, Sierra Leone, and the Gambia. Its main aim was to unite the four British West African colonies into a kind of a federation and put pressure on the British government to grant the colonies the right of self-determination. Its branch in Nigeria was critical of the composition and role of the Nigerian Council set up by Lord Lugard after the 1914 amalgamation.

At the inaugural conference of the Congress, members adopted a number of resolutions which were subsequently embodied in their memorandum submitted to the Secretary of State for the Colonies in 1920. Among other things, the Congress asked for a Legislative Council in each territory, half of whose members would be elected and the other half nominated; a House of Assembly composed of members of the Legislative Council together with six other representatives elected by the people to control taxation, revenue and expenditure; separation of the judiciary from the legislative branch of the government and the appointment of Africans to judicial offices; appointment and deposition of Chiefs by their own people; abolition of racial discrimination in the civil services; development of municipal governments; repeal of certain "obnoxious" ordinances; regulation of immigration of Syrians and other non-Africans and the establishment of a university in West Africa.

The Secretary of State, Lord Milner, having received unfavorable reports on the delegation from the governments of the British West African Colonies, rejected their demands. But owing to continuous pressure in Nigeria, the Colonial Secretary agreed to the Clifford Constitution of 1922 which abolished the old Legislative Council and the Nigerian Council and which introduced for the first time in British West Africa, the elective principle into the Nigerian Constitutional development, whereby Lagos City elected three representatives and Calabar elected one representative to the Legislative Council.

NATIONAL CONVENTION OF NIGERIAN CITIZENS (NCNC). The National Convention of Nigerian Citizens was the new name given to the National Convention of Nigeria and the Cameroons, which was founded in 1944. This new name was given to the NCNC in 1961, after the plebiscite in which the people of Southern Cameroon declared their intention to join the Cameroon Republic. The leader of the National Convention of Nigerian Citizens was Dr. Michael Okpara, Dr. Nnamdi Azikiwe quit partisan politics sometime before his appointment as Governor-General in October 1960. The party was in firm control of both the Eastern and the Mid-Western regions during the First Republic. It was however dissolved in 1966 when the military took over the government. See also NATIONAL COUNCIL OF NIGERIA AND THE CAMEROONS.

NATIONAL COUNCIL OF NIGERIA AND THE CAMEROONS (NCNC). In 1944 a conference was called in Lagos for the purpose of organizing a national council which would bring the diverse peoples of Nigeria together. Accordingly, on August 26, 1944 the inaugural meeting of the conference was held in the Glover Memorial Hall in Lagos. It was attended by various organizations--trade unions, political parties, professional associations, clubs and tribal unions.

Because the Cameroonian associations in Lagos wanted to affiliate with the Council, its name was changed to National Council of Nigeria and the Cameroons. At the Conference Herbert Macaulay, who was leader of the Nigerian National Democratic Party (NNDP), and whose party was represented at the conference, was elected President of the Council while Dr. Nnamdi Azikiwe was the General Secretary.

Until 1951, membership in the party was restricted to organizations, trade unions, political parties, clubs and tribal unions, among which was the Ibo Federal Union. However in 1951 individuals became members. The party's main aims were to extend democratic principles and advance the interests of the people of Nigeria and the Cameroons, to educate the people with a view to achieving self-government and to provide its members with a means of political expression so that they might be able to secure their political freedom, economic security and social and religious tolerance in Nigeria and the Cameroons. When the party was being formed, Dr. Nnamdi Azikiwe was seen as a dynamic educated young nationalist who brought to bear on Nigerian politics the experiences and the education he had received in the United States. He was therefore a popular person, not only in his home region but in Lagos and the Western Region. But even though the party got much support from Lagos and the West, its base of support was in the Eastern Region, which was predominantly Igbo and it began to be seen more as a regional party. After the 1959 federal elections, the NCNC formed a coalition with the NPC to rule Nigeria. This coalition broke down in the 1963/64 census crises.

After the plebiscite that determined whether or not the Southern Cameroon was to be separated from Nigeria in 1961, the name of the party changed to National Council of Nigerian Citizens. The party was one of those banned in 1966 when the military came to power.

NATIONAL COUNCIL OF TRADE UNIONS OF NIGERIA (NCTUN). With the breakup of the All-Nigerian Trade Union Federation (ANTUF) in 1957, the NCTUN was formed. Its principal officers were N. A. Cole, President, and Lawrence L. Bortha, General Secretary. Its aims, among others, were to provide an effective central trade union body, independent of ideological influences, and to promote the interest of the working people in the country. It would encourage workers to organize free and democratic labor unions, aid in the establishment of trade unions in all industries, promote and foster legislation in the interest of the working class and cooperate with free and democratic international trade union federations whose aims were acceptable to the Council. In 1957 the NCTUN applied for affiliation to the International Confederation of Free Trade Unions (ICFTU), just as the ANTUN had done. But in 1958, since the ICFTU could accept only one application and no reconciliation between the ANTUN and the NCTUN was possible, the ICFTU accepted the application of the NCTUN. In 1958 a National Labor Peace Committee was formed to try to bring about a reconciliation between the two unions. In January 1959, the two came together under the umbrella of the Trades Union Congress of Nigeria.

NATIONAL ECONOMIC COUNCIL. After the country became a federation of three regions and following the recommendation of the International Bank for Reconstruction and Development in 1954, the agreement was reached that there should be a body in which representatives of the regions would meet and discuss common problems. The result was the creation of the National Economic Council (NEC). It consisted of the Prime Minister, Premier of the regional governments and all the ministers of Finance and Economic Development. One of the tasks of the National Economic Council was reaching agreements about the locations of new projects and the distribution of foreign aid. For effective programming of the work of the Council, the NEC set up the Joint Planning Committee, manned by the Permanent Secretaries from the several ministries of finance and economic development. The Council also formulated and reviewed the progress of the development plan embarked upon by the government. During the military era, the National Economic Council was one of the forums in which all the state governors and the Head of State conferred on the economic development of Nigeria. Under the 1979 constitution, the National Economic Council became entrenched, and it was then made up of the Vice-President as Chairman, the Governors of the states and the Governor of the Central Bank of Nigeria. The constitution gave it power to advise the President on economic affairs of the federation and in particular on measures necessary for the coordination of the economic planning efforts of all the various governments in the federation.

NATIONAL ELECTRIC POWER AUTHORITY (NEPA). A public corporation established under Decree Number 24 of 1972. It was empowered to develop and maintain an efficient, coordinated and economical supply system of electricity for all parts of the federation. It replaced the Electricity Corporation of Nigeria (ECN) and inherited all its assets and liabilities.

NATIONAL EMERGENCY COMMITTEE. The National Emergency Committee was formed in November 1949 by leaders of the National Council of Nigeria and the Cameroons (NCNC) and the Nigerian Youth Movement (NYM) as a result of the shooting of coal miners at Enugu by the police during their go-slow strike action in which the government ordered the removal of the explosives from the mines in order to prevent the workers from causing trouble with the explosives. During the riots, 21 of the miners were killed. The Committee protested vigorously against the shooting and they demanded that the European Assistant Superintendent of Police who ordered the shooting, Mr. F.S. Phillip, should be punished for recklessly wounding and taking the lives of harmless miners. The Committee was disbanded in September 1950 because of rivalry among its leaders.

NATIONAL EXECUTIVE COUNCIL. With the promulgation of the Unification Decree Number 34 of 1966, the Federal Executive Council was changed to the National Executive Council because Nigeria ceased to be a federation from that date. The composition of the National Executive Council was: the Head of the National Military Government who was the President; the Head of the Nigerian Army; the Head of the Nigerian Navy; the Head of the Nigerian Airforce; the Chief of Staff of the Armed Forces; the Chief of Staff of the Nigerian Army; the Attorney General of the Republic; and the Inspector-General and the Deputy Inspector-General of the Nigerian Police.

With the change of government in July 1966, and the promulgation later of the decree reestablishing the federal system of government, the National Executive Council reverted to its former name, the Federal Executive Council.

NATIONAL FLAG. Designed by Taiwo Akinkunmi, a Nigerian student in London, the flag is divided vertically into three equal parts, green, white and green. The green outer parts represent the agricultural wealth of the country and the central white part represents unity and peace.

NATIONAL GOVERNMENT. On September 2, 1957, Alhaji Abubakar Tafawa Balewa, Deputy Leader of the Northern People's Congress (NPC) and Federal Minister of Transport, was appointed Nigeria's first Prime Minister by Governor-General Sir James Robertson. He immediately formed a national government, consisting of six ministers from the National Council of Nigeria and the Cameroons, four from the Northern People's Congress, two from the Action Group and one from the Kamerun National Congress (KNC). Explaining why he formed a national government, the Prime Minister stated that he regarded the period before independence as a time of national emergency when Nigerians must show the world that they were united and could work together for their common good. He argued that if Nigeria was to achieve independence in 1960, it was most essential that the three major political parties in the country should work together in close cooperation on all matters of policy and planning.

NATIONAL INDEPENDENCE PARTY (NIP). On February 23, 1953, during the Eastern Regional Crisis, the National Independence Party was formed and led by Professor Eyo Ita, who was previously the leader of the Eastern Regional government but expelled from the National Convention of Nigeria and the Cameroons (NCNC). The initial members of the party were the central ministers, expelled from the party for their intransigence, regional ministers who supported them and others from outside the two legislative houses in the center and in the region.

    The party, with the aid of Alvan Ikoku's United National Party, formed the opposition to the NCNC government in the region. The NIP did not take sides in the "self-government in 1956" issue, but acted rather as a bridge between the NPC in the north and the Action Group in the south. The party was represented at the 1953 Constitutional Congress in London in spite of the objection of the NCNC and AG parties which had formed a hurried alliance after the "Self-government in 1956" issue. The party was regarded as being made up of imperialist stooges. At the Conference, the party warned against the dangers of strong regional governments and a weak center which the AG and the NPC favored.

    The name of the party was later changed into the United Nigeria Independent Party and became an ally of the Action Group in the 1954 federal elections.

NATIONAL INSURANCE CORPORATION OF NIGERIA (NICON). Established by Decree Number 22 of 1969, NICON is a public corporation owned by the federal government. It has power to carry on all kinds of insurance business for the government, its companies or corporations and for the public. It is also charged with the responsibility to act as insurance agent or broker in relation to any insurance and to assist in organizing training schemes to employees of any registered insurance company.

NATIONAL INVESTMENT AND PROPERTIES COMPANY LIMITED
see COKER COMMISSION OF INQUIRY

NATIONAL MANPOWER BOARD. Following the recommendations
of the Ashby Commission's report on postschool certificate
and higher education in the country, the National Manpower
Board was set up in 1964. It was charged with the duty of
analyzing the quality and the distribution of available manpower
resources so that policies for a balanced development might be
formulated. It was also to indicate areas in which additional
training of essential manpower was needed from time to time
and to coordinate the work of all the ministries concerned with
manpower development. The Board was directly responsible
to the National Economic Council, but it could also make recommendations to the ministries concerned with manpower development, like the ministries of Labour, of Education and of
Economic Planning. The scholarship policy of the federal Ministry of Education generally took cognizance of the Board's
annual recommendations. To help the Board in its work in the
regions, regional manpower committees were set up to liase
between the Board and regional governments.

NATIONAL MILITARY GOVERNMENT. The national military government came into being on May 24, 1966 following the promulgation of Unification Decree Number 34 of 1966, which abolished
the existing federal structure of government. On that day Nigeria ceased to be a federation and became just the Republic
of Nigeria with a unitary government. As such, the federal
military government became known as the national military
government. The idea of the national military government only
featured prominently during the later months of General Aguiyi-
Ironsi's regime. General Yakubu Gowon, who succeeded him
in August 1966, issued Decree Number 59 of 1966, which returned the country into a federation.

NATIONAL ORIENTATION COLLEGE. During the Biafran War, the
novelist Chinua Achebe and some intellectuals formed what
they called the Political Orientation Committee to work on the
future structure of Biafran society after the civil war. On
June 1, 1969, Lt. Col. Ojukwu came up with the Ahiara Declaration, which launched what he called the "Biafran Revolution."
The Ahiara Declaration set up a National Orientation College
which was given the responsibility of politicizing and recon-
structing the Army and the administration.

NATIONAL PARTY OF NIGERIA (NPN). Formed in 1978, the National Party of Nigeria was the third political party to emerge
after the ban on politics was lifted in September of the same
year. Its main aims were: to bring about social justice and
social welfare; guarantee equality of opportunities for all, fundamental rights and freedom and free electoral system; promote
self-respect and self-reliance and bring about the unity of Nigeria. Realizing that the country was still regionally divided,

it adopted a zoning system of selecting party officials on a ro-
tational basis.   They then resolved that the presidential candidate of the party should come from the northern zone, while
the vice-presidential candidate was to come from the east and
the Chairman of the party from the west.   At the 1979 national
elections, Alhaji Shehu Shagari from Sokoto State was elected
the first Executive President while Dr. Alex Ekueme from the
east became his Vice-President.   The party also won the gubernatorial election in seven of the 19 states and won 36 out
of the 95 seats in the Senate and 168 out of the 450 in the
House of Representatives.   However since it could not win a
majority of the seats in both houses, an accord with the Nigerian People's Party (NPP) was reached under which the country
would be governed.   This accord was reminiscent of the 1959
coalition between the Northern People's Congress (NPC) and the
National Council of Nigerian Citizens (NCNC).   The accord
broke down in 1981.   In the 1983 general elections, which were
characterized by massive rigging at different levels, the party
won the presidential election and 13 out of the 19 gubernatorial
elections, while it considerably improved its strength in the
federal and state legislative houses.   However its victory was
short-lived, for on December 31, 1983 the Army seized power
in a bloodless coup.   The party, like all the others, was later
banned.

THE NATIONAL PROVIDENT FUND.   Established by an Act of Parliament in 1961, it is governed by that Act, the Amendment
Act of 1964 and Decree Number 40 of 1967.   The National
Provident Fund is a compulsory savings scheme to which non-
pensionable workers and their employers are required to contribute equal proportions on a monthly basis for the overall
benefit of the workers.   The present rate is 3k on every complete wage of 50k up to a maximum of ₦4 in any one month.
Members who can receive benefit payments are those
who have reached the retirement age of 55, those who are
physically or mentally declared to be medically invalid, de-
pendents of a deceased member, or non-Nigerian members
who are emigrating from the country.
All employers of labor, both public and private, employing not less than ten workers are required to be registered
under the scheme.   To enforce this rule, the National Provident Fund has branches in all the states, manned by compliance
inspectors who have power to enter premises or places where
workers are employed.

NATIONAL RECONCILIATION COMMITTEE   see   NATIONAL CON-
CILIATION COMMITTEE.

NATIONAL RECONSTRUCTION AND DEVELOPMENT SAVINGS FUND.
Established in January 1968 by the federal military government
to finance reconstruction and development programs of the federal government from sources other than from the general revenue of the federation.   It is a special fund which consists of

contributions made from the incomes of workers. Thus an employer is liable to contribute to the fund with respect to any worker employed by him. The amount was 5 percent per annum of the wages of each worker.

NATIONAL RECONSTRUCTION COMMITTEE. The National Reconstruction Committee was formed in October 1961 by Chief Obafemi Awolowo. Membership included many university lecturers and professors, some of them not actually members of his Action Group Party but sympathizers. The Committee presented a number of working papers to the Federal Executive Committee in December 1961 on the case for austerity measures in government, the implication of the party's commitment to democratic socialism, economic planning and on Pan-Africanism.

NATIONAL UNION OF NIGERIAN STUDENTS (NUNS). A federal union made up of all student unions in Nigeria and abroad. It was affiliated with the International Union of students. It had no official ideology and each branch was free to take any position on issues without reference to the central body. It was also supposed to maintain a neutral position on partisan issues. In the early 1960's it was outspoken on a number of issues like the Defence Pact between Britain and Nigeria and the Preventive Detention Act. In 1977 the organization was represented on the Constituent Assembly, which put finishing touches to the 1979 constitution. In 1978, during the "Ali-Must-Go" crisis, over the issue of democratization of education in the country against the then-elitist educational system, it clashed with the federal military government and was proscribed. It however reorganized in 1980 under a new name, the National Association of Nigerian Students (NANS) which still consists of all students in the Nigerian universities, colleges of technology, polytechnical schools and colleges of education.

NATIONAL UNIVERSITIES COMMISSION. The National Universities Commission (NUC) was set up in 1962 as an administrative body after the government had agreed to implement most of the recommendations of the Ashby Commission's Report on Higher Education in Nigeria. Its responsibilities are mainly to: inquire into and advise the federal government on the financial needs of universities; assist in planning a balanced and coordinated development of universities; receive annually a block grant from the federal government and disburse it on criteria the Commission thinks appropriate; serve as an agency for channelling all external aids to the universities and conduct investigations relating to higher education in Nigeria and publish information relating to university finances and education at home and abroad, making recommendations to the government or the universities as the Commission may consider to be in the nation's interest. When the Commission was set up, there were only five universities in the country, two of which, Ibadan and Lagos universities, were federally owned while the remaining three in Ife, Nsukka and Zaria were owned by the three regional governments. However during the regime of Murtala and Obasanjo, all nonfederally owned universities in Nigeria were taken over by the federal government and new universities were later created and are still being created, including state-owned universities.

NATIONAL YOUTH SERVICE CORPS (NYSC). Established under Decree Number 24 of 1973, the NYSC seeks to: inculcate discipline in the Nigerian youth; raise their moral tone; develop common ties (and by so doing, promote national unity); encourage individual youth corpers to seek employment in states other than their own and so promote mobility of labor and to induce employers to employ Nigerians irrespective of their state of origin and finally to enable them to acquire a spirit of self-reliance. The idea of a Youth Corps was first mentioned in the Second National Development Plan in which the Federal Military Government planned for the establishment of a Youth Corps Organization. On October 1, 1972, the 12th Independence Anniversary, Head of State, General Yakubu Gowon announced that the proposed NYSC was meant to transcend political, social, state and ethnic loyalties and that it would form one of the bases of fostering loyalty to the nation. The scheme was finally launched on June 4, 1973 by the Head of State and the first groups of students to be inducted in July 1973 were university graduates. At present, graduates from the universities and polytechnical schools at home or from abroad are required to serve the nation for one year in a state other than their own. An exception to this rule is the case of married women who are allowed to serve in the states where their husbands are. As such, the scheme offers young men and women an opportunity to know the country and understand some of the problems of the various peoples.

However, some youth corpers in many states complain of underemployment where they are posted, and that even though some would want to work where they served, they were not offered jobs.

Employers require evidence of having served and being duly discharged before a graduate is employed.

The NYSC scheme has been entrenched into the 1979 constitution.

NATIVE ADMINISTRATION. The system of local administration established by the colonial authorities through which they ruled the indigenous population. A native administration had a treasury and was under the authority of the Paramount Chief, or Emir and his councils. Each was empowered to provide a variety of services from road building and maintenance to provision of health care and education to their citizens. Native authority revenues came largely from poll tax, community tax or cattle tax. Each native authority had its native court, its police force and its prison. In the south, the system gave way to the British type of local administration in the early

1950's while it continued to the period after independence in the north. See also INDIRECT RULE.

NATIVE AUTHORITY   see   NATIVE ADMINISTRATION and INDIRECT RULE.

NATIVE COURTS.   In the early years of colonial administration in Nigeria, two systems of judicial administration existed side by side.   There was the British system of judicial administration beginning from the magistrate courts to the Supreme Court. These courts had jurisdiction over natives and nonnatives and applied the statutory laws and the common law of England. The second system of court consisted of the native or customary courts which administered the native law and custom prevailing in their area of jurisdiction.   They were organized into grades A, B, C or D, and they had power to impose fines and punishments with the exception of mutilation, torture or any other punishment repugnant to natural justice and humanity. Appointments to these courts were made by the Head Chief or the Emir, but with the approval of the colonial officers in charge of the area.   In the north the Moslem courts fell into this category, but the colonial official was vested with the power of appointing members to the court.   Native courts had no jurisdiction over nonnatives and they were under the supervision of British officials.   Later on in 1933, a hierarchy of appeals was set up, beginning from native courts to native courts of appeal and, if necessary, to British-type courts. However appeals from Moslem courts on matters governed by Moslem law lay to the Moslem Court of Appeal, which was later replaced in 1958 by the Sharia Court of Appeal.   In the early 1950's the term "customary" replaced the word "native" in native courts and native law in both the Eastern and the Western regions.

Native courts were of great importance in the colonial administration of the local people for maintaining law and order and in settling local disputes which the British types of courts were not equipped to handle.   Today the courts still handle a high proportion of the work of the judicial system.

NATIVE LAND ACQUISITION PROCLAMATION.   A law enacted in 1900 for the Protectorate of Southern Nigeria for the purpose of preventing the exploitation of native landowners by expatriate aliens, and thus controlling the activities of such aliens in the protectorate.

NATIVE LAW AND CUSTOM.   Native law and custom is a term used by the colonial authorities to distinguish local customary law from the imposed British statutory and common law.   It is the law that has its origin in the custom of the people.   In fact it is the "common law" of the people of the area.   Native law and custom were enforced by the local authorities and customary courts.   They deal mainly with succession, marriage and divorce.   In the early 1950's the word "native" was replaced by "customary" and so native law and custom became customary law.

NATIVE TREASURIES. By the Native Revenue Proclamation of 1906 the colonial government in the northern provinces tried to rationalize the various forms of tax assessment and collection that were in existence. But more importantly, the government laid down the principle of sharing the tax so collected between the government and its native authorities. By the Native Authority Proclamation of 1907, the government conferred upon some recognized chiefs responsibilities for law and order in their areas. Subsequent to this, the government began to prepare the ground for the establishment of Native Treasury, into which tax would be diverted from the taxes that the chiefs collected. Such money was to be used for the benefit of the new administration under the Chief, and be properly accounted for. In 1911, the first native treasuries were established and they were gradually extended to the rest of the country, especially after the 1914 amalgamation.

NIGER COAST CONSTABULARY. In 1891, parts of the present Bendel, Rivers and Cross River States were declared as the Oil Rivers Protectorate with its headquarters in Calabar where an armed constabulary was formed. In 1893 the area was proclaimed the Niger Coast Protectorate and in 1894, the existing armed constabulary was reconstituted as the Niger Coast Constabulary.

NIGER COAST PROTECTORATE. The Niger Coast Protectorate was established in 1893 when the Oil Rivers Protectorate, established after the 1885 Berlin Conference and covering mainly the coastal districts, was extended over the hinterland. The new Niger Coast Protectorate covered the former Oil Rivers Protectorate and the hinterland. It extended from the delta to Calabar and up to Benin City. The protectorate maintained a force called the "Niger Coast Constabulary," which was used against any aggression or hostility on the part of the indigenous population, like the Akassa Massacre of 1895 and the Benin Massacre of 1897. In 1900, when the charter of the Royal Niger Company was revoked, the Niger Coast Protectorate became the Protectorate of Southern Nigeria.

NIGER DELTA CONGRESS (NDC). The Niger Delta Congress (NDC) was an outgrowth of the Chiefs and Peoples Conference in the Rivers Area. It was primarily an Ijaw Party which was led by Chief Biriye and Mr. M. O. Ikolo. During the campaign for the 1959 federal elections, NDC, allied with the NPC, said that its aim was to make the Niger Delta a federal territory. It won one seat in the Federal House of Representatives. In preparation for the 1964 elections, new alignments were brought about and the NDC allied with the NPC, NNDP and MDF to form the Nigerian National Alliance (NNA). The party later broke up and the two leaders, Chief Biriye and Mr. Ikolo were expelled for aligning with the NNA.

The party was banned in 1966 together with all other
parties when the military took over the government.

NIGER DELTA DEVELOPMENT BOARD. Following the recommendation of the Minorities Commission of 1957, the 1958 Constitutional Conference in London agreed to establish the Niger Delta
Development Board to look after the physical development of
the area and allay the fears and complaints of the Ijaw people.
Thus the Board was to survey the area to: ascertain what was
needed for land improvement and drainage, the improvement of
communications and to investigate questions of agriculture, fisheries land tenure and forestry; draw up schemes of development
based on the findings of the survey and estimate the costs; conduct an initial survey and produce annual reports on its progress in implementing its proposals and present these to the
federal and regional legislative houses; and finally to advise
the government concerned how to plan and achieve the desired
development of the area. The Board was to exist for an initial period of ten years, after which the federal and regional
governments concerned would review the progress so far made.
The Board was to consist of a full-time Chairman, appointed
by the federal government, one representative of each regional
government and other representatives of the people of the area.
The Secretary was also to be a full-time member. The funds
to execute its duties were to be provided by the federal government.

NIGERIA ADVANCE PARTY. Launched on September 28, 1978 by
Mr. Tunji Braithwaite, a Lagos lawyer, the Nigeria Advance
Party told the people of the country that their destiny was in
their own hands. The symbol of the party was the map of Nigeria in a globe carried with both hands. Its flag was made
up of white, orange, green and black. The party, if elected
into power, promised to revolutionize the educational system
and make it really practical. It promised to take over agricultural lands and compensate the owners and evolve a communal system whereby everyone would be involved. The party
would see to the production of food so that the country could
export the surpluses. The party did not meet the conditions
of the Federal Electoral Commission in 1979 and so it could
not be registered for the 1979 elections and could not take part
in it. However in 1982 it obtained FEDECO's recognition and
so it became the sixth recognized party in the Second Republic
and a contestant in the 1983 elections. However the party did
not win any seat in the national elections and when the military
took over power in December 1983, it was one of the parties
banned.

NIGERIA AIRWAYS. Nigeria Airways was formed in 1959. Before
this time air services in Nigeria were operated under the West
African Airways Corporation (WAAC), formed by Nigeria, Ghana,
Sierra Leone and the Gambia. Nigeria Airways operates both
international and domestic flights. Its domestic flights are being

expanded to all state capitals. The airways is a public company, and its fleet includes B-707, B-737 and DC-10 planes.

NIGERIAN AGRICULTURAL BANK. Established in 1973, the Nigerian Agricultural Bank (NAB) was set up with the objective of
improving the rural life and economy of the country. To this
end, it provides credit and loans for agricultural development
and so helps to raise production and productivity of the rural
population. Loans are therefore available, all conditions being
satisfied, for development of poultry, farming, fisheries, animal husbandry and also for storage, distribution and marketing
of such projects.

NIGERIAN AIR FORCE. Established by the Air Force Act of 1964,
the Nigerian Air Force is charged with the defense of the Nigerian airspace. During the civil war it grew fairly rapidly.

NIGERIAN ARMY. When the Royal Niger Company received its
charter to administer the northern part of the country, it organized the Royal Niger Constabulary with special emphasis on
military activities. The Constabulary consisted of five British
and two African Officers and about 400 men from Nigeria and
the Gold Coast (now Ghana). Because of the French encroach-
ment on the territory of the Royal Niger Company between 1894
and 1897, the British Government decided to raise a local force
to protect its area of influence. The Government sent Colonel
(later, Lord) Frederick Lugard to come to Nigeria, to raise
and command the force. By the beginning of 1900 when all of
Nigeria came under the British authority, the force had become
well organized and well disciplined.
    In 1901, all the colonial military forces in British West
African colonies were constituted into the West African Frontier Force. Each territory was however responsible for its
force. The Nigerian force consisted of the Northern Nigeria
Regiment, the Lagos Constabulary, which became the Lagos
Battalion, and the Southern Nigeria Regiment. When in 1906
the Colony of Lagos was merged with the Protectorate of Southern Nigeria, the Lagos Battalion became the Second Battalion
of the Southern Regiment. However on January 1, 1914, when
the Northern and Southern Protectorates were merged, the two
regiments were also merged and they both became the Nigerian
Regiment. The Nigerian Regiment, as part of the West African
Frontier Force, fought gallantly in the First and Second World
Wars and they won many Distinguished Conduct Medals, military
medals, British Empire Medals and many certificates of good
services. In 1955 the Nigerian Army was constituted into a
separate command and on April 1, 1958, the control of the Nigerian Military Forces was surrendered by the British government to the Government in Nigeria which still was under British rule. The Nigerian Army served in the Congo (now Zaïre)
as members of the United Nations Peace-Keeping Force in 1960,
and in 1963 they were sent to Tanganyika (now Tanzania) to help
maintain order after the Tanzanian troops had mutinied. In

1966, the army seized power by overthrowing the civilian government of Alhaji Sir Abubakar Tafawa Balewa. They surrendered power to an elected government on October 1, 1979, after being in power for 13 years. However, on December 31, 1983 the army struck again, toppling the administration of Alhaji Shehu Shagari, which was accused of mismanagement of the economy, corruption and electoral malpractices.

During the civil war, the army grew very rapidly but efforts have been made to reduce the number. The army has three divisions, and the training facilities for the armed forces are increasing and growing.

NIGERIAN ATOMIC ENERGY COMMISSION. The Nigerian Atomic Energy Commission was established by the federal military government in August 1976. The Commission is charged with the responsibility of promoting the development of atomic energy and for all matters relating to the peaceful uses of atomic energy in the nation. The Commission is to prospect for and mine radioactive minerals, construct and maintain nuclear installations for the purpose of generating electricity. It is also to produce, use and dispose of atomic energy as well as carry out research into matters connected with the peaceful uses of atomic energy.

NIGERIAN BANK FOR COMMERCE AND INDUSTRY. Established in April 1973 by the federal military government, to provide equity and loan capital to indigenous businessmen and women who are interested in setting up or expanding small-, medium- and large-scale commercial and industrial ventures. It also provides other services like opening of letters of credit, discounting of bills and acceptance of documentary bills for collection. It is a multipurpose bank to advance the rapid industrialization of the country by giving assistance to genuine indigenous entrepreneurs.

NIGERIAN CHRONICLE. The Nigerian Chronicle was established in 1908 as the first newspaper that used Nigeria as its prefix. It was established by Mr. Christopher Kumolu Johnson, but it became defunct in 1915.

NIGERIAN COLLEGE OF ARTS, SCIENCE AND TECHNOLOGY. The establishment of the Nigerian College of Arts, Science and Technology came as a result of the Thorp and Harlow Report of 1949. The college was established on a tripartite basis, one branch to be in each of the three regions that made up the federation. The college was to have a principal, three assistant principals--one in each branch--heads of departments and lecturers. The constitution of the college also provided for a council or board of trustees made up of 15 members. The first branch of the college was opened in Zaria, in the Northern Region in 1952. It offered courses in civil engineering, architecture, local government and secretarial work. The second branch was opened at Ibadan, Western Nigeria in 1954 and courses offered included agriculture, forestry, bookkeeping and accountancy, education, arts, sciences and engineering. The third branch was opened in 1955 in Enugu, Eastern Nigeria in 1955 and offered courses in mining, surveying, science and arts. The college, however, was closed down in 1962, ten years after its first branch came into existence and its assets were taken over by the three regional universities of Ahmadu Bello in Zaria, Ife and Nsukka.

NIGERIAN COUNCIL. The Nigerian Council was created by Lord Lugard after the amalgamation of the Northern Protectorate with the Southern Protectorate in 1914. Because it was designed to advise the governor on a nationwide basis, it was composed of representatives from all parts of the country. Its 36 members included the Governor, members of his Executive Council, Residents, Political Secretaries, seven unofficial Europeans and six unofficial Nigerians to represent various interests. There were also six traditional rulers and a member each to represent the Lagos, Calabar and Benin/Warri areas. Because of the little interest the traditional rulers had in its proceedings--as shown by their not attending its meetings--and owing to the fact that it was not popular, it had to be abandoned in 1922 when the Clifford Constitution replaced it with a Legislative Council to legislate for Lagos and the Southern provinces of Nigeria.

NIGERIAN COUNCIL FOR MEDICAL RESEARCH. Established by the federal military government in 1966, it consisted of 15 members and had the function of coordinating medical research in the country as well as initiating and carrying out research. It was also to support other persons' efforts to carry out research, train medical research workers, collect and disseminate information relating to medical science and to encourage and promote collaboration between those engaged in medical research in Nigeria and other countries.

NIGERIAN COUNCIL FOR SCIENCE AND TECHNOLOGY. Established in 1970 with the objective of determining priorities for scientific activities in the federation in relation to the economic and social policies of the country and its international commitments; advising the federal military government on a national science policy, including general planning and the assessment of the requisite financial resources, and ensuring the application of the results of scientific activities to the development of agriculture, industry and social welfare. The Council consists of 11 ex-officio members--permanent ministers of federal ministries--and 24 appointed members, 12 of whom represented the states, with the remaining 12 representing fields of scientific knowledge like agriculture, industry, medicine, environmental sciences, social sciences and the natural sciences.

THE NIGERIAN COUNCIL FOR SCIENTIFIC AND INDUSTRIAL RESEARCH. Established in 1966 by the federal military government with the following general functions: encourage, support and coordinate scientific and industrial research of all kinds in Nigeria; advise the government of the federation and through it those of the regions on national policy relating to the application of science and technology to the development of the national economy; and encourage and coordinate the survey and appraisal of the natural resources of the nation and develop such resources through applied research designed to develop the national economy and finally to encourage the study of all sciences and technology.

NIGERIAN EDUCATIONAL RESEARCH COUNCIL. Established in 1972, it is charged with the function of encouraging, promoting and coordinating educational research programs carried out in Nigeria. It is to identify educational problems on a periodic basis and to establish an order of research priority. It commissions and cooperates in financing research projects and complies and publishes the results of educational research, particularly in relation to Nigerian problems. It also sponsors national and international conferences, maintains relationships with corresponding educational research bodies in and outside Nigeria, and assembles, maintains and extends collection of books and publications in libraries and other reading facilities.

NIGERIAN ENTERPRISES PROMOTION BOARD. The Nigerian Enterprises Promotion Board was established by the federal military government in 1972 for the purpose of developing and promoting enterprises in which Nigerian citizens would participate fully and play a dominant role. The Board advises the Federal Minister of Industries on guidelines to promote Nigerian enterprises and on any other related matter that the Minister may refer to it. The Board is assisted by Nigerian Enterprises Promotion Committees established in all the states.

NIGERIAN EXTERNAL TELECOMMUNICATIONS LIMITED (NET). Incorporated in 1963 as a partnership between the federal government, with 51 percent of the shares and the Cable and Wireless Limited, with 49 percent of the shares. In 1972 the company was nationalized by the federal government by buying all the shares of Cable and Wireless Limited. NET is responsible for the planning, provision, operation and maintenance of international and intracontinental telecommunication services in Nigeria. The services offered include: telephone, telex, leased telegraph channels, and TV program reception through satellite. Its headquarters is in Lagos but it has branches in the states.

NIGERIAN HOUSING DEVELOPMENT SOCIETY LIMITED. Incorporated in 1956, the Nigerian Housing Development Society, otherwise known as the Nigerian Building Society, commenced business in 1957. Its main objective is to help as many Nigerians as possible to own their own houses. As such, it promotes thriftiness and savings among the members. It is wholly owned by the federal government and the former Eastern Nigeria government. The society has now been turned into a mortgage bank known as the Nigerian Mortgage Bank.

NIGERIAN INSTITUTE OF INTERNATIONAL AFFAIRS (NIIA). Established in 1963 as an independent nonprofit research institution to encourage and facilitate the understanding of international affairs, especially the factors and the circumstances that condition the attitude and behavior of other countries and their people. It also provides information on international problems and promotes the study of such problems by organizing conferences, lectures, discussion and publication of their study.

Furthermore the institute provides facilities for the training of diplomats and personnel for the foreign office.

NIGERIAN INSTITUTE OF SOCIAL AND ECONOMIC RESEARCH (NISER). Established at the University of Ibadan in 1962 under the 1962 University of Ibadan Act; it replaced the old West African Institute of Social and Economic Research (WAISER). In 1977 the Institute was taken over by the federal government under Decree Number 77 of 1977. According to the decree, the Institute is to provide consultancy services to the federal and state governments, and their agencies in the field of economic and social development. It is to conduct research into the economic and social problems of the country with a view to the application of the results, to organize seminars and conferences on economic and social problems of the country and to cooperate with Nigerian universities, other research institutes and institutions so as to mobilize all of the country's research potential for the task of national development and disseminate research findings for the use of policymakers. The Decree also established the Nigerian Institute of Social and Economic Research Council to take care of the management of the institute.

NIGERIANIZATION. Nigerianization was the policy of the colonial government that suitable Nigerians should be appointed to the senior service in the government as fast as possible. By this policy, government was committed to set up a body that would determine the suitability of the candidates. Furthermore, if government was to have suitable candidates, it had to provide scholarship and training opportunities to interested persons. This policy led to the setting up in 1948 of the Foot Commission of Inquiry, charged with making recommendations on the steps government had to take to execute this policy. The Commission laid down the principle that only where no Nigerians had relevant qualifications for a post should a non-Nigerian be considered for it.

Before the Nigerianization policy was adopted in 1949, Nigerians in the senior service constituted about 10 percent while the rest were Europeans. In 1952, the figures for Nigerians had risen to about 19 percent.

NIGERIANIZATION COMMISSION. Set up in 1948 to inquire into the best and quickest methods of recruiting substantial numbers of Nigerians into the senior service. The Commission was made up of ten members: a European chairman, two other European civil servants, four Nigerian unofficial members of the Legislative Council, two Nigerian trade union representatives and a woman representative.

In August, the Commission submitted its recommendations:

a. that no non-Nigerian should be recruited for any government post except when no suitable and qualified Nigerian was available;

b. all senior service posts should be advertised only when there were no suitable Nigerian candidates already available for promotion within the civil service;

c. there should be no discrimination with regard to promotion against Nigerians and non-Nigerians already in the service;

d. an independent body, like a civil service commission should be set up to select candidates for senior posts;

e. junior service personnel should be reviewed annually with a view to selecting promising young people for special training and accelerated promotion; and

f. 385 scholarship and training scheme awards should be made for the initial period of three years of the policy implementation (i. e. , 1949-1951). These awards were to be distributed as follows: 100 in education and general degrees; 108 for professional courses in engineering, agriculture, medicine and forestry; 127 in technical courses; 30 in courses reserved exclusively for women and 20 "nongovernment" scholarships. Other scholarship awards were recommended to assist impoverished students in high schools and Ibadan University. The government accepted the recommendations, appointed a civil service commission, a public service commission, four public service boards, one for the national government and three for the emerging three regions and many other departmental boards and promotion committees.

NIGERIAN LABOUR CONGRESS (NLC). Inaugurated on May 26, 1950, as a result of the reconciliatory move between the Trade Union Congress (TUC) and the Nigerian National Federation of Labour (NNFL). The principal officers of the Union were M. A. O. Imoudu as the President and Nduka Eze as the General Secretary. The organization entered into difficulties almost immediately, leading to its disintegration. It sponsored the Mercantile Workers' strike in December 1950 which was a failure, and many affiliated unions decided to quit the Congress. Worse still, in 1951 the Congress opposed the visit of the delegation of the International Confederation of Free Trade Unions (ICFTU) to Nigeria, leading to the ICFTU choosing Accra, Ghana as the base for its operation in West Africa. That put an end to the NLC.

However in 1978, the NLC had a rebirth as a result of the federal military government's effort to reorganize all the existing central labor organizations in the country. In 1976, the government issued Decree Number 44 which provided for the cancellation of the four existing central labor organizations and set up the office of an Administrator of Trade Union Affairs. In 1977 the constitution of the NLC, as the only central labor union for all of Nigeria, was drafted and adopted in 1978. It is to this union that all other labor unions organized on industrial line are affiliated. The NLC can only affiliate with an African body and is presently affiliated with the All-African Trade Union Federation.

NIGERIAN LABOUR PARTY. Formed in 1964, by Chief Michael Imoudu, it was intended to bring together all the Nigerian workers into a political party. The party met with great opposition from other labor leaders like Alhaji H. P. Adebola of the United Labour Congress (ULC), Mr. Wahab Goodluck and S. U. Bassey of the Nigerian Trade Union Congress (NTUC). The party therefore was short-lived.

NIGERIAN NATIONAL ALLIANCE (NNA). As the 1964 general election to the Federal House of Assembly approached, the major political parties began to seek alliances with other parties so as to be sure of victory. The Nigerian National Alliance was one of the two major alliances formed before the election. It was made up of the Northern People's Congress (NPC) Mid-West Democratic Front (MDF), the Nigerian National Democratic Party (NNDP) and the Niger Delta Congress (NDC). The leader of the alliance was Sir Ahmadu Bello, the Sardauna of Sokoto and the leader of the NPC.

At the close of nominations on December 19, 1964, sixty NNA candidates had been returned unopposed. The NNA won 36 out of the 57 seats in the west and 162 seats out of the 167 seats in the north. Thus the NNA had a comfortable majority in the House of Representatives. The alliance's leader in the house, Alhaji Tafawa Balewa, was called to form the government and he was made the Prime Minister in 1965.

NIGERIAN NATIONAL CONGRESS. A political party launched on September 26, 1978, in Lagos by Alhaji Mohammed Idirisu. The party, referred to as "the new breed," was to be run in complete exclusion of old politicians (people who participated in the premilitary government) but it set no age limits to its membership. It intended to correct the ills and blunders that led to the fall of the First Republic. The party would build a new national economy and social order geared to the needs of the people by fighting for the economic emancipation of Nigeria from foreign domination. It would build a society where no man would be oppressed, a society free of hate, avarice, greed and exploitation. It would bring the benefit of modern civilization to the rural and urban poor in forms of pipe-borne water, free health services, electricity, modern housing and recreational facilities. It would pursue a positive agrarian policy to guarantee abundant food for all Nigerians. There would also be freedom for the people: freedom of the press, of movement, of religion and of conscience.

NIGERIAN NATIONAL DEMOCRATIC PARTY. The Nigerian National
Democratic Party was founded by Herbert Macaulay (1864-1946),
an engineer turned politician and nationalist after the introduction of the elective principle by the 1922 constitution. The
party was the most powerful of all those formed at the time,
for not only did it win all the three Lagos seats in the Legislative Council in 1923, 1928 and 1933, it also won the elections
into the Lagos City Council during that period. One of the
weaknesses of the party was that it was a Lagos party, that
is, based in Lagos and concerned for the most part with the
affairs of Lagos, especially the restoration of the ruling house
of Dosunmu, and therefore could not attract much following
outside the city. In 1944, the NNDP became one of the organizations that made up the National Council of Nigeria and the
Cameroons (NCNC) and Herbert Macaulay became the President
of the new party.

Twenty years later, in March 1964 after the Action
Group crisis and during the political instability in Western Nigeria, the United People's Party (UPP), led by Chief S. L.
Akintola, a faction of the NCNC in the Western Region, led by
Chief R. A. Fani-Kayode and Chief Richard Akinjide, and the
Southern People's Congress (SPC) formed a new party by the
same name, the National Democratic Party (NNDP), with Chief
S. L. Akintola as Chairman. Its symbol was the hand. They
claimed later that their membership in all other parties had
been renounced. Their purpose was to put an end to the dis-
unity and political unrest in Western Nigeria brought about by
the Action Group crisis of 1962.

It was believed then that the emergence of the new
party was brought about by the disagreement over the census
by the UPP and NCNC. UPP accepted the figures while the
NCNC government rejected them.

During the political realignment of 1964, before the December federal elections the NNDP joined with the Northern
People's Congress, NPC, to form the Nigerian National Alliance.
The party was banned in 1966 after the military came into
power.

NIGERIAN NATIONAL FEDERATION OF LABOUR. As a result of
the decision of the General Council of Trade Union Congress
(TUC) to affiliate with the National Council of Nigeria and the
Cameroons in 1947 a crisis in the central trade union movement emerged. At the Sixth Annual Delegates Conference of
the TUC in December 1948, the motion for affiliation was debated and defeated. As a result of this a large number of affiliated unions which supported affiliation pulled out of the TUC.
In March 1949, these splinter unions met to form the Nigerian
National Federation of Labour (NNFL). Its aims were to assist member unions to attain their objectives, to foster a spirit
of working-class consciousness among workers, fight for the
realization of the social and economic security of workers and
advance their educational aspirations. It was also to press for
the socialization of many important industries with a view to

realizing a socialist government, and to cooperate with democratic federations of trade unions all over the world.

The leaders of the NNFL were M. A. O. Imoudu as President and Nduka Eze as General Secretary. The union launched a weekly newspaper in 1950, The Labour Champion, its official organ. In the same year, as a result of the effort to reconcile the TUC and the NNFL, a merger was agreed upon and both formed the Nigerian Labour Congress (NLC).

NIGERIAN NATIONAL OIL CORPORATION. A public corporation established in April 1971, it is directed by a Board of Directors made up of the Permanent Secretary to the Federal Ministry of Mines and Powers who was the Chairman, and eight members, some of whom were government officials, and others with necessary ability, experience or special knowledge of the oil industry. The Corporation has the job of exploring and prospecting for petroleum and possessing and disposing of petroleum. It could purchase petroleum and its by-products and market it. The corporation is managed by a General Manager.

In 1972, the corporation became the sole beneficiary of all oil concessions though it could use private companies as contractors or minority partners.

In 1977 it was amalgamated with the Ministry of Petroleum to form the Nigerian National Petroleum Corporation (NNPC).

NIGERIAN NATIONAL PETROLEUM CORPORATION (NNPC). In 1977 the Nigerian National Oil Corporation (NNOC) and the Federal Ministry of Petroleum Resources were merged to form the Nigerian National Petroleum Corporation. The new corporation is empowered to engage in all commercial activities relating to petroleum industry. There is an independent department known as the Petroleum Inspectorate, which enforces the regulatory measures relating to the general control of petroleum product. The business of the corporation is under the direction of a seven-man Board of Directors with the Federal Minister for Petroleum as its Chairman.

THE NIGERIAN NATIONAL SUPPLY COMPANY. The Nigerian National Supply Company was established by the federal military government in 1972 for the purpose of making bulk purchases of scarce commodities and selling these to government ministries, corporations and institutions. It also served as an instrument of price control and stabilization.

NIGERIAN NAVY. The Nigerian Navy was formally established by an Act of Parliament in 1958, then called the Royal Nigerian Navy. However, before this time naval forces had been taking part in many campaigns along the Nigerian Coast, especially during the two world wars. During the Second World War, a section of the Government Department of Marine was formed into a Naval Defense Force, responsible for the security of Nigerian harbor entrances and to patrol the coast. In 1955

when Parliament approved the establishment of the Nigerian
Ports Authority, the former Marine Department was split into
three separate departments: the Ports Authority, the Inland
Waterways Department and a Naval Defense Force. In 1958
the Naval Defense Force was constituted as the Royal Nigerian
Navy. In 1963 when Nigeria became a republic, it became the
Nigerian Navy. Operational control of the Nigerian Navy is
vested in the Chief of Naval Staff, subject of course to the
overall direction of the Head of State who is the Commander-
in-Chief of the Armed Forces.

NIGERIAN PEOPLE'S PARTY (NPP). The Nigerian People's Party
(NPP) was formed in September 1978 after the ban on politics
was lifted. Its major aims included efforts to promote the
unity of the country and uphold its territorial integrity, work
for the integration and equality of all the peoples of the country, full employment and equal opportunity, promote equitable
distribution of the nation's resources, work for free and high
quality of education, and a secular state which would uphold
democracy and the rule of law.
    Among the foundation members of the party were Alhaji
Waziri Ibrahim, Dr. Ben Nzeribe, Chief T.O.S. Benson, Mr.
Paul Unongo, Chief Kola Balogun, Alhaji Ado Ibrahim, Chief
Samuel Onitiri and Chief Ogunsanya. During the struggle for
the presidential candidate, a dispute arose on whether or not
the position of Chairman of the party should also be combined
with being a presidential candidate. As a result Alhaji Waziri
Ibrahim, at the time the Chairman and the party's main financial supporter, wanted to keep the chairmanship while he ran
for the presidency. Because many other important members
disagreed with him, he pulled out of the party to form the
Great Nigerian People's Party (GNPP). After Waziri's exit,
the party leaders invited Dr. Nnamdi Azikiwe to be its presidential candidate, a position which Dr. Azikiwe accepted.
Chief Olu Akinfosile was then elected as Chairman of the party
at the party's first convention.
    The party was one of the five registered parties for the
1979 general elections. It lost the presidency but won the gubernatorial elections in three states--Plateau, Imo and Anambra,
the last two being made up mainly of the Igbo people. During
the postelection politicking, the party and the National Party
of Nigeria (NPN) came to an accord at the federal level to
work together and share the spoils of office. At the 1980
party convention, Chief Ogunsanya was elected Chairman while
Dr. Azikiwe was elected Party Leader. Some people saw the
accord between the NPP and NPN as reminiscent of the coalition between the NCNC and the NPC after the 1959 federal elections. The accord broke down in 1981. In the realignment effort to prepare for the 1983 elections and wrest power away
from the National Party of Nigeria (NPN), the NPP joined the
Unity Party of Nigeria (UPN) together with a faction of the
Great Nigerian People's Party (GNPP) and the Imoudu faction
of the People's Redemption Party (PRP) to form the Progressive

Parties Alliance (PPA). However since the alliance could not present common candidates for the elections, not even for the presidential election, the NPP, just like other parties, fielded its own candidates and was badly defeated in many places, including at the center. The party was banned after the December 1983 coup d'état.

THE NIGERIAN PIONEER. The Nigerian Pioneer was launched in 1914 as a newspaper by Sir Kitoyi Ajasa. However, the paper never saw the grateful eyes of the Nigerian nationalists. This was because, unlike the Lagos Weekly Record, owned by Jackson, the Nigerian Pioneer was actively in support of the colonial government's policies. In fact it used to be regarded as "His Master's Voice." Some people used to think that it was a government paper because of its progovernment posture. In reply to the allegation of Pioneer's collusion with the government, Sir Kitoyi said that the paper existed in order to interpret thoroughly and accurately the government to the people and the people to the government.

NIGERIAN PORTS AUTHORITY. An autonomous public corporation created by the Ports Act of 1954. The Authority commenced operation on April 1, 1955, when it assumed the responsibility for the ports and harbors previously under eight different government departments.

The statutory duties of the authorities include: responsibility for the provision and operation of cargo handling and quay facilities, maintaining, improving and regulating the harbors in all ports in Nigeria, dredging to desired depths and providing and maintaining pilotage services, lighting lighthouses, buoys and navigational aids in all Nigerian ports. It is also responsible for identifying and satisfying demands for port facilities and services at minimum costs to the nation, and to use net revenues from previous years for new project developments and rate stabilization.

The governing body is a board composed of a chairman and nine other members appointed by the federal government. It formulates the policy of the Authority, though the Federal Minister of Transport can issue to it directives of a general character on matters affecting public interests and specific directives for the purpose of remedying particular defects. The day-to-day administration is under the supervision of the General Manager, who is also the Chief Executive of the Authority.

Due to the oil boom and improved economic situation between 1975 and 1980, there was a sharp increase in Nigerian international trade. During the 1975-76 period, about 9.3 million tonnes of cargo passed through the various ports as against the 4.1 million tonnes they were designed for. Hence, there was a lot of port congestion. At its height there were over 450 vessels waiting to berth at the Lagos Port alone. Because of this, the Third National Development Plan of 1975-80 provided for port development programs consisting of short-term and long-term measures. By 1980, most of these developmental measures had been accomplished and ships no longer had to wait beyond the normal maximum international period of ten days.

NIGERIAN PRESS COUNCIL. The Nigerian Press Council, established in 1978 under Decree Number 31, was charged, among other things, with the following duties: preparing and enforcing a code of conduct for the guidance of the press and journalists, inquiring into complaints about the conduct of the press, reviewing developments that might restrict supply of information through the press and fostering the achievements and maintenance of high professional and commercial standards by the Nigerian Press. However the decree was not very satisfactory to the press, who believed that they were capable of monitoring their own activities without government intervention.

NIGERIAN RAILWAY CORPORATION. Railway construction began in 1898 and was, from then on, operated and managed as a government department until October 1955, when it was established as a public corporation. The Corporation, with headquarters in Lagos is headed by a Chairman appointed by the federal government and is in its day-to-day operation under the management of a General Manager. The Corporation is charged with the function of providing technically competent transportation services to the nation. The Corporation maintains two main lines linking the two major ocean ports, Lagos and Port Harcourt with the states' headquarters and commercial centers all over the nation. The two lines from Lagos and Port Harcourt meet in Kaduna, from where one line runs to Kano and then to Nguru near the border with the Niger Republic. The other branches from Kuru on the Kafanchan-Jos line and run through Bauchi to Maiduguri, the capital of the Borno State near the border with the Chad Republic. The railway system still remains single tracked and consists of two main routes. However decisions have been reached to construct standard gauge railway track in three phases, linking some parts of the country, especially Sokoto through Kaura Namoda. The first phase will link Apapa to Lagos in Lagos State, followed by the Kaduna to Kafanchan and finally from Kafanchan to Port Harcourt lines.

NIGERIAN SECURITY ORGANIZATION (NSO). Established in 1976 by Decree Number 16. The organization has responsibility for the prevention and detection of any crime against the security of the country, and the protection and preservation of classified materials concerning or relating to the security of the country. It can also be used for any other purposes, whether in Nigeria or outside it, that the President may deem necessary for the maintenance of the security of the nation. (Continued on p. 389.)

NIGERIAN SOCIALIST GROUP. Based in Enugu, Anambra State, the Nigerian Socialist Group was founded in 1960 as a nonpolitical organization, drawing its members from various political parties and many others. The group favored a militant form of pan-Africanism and believed that the fight against western imperialism could only be won by the united efforts of all African states. The group directed most of its effort to foreign policy. Believing that the sufferings of the African people everywhere were caused by the west, it advocated a policy of nonalignment for Nigeria so that Nigeria could be free to deal with both east and west without any discrimination. The group was one of those banned in 1966 when the military came to power.

THE NIGERIAN STANDARDS ORGANIZATION. The Nigerian Standards Organization was established in 1971 as an integral part of the Federal Ministry of Industries. The decree setting it up also established the Nigerian Standards Council to be the governing body of the organization. The main functions of the organization are to standardize methods and products in industries in Nigeria and ensure that federal and state government comply with the national policy on standardization. It also awards certification marks under those standards.

NIGERIAN STEEL DEVELOPMENT AUTHORITY. Established in 1971 to construct, operate and maintain national iron and steel plants; procure materials for the construction, operation and maintenance of the plants; and develop the application and use of iron and steel generally. The Authority consists of ten members representing government and others who had special knowledge and can contribute to the work of the Authority.

NIGERIAN TRADE UNION CONGRESS (NTUC). Formed in April 1960 as a result of the suspension of Chief Michael Imoudu from the Trade Union Congress of Nigeria (TUCN), with Michael Imoudu as its President and Gogo Nzeribe as its Secretary. There were a series of attempts to reconcile the NTUC and TUCN, including the intervention of the Prime Minister of the Federation Alhaji Tafawa Balewa, but all to no avail. In 1961, further attempts were made. In 1962, the NTUC and the TUCN agreed to merge into the United Labour Congress and in May 1962 both organizations stood dissolved.

NIGERIAN UNION OF STUDENTS. A nationalist organization, founded in 1939 at the Abeokuta Grammar School and led by secondary-school graduates and young educated Nigerians. Its purpose was to spearhead the drive toward self-government for the country. In November 1943, it sponsored a youth rally at Ojokoro, at which members were addressed by prominent Nigerians like Bode Thomas, Rotimi Williams, H.O. Davies and Dr. Nnamdi Azikiwe. The rally passed a resolution affirming the need for the formation of a national front. The occasion for the formation of such a front came in the spring of 1944, when students at the King's College resorted to a strike action in protest against the continued use of their dormitories by soldiers during the war while they were made to live in the town in disagreeable lodging places. As a result of the protest,

75 of the student leaders were expelled while eight of them were drafted into the army.

In August 1944, prominent members of the NUS met Dr. Nnamdi Azikiwe and complained to him that the youth of the country were ready to be led but there was no leader. They later called a meeting of various organizations at the Glover Memorial Hall in Lagos for the purpose of forming a national council which would weld together all the heterogeneous masses of Nigeria into a solid block. The conference of the various organizations met on August 26, 1944 and they formed the Nigerian National Council with Herbert Macaulay as President and Dr. Azikiwe as its General Secretary. Thus came into being a political party later known as the National Council of Nigeria and the Cameroons (NCNC), which played a prominent role in Nigeria's political development before and after independence.

NIGERIAN UNION OF TEACHERS (NUT). The Nigerian Union of Teachers (NUT) was formed in 1931 for the purpose of fighting for the betterment of its members. Originally, it was made up of teachers from government and mission schools all over the country, but now its membership includes all grades of teachers from grade II teachers to university graduates. Its membership however does not include university teachers or lecturers, who have their own separate union.

NIGERIAN YOUTH CHARTER. The Nigerian Youth Charter embodied the official program of the Nigerian Youth Movement (NYM). According to the Charter, the aim of the NYM was the development of a united Nigerian nation out of the conglomeration of peoples that inhabit Nigeria, to encourage forces that would serve to promote understanding and a sense of common nationalism among the different elements that made up the country, to be a critic of the government as it was then constituted, working for the removal of inequality of economic opportunities and correcting abuses which militated against the cultural progress of the people.

The Charter was divided into three sections, the political, the economic and the cultural. The Political Charter was aimed at complete autonomy within the British Empire and equal partnership with other member states of the British Commonwealth of nations, abolition of property or income qualifications for the exercise of the franchise and the substitution of universal suffrage. It also aimed at the separation of the administration of the judiciary from the executive.

The Economic Charter demanded for Nigerians economic opportunities equal to those enjoyed by foreigners. The movement would encourage and support all forms of local industry, work for the amelioration of the welfare of the people, better pay for Africans in the civil service, the appointment of Africans into executive posts within the civil service and more Africans in the administrative branch of the civil service.

The cultural and social charter expressed its belief

that mass education should be the pivot of the government's education policy. The NYM would urge government to make education progressively free and compulsory.

The NYM pursued these objectives vigorously. It fought for the Africanization of the civil service, for the abolition of the discriminatory practices of regarding some posts as European posts. It demanded minimum wage for the workers and stimulated the organization of labor unions.

NIGERIAN YOUTH CONGRESS (NYC). Established in 1960 as a non-political movement, the Congress drew its membership from young Nigerian intellectuals, educated elites and the major political parties. It was ideologically socialist and antiwest. It campaigned against what it regarded as neocolonialist powers which members saw as subverting Nigeria's independence. Thus, in November 1960, the Congress criticized the defense agreement entered into between Nigeria and Britain, contending that the government was trying to bring Nigeria into the Western bloc. In December the Congress organized demonstrations against the agreement, leading to the arrest of some of its members. It also organized demonstrations in support of Patrice Lumumba in the Congo (now Zaïre), putting pressure on the government to support his cause. In 1963 it campaigned against the introduction of the Preventive Detention Act in Nigeria. The demonstration often became violent and the National Council of Nigerian Citizens (NCNC) and the Action Group (AG) parties had to ask their supporters to resign from it. The President of the Congress was a Lagos medical practitioner, Dr. Tunji Otegbeye. The Congress was one of the organizations banned in 1966 when the military came to power.

NIGERIAN YOUTH MOVEMENT. In 1934, four Nigerians--Samuel Akinsanya, Ernest Ikoli, H.O. Davies and Dr. J.C. Vaughan-- formed the Lagos Youth Movement to oppose the government's education policy with regard to the alleged deficiencies of the Yaba Higher College. In 1936, to make the organization truly national, the name was changed to Nigerian Youth Movement (NYM). Its aim was "the development of a united nation out of the conglomeration of the people who inhabit Nigeria." It endeavored to bring about understanding and a sense of common nationality among the different peoples of the country, and by 1937 the NYM had come to the forefront of the nationalist struggle for self-government in the country. In 1938, Dr. Nnamdi Azikiwe became a member, and the organization became so popular in the capital city of Lagos that it won all the elections to the Lagos Town Council and the three Lagos seats on the Legislative Council. However in 1941 the movement had a nerve-racking crisis from which it never recovered. When Dr. K.A. Abayomi, the president of the organization resigned from the Legislative Council, Ernest Ikoli, an Ijaw man, and S.A. Akinsanya, an Ijebu Yorubaman, vied for the vacant seat. Dr. Azikiwe supported Akinsanya but others supported Ikoli, who finally won. Azikiwe felt hurt and disappointed and so withdrew

from the organization, accusing the leadership of tribal prejudice against his candidate. As a result of this the organization
became moribund and its leaders later left it, one by one, to
engage in other affairs.

NIGERIA POLICE FORCE. The Nigeria Police Force is headed by
an Inspector-General of Police who is supported by a Deputy
Inspector-General of Police and Commissioners in each state.
The Inspector-General is appointed and can be dismissed by
the President after due consultation with the Police Service
Commission, and Police Commissioners can be dismissed by
the Police Service Commission. State Governors and Commissioners (ministers) acting for them can issue lawful directives
to Police Commissioners, but a Police Commissioner may ask
that the directives be referred to the President. At present
the total strength of the police is about 80,000 men and women
in over 1,300 stations. There is the Nigeria Police Council,
which has the responsibility for policy, organization and administration of the police force, including establishment and financial matters. For appointment, promotion and discipline there
is the Police Service Commission, members of which are appointed by the President subject to the approval of the Senate.

NIGERIA'S ARMORIAL BEARING. The coat of arms has an eagle
mounted on a shield bisected by two wavy silver bands. Two
white chargers support the shield. The base of the shield is
a wreath of flowers. The black shield is supposed to represent
Nigeria's fertile soil, the wavy silver bands are the rivers Niger and Benue; the eagle stands for the country's strength while
the chargers are Nigeria's symbol of dignity. The wreath de-
picts the national colors of green and white. The motto be-
neath all this is "Unity and Faith."

NIGER RIVER. Nigeria takes its name from River Niger. The Niger rises in the mountains northeast of Sierra Leone about 150
miles from the sea. It then flows northeasterly until it reaches
Timbuktu. From there it flows eastward for about 200 miles
and veers south toward Lokoja where it joins its greatest tributary, the Benue River. The exploration of the Niger River
was one of the main objectives of the European explorers who
were desirous of opening up trade in the interior of Africa.
Mungo Park was the first to tell the world how the Niger flowed
and it was on it that he died during his second voyage.

NIGER STATE. Created in February 1976 out of the former North-
Western State, it comprises most of what was known as the
Niger Province. It shares borders with Kaduna State on the
east, Plateau State on the southeast, Sokoto State on the north
and Kwara State on the south. The state is about 65,037 sq.
km. in area with a population of about 1.2 million people. The
ethnic groups that make up the state can be classified into the
Afro-Asian and the Kwa linguistic families. The Afro-Asian
group is made up of the Koro, Kadara, and the Bassas while

the subbranch of the Kwa group is made up of the Nupe, Gwari
and the Kamuku.   Other language groups in the state include
the Hausas, the Kambari and the Fulani.

Most of the people of the state are farmers, growing
food crops like guinea-corn, rice, yams, millet, groundnuts
and cotton.   There is also a large quantity of mineral resources like glass sands, marble and Kaolin.   A substantial
proportion of the people of the state are craftsmen, producing
handmade pottery, glass beads and bangles, mats, brassworks,
embroidery and dyed cloth.

The new capital of Nigeria, Abuja, is located in the
state while the state capital is Minna.   Other towns include
Bida, Agaie, Wushishi, Kuta, Lafiagi and Suleija.

NIGER SUDAN.   The region lying between Lake Chad and the Niger
River, it extended from the present Borno State to Sokoto State.

NJOKU, PROFESSOR ENI.   Born on November 6, 1917 in Ebem,
Ohafia in Imo State, he attended the Ebem Primary School and
the Hope Waddell Training Institute in Calabar from 1933 to
1936.   He then proceeded to Yaba Higher College in Lagos.
Later on he went to the University of Manchester in England
to study Botany, where he graduated with first-class honors in
1947.   In 1948 he received his M.A. degree there and in 1954
he obtained a Ph.D. degree from the University of London.
Dr. Njoku was appointed Chairman of the Electricity Corporation of Nigeria (ECN), now National Electric Power Authority
(NEPA).   In 1962, he became the first Vice-Chancellor of the
University of Lagos.   He resigned in 1965, following a crisis
over his proposed reappointment, and went to Michigan State
University as a visiting professor.   In 1966 he was appointed
the Vice-Chancellor of the University of Nigeria, Nsukka.
During the civil war of 1967-1970, he supported the Biafran
cause.   After the war he returned to teach Botany at the University of Nigeria, Nsukka.   Professor Njoku was not only an
academician, he also took part in politics.   He was elected to
the Eastern House of Assembly in 1952 and from there to the
Federal House of Representatives in Lagos where he became
the Minister of Mines and Power 1952-53.   He was therefore
intimately involved in the Eastern Regional Crisis of 1953.   He
also became a member of the Senate in 1960.

Professor Njoku received honorary degrees of Doctor
of Science from the University of Nigeria, 1964, and from the
University of Lagos in 1973.   Michigan State University also
conferred on him an honorary degree of Doctor of Law.   He
also served on the Boards of the Commonwealth Scientific Committee, on the United Nations Advisory Committee on the Application of Science and Technology, on the UNESCO Advisory
Committee on Natural Sciences and on the Councils of the Universities of Zambia and Zaïre.   He died in London on December 22, 1974.

NJOKU, RAYMOND AMANZE.   A lawyer and a politician, Raymond

Njoku was born in August 1915 in Emekuku in Owerri Division
of Imo State. He attended Our Lady's School in his hometown
and from there to the Ahiara Catholic Secondary School 1929-
1936. He then went to St. Charles College at Onitsha to train
as a teacher. He taught at the same school in 1939 but left
in 1943 for St. Gregory's College in Lagos. In the same year
he left Nigeria to study law at the University of London. He
was called to the bar at the Middle Temple in 1947.

Upon arrival in Nigeria in 1947, he set up a private
legal practice in Aba and also became interested in politics.
He later joined the National Council of Nigeria and Cameroon
(NCNC) and was Chairman of the party's Eastern Region Working Committee. He tried to get elected to the Eastern House
of Assembly in 1951 and failed. In the 1954 federal elections,
however he was elected into the Nigerian Legislative Council
in Lagos where he became Minister of Commerce and Industry
in the federal council of ministers. In 1955, he became Federal Minister of Trade and Industry and in October 1955, he
had become the second national Vice-President of the NCNC.
In the federal elections of 1959, he was also elected and he
became Minister of Transport in the coalition government of
the Northern People's Congress (NPC) and the NCNC under
Prime Minister Alhaji Tafawa Balewa. In 1964 he became
Minister of Communications and Aviation. When the military
took over in 1966, he went into private practice. He was
chairman of the National Catholic Laity Council of Nigeria and
was knighted by Pope John XXIII with the Knight Grand Cross
of the Order of St. Gregory the Great. His services to the
country were also duly recognized when he became the recipient of the national honor of the Commander of the Federal
Republic of Nigeria. He died September 21, 1977.

NKRUMAH, DR. KWAME. A Ghanaian nationalist, a Pan-Africanist,
the first Premier of independent Ghana and its first President.
Born in 1909, he was educated in the United States and, upon
his return into Ghana, he became a politician. He later founded
his own party, the Convention People's Party (CPP), which
fought for Ghana's independence from the British and got it in
1957. From then on Ghana's independence became a symbol
for all of Africa. But Nkrumah's Pan-Africanism was more
militant than that of Nigerian leaders.

In 1960 Nigeria became independent with Sir Abubakar
Tafawa Balewa, a moderate Pan-Africanist, as the Prime Minister and Chief Obafemi Awolowo, leader of the Action Group,
as the Leader of Opposition. Nkrumah began to court the support of the opposition party in Nigeria to support his African
position. In June 1961, Chief Awolowo visited Ghana for discussion with the Ghanaian President, and upon his return Chief
Awolowo's criticism of Nigerian foreign policy became much
louder and showed that he was leaning towards Nkrumah's Pan-
Africanism. After the visit many Action Group members went
to Ghana for one kind of training or another: some went to
train in party organization while others went to train in the

use of firearms. Furthermore, when Chief Anthony Enahoro, an Action Group Party leader, escaped from Nigeria when he was to be arrested for treasonable felony, he went first to Ghana before proceeding to London, and Mr. Sam Ikoku, another AG leader, took refuge in Ghana under Nkrumah.

Dr. Nkrumah was removed from power on January 24 by the military, just over a week after the Nigerian coup of January 15, 1966. He died later in the Ivory Coast.

NOK CULTURE. The Nok culture was developed in the Nok Valley, north of the Jos Plateau in Plateau State. The valley was surrounded by rocks out of which tin had been eroded and concentrated into alluvial deposits. Some of the artifacts found there include stone axes, terra-cotta figurines and other iron materials. The Nok culture is said to have a common element in the production of figurines: human heads were usually portrayed with triangular eyes and perforations for the pupils, nostrils and the mouth.

NONALIGNMENT. Nigeria follows a policy of nonalignment in her relations with the superpowers. It maintains cordial relations with the countries of both east and west as well as other countries of the world in Asia, Latin America and Africa.

NORDCHURCHAID. A Scandinavian relief organization during the Nigerian civil war. The organization was set up by Scandinavian churches, and it flew relief materials to the beleaguered Biafrans fighting against the federal government.

NORTH-CENTRAL STATE. One of the six states created in Northern Nigeria in May 1967, North-Central State occupied the same land area as the present Kaduna State and its name was changed into Kaduna State in 1976 when the country became a federation of 19 states. It was then the policy of the federal military government not to designate any state with its geographical location of north, west or east.

The capital of the state was Kaduna. See also KADUNA STATE.

NORTH-EASTERN STATE. The largest of the six states created in the north in 1967, it was made up of the Bornu, Bauchi, Adamawa and Sardauna provinces. It had an area of about 271,950 sq. km. and with a population of about 7.9 million people. In 1976, the state was divided virtually into three states, Borno, Gongola and Bauchi States.

The capital of the state was Maiduguri. See also BAUCHI, BORNO and GONGOLA STATES.

NORTHERN ELEMENT PROGRESSIVE ASSOCIATION (NEPA). Formed in Kano in 1945 by Mallam H.R. Abdallah, the Northern Element Progressive Association was a northern extension of Dr. Nnamdi Azikiwe's nationalist struggle. In fact, the same Mallam Abdallah organized the branch of the Zikist

Movement in Kano and became its National President. The
Kano authorities were opposed to NEPA and it was therefore
short-lived.

NORTHERN ELEMENT PROGRESSIVE UNION (NEPU). A political
party formed in 1950 by Mallam Aminu Kano, previously a
member of the Northern People's Congress (NPC). Being dissatisfied with the moderate attitude of the NPC toward traditional rulers and the lot of the ordinary people in the country,
he broke away to found the NEPU. As a political party, it
allied itself with the masses against the authority of the Emirs,
traditional rulers whose authority is exercised through the Native Authority. As such they saw a class struggle between the
masses and the Native Authorities and their interest was to
organize the masses for the conquest of the powers of government. Though based in the north, its program aimed at a
united Nigeria, which was patently different from the regional
separatism of the NPC. It allied itself with the National Council of Nigeria and Cameroon (NCNC), based in the south, which
opened it to the charges that it was an agent of southern domination. The party's support came mainly from Kano Province
and the areas around, and it was no match for the NPC, which
effectively controlled political power in the north. The party
was banned in 1966 after the military takeover.

NORTHERN HOUSE OF ASSEMBLY. The Richards Constitution of
1946 created the Northern Regional Council, consisting of two
chambers: the House of Chiefs and the House of Assembly.
The House of Assembly consisted of the Senior Resident as
President, 18 other official members and 20-24 unofficial members, 14-18 of whom were selected by the Native Authorities
and six to be appointed by the Governor to represent interests
and communities inadequately represented. In 1951 the house
consisted of the President, four official members, 90 elected
members and not more than ten special members. In 1966,
after the military takeover, the house ceased to exist.

NORTHERN HOUSE OF CHIEFS. The Northern House of Chiefs was
created under the Richards Constitution of 1946 as the second
chamber of the then Northern Regional Council. The House of
Chiefs consisted of the Chief Commissioner as President, all
First-Class Chiefs and not less than ten Second-Class Chiefs
selected by the chiefs themselves in accordance with the rules
laid down by the Chiefs themselves. In the Macpherson Consti-
tuion of 1951, the House consisted of the Lieutenant-Governor
as President, three official members, all First-Class Chiefs,
37 other Chiefs and an adviser on Moslem Laws. The house
ceased to exist in January 1966 when the military took over
power.

NORTHERNIZATION POLICY. After Northern Nigeria became self-
governing in internal affairs in 1959, it embarked on a northernization policy. This was basically a recruitment policy

designed to keep the southerners out. Expatriates were often engaged, though at great cost, in preference to Nigerians of non-Northern origin. Any non-Northerners recruited, be they expatriates or Nigerians, were recruited on a contract system, that is, the contract would not be renewed if persons of Northern Nigerian origin became available.

NORTHERN NIGERIA MARKETING BOARD. Established in 1954 as a corporate body, the Northern Nigeria Marketing Board was charged with the function of securing the most favorable arrangements for the purchase and evacuation of produce intended for export, and by so doing, promote the development of the producing industries concerned for the benefit of the producers. It was given power to fix prices to be paid to producers and to appoint licensed buying and storage agents. It also had power to undertake investment projects. The Board was, however, dissolved in 1977 after the establishment of the Commodity Boards. The most important crops handled by the Board were groundnuts (peanuts) and cotton.

NORTHERN NIGERIA POLICE FORCE. In 1900 the British government revoked the charter of the Royal Niger Company and proclaimed the area under the administration of the Protectorate of Northern Nigeria. The Royal Niger Constabulary was split into two: the Northern Nigeria Police Force and the Northern Nigeria Regiment.

NORTHERN PEOPLE'S CONGRESS (NPC). Following the pattern of ethnic group organizational activities going on in the south as seen by the establishment of a Pan-Ibo Federal Union in 1944 and Egbe Omo Odudua, a Yoruba cultural group, first in London in 1945 and later on in Nigeria in 1948, people in the north too began to think of a Pan-Northern Nigerian cultural organization. The organization was formed in 1949 and was called Jami'yya Mutanen Arewa, which means Northern People's Congress. The leaders of the organization included the three leaders of the Bauchi Improvement Union: Mallam Sa'ad Zungur, the first Northern Nigerian to attend Yaba Higher College, Mallam Aminu Kano, a Fulani school teacher who returned from London in 1947, Mallam Abubakar Tafawa Balewa, the headmaster of Bauchi Middle School, together with Dr. A. E. B. Dikko and Mallam Yahaya Gusau. The aims of the organization were clearly innocuous: it wanted to unite the peoples of the north into one organization to preserve northern regional autonomy within a united Nigeria; it did not intend to usurp the authority of the traditional rulers, in fact, it intended to enhance it whenever possible. It believed that the north could be saved only by the northerners but it still wanted to be friendly with the other peoples of Nigeria.

Because of this conservative attitude of the organization and their deference to the Emirs and to the status quo, some more radical elements broke away. They felt they did not want an organization that would unite the north against the feared domination of the south, but rather an organization to which other people from other regions could join, and which would aim first and foremost at Nigerian Unity. It was led by Mallam Aminu Kano, and they all formed another organization known as the Northern Element Progressive Union (NEPU). Because of the successes of NEPU in the Kano Area, a party which was allied with the National Council of Nigeria and the Cameroons and which the NPC saw as a symbol of southern domination, the Jami'yya, which had appeared to be in limbo, began to regroup to fight NEPU in the forthcoming election to usher in the Macpherson Constitution in 1951. The remaining leaders of the organization together with the late Sir Ahmadu Bello, the Sardauna of Sokoto, renamed it the Northern People's Congress and decided to contest the elections under its platform. Alhaji Sir Ahmadu Bello was elected leader of the party while Mallam Abubakar Tafawa Balewa became deputy leader of the party.

The party's aims were imbued with the fear of southern domination, which the people saw as a great threat. The aims included regional autonomy within a united Nigeria, local government reforms without doing much violence to the traditional emirate system, initiating a drive for education throughout the region while at the same time preserving and increasing the cultural influence on the people, retention of the traditional system of appointing the Emirs but with a wider representation on the Electoral Committee, inculcation in the northerners of a genuine love for their region, with the motto "One North, One People," irrespective of religion, tribe or rank to fight for eventual self-government for Nigeria and to seek the cooperation of any organization in or out of the northern region whose aims and aspirations coincided with those of the party.

The party became very powerful and overbearing. It not only effectively controlled the whole of Northern Nigeria, but it was the major coalition partner in the federal government until 1966, when the military came into power and disbanded all political parties.

NORTHERN PROGRESSIVE FRONT. The Northern Progressive Front (NPF) was formed in 1963 as an alliance between the Northern Elements Progressive Union (NEPU) and the United Middle Belt Congress (UMBC). They agreed on a single list of candidates and a common program. The leader of the Northern Progressive Front was Mallam Aminu Kano. For the 1964 general elections the NPF joined the United Progressive Grand Alliance (UPGA), made up principally of NCNC and the Action Group parties.

NORTHERN PROVINCES LAW SCHOOL. A Moslem school set up by Alhaji Abdullahi Bayero, the Emir of Kano after his return from Mecca in 1934. It was to train the Alkalis in the Moslem common law known as the Sharia. In 1947 it became the School for Arabic Studies and came under government control. The school then trained teachers in Arabic and Islamic subjects as well as English, arithmetic and other subjects.

NORTHERN REGION. The Northern Region, made up of the old
Protectorate of Northern Nigeria, consisted of over three-
quarters of the total land area of the country and, according
to the 1963 census, more than half the population. Though
culturally heterogenous, it had the integrative bond of Islam
and the former Fulani empire gave much of the area some
feeling of identity. The Hausa language, which became the
lingua franca of the people in the region, also gave the area
a sense of identity. This was why people from the north, in
spite of their ethnic differences were generally referred to in
the south as Hausas. Though Islamic religion is strong in the
north, all of the region did not accept Islam. There is the
non-Muslim area of the Middle-Belt which escaped the Fulani
conquest of the nineteenth century and have therefore been open
to greater influence from the Christian missionaries and western education. These people have only been partially integrated
into the dominant culture and they have been famous for their
struggle for political freedom from the Hausa-Fulani hegemony.
These people included the Tiv, Gwarri and the Nupe. The
major towns in the region were Kano, Sokoto, Ilorin, Zaria,
Guasau, Katsina, Yola, Borno, Jos, Minna and Kaduna, which
was the capital city.
      Because of the preponderance of the Northern Region
in the federation as seen by its land area and its population,
and because of the fact that only one party, the Northern People's Congress (NPC), effectively controlled the region, fears
began to be felt and expressed that for the forseeable future,
the north would dominate the politics of the whole federation.
As such, demands began to be made that the north should be
divided into more regions or states, but nothing was done about
this by the colonial, postindependence, and the first republican
governments until after the military took over power in January
1966. In 1967, before the outbreak of the civil war, General
Yakubu Gowon divided the nation into 12 states--six in the south
and six in the north. The six northern states were Benue-
Plateau, Kwara, North-Western, North-Eastern, North-Central
and Kano states. In 1976, these six states were further subdivided into ten states: Kano, Sokoto, Kaduna, Borno, Gongola,
Bauchi, Kwara, Niger, Plateau and Benue states. The Northern Region falls within the savannah, which has made it a
suitable place for animal husbandary (cattle, ship and goats).
Thus a large percentage of the population engage in cattle rearing and the keeping of other livestock. A good number of the
others are farmers or traders. Among the most important
food crops in the north are groundnuts (peanuts), millet, rice,
guinea-corn, beans and maize. The administrative capital of
the region was Kaduna. Before the military took over in 1966,
the administration of the region was dominated by the Northern
People's Congress (NPC) from the time it was formed in 1951.
The leader of the party was Sir Ahmadu Bello, the Sardauna
of Sokoto, and the first and only Premier of the region. In
1961, the region established the Ahmadu Bello University in
Zaria.

NORTHERN REGION DEVELOPMENT CORPORATION. This Corporation was established in 1955 and, like its counterparts in the east and west, its purpose was to speed up the economic development of the region. To this end, it made most of its funds available for agricultural land settlement, agricultural production development, water supplies, irrigation and communications and the control of animal pests like the tsetse fly. The Corporation also granted loans to native authorities for the development of markets, motor parks and abattoirs. Businessmen also benefitted from its loans.

NORTHERN TEACHERS' ASSOCIATION. Established in London in 1947 by Mallam Aminu Kano, who later became the leader of the Northern Elements Progressive Union. In 1948, Mallam Aminu Kano convened the first meeting of the Association in Nigeria. It was the first northern labor union in history.

NORTH-WESTERN STATE. One of the 12 states created in May 1967, North-Western State shared common borders in the north with the Republic of Niger, in the south with Kwara and Benue Plateau states and in the east with the North-Central State. It had an area of about 168,770 sq. km. and a population of about 5.7 million people. In 1976 the state was divided into Sokoto and Niger states. The capital of the state was Sokoto. See also SOKOTO and NIGER STATES.

NPN-NPP ACCORD. When Alhaji Shehu Shagari's election as President had been confirmed by the Supreme Court in September 1979, the President-elect invited the leaders of the other four parties to join him in a broad-based government, and asked them to allow their party members to accept any positions that he might offer them in his government. Only the Nigerian People's Party (NPP) agreed to join in his government. The two parties drew up an agreement which was later known as the NPN-NPP Accord.

According to the accord, a special development agency would be set up to ensure the rapid economic development of those states whose social and economic development were lagging behind the other states or had suffered serious setback arising from natural disasters, war or the difficult nature of their terrain. They would also set up a constitution study and review committee, as a matter of urgency in order to ensure permanent stability by removing likely causes of friction arising from various types of ambiguities and conflicts in the new constitution. The committee would, among other things, examine the creation of more states, Land Use Decree, issue of adequate compensation for properties compulsorily acquired, and local government. It would also initiate a workable program based on the manifestos of the cooperating parties within the first 90 days of the new administration and recommend same for adoption by the federal government. The two parties also agreed on their conduct of foreign affairs and their approach to religious issues: to abide by the 1979 constitutional provisions that forbid adoption of state religion, that guarantee freedom of thought, conscience and religion, and freedom from discrimination. Because the two parties were lacking in agreement on common economic and social programs, the accord broke down in July 1981.

NSUKKA. A university city, the home of the second Nigerian university, the University of Nigeria, Nsukka.

NUPE. Living mainly in Niger State, the Nupe are divided into many subgroups like Batau, Beni, Kyedye, Eghagi, Ebe, Benu and many others. However they speak related Nupe languages. Their main towns are Bida, Mokwa and Jebba. They are famous for their glass, silver, bronze and brass works and their craftsmen are organized into societies and guilds according to their work. Many others are farmers, growing such crops as rice, guinea corn, millet and yams.

Nupe State was said to have been founded by Tsoede, the son of the Ata of Igala whose capital was Idah. The state became very powerful between the sixteenth and the eighteenth centuries, during which it waged successful wars against Oyo empire (q.v.). The Fulani Jihad of the early nineteenth century had great difficulty in getting a foothold in the state through one Mallam Dendo, who became effective ruler of the state, and his successors, taking the title of Etsu Nupe (Chief of Nupe), established themselves in Bida and ruled from there. At the end of the century British rule was established through the activities of the Royal Niger Company.

NWAFOR-ORIZU, DR. AKWEKE ABYSSINIA. Born in July 1920, he attended St. Thomas Central School and Onitsha Central School between 1924 and 1931. By taking private lessons he passed the Junior Cambridge in 1937. In 1938 he secured a scholarship to study at Achimota College in Ghana and in 1939 he went to the Lincoln University in Pennsylvania in the United States, where he met the late Dr. Kwame Nkrumah of Ghana. He later transferred to Howard University in Washington D.C. where he studied Political Science.

In 1940 he became a member of the Marcus Garvey Movement in New York City and in 1941, he, together with people like John Karefe-Smart of Sierra Leone, Dr. K.O. Mbadiwe and Mazi Mbonu Ojike, founded the African Students Association of the United States and Canada under the International Students Union of the university. In 1944, he obtained his M.A. degree in Public Law and Government from Columbia University in New York. He was Editor of the Negro Digest, and Contributing Editor to the Pittsburgh Courier. With Dr. Nkrumah as the President of the African Students Association of the United States and Canada, he was elected Vice-President, and he later became the President of the Association. In 1944, he published his book, Without Bitterness.

Back in Nigeria in 1949, he championed the cause of the Nigerian mine workers during the Enugu massacre of 21 miners and was placed under house arrest for 14 days by the colonial government. In 1951 he became a member of the Eastern House of Assembly, from which he was elected to the membership of the Federal Legislative House in Lagos. Before independence, he, at different periods, occupied many political posts, including that of the Chief Whip of the NCNC party in both regional and national legislative houses. In 1960 he was appointed the first Senator to represent Onitsha Province in the Senate. In 1964, he became the President of the Senate, a position he was holding when the military intervened in politics in January 1966, a fact which explained why it was he who was responsible for handing over federal power to the federal military government during the coup of January 1966. After the civil war, he became a private person. When party politics began in 1978, he joined the National Party of Nigeria but was not a very active member.

NWOKEDI COMMISSION. The Nwokedi Commission was the one-man commission under Mr. F.C. Nwokedi appointed in March 1966 by the then Head of State General Ironsi who took over after the January 1966 coup. The Commission was to look into the problem of unifying the civil services of the federation and make recommendations. As a result of its proposals, Unification Decree Number 34 of 1966 came into being.

NZEOGWU, MAJOR PATRICK CHUKWUMA KADUNA. Leader of the first Nigerian coup d'état of January 15, 1966, Major Nzeogwu was born in 1937 in Kaduna, in the Northern Region where his parents, both Ibos from Eastern Nigeria, lived. He attended St. John's College in Kaduna, 1950-1955. He later joined the Nigerian Army as a cadet and was sent to Sandhurst where he became a commissioned officer. By January 1966, he had risen to the position of a Major.

The plot to overthrow the government of Alhaji Sir Abubakar Tafawa Balewa was hatched in 1965 by Major Nzeogwu, Major Emmanuel Ifeajuna, Major D.O. Okafor and Captain E. N. Nwobosi. The plot became effective on January 15, 1966. Nzeogwu, the leader of the plot, was in charge of the Kaduna operation, that is, eliminating leading figures in the Northern People's Congress (NPC) which, at the time, dominated not only the politics of the Northern Region, but also of the federation. As such, it was he who led his forces to the leader of the party, Sir Ahmadu Bello, the Sardauna of Sokoto and Premier of the Northern Region. The Premier was killed, and on January 15, Nzeogwu broadcast a message to the nation that no citizen needed to fear as long as he was law abiding. The type of people his "Supreme Council of the Revolution" was after were political profiteers, swindlers, the men who received bribes and demanded ten percent of contracts awarded, the tribalists and the nepotists.

The main aim of the coup, he said, was to establish a strong united and progressive nation, free from corruption and internal strife.

Unfortunately for his revolution, many of the people entrusted with operations in the other parts of the country did not creditably discharge their duties. They were able to get to the Prime Minister in Lagos and they killed him. They got the Premier of Western Nigeria, Chief S. L. Akintola, and killed him and they also killed Chief Festus Okotie-Eboh, the Federal Minister of Finance, together with other senior military officers. They did not get General Johnson T. U. Aguiyi-Ironsi and in the Eastern Region, the operation was a complete failure. As such, they did not succeed in taking complete control of the country, but they got rid of the regime which most people had begun to hate, and Nzeogwu became a hero to many people. Not being in complete control, he and his men had to surrender to General Ironsi, to whom the federal cabinet had submitted power. On January 19, 1966, Nzeogwu went to submit to General Ironsi in Lagos. He was detained first in Lagos and then later in Eastern Nigeria. Colonel Ojukwu released him in March 1967 before the Eastern Region declared its secession of Biafra from the rest of the country. Though he disagreed with Colonel Ojukwu on secession, he fought on the side of Biafra and was killed in action on July 26, 1967. The federal troops discovered his body and it was buried with full military honors in Kaduna, where he was born. Nzeogwu was a nationalist and beloved by his men.

-O-

OBA. Oba is the term for "king" among the Yoruba people and the title of the ruler of the Edo-speaking kingdom of Benin. The Oba of each Yoruba kingdom is known by a specific title like the "Alaafin of Oyo" or the "Ooni of Ife," and so on. All the principal Obas in Yorubaland, including the Oba of Benin claim their descent from Odudua, the mythical ancestor of the Yorubas. Both the Benin and the Yoruba Obas were "divine" Kings who, in the past, exercised great spiritual and political powers in their kingdoms, but whose authority was nonetheless checked by Councils of Chiefs or some secret societies like the Ogboni Society, composed of traditional religious and political leaders.

OBASANJO, GENERAL OLUSEGUN. Former Head of State, head of the federal military government and Commander-in-Chief of the Armed Forces from 1976 to 1979, General Olusegun Obasanjo was born on March 5, 1937 at Abeokuta in Ogun State. After his primary education he went to Abeokuta Baptist High School. He enlisted in the Nigerian Army in 1958 and was later sent to Mons Officer Cadets' School in England. He returned to Nigeria and was commissioned in 1959. He was promoted to full Lieutenant in 1960 and later served with the United Nations forces in the Congo. He later joined the Engineering Unit of the Nigerian Army and was promoted to Captain in 1963 and Commander of the Engineering Unit. He was sent to the Royal Engineering Young Officers course at Shrivenham

in England and in January 1965 he was promoted to Major.
In the same year he attended the Indian Staff College, and was
later on attachment to the Indian Army Engineering School at
Kirkee.   In 1967 he was promoted to Lieutenant Colonel and
was Commander of the Second Area Command of the Nigerian
Army, Commander of the Second Division (Rear) Ibadan and
Commander Ibadan Garrison, 1967-1969.   He was promoted to
Colonel in 1969 and later commanded the Third Marine Commando Division operating on the South-Eastern front of Biafra
during the civil war.   He accepted the surrender of the Biafran forces in January 1970.   In the same year he was appointed Commander, Engineering Corps.   In 1972 he was promoted Brigadier and he later went on to further studies at the
Royal College of Defence Studies in London, 1973-1974.   He
was appointed Commissioner for Works and Housing, January-
July 1975.   Following the coup d'état of July 29, 1975, he became Chief of Staff Supreme Headquarters under the late General Murtala Muhammed.   After the attempted coup of February
13, 1976, staged by Lt. Col. B.S. Dimka, in which General
Muhammed was assassinated, he was appointed Head of State
and Commander-in-Chief of the Armed forces and Chairman
Supreme Military Council.   He faithfully carried out the military program of disengagement and handed over power to Alhaji Shehu Shagari, the newly elected President of Nigeria in
1979.   He retired from the army in 1979 to become a farmer.
In 1980 he was honored with the title of Grand Commander of
the Order of the Federal Republic of Nigeria.   He wrote My
Command, an account of his activities and those of his division during the Nigerian civil war.

OBI, PROFESSOR CHIKE.   A mathematician and a politician.   Born
on April 7, 1921 in Zaria, he was educated in Zaria, Onitsha
and at the Yaba Higher College in Lagos.   He later went to
Britain for further studies.   Upon his return to Nigeria, he
lectured in mathematics at the University of Ibadan in 1951.
In 1971, he was appointed Professor of Mathematics at the
University of Lagos.   Professor Obi was the founder and the
leader of the defunct Dynamic Party of Nigeria.

ODEBIYI, CHIEF JONATHAN AKINREMI OLAWOLE.   Leader of the
Unity Party of Nigeria in the Senate, 1979-1983.   He was born
in 1923 at Ipaja, Lagos State, attended St. Andrew's School,
Ipaja, CMS Grammar School, Lagos and in 1944 proceeded to
Fourah Bay College in Freetown, Sierra Leone to study Arts,
and received a B.A. degree from the University of Durham in
Britain.
          In 1951 he was elected Action Group member of the
Western House of Assembly and in 1956 he became Minister
of Education under Chief Obafemi Awolowo, who was Premier,
and later was the Minister of Finance and leader of the House
until the Action Group crisis of 1962, in which he took a prominent part.   It was when he was about to move the first business motion of the day that Mr. E. O. Oke, member for Ogbomosho

South West constituency, raised an alarm and started to fling a chair across the floor of the House. In 1978, when the ban on political activity was lifted, he became a member of the Unity Party of Nigeria and was elected a Senator for Egbado North/South Senatorial District.

ODUDUWA. There are two stories as to the origin of Oduduwa. According to the Yoruba creation myth, Oduduwa, the son of Olorun, the Supreme God, was sent down from heaven with a handful of earth, a cockerel and a palm nut. Upon arrival on the water-covered Earth, he scattered the earth he brought with him over the water, the cockerel scratched it and the palm nut grew into a palm tree. The very place where the earth was created is called Ile-Ife, from where the Yoruba people migrated to other parts of the world. The second story says that Oduduwa was a prince from Mecca, the son of a king named Lamurudu. He was driven out for his idolatrous worship and after wandering for a long time, settled at Ile-Ife. He had many children and grandchildren who spread out to other parts, where they established their own kingdoms. These two stories go on to explain the Yoruba belief that Oduduwa was their ancestor. It is also important to note that all the Yoruba Obas and the Oba of Benin like to trace their ancestral line to Oduduwa. It is also believed that Oduduwa brought the Ifa religion to Ile-Ife, established it there, and also founded the Ogboni cult, devoted to the worship of the earth, to protect the ancient customs and institutions of his people. There is today a shrine in Ile-Ife, devoted to the worship of Oduduwa, and many institutions and places have been named after him, e.g. Oduduwa College in Ile-Ife and Oduduwa Hall at the University of Ife in Ile-Ife.

OFF-SHORE OIL REVENUES. From April 1, 1971, the ownership of and the title to the territorial waters and the continental shelf was vested in the federal government. Further, all royalties, rents and other revenues derived from oil accrue to the federal government.

"OGBANJE" See "ABIKU"

OGUNDIPE, BRIGADIER BABAFEMI OLATUNDE. Brigadier Babafemi Olatunde Ogundipe was the number-two man at the Supreme Headquarters as Chief of Staff in January 1966 when the military took over power. His senior, General Aguyi-Ironsi became Head of State after the military takeover.
    Brigadier Ogundipe was born on September 6, 1924. He attended the Wesley and Banham Memorial School in Port Harcourt and in 1943 he enlisted in the army and was posted to India and Burma, where he served the British during the Second World War. He had training in England and was commissioned in 1953. He served with the British forces in Germany before coming to Nigeria, and later served in the United Nations Peace-Keeping Forces in the Congo (now Zaïre), 1960-1963.

Upon his arrival in Nigeria he became Commander of the Second Brigade of the Nigerian Army. He was later sent to London as military adviser to the Nigerian High Commissioner.

The second military coup of July 1966, in which General Ironsi was killed, left Brigadier Ogundipe as the most senior officer in the army. In normal circumstances, he should have succeeded the late Head of State, but things were not normal. The new coup-makers preferred Colonel Gowon as Head of State. One of the reasons why Lt. Colonel Ojukwu refused to accept General Gowon as Head of State and Supreme Commander was that a more senior officer was still available and it was he who should have assumed the post. He was however posted by Gowon to London as Nigeria's High Commissioner, where he served during the civil war. After the war, he was replaced, but he died in London on November 20, 1971 and was buried in Nigeria.

OGUNSANYA, CHIEF ADENIRAN. A lawyer and a politician, Chief Adeniran Ogunsanya was born on January 31, 1918 at Ikorodu, Lagos State. After his primary education he went to the Lagos Government School and King's College, Lagos. He later proceeded to the University of Manchester in England in 1945 and the Gray's Inn School of Law in London where he was called to the bar.

Between 1956 and 1959, Chief Ogunsanya was the Chairman of the Federal Government Industrial Board. In 1959 he became a member of Parliament and was later appointed the Secretary of the Federal Parliamentary Party of the National Council of Nigeria and Cameroons (NCNC) and Federal Minister of Housing and Surveys in 1965. In 1968 he was appointed Attorney-General and Commissioner for Justice in Lagos State and was later made a Commissioner for Education in the same state. In the wake of political activities in 1978, he became a foundation member of the Nigerian People's Party (NPP) and ran for the governorship of the Lagos State in 1979, but lost to Alhaji Lateef Jakande. He later became Chairman of his party, NPP.

OGUN STATE. Ogun State was created in February 1976 as part of the nationwide state creation exercise when some of the then existing 12 states were divided into new states. The state, made up of the former Ijebu and Abeokuta provinces of Western Nigeria, is one of three states carved out of the former Western State, the others being Ondo and Oyo states. The state covers an area of 16,762 sq. km. with a population of about three million, according to the 1963 census. It is bounded in the north by Oyo State, in the south by Lagos State, in the east by Ondo State and in the west by the Republic of Benin. The main inhabitants of the state are the Egbas, the Aworis, the Egbados and the Ijebus, all Yoruba-speaking people. These people engage mainly in agriculture and their major food crops include yams, plantain, rice, cassava, maize and bananas, while their main cash crops include

cacao, kola nut, rubber, palm oil, palm kernel and timber.
Owing to its agricultural and mineral resources, like limestone, chalk, phosphate, clay and stone, Ogun State is also
making progress in industrial development. Among the industries operating in the state are: food canning, rubber foam,
cement and paints manufacturing, the Niger Group Ceramics
Industry, West African Aluminum Products, the Nigeria Federal Cork and Seal and the Midland Galvanizing Industry. In
the field of education in Nigeria, the pioneering role of the
Abeokuta and Ijebu provinces that make up the state is well
known. In 1983 the state had over 150 secondary schools,
seven Teacher Training Colleges, many colleges of education
and a polytechnical college. Ogun State is popularly known as
the "gateway" to Nigeria because of its Idi-Iroko border with
the Republic of Benin, through which thousands of foreigners
come into the country by land. The capital of the state is
Abeokuta with its many tourist attractions, including the Olumo
Rock, which served as a refuge for the early Egba settlers;
the Oba's palace, built in 1854, where there are many antiquities and relics; and the Centenary Hall.

OIL PALM. The oil palm is the palm tree from whose fruit red
oil is extracted. This tree is of great importance in the
economy of the country. Besides the oil, which is called palm
oil, there is palm kernel, which is extracted after the oil has
been taken out, from the hard shell that covers it. The hard
shell is locally used as fuel for cooking. Beautiful baskets
and traditional brooms are made from the palm leaves. The
palm tree is also the producer of the indigenous palm wine,
an alcoholic drink that comes directly from the tree. In fact,
when the British were looking for legitimate trades to take the
place of slave trade, the first they found was the products of
oil palm: palm oil and palm kernel. Thus they became the
oldest legitimate exports of Nigeria and perhaps the first indigenous agricultural export crop. It is this oil that gave the
area from which it was first obtained for export its name, Oil
Rivers.

OIL REFINERY. Petroleum refinery began in Nigeria as a joint
venture of the federal government and the Shell and BP companies at Port Harcourt in 1965. In 1978 a second refinery
was opened at Warri in Bendel State. In 1980, another was
opened in Kaduna. From these centers pipes are built to link
other major population centers.

OIL RIVERS. Oil Rivers was the name given by British merchants
to the delta region of River Niger and its surroundings. This
area extended from Benin River to the Cameroon. The area
got its name from the fact that there was an abundant supply
of palm oil which was needed in the soap factories in Liverpool. Trading in palm oil started very early. By 1806 about
150 tons of palm oil were shipped to Liverpool and the figures
rapidly increased as palm oil and palm kernel began to take

prominence over slave trade. In 1884 the British entered into treaties with the chiefs of the area who feared that the treaties might undermine their middleman role. But in the end they yielded. In 1885 the British proclaimed the area to be under its protection and called it Oil Rivers Protectorate. In 1886 the British also gave a charter to the National African Company, later known as the Royal Niger Company, a trading company in the area to ensure the smooth running and administration of the Oil Rivers. In 1893 the Oil Rivers Protectorate became the Niger Coast Protectorate.

OIL RIVERS PROTECTORATE. The area previously known as the Oil Rivers came under British protection in 1885 and was known as the Oil Rivers Protectorate. In 1893, the same area became Niger Coast Protectorate. See also OIL RIVERS.

OJIKE, MAZI MBONU 1912-1956. A politician and a cultural nationalist, Mbonu Ojike was born in 1912 in Akeme in Arochukwu in Eastern Nigeria. He attended Arochukwu Primary School and after leaving the school he took a teaching appointment in 1926. He entered college in 1929 and trained as a teacher at the CMS Training College, Awka. He left college in 1931 and became a teacher at the Central School in Abagana. In 1933 he joined Dennis Memorial Grammar School in Onitsha as a teacher. In 1938 Ojike met Dr. Nnamdi Azikiwe and they became friends. In the same year he left for the United States to study at the Lincoln University. While in the States, he met people like Dr. Kwame Nkrumah and together they formed the African Students' Association of America and Canada in 1941. The Association campaigned against colonialism in Africa and for justice for the black people. Ojike became its president. When Ojike came back to Nigeria he became a member of the National Council of Nigeria and Cameroon (NCNC) and began to write in the West African Pilot, which had become the organ of the NCNC in its fight for independence. Ojike was a member of the 1953 Constitutional Conference in London, and in 1954 he became Minister of Finance in the NCNC controlled Eastern House of Assembly. He published his book, My Africa, where his philosophy was carefully ennunciated. He encouraged Africans to use their traditional names and dresses. He was the author of the slogan "Boycott all Boycottables." His campaign for cultural pride and awareness bore much fruit, but he died in 1956, just a few years before Nigeria became independent. In his honor, there is now Ojike Memorial Medical Center at Arondizuogu in Imo State.

OJUKWU, CHIEF CHUKWUEMEKA ODUMEGWU. Leader of the Biafran secession, he was born on November 4, 1933 at Zungeru in Northern Nigeria. He was educated in Lagos, finishing at King's College, before going to Epsom College Surrey, Lincoln College, and the University of Oxford in England where he studied history.

Returning to Eastern Nigeria in 1955, he became an

Administrative Officer and in 1957, he joined the army. He did a two-year officer training course at Eaton Hall, Chester in England and returned to join the Fifth Battalion in 1958. He was promoted to Major in 1961 and was among the Nigerian contingents in the United Nations Peace-Keeping Force in the Congo. He became Lieutenant-Colonel in January 1963, and was put in command of the Fifth Battalion in Kano. He did not participate in the January 1966 coup and was rewarded by being made the Military Governor of the Eastern Region by General Ironsi.

After the second coup of July 29, 1966, staged mainly by northern soldiers, which brought General Gowon to power, Ojukwu refused to accept the leadership of General Gowon because he was not the most senior officer available at the time. According to him, General Ogundipe should have succeeded to General Ironsi, who was killed during the coup.

After the October 1966 Massacre of Ibos in the north, and the great exodus of the Ibos from the north to the east, Ojukwu asked Gowon to remove northern troops from Eastern Nigeria and he began to train his own troops and to arm them. In January 1967, he met General Gowon and other top military leaders at Aburi in Ghana in an effort to find an amicable solution to the problems between the east and the federal government. The Aburi Agreement was drawn up, but owing to different interpretations of the Agreement, the problems remained. On May 27, Ojukwu was mandated by the Consultative Committee called at his behest to declare Eastern Nigeria a sovereign state by the name of Biafra. On the same day General Gowon declared a state of emergency throughout the federation and divided the country into 12 states with Eastern Nigeria being divided into three states, two of which were for the minority areas while the third, the East-Central State consisted mainly of Ibo people. Two days later, Ojukwu declared Eastern Nigeria the soverign Republic of Biafra. A month after this, war broke out, which lasted till January 1970 when Ojukwu left Biafra into exile, "in search of peace," and Biafran soldiers surrendered to the federal military government in Lagos. Ojukwu was granted political asylum in the Ivory Coast. He remained in exile until 1982 when he was pardoned by President Shehu Shagari and he returned home. He later became a member of the National Party of Nigeria (NPN), under the banner of which he contested for the post of a senator in Anambra State. He lost. After the December 1983 coup d'état, he was put in detention for security reasons. He was released in October 1984.

OJUKWU, SIR LOUIS ODUMEGWU. A businessman, politician and father of Lt. Col. Chukwuemeka Odumegwu Ojukwu, Military Governor of Eastern Nigeria, who later declared the secession of that region from the rest of Nigeria as the Republic of Biafra. Born in 1909 in Nnewi in Anambra State, he became a produce examiner in 1928 after leaving school. He joined the John Holt Company as a clerk. It was here that he developed his business interest. He resigned from the John Holt Company in 1934 and started a transport business that grew into a multi-million dollar business all over Nigeria.

In 1951 he joined the National Council of Nigeria and Cameroon (NCNC) under the leadership of Dr. Nnamdi Azikiwe. He was later elected to the Federal House of Representatives, but he resigned in 1956 to become Chairman of the Eastern Nigerian Development Corporation. From this time on he was at the head of many business concerns like the Eastern Nigerian Marketing Board, the Nigerian Cement Company and the African Continental Bank (ACB). He was honored at home and abroad for his contributions to Nigerian development. He received an honorary degree of Doctor of Law from the University of Nigeria, Nsukka, was awarded the Queen Elizabeth II Coronation Medal in 1953 and was knighted in 1960. He died on September 13, 1966 while his son, Lt. Col. Ojukwu, Governor of the Eastern Region, wrestled with the problems created by the influx of refugees from other parts of the nation following the massacre of many Ibo people in the north after the second military coup of July 1966.

OKEZIE, DR. JOSIAH ONYEBUCHI JOHNSON. A physician and politician born on November 24, 1926 at Umuahia Ibeku, Imo State, he was educated at the Higher College, Yaba, Achimota College, Ghana, Yaba College of Medicine and University College, Ibadan. He served in many important positions as a medical officer from 1950 to 1961. From 1961 to 1966 he was a member of the Eastern Nigeria House of Assembly and was the leader and the founder of the Republican Party in August 1964, a time when political parties were realigning themselves for the upcoming federal elections of 1964. He was a member of the Nigerian Medical Council 1965-68. He represented the East-Central State at the Federal Executive Council in 1970 and was Federal Commissioner for Health, 1970-71 and Federal Commissioner for Agriculture and Natural Resources, 1972-75.

OKIGBO COMMISSION. President Shehu Shagari, keeping to his election promises, rejected the Aboyade Committee's report on revenue allocation, which he described as too technical to be applied and out of tune with the present political realities. In November 1979 he appointed a six-man Revenue Allocation Commission headed by Dr. Pius Okigbo, a former economic adviser to the government during the First Republic and the Chairman of the Constitution Drafting Committee's (CDC) subcommittee on the economy, finance and division of powers, who also was a member of the Constituent Assembly in that capacity. Other members of the Commission were Professor Dotun Phillips of the Department of Economics, University of Ibadan, Alhaji Talib, Alhaji Balarabe Ismaila, Alhaji Muhammed Bello and Dr. W. Uzoagaa.

The Commission was asked to examine the formula for revenue allocation with regard to such factors as the national interest, derivation, population, even development, equitable distribution and equality of states. The Commission was to

recommend new proposals considered necessary for revenue
allocation between the federal, state and local governments.
It was also to offer broad guidelines on the distribution of
revenue among local governments within the states, and finally
make any other recommendations on any related matter as may
be found necessary.

The Commission recommended that the federal government should have a share of 55 percent of the national revenue,
the states 30 percent, the local governments, 8 percent and 7
percent to go into a special fund. In January 1982 President
Shehu Shagari signed into law a new Revenue Allocation Bill,
giving the federal government 55 percent, the states 35 percent
and the local governments 10 percent.

OKOGIE, ARCHBISHOP ANTHONY OLUBUNMI. A Catholic clergyman, Archbishop Okogie was born in 1936 in Lagos and had
his education in Lagos, St. Theresa's Seminary Oke-Are, Ibadan and Sts. Peter and Paul Seminary Bodija, Ibadan. He was
ordained in 1966 and served in many roles in the Catholic Archdiocese of Lagos. In 1971 he was consecrated Auxiliary Bishop
of Oyo Diocese, but in 1972 he became auxiliary Bishop to the
Archdiocese of Lagos. In May 1973, he was consecrated the
Catholic Archbishop of Lagos, where he presently works.

OKOTIE-EBOH, CHIEF FESTUS SAMUEL. A businessman and a
politician, born in Jakpa, Benin River, Bendel State in July
1912, Chief Okotie-Eboh was educated at the Baptist School in
Sapele and later served as an assistant clerk in the Sapele
Township Office from 1930 to 1931. He taught from 1931 to
1935 when he joined the Bata Shoe Company as a clerk, and
through private studies he rose to the position of Accountant
and Chief Clerk at the Lagos Office in 1942. He later became
the Deputy Manager of the Sapele branch of the Company, which
sent him to Czechoslovakia where he obtained a diploma in
Business Administration and Chiropody.

Upon his return to Nigeria, he decided to start out on
his own. He became a timber and rubber merchant and opened
up many schools and enterprises. Through all these he became a very wealthy man.

Chief Festus Okotie-Ebor was the first Secretary of
the Warri National Union and Secretary General of the Itsekiri
National Society. He became interested in politics and was
elected to the Western Regional House of Assembly in 1951.
In 1954 he won the Warri Division seat to the Federal House
of Representatives and was made the national treasurer of his
party, the National Council of Nigeria and the Cameroons
(NCNC). In the House, he became the Federal Minister of
Labor in 1958 and later the Finance Minister and leader of the
NCNC parliamentary party. He continued as Minister of Finance until he was killed on January 15, 1966 when the military
forcefully seized power and killed some leading politicians and
military officers.

OKPARA, DR. MICHAEL IBEONUKARA. A politician born in December 1920, he was educated at the Yaba Higher College in Lagos and later proceeded to the Nigerian School of Medicine, where he qualified as a doctor. He worked as a medical officer in Lagos and Maiduguri before setting up a private practice at Umuahia.

He entered politics in 1950 and was elected to the Eastern Regional House of Assembly under the banner of the National Council of Nigeria and the Cameroons (NCNC) in 1953. He later became Minister without Porfolio. From then on he moved up very rapidly and when Dr. Azikiwe decided to go to the Federal House of Representatives as leader of his party (the NCNC) in 1959, Dr. Okpara was elected leader of the party in the Eastern Regional House of Assembly and consequently became the Premier of the region. In 1960, when Dr. Azikiwe withdrew from party politics in preparation for his being appointed as the Governor-General of Nigeria, Okpara became the national President of the NCNC.

During the Action Group crisis of 1962, the NCNC, under Dr. Okpara, supported the Akintola faction. But after the breakdown of the Northern People's Congress (NPC) and the NCNC coalition government in 1964, Dr. Okpara, in the realignment effort to prepare for the 1964 federal elections, allied his party with the remnants of the Action Group in the west to form the Southern Progressive Front, which in turn allied with the Northern Progressive Front to form United Progressive Grand Alliance (UPGA). In December 1964 he led a delegation to the President, Dr. Nnamdi Azikiwe, to ask for a postponement of the December 30th elections because of alleged irregularities, but the postponement was not granted, leading to a boycott of the elections in the Eastern Region controlled by his party, the NCNC.

During the Biafran War (1967-1970) Dr. Michael Okpara supported Biafran cause, but he came back after the war. He later joined the National Party of Nigeria. He died in December 1984.

OKUNNU, LATEEF OLUFEMI. A lawyer born in February 1933 in Lagos, he started his education at the Ansar-Ud-deen School, Alakoro in 1947 and later went to King's College, Lagos. He went to the University of London, where he studied law and graduated with an LL. B. degree in 1958. While in Britain, he was the President of the Nigerian Union of Great Britain in 1959 and in 1960 he was the Publicity Secretary of the Committee of African Organizations, which often demonstrated on events in Rhodesia. He returned to Nigeria in 1960 and joined the Nigerian Youth Congress where he agitated against the Anglo-Nigerian Defence Pact and the Detention Act. He became editor of the Nigeria Bar Journal from 1964 to 1968 and member of the Executive Committee of the Nigerian Bar Association. In 1967 he was made Federal Commissioner for Works and Housing and was one of the leaders of the Nigerian delegation to the peace talks in Niamey, Addis-Ababa and Monrovia during the Biafran War. He was also a member of the Constitution Draft Committee in 1975.

OLDMAN COMMISSION. Set up in 1961 by the Northern Regional
government to look into the financial and administrative problems that would arise if the Northern Region should embark
on universal primary education. The Commission was to look
into the form which local contribution to the cost of primary
education should take, whether the control of primary education should be delegated to Local Education Authorities, amendment to the education law and the grants-in-aid regulations, if
necessary, and the future development of primary school inspectorate and the administrative machinery that would be required by Universal Primary Education.

The Commission recommended that a system of primary
education should be developed in partnership between the government, native authorities and voluntary agencies. It recommended the establishment of Local Education Authorities and
Local Education Committees, transfer of voluntary agency primary schools to local authorities while the voluntary agencies
would retain the right to inspect religious teaching and approve
the names of teachers proposed for appointment, training
courses for education officers, amendment to the Education
Law to give effect to the recommendations, an inspectorate
organization for primary schools run by the government and
the appointment in each province of a Provincial Education
Secretary. These recommendations were accepted and embodied in the 1962 Education Law.

OLORUN-NIMBE, DR. ABUBAKAR IBIYINKA. Born in Lagos in
1908, he attended the Tinubu Methodist School and the Aroloya
Government Moslem School. He then proceeded to the CMS
Grammar School and King's College in Lagos from which he
graduated in 1928. He later went to the University of Glasgow
to study medicine and received his degree in 1937. Upon his
return to Nigeria he joined Government Medical Services.

Dr. Olurun-Nimbe became active in politics. He joined
Herbert Macaulay's Nigerian National Democratic Party (NNDP),
which later became an affiliate of the National Council of Nigeria and Cameroon (NCNC) in 1944. He was elected to the
Legislative Council in Lagos in 1947 and the same year he
was a member of the NCNC delegation to London. In 1950 the
NCNC/NNDP alliance in the city of Lagos won 18 out of the
24 seats on the Lagos Town Council and Dr. Olorun-Nimbe became the Mayor of Lagos. In 1951, while still the Mayor, he
contested one of the five seats to the Western House of Assembly (Lagos was then in the Western Region) and he won. Out
of the five members including Dr. Nnamdi Azikiwe, NCNC party
leader, two were to be selected by the Western House of Assembly to represent Lagos in the Central Legislative House.
Dr. Azikiwe was interested, so were two other members,
Adeleke Adedoyin and Dr. Olorun-Nimbe. Neither of these
two men agreed to step down for Dr. Azikiwe. For his un-
yielding attitude, Dr. Olorun-Nimbe was expelled from the
NCNC. From then on, things were not the same again with
him. He was at odds with his colleagues on the City Council

and was the subject of opposition criticism. His administration of the Lagos Town Council was accused of malpractices and organized corruption. An inquiry conducted by Mr. Bernard Storey, Town Clerk for Norwich, England, was instituted to look into the allegations. It reported in 1953 that there was corruption along with other irregularities in the administration of the Council. The Council was later dissolved, but before the election took place a new law had been passed, abolishing the position of Mayor and making the Oba of Lagos the President of the Council. Dr. Olorun-Nimbe later retired from active politics. He died on February 5, 1975 in Lagos.

OLUNLOYO, DR. VICTOR OMOLOLU SOWEMIMO. Mathematician and politician, born on April 14, 1935 in Ibadan Oyo State. He was a very bright student, even from his primary school days, for in 1946 and 1947 he took the first position in examinations held for pupils in standards IV and V in all the schools in Ibadan Province. He entered the Government College in Ibadan with a scholarship and came out in the first division. He attended University College Ibadan, 1953-55 and the University of St. Andrew in Scotland, 1955-61 and obtained a B. Sc. first-class honors degree in Mechanical Engineering and Mathematics in 1958 and a Ph. D. in Applied Mathematics in 1961. He was a five time medalist in mathematics and Mechanical Engineering. He was Assistant Lecturer at the University of Ibadan in 1961 but moved the same year to the University of Ife as a lecturer. He became Senior Lecturer in Mathematics at the University of Ibadan in 1965.

In 1962 during the emergency administration in the Western Region he was appointed Commissioner for Economic Planning and Community Development and in 1967 he became a Civil Commissioner for Special Duties and Chairman of the Board of Directors for Western Nigeria Development Corporation (WNDC). In November of the same year he was appointed Commissioner for Education (1967-70 and 1971). Between 1970 and 1971, he was Commissioner for Local Government and Chieftaincy Affairs. He later went back to teaching at the University of Lagos. When the ban on political activities was lifted in 1978, he joined the National Party of Nigeria and became a gubernatorial candidate for Oyo State in the 1983 elections. He won against the incumbent, Governor Bola Ige. His administration, however, was short-lived, for the army took over the government of the country when he had been only three months in office.

During his short tenure in office he took positive steps to resolve some long-festering problems like conflicts between the traditional rulers in Oyo State as to the Chairmanship of the Council of Obas, and the Ife-Modakeke dispute, which led to the loss of many lives and property during the communal disturbances of April 1981.

OLUWASANMI, PROFESSOR HEZEKIAH ADEDUNMOLA. An agricultural economist and former Vice-Chancellor of the University of Ife who, as Vice-Chancellor, worked very hard to build the newly established university both intellectually and physically so that today the University of Ife is one of the best academic institutions in Africa, and a very beautiful one for that matter. Born on November 12, 1919 at Ipetu-Ijesha, he was educated at St. Paul's School, Ipetu Ijesa, Ilesha Grammar School, Ilesha, Abeokuta Grammar School, Abeokuta and later went to Morehouse College, Atlanta (1941-1951), and Harvard University, Cambridge, Massachusetts (1951-1955). Upon his return to Nigeria, he became a lecturer in the Department of Agricultural Economics at the University of Ibadan, where he rose to the position of Professor and Head of the Department and later Dean of the Faculty of Agriculture. In 1966 he was appointed Vice-Chancellor of the University of Ife, a post he occupied until 1975. He lived to see himself honored by naming the University of Ife Library, Hezekiah Oluwasanmi Library in 1980. He died in 1983.

ONABAMIRO, PROFESSOR SANYA. Born May 24, 1916 at Ago Iwoye, Ogun State, he went to the Wesley College in Ibadan, then to the Higher College, Yaba, later to University of Manchester, England and the University of Oxford, England where he studied chemistry and biology. He was a member of the Western House of Assembly for Ijebu North and later became Minister of Education of the Western Region. He later left to become a Senior Research Fellow, Parasitology, University College, Ibadan. He was later appointed Professor of Parasitology, University of Njala, Sierra Leone.

A former member of the Action Group, former member Federal Scholarship Board, former Chairman, Land Utilization Committee, Ministry of Agriculture and Natural Resources and a former member of the Federal Higher Education Committee.

In 1960, he was appointed--as a member of the Action Group--Minister of Education for Western Nigeria. In 1962 he resigned from the Action Group and he was one of those who gave evidence for the government in the treasonable felony case, saying that Chief Awolowo had formed a Tactical Committee and he himself had attended some of its meetings. Chief Awolowo later denied that Dr. Onabamiro had been a member of of the tactical committee. In 1963 he became Minister of Agriculture in Western Nigeria under the government of Chief S. L. Akintola.

ONABANJO, CHIEF VICTOR OLABISI. A journalist and a politician, born on February 12, 1927 in Lagos, he was educated at the Baptist Academy, Lagos. From 1950 to 1951 he studied journalism at the Regent Street Polytechnic School of Modern Languages in London, where he earned a diploma. From 1951 until 1959, Chief Onabanjo held a number of editorial positions which included the Nigerian Citizen in Zaria, the Radio Times of Nigeria and Deputy Editor-in-Chief of the Nigerian Broadcasting Service. In 1960 he became the Editorial Director of the Express Group of Newspapers. In 1964 he became an

Action Group member of Parliament and was there until the military took over power in 1966.   In 1967 he was appointed a Civil Commissioner for Home Affairs and Information and later for Lands and Economic Planning.   He was in the Western State Executive until 1970.   He was a member of the Constituent Assembly, 1977-78 and when the ban on politics was lifted, he joined the Unity Party of Nigeria (UPN) and was elected Governor of Ogun State under its banner.   He was arrested after the December 1983 military takeover, detained and was accused, together with Governor Bola Ige of Oyo State and Governor Michael Ajasin of Ondo State, of illegally enriching the Unity Party of Nigeria by accepting a kickback of ₦2.8 million on a contract and passing it to the party.   He was found guilty while the other two accused governors were acquitted.   He was sentenced to 22 years' imprisonment.

ONDO STATE.   Ondo State came into being as a result of the creation of more states out of the 12 existing states in February 1976.   The state is one of the three states carved out of the former Western State and with only slight modifications it is made up of the old Ondo Province.   Today the state is one of the 19 states in the federation.   The state lies south of Kwara State, west of Bendel State, east of Ogun and Oyo states, while its southern boundary is made up of the Bight of Benin and the Atlantic Ocean.   With about 21,000 sq. km. in area, the population of the state, according to the 1963 census, was 2,729,690.

Most of the people in the state are Yorubas but there exist subethnic groups like the Ilajes and the Ijaws.   The main occupation of the people is farming, but a good number of them engage in trading, weaving, hunting, pottery, tailoring and so on.   The state's major cash crops are cocoa, palm oil and palm kernel, timber, rubber, coffee and tobacco and their food crops include yams, cassava, rice, plantain, beans, maize, pineapples, oranges, livestock production and so on.

Topographically the area is composed of low lands and rugged hills with granite rocks in many places.   Among the famous hills in the state are the Idanre Hills, Ikere-Ekiti Hills, Akoko Hills and Ado-Ekiti Hills.   The climate is tropical and has two distinct seasons: rainy and dry.   The annual rainfall varies from 2,000 milimeters in the south to 1,150 milimeters in the north.

Educationally, Ondo State has made great progress. The state recently established a multicampus university, Obafemi Awolowo University (OAU), now called Ondo State University (OSU) and the federal government has also established a University of Science and Technology at Akure, the state capital.

Even though many of its tourist attractions are still underdeveloped, tourists can enjoy a warm bath in the Ikogosi warm spring with rest houses for the guests.

ONITSHA.   An Ibo town on the Niger River which tradition says was founded during the migration from Benin.   It has strong Benin influences as seen in its political structure.   The town, like Benin, has a King (Obi), which most Ibo societies do not have. The town is famous for its many educational institutions, which is a result of its early contact with the Church Missionary Society (CMS) through Bishop Ajayi Crowther, who became the Bishop of the Niger. Onitsha produced the first CMS Bishop, the first Catholic Bishop and is the home town of Dr. Nnamdi Azikiwe and because of all this, has produced a large number of Ibo elites. Onitsha Ibos, in fact, regard themselves as superior to all other Ibos.

Onitsha is also a commercial center and is famous for its multimillion dollar market. A bridge across the River Niger links the town to Asaba in Bendel State on the western side of the river and from it a good system of roads connect the town to other major population centers in the area.

ONWU, DR. SIMON EZIEVUO. Born in 1908 in Affa, Anambra State, Dr. Onwu attended the Government School in Udi, St. Mary's School in Onitsha, the Wesley Boy's High School and the King's College in Lagos. He later entered Edinburgh University Medical School and became a doctor in 1932; the first medical doctor from the Ibo ethnic group. Upon his return in 1933, he joined the government service and was posted to Port Harcourt. He was given a most enthusiastic welcome by the Ibo people in Port Harcourt. The reception was so successful that the Reception Committee was transformed into Ibo Union, embracing all Ibo elements in Port Harcourt. The Ibo Union provided an incentive to Ibos in other towns to form such cultural organizations, all of which in later years became the Ibo Federated Union.

As a medical doctor, Dr. Onwu worked in many parts of the country and was appointed to a number of public agencies including the Eastern Nigerian Housing Corporation. In 1953 he was awarded the Queen Elizabeth II Coronation Medal and in 1954 the Queen conferred upon him the Order of the British Empire (OBE) and in 1956 he became a member of the Royal Victorian Order (MVO). Pope Paul VI also conferred upon him the Order of the Knight of Saint Sylvester in 1965. In 1968 his name became enrolled in the Papal Scroll of Honour. Dr. Onwu died on June 4, 1969.

OPERATION BIAFRAN BABY. The name given to the raids on the airfields of Port Harcourt, Benin and Enugu, under federal hands in May 1969 during the Biafran War. It was led by Carl Gustaf Von Rosen, a Swedish pilot who was once a relief pilot but later became a fighter pilot on the Biafran side.

OPERATION DO OR DIE. After the general elections of December 1964, the Action Group met and decided to launch Operation Do or Die, aimed to unseat Chief S. L. Akintola's government in Western Nigeria in the forthcoming Western Regional election. Akintola's Nigerian National Democratic Party (NNDP) was declared the winner in the 1965 October election to the Western House of Assembly. Most people became so frustrated that they later took the law into their hands. The chaos continued until the military put an end to it in January 1966.

OPERATION FEED THE NATION (OFN). OFN was a national campaign launched in May 1976 by General Olusegun Obasanjo, former Nigerian Military Head of State, to make the country self-sufficient in its basic food needs. It was also to encourage general pride in agriculture, especially backyard gardening and poultry. The government was to make artificial fertilizers, improved planting materials, insecticide and other materials available to farmers at subsidized prices and to persuade them to use them. However government effort at persuasion was greatly hampered by scarcity of sufficient number of agricultural extension officers. What is more, the effort was also hampered by various shortcomings in the distribution of fertilizers and other imputs, which often did not reach the farmers or reached them very late.

On February 1, 1980, the Shagari administration abolished the scheme and replaced it by the National Council on Green Revolution which coordinated the activities of all the ministries and organizations having to do with agricultural production, processing, marketing and research.

Before the scheme was abolished, however, many people responded positively to the call by taking to gardening and small backyard poultry to supply family needs.

ORACLES, CONSULTATION OF. The practice of consulting an oracle is a fairly common one in Nigeria, especially in the south, even at the present time. The purpose is to seek light and information about certain events, past, present or future. It is also sought to explain what people regard as supernatural events and to make misfortunes understandable and more acceptable. The oracle may prescribe certain activities and sacrifices meant to control the activities of the supernatural. Among the Ibos there is the famous Aro Chukwu and among the Yorubas, the Ifa oracles.

ORAL TRADITION. In many societies that had no written languages before the arrival of the Birtish, there were certain members in each community whose duty was to remember, off the top of their heads, the history of the community or their rulers and the events that had taken place during their reign. For example, among the Yorubas, many Obas retained professional oral historians who gathered their information from various sources such as titles and names, poetry, genealogical lists, tales and commentaries. There are difficulties, however, in accepting and interpreting such tradition. The stories were open to distortion to please the reigning Oba and there could be distortion of memory.

ORANMIYAN see OYO EMPIRE

ORDINANCE FOR THE PROMOTION AND ASSISTANCE OF EDUCATION FOR THE GOLD COAST COLONY (1882). The first government law to affect Lagos, for at the time (1882) Lagos Colony was still being administered jointly with the Gold Coast Colony. It provided for a general Board of Education which had the power to establish local boards which would advise the general Board on the opening of new government schools, freedom of parents as to religious instruction for their children, grants-in-aid to schools for buildings and for teachers' salaries, conditions of grants-in-aid to private schools, granting of teachers' certificates, admission of children to government schools and the establishment of an Inspectorate of Education to cover the four British colonies of Lagos, Gold Coast, Sierra Leone and the Gambia. In 1886, when Lagos was separated from the Gold Coast and became the Colony and Protectorate of Lagos, a new law was made in 1887 which amended the 1882 law and applied it specifically to Nigeria.

ORGANIZATION OF AFRICAN UNITY (OAU). As the countries of Africa became independent in the late 1950's and early 1960's, there were debates as to how best to forge African unity, protect the independence of Africa and keep colonialism at bay. Two schools of thought emerged: one known as the Casablanca Group and the other the Monrovia Group. The Casablanca Group, made up of Ghana, Guinea, Mali, the United Arab Republic and Morocco, believed in political union as a first step. They believed that a Union Government of Africa which would have authority over all the member states, have its own civil service, an African High Command and a court of justice should be set up. The Monrovia Group, made up of Nigeria, Cameroon, the Central African Republic, Chad, the Congo or Leopoldville, Dahomey, Ethiopia, Niger, Gabon, Ivory Coast, Liberia, Malagasy, Senegal, Mauritania, Sierra Leone, Somalia, Togo and Tunisia, together with the French-speaking African countries known as the Brazzaville Twelve, believed that political union of Africa should be gradual. They argued that because of poor communication and language barriers on the continent of Africa, they should start first on regional economic, social and cultural cooperation, which in the long run would bring about a political unity of Africa. In May 1963, at the invitation of Emperor Haile Selassie of Ethiopia, heads of 32 independent African states met in Addis Ababa to discuss how best to bring about a single political organization for the whole of Africa. Countries from the Casablanca, Monrovia and Brazzaville Twelve were in attendance. The view of the Monrovia Group prevailed and on May 25, 1963 the Organization of African Unity (OAU) was born in Addis Ababa. Other independent African states have since joined the organization.

According to Article II of the Charter of the OAU, the aims of the organization are to promote the unity and solidarity of African States, to coordinate and intensify that cooperation and efforts to achieve a better life for their people, to defend their sovereignty, their territorial integrity and independence, to eradicate all forms of colonialism from Africa, and to promote international cooperation, having regard to the

Charter of the United Nations and the Universal Declaration of Human Rights.

To accomplish these aims the Organization set up four organs for effectively running its affairs:

1. The Assembly of Heads of State and Government. This supreme organ of the OAU meets at least once a year to discuss matters of common interest to Africa with the purpose of coordinating general policy. Chairmanship of the Assembly is by rotation. The Assembly can call emergency sessions.

2. The Council of Ministers. Made up of the foreign ministers of each member state, meets at least twice a year and is responsible to the Assembly for preparing the agenda for the conferences of the Assembly; to implement the decisions of the Assembly and to coordinate inter-African cooperation in accordance with the instructions of the Assembly.

3. The Secretariat. The headquarters of the organization is at Addis Ababa, Ethiopia. The General Secretary is the administrative officer in charge of the Secretariat. He is appointed by the Assembly on the recommendation of the Council of Ministers and he holds office for three years, but he may be reelected.

4. The Commissions. To facilitate the work of the organization, a number of Commissions were set up. Because member states pledge to settle their disputes among themselves by peaceful means, they set up a Commission on Mediation, Conciliation and Arbitration. Other specialized Commissions are the Economic and Social Commission, Education and Cultural Commission, Health, Sanitation and Nutrition Commission, Defence Commission and the Scientific, Technical and Research Commission.

During the Nigerian civil war, the Organization tried to find peaceful solution to the crisis. It held various peace talks in Kampala, Uganda in May 1968 and in Addis Ababa in August 1968. In 1974 General Yakubu Gowon, the Nigerian Head of State, was the Chairman of the organization. In 1982, the Organization could not hold its annual meeting in Libya for lack of a quorum because of division among its members over the representation of the Western Sahara (SADR), which was recognized by a considerable number of OAU members and had become a de jure member of the Organization, and which Morocco vigorously opposed. However the rift was patched up in 1983 when the Organization met in Addis Ababa and the SADR Delegation temporarily and voluntarily withdrew from the meeting in the interest of African unity.

OSADEBAY, DENNIS CHUKADEBE. A lawyer and politician, the first premier of Mid-Western Nigeria, born on June 29, 1911

at Asaba in Bendel State, he was educated at the Government
School in Asaba and at the Hope Waddell Training Institute in
Calabar. In 1942 he was a supervisor of customs and in 1946
he proceeded to the University of London in England where he
was called to the bar at the Lincoln's Inn in 1949.

Coming back home he became a private legal practitioner
in 1949 and in 1951 he was elected to the Western House of Assembly as a member of the National Council of Nigeria and
Cameroons (NCNC) and in 1952 he was a member of the House
of Representatives in Lagos. In 1954 he was leader of the
NCNC opposition in the Western House of Assembly and became
the Deputy Speaker of the House in 1956.

In 1960 he was President of the Senate and in 1961 he
acted as Governor General of Nigeria. When the Mid-Western
Region was created in 1963, he was appointed Administrator of
the region and in 1964, he became the first Premier of the region, a position he was in when the military seized power. In
the same year he was chosen as the national Vice-President of
the NCNC. After the military suspended the office of Premier,
he went back to his private legal practice.

Chief Osadebay has been awarded many honors and tra-
ditional titles. He is the Ojiba of Asaba, the Odoguwu of
Ashara, the Grand Commander of the Order of the Niger
(GCON) and Commander of the Order of Senegal (COS). He
was also awarded an honorary Doctor of Law (LL.D.) at the
University of Nigeria, Nsukka.

OTEGBEYE, DR. OLATUNJI. A medical practitioner and a politician. Born on June 4, 1929 at Ilaro in Ogun State, he was
educated at the Government College, Ibadan, University of Ibadan, and at the Middlesex Hospital Medical School in London.
While in London he was the Secretary-General and President
of the Nigerian Union of Great Britain and Ireland. And when
he came back home he became President of the Nigerian Youth
Congress. He was also appointed Secretary-General of the
Socialist Workers and Farmers Party of Nigeria. He is in
private medical practice, and a member of the Council of
Nigerian Medical Association.

OVENRAMWEN, OBA OF BENIN. The last Oba of Benin before the
British declared Southern Nigeria the Protectorate of Southern
Nigeria. He became Oba in December 1888 with the ambition
to put all the chiefs under him in their places and to extend
the Benin empire to its previous dimension if possible. But
at the time he was pursuing this twin objective, the British
became interested in the exploitation of the wild rubber forest
in his domain and he resisted. In 1892 the British were able
to persuade him to sign a treaty to place Benin under British
protection, abolish human sacrifice and slave trade in his kingdom and open up trade. But the treaty did not last long. In
1897, Acting Consul General Phillips decided to visit the
King and without waiting for a reply he set off on his journey
with many of his officials together with an escort of about 200

men. The time was inappropriate, for the Benis were cele-
brating a festival during which the Oba must not see someone
who was not a Beni. Phillips was met by the Oba's messen-
gers. Fighting broke out in which Phillips and most of his
men were killed. The British then sent a punitive expedition
to Benin which conquered Benin and set the town on fire. Oba
Ovenramwen fled but was later delivered up to the British who
tried him, deposed and deported him to Calabar, where he
died in January 1914. Thus with the fall of Benin came the
end of any major resistance to the British occupation of Southern Nigeria.

OVIE-WHISKEY, JUSTICE VICTOR EREREKO. A jurist, born on
April 6, 1924 at Ikiwewu, Agbarho in Bendel State, he was educated at the Yaba Higher College in Lagos, University of Ibadan and at the University of London in England. He was called
to the bar at the Middle Temple in London in 1958. Upon his
return to Nigeria he served in many roles as Magistrate, Commissioner of Customary Courts, Director of Public Prosecution,
judge of the High Court and later the Chief Justice of the High
Court in Bendel State. In 1980, he was appointed Chairman of
the Federal Electoral Commission charged with the responsibility of organizing and supervising the 1983 elections. He is
a Grand Knight of the Order of St. Gregory the Great.

OYO EMPIRE. The Oyo empire was founded by Oranmiyan, who,
tradition says, was an Ife Prince, one of the sons of Oduduwa,
the mythical ancestor of the Yorubas. The capital of the empire was Oyo, a town situated in the savannah region, south
of the River Niger. The traditional ruler of the empire was
the Alafin of Oyo, who ruled with the assistance of a Council
of Chiefs called Oyo Mesi. These chiefs were, and still are
the king makers of Oyo.
    The Oyo empire extended to the present Republic of
Benin, Nupe in Kwara State in Nigeria, down to the coast,
through Egba and Egbado kingdoms. The Alafin administered
the capital city, Oyo, while he allowed the conquered kingdoms
to govern themselves, but they had to pay to him annual trib-
utes or royalty.
    The empire had a standing army under the leadership
of the Are-Onakakanfo. It was a rule that the army leader
should not live in the capital city with the Alafin. He was
therefore sent to a neighboring town to stay as the Governor
of the place. This was one of the factors that led to the total
collapse of the empire in the early nineteenth century, when
Afonja, Alafin's Army Commander in Ilorin, set himself up
with the assistance of the Fulanis as the independent ruler of
Ilorin. The capital itself fell and Oyo Town had to be resettled a little south of the old capital. Before this time however,
the empire had been declining. In the eighteenth century, Alafin's army was defeated by the Bariba of Borgu in 1783 and
by the Nupe in 1791. The Egbas, who were Yorubas south of
Oyo before this time, had gained their independence and Dahomey

had refused to be paying the annual tribute. Afonja's rebellion came in 1817-1818 and in 1818, Dahomey declared itself independent. This chaotic situation encouraged other kingdoms to revolt and the empire totally collapsed.

OYO STATE. Oyo State was one of the seven states created in the federation in 1976. It used to form part of the former Western State which was divided into three in 1976--Ogun, Ondo and Oyo States. The capital of the state is Ibadan, which has always been the administrative center of all of the Western Region. As such, Oyo State is the inheritor of all the administrative facilities built in the capital city from the colonial days. The state has a population of over five million people, according to the 1963 census, on an area of about 42,862 sq. km. It is inhabited predominantly by the Yorubas with the Oyo, Ibadan, Oshun, Ife, Ijesha and Ibarapa as subgroups. Being an agricultural state it is rich in timber, cocoa, kola nuts, palm produce and food crops like maize, rice, yams, cassava and plantain. The state is also developing its manufacturing potential. Educationally two universities are situated within the state, the University of Ibadan, established in 1948 and the University of Ife, established in 1961. It also has other higher-educational institutions. Among the important towns in the state are Ibadan, Oyo, Shaki, Ogbomosho, Osogbo, Ede, Ile-Ife and Ilesha. Important places of interest include the Erin-Ijesha Waterfall, the Oshun Shrine in Osogbo and the Ife Museum.

-P-

PAGANS. A term used by Europeans to describe Africans who follow African traditional religions. Before the coming of the Europeans in Nigeria, most Nigerians were believers in God, whom they generally worshipped through intermediaries. For example, the Yorubas believed in Orisas, whom they regarded as their intermediary or spokesman with the Supreme God whom they called Olorun.

Upon their arrival the Europeans began to encourage Africans to abandon their religion in favor of their own Christian religion. Those who refused to embrace this new religion were initially regarded as pagans, i.e., people who did not believe in God. The word pagan began to be used pejoratively to mean nonbelievers in the Christian religion.

However it must be stated that Nigerians do believe in a Supreme Being just like Christians and Moslems do; and like Christianity which has Jesus as a kind of intermediary with God, so also do Africans in their traditional religion have their own intermediaries with God.

PAM, HONORABLE JOHN WASH. Deputy President of the Senate in the Second Republic, Pam was born in 1940 in Foron, Barakin Ladi Local Government area of Plateau State. After his primary education he went to the Gindiri Boys' Secondary School 1956-1960 and then to King's College, Lagos and later to Ahmadu Bello University in Zaria, where he obtained a B.A. degree in International Affairs in 1966. Mr. Pam worked as a Clerical Officer in the Prime Minister's Office in Lagos before entering the University in 1963 and as Assistant Secretary for Political Affairs in the Military Governor's Office in Kaduna, 1966-1977. In 1968 he was sent to Freetown, Sierra Leone as a member of the diplomatic corps and in 1969 he was returned to the Ministry of External Affairs in Lagos. He also worked in many other capacities in the government service. He was in the Ministry of Transport (1970-1971), served on the Statutory Corporations' Service Commission in Lagos (1971-1972), the Ministry of Mines and Power (1972) and the Nigerian Industrial Development Bank in Lagos (1972-1975). When local government councils were reformed and created in 1976, he became a member of the Barakin Ladi Local Government Council in Plateau State in 1976-1979, from where he was chosen to go to the Constituent Assembly in Lagos, 1977-1978. In 1979 he was elected to the Senate and became the Deputy President of the Senate in 1979. He wrote "Customary Land Tenure System in Northern Nigeria."

PAN-AFRICANISM. The belief entertained by some Africans and people of African descent that the whole continent of Africa is a national homeland. They therefore aspire to put an end to the colonial fragmentation of Africa by seeing it united and independent under African leadership. They also want to direct their activities towards the spreading of that belief and their desire. Early Pan-Africanists, like Dubois and Marcus Garvey, had great influence on many Nigerian nationalists like Ladipo Solanke and Dr. Nnamdi Azikiwe.

PARAMOUNT CHIEFS. A term applied by the colonial authorities to the traditional ruler of a town, a city-state, a division or a kingdom in contradistinction to the more appropriate word "King," which they did not want to use for the subjugated African Kings.

PAYNE, JOHN AUGUSTUS OTUNBA (1839-1906). Born in August 1839 in Sierra Leone, the son of a freed slave resettled in that country, he was originally a Nigerian from Ijebu Ode, now in Ogun State. He attended the CMS Grammar School in Freetown and came to Lagos about 1862. In that year he entered government service as a Police Clerk. He became Commissioner in Petty Debt Court and later Registrar of Births and Deaths, 1866-1869. In 1869 he became Chief Registrar and Taxing Master of the Supreme Court in Lagos. In 1881, he was commissioned to take a census of Lagos. From 1874 he began to produce Payne's Lagos and West African Diary and Almanack, published annually until a year after his death. In 1890 he organized the visit of Edward Wilmot Blyden, who stayed with him. He retired in 1899 and died in 1906.

PEOPLE'S REDEMPTION PARTY (PRP). A political party formed after the ban on political activities was lifted in 1978. The party leader was Alhaji Aminu Kano, the former leader of NEPU. Ideologically the party was a collection of radical leftist elements who could not find places in the other major parties. Their analysis of the Nigerian society was based on class conflict and they saw the country as moving towards a major social transformation. According to them, there were two major types of forces struggling for survival and ascendancy in the country: the forces of privilege, which were resolved to protect their interests under the existing social order, and the forces of the people, which were determined to replace the existing social order and which they saw themselves as representing.

The party contested the 1979 general elections. It failed to win the presidency but it controlled two state houses, Kano and Kaduna states. However the party did not win a majority of the seats in the Kaduna State House of Assembly.

Not long after the elections, fissiparous tendencies began to manifest themselves within the party. Party leaders disagreed on whether or not the party should join in a national government which the President-elect was asking for. They also disagreed on whether or not the two PRP governors should be attending the periodic Nine Progressive Governors meeting, organized by the Unity Party of Nigeria and consisting of the five UPN Governors, two PRP Governors and two GNPP Governors. The party had to break up into two major factions, one led by the party leader, Alhaji Aminu Kano and the other led by Chief Michael Imoudu, the Veteran Labour Unionist. The rift was later patched up. However in the 1983 general elections, the party could win the gubernatorial elections only in Kano State. In January 1984, after the military had taken over power on December 31, 1983, the party, like all others, was banned.

PEPPLE, KING WILLIAM DAPPA. Born in 1817 in Bonny, a trading post in the Niger Delta now the Rivers State. King William Dappa Pepple, the son of King Opobo Pepple who died in 1830, succeeded to his father's throne in 1837. Because he was a young Prince at the time of his father's death, there was a period of regency. The Regent not only refused to relinquish his claim to the throne but also supported the Spanish slavers against the British Anti-Slavery Patrol. In 1837, William Dappa Pepple, supported by the British, declared war on the Regent and had him deposed and he became King of Bonny.

In 1839, the new King signed a treaty abolishing the slave trade and giving the British more trading concessions in Bonny. But the treaty was never ratified. The British believed that if they paid the compensation agreed upon, it would be used to finance the slave trade. In 1841, another treaty was negotiated, abolishing the slave trade and with a proviso that if Britain should permit slave trade to be carried on, King Pepple was also free to do the same. The treaty was never ratified because the British never paid him the compensation agreed upon. The British patrol on the mouth of the River Bonny prevented the King from carrying on the trade openly and so he and his people rerouted their exports through the State of Brass, which exported slaves to West Indies. By 1844 King Pepple was becoming tired of the British, his erstwhile friends and supporters. Tension later rose in Bonny and some European traders were attacked, at which time they lost a lot of property. The British, believing that the King engineered the attacks, retaliated. King William Pepple himself was tried in the Court of Equity, presided over by the Consul John Beecroft and was found guilty. He was dethroned and exiled in 1854, first to Fernando Po and finally to London. He was allowed to return home in 1861 but he died in 1865.

PETROLEUM. The story of oil in Nigeria dates back to 1937 when the first search for oil began. The first showing of oil was first announced in 1953 and the first export of crude oil was made in 1958.

Large deposits of crude petroleum have been discovered in Nigeria both on land and offshore. In 1972 Nigeria exported almost 700 million barrels of oil. Today, Nigeria is the sixth largest oil producing country in the world and the second in Africa after Libya.

Since 1958, several oil fields have been discovered in the Niger Delta areas of the country and offshore. There were in 1972 about 15 companies prospecting for oil in the country. A ₦21 million refinery, the first in the country was built at Elesa-Eleme, near Port Harcourt in the Rivers State, and was commissioned in 1965. This refinery, with just a capacity for 60,000 barrels per stream day, has been further expanded. Other oil refineries have been built in Warri and Kaduna. Nigeria depends heavily on oil which accounts for over 80 percent of its export earnings.

PHELPS-STOKES COMMISSION. Set up on the initiative of the American Baptist Foreign Missionary Society to study the needs and resources of West, South and Equatorial Africa with special reference to the quality and quantity of education being provided. The Commission was funded by the Phelps-Stokes Funds, which was a voluntary philanthropic organization with interest in the education of black people in Africa and the United States. The Commission was to look into the educational work being done in the areas under consideration, to investigate the educational needs of the people with reference to religious, social, hygienic and economic conditions, to ascertain the extent to which these needs were being met and to make a full report of its study. The Commission was headed by Dr. Thomas Jesse Jones, a sociologist from Hampton Institute in Virginia.

The report of the Commission, entitled Education in Africa, came out in 1922. The Commission criticized the colonial government education system and said that even though missionaries had played an important role in the education of

Africa, they did not completely realize the full significance of education in the development of the people of Africa. It urged the adaptation of education to meet the needs of the people and the conditions of their environment and it claimed that many of the failures in the educational systems were due to poor organization and supervision. Governments and missions in Africa had failed to apply sound principles of administration to the work of education.

PHILLIPSON-ADEBO COMMISSION. After the Nigerianization Policy had been on for three years, the government, in 1952, decided that it was necessary to review the policy and the machinery for implementing it. In April 1952, the government appointed two civil servants to do this, one a Nigerian and the other a European. This was the Phillipson-Adebo Commission, set up to review the progress made thus far in the Nigerianization Policy since 1948.

The Commission submitted its report in April 1953 but it was not immediately made public. Among its recommendations were that the qualifications or standards already prescribed for appointment to the senior service should not be lowered, that where vacancies occurred and no Nigerian was immediately qualified for promotion to them, such vacancies should be advertised for Nigerians at home and abroad and their applications should be considered before non-Nigerians were recruited, and non-Nigerians thus recruited should be on contract renewable until there were suitable Nigerians.

In 1954, the government released the report to the public, but the government made it clear that the report had been overtaken by political development which that year was to usher in a federal system of government.

PHILLIPSON COMMISSION. With the concept of regionalism being written into the 1946 constitution, the problem of how the services to each of the regions would be financed arose. To look into this problem the Sidney Phillipson Commission was set up. The Commission recommended the principle of derivation and even progress as a way of dealing with this problem. Under this principle central government grants to the regions would be related to the contribution by each of the regions to the government revenue. To obviate the natural effects of this by making the richer regions to grow richer and the poorer, poorer, the Commission recommended that principle of derivation be tempered by that of even progress. According to this, relatively poor regions would receive a little more than would be due to them under the first principle. Allocation of revenue to the three regions was based on this recommendation during the period of 1948-1951.

PLATEAU STATE. Plateau State was one of the seven states created in 1976. It was carved out of the former Benue Plateau State, which was one of the six states created from the former Northern Region in 1967. Its population is a little over two

million people and it has an area of about 58,030 sq. km.
The state presents a beautiful panorama of undulating highlands
averaging 2,500 meters above sea level. The state is rich in
mineral deposits like columbite, zinc, gold and tin, which
dominates the industrial life of the state. Plateau is also
blessed with picturesque waterfalls, which are beautiful attractions for tourists.

The state is bounded by Gongola State on the east,
Bauchi and Kaduna states on the north, Kwara State on the
west and Benue State on the south. The peoples of the state
are varied and include the Vergam, the Ankwei, the Angas,
the Jawara, the Birom, the Mungo, the Eggen, the Hausa and
the Fulani. Agriculture is widely practiced in the state. They
grow yams, millet, maize, Irish potatoes, cowpeas, rice and
many types of vegetables. Hides and skin are the major export products of the state and there is a veterinary research
center at Vom in the state.

The capital of the state is Jos, which is famous for its
temperate climate almost all year round. Other important
towns in the state are Bukuru, Vom, Wase, Akwanga, Lafia,
Pankshin, Shendam and Nasarawa, all of which were parts of the
old Middle-Belt Area. There is the University of Jos in the
state.

PLEASS, SIR CLEMENT. Born in 1901 in England, he joined the
Colonial Administrative Service in 1924 and was sent to Nigeria the same year. He moved up to become Lieutenant Governor for Eastern Nigeria in 1951. In 1953 he was faced with
the Eastern Region Crisis in which the NCNC turned its majority in the House into an opposition to defeat every bill that was
brought before the House for debate, even the appropriation
bill. The Lieutenant Governor had to use his reserve powers
to decree an appropriation for the running of the government.
In 1954, he became the Governor of Eastern Nigeria, a constituent part of the new federation of Nigeria. He remained
there until 1957 when he retired.

PLEBISCITE ON THE CAMEROONS. The former British Cameroons,
made up of the Northern and the Southern Cameroons, were
United Nations Trust territories, administered by Britain as
an integral part of Nigeria. The Northern Cameroon then
formed part of Northern Nigeria while the Southern Cameroon
had its own separate administration within the Nigerian Administrative System. As independence approached, there was a
United Nations recommendation asking that both parts of the
Cameroons should be constitutionally separated from Nigeria
by October 1, 1960 when Nigeria would become independent,
and that there should be separate plebiscites by March 1961
in each part of the territory to ascertain whether each wanted
to achieve independence as part of Nigeria or as part of the
Republic of Cameroons. As such, a plebiscite was held on
February 11 and 12, 1961. The Northern Cameroon voted for
unification with Nigeria and was formally incorporated into the

federation in June 1961 and was later renamed Sardauna Province. The Southern Cameroon voted to be united with the Federal Republic of the Cameroons and was incorporated into the Cameroon Republic on October 1, 1961 from which time it ceased to be administered as part of the federation of Nigeria.

PLEIAD, THE. The Pleiad was a steamer built by McGregor Laird, a Liverpool merchant, with the purpose of opening up the Niger River to trade. The expedition started under Dr. R. N. Baikie in 1854. Dr. Baikie carefully prepared for the voyage, with a good dose of quinine for the crewmen. The Pleiad ascended the Niger up to Lokoja where River Benue joined it, about 250 miles from the coast. It returned to England after four months in the delta without any loss of life. This was cogent proof that trade with the interior was a possibility and that it could be carried on without undue loss of life. Furthermore, with good precautionary preparations and the use of quinine, the interior of Nigeria could no longer be regarded as the "white man's grave."

POLICE SERVICE COMMISSION. The 1963 Republican Constitution provided for the establishment of the Police Service Commission to see to the appointment, promotion and discipline of Senior Police Officers. The members of the Commission were appointed by the President on the advice of the Prime Minister. Under the 1979 constitution, the Police Service Commission advises the President on the appointment of the Inspector-General of Police, and appoints persons to offices in the Nigerian Police Force. It also has power to discipline and, if necessary, to remove such officers.

POLITICAL ORIENTATION COMMITTEE. During the Nigerian civil war, a group of intellectuals including the famous Nigerian novelist, Chinua Achebe, in Biafra set up what was called the Political Orientation Committee. It was organized to work on the future structure of Biafran society and its institutions after the civil war.

POPULATION. The population of Nigeria at any time has always been a subject of controversy. In fact no one can say with any degree of accuracy how many people live in Nigeria. Nigerians have never been able to count themselves accurately. The 1952-53 census put Nigerians at 30,403,305 people but there were reports that many people were not counted or refused to be counted. The 1963-64 census figures put Nigerians at 55,653,821. This figure engendered a lot of controversy, but was finally accepted. There was another census in 1973. The figure declared from this census generated so much debate and criticism that it had to be cancelled. Thus for planning and administrative purposes, the government is using the projections based on the 1963 population figure of 55,653,821. See also CENSUS.

PORT HARCOURT. The capital of Rivers State and the second
largest seaport in the country, the city is situated on the Bonny
River and is about 60 km. from the Atlantic Ocean. It is one
of the new towns, the construction of which began in 1913 when
the colonial authorities decided to build a railway line from
there to Northern Nigeria through the Enugu coalfields. As a
result of the railway construction, many people went to the
place to work and settle. Today Port Harcourt is one of the
growing industrial cities especially since the establishment of
oil refinery and other petro-allied industries. It has sheet-
metal, cigarettes, tire and aluminum factories. The city is
well connected by air, land and sea and it is the southern
terminus of the North-South-East Railway Line. The University of Port Harcourt is named after the city.

PRESIDENTIAL LIAISON OFFICERS. Appointed early in 1980,
Presidential Liaison Officers were special assistants to the
President, who were to serve as liaison officers between the
President, the state governments and the federal institutions
in the states. They supervised various federal government
projects in the state and reported directly to the President.
They are not an intermediary between the state Governors
and the President.

PRESIDENT OF NIGERIA. In 1963 when Nigeria became a republic,
it adopted a constitutional presidential system in which the
President was only the Head of State but not the Head of Government. This system worked until 1966 when the military
came into power and suspended the office of the President of
Nigeria. However experience during the military era showed
that Nigeria might do better under an executive presidential
system. As such, the 1979 constitution provided for an executive President who must be popularly elected. To win this
election, where there were more than two candidates (as it
happened in 1979), a candidate must not only have the highest
number of votes cast at the election but must also have not
less than one quarter of the votes cast at the election in each
of at least two-thirds of all the states in the federation. If
there was no clear winner, a second election was to be conducted between the candidate with the highest number of votes
and another candidate who had a majority of votes in the highest number of states. This runoff election was to be held in
each House of the National and State Assemblies. In the first
election conducted under these provisions a serious controversy
emerged as to the interpretation of one-quarter of the votes
cast at the election in each of at least two-thirds of all the
19 states in the federation. According to the Federal Electoral Commission (FEDECO) one-quarter of two thirds of 19
states meant 12 states plus one-quarter of the two-thirds of
the votes cast in the thirteenth state. The interpretation was
challenged by Chief Obafemi Awolowo the second-best candidate
who had put his hope for winning in the second ballot, first
before the Electoral Tribunal and finally on appeal to the
Supreme Court which accepted FEDECO's interpretation and

confirmed Alhaji Shehu Shagari, who had the highest number of votes cast and one-quarter of two-thirds of the votes cast in Kano State which was the thirteenth state as the winner.

Before the military withdrew into the barracks, they amended that corruption-prone section of the constitution, providing for a runoff election in the State and National Legislative Houses, and substituted in its place a general election between the two leading candidates by the people of the country within seven days of the first one.

Under the military administration which took over in December 1983, the office of the President was suspended. However, the new military government that succeeded the Buhari Administration in August 1985 decided that the new military Head of State, Major-General Ibrahim Babangida, would be called President.

PREST, CHIEF ARTHUR EDWARD. Born in March 1906 in Warri, Bendel State he was educated at Warri Government School and later at the King's College in Lagos. After graduating in 1926, he joined the police force and rose to the rank of Chief Inspector of Police. He resigned in 1943 to go to London University to study law, and was in 1946 called to the bar at the Middle Temple Inn.

Back in Nigeria he set up a private practice but he was soon attracted to politics and he became a member of the Action Group (AG) Party, the ruling party in the then Western Nigeria which included the present Bendel State. He was elected to the Western House of Assembly and later to the Central House of Representatives in Lagos and there he was made the Minister of Communications, being the first Nigerian politician to occupy that post. In the federal elections of 1954, he was defeated in his constituency by Chief Festus Okotie-Eboh but he was later appointed to the Public Service Commission with his base in London. He later became the Agent-General of Western Nigeria in London. After the creation of the Mid-Western Region in 1963, he became a Judge of the region's High Court. In 1966, when the military came to power, he went back to his private practice in Warri. He died on September 11, 1976.

PREVENTIVE DETENTION ACT. At the All-Party Constitutional Conference of July 1963, a proposal was tabled to empower Parliament, if and when it deemed fit, to enact a law curtailing personal liberty in certain circumstances. This proposal was generally referred to as the Preventive Detention Act. It generated a lot of controversy, both in parliament and on the pages of newspapers.

The proponents of the Act, mainly the leaders of the Northern People's Congress (NPC), the National Council of Nigerian Citizen (NCNC) and the United People's Party (UPP), which broke away from the Action Group Party, argued that the Act was a necessary evil, designed to be an insurance policy against subversion, which they said many African nations and in fact many nations all over the world were making use of. The opposition against the Act was great and massive.

The West African Pilot, joined by other newspapers, led a
fierce opposition to the Act. Opposition to the Act also included student and professional organizations, especially the
Bar Association, which described it as a measure to starve out
liberal democracy in Nigeria. The opposition party in the
House of Representatives condemned the proposal as a move to
curb the fundamental human rights guaranteed by the constitution.

Because of the nationwide opposition to it, the Prime
Minister was persuaded to drop it and so the proposed bill
never came up for debate in the House of Representatives.

PRICE CONTROL. Owing to the nationwide inflation following the
end of the civil war, the government enacted Decree Number
33 of 1970, establishing a Price Control Board. The Board
was empowered to fix the prices of certain commodities like
textiles and clothing, cement, beer and soft drinks, salt, motor
vehicles etc. Price Control Inspectors were appointed throughout the federation to see to the strict observance of the prices
as fixed. Persons who contravened the law were punishable
by fines and forfeiture of the commodities which could be disposed of by the Board as it saw fit. In spite of its efforts,
however, it was ineffective and therefore it was abolished in
1980 because the government saw that in a situation of acute
shortage, it could not work.

PRIME MINISTER OF THE FEDERATION. Before the 1957 Constitutional Conference in London, there was no provision in the
Nigerian constitution for the office of the Prime Minister.
However agreements were reached at the conference for the
creation of the office of the Prime Minister for the federation.
The Prime Minister was to be the Head of Government but not
the Head of State, the Governor-General was to appoint a person who appeared to him to command the support of a majority
of the members in the House of Representatives. He in turn
was to recommend to the Governor-General members of the
House of Representatives and Senate whom he wanted as ministers in his cabinet. The ministers were to serve at his dis-
cretion. On September 2, 1957, Alhaji Abubakar Tafawa Balewa, deputy leader of the Northern People's Congress and
Minister of Transport in the Federal Council of Ministers,
was appointed the first Prime Minister of the Nigerian Federation. In 1966 when the army took over government, the
post of the Prime Minister was suspended. The 1979 constitution, however, has no provision for the post of the Prime
Minister.

PROGRESSIVE GOVERNORS' MEETING. After the victory of the
National Party of Nigeria (NPN) in the presidential elections
of 1979 and the signing of the accord between the NPN and the
Nigerian People's Party (NPP), the leadership of the Unity
Party of Nigeria (UPN) began to organize the nine state Gov-
ernors--five from the UPN, two from the People's Redemption
Party (PRP) and two from the Great Nigerian People's Party

(GNPP)--into a kind of opposition group to the federal government as part of its strategy to win the 1983 presidential elections. The nine Governors met regularly to discuss matters of common and national importance. In July 1981, when the NPN/NPP accord broke down, the three NPP Governors also joined the nine Governors, and they all formed an unofficial opposition to the federal government.

PROGRESSIVE PARTIES ALLIANCE. After the breakdown of the accord between the National Party of Nigeria (NPN) and the Nigerian People's Party (NPP) in July 1981, the three NPP Governors began to attend the Progressive Governors' Meetings (q. v.), which, before then were attended only by the five Governors of the Unity Party of Nigeria (UPN), two Governors of the People's Redemption Party (PRP) and two Governors of the Great Nigerian People's Party (GNPP). Talks then began about a realignment of the UPN, GNPP, NPP and the Imoudu Faction of the PRP. In March 1982, at the summit meeting of the leaders of the four parties at Maiduguri, Borno State, agreement was reached to form the Progressive Parties Alliance (PPA) in an effort to win the 1983 elections against the National Party of Nigeria (NPN). The Alliance, in May 1982, decided to present a common list of candidates for the five elections to be held in 1983, but it later could not agree on a common list for any of the elections, not even for the presidential elections. The two major leaders of the alliance, Chief Obafemi Awolowo and Dr. Nnamdi Azikiwe could not agree to step down, one for the other, as each of them became a candidate for the election. They both lost to the incumbent president, Alhaji Shehu Shagari of the National Party of Nigeria. The Alliance failed to agree on a presidential candidate because of personal ambition and animosity, together with personal and ethnic rivalry.

PROGRESSIVE PEOPLE'S PARTY. A proposed reunion of the Nigerian People's Party (NPP) and the Great Nigerian People's Party (GNPP). In 1978 after the ban on politics was lifted, the Nigerian People's Party (NPP) was formed, but it soon broke into two factions, one retaining the old name and the other, led by Alhaji Waziri Ibrahim becoming the Great Nigerian People's Party (GNPP). These two parties were among the four that formed the Progressive Parties Alliance in March 1982. But soon after, disillusionment set in, and a new alliance was proposed, the Progressive People's Party (PPP), which was to be a union of the NPP and the GNPP. The PPP applied to the Federal Electoral Commission (FEDECO) for recognition as a political party, but its application was rejected.

PROTECTORATE. In 1861, Lagos became a British Crown Colony, and from there, British officials extended their influence into the interior of Nigeria. They began to enter into "treaties" with the local chiefs, granting them trade privileges with their people, opening up trade routes from the interior to the coast and guaranteeing the chiefs British protection against foreign influence or attack from neighboring people. The competition between Britain, Germany and France for colonies in Africa led to the Berlin Conference of 1885, at which the areas around the Niger where the British had made treaties with the local chiefs were conceded to be under her influence. In 1887 the British proclaimed its zones of influence in the coastal districts in the Niger Delta the Oil Rivers Protectorate. In 1893, the protectorate was extended into the interior and was renamed the Niger Coast Protectorate. In 1900, when the charter of the Royal Niger Company was revoked, the company territories became the Protectorate of southern Nigeria while the territory north of Idah became the Protectorate of Northern Nigeria, each under the administration of a High Commissioner. In 1906 the Colony of Lagos was merged with the Protectorate of Southern Nigeria to become the Colony and Protectorate of Southern Nigeria. In 1914 the Protectorate of Southern Nigeria was merged with the Protectorate of Northern Nigeria to form the Colony and Protectorate of Nigeria.

PROVINCES. A province was an administrative subdivision of the country under the colonial administration. These subdivisions were, in most cases, based upon the territorial boundaries of the indigenous political units. In areas where this was not feasible, colonial authorities resorted to administrative convenience. Each province was divided into divisions and districts. The administrative head of a province was the Resident while that of a division was a District Officer (D.O.).

PROVINCIAL ADMINISTRATION. For the purposes of administration, the colonial authorities divided the whole country into provinces--13 in the Northern Region, 12 in the Eastern Region and eight in the Western Region. Each province was further subdivided into a number of divisions and each division into districts. In charge of each province during the colonial era was the Resident and in charge of the division or the district was a Divisional or District Officer. When the British system of local government was adopted, Provincial Commissioners who were political appointees with a cabinet rank were put in charge of the provinces. They were assisted by the Provincial Secretary, who was an administrative officer. Some of the functions of the Provincial Secretary included the supervision of local governments and local government treasuries in his province.

PROVINCIAL COURTS. Set up by the colonial administration in each of the provinces during the early years of the protectorate, they were presided over by the Residents who were the administrative heads of the provinces.

PUBLIC ACCOUNTS COMMITTEE. One of the parliamentary committees in the Federal Legislatures, it was introduced under the Lyttelton Constitution of 1954.

The Committee was established to allow the parliament to control government finances. The Committee looked into the finances of the government and reported any irregularities to the Parliament. For instance in 1958-59, it was revealed that £7.5 million was spent without the authority of a warrant from the Ministry of Finance. Although this system of examining public accounts did not give the legislature any control over public finances in the true sense that it could punish or dismiss any Head of Department who had misused funds, it nonetheless deterred them from careless use of funds in that no Head of Department would want to be criticized publicly in the Public Account Committee Reports.

PUBLIC BOARDS see PUBLIC CORPORATIONS

PUBLIC COMPANIES. Apart from public corporations, which are set up primarily to serve the public in their economic and social lives and which are financed by the government if they are unable to make ends meet, there are also public companies. These companies are set up by the government to operate on a purely commercial basis, partly to break the monopoly of foreign companies and partly to meet the needs which are not being sufficiently met by private financial arrangements. These companies include the Commodity Board, the Nigerian National Shipping Lines, the National Insurance Corporation of Nigeria, the Nigerian External Telecommunications Limited, the Industrial Development Bank, the Bank for Commerce and Industry, the Nigerian Agricultural Bank, the Nigerian Mortgage Bank, the National Supply Company and the Nigerian Re-Insurance Corporation.

PUBLIC CORPORATIONS. Public corporations, both at the federal and state levels, are statutory bodies established and financed by the government that creates them to operate certain public utilities. These corporations (or boards as some of them are called) have their own staff distinct from the civil service and are independent in their day-to-day activities of the government officials. However they are accountable to certain ministries on a number of issues like policy matters. While most of them are expected to operate along commercial lines, their major duty is service to the people: they are to function effectively in the overall interest of the economy and the social needs of the people. However some of them, like the National Electric Power Authority, are better known for their gross inefficiency as demonstrated by incessant power failures and complete blackouts for days and weeks in some parts of a city. Federal public corporations include the Nigerian Railway Corporation, the Federal Radio Corporation of Nigeria, the Nigerian Ports Authority, the Nigerian Airways, the Nigerian Coal Corporation, the National Electric Power Authority, the Nigerian Steel Development Authority, the National Mining Corporation, the Nigerian National Petroleum Corporation, the Nigerian Television Authority, the Nigerian Airport Authority and the

Federal Housing Authority. All the utilities which these operate are exclusively the property of the federal government.

PUBLIC LAND ACQUISITION ACT. Promulgated in 1917, the law
empowered the government of Nigeria to acquire land compulsorily for public use but subject to the payment of compensation to the person expropriated of his land. Such lands became "crown" or "state lands."

PUBLIC ORDER DECREE NUMBER 34 OF 1966. Issued on May 24,
1966 it dissolved all the 81 existing political parties and 26
tribal unions and cultural organizations. It also prohibited
the formation of all such parties, associations or organizations. The decree also banned party slogans and gave power
to the police to enter buildings or places where political meetings were suspected to be taking place and arrest persons
found in such places. The police were also given power to
disperse unlawful processions. This ban was lifted in September 1978 in preparation for elections to usher in the Second
Republic.
In addition, Nigeria, under the decree, ceased to be a
federation and became simply the Republic of Nigeria. See
also UNIFICATION DECREE.

PUBLIC SERVICE COMMISSION. Set up in 1952, the Public Service
Commission evolved from the Lagos Civil Service Commission
of 1948. In 1954 the Commission was decentralized as a result of the adoption of a new federal constitution. Each region
in the federation had its own Public Service Commission with
the power of appointments and promotions in the respective
services. Each Commission is expected to be politically independent of the executive and well insulated from politics.
Under the 1979 constitution, members of the Commission must
be approved by the Senate (in case of the federal) or the State
Legislature (in case of the state).

PURGE, THE MASS see MASS PURGE

-R-

RAILWAY WORKERS UNION (RWU). Founded in 1931 by Michael
Imoudu (q. v.) in opposition to the introduction of hourly payments of the railway employees, the Union was inaugurated in
1932 with Messrs. Babington A. Macaulay as President and
E. T. Z. Macaulay as Secretary. As the Union grew in strength,
the railway management tried to weaken it by transferring Babington Macaulay to Zaria and E. T. Z. Macaulay to Kafanchan
in 1939. In 1940, after the death of Babington, Michael Imoudu
was elected President of the Union. The same year, following
the promulgation of the Trade Union Ordinance, the RWU was
recognized, and was granted some concessions, including paying workers for the loss they had sustained by the 1931 conversion

into hourly payment. In October 1941, the hourly rate was abolished.

RAISMAN COMMISSION.   A fiscal review commission appointed after the London Constitutional Conference of 1957 by the Secretary of State for the Colonies, Mr. Alan Lennox-Boyd, to examine the division of powers to levy taxation and the system of revenue allocation.   The Commission, headed by Sir Jeremy Raisman, was to consider the country's experience with the existing system, the allocation of functions between the regional and federal governments, the desirability of each government collecting the maximum proportion of its income, the allocation of funds from the federal government to the regions, the special taxation problems of Lagos, fiscal arrangements for the Southern Cameroons, which were still part of the federation, and the adequacy of the government's loan policy on government borrowing and capital issues.

The Commission combined the operation of independent revenues, derived revenues, and allocation from the Distributable Pool to come out with the distribution of revenue that would assist in bringing about balanced development of all the parts of the federation.   In making its recommendation it sought to see that the financial stability of the federal government would be guaranteed so that it could readily come to the aid of needy regions.

The Commission therefore recommended that the constitution should provide for the federal government, after consultation with the regional governments, to appoint, from time to time, a Fiscal Review Commission in light of the general revenue situation of the country.   Since the north was not getting its fair share of revenue from import duties, the federal government should pay a bulk sum of money to it from the 1958-59 year.   The constitution should ensure complete freedom of internal trade throughout the federation.   The general power of the federal government to control the tax imports should remain and the federal government should retain jurisdiction over export and excise duties, and jurisdiction to impose sales tax should be federal.   The federal government should have full power to levy taxes on beer, wines and spirits and the principle of derivation in this regard should be discontinued.   The regions should retain jurisdiction over personal income taxes, and jurisdiction over mining royalties and rents should be exclusively federal and the proceeds from them should be shared between the regions of origin, the federal government and all the regions in the proportion of 50 percent to the regions of origin, 20 percent to the federal government and 30 percent to all the regions by way of the Distributable Pool and the Distributable Pool should be shared between the regions in the proportion of 40 percent to the north, 24 percent to the west, 31 percent to the east and 5 percent to the southern Cameroons.

Finally the Commission recommended that external borrowing should be in the federal exclusive list and funds to service the loans on behalf of regions should be deducted from the proceeds of revenues which it collected on their behalf and which were to be paid to them.

RAMADAN. Ramadan is the month in which Moslems usually have their yearly 30-day fast. In Nigeria the fast is observed by having a meal before dawn. There is no food or water during the day until 7 p.m.

RANSOME-KUTI, REVEREND CANON JOSIAH. A clergyman, born in 1855 at Igbein in Western Nigeria, he attended the CMS Training Institution in Abeokuta and later in Lagos. In 1876 he became a teacher at St. Peter's School in Ake, Abeokuta. He later went to the CMS Girls' School in Lagos as a teacher. In 1891 he became a Catechist at the Gbagura Church Parsonage at Abeokuta. In 1895, he became a Deacon and in 1896 he was transferred to Sunren-Ifo District. In 1897 he was ordained a Priest. In 1903 he became the Superintendent of the Abeokuta Church Mission. By 1906, he had seen to the establishment of many churches and schools in the Sunren-Ifo District. In 1911 he became Pastor of St. Peter's Church in Ake. When in 1914, the Egba State lost its independence and became a part of the amalgamated North/South protectorates under British rule, Reverend Ransome-Kuti played a major role in mediating between opponents of the change, and in 1918, when there was an uprising against British rule, he was also called upon to mediate. In 1922 he visited the Holy Land and in the same year he became a Canon of the Lagos Cathedral Church of Christ. He died in 1930.

RANSOME-KUTI, CHIEF (MRS.) OLUFUNMILAYO. A politician and a fighter for women's rights, Mrs. Olufunmilayo Ransome-Kuti was born on October 20, 1900 in Abeokuta and attended the Anglican Church Primary School and later the Abeokuta Girls' Grammar School. She proceeded to Wincham Hall College, Manchester, England to study music and domestic science in 1920. Returning later to Nigeria, she became a teacher at the Abeokuta Girls' Grammar School and there she married Reverend Israel Ransome-Kuti, the son of Reverend Josiah Ransome Kuti. After her marriage, she joined her husband, who was the principal of Ijebu-Ode Grammar School in Ijebu-Ode. Later on Reverend Ransome Kuti came back to Abeokuta with his wife, where he became principal of Abeokuta Grammar School.

Back in Abeokuta, Mrs. Kuti began to organize the women of the town. She founded a Ladies' Club and another club for market women. Adult education for market women was also started. Later, the two clubs were merged to form the Egba Women's Union.

In 1948, the Egba Women's Union became a very powerful force in Abeokuta, so powerful that their campaign against the Alake of Abeokuta, Oba Ademola II, who was the Sole Native Authority in the area, had to lead to the temporary exile of the Oba. The women complained of the hardship created by the Oba's enforcement of the British food trade regulations during the Second World War, which they claimed made market women in the town suffer a great deal. They accused the Oba of abuse of powers. They criticized the imposition of the poll tax on women without any regard for their ability to pay and they complained of discriminatory pay for women in employment and they asked for women's right to vote. On July 29, 1948, the British, in their effort to maintain peace had to temporarily deport the Alake to Oshogbo after which some major reforms were initiated in the taxation policy of the Egba Native Authority.

Mrs. Ransome-Kuti was also a party activist. Early in the founding of the National Council of Nigeria and Cameroons (NCNC), Mrs. Ransome-Kuti joined that party and was the only woman in the party's delegation to London in 1947 to protest against the Richards Constitution. She later held important party posts such as Treasurer of the party in the Egba Division and was also a member of the National Executive.

Mrs. Ransome-Kuti travelled far and wide, not only in Africa, but in Europe and North America, representing women's interests in various international conferences. For her contribution, she was honored with many awards: the Order of the Niger in 1963, Doctor of Laws by University of Ibadan in 1968, Lenin Peace Prize in 1968 and was later awarded an honorary chieftaincy title. She died on April 13, 1978, leaving four famous children behind, among whom are Fela Anikulapo-Kuti, one of Nigeria's renowned musicians, and two medical doctors.

REGIONALIZATION OF THE CIVIL SERVICE. Until 1954, when Nigeria became a federation of three regions, there was a national civil service system in accordance with the unitary system of government then in operation. However under the Lyttelton Constitution of 1954, which ushered in a federal system of government, each regional legislature was given power to provide for new posts in the regional civil service and fix their salaries, allowances and conditions of service. Furthermore the recruitment, transfer and discipline of civil servants were to be under the control of the regional Governor, who was to be advised by the Regional Public Service Commission. The effect of this was that many capable senior civil servants in the previous unitary public service transferred their services to their regions of origin, thereby leaving the federal civil service in a poorer situation than before.

RENASCENT AFRICA. Renascent Africa, written by Dr. Nnamdi Azikiwe, was published in 1937. Its theme is that renascent Africa must be reckoned with as an important factor in the peace of the world. Africa should cultivate spiritual balance, social regeneration, economic determinism and mental emancipation. Renascent Africa is said to be Azikiwe's basic social philosophy.

RENT CONTROL PANEL. As a result of the recommendation of

the Anti-Inflation Task Force, headed by Professor N.M.A. Onitiri, the federal military government in 1976 appointed a panel to look into the housing situation in the cities and to suggest appropriate remedial measures for solving the rent problem in the country, with particular reference to the low- and medium-income groups. The panel, chaired by Dr. M.O. Omolayole, submitted its report and a government white paper was issued on it. The government later announced several measures to curb the perpetual rise in rents. Today evidence is hard to come by that the rent edict has been successful in curbing the growing rise of rent. What the measure failed to take into consideration was the problem of scarcity in the big industrial cities like Lagos.

REPUBLICAN PARTY. The Republican Party was formed in 1963 by Dr. Josiah Onyebuchi Johnson Okezie, who was a former NCNC member. It had its foothold in the former Eastern Region. During the 1964 alliance formation, the party joined the Nigerian National Alliance. In the Little election of 1965 it contested in 13 constituencies and was badly beaten. It was banned along with others in 1966 after the military took over power.

RESIDENT. The Resident was the most important of the subordinate officials in the groups of provinces in Nigeria during the colonial era. He was in charge of the various activities in a province. Under him were District Officers and other minor administrative officers. He had responsibility for a number of things. He was responsible for law and order, he was required to keep the account of the province and he was expected to supervise government construction of roads and buildings. He directed the postal system in his area, collected revenue and compiled statistics with respect to population, crime and trade, and he was to write reports on native organizations, tribal customs, languages and taxation. He also served as Judge, Counsellor and Adviser to Chiefs. He was said to be the "backbone" of the colonial administration.

REVENUE ALLOCATION. From 1946 to 1979, the government of Nigeria had set up eight different revenue allocation commissions--Phillipson (1946), Hick-Phillipson (1951), Chicks (1953), Raisman (1958), Binns (1964), Dina (1968), Aboyade (1978) and Okigbo (1979)--to look into the problem of revenue sharing among the constituent parts of the country and the national government. The problem of revenue allocation arose from the fact that even though regional and later state governments had independent sources of revenue, they were not commensurate with their constitutional responsibilities and the national government controlled most of the important revenue sources like import and export duties, excise taxes, mining rents and royalties from offshore oil production.

The major principles that have figured prominently in revenue sharing in the country as recommended by the various commissions were equality of status among the regions or states, derivation, needs, national interest, even development and geographical peculiarities. However the most important of these was the principle of derivation which was subject to a more precise measurement. According to this principle, each region and later state would share in the distributable revenues put in the distributable pool account in accordance with the proceeds derived from the relevant taxed transactions within its borders.

Under the 1979 constitution, there was a distributable pool account called the Federation Account into which almost all revenues collected by the federal government were paid, and it was to be shared between the federal, state and local governments on the terms that the National Assembly prescribed. Until December 1983 the federal government got 55 percent, all state governments got 35 percent and local governments got 10 percent.

REVOLVING LOANS FUND. Established by the Nigerian federal government in 1959 under the Industry Ordinance No. 16 of 1959 with an initial capital of £2000,000. The fund was to be used to provide loans to assist in the establishment, expansion or modernization of industrial enterprises of a productive character, including provision of services, within the Federation of Nigeria. The loan was to be made to private or public limited liability companies incorporated in Nigeria, or registered partnerships, which have Nigerian participation in their direction and provide reasonable training facilities for Nigerians in management and technical skills. The loan was payable within ten years. The fund was placed under the Federal Minister of Industries.

RIBADU, ALHAJI MUHAMADU (1910-1965). Born in 1910 at Balala, Gongola State, Alhaji Muhamadu Ribadu was educated at Yola Middle School after which he taught for some time at the school. In 1931 he joined the Yola Native Administration as an Accountant. In 1936 he was made district head of Balala and the Treasurer of Adamawa Native Authority Treasury. In 1946 he was sent on a local government training course to Britain.

Back in Nigeria, he became interested in politics. Following the coming into effect of the Richards Constitution he entered the Northern House of Assembly in Kaduna in 1947. When the Northern People's Congress (NPC), originally a cultural organization, became a political party in 1951, he became prominent in it and rose very rapidly. In the 1951 elections to usher in the Macpherson Constitution, Alhaji Ribadu was elected to the Northern House of Assembly and later to the Central House of Representatives, where he was appointed Minister of Natural Resources. In 1954, after Nigeria became a federation, he was appointed Federal Minister of Land, Mines and Power. In 1957 he was made Minister for Lagos Affairs (Lagos then had ceased to be part of Western Nigeria and had become a federal territory). In 1960, he was appointed Federal Minister of Defence.

Alhaji Ribadu was an influential leader in the NPC, which dominated the politics of Nigeria before the military took over in 1966. He was Second Vice-President of that party and a powerful person in the federal government of Alhaji Sir Abubakar Tafawa Balewa. In fact, he was so powerful that he was later described by a former colleague as the only person in the NPC who could face the party leader and Premier of the Northern Region, the Sardauna of Sokoto, Sir Ahmadu Bello, squarely, tell him off and get away with it. For some time Ribadu was the recognized link between Sardauna and the Prime Minister in Lagos. He died in May 1965.

RICHARDS CONSTITUTION. The Richards Constitution came into being in 1946. Its aim was to promote the unity of the country, provide adequately within that unity for the diverse elements in the country and to secure for the Africans greater participation in the discussion of their own affairs. As such, the constitution set up a Legislative Council of 45 members, 28 of whom were Nigerians, four of whom were elected from Lagos and Calabar while the remaining 24 were nominated. The constitution set up a Regional Council for each of the three regions made up of only one chamber in the Eastern and the Western regions, and two chambers in the Northern Region, the House of Chiefs and the House of Assembly. The Regional Legislative Assemblies were to consider and advise the governor on matters referred to them, or introduced by a member in accordance with the constitution. Thus the regional councils did not have legislative powers. With regard to the Executive Council, the constitution provided no changes in representation. This constitution brought for the first time representatives of the northern provinces into the Legislative Council which had the power to make law for the whole country, unlike in the past when the Governor made laws for the north by proclamations. Furthermore the constitution, for the first time in Nigeria, provided for unofficial members of the Legislative Council to be in the majority.

However the constitution did not differ from the Crown Colony type of government that had previously been in existence. Effective power still resided in the Governor, the Executive Council and the administrative staff who were mainly British officials. Because of the shortcomings of this constitution, the NCNC bitterly attacked it and sent a delegation to the Secretary of State for the Colonies in London in 1947. According to the NCNC, once regions were created, they would help to crystallize the disintegrative tendencies in the country. The party also complained that the constitution was the work of one man without the consent of the millions of people who were to live under it. The new constitution should not only seek to secure greater participation by Africans in the discussion of their own affairs, but it should enable Africans to secure greater participation in the management of their affairs. Finally, the

party objected to the continued practice of nominated members
and suggested that it should be replaced by popular representation based on adult suffrage.

RIGGING, ELECTION. Rigging is a popular term used in Nigeria
to describe election malpractices such as buying ballot papers
and stuffing them illegally into the ballot boxes of party candidates and manipulating election figures in favor of one party.
While many allegations can be substantiated and have been substantiated, even in court, many others cannot be so substantiated. It is common for the loser to allege that the elections
were rigged, even in areas where they have little or no support. Generally, the winner does not allege there is rigging
where he wins, even though he may have been guilty of the
same offense. See also ELECTORAL MALPRACTICES.

RIGHT OF OCCUPANCY. The right of an individual to use and occupy a piece of land. This could be statutory or customary.
A statutory right of occupancy is one granted by the Governor
or his delegate under powers conferred upon him by the Land
Use Act. This statutory right can be granted to natives of the
state as well as to nonnatives. A customary right of occupancy used to be one derived by force of customary law. Under the Land Use Act, local government is enpowered, with
respect to land in rural areas, to grant customary rights of
occupancy to any person or organization for agricultural,
residential or other purposes.

RIMI, ALHAJI MOHAMMED ABUBAKAR. The first Kano State Governor in the Second Republic, born in 1940 in the Wudi Local
Government Area in Kano State, he was educated at Sumaila
Junior Primary School, Birmin-Kudu Senior Primary School,
Clerical Training Center in Sokoto, Institute of Administration
in Zaria (1961-1962) and University of London and University
of Sussex, Brighton (1972-1975).
He worked in many capacities before entering into politics in 1978. He was an instructor at the Institute of Administration in Zaria, and at the Clerical Training Center in Sokoto, 1962-1964. He also worked at the Kano local government
in 1965 and at the Federal Ministry of Information in Lagos
from 1966 to 1970. He was the Cultural Attaché at the Nigerian Embassy in Cairo, 1970-1972 and in 1976 he worked at the
Nigerian Institute of International Affairs.
He was a member of the Constituent Assembly in 1977
and when the ban on politics was lifted he was elected the
PRP's (People's Redemption Party) Governor for Kano State
in 1979.
In the party realignment for the 1983 elections, he
joined the Nigerian People's Party. He was however not
elected into power in 1983.

RIVER BASIN AUTHORITIES. There are 11 statutory River Basin
Development Authorities, created by the federal government

for the purpose of using the major rivers in the country for agriculture through irrigation for year-round cultivation. These authorities are at Sokoto-Rima, Hadejia Jama'are, Chad Basin, Upper Benue, Lower Benue, Cross River, Anambra-Imo, Niger Delta, Niger River, Ogun-Oshun, and Benin River. They undertake comprehensive development of underground water resources, control of floods and erosion, water-shed management, and construction and maintenance of dams, dykes, wells, boreholes, irrigation and drainage systems. They also develop irrigation for crops and lease irrigated land to farmers.

RIVERS CHIEFS AND PEOPLES CONFERENCE see RIVERS STATE

RIVERS STATE. The agitation for the creation of the Rivers State began in the early 1950's, when plans were on the way to give Nigeria its first federal constitution. As such, minorities in each of the regions began to express fear of domination, oppression and victimization. There was in 1954 the Rivers Chiefs and Peoples Conference, which submitted a memorandum for the Nigerian Constitutional Conference for their felt need for a separate state. Also, in 1957, the people of the area submitted memoranda to the Minorities Commission, set up to inquire into the fears of the minorities and the means of allaying them. As a result of the report of the Commission, the Niger Delta Development Board was set up in 1961 to monitor and incorporate the development of the area now known as the Rivers State. In 1967, when General Yakubu Gowon's administration decided to create new states in the former regions, the Rivers State was carved out of former Eastern Region and the Government made Port Harcourt its capital. The state has a population of about 2.23 million people with an area of about 21,850 sq. km. about two-thirds of which is mostly swamp. The state is bounded on the west by Bendel State, on the east by the Cross River State, on the north by Imo State and on the south by the Atlantic Ocean. The state is linked up by many rivers and many tributaries. The area used to be known as the "Oil Rivers" because of the palm oil, which used to be plentiful on the rivers. But today it is in a more important sense the Oil Rivers, for the state produces about 60 percent of all the crude oil produced in the country.

Small as the state is, it contains ancient kingdoms and autonomous communities like the kingdoms of Bonny, Kalabari, Nambe, Ogbakiri, Opobo, Andoni, Okrika, Abua, Amassom and Ikwerre. The people of the state are farmers and fishermen. They produce palm oil, rubber, rice, coconut and cassava. The state is also growing industrially; there is the Nigeria Tobacco Company, oil refinery and many other firms producing a variety of goods. Some of the main towns are Ahoada, Bonny, Bori, Brass, Buguma, Degema Amassoma, Odi, Okrika, Oporoma and Yenagoa.

ROBERTSON, SIR JAMES. First Governor-General of independent Nigeria, born on October 27, 1899, he was educated in Edinburgh and at Oxford. In 1922 he entered the Sudan public service and held such important posts as Governor of various provinces. In 1955 he was appointed Governor-General of the Federation of Nigeria, a post he occupied until November 1960, two months after Nigeria became independent. It was therefore his lot to pilot the young federation to independence. He was succeeded in office by Dr. Nnamdi Azikiwe, the first Nigerian to become Governor-General of the federation. He died in 1983.

ROSIJI, CHIEF AYOTUNDE. A foundation member of the Action Group Party, he was born in January 1917 in Abeokuta. He attended Ibadan Grammar School and Ibadan Government College. He later went to the Yaba Higher College where he studied civil engineering. He later went to London to study law from 1944 to 1947. As a member of the Action Group, he held many important positions, including being a member of the Western Region Education Advisory Board and the Electricity Corporation Advisory Board in 1953. In 1954 he was appointed the General Secretary of the party and its legal advisor. He was also elected to the Federal House of Representatives the same year. In 1957 he was appointed Minister of Health in the National Government formed by the Prime Minister Sir Abubakar Tafawa Balewa. After the 1959 general elections, the Action Group became the Opposition Party and Chief Rosiji became a member of the Opposition Shadow Cabinet. During the Action Group crisis of 1962, he supported Chief S. L. Akintola's faction. He spoke in the Federal Parliament in favor of the declaration of the state of emergency in the Western Region and in 1963 he became the Deputy Leader of the United People's Party. In 1964 after the federal elections, he became the Minister for Information.

ROYAL EXCHANGE INSURANCE (NIGERIA) LIMITED. A subsidiary of the Royal Exchange Assurance Limited of London. Founded in Nigeria on February 28, 1921 when Mr. C. C. Alldridge, the first full-time insurance official in West Africa, reported his arrival in Lagos to the General Manager of the home company in London. This also was the beginning of the insurance industry in West Africa. The company has grown, with branches all over the nation. At present, the federal and state governments own a majority of the shares, even though the Company still retains a link with the parent company, which is allowed to retain a minority shareholding in the name of their successor, Guardian Royal Exchange Assurance Limited of London. In the Company's history, the first Nigerian to become its Chief Executive was Mr. K. A. Onalaja, who was appointed in 1980, but who joined the Company in 1949.

ROYAL NIGER COMPANY (RNC). In 1886, the British Government granted the National African Company (NAC) the charter it had long sought and it was renamed the Royal Niger Company. The Company was authorized to hold and retain the benefit of the several treaties already signed and to administer the areas and preserve public order; it was to interfere as little as possible in the affairs of native Chiefs. The Company made regulations for the area which was known then as the Oil Rivers Protectorate and established an armed constabulary of three British officers and about 150 local people. The Company moved ahead, acquiring more territories, and in 1893 the Oil Rivers Protectorate was renamed the Niger Coast Protectorate. The Company met with local resistance as it extended its influence over the rest of the country, and strong competition from the French, who were established on the frontiers of the Company's area of interest. In 1898, the British government sent Captain Frederick Lugard, who later became Lord Lugard, to the country to raise troops to help to uphold its authority. He raised a force which later became West African Frontier Force, which was independent of the Royal Niger Company. On December 31, 1889, the British government revoked the charter of the Company and all the areas under it came under British protection on January 1, 1900. The administration of the Niger Coast Protectorate was merged with the area south of Idah under the company's control and was named the Protectorate of Southern Nigeria, while the area north of Idah under the Company, became the Protectorate of Northern Nigeria, with Captain Lugard as its High Commissioner. Thus the Royal Niger Company reverted to its private role after laying the foundation for a united Nigeria.

ROYAL NIGER CONSTABULARY. After the British government granted the Royal Niger Company a charter to administer the northern parts of the country in 1886, the company set up the Royal Niger Constabulary in 1888 with its headquarters at Lokoja, the confluence of River Niger and River Benue. The Royal Niger Constabulary was modelled on the Hausa Constabulary but emphasis was placed more on their military role.

RUBBER. Apart from cocoa, Nigeria's other major agricultural export in recent years is rubber, of which Nigeria is the major African producer. But production is declining. Rubber is now under the marketing board system, which means farmers can be sure of a market and a minimum of price for their product. About one-third of the rubber produced is used locally.

-S-

SABON-GARI. Sabon-Gari is the area set aside in the Moslem north for Nigerians who were regarded as strangers or "aliens." These people generally were of southern origin (east and west). In the south, especially in the Yoruba towns, there are such residential areas set aside for the "Hausa" people.

SALEM, ALHAJI KAM. Inspector General of Police in General Gowon's administration, born in 1924 in Dikwa Borno State, he was educated at Dikwa and Bornu Middle School in Maiduguri. He joined the Police Force in 1942 and from there rose fairly rapidly. In 1962 he became Commissioner of the Northern Region and in 1965 he was Deputy Inspector General of Police. After January 1966, and the retirement of the then Inspector General of Police, Mr. Louis Edet for health reasons, he was promoted to Inspector General of Police with a place in the Federal Executive Council and in 1967 became the Federal Commissioner for Internal Affairs. In 1975, after the July coup which brought Brigadier Murtala Muhammed to power, he was retired, succeeded by Alhaji M. D. Yusuf. When the ban on politics was lifted in 1978, he became a foundation member of the National Party of Nigeria (NPN).

SARAKI, HON (DR.) ABUBAKAR SOLA. Physician and politician, leader of the National Party of Nigeria (NPN) in the Senate during the first term in the Second Republic. Born in 1933, he attended the Edward Blyden Memorial School and Eko Boys High School in Lagos. He later went to the College of Technology, Chatam University College and St. George's Hospital Medical School in London. In 1962, he was a House Surgeon in St. George's Hospital, but he returned home in 1963 to the General Hospital in Lagos and then went on to the Creek Hospital in Lagos in 1964. He was a member of the Constituent Assembly, 1977-1978, became an NPN Senator in 1979 and was chosen as leader of the NPN in the Senate. He was a National Vice-Chairman of the party's Chairman in Kwara State. After the military ousted the Shagari administration in December 1983, he, like many other politicians, was arrested and detained. In August 1985 the Babangida administration released him.

SEASONS. Generally, Nigeria has two main seasons, the rainy season and the dry season. The rainy season begins in March in the south (May in the north) and lasts until October or November. The dry season starts in November and ends in March. In the south, the prevailing wind during the rainy season is from the southwest and with it comes the rain, which is generally heavy along the coast and progressively decreases as it travels inland and north. The annual rainfall varies from place to place. In the southwest the average annual rainfall is about 177. 8 cm. while in the southeast, it is about 431. 8 cm. In the central part of Northern Nigeria it is about 127 cm. while it is about 50. 8 cm. in the far north. Lightning and thunder often accompany rains in April, May, September and October.

SECESSION THREATS. The three major regions of Nigeria--Northern, Eastern and Western--have each made secession threats at one time or another, but it was the Eastern Region that carried out its threat. Following the independence-in-1956 Constitutional Crisis of 1953 the Northern Region put forth an eight-point program which, if accepted, was tantamount to a demand for secession. At the London Conference of 1953, the north accepted a compromise on a federal system and gave up its eight-point program. However the west was angry over the Lagos issue.

The Action Group Party, which controlled the west, wanted Lagos, the capital of Nigeria, to be a territorial part of the Western Region (the slogan then was "Lagos belongs to the West" as it was under the 1951 Macpherson Constitution) but the Northern People's Congress (NPC) and the National Council of Nigeria and Cameroons (NCNC) wanted a neutral capital, as is the case in many federal countries. When the Action Group could not get what it wanted, it declared that if the north had to lay down conditions before joining the federation, the west would like to be counted out of the federation.

Again after the 1963-64 census, and the Supreme Court's decision disallowing the appeal of Eastern Nigeria, it was alleged that the east was contemplating secession. This was not proved but events in 1966 led to a real threat of secession. After the second coup in July 1966 and the mass killing of the Ibos in the north, many Ibo leaders began to think and believe that no part of the federation was safe for them. All people of Eastern Nigeria origin went back to the east, and in May 1967, Col. Ojukwu declared the secession of the east and a proclamation of the Republic of Biafra. This led to a 30-month civil war which finally reunited all the peoples of the country again.

SECONDARY MODERN SCHOOLS. The Secondary Modern School, introduced in the former Western Region of Nigeria in 1955, was a three-to-four year course. Its objective was to provide a means whereby primary school graduates who could not be admitted into grammar schools could be prepared for vocational and professional training. In the school, students took a good number of courses. Those who offered commercial subjects spent four years while those who offered basic courses took three years. Products of these schools were generally admitted into three-year grade II teacher training colleges and to trade centers. Some graduates also found their way into grammar schools. In 1978 government began to phase them out and by the beginning of the 1980-81 academic year, none of them was still in existence. Most of them had been converted into full-fledged secondary grammar schools and others into primary schools. It must be noted that the experiment existed only in the former Western Region of Nigeria and the states created from it.

SECOND NATIONAL DEVELOPMENT PLAN 1970-74. This plan was launched shortly after the civil war as a means to reconstruct the facilities destroyed during the war, and to promote the economic and social development of the country. The plan aimed to spend over ₦3 billion during the four years. This amount was distributed between public and private sectors. The average growth rate expected throughout the plan period was 7 percent per annum.

There were a number of important achievements during the plan. Agricultural farms abandoned during the civil war-- especially in the East-Central and South-Eastern states--were rehabilitated and brought back into production. Government distributed fertilizers to farmers and brought more acres of land into cultivation. In industrial development, a number of manufacturing establishments, damaged during the war, were reactivated and new ones were set up. In transportation, over 3,000 km. of roads were built while work was progressing over 2,000 km. more. Airports were built and damaged ports were reconstructed. In education the story is very much the same. Enrollment in primary schools went up from 3.5 million in 1970 to 4.5 million in 1973. In secondary schools, enrollment nearly doubled from 343,000 in 1970 to 649,000 in 1973. Many higher institutions were also built, all geared to the technological development of the country.

SECOND REPUBLIC. The struggle to capture governmental power during the Second Republic started in earnest in September 1978, when the ban on political activities had been lifted and the Republican Constitution, which was to take effect on October 1, 1979, had been approved by the Supreme Military Council. Political parties began to emerge and out of about 50 such parties, only five of them satisfied the criteria laid down by FEDECO for recognition. Thus the major parties that juggled for power during the Second Republic were the National Party of Nigeria (NPN), the Unity Party of Nigeria (UPN) the Nigerian People's Party (NPP), the Great Nigerian People's Party (GN PP) and the People's Redemption Party (PRP).

The Second Republican Constitution was modelled on the American presidential system, which laid down a system of checks and balances. The President was nationally elected and was given power to execute the law of the land. The National Assembly was given power to make laws and the Judiciary was to enforce and interpret the law.

Elections to national and state offices took place between July and August 1979. The election returns favored the NPN, in that that party, by judicial interpretation, won the presidential elections, and won 7 out of the 19 state gubernatorial elections. It also had more seats in the national assembly than any one of the other four parties. The President-elect, in an effort to promote national unity, called all the other parties to join him in forming a national government, but it was only the NPP that acceded to his call by coming into an accord to work together without any party losing its identity. The other parties began to get together, and they formed a kind of an unofficial opposition.

The politicians of the Second Republic were more concerned about their personal interests than the interest of the generality of the people. At the national level, corruption was rampant and the President was too weak to moderate it. At the state level the story was not much different except that state officials had less access to public money and so they misappropriated less than their national counterparts. Politicians and public officials got bribes and kickbacks in millions of naira, which they carefully syphoned away to Europe and

America. The economy was in a terrible state of affairs and
the government had to resort to austerity measures to keep
the country afloat.

Added to this economic malaise was the farce of election processes that the country went through in 1983. Because
the stakes were high, i. e. , because the opportunity to loot the
public treasury was wide open to government functionaries,
the struggle for power was desperate and vicious; people killed
and maimed opposition members and destroyed their property
with great zest, and the major parties heavily rigged the elections in a way unparalleled in the history of the country.
Again, the governing NPN party, which had full control of the
police, won not only the presidency but it also improved its
position in the states, winning 13 out of the 19 state elections
and having an overwhelming majority in the National Assembly.

The President and the Governors that had been declared
winners were sworn in on October 1, 1983, but just three
months after, on December 31, 1983, a coup d'etat put an end
to the Shagari administration and suspended many parts of the
Second Republican Constitution.

SECRETARY OF STATE FOR THE COLONIES. The Secretary of
State for the Colonies was a Minister of cabinet rank in the
British government. It was he who was in charge of the colonial office in London and oversaw the various activities and
developments in the colonies and overseas territories. However
his power was limited by the circumstances in which a particular territory had been acquired or by the constitutional arrangements reached by his predecessors. Governors of the colonial
territories were responsible to him and they kept him constantly informed. In the history of Nigeria's constitutional development, various Secretaries of State for the Colonies played
important roles. In 1920, a delegation of the National Congress of British West Africa went to London to see the Secretary of State Lord Milner on the need for increased participation of Africans in their own affairs, and even though the demands were rejected, two years later, the government yielded
to the demand for elected members on the Legislative Council.
In 1947, the NCNC Delegation to London had a meeting with
the Secretary of State Lord A. C. Jones on the revision of the
Richards Constitution. When Sir John Macpherson in 1948 succeeded Richards, he promised a review of the constitution in
1950. The Secretary of State held constitutional conferences
with the Nigerian leaders from 1953 to 1960 on the Nigeria's
self-government and independence issue.

SEGREGATION. The white man in Nigeria lived segregated from
the people he came to rule, carving out a separate residential
area for himself and a few Africans of the same standing.
These areas were referred to as "government reservations"
and could be found in all the capital cities. The reason the
white man generally gave for this was the incidence of malaria,
which he said was prevalent among the indigenous population.
The practice was highly resented and has long been abandoned.

SELF-GOVERNMENT MOTION CRISIS. In March 1953, an Action Group member, Chief Anthony Enahoro, tabled a private member's motion in the Central Legislature for self-government in 1956. This was resented by northern representatives, even though it resulted in a temporary alliance between the Action Group (AG) Party, which controlled the west and the National Council of Nigeria and the Cameroons (NCNC), which controlled the east. The Northern Delegation, believing that 1956 was too early, moved a counter motion with the phrase "as soon as possible" instead of "in 1956." Because of failure to agree on a motion, the Action Group members and the NCNC members walked out of the House. This was the death blow to the Macpherson Constitution. The north later presented its Eight-Point Program which, if carried out, would amount to a virtual secession from the rest of the country. In the Constitutional Conference of 1954, the British Government helped to resolve the crisis by agreeing to give self-government to those regions, constituent members of the federal system of government that was to be set up, which desired it. At the Constitutional Conference held in London in 1957, arrangements were completed for the Eastern and Western regions to become self-governing later in the same year. In 1958 there was another Constitutional Conference in London at which agreements were reached that the Northern Region should also become self-governing in 1959. Her Majesty's Government also agreed that if a resolution asking for independence was passed by the Federal Parliament which would come into being in early 1960, her Majesty's Government would agree to that resolution and would introduce a bill in Parliament in London to make Nigeria a fully independent country on October 1, 1960.

SENATE. Even though Nigeria became a federation in 1954, it did not have a second Legislative House until after the 1957 Constitutional Conference, at which a decision was reached to establish a second chamber in the center. The first set of Nigerian Senators were appointed toward the end of 1959 and the first sitting of the Senate took place in January 1960. According to the Independence Constitution of 1960, each region was to be represented by 12 senators selected at a joint sitting of the Legislative Houses of each region. In addition, four senators were appointed to represent the federal territory of Lagos and four others were appointed by the governor on the advice of the Prime Minister. The power of the Senate was very limited, much like the British House of Lords. It could not amend money bills unless the House of Representatives agreed, and it could not delay money bills for more than one month and other bills for more than six months. During the Second Republic, the constitution, following American practice, gave greater powers to the Senate. In the first place, members of the Senate were elected, five from each state. The Senate's consent was required on all legislations and it had other constitutional powers to give or refuse its consent to certain presidential appointments like those of Cabinet Ministers, Ambassadors and members of certain commissions. The constitutional provision for the Senate was suspended after the December 1983 coup d'etat.

SHAGARI, ALHAJI SHEHU ALIYU USMAN. The first Executive President of Nigeria, Alhaji Shehu Shagari, was born in May 1924 in Shagari Village in Sokoto State and was educated at the Zaria Middle School to become a teacher. In 1945 he became a science master in Sokoto Middle School. After further training courses at the Bauchi Teachers College he became the Headmaster of the Senior Primary School at Argungu from 1951 to 1952, and later a Visiting Teacher for Sokoto Province from 1953 to 1956. He then proceeded to the United Kingdom to study.

Alhaji Shehu Shagari has always been interested in politics, which he sees as the best way to serve the people. He founded and became the Secretary of the Sokoto Branch of the Northern People's Congress (NPC), which originally was a cultural organization in 1949, but which became a political party in 1951. In 1954 he was elected into the Federal House of Representatives in Lagos and was a member of the Scholarship Board (1954-1958). In 1958 he was appointed Parliamentary Secretary to the late Prime Minister Sir Abubakar Tafawa Balewa and in 1959 he was appointed Minister of Commerce and Industry and Minister of Economic Development the same year. In 1960 he became Federal Minister of Pensions, Establishment and Training. He later held the post of Federal Minister of Internal Affairs and Communications and Federal Minister of Works, a post he was holding when the military took over power in 1966. In fact he was prominent at the negotiations that led on to the cabinet handing over power to General Ironsi after it was clear that the Prime Minister had been killed in the coup. He later retired to his farm in Sokoto.

Soon after, he became Secretary to the Sokoto Provincial Education Development Fund and in 1968 he was appointed Commissioner for Establishments in the North-Western State and in 1969, Commissioner for Education. In 1970 General Gowon appointed him Federal Commissioner for Economic Development, Rehabilitation and Reconstruction and in 1971 he succeeded Chief Obafemi Awolowo who had resigned as Federal Commissioner for Finance, a post he was at until 1975, when the Gowon administration was overthrown. Alhaji Shehu Shagari again went back to his farm. But in 1977 he was elected into the Constituent Assembly, and when the ban on politics was lifted in 1978, he became a foundation member of the National Party of Nigeria (NPN), which nominated him as its presidential candidate for the 1979 election. He won the election and became the first Executive President of the Second Republic. He also sought reelection for a second term. He was nominated by his party, and he won.

He was sworn in on October 1, 1983, and two days after giving his budget speech to the National Assembly the army struck on December 31, 1983. He was later arrested and detained.

Alhaji Shehu Shagari is the Turakin of Sokoto and he
has an honorary Ph. D. from the Ahmadu Bello University in
Zaria.

SHANGO.   Shango was the son of Oranmiyan, who was the son of
Oduduwa, the mythical ancestor of the Yorubas.   Shango
was the fourth King of the Yorubas.   Shango was reputed for
his magical powers.   He had the habit of emitting fire and
smoke out of his mouth, a feat which greatly increased the
dread his subjects had for him.   He reigned in Yorubaland
for seven years, during which he fought many battles.   Shango
was reputed to have the power to attract lightning.   One day,
having made the charm, he ascended a hill with some relations
and tested his charm on his own palace.   Very soon a storm
gathered and before the King and his followers could get back
to the palace, the palace had been struck by lightning and was
set on fire, in which many of his wives and children died.
Shango was filled with remorse.   He abdicated the throne and
decided to retire to the court of his maternal grandfather,
Elempe, the King of the Nupes.   On the way, his followers
deserted him and because he could not proceed alone or for
shame, he returned home, climbed a tree and hanged himself.
Shango was later deified and is worshipped today in Yorubaland and in some parts of South America as the god of thunder
and lightning.

SHARIA.   Sharia is the law of Islam which applies to all human activities.   In Northern Nigeria, it deals mostly with civil cases,
but it is in the area of family law and succession that it is
strongest and most important.   Sharia law is recognized by
the Nigerian Constitution as a law which is applicable to Moslems.
        The Sharia is said to have four main sources: the
Koran, which is considered as the ultimate source of the
Sharia; the Sunna or the tradition which deals with the pre-
cepts and customs of the Prophet Mohammed himself and which
are used to explain and interpret the Koran; the Kiyas or an-
alogical deductions, from established principles in the Koran
or the Sunna, and Ijma or the consensus of Moslem jurists.
        The law in Northern Nigeria is administered by Sharia
Courts.   Under the 1979 Constitution, appeals lie from the
Sharia Court of Appeal to the Federal Court of Appeal in any
civil proceedings with respect to any question of Islamic law.

SHUGABA, ALHAJI ABDURAHMAN DARMAN.   Majority Leader in
Borno State House of Assembly and a member of the Great
Nigerian People's Party.   On January 29, 1980, the Federal
Cabinet Office stated that President Shuhu Shagari had approved
the deportation of Alhaji Abdurahman Shugaba because he was
not a Nigerian and was a security risk.   The government also
stated that it had set up a judicial inquiry to determine whether
or not the deportee was a Nigerian, and Mr. Justice Tunji
Adeyemi of the Oyo State High Court was appointed the Sole

Commissioner. The deportation order aroused great concern
and outcry. The new government was seen as beginning to
eliminate its opponents in a most crude way, without a hearing.
Shugaba himself challenged the order in court. Many lawyers,
especially from the Unity Party of Nigeria (UPN), offered their
services.

Justice Oye Adefila declared in his judgement that Shugaba was a Nigerian. The deportation order was ultra vires
and so void. The order was a violation of Shugaba's constitutional rights to personal liberty, privacy and freedom of movement. It awarded damages of ₦350,000.

SIERRA LEONE. One of the British colonies in West Africa into
which freed slaves were settled, beginning from 1787. Among
the ex-slaves were many Nigerians, like Bishop Ajayi Crowther, who later came back to Nigeria either as missionaries
or as traders and therefore were of great importance in the
educational development of the Yorubas of Western Nigeria.

In 1866 the Crown Colony of Lagos was placed under
the British administration in Sierra Leone, even though it retains its own separate Legislative Council and administrator
and was responsible for its affairs. Furthermore, the oldest
higher-educational institution, the Fourah Bay College, was
situated in Sierra Leone. A lot of Nigerians were educated
at the college.

SLAVE TRADE. The first slaves from Africa landed in Lisbon,
Portugal in 1441 and by 1472, the Portuguese, in their effort
to open up trade with people on the coast of West Africa, had
reached the Bight of Benin and their vessels had safely an-
chored in the Niger Delta. In 1482, they built a fort at El-
mina on the Gold Coast, now Ghana, and in 1485, John Affonso
d'Aveiro had visited Benin City and opened up trade in ivory
and pepper in exchange for European goods. Other nations
soon joined in opening up trade with the West African countries. By 1553 the first English ships had reached the Benin
river.

The first slaves to Portugal were used on São Tomé,
but with the discovery of America and the establishment of
Spanish colonies in the West Indies, there were great demands
for African slaves to replace the aborigine Indians who were
unable to cope with the hard work demanded in Spanish mines
and plantations. The Portuguese served then as their main
suppliers since they themselves, in deference to the Papal
Bull of 1493, which divided the undeveloped parts of the earth
between Spain and Portugal and assigned the greater part of
Africa to Portugal, could not go to Africa for their slave supplies. But the British soon entered into the trade and in 1562
Sir John Hawkins, said to be the first Englishman to engage
in slave trade was reported to have taken 300 slaves from
Sierra Leone to Haiti. British, Dutch, French and Portuguese
nationals, encouraged by their governments, entered into keen
competition to secure a monopoly of the trade. Thus, by the

eighteenth century the Nigerian coastlines were strewn with slave trading posts--Lagos, Brass, New Calabar (Kalabari), Bonny and Old Calabar--all which became thriving centers of the slave trade. Trade routes from these centers extended to the hinterland, even to the Hausa states of the north. The trade led to a lot of intertribal warfare in an effort to secure the trade routes to the coast, and by destroying the able-bodied young men and women either through fruitless wars or by being sold into slavery it contributed immensely to the political and economic underdevelopment of the area. However, opinions in Britain against the slave trade were gradually growing. In 1727, the Quakers denounced it and in 1787, the Society for the Abolition of the Slave Trade was formed in London but bills presented to Parliament between 1788 and 1796 to stop the trade were all defeated. As the nineteenth century began, opinions were changing in many nations against the trade. In 1802 the Danish government declared it illegal. In 1804 the importation of slaves into the United States was prohibited, even though slaves were still getting in until the American Civil War. In 1807 an Act of the British Parliament prohibited British ships from carrying slaves or other ships from landing slaves in British colonies from March 1, 1808.

In spite of all these efforts on the parts of various governments, the trade still continued, not only because Europeans derived great profit from it but also because many Africans had become dependent on trade. It was therefore not an easy task for British merchants in Nigeria, who were turning their efforts to what they called legitimate trade in palm oil, gold and other goods to persuade many Nigerians and their Chiefs to give up their lucrative trade.

The effects of slavery on the development of the West African countries are many. It drained the population of a considerable number of able-bodied men and women, in their prime of life, leaving behind old men and women. It destroyed many villages and flourishing towns and created distrust and hatred between various ethnic groups and even within the same ethnic groups, especially as seen by the Yoruba civil wars. Still important is the fact that it diverted West African efforts away from agriculture and industries. And finally the suppression of the slave trade gave the European empire builders a good opportunity to intervene in local African affairs, support one group against the other and finally subjugate all of them.

SLESSOR, MARY MITCHELL. Miss Mary Mitchell Slessor, a Scot by birth, was a Presbyterian medical missionary who lived in the Eastern Province from 1876 to 1915 and died at Itu on January 13, 1915. She devoted much of her time to saving twins and their mothers from the death that ancient superstition condemned them to. She was loved and admired all over the area. In 1890 she was appointed Vice-Consul for Okoyong, among the people she had worked so hard to convert and serve.

SOCIALIST WORKERS AND FARMERS PARTY. The Socialist Workers and Farmers Party (SWAFP) was launched under the leadership of Dr. Tunji Otegbeye, a medical practitioner in 1963
at Enugu, capital of Anambra State. The aim of the party
was to mobilize the support of the workers and the farmers to
improve their welfare. The party had official support from
almost all the major trade unions, but this support was not
translated into votes in the 1964 federal elections, for it won
no seats. In 1966, after the military takeover, the party was
banned with all the other parties.

SOCIETY FOR THE ABOLITION OF THE SLAVE TRADE. Formed
in London in 1787 to fight against the slave trade in which
many European countries were engaged. Granville Sharp,
the Chairman and Thomas Clarkson were the most active members of the organization. They saw to it that many bills were
presented to Parliament on the issue, but success did not crown
their effort until they had sufficiently educated the people and
until Parliament, in 1807, 20 years after the foundation of the
Society, passed a bill for an Act prohibiting the slave trade.
The Act took effect from March 1, 1808.

SOKOTO EMPIRE see FULANI EMPIRE

SOKOTO STATE. Carved out of the former North-Western State
in 1976, it is a fairly large state with a population of about
4. 5 million people. The major ethnic groups in the state are
the Fulanis, Hausas, Zabarmas and the Dakarkaria. Most of
these people are Moslems--Christianity has not been able to
make any appreciable penetration. This is understandable
since it was in Sokoto, the capital of the state, that Lord Lugard in 1903 laid down the policy that the colonial government
was not to interfere with the Moslem religion. Agriculture is
the main revenue-yielding industry in the State--over 70 percent of economically active population are engaged in one type
of farming or another, including the rearing of cattle. Cli-
matically, the average annual rainfall is 20 inches and rain
falls between May and October. The harmattan winds blow
from the Sahara Desert in the northeast between December
and February. This wind is laden with dust and fog, all of
which makes the air very uncomfortable. The weather is very
cold in the night and in the morning but hot during the day.
Sokoto State has the second largest concentration of livestock
in the country and is the leading exporter of hides and skin
in the nation. The capital of the state is Sokoto, the capital
of the former Fulani empire. Other important towns are Argungu, Bagddo, Birnim-Kebbi, Bunza and Gusau, to name just
a few. The state has a university, the University of Sokoto.

SOLANKE, OLADIPO. A lawyer and founder of the West African
Student Union (WASU) in Britain, Mr. Solanke was born in
Abeokuta in 1884. He attended Ake Primary School in Abeo-
kuta and after his high school education went to Fourah Bay

College in Sierra Leone, where he obtained a B. A. degree from Durham University in England. In 1917 he taught at Leopold Educational Institution in Freetown. In 1922 he went to Britain to study law. In 1924 he founded the Nigerian Progress Union, but the Union was replaced in 1925 by WASU, also founded by him and to which he devoted most of his active life.

Solanke in 1927 wrote his book, United West Africa at the Bar of the Family of Nations, in which he attributed the decline of West Africa to the slave trade. He saw a conflict between British imperialism and African nationalism. He encouraged Africans to drop foreign names. He asked the British political officers not to think that educated Africans were enemies--they were copartners in the guardianship of Africa and sooner or later educated Africans and the traditional rulers would join together and fight the white man. Solanke died on September 2, 1958 in London and was buried there.

SOLE NATIVE AUTHORITIES. Under the indirect rule system, the British governed the local population through their traditional rulers called Chiefs or Emirs or Obis. In some local government areas each such Chief or any other person was constituted into a Sole Native Authority. This meant that the decision of the Chief was supreme in his area, although in most cases he was advised by a traditional council.

SOUTHERN ALLIANCE. An alliance between the two major parties, the National Council of Nigeria and the Cameroons (NCNC) and the Action Group (AG) in the south in 1953. It was hurriedly formed during the 1953 crisis on "Self Government in 1956" motion. In the preparation for the Constitutional Conference in London in 1953, the Alliance agreed on common proposals to be put before the Conference. These included:

1. the exclusion of special members from the central and regional legislatures;
2. uniform electoral laws for election to the federal legislature based on universal adult suffrage; and
3. delimiting the boundaries of the regions into practically equal units so as to avoid the fear of domination by one region over others.

Both parties, however, agreed on a federal type of constitution and they also agreed that the issue of Lagos would not be raised at the Conference, but when the Northern People's Congress (NPC) asked for the neutralization of Lagos as a federal territory, the NCNC supported the NPC. As a result the Alliance broke down immediately. Dr. Nnamdi Azikiwe later accused the Action Group of "overt acts which stultified the freedom of Nigeria" and the Action Group countered by saying that the NCNC had stabbed them in the back.

SOUTHERN NIGERIAN CIVIL SERVICE UNION. Inaugurated on

August 18, 1912, it was the first trade union in Nigeria. In 1914, after the amalgamation of the Southern and Northern protectorates, it changed its name to the Nigerian Civil Service Union.

SOUTHERN NIGERIA POLICE FORCE. In 1900 when the Protectorate of Southern Nigeria was proclaimed, the Lagos Police Force and part of the Niger Coast Constabulary became the Southern Nigeria Police Force, while the remaining part became the Southern Nigeria Regiment.

SOUTHERN NIGERIA REGIMENT see SOUTHERN NIGERIA POLICE FORCE.

SOUTHERN PROGRESSIVE FRONT (SPF). This was an alliance signed in Ibadan on June 3, 1964 by Dr. Michael Okpara, leader of the National Council of Nigerian Citizens (NCNC) with the Action Group Party (AG). It was a reaction to the formation of the Nigerian National Democratic Party (NNDP) of Chief S. L. Akintola, made up of the breakaway faction of the Action Group known then as the United People's Party (UPP) and another faction of the NCNC led by Chief R. A. Fani-Kayode. Since the NNDP was effectively in power, the remnants of the AG and NCNC in opposition had no choice but to come closer together to form a kind of an alliance. Okpara's signature on June 3, 1964 only formalized this informal arrangement. The alliance decided to present a common list in the forthcoming federal elections. This alliance came to be known as the United Progressive Grand Alliance. See also UNITED PRO-GRESSIVE GRAND ALLIANCE.

STATE BOUNDARIES DELIMITATION COMMISSION. Appointed after the creation of the 12 states in 1967, its job was to adjust, where necessary, the boundaries of states with regard to districts, provinces or ethnic groups as the case might be.

STATE ELECTORAL COMMISSION. A State Electoral Commission, set up by the 1979 constitution, was composed of a Chairman and five to seven members. It had the power to organize, undertake and supervise all elections to local government councils within the state and to tender advice to the Federal Electoral Commission on the compilation of the register of voters insofar as the register was applicable to local government elections in the state.

STATE HOUSE DIARY. Refers to the records of events in the State House in Lagos. For example, during the election crisis of December 1964, it recorded among other things that Dr. Michael Okpara, leader of the United Progressive Party Alliance (UPGA), when he led a delegation to the President to ask for a postponement of the elections, had threatened the secession of the Eastern region from the federation. It also recorded that in the December 29, 1964 meeting held by the President at the State House with the Prime Minister, Premiers and Governors of the country, the Northern and Western Premiers and Governors absent, the President had expressed the view that UPGA boycotting of the elections would be a tactical error, because it could not have any legal effect on the outcome of the election. The Diary also stated the legal advice given to the President by the Eastern Nigeria Solicitor-General, Mr. D. O. Ibekwe, that the President had no constitutional powers to form an interim government or assume power himself.

STATE JUDICIAL SERVICE COMMISSION.   This is the state counterpart of the Federal Judicial Service Commission.   Under the 1979 constitution it is responsible in each state to advise the Governor of the state on the appointment of judges to the High Court of a state but the appointment needs the approval of a simple majority vote in the State House of Assembly.   The Commission also can recommend removal of judges for inability to discharge duties or for misconduct or contravention of the Code of Conduct.

STATES.   The demand for the creation of states in Nigeria appears to be a perennial one.   It arose in the 1950's when the regions were being given self-government and the minorities in each region, fearing discrimination and oppression began to agitate for their own states.   The areas that were much affected were the Middle-Belt in the Northern Region, the Mid-West in the Western Region and the Calabar-Ogoja-Rivers areas in the east. Furthermore, because of the population of the Northern Region, which was said to be slightly more than that of the south, and because of the land area of the north being about three-quarters of the land area of the whole country, many people believed that the federation was too lopsided, for a constituent part, if united could dictate the political tune of the nation for the unforeseeable future.   The north, under the Northern People's Congress (NPC), was fairly united and it was not easy for southern parties to penetrate it.

The Action Group Party got most of its support in the Middle-Belt because of its support for their aspiration for their own state.   The National Council of Nigeria and Cameroon (NCNC) went into an alliance with the Northern Element Progressive Union (NEPU) a northern party, but the NPC controlled the government not only at the regional level but also at the local level.   As such the north appeared impregnable, and so the demand was loud in the south for breaking up the north.

These demands led to the setting up of the Minorities Commission in 1957 by the British government.   But the British had already told the nation and the Commission the kind of recommendation that the British were willing to hear: state creation should be a last resort, for if new states or regions were created, then independence might not be possible in 1960. The Commission therefore did not recommend creation of more states but rather some amendment to the constitution which would protect minorities' interests. But these amendments amounted to little more than cosmetic changes.

Two years after independence, during the Action Group crisis of 1962, the NCNC, thinking that it would have a second region under its control, and the NPC (the major coalition partner at the center), believing that the opportunity had offered itself to clip the wings of the Action Group in the Mid-West (which was predominantly NCNC), decided to accede to the demand of the people of the area for their own region in the federation. The reinstated Akintola government in the west, which owed its existence to the NCNC/NPC coalition at the center, also supported the move and the Mid-Western Region was created in 1963. This event spurred on the agitation of other areas for their own states and the need to create more states in the north to have a more balanced federation. This demand was not met until 1967, during the crisis between the former Eastern Region, headed by Lt. Colonel Odumegwu Ojukwu and the federal government, headed by General Yakubu Gowon. The crisis was inescapably leading to a civil war, and partly in an effort to create disaffection in the support Ojukwu was getting in all of the Eastern Region, the federal government decided to create 12 states in the country. Three of these were in the east, two of which gave the minorities what they wanted while the majority Ibos were confined to the East-Central State. The north was divided into six states while the Lagos State was created from the Western Region.

This move was very popular but it did not satisfy the demands of people who saw state creation not only as a means to satisfy genuine minorities demands or the fear of domination but more importantly as a means of "regional" and local development and as a means of sharing effectively in the sudden petronaira. Their demands were again acceded to in February 1976, when out of the 12 existing states, seven others were created, making the total 19. The hope then was that these 19 states would do it: there would be no more agitation that would be worth anybody's consideration. But the cry went on. In 1983, the House of Representatives and the Senate were thinking of whether or not Nigeria should not be broken up into as many as 40 states.

STATE SECURITY (DETENTION OF PERSONS) DECREE. The State Security (Detention of Persons) Decree was enacted in January 1966. This decree dealt with the detention of certain specified persons in the interest of the security of the country for a period not exceeding six months in places where the Head of the National Military Government might, from time to time, direct. Persons so detained were entitled to make representations in writing to the national military government which might, if it thought it fitting, constitute a tribunal for that purpose under conditions laid down in the Decree. Furthermore the Decree suspended Chapter III of the Republican Constitution of 1963, which dealt with fundamental human rights.

STATUTORY CORPORATIONS SERVICE COMMISSION. Established in 1968, it consisted of a Chairman and two to four other members. It was to have the powers, the immunities and the functions allocated to the Public Service Commission. Some of the powers allocated to it were power to appoint persons to hold or act in offices in any of the following statutory corporations: Electricity Corporation of Nigeria (ECN), now National Electric Power Authority (NEPA), the Nigerian Broadcasting Corporation (NBC), the Nigerian Railway Corporation and the Nigerian Ports Authority together with the following companies: the Nigerian National Shipping Line Limited and the West African Airways Corporation (Nigeria) Limited. It also has the power to promote, transfer and confirm appointments and the power to dismiss and exercise disciplinary control over persons in those corporations or companies.

STATUTORY RIGHT OF OCCUPANCY see RIGHT OF OCCUPANCY.

SUDAN INTERIOR MISSION. Canadian missionaries were permitted by Lord Lugard to set up in the Northern Nigeria about the end of the nineteenth century. The mission's initial aim was to set up industrial education in the area. As such they set up farms at Pategi, Bida and other places.

SUPER TAX. A profit tax established by the federal military government in 1967. It was to be paid by certain companies and calculated at 10 percent on the amount by which a company's profit for a particular year of assessment exceeded the standard deduction for that year. The standard deduction was 15 percent of the company's paid up share capital or ₦10,000, or whichever is the greater.

SUPREME COUNCIL OF THE REVOLUTION OF THE NIGERIAN ARMED FORCES. On Saturday January 16, 1966, when Major Chukwumah Nzeogu seized power in the Northern Region, he went on the air to announce the coup in the name of the "Supreme Council of the Revolution of the Nigerian Armed Forces." The aim of the Council was to establish a strong, united and prosperous nation which would be free from corruption and internal strife. The name was coined by the coupmakers, but unfortunately they were not allowed to carry out their revolution since the coup in the south was not very successful. General Ironsi, quickly reacting to the coup, took over the rein of affairs after the rump of civilian government had handed over power to him and he ordered the detention of the coupmakers in prison.

SUPREME COURT. Following the abolition of appeals to the Judicial Committee of the Privy Council in London under the 1963 Republican Constitution, the Supreme Court, composed of the Chief Justice and not more than 15 justices with five or in special cases seven, of them forming a quorum has been made the highest court of the land. Its jurisdictions are both original and appellate. The original jurisdiction covers cases of dispute between a state and the federal government or between one state and another. In addition, the House of Assembly could confer further original jurisdiction on it provided it is not with respect to criminal matters. Its appellate jurisdiction includes appeals from the decision of the Federal Court of Appeal, either as of right or with leave of the Federal Court of Appeal. Being the final interpreter of the law and the Constitution for the nation, the Supreme Court carries a lot of responsibility for maintaining the integrity of the federation.

SUPREME MILITARY COUNCIL (SMC). Established by Decree Number 1 of 1966. The Council was the highest policy-making body in the nation. It consisted of the Head of the Federal Military Government who was the President of the Supreme Military Council, the Heads of the Nigerian Army, Navy and Air Force, the two Chiefs of Staff of the Armed Forces and of the Nigerian Army, the Military Governors of the four regions that made up the federation and the Attorney General of the Federation. In 1967, the Secretary to the Federal Military Government and other appropriate officials of the federal and state governments could attend its meetings in an advisory capacity. But in 1975, after the third military coup which overthrew General Gowon's administration, military governors were no longer members of the Council and government officials could no longer attend its meetings. After the 1983 coup d'état the Supreme Military Council consisted of 19 members, made up of the Head of State, Heads of various military units, other military members, the Inspector General of Police and his Deputy, the Director General of the Nigerian Security Organization and his Deputy, and the Secretary to the Federal Military Government, who was also the Head of the Civil Service. The SMC became the Armed Forces Ruling Council (AFRC) in August 1985 after Major-General Babangida came to power.

-T-

TACTICAL COMMITTEE. After the federal election of 1959 at which the Action Group Party won only 75 out of the 312 seats, Chief Obafemi Awolowo became the leader of the opposition rather than the Prime Minister in the Federal House of Assembly. Fearing that the federal government after independence in 1960 might want to use its powers to declare a state of emergency in the Western Region (which was the stronghold of the Action Group Party) and impose a caretaker administration to replace that of the Action Group, the Federal Executive Council of the party in September 1960 decided to set up what it called the Tactical Committee.

Chief Awolowo was given power to be solely responsible for the functioning of the Committee and its members were to remain secret. As the treason trials showed, Chief Awolowo appointed three members: Chief Anthony Enahoro, who was then a federal Vice-President of the party and Chairman of

of the party's regional organization in the Midwest; Chief Ayo
Rosiji, the party's Federal Secretary and Chief S. L. Akintola,
Deputy Leader of the party and Premier of the Western Region.
But as Professor Sanya D. Onabamiro testified at the treason
trial, rather than Chief Akintola and Chief Rosiji being mem-
bers, it was he himself and Sam Ikoku who were members.

The purpose of the Committee was to devise ways and
means of protecting the party base in the Western Region and
to forestall any federal government plan to assail democracy
and the rule of law. This the Committee planned to do in the
following ways:

1.   To ensure that the party's field organization in the West-
     ern Region was maintained in a state of constant prepared-
     ness to deal with any attempt by the National Council of Ni-
     gerian Citizens (NCNC) to provoke acts of lawlessness which
     might be used as a pretext for a takeover.
2.   To conduct publicity in Nigeria and abroad so as to dis-
     credit any attempt by the federal government to take over
     Western Regional government by any means other than elec-
     tions.
3.   To make overtures to the NCNC with a view to cooperating
     on a nationwide basis in order to enhance the security of
     the Action Group in the Western Region and the likelihood
     of success of the progressive elements in the future federal
     elections.
4.   To intensify organizational efforts in the Northern and
     Eastern regions so as to extend Action Group popular sup-
     port and at the same time relieve pressure on the Western
     Region.

In March 1962, after Chief Awolowo had alleged at the
peace meeting of party elders that S. L. Akintola had been
spreading the rumor that he was planning to overthrow the
federal government by means of a coup d'etat, Chief Awolowo
asked the Federal Executive Council to dissolve the Committee
because its work and its purposes were being misrepresented.

TARKA, JOSEPH SARWUAN.   Born on July 10, 1932 at Igbor in
     the Tiv Division of Benue State, he attended Gboko Primary
     School, the Katsina-Ala Middle Secondary School and Bauchi
     Teachers' Training College.
          Being interested in politics early in his life, he formed
     the United Middle Belt Congress (UMBC) and became its Pres-
     ident.   The aim of the party was to campaign for the Middle-
     Belt Region.   In 1954, he won a seat in the Federal House
     of Representatives for the UMBC.   While in the Federal Par-
     liament, he allied his party with the Action Group (AG) of
     Chief Obafemi Awolowo.   Both parties presented a coordinated
     opposition to the government of Alhaji Tafawa Balewa.
          Tarka led his party's delegation to the constitutional
     conferences of 1957 and 1958 in London.   After the federal
     elections of 1959, Tarka acted as the shadow cabinet for

commerce and industry. In 1962 he was arrested with prominent Action Group members, including Chief Awolowo, charged with plotting to overthrow the federal government, but was later discharged for want of sufficient evidence. In 1964, his party joined the so-called Southern Progressive Parties and, under the alliance known as the United Progressive Grand Alliance (UPGA), he fought the elections. The UPGA lost, but he continued his campaign for a separate Middle-Belt State. On May 27, 1967, his wishes came true when General Gowon's administration created the Benue Plateau State as one of the 12 states created out of the former four regions.

In 1966, after the military came to power, Tarka was appointed member of the northern delegation to the All-Nigeria Constitutional Conference. In June 1967 he became a member of the Federal Executive Council, where he served first as Commissioner for Transport and later, in 1971, as Commissioner for Communications in the regime of General Yakubu Gowon. In 1974, he had to resign following allegations of corruption and abuse of office. He then went into private business. In 1978, when the ban on politics was lifted, Tarka went back into politics and became a member of the National Party of Nigeria (NPN). He was elected Vice-Chairman of the party and later won a seat in the Senate on the party's ticket. He died in London on March 30, 1980 and was buried in his hometown.

TELEVISION BROADCASTING. Television broadcasting in Nigeria started in October 1959 when the Western Nigerian Television Service (WNTV) was launched. It was the first television service in the whole of Africa and WNTV proudly described itself as "First in Africa." A year later the Eastern Nigeria Television Service (ENTV) came into operation and in 1962 the Northern Region Television Service (NRTV) joined them. It was not until 1963 that the Nigerian Television Service (NTV) began operation. In 1978 television broadcasting in the country was placed under the Nigerian Television Authority (NTA) by the military administration. Thus NTA took over all the television stations in the country, but each station in the states was allowed to draw up its own programs. However it was required to relay the national network programs.

With the return of the civilian administration, states began to set up new state television stations. The state television operates on UHF while NTA stations are allocated channels on VHA.

THOMAS, CHIEF BODE. A lawyer and a politician, born in 1919 in Oyo, Oyo State. He was a foundation member of the Action Group Party, whose ideas that the country should be organized on a regional basis, both for government and party purposes, greatly influenced government and party development in the country. Before his death in 1953 he was the deputy leader of the Action Group, and the Minister of Transport in the central government in Lagos. He was also awarded the chieftaincy title of Balogun of Oyo.

THORP AND HARLOW COMMISSION. The Commission, consisting of F. J. Harlow, Principal of Chelstea Polytechnic in London and W. H. Thorp, Nigerian Deputy Director of Technical Education, was appointed to look into the possibilities of setting up technical institutions in Nigeria. The Commission submitted its report in April 1949. It recommended that technical colleges should be set up, which would cater to the needs of secondary school leavers for additional education. The Commission recommended that a Nigerian College of Arts, Science and Technology be set up on a tripartite basis with a branch of the college in each of the three regions into which the country was divided. Government accepted the report and by 1952 the first branch of the college had been set up in Zaria in Northern Nigeria.

THUGGERY. An important feature of Nigerian politics in 1964 and 1965 was thuggery. Each political party operating in Nigeria between 1964 and 1966 had a quasi-military corps called "thugs." These thugs went about, especially during electioneering campaigns, molesting innocent citizens and their party opponents. There were situations where thugs of different political parties clashed. Thuggery became more pronounced in the west in 1965, at the approach of the Western Regional election. They disrupted the campaigns of opposing parties and engaged in acts of vandalism, wanton destruction of property and lives. After the announcement of the Western Regional election results of 1965, thugs of opposing parties engaged in open battles. They began "Operation Wet E, " that is, "operation wet it, " in which petrol was sprayed on opponents and they were set on fire. It is important to note that the 1979 constitution banned the operation or inclusion of any quasi- or para-military corps or institution in any political party.

TIN MINING. Tin mining had long been one of the indigenous industries in Northern Nigeria. However in 1900, when the Royal Niger Company gave up its charter to administer Northern Nigeria, it was allowed to keep a share of the mineral rights in the area lying north of rivers Niger and Benue. The company, having discovered long before then that the tin the Hausas used for their brassware was being mined in the Bauchi Plateau, sponsored expeditions to locate tin in commercial quantity in the area. In 1906, the company began tin mining operations on a commercial basis, and other companies soon joined in. By 1913, investment by individual non-Nigerians and companies had exceeded £4 million. To facilitate transportation of the tin ore to the sea, some of the companies agreed to invest in building roads to link the centers of production with the major roads and with the railway line. In 1914 the railway was extended to the Bauchi Plateau and so it aided in the expansion of the mines. Nigeria later became the fourth largest tin-producing nation in the world. At present tin is Nigeria's most important mineral export after oil. However it earns very little, compared to other export products.

In 1978 it earned only ₦22 million. The tin was managed by the Nigerian Mining Corporation (NMC), which engages in direct exploration and joint ventures with mining companies.

TINUBU, MADAM. A nineteenth-century prominent businesswoman, born in Abeokuta in Ogun State. She served as a business apprentice to her mother, after which she went to Badagry, near Lagos, to set up her trading business in tobacco and salt. She came in contact with the European slave dealers and served as a middle woman.

In 1846, when King Akintoye of Lagos was deposed, he went to Badagry seeking Madam Tinubu to use her influence to organize support for Akintoye to regain his throne. In 1851 Akintoye regained his throne in Lagos and Madam Tinubu was asked to come to Lagos. She later transferred her trading business to Lagos, serving, as before, as an intermediary between the Europeans and the Nigerians of the interior. In Lagos, she soon became a prominent and powerful woman, so powerful that people believed that she was the power behind the throne, a situation which led to rebellion among some chiefs. In 1853, Akintoye died and was succeeded by his son Dosumu. During the reign of Dosumu, whom historians described as a weak king, the influence of Madam Tinubu grew. In 1855 she organized a campaign against wealthy immigrants who were from Brazil and Sierra Leone, using their wealth and power against the king. She accused them of an attempt to destroy the tradition and custom of the people of Lagos. The immigrants did not fold their arms; they struck back and Tinubu together with her supporters had to be expelled from Lagos and they went to Abeokuta where her business enterprises grew. In Abeokuta she became a prominent and powerful woman. In recognition of her contribution to the peace and progress of Abeokuta, she was made Iyalode of Abeokuta by the Alake of Abeokuta in 1864. She died in 1887. A monument was created in her name in Abeokuta and in memory of her patriotism, Tinubu Square, which is the focal point of the city of Lagos, is named after her.

TIV RIOTS. An ethnic group with a tradition of common descent living mainly in an area south of the Benue River in the present Benue State, the Tivs constituted an important group in the former Northern Nigeria. The Tivs were never conquered by the Fulani during the Jihad.

The Tiv riots occurred in March 1960 as a result of the people's dissatisfaction about the Native Authority System. The riot also had a political overtone in that the Tivs were mainly members of the United Middle Belt Congress (UMBC), which opposed the rule of the Native Authorities which supported the Northern People's Congress (NPC), the ruling party in the Northern Region. The riots were precipitated by the speech made by a Clan Chief, which was regarded as anti-Action Group (AG) Party with which the UMBC was in alliance. The riots started in Yander and, a week later, moved to other

places in the area and lasted until October 1960. The UMBC
Party supporters went out in a rampage and burnt the houses
of the NPC supporters including those of local chiefs who supported the NPC. The police had to open fire and many people
were injured or killed. The Resident in the area appealed to
the leaders of the two parties, Mr. J. Tarka for UMBC and
Mr. Anja, NPC local leader, to assist in putting an end to
the violence. They agreed to tour the area in an effort to
appeal for peace and calm. The Resident later met with the
Northern Regional Cabinet where it was resolved that the Native Authorities in the area should be dissolved, and their powers temporarily were vested in District Officers.

In February 1964 another uprising was started in the
Tiv Division in which not less than 11 people were killed. The
situation became so grave that the maintenance of law and order was handed over to the army.

TOWNSEND, REVEREND HENRY. A lay minister of the Church
Missionary Society (CMS) sent to Abeokuta, Ogun State on January 4, 1743, accompanied by two freed Egba slaves from
Sierra Leone, to explore the possibility of establishing a mission in Abeokuta. He saw to the opening of mission stations
and schools in Badagry and Abeokuta.

TRADE UNION CONGRESS OF NIGERIA. Formed in 1943, its aims,
among other things, were to unite all trade unions into one
organized body, deal with general labor problems affecting
workers in Nigeria, protect the rights of trade union organizations and see to the proper organization of trade unions.
The TUC was accorded recognition by the government soon
after its formation. The organization became very successful
soon after its formation, influencing labor legislations and showing great interest in worker's education.

Problems, however, arose in 1947 over the decision by
the General Council to affiliate with the National Council of Nigeria and Cameroon (NCNC), a political party. At the Sixth
Annual Delegates Conference of December 1948, the decision
was put to a motion and was defeated. As a result of this
disaffiliation vote, many affiliated unions withdrew their membership, leading in March 1949 to the formation of the Nigerian
National Federation of Labor (NNFL). In May 1950 the TUC
and the NNFL agreed to merge into a central union, the Nigerian Labour Congress (NLC). Not much was heard again
of the TUC until 1959, when the All-Nigerian Trade Union Federation (ANTUF) and the National Council of Trade Union of
Nigeria (NCTUN) agreed to unite under the umbrella of the
Trade Union Congress of Nigeria. However the merger did
not last long. In 1960 the organization split again over the
suspension of Michael Imoudu, who called a conference to
form the Nigerian Trade Union Congress. However the two
organizations agreed in 1962 to merge together again under
the United Labour Congress.

TRADE UNION MOVEMENT. In pursuance of the British government
policy to encourage the growth of labor union organizations in
its colonies, the colonial government helped in no small way
to foster the development of trade unionism in Nigeria. The
government, even before the Second World War, had passed
legislations dealing with the registration of unions. The first
trade union in Nigeria, the Southern Nigeria Civil Service Union, was formed in 1912. In 1914, after the amalgamation of
the Northern and the Southern protectorates, its name was
changed to the Nigerian Civil Service Union. In 1931, the
first effort to organize workers in the private sector was that
of the Nigerian Union of Teachers, which was composed of
teachers in voluntary agency schools as well as some government schools. The same year the Railway Workers Union was
founded. In 1936 the Marine Daily Paid Workers' Union was
formed--its name was changed in 1937 to Nigerian Marine
African Workers' Union. In 1941 the existing trade unions in
the public services merged into the African Civil Servants and
Technical Workers' Union (ACSTWU), with the aim of protecting the interests of African technical workers and establishing
better understanding between them and the government. In
1942 another attempt was made to establish a central labor
movement. This gave birth to the Federated Trade Unions
of Nigeria, but its name was changed in 1943 to the Trade
Union Congress of Nigeria, which the government recognized
as the legitimate representative of the workers' interests.
Among the main objectives of the Congress was to unite all
trade unions into one organized body, protect the rights of
trade unions and their members and establish a newspaper
which they called The Nigerian Worker. In 1949 a group of
members became disaffected. They broke away and formed
the Nigerian National Federation of Labour (NNFL), led by
Chief Michael Imoudu, who became president, and Nduka Eze,
who was the General Secretary. Following this rift, other
trade union organizations emerged: All-Nigeria Trade Union
Federation (ANTUF) in 1953 and National Council of Trade Unions of Nigeria (NCTUN) in 1957. These two merged in 1959
into the Trade Union Congress of Nigeria (TUCN). In 1960
Nigerian Trade Union Congress (NTUC) was formed and in
1962 United Labour Congress (ULC) was formed. On the
same day that the ULC was formed, Imoudu's supporters
formed the Independent United Labour Congress (IULC). This
division continued even when the military took over power and
it was not until 1978 when, through the efforts of the federal
military government, major differences were reconciled
and a restructuring of the existing labor unions was carried
out. At present there is a central labor organization, The
Nigerian Labour Congress, to which all labor unions have to
affiliate. Some of the reasons responsible for past instability
in the movement were problems of ideology, personal ambition
and political alignment.

TRADE UNION ORDINANCE. As a follow-up to the directive of

September 1930 issued by the Secretary of State for the Colonies, Lord Passfield (formerly Sidney Webb) asking colonial governments in British dependencies to take steps to smooth the passage of labor union organizations into constitutional channels rather than allowing them to be taken over and dominated by disaffected persons, the 1939 Trade Union Ordinance, was proclaimed. Under the Ordinance, a union, in order to engage in collective bargaining with its employer, must first be registered.

TRANSPORTATION. The transportation sector has for many years been a major area of government investment. In the Third National Development Plan it was next to industries, attracting the highest investment with a total of ₦7.3 billion. This represented 24.3 percent of the total investments for the Plan period.

Transportation in Nigeria is basically through four means--road, air, water and rail. The roads in Nigeria are divided into three categories: Trunk "A" roads, which are maintained by the federal government, cut across state boundaries; Trunk "B" roads, maintained by the state government, link the towns in the state; and Trunk "C" roads, composed of urban and rural roads, are maintained by local government in their areas.

The second means of transportation in Nigeria is by rail. The railway system comprises a total of 3,505 km. route of 1,067 mm. (3 ft. 6 ins.) gauge and runs through the states of Nigeria except Bendel, Ondo and Cross River. The railway is single-tracked and consists of two main routes, linking the two major ocean parts of Lagos and Port Harcourt with the state capitals, industrial and commercial centers in the country.

The third means of transportation in Nigeria is by water or sea. The transportation by sea is controlled by the Nigerian Ports Authority, which established harbors at Lagos, Port Harcourt (two major ports), Calabar, Akassa, Bonny, Warri, Sapele, Burutu and Degema. Ships from Nigeria and other countries load and off-load at these harbors. There is Inland Waterways, which is made possible by the use of River Niger.

The last and the latest means of transport in Nigeria is air travel. Flights in Nigeria are operated both locally and internationally. The Nigerian Airport Authority has built airports in some major towns in Nigeria and has plans to connect all state capitals by air. There are two International Airports --Kano and Ikeja--with a number of ports in others. The management of these ports are under the control of Nigeria Airport Authority.

Flights to and from Nigeria are carried on by the Nigerian Airways and some other foreign airways but Nigerian Airways maintains a monopoly over domestic flights while it competes with other foreign firms on international flights. The biggest Airport in Nigeria is the Murtala Mohammed Airport at Ikeja.

TRANS-SAHARAN ROAD PROJECT. The Trans-Saharan Road Project is a continental road system to link Algiers in Algeria to Lagos in Nigeria. Nigeria became a full member of the committee working on the road system in October 1977.

TREASON TRAIL. On October 1, 1962, Prime Minister Alhaji Sir Abubakar Tafawa Balewa announced to the nation that the government was aware of the intention of some people in the country to violently overthrow the government. The police, in September, had searched a house in Mushin, Lagos and found a large quantity of firearms, including submachine guns, automatic pistols, revolvers and plenty of ammunition. Later, on October 5, 1962, the police reported that they had found three stores of arms during their search of the homes of some Action Group leaders. On November 2, 1962 Chief Obafemi Awolowo was charged, along with 26 other persons, with conspiring to overthrow the federal government. The prosecution alleged that the accused had, between December 1960 and September 1962 in Lagos and in many other places in Nigeria, formed an intention to levy war against the Queen within Nigeria in order to compel the Queen to change her measures or her counsels and had manifested such intention by overt act, treasonable felony. Similar charges were made against Anthony Enahoro and Samuel Ikoku, both of whom had fled the country and were wanted persons.

Among the accused were Dr. Oladipo Maja, Alahaji Lateef Jakande, Mr. Olabisi Onabanjo, J. S. Tarka, Mr. Josiah Olawoyin and Mr. Michael Omisade. Charges against Oladipo were later withdrawn for lack of evidence, but he later gave evidence for the prosecution. Chief Awolowo's counsel, Mr. E. F. N. Gratiaen from the United Kingdom, was refused permission to enter Nigeria to defend him and so he had to defend himself. On December 6, 1962, a Bill was passed forbidding non-Nigerians to enter Nigeria to practice any profession without the written consent of the Minister for Internal Affairs. The law was supported by the Nigerian Bar Association, for on November 10, it had called on the government to pass laws against expatriate lawyers practicing in Nigeria. But the Association did not support the government action with regard to Mr. Gratiaen, Q. C. , since he was a lawyer enrolled to practice in Nigeria. Chief Awolowo challenged the federal government for refusing to allow his lawyer to enter Nigeria, but he lost.

Chief Awolowo and 17 other accused persons were found guilty and were sentenced to varying years of imprisonment: Awolowo to ten years, Jakande and Omisade to seven years each.

TRIBALISM. A term used to denote doing something to favor one's ethnic group or giving apparently undue privilege to people from one's own ethnic group.

Nigeria, as a country, was the creation of the British. It is made up of many ethnic or "tribal" groups who are geographically located and whose languages are quite different from one another. A few of these language groups are the Hausas, Fulani, Kanuri, Tiv, Yoruba, Nupe, Edo, Ibo, Urhobo, Ibibio, Anang, Ijaw, Tikar and many other minority groups scattered in geographical locations all over the country. Most people, even the highly educated ones in the universities, government and business, still feel stronger loyalties and sympathy to their local or ethnic group than to the nation as a whole.

This ethnic or tribal feeling has been often exploited by politicians when campaigning. For example Dr. Nnamdi Azikiwe, one of the architects of modern Nigeria and a presidential candidate in 1979, said while electioneering over his tax problem with the Federal Electoral Commission (FEDECO), that his tribulations came as a result of the fact that he was an Ibo.

The term also has become a convenient word for many Nigerians when they are penalized for certain action, especially when the person in charge is of a different ethnic group from the one who is penalized. It is also used in a scapegoat fashion over failure to secure a post when another person of a different ethnic origin gets the post.

TRIBAL MARKS. Tribal marks were used as a means of identification, especially during the period of intertribal wars and slavery. Thus, in the past, members of most ethnic groups and their subdivisions had facial marks made during infancy by incision or tattooing. The incisions, while being treated, were deliberately kept open so that the scars would remain permanent. Even though some traditionally oriented families, especially in Yorubaland, still continue with this practice, most people have long put an end to it since the need for it is no longer present.

TRIBE. A derogatory term generally applied by Europeans to any nationality or ethnic group of non-European origin in colonial territories of Africa, irrespective of population and sociocultural development Thus the Yorubas, the Ibos and the Hausa-Fulanis, each numbering over five million people when the colonial authorities arrived in Nigeria, were described as tribes. In spite of the inappropriateness of the term, it lingers on, especially in its derivative of tribalism. Today words like nation, ethnic group, group or race are used.

TUDOR DAVIES COMMISSION. The Tudor Davies Commission was set up in October 1945, following the June 1945 General Strike which lasted for about two months. The Commission, consisting of W. Tudor Davies as Commissioner and F. W. Dalley and G. P. W. Lamb as Assessors, was to consider: the government representation with regard to government and native authority employees, an increase in the cost of living allowance for Nigerian workers and making recommendations as to what government should do. The Commission started sitting in November 1945 and continued until March 1946. The Commission recommended that the cost of living allowance existing in July 1945 be increased by 50 percent and that the 50 percent award should apply not only to Africans earning £220 per annum or less but also to the special allowances paid since October 1944 to African employees whose salaries were over £220, except for those receiving local allowances because they held superior posts. It also recommended that the award should remain in force until a new wage structure was set up by a team of statistical officers and nutritionists, which should be set up within two years from the date of the report.

-U-

UDOJI COMMISSION. The Public Service Review Commission, popularly known as the Udoji Commission, was set up in September 1972 under the chairmanship of Chief Jerome Oputa Udoji, a distinguished public servant. The Commission was to carry out a review of the organization, structure and management of the Nigerian public services, including recruitment, career and staff development, pensions and superannuations as well as the grading system. The sectors of the public services covered in the exercise were the federal and state civil services, the public corporations and enterprises, universities, the judiciary, the police, teaching services and the local government administration.

The Commission submitted its report in September 1974 and the government made the report public in January 1975. In its report, the Commission, among other things, called for a new style public service in the country which would be production- or result-oriented, and which would concentrate attention and resources on the purposes for which an institution was set up. With regard to the structure of the public services, the Commission recommended the abolition of the former division into classes which was a source of great conflicts, and asked that a unified grading structure be introduced which would embrace all posts in the civil service from the lowest to the highest and provide equal opportunity for every person to advance to the highest post in the service irrespective of his discipline. The Commission recommended a grading level from 1 to 17 and suggested the salary appropriate to each level to make public servants' salaries commensurate with their responsibilities and comparable to the private sector so as to stem the movement from the public to the private sector.

The government accepted most of its recommendations. It was the time of the oil boom and rather than space out the payment of the salary areas as the Commission had recommended, the government paid all of it at once, leading to skyrocketing inflation.

UNIFICATION DECREE. When General Aguiyi-Ironsi assumed power in January 1966, he set up three important commissions, one of which was the Nwokedi Commission under Mr. F. Nwokedi, who was the sole Commissioner. His responsibility was to put forward proposals for the unification of the regional and federal public services. The military government accepted the recommendations and issued Decree Number 34, which Ironsi said was intended to remove the last vestiges of the excessive regionalism of the recent past and to produce a cohesion in the governmental structure which was necessary to achieve and maintain the paramount objective of national unity. According to the Decree, Nigeria ceased to be a federation and it was known as the Republic of Nigeria. The former four regions of the country were to be known as the Northern, Eastern, Western and the Mid-Western groups of provinces. The federal territory of Lagos became the capital territory. The federal military government became the national military government and the Federal Executive Council became the Executive Council. The federal and regional public services became unified under a National Public Service Commission. The decrees also dissolved the 81 existing political parties and ethnic associations all over the country. The part of the decree setting up a unitary form of government was later revoked by General Yakubu Gowon after the second coup in Decree Number 59 of 1966.

UNION BANK OF NIGERIA LIMITED. One of the leading banks in Nigeria, formerly known as the Barclays Bank DCO (Nigeria) Limited, was formed in 1925 as Barclays Bank Dominion Colonial and Overseas (DCO) and took over the activities of some other banks. The bank has branches all over the country. At present, the federal government together with Nigerian citizens hold 80 percent of its share capital while the Barclays Bank International (BBI) holds the remaining 20 percent. The federal government then terminated the subsidiary relations of the bank to the BBI, and to reflect this changed relationship, its name was changed in 1979 to the Union Bank of Nigeria Limited. The bank still maintains correspondent relationship with the BBI.

UNITED AFRICAN COMPANY (UAC). Formed in 1879 by Mr. George Dashwood Goldie Taubman, later knighted as Sir Taubman Goldie, by the amalgamation of four British firms in the Niger Delta. The firms were West African Company, Central African Company, Miller Brothers and James Pinnock, each competing against the other in the area. Before the merger, the French and the Germans had begun to look for ways to expand their interest in the Niger Delta and the hinterland, and Goldie designed the merger to forestall this. He persuaded the companies that the only cure for overcompetition among them was for all of them to amalgamate.

In 1882 the UAC changed its name to National African Company and applied to the British government for a charter, which was then refused. By this time, two French companies had formed on the Niger and when they refused to join the National African Company, a price war was started which pushed

the two French companies off the market.   After the Berlin
Conference of 1885, which recognized the area around the Niger as being under British protection, Britain finally granted
the company the charter it had long sought for in 1886 and
was renamed the Royal Niger Company.   Under the terms of
the charter, the company was given political authority over
the areas.   The Company set up a governing council subject
to the control of the Foreign Office in London.   In July 1899
the bill divesting the Royal Niger Company of its administrative functions was passed and the Company then became a private concern.   Since then, the UAC has exercised a prominent
role in the country's economy.   In the 1930's it controlled
more than 40 percent of the country's import-export trade and
by 1949 it handled about 34 percent of commercial merchandise
imported into Nigeria.   The UAC was a member of the Association of West African Merchants (AWAM), through which
members made import agreements and allocated export quotas.
Today the UAC is indigenized, with most of its shares owned
by Nigerians and its management in the hands of Nigerians.
The Company has remained one of the biggest commercial
firms in Nigeria.

UNITED LABOUR CONGRESS (ULC).   The United Labour Congress
(ULC) came into being as the result of a merger of the Trade
Union Congress of Nigeria (TUCN) and the Nigerian Trade Union Congress (NTUC) in 1962 during the joint conference of the
two factions.   But disagreements at the conference over the international affiliation of the Congress led to another split: one
faction led by Chief Michael Imoudu who, together with his
supporters, formed the Independent United Labour Congress
(IULC) while others continued with the conference.   At the
conference, Alhaji Adebola was elected the President of the
Congress.

UNITED MIDDLE BELT CONGRESS (UMBC).   The United Middle
Belt Congress was founded in 1955 as a result of a merger
between two previously formed organizations, the Middle Zone
League, founded in 1950 and the Middle Belt Peoples Party,
founded in 1953.   The UMBC later split into two, one part
joined with the Northern People's Congress (NPC) while the
other, under the leadership of Mr. Joseph S. Tarka, retained
the organization and went into an alliance with the Action Group
Party.   The party advocated the creation of a Middle-Belt Region for the area and constantly agitated against the NPC government of the north.   The party, together with all other political parties, was banned in 1966 when the military came into
power.   But in 1967, the people of the Middle-Belt got the state
they had been asking for, the Benue/Plateau State.

UNITED NATIONAL INDEPENDENCE PARTY (UNIP).   The United
National Independence Party (UNIP) was formerly known as
National Independence Party (NIP), a breakaway party from
the National Council of Nigeria and Cameroon (NCNC), and

formed in 1953 by three federal ministers dismissed from the NCNC as a result of the 1953 Eastern Regional Crisis. The party, led by Professor Eyo Ita, joined the Action Group in an alliance with which they both jointly won seven seats in the 1954 federal elections in the Eastern Region. The main stronghold of UNIP were the areas known as COR areas, that is, Calabar-Ogoja and Rivers areas. The party advocated for the creation of separate states for the areas. The party was dissolved along with others in 1966 but in 1967 the areas got their states, known as the South-Eastern and Rivers states.

UNITED NATIVE AFRICAN CHURCH. The church came as a protest to the white-dominated Christian churches. The United Native African Church seceded in 1891 from the Anglican church because the founders believed that Africa was to be evangelized by Africans, since such circumstances as climate and other such influences made it difficult for the Europeans to do so. Furthermore they wanted a purely Native African church that would evangelize the people and be governed by Africans. The group that founded the church was much influenced by the writings of Dr. Edward Blyden and his visit to Lagos in 1890 when he urged African Christians to establish native churches patterned on the black churches in the United States.

UNITED PEOPLE'S PARTY (UPP). The United People's Party was formed after the Action Group crisis of 1962 by Chief S. L. Akintola, who, together with 23 members of the Western House of Assembly who supported him, formed its nucleus. The UPP formed a coalition with the NCNC to run the government of the Western Region after the state of emergency was lifted in 1963 in the region. Chief S. L. Akintola then became the Premier and the leader of the NCNC coalition partner Chief Fani-Kayode became the Deputy Premier. In 1964 members of the UPP and a faction of the NCNC in the west, led by Chief Fani-Kayode and Chief Richard Akinjide, formed the NNDP, Nigerian National Democratic Party with Chief S. L. Akintola as Chairman. During the political realignment of 1964 before the December federal elections, NNDP joined with the NPC (Northern People's Congress) to form the Nigerian National Alliance (NNA).

UNITED PROGRESSIVE FRONT. An alliance of four parties--the Great Nigerian People's Party (GNPP), Nigerian People's Party (NPP), Unity Party of Nigeria (UPN) and People's Redemption Party (PRP)--proposed during the 1979 general elections to stop the National Party of Nigeria (NPN), the leading party, from winning. The alliance helped the PRP to win the gubernatorial elections in Kaduna State which had its legislative house controlled by the NPN with more than two-thirds majority. The alliance did not hold for the presidential elections, which the NPN won.

UNITED PROGRESSIVE GRAND ALLIANCE (UPGA). Formed at Ibadan in June 1964 by the Action Group Party (AG) together with its northern ally, the United Middle Belt Congress (UMBC) and the National Council of Nigerian Citizens (NCNC), together with its ally in the north, the Northern Element Progressive Union (NEPU) which, together with UMBC, had formed the Northern Progressive Front while the NCNC and the AG had formed themselves into the Southern Progressive Front. Thus UPGA was an alliance of the Southern and Northern Progressive fronts.

The purpose of the Alliance of the two erstwhile rival parties was to enable them to win the 1964 federal election. The Alliance ran into difficulties in the west over the nomination of candidates. Both the Action Group and the National Council of Nigerian Citizens wanted to field their candidates on the platform of the Alliance. They finally reached a compromise in which 37 out of the 57 seats in the region were to be contested by the Action Group while the rest went to the National Council of Nigerian Citizens. A few days before the election, the UPGA leaders led a delegation to the President of the federation asking him to postpone the election because of election malpractices in various parts of the federation. They also said that if their request was not granted they would boycott the election. When all efforts to postpone the election had failed, they decided to boycott the election and their decision was broadcast on December 29, 1964, just a day before the election. The boycott succeeded only in the east, while elections were held in the other three regions. When the result of the election was announced, the National Democratic Party, which was in alliance with the NPC to form the Nigerian National Alliance (NNA), won 36 of the 57 seats in the west and an overwhelming victory in the north. Because of the election boycott of the UPGA, another election, called the Little Election, was held in March 1965 in the Eastern Region and the NCNC won the majority of the seats. But overall, UPGA came out the loser. The UPGA was dissolved and banned in 1966 when the army took over.

UNITY PARTY OF NIGERIA. Launched on the 22nd of September 1978, it was the first political party to be formed at the wake of political activities. At the formation of the party, Chief Obafemi Awolowo, who was the leader of the party, highlighted the UPN's four cardinal programs:

1. free education at all levels for all, effective October 1, 1979
2. integrated rural development which would be aimed at boosting food production and feeding the people of the nation
3. the provision of free health facilities for all citizens
4. full employment for all

The party was formed out of the National Committee of Friends, an association formed by Chief Awolowo in anticipation of civilian rule.

At the party's convention, Chief Obafemi Awolowo was selected as the presidential candidate of the party and Chief Philip E. Umeadi was chosen as his vice-presidential running mate. The party submitted its registration forms to FEDECO in December 1978 and was subsequently registered along with four others. Owing to the personality of the founder, Chief Awolowo, and the programs of the party, many people saw the UPN as a rebirth of the former Action Group Party, disbanded in 1966 when the military seized power.

The UPN contested the 1979 elections. It won 28 senatorial seats out of 95 and 110 seats in the National House of Assembly. The party won overwhelming support in the old Western Region (now Lagos Ogun, Oyo, Ondo and Bendel states), and it controlled both the state Executive and Legislative Branches in those states.

The party's presidential candidate, Chief Obafemi Awolowo, lost to the National Party of Nigeria's candidate Alhaji Shehu Shagari. Although he challenged the Federal Electoral Commission's (FEDECO) verdict at both the electoral tribunal and at the Supreme Court of Nigeria, both judicial bodies upheld the interpretation of FEDECO that the constitutional requirement that the winner should have the highest number of votes at the election and must have at least one quarter of the votes cast at the election in each of at least two thirds of the states of the federation.

In preparation for the 1983 elections, because the party did not appear to have enough support in the other, older regions (north and east), to win the presidential election, it was in the forefront of the effort to ally with the other minority parties to defeat the National Party of Nigeria. Thus the UPN, the Nigerian People's Party (NPP), the Imoudu faction of the People's Redemption Party (PRP) and the Mahmud faction of the Great Nigerian People's Party (GNPP) formed themselves into a kind of an alliance, the PPA (Progressive Parties Alliance).

However, the PPA was unable to agree on a common list for the 1983 elections, not even on the presidential candidate, and each party went it alone in all the states. The UPN lost the presidential race to the NPN and lost two of the states it controlled in 1979, Oyo and Bendel, but won the Kwara State gubernatorial election. The party was with all other parties proscribed after the December 1983 Coup which toppled the government of Alhaji Shehu Shagari.

UNIVERSAL PRIMARY EDUCATION (UPE). In 1955, the government of Western Nigeria, under the Action Group Party, launched its Universal Free Primary Education in the region. Two years later the east followed suit but in 1958, owing to financial constraints, the Eastern Region reimposed fees from primary III upward. In the west, the scheme continued until 1976, when the federal military government, under the leadership of General Olusegun Obasanjo, launched the nationwide Universal (Free) Primary Education in Nigeria. The scheme was launched to correct the imbalance between educational development in the south and the north. For example, in 1972 while about 70 percent of the school-age children were in school in the south, only about 10 percent were in school in the north. In 1974 General Gowon, the Head of State and a northerner, announced in the North-Western State that the government had planned to introduce free compulsory primary education throughout the country. But before he could launch the program he had been overthrown and it was the lot of General Olusegun Obasanjo, the then Head of State in 1976, who launched the program of Universal Free (not compulsory) Primary Education all over the nation. As the Head of State said, education in Nigeria was no longer a privilege but a right of every citizen.

Today no primary school children, except those who are attending private schools, are required to pay school fees and tuitions.

UNIVERSITIES, FINANCING OF. All universities in Nigeria are either federally owned or state owned. They all derive most of their income from the federal or state governments. The University of Ibadan, the first University in Nigeria, was jointly financed by the British government and the Nigerian government between 1948 and 1952. The full responsibility of the institution fell on the federal government after 1959. The University of Lagos, established by the federal government, was fully financed by the federal government right from its inception in 1962. The regional University of Nigeria, Nsukka, University of Ife, and Ahmadu Bello University were fully financed by their regions for some years before the National Universities Commission took over part of the financial responsibility on behalf of the federal government. In 1964, the federal government assumed 100 percent financial responsibility for the Universities of Ibadan and Lagos, while it agreed to finance 30 percent of recurrent and 50 percent of capital expenditure for Nsukka and Ife and assumed 50 percent of both recurrent and capital expenditure for Ahmadu Bello. There were other changes in 1967 but the big change came in August 1972 when the federal military government assumed full responsibility for all the then existing universities, and in 1976 the federal government declared that all the Nigerian universities were federally owned and no longer under the state control. However, with the coming into operation of the politicians, not only has the federal government been establishing new universities in the states that had none in 1979, but many state governments have embarked upon setting up state universities, and each government has to look for money to finance them. It is to be remembered that under the 1979 constitution, university, technological and post-primary education is on the concurrent list.

UNIVERSITY COLLEGE OF IBADAN. The University College of Ibadan was established in January 1947 following the recommendations of the Elliot Commission on Higher Education in

1945 in the then British colonies of which Nigeria was one.
The college opened in January 1948 and the students
of the old Yaba College started as undergraduates of the new
institution. The standard of academic instruction was based
upon what was obtained in the London University and students
retained London University degrees. In 1953, work began on
the building of the University College Hospital as a University
teaching hospital. In 1962 the University College of Ibadan became a full-fledged university.

UNIVERSITY OF IFE. Founded by the Western Regional government
in 1961, it was temporarily located on the site of the Ibadan
branch of the Nigerian College of Arts, Science and Technology
when it was formally opened in October 1962 with 244 foundation students.
Its staff came from the incorporated college while others
were from the University College of Ibadan. It was therefore
greatly influenced by Ibadan University, which itself was influenced by the British. The university was taken over in August
1975 by the federal government.

UNIVERSITY OF NIGERIA, NSUKKA. Formerly opened on October
7, 1960 by Her Royal Highness Princess Alexandra, who represented Her Majesty Queen Elizabeth II at the independence
celebration, the University of Nigeria became the second university to be opened in Nigeria. In the 1961-62 session, the
Enugu branch of the Nigerian College of Arts, Science and
Technology was incorporated into the university and was desig-
nated as the Enugu Campus of the university. The university
was different from its predecessor, University of Ibadan, in
certain ways: it was not completely residential and so could
admit a much larger number of candidates, its admission requirements were not as demanding as those of Ibadan University, the range of courses offered were much wider and examination schemes were based on course work similar to that in
the United States, and finally, it awarded its own degrees from
the very start without being affiliated with any university. The
university was regionally owned until it was taken over by the
federal government in April 1973.

UNIVERSITY STUDENT FINANCING. Until 1977, tuition fees were
paid in the Nigerian universities, and other levies included
accommodation, boarding, examination, caution and teaching
practice (education students) fees. In 1978 tuition fees were
removed from among all these fees for Nigerian students while
foreign students still had to pay the tuition fees. Various state
governments assist their indigenes by way of bursaries and
scholarships and the federal government has scholarship
schemes for students in Nigerian universities and those abroad.
In spite of all this, much of the burden of the cost of higher
education is still borne by parents and relatives.

URHOBO. An Edo-speaking minority ethnic group, the Urhobos

live in the Bendel State. They are divided into many smaller groups, each with its own traditional Chief or Ovie. Their main occupation is farming, growing crops like cassava and yams. They also fish and produce and market oil palm products. Some of their old villages, like Sapele and Ughelli, have become large towns and centers of oil and timber industries.

USMAN DAN FODIO. A Fulani, born in 1754 at Marata in Gobir, he was educated in Islamic religion and law. After his education he became a Moslem preacher, preaching for religious and social reforms among the people of Gobir. In 1802 a young man named Yunfa, who had been his pupil, became the King of Gobir, and he decided to put an end to the efforts of his reformist teacher. As Yunfa's persecution of the Moslems increased, the Moslems decided it was time to have their own government. Usman Dan Fodio was therefore elected Caliph and leader of the revolt against the King of Gobir. In 1803, the Jihad began, which removed most Hausa Kings from their thrones except in Bornu and some areas that were inaccessible to the Fulani horsemen. Usman then established himself in Sokoto. He handed over active military and administrative duties to his brother Abdullahi and his son Mohammed Bello. As his lieutenants defeated many rulers, Usman sent his nominees to be installed in office as rulers. Thus when the British came, there were two great Mohammedan empires in the north--Sokoto and Bornu.

-V-

VILLAGE HEADS. Under the Native Authority system in Northern Nigeria, a village was a part of a district and the village was under the authority and leadership of the village head, who had the responsibility for collecting taxes and other forms of revenue. In places where taxes were levied on villages as units, it was the task of the village head to determine how much each taxpayer was to pay. Village heads were members of the District Council.

VON ROSEN, CARL GUSTAF. A Swedish pilot who, during the Biafran War, flew relief materials for the Scandinavian churches (NORDCHURCHAID). He later joined the Biafrans and led the air raid on the Port Harcourt airfield in May 1969. His men also raided Benin and Enugu airfields under federal troops and destroyed many aircraft on the ground.

-W-

WACHUKWU, JAJA ANUCHA. Lawyer and politician, born in 1918 at Mbawsi Ngwa Imo State, he was educated at St. George's School, Mbawsi, Government School Afikpo, Government College,

Umuahia, Yaba Higher College, Lagos and at the Trinity College, University of Dublin in Ireland. He was called to the bar in Dublin and he returned to Nigeria in 1947, and from 1949 to 1952 he was a member of the Ngwa Native Authority Council. In 1951, he was elected into the Eastern House of Assembly and in 1952 to the House of Representatives in Lagos and became the Nigerian Speaker of the Federal House of Representatives in 1960, but in October 1960, he was appointed Federal Minister for Economic Development. In 1962 he was Minister for Foreign Affairs and Commonwealth Relations and in 1965 he was appointed Minister of Aviation. When the military took over power in 1966, he became Managing Director of the Jawach Properties and Development Corporation. He also went back into private legal practice in 1966. In 1978 he joined the Nigerian People's Party (NPP) and was elected Senator for Imo State. He later became the NPP leader in the Senate. He has an honorary LL.D. from the University of Dublin.

WADDELL, REVEREND HOPE MASTERTON. A Presbyterian missionary sent, in 1846, to Calabar in Eastern Nigeria. He and his party of Jamaican Christians landed at Duke Town, Calabar. They set up mission houses and built schools. They worked hard to put an end to some of the traditional practices like the killing of slaves to accompany a dead chief on his way to eternity, and twin murder.

WALLACE-JOHNSON, ISAAC THEOPHILUS AKUNNA. A Sierra Leonian resident in Lagos, Wallace-Johnson was born in 1894 at Wilberforce Village in Sierra Leone. In the late 1920's he came to Lagos and worked on the Daily Times. In 1931 he saw to the organization of the African Workers Union, the first Nigerian Labour Organization and became its General Secretary while at the same time acting as editor of the Nigerian Daily Telegraph and contributing to the Negro Worker. He soon became unpopular with the colonial authorities and he moved to Accra, Ghana and joined Dr. Nnamdi Azikiwe in the publication of a new nationalist paper, the African Morning Post. In 1938 he returned to Sierra Leone, his native country, where he continued the nationalist struggle. He died in May 1965.

WARRANT CHIEFS. These were chiefs created in the former Eastern Region by warrants issued to them by the colonial government. Many Ibo communities in the region did not have the kind of centralized administration that was characteristic of the emirates of Northern Nigeria and the chiefdoms of Western Nigeria. Since the system of Native Administration being extended to the south after the 1914 amalgamation was based on ruling through the indigenous chiefs, the government resorted to creating such chiefs who were given a cap of office and a warrant of authority; hence they were called "Warrant Chiefs." These chiefs were unpopular because in choosing them the colonial authorities (the District Commissioners) did not take into consideration the social and the cultural millieu of the people from which they were being chosen. In some places local traditional rulers were not even considered and therefore, rather than securing the loyalty and confidence of the people, the creation of Warrant Chiefs made for suspicion of British intentions and rule. This suspicion, together with the fact that the Native Courts in which the Chiefs sat were corrupt and the fear that women were to be asked to pay taxes, led to the Aba Riot of 1929, in which many people died and much property was destroyed.

WARRI. Founded in the fifteenth century by an ousted Benin prince together with his followers, Warri is the chief town of the Itsekiri people. Warri was, for long, the center of trade, including slave trade in the area. Today Warri has become the center of administration of many of the oil-producing companies.

WATER CORPORATIONS. Water corporations are public corporations in the various states. They were set up to maintain the existing water supply to the cities and rural areas in the states and to extend them where necessary or design and construct new water supply schemes.

WAYAS, DR. JOSEPH. President of the Senate in the Second Republic. He was born on May 21, 1941 in Basang, Obudu, Cross River State. He attended Central School, Sankwala Obudu, St. Charles School, Obudu, the Central Commercial Academy, Enugu and the Dennis Memorial Grammar School in Onitsha. He later went to the Tottenham Technical College, London, West Bormwich College of Commerce, Science and Technology and Bermingham and Aston University in Bermingham. He has a diploma in Business Administration, a higher diploma in Business Finance and a diploma in Industrial Relations. He also has an honorary doctorate degree in Law and Human Letters. He was Commissioner for Transport in the former South-Eastern State and was appointed later to the Constituent Assembly. Until his election to the Senate, he was Director and Managing Director of many companies.

The December 31, 1983 coup d'état, which removed the government of Alhaji Shehu Shagari from power, met Dr. Wayas safely in the United States, where he preferred to remain for some time. Dr. Wayas has authored Nigeria's Leadership Role in Africa.

WEST AFRICAN AIRWAYS CORPORATION (WAAC). The West African Airways Corporation was an Interterritorial statutory corporation which was established in 1946 to serve Nigeria, Ghana (Gold Coast), the Gambia and Sierra Leone on air transportation. The governing body which controlled the activities of the corporation and which formulated its general policies was the West African Air Transport Authority. Members of the authority consisted of representatives of the governments of Nigeria, the Gold Coast, Sierra Leone and the Gambia. West African Airways Corporation operated internal services in Nigeria and the Gold Coast and an intercolonial service from Lagos to Dakar. With this Corporation, the air transportation in Nigeria became developed. The Corporation developed 28 airports and landing grounds in Nigeria, including the International Airports of Lagos and Kano. The activities of the West African Airways Corporation in Nigeria was taken over by the Nigerian Airways when it was established in 1958.

WEST AFRICAN CURRENCY BOARD. The West African Currency Board was established in 1912 with the functions of providing and controlling the supply of currency issued to the West African colonies and protectorates of Nigeria, the Gold Coast, the Gambia and the Sierra Leone. It was also to make arrangements to withdraw notes from circulation so that they could be destroyed when necessary, and finally to make arrangements to mint coins for circulation. The activities of the Board were wound up in Nigeria with the establishment of the Central Bank of Nigeria in 1958.

WEST AFRICAN FRONTIER FORCE. After the Royal Niger Company had received its charter in 1885, it organized a small constabulary force made up of five British and two African officers and about 400 rank and file, most of whom were drawn from the Gold Coast, now Ghana. But with the French pressure on the company's territory between 1894 and 1897, the British decided to send Sir Frederick Lugard to Africa to raise and command a local force. By 1900, it had become a very disciplined force which helped the British in their campaign in the Ashanti.
In 1901, all the colonial military forces in West Africa were constituted into the West African Frontier Force (WAFF), but each territory was responsible for the maintenance of its own force. In Nigeria the force initially consisted of the Northern Nigerian Regiment, the Lagos Battalion and the Southern Regiment, made up of the Niger Coast Protectorate Force and the Niger Company Constabulary. When Lagos and Southern Nigeria were amalgamated in 1906, the Lagos Battalion became the Second Battalion of the Southern Nigeria Regiment. In 1914 when the Northern and Southern protectorates were amalgamated, the two regiments became known as the Nigerian Regiment.

WEST AFRICAN INSTITUTE OF SOCIAL AND ECONOMIC RESEARCH. Set up in 1950, it was meant to be an institute of social and economic research with no teaching commitments. Its job was to coordinate the social and economic research being carried on in all the British West African territories and to cooperate with other such bodies working on African affairs outside the area. In 1951 the name was changed to the Institute of Social and Economic Research. This was later converted into the Nigerian Institute of Social and Economic Research (NISER). The Institute is located at the University of Ibadan campus.

WEST AFRICAN PILOT. The West African Pilot, a daily newspaper, was set up in 1937 by Dr. Nnamdi Azikiwe who, between 1934 and 1937, was the editor of the African Morning Post in Accra, Ghana. The Pilot was the first Nigerian newspaper whose editor and proprietor was a Nigerian with a diploma in journalism and a graduate degree in political science and anthropology. With the arrival of the Pilot on the scene, the general trend among the existing papers changed considerably: they became more nationalist and harped on the evils of colonial rule in the country.

WEST AFRICAN STUDENT UNION (WASU). West African Student Union was founded in London in 1925. It replaced the Nigerian Progress Union, founded previously by Ladipo Solanke, a law student from Abeokuta, the capital of the present Ogun State. The organization was of great importance to Nigerian students in the United Kingdom, for it was the social and political center for them. Its objectives, among others, were: to act as a center for information and research on African history, culture and institutions; to promote good will and understanding between Africans and other races, fostering a spirit of national consciousness and racial pride among its members; to provide and maintain accommodation in London for students from West Africa; and to publish a monthly magazine called WASU. The organization served as a pressure group against alien rule in Africa, but its main achievement was in stimulating among its members political and racial consciousness.

WESTERN HOUSE OF ASSEMBLY. Established under the Richards Constitution in 1947, the Western House of Assembly consisted of the Chief Commissioner as President, 13 other official members and 15-19 unofficial provincial members, 7-11 of whom were to be selected by the native authorities while five were nominated by the Governor to represent interests and communities inadequately represented. In addition, three Head Chiefs were nominated by the Governor after consultation with the Head Chiefs in the region. In 1951, there was added a House of Chiefs with the Lieutenant Governor as President, three official members and not more than 50 Chiefs. The House of Assembly consisted of a President, four official members, 80 elected members and not more than three special members. Under the federal constitution of 1954, the bicameral legislative system was retained but the House of Assembly was presided over by a Speaker. The House was dissolved in 1966 when the military seized power.

WESTERN HOUSE OF CHIEFS. The Western House of Chiefs was established following the adoption of the Macpherson Constitution of 1951. According to the Constitution, the membership of the House of Chiefs comprised the Lieutenant Governor as President, three official members appointed by him and not more than 50 Chiefs and Head Chiefs. The House exercised legislative power similar to the House of Assembly and apart from the Finance Bill, the House could initiate any bill. The 1954 constitution removed the Lt. Governor from the presidency of the House of Chiefs. The Chiefs were then empowered to appoint a President from among themselves. The first President of the Western House of Chiefs was Oba Adesoji Aderemi, the Ooni of Ife. Ministers were also appointed from the members of the House of Chiefs. The House of Chiefs was dissolved following the military takeover in 1966. The 1979 constitution did not make any provision for the House of Chiefs.

WESTERN NIGERIA AGRICULTURAL CREDIT CORPORATION. Established in 1964, the Corporation was responsible for the provision of supervised credit to farmers in Western Nigeria in order to improve and develop Western Nigeria farms by making it possible for the farmers to purchase new tools, seeds, fertilizer, better livestock and to adopt improved farming methods. The Corporation provided credit to farmers with guidance in farm, home and financial management and on sound economic basis at reasonable rates and terms.

    With the creation of Oyo, Ogun and Ondo states out of the former Western State in 1976, the Corporation has since then ceased to function.

WESTERN NIGERIA DEVELOPMENT CORPORATION (WNDC). Western Nigeria Development Corporation was established under the Western Nigeria Law No. 5 of 1959. The objective of the Corporation was to foster the economic development of the region by promoting, establishing, operating or giving assistance to approved agricultural, industrial and commercial projects. However the Corporation ceased to exist in 1973 by the promulgation of the Western State Law No. 11 of 1973, which replaced it with the Western State Industrial, Investment and Credit Corporation (IICC).

WESTERN NIGERIA FINANCE CORPORATION. Known as the Western Region Finance Corporation, 1954-1964, the Corporation was established to give economic aid in the form of loans to government-owned companies, private firms and individuals pursuing small-scale industrial projects. The Corporation also bought shares in companies like the Epe Boatyard Company. But it ceased to function since 1976, when the old state was split up into three new states.

WESTERN NIGERIA GOVERNMENT BROADCASTING CORPORATION. The Corporation was established in 1959. In partnership with the Overseas Rediffusion (Service), it formed the Western Nigeria Radiovision Service Limited. However the company later became fully owned by the Western Regional government. The Corporation had two broadcasting services: the Western Nigeria Broadcasting Service (WNBS) and the Western Nigeria Television Service (WNTV), which was the first television service in black Africa and is popularly called "First in Africa." The WNTV made its first broadcast on October 31, 1959 while the WNBS commenced its commercial broadcasting in May 1960.

The Corporation has ceased to function since 1976, when the former Western State was divided into three states, with each state having its own radio station and the federal government taking over the WNTV.

THE WESTERN NIGERIA HOUSING CORPORATION. The Western Nigeria Housing Corporation, formerly known as the Western Region Housing Corporation, was established by law in 1958. The main function of the Corporation is to develop housing estates in the region for acquisition by members of the public. It also grants loans to enable individuals to build houses to their own taste and specification in any part of the region. In 1960 the Corporation was further empowered to undertake industrial development and management of industrial estates. As a result its largest estates are in Bodija, Ibadan, capital of the region, and Ikeja, now capital of Lagos State. The Corporation later spread its activities to Abeokuta, Akure and Ijebu Ode. With the creation of states in 1967 and 1976, the Corporation had to be dissolved and its properties were divided between the new states which had established their own housing corporations. In Oyo State the Corporation is now known as Property Development Corporation of Oyo State and its headquarters is in Bodija, the headquarters of the former Housing Corporation.

WESTERN NIGERIA MARKETING BOARD. The Western Nigeria Marketing Board was established in 1954 to secure the most favorable arrangements for the purchases and exports of Western Nigerian agricultural products. It bought and exported major cash crops like cocoa, found in the region. It also invested in cocoa industries and in office complexes like the Cocoa House in Ibadan. The Board ceased to function with the promulgation of Decree Number 29 of 1977, which established the Commodity Board. The Decree vested the functions of the Marketing Board on the Commodity Board.

WESTERN NIGERIA WATER CORPORATION. The Western Nigeria Water Corporation, a public corporation, was established by law in 1964 with the duty to control and manage all waterworks in the region and to extend these waterworks where necessary. It was also to develop new waterworks, see that potable water is supplied to the consumers at reasonable charges and conduct necessary research. The Corporation had area offices in Abeokuta, Ibadan, Osogbo and Akure. When, in early 1976, the Western State was divided into three states, Abeokuta, Ibadan and Akure became the headquarters of the new state water corporations.

WESTERN REGION. The Western Region came into being with the adoption of the Richards Constitution of 1946, which provided for regional councils. The region was comprised of the former

Ondo, Oyo, Ibadan, Abeokuta, Ijebu colony, Benin and Delta provinces. The region was estimated at 6,085,065 in population in the 1952-53 census but during the 1963-64 census, the region was estimated to be 12,811,837 in population. The people of the region were predominantly Yoruba. Other ethnic groups in the region were the Edos, the Ijaws, the Urhobo, and the Itsekiris. Because the Yorubas, the predominant ethnic group, were noted for their high degree of urbanization, the region contained some of the largest towns in the country like Ibadan, Ogbomoso, Osogbo, Ife, Iwo, Abeokuta, Ilesha, Benin city, Oyo and Iseyin.

The religion of the people varied from people to people. But Christianity and Islam had strong adherents while adherents of traditional religions still abound. In fact, the region was singular in that adherents of Christian, Islamic and traditional religions might live in the same household without any religious friction.

The region was an agricultural region and proceeds from the export crops in the region used to form a great share of the the government external earnings. These crops included cocoa, rubber, palm produce, yams and many others. The region was also blessed with thick forests providing timber for use in both furniture and house building and also for export.

The seat of the regional government was Ibadan. The first regional government was formed in 1951 by the Action Group Party, led by Chief Obafemi Awolowo, under whom the region became noted as the initiator of many development programs in the country. For instance, the free primary education started successfully in the region in 1955--other regions were not able to execute theirs until 1976 when the federal military government stepped in. Furthermore, the first television station in the whole of black Africa was established in the region in 1959 and the premier stadium in Nigeria, the Liberty Stadium in Ibadan was opened in 1960. Even before the Action Group Party came into power, the colonial government in 1948 had made Ibadan the seat of the first university in Nigeria, the University of Ibadan. Also in 1961 the Action Group government in the region established a regional university in Ile-Ife, the University of Ife.

However in 1962, things began to fall apart when an intraparty crisis erupted in the Action Group Party. The resultant effect of the crisis was the state of emergency declared upon the region in May 1962. The crisis led to the split in the Action Group--one faction led by Chief Awolowo and another faction led by the premier, Chief S. L. Akintola. Chief Akintola was removed from office as Premier but at long last he was declared victorious and he continued his premiership until the military took over power in January 1966. During the period of emergency, Dr. Majekodunmi was the Administrator of the region.

In 1963, a region was carved out of the Western Region, that is, the Mid-Western Region, made up of the former Benin and the Delta provinces. In 1965, trouble started again in the region after the Western Regional election. There were allegations of gross election malpractices. The people swiftly reacted to the election result, which gave victory to the Nigerian National Democratic Party (NNDP) instead of giving it to the Action Group. The people took the law into their hands and began to commit arson, looting and rioting that led to many deaths. The crisis continued until January 1966, when it became obvious that the Government had lost control of the region. This and many other factors led to the army takeover of 1966. The region was changed to the Western State with some minor boundary adjustments (e. g. , the colony became Lagos State) in May 1967 and the state was in turn divided into Oyo, Ogun and Ondo states in 1976.

WESTERN REGION FINANCE CORPORATION. Established in 1955, it took over the functions of the former Western Nigeria Development (Loan) Board. The Corporation granted loans for industrial, agricultural and commercial projects.

WESTERN STATE. Created in May 1967, the Western State was bounded on the north by the Kwara State, on the east by Bendel State, in the south by Lagos State and the Atlantic Ocean and in the west by the Republic of Benin (previously known as Dahomey). It was about 29,100 square miles in area and had a population of about 9. 5 million people. In May 1967, the Western State was one of the three states created out of the old Western Region--the other two were the Mid-Western State, which was originally created in 1963, during the Action Group crisis, and the Lagos State.
The state abounded in a wide variety of natural resources: fertile agricultural land, mineral deposits and ocean fishing. The state was a large producer of cocoa and timber, and it exported also rubber, palm oil, coffee and large quantities of citrus.
The state was blessed with two good universities, the University of Ibadan and the University of Ife. The capital of the state was Ibadan, the largest town in West Africa.
The people of the state are predominantly Yorubas, the most urbanized people in all of Nigeria. As such there are, in addition to Ibadan--the largest city in West Africa--many large cities like Ogbomoso, Abeokuta, Oshogbo, Iwo, Ile-Ife, Ilesa, Oyo and Iseyin.

WEY, JOSEPH EDET AKINWALE (VICE-ADMIRAL). A naval officer and marine engineer, born on March 7, 1918 in Calabar, Cross River State, he went to the Holy Cross School, Lagos, Methodist School, Ikot Ekpene and St. Patrick's College, Calabar. In 1939 he joined the Marine Department as a Trainee Technical Apprentice, becoming a Junior Engineer at the end of his training and in 1949 he attended the London County School of Technology for Marine Engineers. In 1950 he became a Marine Engineer Second Class and in 1956 he became a Sublieutenant and Engineer for the navy. In 1960 he was made Lieutenant

Commander and Fleet Engineer Officer and Commander in
Charge of the Apapa Naval Base in Lagos. In 1963 he served
in India as Captain on Commonwealth exercises. He returned
in March 1964 to become Commodore and head of the Nigerian
Navy. In 1966 he was appointed to the Supreme Military Council. He attended the Aburi Conference in January 1977 between
Gowon and Ojukwu in an attempt to ward off any future hostilities. When the civil war started, the Nigerian Navy under
him effectively blockaded the Biafran ports throughout the war.
On July 27, 1967, the navy captured Bonny and blocked Biafra's
route to the sea.

He was promoted to Rear Admiral on January 2, 1967
and in 1971 he became Commissioner for Establishments. He
also acted as Commissioner for Labour in 1971 and was appointed Vice-Admiral in the same year. In 1973 he was appointed Chief of Staff, Supreme Headquarters and was also the
Chairman of the Administrative Committee of the Nigerian Defence Academy and responsible to the Commander-in-Chief of
the Armed Forces. He retired in 1975.

WHITLEY COUNCIL. Following the Cowan Report of 1948, asking
the government to provide facilities for consultation and negotiation between the government, its departments and trade unions, government set up Whitley Councils with the function of
determining the general principles governing conditions of service such as recruitment, remunerations, hours of work, promotion, discipline and tenure. Decisions were to be taken by
agreement and not by voting, but such decisions required the
approval of the Governor.

WILLIAM, CHIEF FREDERICK ROTIMI ALADE. A constitutional
lawyer who has had great influence on the constitutional development of the country since the 1950's. Born on December 16, 1920 in Lagos, he was educated at the CMS Grammar
School in Lagos and at the University of Cambridge in England
and was later called to the bar. Returning to Nigeria, he
served in many important positions in the former Western Regional government including those of the Attorney General and
Minister of Justice. In 1975 he was appointed Chairman of
the Constitution Drafting Committee, which drafted the Second
Republican Constitution of 1979. He is in private legal practice and a member of the Senior Advocate of Nigeria (SAN).

WILLINK COMMISSION. As a result of the ethnic minorities' demands for separate regional identity to remove the fear of
domination by the ethnic majorities in each of the three regions that made up the federation, the British government
agreed to set up in 1957 a Minorities Commission to look into
the fears of ethnic minorities in all parts of the country and
to propose means of allaying the fears whether or not they
were well founded. The Commission was chaired by Sir Henry
Willink, a lawyer and former member of Parliament in London,
and it is sometimes called the Willink Commission. The

Commission reported in July 1958, but did not recommend the
creation of new regions as a means to allay those fears.
Rather it, among other things, recommended the inclusion of
the fundamental human rights in the federal constitution. See
also MINORITIES PROBLEM.

-Y-

YABA COLLEGE OF TECHNOLOGY. Established in 1969 to succeed Yaba Technical Institute with the function of providing
courses of instruction, training and research in applied science, technology, commerce, management and such other fields
as the governing council might determine. The college is governed by a council consisting of 13 members selected from
various institutions, government and business.

YABA HIGHER COLLEGE. The Yaba Higher College was opened in
Lagos in 1934 with only 18 students. The college was to provide the manpower needed to fill the government technical departments. Unlike the Fourah Bay College in Sierra Leone,
the Yaba College was not affiliated with any English University;
hence the college awarded its own diplomas and certificates.
Thus examination standards were Nigerian and educated Nigerians resented that it was only a Nigerian diploma recognized
in Nigeria that would be obtained from the college. This and
other deficiencies in the institution led to the formation of the
Nigerian Youth Movement in 1934.
Besides the medical school, opened in 1930, Yaba Higher
College was the first post-secondary institution in Nigeria.
The products of the college were among the early nationalists
in Nigeria. The name of the college was changed in 1969 to
Yaba College of Technology. The College offers courses lead-
ing to the award of both Ordinary National Diploma (OND) and
Higher National Diploma (HND).

YAR'ADUA, MAJOR GENERAL SHEHU MUSA. Born in 1943 in Katsina, Kaduna State, Major General Shehu Musa Yar'Adua attended the Government Secondary School in Katsina, then the
Nigerian Military Training College in Zaria, the Royal Military
College, Sandhurst and the Command and Staff College in England. He was a Platoon Commander between 1964 and 1965,
a Battalion Adjutant 1965-1967, Assistant Adjutant General,
Second Division in 1967 and Commander, Sixth Infantry Brigade
in the Second Infantry Division in 1968 and became Commander,
Ninth Infantry Brigade in 1969. After the 1976 abortive coup,
during which the Head of State, General Murtala was killed, he
became the Chief of Staff Supreme Headquarters and also the
Vice-Chairman of the Supreme Military Council, posts which
he occupied until his retirement when the army, in October
1979, handed over power to the civilians.

YERO, BUBA. Buba Yero was born in about 1762 near Mada in

what is now known as Numan District. He was of Fulani descent and during his youth, he was a student under Shehu Usman Dan Fodio at Gobir. He later became a mallam and a preacher. On hearing about Shehu's Jihad in 1804, he came to Gobir, where Usman was staying. It was there he received a flag from Shehu Usman Dan Fodio as one of the 14 flag bearers he sent to conquer the Hausa states. He was asked to go to Gombe and became the first Emir of Gombe in 1804. During the Jihad, he conquered the Muri people and the areas in the valleys of the Gongola and Kilengi rivers. He died in 1841 and was succeeded by his son, Sule, who died just three years later.

YOLA. Yola is the capital of Gongola State in the northeastern part of the country. It is not only an administrative center but also a commercial center.

One of the important festivals in Yola is the fishing festival called "Njuwa," which is celebrated annually and which attracts a lot of tourists. The town has a number of higher educational institutions like the Federal Advanced Teachers College and the College of Preliminary Studies.

YORUBA. One of the three largest ethnic groups in the country, they live mainly in Lagos, Oyo, Ogun, Ondo and Kwara states, and some of them live in the Republic of Benin. There are many subgroups of Yoruba, like the Oyo, Ekiti, Ife, Egba, Ijesha, Ijebu and so on, all speaking dialects of the same language.

The origin of the Yorubas is not clearly known, but tradition has it that they are descendants of Oduduwa who migrated from the East, probably from Upper Egypt or Nubia, and settled in Ile-Ife. This appears to be confirmed by the similarities observed between the Egyptian sculptures and the Ife marbles seen in Ile-Ife. According to tradition, Oduduwa, the mythical founder of Ile-Ife, had seven children from whom grew the various "tribes" that made up the Yoruba nation. These were Owu, Ketu, Benin, Ila, Sabe, Olupopo of Popo and Oranmiyan who settled in Oyo (later becoming the center of the powerful Oyo empire). The Fulani Jihad destroyed much of the empire, causing the Yorubas to move southward into the forest areas.

In the nineteenth century, competition among Yoruba states for trade with the Europeans was the cause of wars all over the Yoruba states, leading to the establishment of towns like Ibadan and Abeokuta. As a result of these wars, trade and normal life were interrupted for decades, until peace was restored as the British government established their authority over the fragmented Yoruba states and towns and by 1896, most Yoruba areas of the country were under British control.

Thus, before the arrival of the British the Yorubas had developed fairly large political organizations and traditional and constitutional monarchy. Of all the peoples of Nigeria the Yorubas were the most urbanized. They have been exposed to more intensive westernization than the rest of the country.

YORUBA TOWNS. Most Yoruba towns, according to Samuel Johnson, have certain identifiable features. They each have a founder who first settled there and attracted others to settle with him. The towns were either farmsteads or rest places where people could have some refreshments and if it was a popular place or a crossroad, a market could spring up. When houses were built and what might be called a village or small town was formed, the original founder was made the Baale (father of the land). The Baale then appointed his chiefs like Otun, right-hand man, Osi, left-hand man and Balogun, the War Chief. In most Yoruba towns, the principal marketplace is in the center of the town and in front of the Oba's or King's palace. For defensive purposes, many Yoruba towns had walls around them--this was a ditch or moat dug around the towns.

YUSUF, BELLO MAITAM. Minister for Commerce in the Shagari administration during the Second Republic. Born on April 22, 1945 in Gwaram, Kano State, he received an LL.B. degree from Ahmadu Bello University in Zaria in 1973 and was called to the bar in 1974. In 1979 he was appointed Minister for Internal Affairs, and while in that office, he ordered the deportation of Alhaji Abdurahman Shugaba, the Great Nigeria People's Party (GNPP) Majority Leader in the Borno State House of Assembly because he was said not to be a Nigerian, and was therefore a security risk.

-Z-

ZARIA. An ancient town, it is situated at a railway junction in Kaduna State where the two railway lines from the south meet and pass on to Nguru and Kaura Namoda. It is a university city, being the home of Ahmadu Bello University.

ZIKIST MOVEMENT. In 1945, Dr. Nnamdi Azikiwe announced that there was a plot to assassinate him. Many people were critical of this so-called plot and in February 1946 three young admirers of his (Mr. Kolawole Balogun, Mr. M.C.K. Ajuluchuku and Abiodun Aloba) began to form the Zikist Movement to defend their hero. The Movement had a philosophy which they called Zikism, which aimed at redeeming Africa from political servitude and economic weakness. Because of its militancy against and uncompromising attitude toward colonial rule, the government saw it as an organization whose purposes and methods were dangerous to the good of the colonial government and it was thus banned in 1950 after a Zikist member had made an unsuccessful attempt on the life of the government's Chief Secretary, Mr. Foot. But soon after, its members regrouped to form themselves into another organization, the Freedom Movement.

"ZIK MUST GO." A call by 31 members of the National Council of Nigerian Citizens (NCNC) on Dr. Nnamdi Azikiwe (Zik) to resign as the Eastern Regional Premier and party President. The leaders of this call were Dr. K. O. Mbadiwe, who was then Federal Minister of Commerce and Chief Kolawole Balogun, Federal Minister of Information. They accused Zik of splitting the party asunder and of losing interest in the party. Rather than Zik going, it was these leaders and some others who were expelled by the National Executive Committee of the NCNC Party.

ZONING. According to the constitution of the National Party of Nigeria (NPN), zoning refers to the convention in recognition of the need for adequate geographical spread in the allocation of offices within the party. The country was divided into four zones, Northern, Western, Eastern and Minority. In 1978, the presidency went to the Northern Zone, the vice-presidency to the Eastern Zone, the chairmanship of the party to the Western Zone and the presidency of the Senate to the Minority Zone. By this means, all the major ethnic groups were brought together at the top-most level of decision making in a kind of consensus. In fact zoning is the NPN's practical interpretation of the constitutional requirement of the federal character in the governing body of political parties. The offices that are zoned at the national level are those of the national Chairman, the President, Vice President, President and Deputy President of the Senate, National Secretary, Speaker and Deputy Speaker of the House of Representatives, the Senate Leader and Majority Leader of the House of Representatives. The idea is that these offices will rotate periodically among the zones.

ZUNGERU. A town on the Kaduna River, chosen in 1902 as the headquarters of the Northern Provinces of Nigeria. In 1917, the colonial authorities moved the headquarters from there to Kaduna, leaving the town practically abandoned.

ZUNGUR, MALLAM SA'AD. The first northern student to attend the Yaba Higher College and to come in contact with nationalist activities in Southern Nigeria. With two other Northern Nigeria teachers in Bauchi, he formed in 1943 the Bauchi General Improvement Union (BGIU), the first of such pressure group organization in the north. He became an ardent supporter of Dr. Nnamdi Azikiwe, joined the National Council of Nigeria and the Cameroons (NCNC) and rose to become the party's General Secretary.

BIBLIOGRAPHY

General Works

Ananaba, Wogu. The Trade Union Movement in Africa: Promise and Performance. London: C. Hurst, 1979.

Arikpo, Okoi. The Development of Modern Nigeria. Harmondsworth: Penguin Books, 1967.

Austin, Dennis. West Africa and the Commonwealth. London, 1957.

Bown, Lalage and Crowder, Michael, eds. Proceedings of the First International Congress of Africanists. London, 1964.

Buchanan, K.M. and Pugh, J.C. Land and Peoples of Nigeria. London: University of London Press, 1955.

Cary, Joyce. Britain and West Africa. London, 1940.

_____. The Case for African Freedom. London: Secker and Warburg, 1941.

Cervanka, Zdenek. The Organization of African Unity and its Charter. London: Hurst & Co., 1969.

Cowan, L. Gray. West African Local Government. New York: Columbia University Press, 1958.

Du Bois, Woe, Burghardt. The World and Africa. New York: Viking, 1947.

Duignam, Peter and Gann, Lewis H. eds. Colonialism in Africa, 1870-1960 Vol. II. Cambridge: Cambridge University Press, 1970.

Fage, J.D. An Introduction to the History of West Africa. Cambridge: Cambridge University Press, 1955.

Garvey, Amy Jacques, ed. Philosophy and Opinions of Marcus Garvy. New York: Universal Publishing House, 1923.

Graf, W.D., ed. Towards a Political Economy of Nigeria: Critical Essays. Benin City: Koda Publishers, 1981.

Hailey, Lord. An African Survey Revised. London: Oxford University Press, 1938.

_____. Native Administration in British African Territories, 5 Vols. London, 1951.

Haives, C. Grove, ed. Africa Today. Baltimore: Johns Hopkins Press, 1955.

Hancock, W. K. Survey of British Commonwealth Affairs, 2 Vols. London: Oxford University Press, 1952.

Hargreaves, J. O. Prelude to the Partition of West Africa. London, 1963.

Hodgkin, Thomas. Nationalism in Colonial Africa. London, 1956.

Horton, James Africanus B. West African Countries and Peoples and a Vindication of the African Race. London: W. J. Johnson of 121 Fleet Street, 1868.

Hovet, Thomas Jr. Africa in the United Nations. Evanston, IL: Northwestern University Press, 1963.

Jennings, W. Ivor. The Approach of Self-government. Cambridge: Cambridge University Press, 1956.

Krik-Green, A. and Rimmer, D. Nigeria Since 1970: A Political and Economic Outline. London: Hodder and Stoughton, 1981.

McPhee, Allan. The Economic Revolution in West Africa. London, 1926.

Mair, L. P. Native Policies in Africa. London, 1935.

Melson, R. and Wolpe, H., eds. Nigeria Modernization and the Politics of Communalism. East Lansing: Michigan State University Press, 1971.

Morel, E. D. Nigeria, Its Peoples and Problems. London: Frank Cass and Company Ltd., 1968.

_____. Trading Monopolies In West Africa. Liverpool: Richardson and Sons, 1901.

Murdock, G. P. Africa--Its Peoples and Their Culture History. New York: Dakar, 1961 (1959).

Nuffield Foundation and Colonial Office. African Education: A Study of Educational Policy and Practice--British Tropical Africa. Oxford, 1953.

Odetola, T. O. Military Politics in Nigeria: Economic Development and Political Stability. New Brunswick, NJ: Transaction Books, 1978.

Oyediran, ed. Survey of Nigerian Affairs 1975. Lagos: OUP, 1978.

Padmore, George. Africa: Britain's Third Empire. London, 1949.

_____. How Britain Governs Africa. London, 1936.

_____. Pan Africanism or Communism? London, 1956.

Pedlay, F. J. West Africa. London: Methuen, 1951.

Perham, Margery. Africans and British Rule. Oxford: Oxford University Press, 1941.

Phelps-Stokes Fund. The Atlantic Charter and Africa from American Standpoint. New York, 1942.

Record, Wilson. The Negro and the Communist Party. Chapel Hill: University of North Carolina Press, 1949.

Robinson, K. and Madden, F. , eds. Essays in Imperial Government. Oxford: Oxford University Press, 1963.

Royal Institute of International Affairs. Nigeria: The Political and Economic Background. London, 1960.

Senghor, Leopold, Seder. On African Socialism. London and Durmow: Pall Mall Press, 1964.

Shagari, S. My Vision of Nigeria. London: Frank Cass, 1981.

William, G. , ed. "Nigerian Issue," Review of African Political Economy, Vol. 13 (1979).

_____. State and Society in Nigeria. Lagos: Afrographika, 1980.

_____ and Turner, T. "Nigeria," in West African States, edited by J. Dunn. Cambridge: Cambridge University Press, 1979.

Economics

Aboyade, O. Foundations of an African Economy. New York: Praeger, 1966.

Adedeji, Adebayo. Nigerian Federal Finance. New York, 1969.

Adegboye, R. O. et al. "Impact of Farm Settlement on Surrounding

Farmers" Nigerian Journal of Economic and Social Studies, Vol. 11, No. 2 (1969).

Adeoye, Tafa. Agbe-Ko-Ya: Farmers Against Oppression. Lagos: Lagos International Press, 1970.

Akeredolu-Ale, E. O. The Underdevelopment of Indigenous Entrepreneurship in Nigeria. Ibadan: Ibadan University Press, 1975.

Apeldoorn, G. J. Perspectives on Drought and Famine in Nigeria. London: Allen & Unwin, 1981.

Ayida, A. A. "Contractor Finance and Supplier Credit in Economic Growth" Nigerian Journal of Economic and Social Studies, Vol. 7 (1965).

Ayida, A. D. and Onitiri, H. M. A. , eds. Reconstruction and Development in Nigeria. Ibadan: Oxford University Press, 1971.

Baldwin, K. D. S. The Marketing of Cocoa in Western Nigeria. New York: Oxford University Press, 1954.

_____ et al. Nigerian Cocoa Farmers--An Economic Survey of Yoruba Cocoa Farming Families. Oxford: Oxford University Press, 1956.

Bauer, P. T. West African Trade--A Study of Competition, Oligopoly and Monopoly in a Changing Economy. Cambridge: Cambridge University Press, 1954.

Berry, S. S. Cocoa, Custom and Socioeconomic Change in Rural Western Nigeria. Oxford: Oxford University Press, 1975.

Bienen, H. and Diejomoah, V. P. eds. The Political Economy of Income Distribution in Nigeria. New York: Africana, 1981.

Biersteker, T. J. Distortion or Development: Contending Perspectives on the Multinational Corporation. Cambridge, Mass: MIT Press, 1978.

Bohannan, Laura and Paul. The Tin of Central Nigeria. London: International African Institute, 1953.

Brown, Charles V. Government and Banking in Western Nigeria. Ibadan: Oxford University Press, 1964.

Buxton, T. F. The African Slave Trade and its Remedy. London, 1839.

Callaway, Achibald. "From Traditional Crafts to Modern Industries, " Odu, Vol. 2, No. 1 (July 1965).

Callaway, B. "The Political Economy of Nigeria" in The Political

Economy of Africa, edited by R. Harris. New York: Schenkman, 1973.

Central Bank of Nigeria (Lagos). _Annual Report Economic and Financial Review_ (various issues).

_____. _Annual Report and Statement of Accounts._

Chubo, L. T. _Ibo Land Tenure_, 2nd ed. Ibadan: Ibadan University Press, 1961.

Clough, P. "Farmers and Traders in Hausaland," _Development and Change_, Vol. 12, No. 2 (1981).

Collins, Paul. "The Policy of Indigenization: An overall View," _Quarterly Journal of Administration_, Vol. IX, No. 2 (January 1975).

_____. "The Political Economy of Indigenization: The Case of the Nigerian Enterprises Promotion Decree," _The African Review_, No. 4 (1976).

_____. "Public Policy and the Development of Indigenous Capitalism: The Nigerian Experience," _Journal of Commonwealth and Comparative Politics_, Vol. XV, No. 2 (July 1977).

Cook, Arthur N. _British Enterprise In Nigeria._ Philadelphia: University of Pennsylvania Press,

Davies, F. _The Royal African Company._ London: Longman, 1957.

Dean, E. _Plan Implementation in Nigeria 1962-66._ Ibadan: Oxford University Press, 1972.

Diejomoah, V. P. "The Economics of the Nigerian Conflict" in J. Okpaku, ed. _Nigeria: Dilemma of Nationhood._ New York: Third Press, 1972.

_____. "Industrial Relations in Nigeria" in _Industrial Relations in Africa_, edited by U. K. Damachi _et al._ London: Macmillan, 1979.

Economic Commission for Africa. _Multinational Corporations in Africa._ Addis Ababa: ECA, 1979.

Eicher, C. K. and Leidholm, C., eds. _Growth and Development of the Nigerian Economy._ East Lansing: Michigan State University Press, 1970.

Ekundare, R. O. _The Economic History of Nigeria, 1860-1960._ London: Methuen, 1973.

Famoriyo, Segun. _Land Tenure and Agricultural Development in Nigeria._ Ibadan: NISER, Ibadan University Press, 1979.

F. A. O. Agricultural Development in Nigeria, 1965-1980. Rome, 1966.

Fashoyin, T. Industrial Relations in Nigeria. London: Longman, 1981.

Forde, Daryl, ed. Efik Traders of Old Calabar. London, 1956.

Forrest, T. "Recent Developments in Nigerian Industrialization" in Industry and Accumulation in Africa, edited by M. Fransman. London: Heinemann, 1982.

Frennd, W. Capital and Labour in the Nigerian Tin Mines. London: Longman, 1981.

Galletti, R., Baldwin, K. O. S. and Oina, I. O. Nigerian Cocoa Farmers. London: Oxford University Press, 1956.

Goddard, A. D. "Land Tenure and Agricultural Development in Hausaland," Samaru Agricultural Newsletter, Vol. 12, No. 2 (1971).

Graf, W. D., ed. Towards a Political Economy of Nigeria: Critical Essays. Benin City: Koda Publishers, 1981.

Hakam, A. N. "The Motivation to Invest and the Locational Pattern of Foreign Private Investment in Nigeria," Nigerian Journal of Economic and Social Studies, Vol. 8, No. 1 (1976).

Hawkins, E. K. "Marketing Boards and Economic Development in Nigeria and Ghana," Review of Economic Studies, Vol. 26 (1) No. 69 (October 1958).

Hazlewood, Arthur. The Finances of Nigerian Federation. London: Oxford University Press, 1956.

Helleiner, G. K. "The Eastern Nigeria Development Corporation: A Study in Sources and Uses of Public Development Funds, 1949-1962," Nigerian Journal of Economic and Social Studies, Vol. 6, No. 1 (March 1964).

_____. "The Fiscal Role of the Marketing Boards in Nigerian Economic Development 1947-61," Economic Journal, Vol. 74, No. 295 (September 1964).

_____. "Marketing Boards and Domestic Stabilization In Nigeria," Review of Economic and Statistics, Vol. 48, No. 1 (February 1961).

_____. "The Northern Region Development Corporation: Wide-ranging Development Institution, 1949-52," Nigerian Journal of Economic and Social Studies, Vol. 6, No. 2 (July 1964).

_____. Peasant Agriculture, Government and Economic Growth in Nigeria. Homewood: R. D. Irwin, 1966.

Hill, P. Population, Prosperity and Poverty: Rural Kano 1900 and 1970. Cambridge: Cambridge University Press, 1977.

_____. Rural Hausa. Cambridge: Cambridge University Press, 1972.

Hodder, B. W. "Rural Periodic Day Markets in Parts of Yorubaland, Western Nigeria," Transactions and Papers of the British Institute of Geographers, No. 29 (1961).

Hopkins, A. G. An Economic History of West Africa. London: Longman, 1972

Imade, U. O. et al. Directory of Management Development Programmes in Nigeria 1982. Lagos: Center for Management Development.

International Bank for Reconstruction and Development. The Economic Development of Nigeria. Baltimore: Johns Hopkins Press, 1955.

International Bank for Reconstruction and Development. Options for Long Term Development of Nigeria. Washington, D. C., 1976.

International Monetary Fund. Surveys of African Economics, Vol. 6 (Washington: IMF, 1975).

Jemibewon, D. M. The Land Use Decree and You. Ibadan: Ministry of Local Government and Information.

Jones, G. I. "Native and Trade Currencies in Southern Nigeria During the 18th and 19th Centuries." Africa, xxviii, 1 (1958).

_____. The Trading States of the Oil Rivers. London, 1963.

Kayode, M. O. and Teriba, O., eds. Industrialization in Nigeria. Ibadan: Ibadan University Press, 1977.

Kilby, P. Industrialization in an Open Economy: Nigeria 1945-66. Cambridge: Cambridge University Press, 1969.

Kirk-Green, A. and Rimmer, D. Nigeria Since 1970: A Political and Economic Outline. London: Hodder and Stoughton, 1981.

Koll, M. Crafts and Cooperation in Western Nigeria. Freiburg, Germany: Arnold-Bergstraesser-Institute, 1969.

Le Vine, R. A. Dreams and Deeds: Achievement Motivation in Nigeria. Chicago: University of Chicago Press, 1966.

Lewis, W. Arthur. Reflections on Nigeria's Economic Growth. Paris: O. E. C. D., 1967.

Mannix, Daniel P. and Cowley, Malcolm. Black Cargoes. London, 1963.

Martin, Ann. The Oil Palm Economy of the Ibibio Farmer. Ibadan: Ibadan University Press, 1956.

Meek, C. K. Land Tenure and Administration in Nigeria and the Cameroons. London: HMSO, 1957.

Morel, E. O. Trading Monopolies in West Africa. Liverpool: Richardson and Sons, 1901.

Nafzinger, E. W. African Capitalism: A Case Study in Nigerian Entrepreneurship. Stanford: Hoover, 1977.

Newlyn W. T. and Rowan, D. C. Money and Banking In British Colonial Africa. Oxford: Clarendon Press, 1954.

Nigerian Economic Society. Poverty in Nigeria. Ibadan, 1976.

Nigerian Ports Authority. Lagos: Management Service Division, 1981.

Norman, D. W. et al. Technical Change and the Small Farmer in Hausaland. East Lansing: Michigan State University, 1979.

Oculi, O. "Dependent Food Policy in Nigeria 1975-79," Review of African Political Economy, 15/16 (1979).

Ogunpola, G. A. "The Pattern of Organization in the Building Industry--A Western Nigeria Case Study," Nigerian Journal of Economic and Social Studies, Vol. 10, No. 3 (1968).

Okediji, F. Olu. "Indigenization Decree and Income Distribution: The Social Implications," Quarterly Journal of Administration, Vol. IX, No. 2 (January 1975).

Okigbo, Pius N. African Common Market. London: Longman, Green and Co. Ltd., 1967.

_____. Nigerian National Accounts, 1950-57. Enugu: Government Printer, 1962.

Olatunbosun, Dupe. Nigeria's Neglected Rural Majority. Ibadan: Oxford University Press, 1975.

Olayide, S. O., ed. Economic Survey of Nigeria, 1960-75. Ibadan: Aromolaran Publishing Co., 1976.

Oluwasanmi, H. A. Agriculture and Nigerian Economic Development. Ibadan: Oxford University Press, 1966.

_____ and Alao, J. A. "The Role of Credit in the Transformation of Traditional Agriculture," Nigerian Journal of Economic and Social Studies, Vol. 7, No. 1 (March 1965).

Omotola, J.A., ed. The Land Use Decree: Report of a National Workshop. Lagos: Lagos University Press, 1982.

Oni, Ola and Onimode, B. Economic Development of Nigeria--The Socialist Alternative. Ibadan: The Nigerian Academy of Arts, Sciences and Technology, 1975.

Onimode, B. "Imperialism and Multinational Corporations--A Case Study of Nigeria" in Y. Yansane, ed. Decolonization and Dependency--Problems of Development of African Society. Westport, CT: Greenwood Press, 1980.

_____. Imperialism and Underdevelopment in Nigeria. London: Macmillan, 1983.

Onitiri, H.M.A. and Olatubosun, D., eds. The Marketing Board System. Ibadan: NISER, 1974.

Onoh, J.K., ed. The Foundation of Nigeria's Financial Infrastructure. London: Croom Helm, 1980.

Onyemelukwe, C.C. Problems of Industrial Planning and Management in Nigeria. London: Longman, 1966.

Oyejide, T.A. Tariff Policy and Industrialization in Nigeria. Ibadan: Ibadan University Press, 1975.

Pearson, S.R. Petroleum and Nigerian Economy. Stanford: Stanford University Press, 1970.

Perham, M., ed. Economics of a Tropical Dependency, 2 vols. London: Faber, 1946.

Perham, Margery, ed. Mining Commerce and Finance in Nigeria. London: Faber, 1948.

_____. The Native Economies of Nigeria. London: Faber, 1946.

Phillips, A.O. "Revenue Allocation in Nigeria 1970-1980," Nigerian Journal of Economic and Social Studies (1976).

Phillips, Adedotun. "Nigeria's Federal Financial Experience," Journal of Modern African Studies, 9 (1971).

Prest, A.R. and Stewart, I.A. The National Income of Nigeria. London, 1953.

Schatz, Sayre P. Development Bank Lending in Nigeria--The Federal Loans Board. Ibadan: Oxford University Press, 1964.

_____. Nigerian Capitalism. Berkeley: University of California Press, 1977.

_____. "Under-Utilized Resources, Directed to Demand and Deficit Financing, Illustrated by Reference to Nigeria," Quarterly Journal of Economics, Vol. 73, No. 4 (November 1959).

Schatzl, L. H. Industrialization in Nigeria--A Spatial Analysis, Munchen: Weltforum Verlag, 1973.

_____. The Nigerian Tin Industry. Ibadan: Oxford University Press, 1971.

_____. Petroleum in Nigeria. Ibadan: Oxford University Press, 1969.

Smith, M. G. The Economy of Hausa Communities of Zaria. Colonial Research Studies No. 16. London: HMSO, 1955.

Smock, A. C. "Ethnicity and Attitudes toward Development in Eastern Nigeria," Journal of Developing Areas, 1969.

Stolper, W. Planning Without Facts. Cambridge, MA: Harvard University Press, 1966.

Teriba O. "Nigerian Revenue Allocation Experience 1952-65: A Study in Inter-governmental Fiscal and Financial Relationships," Nigerian Journal of Economic and Social Studies, Vol. 8 (1966).

_____ and Kayode, M. O. , eds. Industrial Development in Nigeria. Ibadan: Ibadan University Press, 1977.

Tiffen, M. The Enterprising Peasant: Economic Development in Gombe Emirate. London: HMSO, 1976.

Uvieghara, E. E. Trade Union Law in Nigeria. Ethiopia, 1976.

Wallace, T. Rural Development through Irrigation: Studies in a Town on the Kano River Project. Zaria: ABU Center for Social and Economic Research, 1979.

Wells, J. C. Agricultural Policy and Economic Growth in Nigeria 1962-68. Ibadan: Ibadan University Press, 1972.

Williams, G. , ed. Nigeria: Economy and Society. London: Collins, 1976.

World Bank Report. Nigeria: Options for Long-Term Development. Baltimore: Johns Hopkins University Press, 1974.

Yesufu, T. M. Industrial Relations in Nigeria. Ibadan: Oxford University Press, 1962.

Education

Alauja J. Bala. "Koranic and Master Law Teaching in Hausa Land," Nigeria, 37 (1951).

Ashby, Eric. Universities: British, Indian, African. Cambridge, MA: Harvard University Press, 1966.

Asiwaju, A.I. "Ashby Revisited, A Review of Nigeria's Educational Growth, 1961-1971," African Studies Review, Vol. MV, No. 1 (April 1974).

Awokoya, S.O. "Curriculum Development in Nigeria," West African Journal of Education, Vol. VIII, No. 3 (October 1954).

Burns, D.G. African Education. London: Oxford University Press, 1956.

Beckett, P. and O'Connell, J. Education and Power in Nigeria: A Study of University Students. London: Holder & Stoughton, 1977.

Callaway, A. and Musone, A. Financing of Education in Nigeria. Unesco, 1968.

Fafunwa, A.B. The Growth and Development of Nigerian Universities. Washington: Overseas Liaison Committee, American Council on Education, 1974.

_____. History of Education in Nigeria. London: Allen & Unwin, 1974.

_____. A History of Nigerian High Education. Lagos: Macmillan, 1971.

_____. An Historical Analysis of the Development of Higher Education in Nigeria. New York: New York University, 1955.

Gbadamosi, G.O. "The Establishment of Western Education among Muslims in Nigeria, 1896-1926," Journal of the Historical Society of Nigeria, Vol. IV, No. 1 (February 1967).

Graham, Sonia F. Government and Mission Education in Nigeria, 1900-1919. Ibadan: Ibadan University Press, 1966.

Groves, C.P. The Planting of Christianity in Africa, Vols. I-IV. London: Lutterworth Press, 1954.

Hilliard, F.H. A Short History of Education in British West Africa. Edinburgh: Nelson, 1957.

Ikejiani, O., ed. Nigerian Education. Ikeja: Longmans of Nigeria, 1964.

ILO. Report to the Government of the Federation of Nigeria on Co-operative Education. Geneva, 1963.

Kilby, P. "Technical Education in Nigeria," Bulletin of the Oxford University Institute of Economics and Statistics. Vol. 26, No. 2 (1964).

Lewis, L. J. and Loveridge, A. J. The Management of Education. London: Pall Mall Press, 1951.

Mellanby, Kenneth. The Birth of Nigeria's University. London: Methuen, 1958.

Murray, A. Victor. The School In the Bush. London: Longmans, 1929.

Nduka, O. Western Education and the Nigerian Cultural Background. Ibadan: Oxford University Press, 1964.

Nuffield Foundation and the Colonial Office. African Education: A Study of Education Policy and Practice in British Tropical Africa. London: Oxford University Press, 1953.

Ogunsola, A. F. Legislation and Education in Northern Nigeria, Ibadan: Oxford University Press, 1975.

Okafor, I. Ndukar. The Development of Universities in Nigeria. London: Longman, 1971.

Okeke, P. U. Educational Reconstruction in an Independent Nigeria. New York: New York University Press, 1956.

Okongwu, J. N. History of Education in Nigeria 1842-1942. New York: New York University Press, 1946.

Phelps-Stokes Fund. Education in Africa. New York, 1932.

_____. A Survey of African Students Studying in the United States. New York, 1949.

Phillipson, Sydney. Grants in Aid of Education in Nigeria. Lagos: Government Printer, 1948.

Read, Margaret. Education and Social Change in Tropical Areas, 2nd ed. Edinburgh: Nelson, 1956.

Smyke, Raymond J. and Stover, Denis C. Nigeria Union of Teachers, an Official History. Ibadan: Oxford University Press, 1974.

Solaru, T. T. Teacher Training in Nigeria. Ibadan: Ibadan University Press, 1964.

Stock, Eugene. The History of the Church Missionary Society. London: C. M. S., 1899.

Taiwo, C. O. "The Administration and Control of Education in Nigeria," West African Journal of Education, Vol. XIX, No. 1 (June 1972).

_____ and Carr, Henry. An African Contribution to Education. Ibadan: Oxford University Press, 1969.

_____ and _____. The Nigerian Education System, Past, Present & Future. Nigeria: Thomas Nelson Ltd., 1980.

Taylor, O. W. "Reflections of an American Teacher after Seven Years in Nigeria," West African Journal of Education, Vol. VI, No. 2 (June 1962).

Ukeje, B. O. Education for Social Reconstruction. London and Lagos: Macmillan, 1966.

Van Den Berghe, P. L. Power and Privilege at an African University. London: Routledge, 1973.

Wheeler, A. C. R. The Organization of Educational Planning in Nigeria. 1968 (African Research Monographs).

Williams, D. H. A Short Survey of Education in Northern Nigeria. Kaduna: Ministry of Education, Northern Region of Nigeria, 1960.

Wise, Colins. A History of Education in British West Africa. London: Longman, 1956.

History

Abdulkadir, D. The Poetry, Life and Opinions of Sa'adu Zungur. Zaria: Northern Nigeria Publishing Corp., 1974.

Adeleye, R. A. The Sokoto Caliphate. Ibadan: Ibadan University Press, 1975.

African Journal Ltd. Africa Who's Who. African Books Ltd., 1981.

_____. Makers of Modern Africa: Profiles in History. African Books Ltd., 1981.

Ajayi, J. F. Ade. "The British Occupation of Lagos 1851-1861," Nigerian Magazine, No. 69 (August 1961).

_____. Christian Missions in Nigeria, 1841-1891. London: Longman, 1965.

_____. Milestones in Nigerian History. Ibadan, 1962.

_____. "Nineteenth Century Origins of Nigerian Nationalism,"
Journal of Historical Society of Nigeria, Vol. II, No. 2 (1961).

_____ and Epie, Ian, eds. A Thousand Years of West African
History. London: Nelson for Ibadan University Press, 1958.

_____ and Smith, Robert. Yoruba Warfare in the Nineteenth Century. London and Ibadan, 1964.

Akinjogbin, I.A. "A Chronology of Yoruba History," Odu 2 (2).

_____. "The Prelude to the Yoruba Civil Wars of the Nineteenth
Century," Odu, No. 2.

Alagoa, E.J. The Small Brave City State--A History of Brass-
Nembe in the Niger Delta. Ibadan, 1964.

Alimen, H. The Prehistory of Africa. London, 1957.

Ananaba, Wogu. The Trade Union Movement in Nigeria. 1969.

Anene, J.C. "The Southern Nigerian Protectorate and the Aros,
1900-02," Journal of Historical Society of Nigeria, Vol. II, No.
1 (1960).

Arikpo, Okoi. The Development of Modern Nigeria. New York:
Penguin Books, 1970.

Arnold, Guy. Modern Nigeria. London: Longman Group Ltd.,
1977.

Aronson, D.R. The City is Our Farm: Seven Migrant Ijebu Yoruba
Families. Cambridge, MA: Shenkman, 1978.

Atanda, J.A. The New Oyo Empire: Indirect Rule and Change in
Western Nigeria 1894-1934. London: Longman, 1973.

Awolowo, Obafemi. Awo, The Autobiography of Chief Obafemi Awolowo. Cambridge: Cambridge University Press, 1960.

Ayandele, E.A. African Historical Essays. London: Frank Cass,
1979.

_____. Holy Johnson, Pioneer of African Nationalism 1836-1917.
London: Frank Cass, 1970.

_____. The Missionary Impact on Modern Nigeria, 1842-1914.
London: Longman, 1966.

Azikiwe, N. My Odyssey. London: Hurst, 1970.

Balewa, Alhaji Sir Abubakar Tafawa. Nigeria Speaks. Cambridge:
Cambridge University Press, 1962.

Beier, Ulli. "Before Oduduwa," Odu 3, 1956.

Beier, Ulli and Biobaku, S.O. "The Use and Interpretation of Myths," Odu, 1 (1955).

Bello, Alhaji Sir Ahmadu. My Life. Cambridge: Cambridge University Press, 1962.

Biobaku, S.O. The Egba and their Neighbours 1832-1872. London, 1957.

_____. "The Problem of Traditional History with Special Reference to Yoruba Traditions," Journal of Historical Society of Nigeria, Vol. 1, No. 1 (1959).

_____. The Origin of the Yorubas. Lagos, 1955.

Boahen, Adu. Britain, The Sahara and the West Sudan 1788-1861. London, 1964.

Bourdillon, Sir Bernard. The Future of the Colonial Empire. London, 1945.

_____. Memorandum on the Future Political Development of Nigeria. Lagos, 1939.

Bovill, E.W. Caravans of the Old Sahara. London: Oxford University Press, 1933.

Bowen, T.J. Adventures and Missionary Labours in Several Countries in the Interior of Africa. Charleston, SC: Southern Baptist Publication Society, 1857.

Bradbury, R.E. The Benin Kingdom and the Edo-Speaking Peoples of South-Western Nigeria. London: International African Institutes, 1957.

Bradbury, R.E. and Lloyd, Peter C. The Benin People and Edo Speaking Peoples, etc., plus the Itsekiri. London, 1959.

Burns, Alan. History of Nigeria 4th ed. London: George Allen & Unwin, Ltd., 1948.

_____. In Defence of Colonies. London: George Allen & Unwin, 1957.

Buxton, T.F. The African Slave Trade and Its Remedy. London, 1839.

Clapperton, Hugh. Journal of a Second Expedition into the Interior of Africa, etc. London, 1829.

Crowder, M. The Story of Nigeria. London: Faber and Faber, 1973.

_____. West Africa under Colonial Rule. London: Hutchinson, 1968.

_____ and Ikime O., eds. West African Chiefs: Their Changing Status under Colonial Rule and Independence. Ile-Ife: University of Ife Press, 1970.

Crowther, S. A. Journals of an Expedition up the Niger and Tshadda Rivers etc. London, 1855.

Daily Times. Nigerian Year Book (different editions from 1973 to 1984). Lagos.

_____. Who's Who in Nigeria (different editions up to 1983). Lagos.

Davidson, Basil. Black Mother. London, 1961.

_____. Old Africa Rediscovered. London, 1959.

_____ and Adenekan Ademola, eds. The New West Africa. London: Allen & Unwin, 1953.

Davies, O. West Africa Before the Europeans. London: Methuen, 1967.

Dickie, John and Rake, Alan. Who's Who in Africa: The Political, Military and Business Leaders of Africa. London: African Buyer and Trader, 1973.

Dike, K. Onwuka. 100 Years of British Rule in Nigeria 1851-1951. Lagos, 1957.

_____. Origins of the Niger Mission, 1841-1891. Ibadan: Ibadan University Press, 1962.

_____. Trade and Politics in the Niger Delta 1830-1885. London, 1956.

Eades, J. S. The Yoruba Today. Cambridge: Cambridge University Press, 1980.

Egbarevba, J. U. A Short History of Benin. Ibadan: Ibadan University Press, 1960.

Enahoro, Anthony. Azikiwe--Saint or Sinner? Lagos, 1946.

English, M. C. An Outline of Nigerian History. London, 1959.

Fage, J. D. An Introduction to the History of West Africa. London, 1955.

Feinstein, A. African Revolutionary: The Life and Times of Nigeria's Aminu Kano. New York: Quadrangle, 1973.

Flint, J. E.   Sir George Goldie and the Making of Nigeria.   London: Oxford University Press, 1960.

Forde, Daryll.   The Yoruba-Speaking Peoples of South-Western Nigeria.   London: International African Institute, 1951.

_____, ed.   Efik Traders of Old Calabar.   London: Oxford University Press, 1956.

_____ and G. I. Jones.   The Ibo and Ibibio-Speaking Peoples of South-Eastern Nigeria.   London: International African Institute, 1950.

Fortes, M.   "The Impact of British War on West Africa," International Affairs (April 21, 1945).

Freeman, Thomas Birch.   Journal of Various Visits to the Kingdom of Ashanti, Aku and Dahomi in Western Africa.   London: Frank Cass, 1968.

Gollmer, Charles, H. V.   Charles Andrew Gollmer--His Life and Missionary Labours in West Africa.   London: Hodder and Stoughton, 1881.

Groves, C. D.   The Planting of Christianity in Africa, 3 vols.   London: Lutterworth Press, 1955.

Gunther, John.   Inside Africa.   New York: Harper's, 1955.

Hargreaves, J. D.   Prelude to the Partition of West Africa.   London, 1963.

Harris, John.   Books About Nigeria, 4th ed.   Ibadan, 1963.

Hinden, Rita.   Empire and After.   London: Essential Books, 1949.

Hinderer, Anna.   Seventeen Years in the Yoruba Country.   London: Seely, Jackson and Halliday, 1873.

Hodgkin, Thomas.   "Uthman dan Fodio" in "Nigeria 1960," a Special independence issue of Nigeria Magazine (October 1960).

Hodgkin, Thomas et al.   The New West Africa.   London, 1953.

Hogben, S. J.   The Muhammedan Emirates of Nigeria.   London, 1930.

_____ and Kirk-Greene.   The Emirates of Northern Nigeria.   London: Oxford University Press, 1966.

Howard, C. and Plumb, J. H.   West African Explorers.   London, 1952.

Hussey, E. R. J.   Tropical Africa, 1908-1944.   London: St. Catherine Press, 1959.

Igbafe, P. A. Benin Under British Administration 1897-1938. London: Longman, 1979.

Ikime, O. "Colonial Conquest and Resistance in Southern Nigeria," Journal of Historical Society of Nigeria, Vol. 4, No. 3 (December 1972).

_____. Merchant Prince of the Niger Delta: The Rise and Fall of Nana Olomu, Last Governor of the Benin River. London: Heinemann, 1968.

The International Who's Who 1981-1982. Europa Publications Ltd., 1981.

Isichei, Elizabeth. A History of the Igbo People. London: Macmillan, 1976.

Johnson, Samuel. The History of the Yorubas. Lagos: C. M. S. Bookshop, 1937.

Jones, G. I. The Trading States of the Oil Rivers. Oxford: Oxford University Press, 1963.

Jones-Quartey, K. A. B. A Life of Azikiwe. Harmondsworth: Penguin, 1956.

Kingsley, Mary H. Travels in W. Africa. London: Macmillan, 1900.

_____. West African Studies. London: Macmillan, 1899.

Kirk-Greene, A. H. M. Adamawa, Past and Present. London, 1958.

_____. Barth's Travels in Nigeria. London, 1962.

_____. "Who Coined the name Nigeria?" West Africa (December 22, 1956).

_____. Lugard and the Amalgamation of Nigeria. London: Frank Cass, 1968.

Laird, Macgregor and Oldfield, R. A. K. Narrative of an Expedition to the Interior of Africa in 1832, 1833 and 1834. London, 1837.

Lander, Richard and John. Journals of an Expedition to Explore the Course and Termination of the Niger. London, 1832.

Legum, Colin, ed. African Contemporary Record: Annual Survey and Documents 1976-1977. London: Rex Collings, 1977.

Lewis, L. J. Henry Carr. London: Oxford University Press, 1949.

Lipschutz, Mark R. and Rasmussen R. Kent. Dictionary of African Historical Biography. London: Heinemann, 1978.

Livingstone, W. P.   Mary Slessor of Calabar.   London, 1933.

Lloyd, P. C.   "Conflict Theory and Yoruba Kingdoms" in I. M. Lewis, ed.   History and Social Anthropology.   London: Tavistock Publications, 1968.

_____ and Ryder, A. F. C.   "Don Domingos, Prince of Warri-- Portuguese Contact with the Itsekiri,"   Odu (1954).

Lugard, F. D.   The Dual Mandate in British Tropical Africa.   1922.

_____.   Political Memoranda.   London, 1906.

_____.   Report on the Amalgamation of Northern and Southern Nigeria and Administration.   London, 1920.

Lumley, Frederick, ed.   Nigeria, the land, its art and its people.   1974.

MacCartney, William M.   Dr. Aggrey.   London: S. C. M. Press, 1949.

MacFarlane, Donald M.   Calabar: and the Church of Scotland Mission 1846-1946.   London, 1946.

Mair, Lucy P.   Native Policies in Africa.   London: George Routledge, 1936.

Mannix, D. P. and Cowley, M.   Black Cargoes: A History of the Atlantic Slave Trade 1518-1865.   London, 1963.

Martins, E. C.   The British West African Settlements, 1750-1821.   London: Longman, 1927.

Maxwell, J. Houvif.   Nigeria, the land, the people and Christian Progress.   London: World Dominion Press, 1931.

Meek, C. K.   The Northern Tribes of Nigeria.   London: Oxford University Press, 1925.

_____.   A Sudanese Kingdom.   New York, 1958.

Mefarlaw, Donald M.   Calabar.   Edinburgh: Nelson, 1946.

Miller, W. R. S.   Reflections of a Pioneer.   London: C. M. S., 1936.

_____.   Yesterday and Tomorrow in Northern Nigeria.   London: S. C. M., 1938.

Newbury, C. W.   The Western Slave Coast and its Rulers.   Oxford, 1961.

Nigeria Handbook, 1953.

Niven, C. R. A Short History of Nigeria. London, 1937.

_____ . A Short History of the Yoruba Peoples. London, 1958.

Nwabara, S. N. Iboland: A Century of Contact with Britain 1860-1960. London: Hodder & Stoughton, 1977.

Obi, Chike. My Struggle. Lagos, 1954.

_____ . Our Struggle. Ibadan, 1953.

Ojo, G. J. A. Yoruba Palaces. London: University of London Press, 1966.

Ojukwu, C. O. Biafra, 2 vols. New York: Harper & Row, 1969.

Okonjo, I. M. British Administration in Nigeria 1900-1950. New York: Nok Publishers, 1974.

Oliver, Roland. Sir Harry Johnson and the Scramble for Africa. London, 1957.

_____ and Fage, J. D. A Short History of Africa. London, 1962.

Orr, Charles. The Making of Northern Nigeria. London: Frank Cass & Co. Ltd., 1965.

Otite, O. Autonomy and Independence: The Urhobo Kingdom of Okpe in Nigeria. London: Hurst, 1973.

Oyediran, O., ed. Survey of Nigerian Affairs 1975. Lagos: OUP, 1978.

Padmore, George. Africa, Britain's Third Empire. London: Dobson, 1949.

_____ . How Britain Rules Africa. London: Dobson, 1936.

_____ . How Russia Transformed her Colonial Empire. London: Dobson, 1949.

_____ . Pan Africanism or Communism. London: Dobson, 1956.

Palmer, H. R. The Bornu, Sahara and Sudan. London, 1936.

_____ . Sudanese Memoirs, 3 vols. Lagos, 1928.

Park, Mungo. Journal of a Mission to the Interior of Africa in the Year 1805. London, 1815.

_____ . Travels in the Interior Districts of Africa, in 1795, 1796 and 1797. London, 1799.

Parrinder, Geoffrey. The Story of Ketu--An Ancient Yoruba Kingdom. Ibadan, 1956.

Pedrarza, H.J. Borioboda-Gha: The Story of Lokoja: The First British Settlement in Nigeria. London: Oxford University Press, 1960.

Perham, Margery. Africans and British Rule. London: Oxford University Press, 1941.

_____. Lugard, the years of Adventure 1858-1898. London, 1960.

Perry, Ruth. A Preliminary Bibliography of the Literature of Nationalism In Nigeria. London: International African Institute, 1955.

Rawling, M.A. Bibliography of African Christian Literature. London, 1923.

Sadler, G.W. A Century in Nigeria. Nashville: Vanderbilt University Press, 1950.

Schoen, Jacob F., and Crowther, S.A. Journals of an Expedition up the Niger River in 1841. London, 1842.

Schram, R. Development of Nigerian Health Services 1460-1960, 500 Years of Medical History. Makerere, 1967.

Schultze, A. The Sultanate of Borno. London: Frank Cass, 1968.

Segal, Ronald. Political Africa: A Who's Who of Personalities and Parties. London: Stevens, 1961.

Shaw, Thurstan. Archaeology and Nigeria. Ibadan, 1964.

_____. Nigeria. London: Thames & Hudson, 1978.

Smith, Edwin W. The Christian Mission In Africa. London: International Missionary Council, 1926.

Smith, M.G. The Affairs of Daura. Berkeley: University of California Press, 1978.

Stock, Eugene, ed. The History of the Church Missionary Society, 4 vols. London: Church Missionary Society, 1899.

Talbot, P. Amaury, and Curzon, G. Nigeria: An Outline. London: Nigeria Office, 1955.

Temple, C.L. Notes on the Tribes, Provinces, Emirates and States of Northern Nigeria. Lagos, 1922.

Todd, J.M. African Mission. London: Burns and Oates, 1962.

Townsend, George. Memoir of the Rev. Henry Townsend. London: Marshall Brother, 1887.

Tremearne, A. J. N. The Niger and the West Sudan: London: Stoughton, 1900.

Trimingham, J. P. The Christian Church and Islam In West Africa. London: S. C. M. Press, 1955.

Trimingham, J. Spencer. A History of Islam in West Africa. London, 1962.

_____. Islam in West Africa. London, 1959.

Tucker, Miss. Abeokuta or Sunrise within the Tropics. London: Nisbet, 1853.

Venn, Henry III. Memoir of the Rev. Henry Venn (II). London: William Knight, 1880.

Waddell, Hope M. Twenty Nine Years in the West Indies and Central Africa. Edinburgh: Nelson, 1863.

Walker, F. D. A Hundred Years in Nigeria. London: Cargate Press, 1942.

_____. The Romance of the Black River. London: C. M. S., 1931.

Wellesley, Dorothy. Sir George Goldie. London: Macmillian, 1934.

Westermann, Diedrich. The African To-day. London: Oxford University Press, 1934.

_____. The African To-day and To-morrow, 3rd ed. London: Oxford University Press, 1949.

Politics

Abernethy, David B. "Nigeria Creates a New Religion," Africa Report, IX, 3 (March 1964).

Adamolekun, L. and Rowlands, L., eds. The New Local Government System in Nigeria. Ibadan: Heinemann, 1979.

Adamu, Haroun and Ogusanwo, Alaba. Nigeria: The Making of the Presidential System, 1979 General Elections. Kano: Triumph Publishing Co. Ltd., 1982.

Adebayo, A. Principles and Practice of Public Administration in Nigeria. Chichester: Wiley, 1981.

Adedeji, A. "The Finances of Nigeria's State Governments," Administration, Vol. 2, No. 4 (July 1969).

_____, ed. Nigerian Administration and its Political Setting. London: Hutchinson Educational, 1968.

Ademoyega, A. Why We Struck, The Story of the First Nigerian Coup. Evans Brothers Nigeria Publishers, 1981.

Adu A. L. The Civil Service in Commonwealth Africa. London: George Allen & Unwin, 1969.

Afigbo, A. E. The Warrant Chiefs--Indirect Rule in South-Eastern Nigeria, 1891-1929. London: Longman, 1972.

Africa Research Group. The Other Side of Nigeria's Civil War. Boston: Africa Research Group, 1970.

Ake, Claude. "Explaining Political Instability in New States," Journal of Modern African Studies, Vol. 11, No. 3 (September 1973).

Akinyemi A. B. Foreign Policy and Nigerian Federation. Ibadan: Ibadan University Press, 1975.

_____. "Nigeria: What Should follow Army Rule--and When?" Africa Report, 16 (1971).

_____, ed. Nigeria and the World. Ibadan: Oxford University Press, 1978.

Akiwowo, A. "The Performance of the Nigerian Military from 1966 to 1970" in M. Janowitz and J. van Doorn eds. On Military Ideology. Rotterdam University Press, 1971.

Akpan, N. The Struggle for Secession, 1966-70. London: Frank Cass, 1971.

Akpan, N. U. Epitaph to Indirect Rule. 1956.

Aluko, O. Essays in Nigerian Foreign Policy. London: Allen & Unwin, 1981.

Aluko, Olajide. Ghana and Nigeria, 1956-70. London, 1976.

Anber, Paul. "Modernization and Political Disintegration: Nigeria and the Ibos," The Journal of Modern African Studies, Vol. 5, No. 2 (September 1967).

Anglin, D. G. "Brinkmanship in Nigeria: The Federal Election of 1964-65," International Journal, Vol. 20, No. 2 (Spring 1965).

Anifowose, R. Violence and Politics in Nigeria: The Tiv and Yoruba Experience 1960-66. Lagos: Nok, 1980.

Arnold, Guy. Modern Nigeria. London: Longman Group Ltd.,
1977.

Atanda, J. A. The New Oyo Empire: Indirect Rule and Change in
Western Nigeria 1894-1934. London: Longman, 1973.

Awa, Eme O. Federal Government in Nigeria. Berkeley: University of California Press, 1964.

Awolowo, Chief Obafemi. The People's Republic.

Awolowo, O. Awo on the Nigerian Civil War. Ikeja: John West
Publications, 1981.

Awolowo, Obafemi. Path to Nigerian Freedom. London: Faber,
1947.

Azikiwe, Nnamdi. Assassination Story: True or False? Lagos,
1945.

_____. Economic Reconstruction of Nigeria, Lagos, 1948.

_____. "Essentials for Nigerian Survival," Foreign Affairs,
XLIII, 3 (April 1965).

_____. Zik, a Selection from the Speeches of Nnamdi Azikiwe.
Cambridge: Cambridge University Press, 1961.

_____. Political Blueprint of Nigeria. Lagos, 1945.

_____. Renascent Africa. Lagos, 1937.

Beer, C. E. F. The Politics of Peasant Groups in Western Nigeria.
Ibadan: Ibadan University Press, 1976.

Blitz, L. F., ed. The Politics and Administration of Nigerian Government. London: Sweet and Maxwell, 1964.

Bohannan, Laura. "Political Aspects of Tiv Social Organization"
in J. Middleton and D. Tait eds. Tribes Without Rulers. London: Routledge and Kegan Paul, 1958.

Bolaji, S. L. Shagari: President by Mathematics. Ibadan: Automatic Printing Press, 1980.

Bretton, H. L. Power and Stability in Nigeria: The Politics of Decolonization. New York: Praeger, 1962.

Brown, Charles V. Government and Banking in Western Nigeria.
Ibadan: Oxford University Press, 1964.

Bull, Mary. "Indirect Rule in Northern Nigeria, 1906-11" in Robinson, Kenneth and Madden, Frederick Essays in Imperial Government. Oxford, 1963.

Cameron, Donald. Principles of Native Administration and their Application. Lagos: Government Printer, 1934.

Campbell, M. J. Law and Practice of Local Government in Northern Nigeria. London: Maxwell, 1963.

Carter, G. M. Politics in Africa: 7 Cases. New York: Harcourt, 1966.

Cohen, A. Custom and Politics in Urban Africa. London: Routledge, 1969.

Cohen, R. Organized Labour in the Nigerian Political Process. London: Heinemann, 1974.

Cole, M. Modern and Traditional Elites in the Politics of Lagos. Cambridge: Cambridge University Press, 1975.

Cole, R. T. and Tilman, R. O., eds. The Nigerian Political Scene. Durham: Duke University Press, 1962.

Coleman, J. S. Nigeria; Background to Nationalism. Berkeley and Los Angeles: University of California Press, 1958.

Coleman, James S. "Emergence of African Political Parties," Africa Today ed. by C. Girovehaines. Baltimore: Johns Hopkins Press, 1955.

_____. "Nationalism in Tropical Africa," The American Political Science Review, Vol. XLVII, No. 2 (June 1954).

_____ and Rosberg, Carl G., eds. Political Parties and National Integration in Tropical Africa. Berkeley and Los Angeles: University of California Press, 1965.

Collins, P., ed. Administration for Development in Nigeria. Lagos: African Education Press, 1980.

_____. "Public Policy and the Development of Indigenous Capitalism: The Nigerian Experience," Journal of Commonwealth and Comparative Politics, 15, 2 (1977).

Cowan, L. Gray. Local Government in West Africa. New York, 1958.

Crocker, W. R. Nigeria: A Critique of British Colonial Administration. London: George Allen and Unwin, 1936.

_____. Self-Government for the Colonies. London: Allen and Unwin, 1949.

Cronje, S. The World and Nigeria: The Diplomatic History of the Nigerian Civil War 1967-70. London: Sidgwick & Jackson, 1972.

Crowder, M. West Africa Under Colonial Rule. London: Hutchinson, 1968.

_____ and Ikime, O., eds. West African Chiefs: Their Changing Status under Colonial Rule and Independence. Ile-Ife: University of Ife Press, 1970.

Crowe, B. E. The Berlin West African Conference, 1884-1885. London: Longmans, 1942.

Daily Times. The Constitution on Trial--Balarabe Musa Vs. The Assembly. Lagos Times Press,

Daily Times. Elections 1983. Lagos, 1983.

Daily Times. The Light and Darkness. Lagos, n. d.

Davies, H. O. Nigeria: The Prospect for Democracy. London: Weidenfeld and Nicolson, 1961.

_____. Nigeria's New Constitution. The West African Review, Vol. xvi, No. 212 (May 1945).

Dent, M. and Austin D., eds. Implementing Civil Rule: The First Two Years. Manchester: Machester University, 1981.

De St. Jorre, J. The Nigerian Civil War. London: Hodder & Stoughton, 1972.

Dudley, B. J. "Federalism and the Balance of Political Power in Nigeria," Journal of Commonwealth Political Studies Vol. v (1966).

_____. Instability and Political Order: Politics and Crisis in Nigeria. Ibadan University Press, 1973.

_____. An Introduction to Nigerian Government and Politics. London: Macmillan, 1982.

_____. "The Military and Development" Nigerian Journal of Economic and Social Studies, Vol. 13, No. 2 (1971).

_____. Parties and Politics in Northern Nigeria. London: Frank Cass, 1968.

_____. "The Political Theory of Awolowo and Azikiwe" in O. Otite ed. Themes in African Social and Political Thought. New York: Africana Publishing Co., 1978.

_____, ed. Nigeria 1965: Crisis and Criticism. Ibadan University Press, 1966.

Duignam, Peter and Gann, Lewis H., eds. Colonialism in Africa,

1870-1960, Vol. II. Cambridge: Cambridge University Press, 1970.

Ekeh, P.P. Citizenship and Political Conflict: A Sociological Interpretation of the Nigerian Crisis" in J. Okpaku ed. Nigeria: Dilemma of Nationhood. New York: Third Press, 1972.

Elias, T.O. Groundwork of Nigerian Law. London, 1954.

_____. Local Government in the Western Provinces of Nigeria. Ibadan, 1951.

_____. The Nigerian Legal System. London: Routledge, 1963.

Enahoro, Chief Anthony. Fugitive Offender: The Story of a Political Prisoner. London: Cassell, 1965.

Ezera, Kalu. Constitutional Developments in Nigeria. Cambridge: Cambridge University Press, 1960.

First, Ruth. The Barrel of a Gun: Political Power in Africa and the Coup. London: Penguin Books, 1969.

Forsyth, Frederick. The Biafran Story. London: Penguin, 1969.

Fortes, M. and Evans-Pritchard, E.E. African Political Systems. London: Oxford University Press, 1940.

Frank, L.P. "Ideological Competition in Nigeria: Urban Population v. Elite Nationalism," Journal of Modern African Studies, Vol. 17, No. 3 (1979).

The Future of Local Government in Nigeria: The Report of the National Conference on Local Government Held at the University of Ife, 1969. Ile-Ife: University of Ife Press, 1969.

Gambari, L.A. Party Politics and Foreign Policy: Nigeria During the First Republic. Zaria: ABU Press, 1979.

Gbulie, Ben. Nigeria's Five Majors. Onitsha: Africana Educational Publishers, 1981.

Geary, William N.M. Nigeria Under British Rule. London: Methuen, 1927.

Graf, W.D. Elections 1979: The Nigerian Citizens' Guide to Parties Politics and Issues. Lagos: Daily Times, n.d.

_____, ed. Towards a Political Economy of Nigeria: Critical Essays. Benin City: Koda Publishers, 1981.

Green, Fred. "Toward Understanding Military Coups," Africa Report, Vol. 11 (1966).

Green, Harry A. "The Theory of Local Government and Managerial Effectiveness," The Nigerian Journal of Public Affairs Vol. iv, No. 1 (May 1976).

Gutteridge, F. F. Military Regimes in Africa. London: Methuen, 1976.

Hailey, Lord. An African Survey. London: Oxford University Press, 1938.

_____. An African Survey revised 1956. London: Oxford University Press, 1957.

_____. Native Administration in the British African Territories, 5 vols. London: H. M. S. O., 1951.

Harris, P. J. Local Government in Southern Nigeria. Cambridge: Cambridge University Press, 1957.

Harris, Richard L. "Nigeria: Crisis and Compromise," Africa Report, X, 3 (March 1965).

Hazelwood A. African Integration and Disintegration. London: Oxford University Press, 1967.

Hodgkin, T. Nigerian Perspectives. London: Oxford University Press, 1960.

Hogben, S. J. and Kirk-Greene, A. H. M. The Emirates of Northern Nigeria. London: Oxford University Press, 1966.

Ibo State Union. "Nigerian Disunity--the Guilty Ones." Pamphlet No. 1, Enugu (c. 1964).

Idang, G. J. Nigeria: Internal Politics and Foreign Policy 1960-66. Ibadan: Ibadan University Press, 1973.

Idang, Gordon J. "The Politics of Nigerian Foreign Policy: the Ratification and Renunciation of the Anglo-Nigerian Defence Agreement," African Studies Review, Vol. xiii, No. 2 (September 1970).

Jemibewon, D. M. A Combatant in Government. Ibadan: Heinemann, 1978.

Keay, E. A. The Native and Customary Courts of Nigeria. London: Sweet & Maxwell, 1966.

Kingsley, Mary. West African Studies. London, 1901.

Kirk-Greene, A. H. M. Lugard and the Amalgamation of Nigeria. London: Frank Cass, 1968.

_____. The Principles of Native Administration in Nigeria Selected Documents, 1900-1947. London: Oxford University Press, 1965.

_____, ed. Crisis and Conflict in Nigeria: a Documentary Source Book 1966-69, 2 vols. London: Oxford University Press, 1971.

Koehn, P. "The Nigerian Elections of 1979," Africa Today, Vol. 28, No. 1 (1981).

Kumu, S. and Aliyu, A., eds. Issues in the Nigerian Draft Constitution. Zaria: Institute of Administration, 1977.

Langa Langa. Up Against it in Nigeria. London, 1922.

Lindley, M.F. The Acquisition and Government of Backward Territory in International Law. London, 1966.

Lloyd, P.C. "Conflict Theory and Yoruba Kingdoms" in I.M. Lewis ed. History and Social Anthropology. London: Tavistock Publications, 1968.

Lloyd, Peter C. "Development of Political Parties in Western Nigeria," The American Political Science Review, Vol. XLIX, No. 3 (September 1955).

_____. "The Traditional Political System of the Yoruba," South-Western Journal of Anthropology, X, V (Winter 1954).

Luckham, R. The Nigerian Army: A Sociological Analysis of Authority and Revolt, 1960-1967. New York, 1971.

Lugard F.D. The Dual Mandate on British Tropical Africa. 1922.

_____. Political Memoranda, 1913-1918. London: Waterlow, 1919, Memo No. 4, para. 1.

_____. Report on the Amalgamation of Northern and Southern Nigeria and Administration. London, 1920.

Lugard, Lady A. Tropical Dependency. London, 1905.

Mackintosh, J.P. "Electoral Trends and the Tendency to a One Party System in Nigeria," Journal of Commonwealth Political Studies, 1 (November 1962).

_____. Nigerian Government and Politics. London: George Allen and Unwin, 1966.

_____. "Politics in Nigeria: The Action Group Crisis of 1962," Political Studies, Vol. XI (June 2, 1963).

Madeibo, A. A.   The Nigerian Revolution and the Biafran War.
Enugu: Fourth Dimension, 1980.

Madunagu, E.   Problems of Socialism: The Nigerian Challenge.
London: Zed, 1981.

Melson, R. and Wolpe, H. , eds.   Nigeria: Modernization and the
Politics of Communalism.   East Lansing: Michigan State University Press, 1971.

Middleton, J. and Tait, D. , eds.   Tribes Without Rulers.   London:
Routledge and Kegan Paul, 1958.

Milley, Walter R.   Have We Failed in Nigeria?   London: Butterworth Press, 1947.

_____.   Success in Nigeria.   London: Butterworth Press, 1948.

Miners, N. J.   The Nigerian Army, 1956-1966.   London: Methuen,
1971.

Mockler-Ferryman, A. F.   British Nigeria.   London, 1902.

Murray, D. J.   The Work of Administration in Nigeria: Case Studies.   London: Hutchinson Educational, 1969.

Ndem, Eyo B. E.   Ibos in Contemporary Nigerian Politics.   Onitsha:
Eludo Ltd. , 1961.

Ngosu, H. N. , ed.   Problems of Nigerian Administration: A Book
of Readings.   Enugu: Fourth Dimension, 1980.

Nicholson, I. F.   The Administration of Nigeria 1900-1960.   Oxford,
Clarendon Press, 1969.

Niven, C. R.   "Can There Be Unity in Nigeria?"   The New Commonwealth, Vol. XXX, No. 2 (July 1955).

_____.   How Nigeria is Governed.   London: Longmans, 1950.

_____.   Nigeria, Outline of a Colony, 2nd ed.   London, 1967.

Nnoli, O.   Ethnic Politics in Nigeria.   Enugu: Fourth Dimension,
1978.

Nwabueze, B. O.   Constitutional Law of the Nigerian Republic.   London: Butterworth, 1964.

Nwankwo, A. A.   Nigeria: The Challenge of Biafra.   London: Rex
Collings, 1972.

Nwigwe, H. E.   Nigeria: The Fall of the First Republic.   London:
Ebony Press, n. d.

Nzimiro, I. Studies in Ibo Political Systems--Chieftaincy and Politics in Four Niger States. Berkeley: University of California Press, 1972.

Obasanjo, O. My Command. Ibadan: Heinemann, 1980.

O'Connell, J. "Authority and Community in Nigeria" in R. Melson and H. Wolpe eds. Nigeria: Modernization and the Politics of Communalism. East Lansing: Michigan State University, 1971.

_____ and Beckett, P. A. Education and Power in Nigeria. London: Hodder & Stoughton, 1977.

Oden, G. W. E. , ed. A New System of Local Government. Enugu: Nwamife Press, 1977.

Odetola, O. PRP Crisis Making and Unmaking the Key, Who Wins? Ibadan: Sketch Publishers, 1981.

Odumosu, Oluwole I. The Nigerian Constitution: History and Development. London: Sweet and Maxwell, 1963.

Ofonagoro, W. I. and Ojo, A. , eds. The Great Debate: Nigerian Viewpoints on the Draft Constitution 1976/77. Lagos: Daily Times, n. d.

Ogunbadejo, O. "Ideology and Pragmatism: The Soviet Role in Nigeria," Orbis, Vol. 21, No. 4 (1978).

Ogunsanwo, G. , ed. The Great Debate. Lagos: Daily Times, 1978.

Ojiako, J. O. Nigeria: Yesterday, Today and.... Onitsha: African Educational Publishers, 1981.

_____. 13 Years of Military Rule, 1966-1979. Lagos: Daily Times, n. d.

Ojo, Olatunde J. B. "Federal-State Relations 1967-1974," Quarterly Journal of Administration, Vol. 10 (January 1976).

Okonjo, I. M. British Administration in Nigeria 1900-1950. New York: NOK Publishers, 1974.

Okpaku, J. , ed. Nigeria: Dilemma of Nationhood. New York: Third Press, 1968.

Oladosu, S. A. Kaduna Essays in Local Government. Kaduna, 1981.

Olusanya, G. O. "The Role of the Ex-servicemen in Nigerian Politics," Journal of Modern African Studies, 6 (1968).

_____. The Second World War and Politics in Nigeria 1939-53. London: Evans, 1973.

Orizu A. Nwafor. Without Bitterness. New York, 1944.

Osoba, S.O. "The Nigerian Power Elite," African Social Studies edited by P.C.W. Gutkind and P. Waterman. London: Heinemann, 1976.

Ostheimer, J.M. Nigerian Politics. New York: Harper and Row, 1973.

Otite, O. Autonomy and Independence: The Urhobo Kingdom of Okpe in Modern Nigeria. London: Hurst, 1973.

Oyediran, O., ed. Nigerian Government and Politics Under Military Rule 1968-79. London: Macmillan, 1979.

_____. Survey of Nigerian Affairs 1976-77. London: Macmillan, 1981.

Oyinbo, J. Nigeria: Crisis and Beyond. London: Charles Knight & Co. Ltd., 1971.

Panter-Brick, S.K., ed. Nigerian Politics and Military Rule: Prelude to the Civil War. London: Athlone Press, 1970.

_____. Soldiers and Oil: The Military and the Political Transformation of Nigeria. London: Frank Cass, 1978.

Park, A.W.W. The Sources of Nigerian Law. London: Butterworth, 1963.

Peil, M. Nigerian Politics: The People's View. London: Cassell, 1976.

Perham, Margery. Lugard: The Years of Authority, 1899-1945. London, 1960.

_____. Native Administration in Nigeria. London: Oxford University Press, 1948.

_____. and Bull, Mary. The Diaries of Lord Lugard. London, 1963.

Phillips, A.O. "Three Decades of Intergovernmental Financial Relationships in Federation of Nigeria," The Quarterly Journal of Administration, Vol. XIV (1980).

Phillips, Claude S. Jr. The Development of Nigerian Foreign Policy. Evanston, IL, 1964.

Phillipson, Sidney and Adebo, S.O. Nigerianization of the Civil Service. Lagos, 1954.

Post, K.W.J. "Forming a Government in Nigeria," Nigerian Journal of Economic and Social Studies, Vol. 2, No. 1 (1960).

_____. "Is There a Case for Biafra?" International Affairs Vol. 44, No. 1 (January 1964).

_____. The Nigerian Federal Election of 1959. London: Oxford University Press, 1963.

_____. "Nigeria's Un-Election," New Society, No. 22 (January 1965).

_____ and Jenkins, George O. The Price of Liberty: Personality and Politics in Colonial Nigeria. Cambridge: Cambridge University Press, 1973.

_____ and Vickers, M. Structure and Conflict in Nigeria 1960-1965. London: Heinimann, 1973.

Quinn-Young, C. T. and Herdman, I. Geography of Nigeria. London: Longmans, 1954.

Royal Institute of International Affairs. Nigeria: The Political and Economic Background. London, 1960.

Schwartz, Walter. Nigeria. Pall Mall, 1968.

Schwarz, Jr., F. A. O. Nigeria, The Tribes, the Nation or the Race --The Politics of Independence. Cambridge: M. I. T. Press, 1965.

Seibel, H. D. Some Aspects of Inter-Ethnic Relation in Nigeria," Nigerian Journal of Economic and Social Studies, Vol. 9, No. 2 (July 1967).

Shagari, S. My Vision of Nigeria. London: Frank Cass, 1981.

Sklar, R. L. "Contradictions in the Nigerian Political System," Journal of Modern African Studies, Vol. 3, No. 2 (1965).

Sklar, Richard L. Nigerian Political Parties. Princeton: Princeton University Press, 1963.

_____. "Nigerian Politics: The Ordeal of Chief Awolowo 1960-65" in Gwendolen M. Carter, Politics in Africa. New York: Harcourt, Brace & World Inc., 1966.

_____ and C. S. Whitaker Jr. "The Federal Republic of Nigeria" in Gwendolen M. Carter ed., National Unity and Regionalism in Eight African States. Ithaca, NY: Cornell University Press, 1966.

_____ and _____. "Nigeria" in James S. Coleman and Carl G. Rosberg, Jr. eds. Political Parties and National Integration in Tropical Africa. Berkeley: University of California Press, 1964.

Smith, M. G. Government in Zazzau. London: Oxford University Press, 1960.

Smith, S. "Colonialism in Economic Theory: the Experience of Nigeria," Journal of Development Studies, 15, 3 (1979).

Smock, A. C. Ibo Politics: The Role of Ethnic Unions in Eastern Nigeria. Cambridge, MA: Harvard University Press, 1971.

_____. "NCNC and Ethnic Unions in Biafra," Journal of Modern African Studies, Vol. 7 (1969).

Stremlau, J. J. The International Politics of the Nigerian Civil War, 1967-70. Princeton: Princeton University Press, 1977.

Tamuno, T. N. Nigeria and Elective Rerepresentation 1923-1947. London: Heinemann, 1966.

_____. The Police in Modern Nigeria 1861-1965. Ibadan: Ibadan University Press, 1970.

Taylor, J. V. Christianity and Politics In Africa. London: Penguin African Series, 1957.

Tilman, R. O. and Cole, T., eds. The Nigerian Political Scene. Durham, NC: Duke University Press, 1962.

Tukur, M. "The establishment of state governments in Northern Nigeria," Journal of Modern African Studies, 8 (1970).

Turner, T. "Multinational Corporations and the Stability of the Nigerian State," Review of African Political Economy, 5 (1976).

_____. "Nigeria: Imperialism, Oil Technology and the Comprador State" in P. Nore and T. Turner eds. Oil and Class Struggle. London: Zed, 1980.

Usman, Y. B. For the Liberation of Nigeria. London: New Bacon Books, 1979.

Uwanaka, Charles U. Awolowo and Akintola in Political Storm. Lagos: Yaba, 1964.

Uwechue, R. Reflections on the Nigerian Civil War. London: O. I. T. H. International Publishers Ltd., 1969.

Waugh, Auberon and Cronje, Suzanne. Biafra: Britains' Shame. London: Michael Joseph, 1969.

Wheare, Joan. The Nigerian Legislative Council. London: Faber and Faber, 1950.

Whitaker, C. S. The Politics of Tradition Continuity and Change In

Northern Nigeria, 1946-66. Princeton: Princeton University Press, 1970.

_____. "Three Perspectives on Hierarchy: Political Thought and Leadership in Northern Nigeria," Journal of Commonwealth Political Studies, III (1 March 1965).

Whiteman, K. "Enugu: The Psychology of Secession" in S. K. Panter-Brick ed., Nigerian Politics and Military Rule. London: Athlone Press, 1970.

Williams, B. A. and Walsh, A. H. Urban Government for Metropolitan Lagos. New York: Praeger, 1968.

Williams, G. "Political Consciousness Among the Ibadan Poor" in E. de Kadt and G. Williams eds., Sociology and Development. London: Tavistock Publications, 1974.

_____. State and Society in Nigeria. Lagos: Afrographika, 1980.

_____. ed. "Nigeria Issue," Review of African Political Economy, 13 (1979).

Wolpe, H. Port Harcourt: Ibo Politics in Microcosm," Journal of Modern African Studies, 7 (1969).

Wolpe, Howard. Urban Politics in Nigeria; A Study of Port Harcourt. Los Angeles: University of California Press, 1974.

Yahaya, A. D. Native Authority System in Northern Nigeria. Zaria: ABU Press, 1979.

Society

Abraham, R. C. The Tiv People. Lagos: Government Printer, 1933.

Achebe, Chinua. No Longer at Ease. London: Heinemann, 1960.

Aderibigbe, A. B. Lagos: The Development of An African City. 1975.

Akinkugbe, O. O. et al, eds. Priorities in National Health Planning. Ibadan: Caxton Press, 1973.

Anderson, J. H. D. Islamic Law in Africa. London: H. M. S. O., 1955.

Arikpo, Okoi. Who are the Nigerians? Lagos, 1958.

382 / Bibliography

Barton, F. The Press of Africa. African Publishing Company, 1979.

Bolaji, L. Anatomy of Corruption in Nigeria. Ibadan: Daystar Press, 1970.

Bradbury, R. E. and Lloyd, Peter C. The Benin People and Edo Speaking Peoples, etc., plus the Itsekin. London, 1959.

Clarke, J. D. Omu Aran, An African Experiment. London: Longman, 1937.

Coker, Increase, Seventy Years of the Nigerian Press. Lagos: Daily Times publication, 1952.

Cooksey, J. J. and A. Mcleish. Religion and Civilisation In West Africa. London: World Dominion Press, 1931.

Daily Sketch. FESTAC 77. Ibadan: Sketch Publishing Company Ltd., 1977.

Daily Times. The Black of the World. Lagos: Times Press, n. d.

Echeruo, M. J. C. and Obiechina, E. N. Igbo Traditional Life, Culture and Literature. Conch Magazine Limited, 1971.

Elias, T. O. Nigerian Land Law and Custom. London, 1950.

_____, ed. Law and Social Change in Nigeria. Lagos: Evans Brothers, 1972.

Enahoro, P. How to be a Nigerian. Ibadan: Caxton Press, 1966.

Fadipe, N. A. The Sociology of the Yoruba. Ibadan: Ibadan University Press, 1970, p. 311.

Fagg, Bernard. "The Nok Culture," West African Review (December 1956).

Fasuyi, T. A. Cultural Policy in Nigeria. Paris: Unesco, 1973.

Forde, Daryll. The Yoruba-Speaking Peoples of South-Western Nigeria. London, 1951.

_____, ed. Efik Traders of Old Calabar. London, 1956.

_____ and Jones, G. I. The Ibo and Ibibio-Speaking Peoples of South-Eastern Nigeria. London, 1950.

_____ et al. Peoples of the Niger-Benue Confluence. London, 1955.

Green, M. M. Ibo Village Affairs. London: Sidgwick & Jackson, 1947.

Greenberg, Joseph H. Studies in African Linguistic Classification. New Haven: Compass Publishing Company, 1955.

Gunn Harold D. Peoples of the Plateau Area of Northern Nigeria. London: International African Institute, 1953.

Hambly, Wilfrid D. "Culture Areas of Nigeria," Chicago: Field Museum of Natural History (Anthropological Series) XXXI, 3 [1953].

Idowu, E. Bolaji. Olodumare--God in Yoruba Belief. London, 1962.

Kasunmu, A. B. and Salacuse, J. W. Nigerian Family Law. London: Butterworth, 1960.

Kuper, Leo & Smith, M. G. Pluralism in Africa. Berkeley: University of California Press, 1969.

Lloyd, P. C. "Conflict Theory and Yoruba Kingdoms" in I. M. Lewis ed. , History and Social Anthropology. London: Tavistosck Publications, 1968.

_____, ed. The New Elites of Tropical Africa. London: Oxford University Press, 1966.

Lubeck, P. "Class Consciousness and Islamic Nationalism Among Nigerian Workers," Research in the Sociology of Work Vol. 1, R. L. and I. H. Simpson, eds. Greenwich, Conn.: JAI Press, 1980.

Mabogunje, A. L. Urbanization in Nigeria. London: University of London, 1968.

Meek, C. K. Law and Authority in a Nigerian Tribe. London: Oxford University Press, 1937.

Nwabara, S. N. Iboland: A Century of Contact with Britain, 1860-1960. London: Hodder and Stoughton, 1977.

Nzimiro, I. The Nigerian Civil War: A Study in Class Conflict. Enugu: Fourth Dimension, 1978.

Ohonbamu, O. The Psychology of the Nigerian Revolution. Ilfracombe, Devon: Arthur H. Stockwell, 1969.

Paden, J. Religion and Political Culture in Kano. Berkeley: University of California Press, 1973.

Parrinder, Geoffrey. West African Religion. London: Harvester Press, 1949.

Peace, A. J. Choice, Class and Conflict. Hassocks: Harvester Press, 1979.

Peel, J. D. Y. Aladura: A Religious Movement Among the Yoruba. London: Oxford University Press, 1968.

_____. "Inequality and Action: The forms of Ijesha Social Conflict," Canadian Journal of African Studies, Vol. 14, No. 3 (1980).

Roth, Henry L. Great Benin: Its Customs, Art and Horrors. Halifax, 1903.

Seibel, H. Dieter. "Some Aspects of Inter-Ethnic Relations in Nigeria," The Nigerian Journal of Economics and Social Studies, Vol. IX, No. 2 (July 1967).

Smith, M. G. "Historical and Cultural Conditions of Political Corruption Among the Hausa," Comparative Studies in Society and History 6 (1964).

St. Croix, F. N., de. The Fulani of Northern Nigeria. Lagos: Government Printer, 1944.

Sufstkasa, N. Where Women Work: A Study of Yoruba Women in the Market Place and Home. Ann Arbor: University of Michigan Press, 1973.

Talbot, P. Amaury. The Peoples of Southern Nigeria, 4 Vols. London: Oxford University Press, 1926.

_____. Tribes of the Niger Delta. London: Sheldon Press, 1932.

Taylor, J. V. Christianity and Politics in Africa. London: Penguin African Series, 1957.

Temple, C. L. Native Races and their Rulers, 2nd ed. London: Frank Cass, 1968.

_____, ed. Notes on the Tribes, Provinces, Emirates and States of the Northern Provinces of Nigeria. Lagos: C. M. S. Bookshop, 1922.

Thomas, Northcote Whitridge. Anthropological Report on Ibo-Speaking People of Nigeria, 1914.

Uchendu, V. C. The Igbo of Southeast Nigeria. New York: Holt, Rinehart and Winston, 1965.

Westermann, Diedrich and Bryan, M. A. Languages of West Africa. London, 1952.

Williams, G. State and Society in Nigeria. Lagos: Afrographika, 1980.

ADDENDA

During the final production stages of this book, the occurrence
of new political developments as well as the availability of additional
information created a need for new entries and a continuation of
some existing entries.

The information contained in this Addenda supplements the
material found in the Dictionary and cross-references are made
from one to the other in instances where additional information has
been added to an entry.

*   *   *

ABACHA, MAJOR GENERAL SANNI.   Chief of Army Staff in the
Babangida administration.   When he was still a Brigadier, he
announced the overthrow of the civilian administration of Alhaji
Shehu Shagari on December 31, 1983.   He was also the first
officer to address the press after the overthrow of Major-
General Muhammadu Buhari had been previously announced by
Brigadier Joshua Dogonyaro.   A Kanuri, born on September
20, 1943, in Kano State, he was educated at the Government
College in Kano and in 1962 started his military training at
the Nigerian Military Training College in Kaduna.   In 1963,
he was sent to the Mons Defence Cadet College in the United
Kingdom in 1963 and in 1976 he went to the School of Infantry
in Jaji, Nigeria.   In 1981, Abacha attended the National Insti-
tute of Policy and Strategic Studies in Kuru, Nigeria and the
Senior International Defence Management course in Monterey,
California, USA in 1982.   Major General Abacha has held many
important military posts among which were Battalion Commander, Brigade Commander, General Staff Officer I, Army
School of Infantry.   He was also Director of Army Training
and General Officer Commanding, Second Mechanized Infantry
Division.   He became a Major-General in 1984 and Chief of
Army Staff in the Babangida administration in 1985.

BABANGIDA, MAJOR-GENERAL IBRAHIM GBADAMOSI (continued
from p. 55).   Between 1966 and 1967 he was at the Royal
Armoured Center in the United Kingdom, and in 1972 he attended the Army Armour School in the United States.   Between
1979 and 1980 he took courses in Senior Executive Management
at the National Institute of Policy and Strategic Studies in Kuru,
Nigeria.

385

General Babangida has held many important military posts. He was Troop Commander from 1964 to 1966, and during the 1967-1970 Nigerian Civil War he commanded the 44th Infantry Battalion called "The Rangers." Between 1970 and 1972, he was Company Commander and Instructor at the Nigerian Defence Academy. In 1973 he was Regiment Commander and in 1975 he became Commander, Armoured Corps. In 1981 he was Director of Army Staff Duties and Plans; in 1984 he became Chief of Army Staff, a position he held until August 27, 1985, when he became the President and Commander in Chief of the Armed Forces after the coup he organized had successfully ousted Major-General Muhammadu Buhari from office. He came to the public limelight when he single-handedly disarmed the mutinous Lt. Col. Buka Suka Dimka, who had taken control of the Radio Nigeria in the abortive coup that attempted to topple the government of the Late General Murtala Muhammed on February 13, 1976.

BAREWA COLLEGE. The school that has educated four Nigerian Heads of State (Alhaji Tafawa Balewa, General Yakubu Gowon, General Murtala Mohammed and Alhaji Shehu Shagari) was founded in 1922. It is the oldest secondary school in all of the Northern part of Nigeria, and the school that many northern elites like Mallam Aminu Kano, Sir Ahmadu Bello, the Sardauna of Sokoto, Alhaji Waziri Ibrahim and Alhaji Umaru Dikko have attended. Its motto was "Man jada-wa-jada," i.e., "He who tries, would succeed."

The school was originally founded in Katsina and called Katsina College. It later became Katsina Higher College, and Katsina Training College. Before the Second World War, the school was moved to Kaduna, the regional capital, and called Kaduna College. After the war, in 1949 it was moved to Zaria and became Zaria College, and later Zaria Secondary School. In 1970 it adopted its present name, Barewa College.

COUP D'ETAT (continued from p. 92). The last successful coup took place on August 27, 1985. A palace coup organized and controlled by Major General Ibrahim Babangida, who became the first military President and Commander in Chief of the Armed Forces, it removed Major General Muhammadu Buhari and his lieutenant, Major General Tunde Idiagbon, both of whom were said to be stubborn and not listening to advice. The new administration changed the name of the Supreme Military Council (SMC) to the Armed Forces Ruling Council (AFRC) and enlarged the number from 19 to 28. The position of the Chief of Staff Supreme Headquarters responsible for general government administration and the administrative functions of the armed forces was abolished and in its place were created the Chief of General Staff (CGS) responsible only for the general administration of government, while the administration of the armed forces was under the Chairman, Joint Chiefs of Staff, both of whom were responsible to the President.

GOVERNMENT (continued from p. 142). The highest policy-making body for the country was the Supreme Military Council (SMC), made up of The Head of State, top military officers, the Attorney-General of the Federation and the Inspector-General of Police. The executive authority of the government was exercised by the Federal Executive Council (FEC), members of which were appointed by the Head of State. The Head of State also appointed military governors to the constituent units of the federation (four regions in 1966, 12 states in 1967 and 19 states in 1976) thus enabling the military to maintain its command structure. In 1979, the military voluntarily gave up power after having successfully drawn up a new Constitution and supervised elections that ushered in the constitution.

Under the 1979 Constitution, Nigeria had an executive presidential system of government, very much like the American system. The Federal Republic of Nigeria was headed by an Executive President who was Head of State, the Chief Executive of the Federation and the Commander-in-Chief of the Armed Forces. He was elected for a term of four years and could be re-elected for a second term. He was assisted by Ministers who were the heads of various federal ministeries. The President, in choosing his ministers, was required to choose at least one member from each of the states that made up the federation and submit his nominations for approval to the Senate.

The Legislative Assembly was made up of two houses: the Senate and the House of Representatives. Members of the legislative assembly could not at the same time be members of the executive authority.

In the states, there were governors who were each the Chief Executives of their respective states. The governor's term of office was four years and he could be re-elected for a second term only. He was assisted by a Cabinet of Commissioners, the appointment of whom had to be approved by the State House of Assembly, which was unicameral. Each state was divided into all-purpose local government authorities. Under the constitution, local governments were given special functions and were required to share in the national revenue collected by the federal government.

This new type of government was not understood by the operators. The legislative assembly did not appreciate its role as a check on the executive authority and its independence of it. Right from the beginning, the Senate yielded to executive pressure by approving some of the presidential nominations for ministerial posts, which it had previously rejected. The executive authority saw this weakness, and exploited it. By the end of the first four years, the executive branch, by all kinds of tactics including corruptive ones, was in virtual control of the houses. The system broke down after the 1983 elections which were perhaps the most rigged elections in the history of the country. On December 31, the soldiers again came into power.

The new military government was based on the same

model as the one the country had during the first period of
military rule. There was the Head of State and Commander-
in-Chief of the Armed Forces. He was also the Chairman of
the Supreme Military Council, the highest policy-making body,
the Chairman of the Federal Executive Council (FEC), and the
National Council of State, a consultative body that included
State Military Governors.

The new administration started with great popular support and enthusiasm. It decided that every person who had
held elective or appointive public offices from October 1979
to 1983 should account for his or her stewardship. Thus, it
asked all former governors and their deputies, political appointees at the federal and state levels and members of federal
and state houses of assembly, together with party officials to
report to security officers. Those who were suspected of having illegally enriched themselves while in office were detained.
Most of these were later set free while some were tried by
military tribunals and if found guilty were sentenced to varying terms of imprisonment.

The government would also be remembered for launching
the campaign of War Against Indiscipline, the Currency Exchange, and its austerity measures. In March 1984, the War
Against Indiscipline (WAI) was launched to inculcate discipline
and instill in all Nigerians orderly and respectable conduct in
every sphere of life. The currency exchange of April 1984
was to stop currency trafficking and reduce the excess money
in circulation by changing the colors of the various denominations of the Naira and thus making worthless about half the ₦6
billion in circulation at the expiry of the change. Finally, the
government austerity measures forced Nigerians to begin to
look for ways to provide locally for their needs rather than
depend on imports.

However, the administration soon began to show signs
of stress. It lost steam and began to drift. The Supreme
Military Council was deeply divided on policy issues and the
economy showed no sign of improvement. On August 27, 1985,
the fifth military coup in Nigeria took place, ousting from
power the regime of Major-General Mohammadu Buhari and
his second in command, Major General Tunde Idiagbon. The
new Head of State became President and Commander in Chief
of the Armed Forces. The second most important position in
the ousted administration, that of the Chief of Staff Supreme
Headquarters was abolished and a new one, Chief of General
Staff (C G S) was created. The CGS was responsible only for
the general administration of the country, but not for the Armed
Forces as was previously the case. The highest policy-making
body was no longer called the Supreme Military Council (SMC),
but the Armed Forces Ruling Council (AFRC). The Federal
Executive Council (FEC) became the National Council of Ministers while the National Council of State retained its name and
its role.

The new administration retained many top leaders of the
ousted one. What really happened was a change of guards: the

majority group in the ruling military council, headed by Major-General Ibrahim Babangida overthrew the minority group, which wielded power, headed by Major-General Muhammadu Buhari and his second in command Major General Tunde Idiagbon who was then at the Mecca pilgrimage, both of whom were accused of being rigid, inflexible, stubborn and not guided by the principle of consultation and cooperation in decision-making. Rather, any effort made to offer any advice was met with stubborn resistance and was viewed as a challenge of authority, and disloyalty.

IDIAGBON, BRIGADIER TUNDE (continued from p. 157). In January 1984, Idiagbon became the Chief of Staff Supreme Headquarters in the Buhari Administration, a position in which he was responsible for both the general administration of government and the administrative functions of the armed forces. He lost this position as a result of the palace coup which replaced Major General Muhammadu Buhari, the Head of State, when he, Idiagbon, was away on a pilgrimage to Mecca. While in power he was seen as a very disciplined, non-smiling and no-nonsense officer. He launched the campaign of War Against Indiscipline to instill discipline in Nigerians and promote unity and patriotism. He also insisted on the accountability of Public Officers of all ranks. He however was accused of stubborness and refusal to listen to advice. His greatest undoing was the wide power he gave to the security officers, the NSO, to arrest and detain, a power which was grossly abused. He was retired in September 1985, after he had come back from his pilgrimage.

NIGERIAN SECURITY ORGANIZATION (NSO) (continued from p. 240). The misuse of the NSO by the Buhari administration (1984-1985) was an important factor in the overthrow of that administration on August 27, 1985. The NSO was accused of making life insecure by indiscriminate arrests, indefinite detention of people without charge or trial, and the wire-tapping of people's telephones, including those of the members of the Supreme Military Council, the highest policy-making body in the country. In his first address to the nation, on August 27, 1985, the new Head of State, President Ibrahim Babangida, promised to overhaul and reorganize the NSO.

UKIWE, COMMODORE EBITU. Chief of General Staff and number two man in the Babangida Administration, Ukiwe was born at Abiriba, Imo State. He was a member of the Supreme Military Council in 1975 and was the Military Governor of Niger State in 1977. In 1978, when the military was preparing to hand over power, he was posted to Lagos State as Military Administrator of the State and Commanding Officer of the NNS Beecroft. In 1979 when the civilian administration came to power, he returned to regular naval duties. In 1980, he was at War College, Rhode Island in the United States and in 1981, he became the Head of the Naval Faculty at the Command Staff College in Jaji. In 1984, he became a member of the Supreme

Military Council under Major-General Muhammadu Buhari and when General Buhari was removed from power, he was appointed Chief of General Staff to take care of the general administration of the Federal Government, but without having responsibility for the military as was the case of the Chief of Staff Supreme Headquarters under the previous military regime.

WAR AGAINST INDISCIPLINE. One of the major problems militating against Nigeria's social, political, and economic development is lack of discipline among many of its people. This lack of discipline is seen in all aspects of life--in the rush and push to board a bus or plane when there are more than enough seats for everyone, in ostentatious living, in election rigging and other malpractices, and generally in various aspects of its economic life. General Olusegun Obasanjo, the former Head of State, in his 1977 Jaji Address clearly identified this problem and called for greater discipline in the nation's private and public life. However, the civilian administration that succeeded him was perhaps the most undisciplined that the nation had ever had. The administration provided the atmosphere of free-for-all, leading to the collapse of the national economy and the Second Republic.

The military administration that succeeded the Shagari administration, which regarded itself as the offshoot of the Murtala/Obasanjo Administration of 1975 to 1979, decided to combat this evil. On March 20, 1984, the Chief of Staff, Supreme Headquarters, Brigadier Tunde Idiagbon, launched a nationwide campaign against indiscipline known as War Against Indiscipline (WAI). The campaign was to bring sanity to the society by replacing indiscipline with discipline in all facets of the nation's life. It involved the propagation of the ideals of national consciousness and patriotism, and it tried to demonstrate the significance of nationhood and national unity by instilling respect for such national symbols as the flag, the anthem, and the pledge. The government intended to use for the campaign the mass media, government information services, community leaders, trade unions, traditional rulers, religious leaders, and many other organizations including youth organizations, that were interested in the objectives of the campaign. The mass media were especially enjoined to set a good example and help instill in the minds of the people the noble ideals of national consciousness and patriotism and to remold and redirect national values and destiny, a task greatly impeded by the Public Officers Protection Against False Accusation Decree Number Four of 1984 which protected public servants against false accusation and the government from embarrassment.

The campaign had limited success. It established what may be called the queueing culture. People began to queue in some public places and they began to conform to the work ethics. The streets also began to be clean. However, the WAI Campaign soon existed more in words than in deeds. Rules and regulations were being circumvented by many people, including even some who carried the WAI patches, and the campaign turned more and more to symbolic events, like competition by states or local government areas for monetary reward for being the cleanest state or local government area in the country. The military administration that succeeded the Buhari administration in August 1985 was aware of this perversion of the campaign. As the new military President, Major-General Ibrahim Babangida said on assuming power: "The War Against Indiscipline shall continue but this time in the minds and conduct of Nigerians, and not by way of symbolism or money-consuming campaigns. This government on its part will ensure that the leadership exhibits proper example."